Voices from Company D

Edited by G. Ward Hubbs

Voices from Company D

Diaries by the Greensboro Guards, Fifth Alabama Infantry Regiment, Army of Northern Virginia

The University of Georgia Press *Athens and London*

© 2003 by the University of Georgia Press

Athens, Georgia 30602

All rights reserved

Set in 10/13 Bulmer by Bookcomp, Inc.

Printed and bound by Maple-Vail

The paper in this book meets the guidelines for permanence

and durability of the Committee on Production Guidelines

for Book Longevity of the Council on Library Resources.

PRINTED IN THE UNITED STATES OF AMERICA

07 06 05 04 03 C 5 4 3 2 1

Library of Congress Cataloging-in-Publication Data

Voices from Company D : diaries by the Greensboro Guards, Fifth Alabama

Infantry Regiment, Army of Northern Virginia / edited by G. Ward Hubbs.

   p. cm.

Includes index.

ISBN 0-8203-2514-7 (hardcover : alk. paper)

1. Confederate States of America. Army. Alabama Infantry Regiment, 5th.

2. Alabama—History—Civil War, 1861–1865—Personal narratives.

3. United States—History—Civil War, 1861–1865—Personal narratives,

Confederate.   4. Alabama—History—Civil War, 1861–1865—Regimental

histories.   5. United States—History—Civil War, 1861–1865—Regimental

histories.   6. Alabama—History—Civil War, 1861–1865—Social aspects.

7. United States—History—Civil War, 1861–1865—Social aspects.

8. Soldiers—Alabama—Greensboro Region—Diaries.   9. Greensboro Region

(Ala.)—Biography.   I. Hubbs, G. Ward, 1952– .

E551.5 5th .V65 2003

973.7'461'0922—dc21

2002152513

British Library Cataloging-in-Publication Data available

For my parents, LaMar and Louise

Contents

The Diarists

JHC	John Henry Cowin
RHA	Richard Henry Adams
SP	Samuel Pickens
JP	James Pickens
HB	Henry Beck
McD	Joel Calvin McDiarmid
JST	John S. Tucker
Vᴇᴛ	Veteran from Co. D, 5th Alabama Regiment

A Note from the Editor

This project began many years ago when Ron Cartee, now of Martinsburg, West Virginia, walked into my office with Dr. Cowin's diary, which he graciously photocopied and allowed me to transcribe. In it I noticed several names that seemed familiar to me. Sure enough, I remembered having seen those names in the typescript diaries of Samuel and James Pickens deposited at the University of Alabama's Hoole Special Collections Library. Later I came to know John McCall, of Mobile, Alabama, whose family owns the original Pickens diaries. John went far out of his way by allowing me to transcribe the Pickens diaries from the originals and by generously assisting me in many other ways.

I originally set out to publish these three diaries and move on to other projects. But the more I discovered about Cowin and the Pickens brothers, the more I was determined to tell the larger story of their company's relationship to Greensboro. The result was *Guarding Greensboro: A Confederate Company in the Making of a Southern Community,* this book's companion volume, also published by the University of Georgia Press. Although *Guarding Greensboro* took a long time to complete, I never doubted that at some point the diaries would also be published, especially after I discovered others.

I found the original of Richard Henry Adams' 1862 diary at the Virginia Military Institute Archives, Lexington; typescripts of both his 1862 and 1865 diaries (when he was no longer a Guard) are deposited at the Alabama Department of Archives and History. A typescript of the Henry Beck diary is in the Birmingham Public Library. The Joel Calvin McDiarmid diary, also in typescript, is located in the Malcolm Macmillan papers, Special Collections and Archives Department, Ralph Brown Draughon Library, Auburn University. Extracts from the John S. Tucker diary were published in the spring 1981 edition of the *Alabama Historical Quarterly,* but I relied on a collection of photocopies and typescripts in the Alabama Department of Archives and History. Finally, "a Veteran from Co. D, 5th Alabama Regiment" was printed weekly in the *Greensboro Alabama Beacon* during February and March 1899.

The transcriptions of the Cowin, the two Pickens brothers, and the Adams diaries are published here without changes, except where indicated by brackets. I have tried to avoid using the intrusive *[sic]* every time a diarist misspelled a word, relying instead on the readers' patience and good judgment. I have used brackets and ellipses [. . .] where material is missing or hopelessly illegible. Dashes, parenthetical material, and question marks are in the original. In the other three diaries (Tucker, Beck, and Veteran), I decided to take more liberties by making punctuation more consistent and by silently correcting many misspelled proper names that earlier transcribers had obviously garbled. In all the diaries, underlined words have been italicized, and A.M. and P.M. have been rendered in small caps. Explanatory notes follow the daily entries and are introduced by *Notes.* Casualty estimates usually come from Thomas L. Livermore's *Numbers and Losses in the Civil War in America: 1861–65* (Bloomington: Indiana University Press, 1957). The other material can be found either in any Civil War encyclopedia or in *Guarding Greensboro.* A biographical dictionary is appended that includes all members of the Guards during the Civil War (designated by an asterisk) and names mentioned by the diarists.

In addition to contributions by John McCall and Ron Cartee, I wish to recognize William Alexander and Fred L. Ray for pointing me to the Beck and McDiarmid diaries. Lexington native Angelika Kuettner and archivist Diane B. Jacob helped me at the VMI Archives. George C. Rable and Alan Pitts tracked down some names and terms that eluded me. James Glen Stovall solved some technical problems of transcription. And Lawrence Frederick Kohl patiently listened to my ideas and then just as patiently straightened them out. Thanks to all of you.

Introduction

This volume brings together into a single narrative eight diaries written by members of the Greensboro Guards (initially Company I, then D), Fifth Alabama Infantry Regiment. Theirs is a well-told tale—of terror and boredom, of regret and pride, of victories and defeats—from the most storied military force ever to fight on American soil: Robert E. Lee's Army of Northern Virginia. The Guards were not mere bystanders, but as part of the famous Rodes' brigade fought in some of the Civil War's hardest battles. The company sustained heavy losses at Malvern Hill, for example. A few weeks later most were captured at South Mountain, where the Guards and a few other companies had been left behind to hold back George McClellan's Army of the Potomac while Lee gathered in his forces at Sharpsburg on Antietam Creek. At Chancellorsville Company D was selected to carry the colors at the head of Stonewall Jackson's corps as it moved to outflank and then smash Hooker's surprised troops ("Never saw such confusion in my life," wrote one Guard, "men scattered & mixed up every way. It was a running fight & difficulty was to keep near enough to Y. to shoot them"). Among the first to reach Gettysburg, the Guards were hit hard once again. Lee personally ordered the Guards into Spotsylvania's bloodiest fighting. And as members of Jubal Early's corps, the Guards looked down on Washington from the Maryland hills one summer's day in 1864. The company spent the last winter of the war in the Petersburg trenches, until they were captured and held in prison camp long after hostilities ended. One lone Greensboro Guard reportedly attended the surrender at Appomattox Court House. Yes, these diarists were firsthand participants in America's greatest crisis.

The Guards, needless to say, did not spend the entire four years ceaselessly fighting Yankees. Much of their time, especially in the beginning, was spent in routine camp duties, including drilling and all the other detested tasks designed to turn civilians into soldiers. In this endeavor they were fortunate to be led by one of the greatest of Lee's lieutenants, Robert E. Rodes, a man historian Douglas Southall Freeman described as like a Norse god or a character in

Beowulf. This West Pointer had come to Alabama as the engineer for the proposed Northeast-Southwest Railroad. When the South seceded the Tuscaloosa
Warrior Guards elected him their captain, and then the Fifth Alabama (which
included the Warrior Guards, the Greensboro Guards, and ten other companies)
elected him colonel. The soldiers at first resented Rodes as a harsh taskmaster,
but then came to respect him—and vice versa—as his brigade emerged to be one
of the finest and most feared in the entire Army of Northern Virginia.

Rodes' brigade was part of Stonewall Jackson's corps, and this afforded the
Guards opportunities to see the famed warrior in action ("& there came Glorious
old Stonewall at a sweeping gallop," one Guard entered in his diary, "hat in hand
on his sorrel horse followed by aids & couriers. All long line troops waved hats
& cheered long & loud"). By contrast, the Guards regarded Robert E. Lee with
deference and respect ("a well set venerable looking man with white hair &
beard . . . he passed in silence—no cheering. All who knew him was inspired
with the utmost confidence & gazed attentively upon him").

These diarists also recorded the long marches along unknown roads that,
although exhausting ("23 ms. we marched to-day . . . I was completely broken
down & my feet hurt me very much"), were not without diversions ("We counted
the number of ladies, who came out to see us pass & there were 159"). But even
more ink was spilled recounting their attempts to fend off the boredom of camp
life. Soldiers had letters to write, the latest rumors to share, and novels to read—
often the fiction popular among Southern patriots, but occasionally obscure
biographies of Reformation leaders. Then came the games of chance, town ball
and something they called "hard ball," and practical jokes. They built cabins for
winter quarters and were occasionally called out to witness a deserter's execution
("Sad & heart-sickening scene! I felt the moment after the volley was fired, an
indescribable & mixed sensation of sickness & horror at the sight").

The war—alternating between drilling, fighting, marching, the boredom and
novelty of camp life—furnished ample material for the Guards' tale. But in the
hands of lesser writers, the material would lie as dead on the page as corpses on
the field. So let the authors be introduced.

John Henry Cowin (designated JHC in the text; his diary runs from April
to December 1861, plus January 1863) was the son of a Greensboro hotelier
who had the means and foresight to provide his son with an excellent education.
Young Cowin first attended the Greene Springs School near Havanna (now
spelled with a single *n*), a few miles up the road from Greensboro and one of
the foremost schools in the South. Its visionary founder, Henry Tutwiler, who
was among the first to earn a master's degree from the University of Virginia,
convinced many of his students, including Cowin, to continue their education
in Charlottesville. Cowin did not end his education there, however, but continued on to graduate from Philadelphia's Jefferson Medical College, at that time
probably the country's best.

National events changed what was otherwise a promising and secure career. When the young physician learned of Abraham Lincoln's election in November 1860, he joined other Southerners in heading back to his native soil. And the day after South Carolina forces began shelling Fort Sumter, he and fifty other Greensborians joined the Guards. Three weeks later the company was in Montgomery, where it was placed in the newly formed Fifth Alabama. Dr. Cowin, who was already an accomplished wordsmith, pulled out a tall hardbound ledger in which he had often copied writings that interested him, or student orations he had given, and opened to a fresh page. In dark ink he titled this new chapter, "A record of events transpiring in the Campaign of the Greensboro Guards, 5th Regt Ala Vols." A preface immediately followed, justifying the Southern states' secession and outlining the Guards' activities after the presidential election. Although entirely his own, both Dr. Cowin's title and his preface (signed "Members of the Greensboro Guards") announced that this was not so much an account of Cowin's personal experiences as a corporate diary. He had melded his individual fate with those of his fellow Guards. Moreover, this would be no mere "record of events," despite its title, for the best of the diarists would use their words to sort out the confusing jumble of impulses, loyalties, and moral justifications that brought them to this point.

Dr. Cowin chose to serve in the Guards as a private rather than use his medical skill as a surgeon. But he did spend weeks nursing his typhoid-stricken best friend. Like the war itself, all his training and efforts came to naught ("With an anxious attention have I watched by his bedside, and administered to his wants. Just before his death he grasped my hand with a warmth that indicated his gratitude and attachment for me"). Dr. Cowin himself would not live to write the end of his "record of events"—that, figuratively speaking, would be left to others. At Chancellorsville a Yankee ball hit his femoral artery, and he bled to death. A few days later the remaining members of Company D would honor their fallen comrade by posthumously inscribing his name on the Confederate Roll of Honor, established in November 1862 by the Confederate Congress to recognize bravery.

Richard Henry Adams (RHA; April and May 1862) joined the Guards along with his two brothers as the company came through Uniontown upon first leaving Greensboro. Adams lasted only a little over a year in the Guards, joining the Partisan Rangers (the Fifty-first Alabama, organized by two officers of the Fifth Alabama, one of whom was a Greensboro Guard) in September 1862. Then his adventures really began. He was captured and kept at various Northern prisons, including Johnson's Island outside Sandusky, Ohio, and Fort Delaware. At one point Adams nearly drowned in an unsuccessful escape attempt. But he survived the war and returned to Uniontown to become a successful planter.

Like Dr. Cowin, Samuel Pickens (SP; July 1862 to July 1865, except for the summer and fall of 1864) also attended Henry Tutwiler's school and the

University of Virginia. Sam was an heir to one of the state's wealthiest families (his widowed mother reported assets of nearly a half million dollars to the 1860 census enumerator). Their fortune came from the cotton grown by over two hundred slaves on the several plantations that an earlier Pickens had acquired while land registrar. The family home, Umbria, lay a few miles west of Greensboro and, while by no means ostentatious, stood out as one of the state's finest.

Sam was not among those who joined the Guards in the wake of Fort Sumter, but by the late summer of 1862 he was preparing to join them in Virginia. With a precise and forceful script, he made the first entry in several small paperbound notebooks that could easily fit in a shirt pocket. Sam jotted down the price he had to pay for a small silk handkerchief ($3.50) when he got off the train in Petersburg that November. Despite this inauspicious start, Sam would prove himself tough, enduring increasing hardships until he was one of only twenty-odd Guards left in the winter of '64. The ink would sometimes freeze, but he continued to write. Sam was among those captured in the trenches of Petersburg only a week before the rest of the army surrendered at Appomattox Court House. Confined to a prison camp, he continued to believe that the South would triumph until the obvious could no longer be denied. Entering "the machine where U.S. citizens are made out of rebel soldiers," he at last stood under an immense American flag stretched into a canopy and bitterly took his oath to the Union.

A more vivid contrast could not be found than Sam's brother James Pickens (JP; March through June 1864). Jamie had grown up alongside his older brother; together the two had attended Greene Springs School, then Gessner Harrison's School in Albemarle County, Virginia, and finally the University of Virginia in 1859. But here all similarities ended. Where Sam became a seasoned veteran of three long years, Jamie spent his three months in the Guards struggling to keep up. Totally unfit to be a soldier, Jamie had a weak constitution, so he was usually to be found in the hospital or in quarters. This confinement gave him an abundance of time for reading novels and for writing in his journal.

Jamie's lengthy and literate diary represents the work of an unusually introspective man unhesitant to describe his feelings of separation from, and devotion to, his mother and siblings ("Trust Sam may be enabled to get a furlough & go home if I go, that we may go together. Oh how happy I would be!"). Jamie's war was no adventure, no chance for glory defending what he cared most for, but rather an ordeal to be avoided. His feelings of homesickness repeatedly overwhelmed his duties as a soldier and even his common sense. During the Battle of Spotsylvania Court House, in May 1864, he deliberately left his gun and cartridge box in the hospital. On another occasion, while pouring out contempt for the Yankees who took him away from his family, Jamie charged the North with having started the war by attacking Fort Sumter. (The reality, of course, was exactly the opposite.) A desire to be home and a reluctance to fight did not imply sympathy for the Union, or even a diminished support for the Confederacy—so long as the fighting excluded him ("Oh, what a terrible scene it is to behold the wounded & dying; & to hear their cries how distressing! I have seen enough of battle"). As atypical as Jamie may have been as a soldier, he displayed well the confusing mixture of personal commitment and physical weakness that many probably felt but seldom expressed.

Henry Beck (HB; March 1864 to February 1865) was one of many Confederate soldiers who served behind the scenes as sutlers, quartermasters, couriers, smiths, or—like Beck—commissary clerks. In many ways he had an easier time of it than those Guards in camp, for his duties took him to new parts of the countryside where he boarded with civilians. Indeed, it was on one such stay that he met his future wife, Lucy Heller. Like many others, Beck moved in and out among different units. He was listed among those who first joined the Guards in April 1861 but served as a clerk in the Jeff Davis Legion (a cavalry unit about battalion size that served under J. E. B. Stuart and included two companies of men with Greensboro connections) until 1864, when he reentered Company D. Little else is known of Beck's life. Born in Germany about 1839, he moved to Greensboro in 1857 and three years later was living in nearby Havanna with his German-born parents and his younger Alabama-born sister. During the war he attended Christian services, although in 1892 his son was listed as Jewish. Beck returned to Greensboro after the fighting ended to resume his career as a merchant, moving with his wife and seven children to Birmingham later in life.

Little out of the ordinary characterized the life of Joel Calvin McDiarmid (McD; May 1864 to June 1865). Two years after his birth in 1836, the family moved from North Carolina to Talladega County, which Alabama had created from Creek Indian lands only five years before. When the Confederates bombarded Fort Sumter, McDiarmid, then clerking in Havanna, eagerly joined the Guards. At times he shared the same mess with codiarist James Pickens, and a comparison of their entries can be revealing. Pickens, for example, observes that in December 1864 McDiarmid was intoxicated on apple brandy—a fact that the latter conveniently fails to mention. McDiarmid managed to survive the war unscathed and returned to Talladega County.

All the surviving entries written by John Henry Cowin, Samuel Pickens, James Pickens, Henry Beck, and Joel Calvin McDiarmid are published here in their entirety. All the entries from Richard Henry Adams' brief career while a Guard are also included. The diaries of two others—John S. Tucker and "a Veteran from Co. D, 5th Alabama Regiment"—are extracted. These two do not match the quality of the other five and are introduced to fill in missing entries or where they give unusually insightful observations. All the evidence suggests that none of the diarists continued to keep a diary after returning home at the war's end.

John S. Tucker (JST) kept a diary throughout most of the war, but it consisted largely of brief notations of weather and location. He received appointment as a commissary clerk in June 1862 and thereafter missed a great deal of the Guards' activities. Occasionally Tucker recorded in his journal the pleasure of receiving a letter from his wife, Annie Nutting Tucker (whose two brothers also served in Company D). At Gettysburg he found his brother dead ("Never shall I forget my feelings when I got to him & found him lifeless. How sudden & heart-rending the change"). Tucker left the Guards April 1, 1864, when he entered the Jeff Davis Legion by exchanging with diarist Henry Beck. Tucker returned to Greensboro after the war to become sheriff and in 1880 was murdered trying to foil a robbery.

Finally, in 1899 "a Veteran . . ." (Vet) published entries from his diary in the local Greensboro newspaper. These scant selections warrant only occasional inclusion.

Clearly these collected journals offer us immediate and vivid insights into the life of the common soldier, a topic that has attracted a growing number of scholars. But even more, when brought together these journals tell a remarkable story of a single company's four years in the Army of Northern Virginia. The course of the war itself heightened the drama. Things would start slowly as the armies marshaled their resources and plotted strategy. Then an inciting incident would lead to fighting, and at some critical moment success—perhaps for their army, perhaps for the cause itself—hung in the balance. The end of the battle brought the inevitable weighing of loss and gain. The boredom of camp life only served to heighten the emotional intensity of the battles. Here was the sort of plot that novelists crave. The diarists realized it, as Dr. Cowin's use of a title and preface demonstrates. They were embarking on an exceptional adventure unlike anything they had ever encountered, a challenge to the routine that had heretofore characterized their lives. Four years later, when Sam Pickens ended his diary upon reaching Greensboro, he knew that their tale had reached its conclusion.

Over and above the drama, these eight surviving journals display an exceptional unity. Readers will immediately be struck by the fortuitous way that they begin and end with little overlap. This is most obvious when Tucker and Beck switched positions, but the sequential entries occur throughout. The diaries, of course, also display the unity of having all been written by members of the same Confederate company. These men camped under the same rain, ate the same gruel, marched down the same trails, charged the same blue lines, and obeyed the same inexplicable orders from the same commanders. But even more held these men together than the common experiences they shared as soldiers in the Greensboro Guards. The eight diarists all hailed from the little town of Greensboro, Alabama, or its environs. (Richard Henry Adams lived farthest away in Uniontown, twenty miles to the south.) All knew each other and were related by blood or acquaintance with most of the other members of the company. This was not merely a dramatic narrative then, but a complex story of intertwining personalities worthy of Dickens, a tale bounded by Manassas and Appomattox— and the covers of this book. Yet *Voices from Company D* is better understood as a chapter—an essential chapter, to be sure—in a much larger story of Greensboro and its Guards.

One might assume that the company sprang into existence during the crisis of the 1860s. But in fact, the Guards had been mustering and drilling since the early 1820s, when Greensboro was just coming into existence. (The story of the Guards from the 1820s into the 1870s is more fully told in the companion volume, *Guarding Greensboro: A Confederate Company in the Making of a Southern Community,* also published by the University of Georgia Press.) People were then settling along the northern edge of what was known as the Canebrake, a portion of the west Alabama Black Belt that was considered the richest soil in the South. Young men—often alone, sometimes with families in tow—descended upon the settlement hoping to make their fortunes growing cotton. Most stayed briefly before continuing westward on their quest for success. But some did stay, and some of them made fabulous fortunes.

Within a few years, Greensboro's busy Main Street and imposing Greek-revival houses bespoke a commercial success that disguised the town's social failings. Letters back home routinely observed Greensborians' lack of community feelings. One young lawyer, after being away six months, complained of finding himself "among strangers." The Panic of 1837 drove the residents even further apart as they began suing each other to collect debts. Community feelings were not about to emerge without deliberate and creative action.

Their solution was typically American. Greensborians formed voluntary associations to advance their own self-interests. They gathered to promote railroads. They joined churches and temperance societies to save their souls. They founded Masonic lodges that would facilitate their making business connections and gaining credit. They enlisted contributions to build schools for their children, ultimately convincing the Methodists to found Southern University within their town limits. By the eve of the Civil War, Greensboro resembled countless small towns across America. Instead of a single community, the townspeople formed a complex web of voluntary ones.

One voluntary association came to stand out from the rest. The Greensborough Light Artillery Guards, as it was formally known, had originated as just another local company in the state's general militia (in which nearly all adult males were automatically enrolled). But the general militia was unreliable, and instead the state began to depend on local volunteer companies that had organized spontaneously. These elite units, which after 1834 officially included the Guards, were given privileges and prestige in return for assuming the role of leading the state's defense.

Alabamians initially believed that they needed protection from foreign invaders and Indians on the warpath. But these concerns gave way to another, especially after 1831 when word came of a major slave uprising led by Nat Turner in rural Southampton County, Virginia. Greensboro's economic success had been built on the backs of the thousands of slaves laboring on Canebrake cotton plantations. But whites feared that those growing numbers of black bondsmen would rise up against them in a brutal race war, a notion kept alive by stories from local Santo Domingan refugees, who had themselves escaped a massive bloodletting earlier in the century.

The Guards knew their role. If and when a slave uprising occurred, the citizens of Greensboro had an organization ready to protect them. Company officers regularly petitioned the governor to establish an armory in Greensboro, arguing that in no other part of the state were whites so vulnerable to a slave uprising. The company's spectacular parades, while dressed in full regalia, were overtly aimed at intimidating the bound population with displays of military might. Many who marched off in April 1861 were sons of Greensboro Guards who had been active in earlier years. Thus Dr. Cowin (who, like others, was the son of a Guard) easily charged the abolitionists of the North with starting the war by electing Abraham Lincoln, the first step in realizing Greensborians' worst fears: the destruction of slavery and an apocalyptic race war.

The Guards differed from Greensboro's other voluntary associations in another important way. Young men had joined the Masons or agricultural societies largely as tools of self-advancement. Membership might provide access to credit, for example, or knowledge that an individual could use to increase his cash crop. The Guards, however, assumed responsibility for their fellow citizens; and by drilling together, by fighting as one, by living closely together for four years—by all these activities and more—the members of the company moved beyond the self-interested voluntarism that had characterized their antebellum society. When our diarists wrote in their journals, they were not writing eight different stories; instead, they were all contributors to one: the Guards' campaign to protect their family and friends.

In this sense, the Civil War became the essential event that transformed Greensborians from individualistic self-seekers into Southerners. Instead of actively encouraging citizens to join voluntary associations, Greensborians in the late 1860s instead began to use participation and support for the Confederacy as a kind of test to determine who was worthy of inclusion in their now-unified community. Those who failed were actively excluded. Support for reform and town-building enterprises declined as Greensboro lost the dynamism that had characterized its first few decades.

If Greensboro is anything like the other small towns throughout the South, and I think it is, then Confederate diaries like those from Company D are more than mere reports of the experiences of individual soldiers between April 1861 and April 1865, more even than exciting tales. Confederate diaries are crucial Southern documents revealing a time when their many stories became one story, when individualists merged their particular fates with others to fight a common foe, when Confederate soldiers created a Southern heritage—a past that is yet present.

Voices from Company D

A record of events transpiring in the Campaign of the Greensboro Guards, 5th Reg^t Ala Vols

After the election of Abraham Lincoln to the presidency of the United States by the abolitionists of the North, it became evident to the people of the South that their rights would not be respected, and that every thing would be done to break down the peculiar institutions of the South, they therefore determined to seperate themselves from a government so inimical to their interests. The gallant state of South Carolina was the first to declare by a unanimous vote of her legislature herself a free and independent state. Alabama followed on the 11th January 1861. Then followed the other Gulf States in quick succession. After the inauguration of Lincoln a demand was made upon him for the evacuation of the forts and arsenals by the U.S. forces in the seceded States. To this demand he did not accede. Therefore the troops of South Carolina under command of Genl Beauregard bombarded and captured Fort Sumpter near Charleston, April 12th 1861, without loss however to either side. Alabama took Fort Morgan near Mobile, also took the Mt. Vernon Arsenal with arms and ammunition. Soon Lincoln made a call upon the northern States for seventy five thousand troops to retake the captured forts. The Confederate Congress then sitting at Montgomery Ala, composed of the states of South Carolina, Georgia, Florida Alabama Mississippi Louisiana Texas, made a call upon these states for troops to defend their homes and firesides from invasions. Each State promptly responded to the call. The Greensboro Guards under command of Capt Allen C. Jones were ordered to Fort Morgan, but only remained there six weeks, when they were discharged and came home.

The U.S. forces still occupied Fort Pickens Florida and refused to give it up. A call was made for twelve months volunteers to serve the Confederate States. The Greensboro Guards immediately reorganized and went into encampment opposite the residence of Mr. Thos K. Carson in the suburbs of the town, April 22^d 1861. An election was held which resulted in placing A. C. Jones in command of the company. G. E. Nelson 1ˢᵗ Lieutenant. M. L. Dedman 2ᵈ and E. L. Hobson 3ᵈ. J. F. Christian 1ˢᵗ Sergeant. Samˡ Cowin 2ᵈ Joseph Borden 3ᵈ and W. J. McDonald 4ᵗʰ. J. D. Webb Jr. J. W. Williams E. P. Jones G. G. Westcott corporals, [. . .] Chadwick company commissary

—Members of Greensboro Guards.

1861

April 22, Monday

JHC: The Greensboro Guards went into encampment in Greensboro to organize and offer their services to the Confederate States of America. While in camp here the ladies supplied us bountifully with every delicacy, and quite a number of the citizens visit the camp every afternoon to witness us drill. Lieu^t E. L. Hobson is the principal drill master. We think now that playing the soldier is a grand thing, but let's see the end of the twelve months, wonder how we will then like it. Report says that the young ladies are to hold a meeting, and pass resolutions to supply with hoop-skirts all those rich young men who some time ago sported the blue cockades but who now refuse to respond to their country's call. Do not think it a good idea, for I fear they would disgrace even the apparel of the fair sex. We are now formed into messes[.] Ours is composed of Father (S. Cowin) Jas E. Griggs, Joe Grigg, J. W. Wynne, A. B. Chapman, brother and myself. Jas D. Webb Esqr is the jolliest man in the company. He marches around in his little blue jacket and grey pants and looks like a little boy. We have prayer morning and evening by the different ministers from the town. James Jack is the ugliest man in the company, but one of the merriest, and has already won for himself the high regard of the company by his gentlemanly deportment, and by contributing greatly to the amusement of the company by his inexhaustible store of funny anecdotes.

April 26, Friday

JHC: a telegraphic dispatch heralds the news of the possession of Arlington Heights by Virginia troops. The heights overlook the city of Washington—

April 27, Saturday

JHC: We have rain and the boys are all in quarters variously engaged. A great many are leaving camp for home to take a last fond farewell of parents, relatives and friends as we expect to leave next week. Father is on guard to night.

We broke up camp several days before we received orders to leave.

May 5, Sunday

JHC: We took leave of our parents relatives and friends to go forth to battle in our country's cause. Many were the burning tears shed by devoted mothers and loving sisters, many were the words of kind advice given by indulgent fathers, proud to see the fire of patriotism burn so brightly in the bosoms of the brave sons, and many were the kind words spoken by friends, and fond hope were indulged in for our safety. The citizens furnished conveyances for us as far as Newbern. Arriving there we partook of the hospitalities of the kind people of the place, after which Capt Jones called us out on drill. At night we were kindly entertained by the citizens who showed us every attention possible. Monday morning we took the cars for Selma, arriving *there* we were met by the Selma Blues and escorted to a ware house on the river. *Here* we remained several days drilling &c. We began now to feel like soldiers, as we had our daily rations issued to us and we did not have the attention paid us that we were accustomed to.

May 9, Thursday

JHC: *Camp Jeff Davis Montgomery Ala*

Arrived in Montgomery yesterday on the Southern Republic, the finest steamer on the river. There were five companies on board. Warrior Guards, Greensboro Guards, Cahaba Rifles, Sumter Rifles and Grove Hill Guards. Father was attacked in Selma night before last with Cholera Morbus and suffered intensely. To day he is better— There were so many on the boat coming up, that we with the Warrior Guards had to take passage with the deck hands and horses, but fortunately the boat arrived here before night, so we were not necessitated to sleep with our black and equine companions.

Remained in Montgomery until Sunday May [12]. In the mean time the regiment was organized, officers elected &c. Capt R. E. Rodes of the Warrior Guards elected Colonel. A. C. Jones Lt Colonel and John T. Morgan Cahaba Rifles Major. J. D. Webb Esqr was appointed Quartermaster and Dr Farley of Cahaba Commissary. The regiment is composed of the following Companies. Mobile Continentals (Artillery) Capt Ketchum, Grove Hill Guards—Capt Hall, Monroe Guards, Capt Goode Warrior Guards Capt Fowler, Cahaba Rifles Capt Pegues Sumter Rifle Guards Capt Blount, Sumter Rifles Capt Dent, Greensboro Guards Capt Hobson, Pickensville Blues Capt Furgeson, Talladega Artillery, Capt Shelley.

NOTE: The initial organization of Fifth Alabama was as follows:

Company A   Grove Hill Guards (Captain Josephus M. Hall)
Company B   Livingston Rifles (Captain John Hubbard Dent)
Company C   Pickensville Blues (Captain Sampson Noland Ferguson)
Company D   Monroe Guards (Captain Giles Goode)
Company E   Talladega Artillery (Captain Charles Miller Shelley)
Company F   Sumter Rifle Guard (Captain Robert P. Blount)
Company G   Cahaba Rifles (Captains John Tyler Morgan and Christopher Claudius Pegues)
Company H   Warrior Guards (Captains Robert E. Rodes and William Henry Fowler)
Company I   Greensboro Guards (Captains Allen C. Jones and Edwin Lafayette Hobson)
Company K   Mobile Continental State Artillery (Captain William H. Ketchum)

The Guards' orderly sergeant, John F. Christian, published the Guards' muster roll in the May 24 edition of the *Greensboro Alabama Beacon,* listing ninety-three privates and thirteen officers.

JHC: Left Montgomery Sunday morning May [12] and had a very fatiguing march from camp to the depot. Arrived at Pensacola Monday morning about day break after a very fatiguing trip. Provisions *being* very scarce on the way, *a number of us* had nothing to eat during the day. Slept on the car floor and then had to almost tie myself into a double bow knot things were so crowded. Soon after arriving we pitched camp, and the next day were put to work to clear up a piece of ground upon which to drill. So here commences our campaign in earnest. Pensacola is the dirtiest place I was ever in. The sand everywhere five or six inches deep. After clearing up the drill ground we had to drill in this deep sand five times daily, which gave us about as much as we could stand up to well. We were mustered into the service of the Confederate States on the 13th May by Co¹ Forney of Gen¹ Bragg's staff to serve for a period of twelve months. We have fine sea bathing here every morning and evening. Get plenty fish from the market which are cheaper here than anything else. The citizens charge the soldiers double price for every thing they get. We buy nearly every thing we eat for we are furnished nothing but pork & sometimes tough beef. Father has been detailed to go home on business for the Company. Expect him back in about a week. Several of the Livingston Rifles have died since we have been here. The Louisiana Zouaves are now in Pensacola, and a hard looking set they are, perfectly regardless of all sense of propriety and gentlemanly deportment[.] Several of them have already been shot by their officers; and several have been killed in fights among themselves. A shocking accident occurred in town on Saturday afternoon. A soldier standing guard on the street was going through the manuel for the amusement of a little boy who was giving the commands. Coming to a charge bayonet, the gun was accidentally discharged the contents, a ball and three buck shot, passing through the brain of the little boy, scattering them over the side walk, and killing him instantly. The jury rendered a verdict of accidental shooting. We are getting tired of Pensacola and desire to be sent immediately on to Virginia, where it is not so warm, and where we think most of the fighting will take place. We expect orders in a few days to return to Montgomery and from there to go on to Virginia

When we came to Pensacola we were in high spirits at the prospects of a brush with the Yankees, and thought Fort Pickens would be attacked as soon as we arrived. Being at leisure one day I indulged in a bit of rhyming, thinking we could easily take the fort if we were only turned loose upon it. Here it is.

There is an abolitionist who in Washington does dwell
    And who at Pensacola wants to cut a swell
He sent around his fleet and I'll tell you the reason why
    For he says he'll hold Fort Pickens or he'll root hog or die

But about that thing we have a word to say
    For when we get started we have our own way
We'll whip 'em like thunder and then you'll hear our cry
    You may have Fort Pickens we'll root hog or die.

Just let Co^l Rodes take the 5$\underline{\text{th}}$ Regt down
    And we'll give the Yankees one good round
We'll soon force 'em out, and then you'll hear 'em cry
    Good bye Fort Pickens we've got to root hog or die.

The Greensboro boys are anxious for a fight
    With Hobson in the lead and Dedman all right
We'll soon show the Yankees if we'll only try
    How quick we can learn 'em to sing, root hog or die.

JHC: Left the hot sands of Pensacola June 2^d for Montgomery. Arriving there, I learned that Father had been there for several days confined to his bed. Went up to see him and found him suffering all the tortures of a man with the gout. Went again the next day to see him and found him much better—We remained only a day or two in Montgomery, when we started for Richmond Virginia. We started and in box cars as crowded as they could be packed. The trip was an awful one. Could get no sleep at all scarcely. We had a very pleasant time during the day, at the different stations looking at the ladies cheering us on, waving flags, throwing us boquets, pieces of poetry &c. Saw some beautiful young ladies on the route and passed through a beautiful country. The mountain scenery was grand. We saw only one union flag on the road and that in Tennessee at a place called Strawberry Plains. Some of our troops were fired into the day before we passed. At all the other stations we were cheered by the gentlemen and the ladies, and even the negro children waved their handkerchiefs. We arrived in Richmond on Sunday night about nine o'clock and were marched up town from the depot to a church near the Exchange Hotel where we slept ~~for~~ all the night. We were turned loose for an hour and a half to hunt up something to eat, but could find nothing, not even a cool drink of water. Soldiers are looked upon in

Richmond as suspicious persons, not to be trusted. Several gave the proprietors of the Exchange Hotel a good cursing about their treatment to soldiers. The next morning we were marched to our place of encampment, a race track, about a mile and a half from the city, a good level place, but pretty hot as there are no shade trees on the ground. While there I met with several of my old friends, Ed Butts of Vicksburg Miss, Ben Briggs, 8th Ala. & Dan Jones Selma Blues. There are some ten or twelve thousand troops stationed around Richmond, but they are being ordered off every day to different portions of the state. We remained here one week and had a pretty rough time of it so far as drilling was concerned. Battalion drill is awful. Col Rodes drills us from two and a half to three hours without stopping. Father and brother having remained in Montgomery on account of the illness of Father did not get to Richmond until a few days before we left. We left on Tuesday 18th for Manassas Junction and had a very hard march from the encampment to the depot. The ~~sun~~ weather being very hot and the road dusty, we got off between nine and ten o'clock and arrived at Manassas Junction the next morning before the break of day. Then commenced hard times. We had to march to a place called Stony bridge on Bull Run creek. The march was awful. The weather hot, roads very rough and broken, up hills and through fields. We however got here all right and pitched our tents. Squire Griggs and myself walked about a mile to get a drink of water, came back and had nothing to eat, so had to walk another mile to buy our supper from an old free negro. When night came we were quite tired, so we retired as early as we could and slept soundly. We are encamped on the land of a Pennsylvanian, thoroughly union at heart. Some of the boys went up to his house and fell afoul of his milk and butter. They drank about twenty gallons of milk and ate all his butter. The old fellow charged around considerably, but it was too late to save his milk and butter. We have to walk nearly a mile for water. We left Stone Bridge Saturday night (22d) at 7 o'clock for Fair fax Court House a distance of thirteen miles it is called, but before we got through with it, it appeared more like twenty. We marched all night until day was breaking. This was a far worse march than the other, as the march was at night and over a very rough, rocky road. We how ever got through with it pretty well, but were well nigh broken down when we stopped. Some stopped on the roadside and slept 'till morning. We stopped about three o'clock and lay down in the bushes to sleep 'till light, with the earth for our bed and the heavens for our covering.

After light we got up went to an old field and pitched our tents. After we arranged every thing, if one could have happened in our camp he could have seen sleeping done up according to the latest agony. If the Yankees had come upon us they could have taken us all prisoners before we could have been aroused. We have the finest water here I ever drank, almost as cold as ice water. We have no place here to drill except an old field full of stumps and ditches, yet Col Rodes puts us through. It is amusing to see the boys tumble over the stumps and in the ditches. We are now within eight miles of the enemy's camp. Our pickets are out all the time. Yesterday Monday June 24th Capt Blounts company was out in four miles of the enemy's camp. Twenty six of our men were also out on guard. Today June 25th our company is out on picket and in four miles of the enemy. I am now sitting down beside a tree, with my gun across my knee, writing these lines. Paul Lavender, Joe Wright and myself are the advanced guard of the company and some distance from it, but close enough for our guns to be heard should any of the enemy's scouts happen to come along. Their scouts are sent out all through the country. Our scouts are also out. Some of ours have been in sight of the enemy's camp. We have taken a great many prisoners and I suppose they have taken some of ours. They are however a little scary and do not venture out as far from camp as we do. Within fifty yards of where I now stand it is said that two of our men were either taken prisoners or else deserted to the enemy for nothing has ~~since~~ been heard from them since they were placed there. To stand picket guard is nothing pleasant, for one has to sit so long at a time, without being allowed to speak with any one, and keeping still all the while. One however soon becomes as much accustomed to it as to any other duty of a soldier. A soldier soon becomes reckless and cares neither for his life nor any thing else. I was never on picket before, and therefore know but little about it, but I suppose I will know a thing or two before my twenty-four hours are up!

Each company remains on picket twenty four hours when we are relieved and marched back to camp distant four miles. There are more cherries in this part of the country than I ever saw. I eat a great many Sunday and they were fine. Saw a great many today, but could not stop to get them as we were in a hurry to get out here. The sun is now sinking behind the western hills, and soon the stilly [*sic*] night will clothe the world in darkness and invite *sweet sleep to the millions,* but not to me, for here I must sit with my gun across my knees, and keep a sharp lookout throughout the long and dreary night, to prevent the lurking foe from surprising our gallant little band, and taking us prisoners. I had almost as soon die as to be a prisoner in the hands of such villains as are at the head of affairs in the United States. It is reported that the Yankees have given our regiment the handsome name of the Alabama blood hounds—we have just halted a gentleman and lady on the road, who seem very fearful of falling in with the Yankees, as they live three and a half miles from here and the enemy are only four. The gentleman told us that he had been a prisoner three days, they having taken him one night from his bed. I suppose he took the oath and they released him. Sat all night with a watchful eye, but saw nor heard nothing to excite suspicions. Do not think there were any of the villains out near here. Being relieved by another company we got back to camp about one o'clock. The weather was quite warm and the march very disagreeable. Quite a storm this afternoon, which prevented Co^l Rodes from having us out on drill. A party of Texas Rangers were out yesterday and were within four miles of Alexandria—they captured two prisoners and shot a third.

Some of our company saw and spoke to them, but could get no information from them.

NOTE: The Mobile Continental State Artillery stayed behind in Pensacola. Company K was replaced by the Barbour Greys.

From Montgomery to Richmond, the Guards traveled along the East Tennessee and Georgia Railway. On June 20 the Fifth and Sixth Alabama infantry regiments were assigned to Richard S. Ewell's brigade.

June 28, Friday

JHC: A number of the Texas Rangers to day captured ten of the enemy, among them a Lt Colonel. They were taken within four miles of Alexandria. The Yankees do not appear to be anxious to fight, for the moment they discover any of our scouts they run for camp, although they may outnumber us. Nothing of importance has transpired today. To night Tom Moore & Chris Sheldon brought in two prisoners, but they were not Yankees. A young man belonging to the Talladega Company died very suddenly this evening

June 29, Saturday

JHC: This morning I am to go on guard and it is now raining with a prospect of its continuing all day. Have just been reading The Greensboro Beacon in which there is nothing of importance, yet I like to read it because it is from home. After reading the Beacon to my great joy I was made the recipient of a letter from home and from my mother. My feelings can better be imaged than described, it is the first I have received since I have been here. After reading her letter with great pleasure, I returned to the Guard tent and after being there a short time, brother brought me another which was from Father. He is at Woodstock with his mother and sister, having gone there on account of another attack of the gout. He left us at Stone Bridge, not being able to make the march. His health is fast improving, and he is anxious to be with us again. Nothing to importance occurred today— A prisoner was carried by here today to Manassas Junction. A New York Zouave, He was taken within two miles of his camp, up a cherry tree. He expressed himself perfectly satisfied at being a prisoner.

June 30, Sunday

JHC: Stood guard last night, nothing of any consequence transpiring to disturb the quiet of the Camp. Relieved this morning at eight o'clock and though I would have a fine mornings nap, but before I had time to wash my face had to go out on inspection, and would have had to stand out an hour or two had it not began raining which caused them to hurry through with it. Capt Webb is now making out our pay roll— No dress parade this afternoon.

July 1, Monday

JHC: Another week's duty begun. We drill now mostly in the double quick step, which gives us about as much as we can well stand up to. We elicited the praise of Rodes, Jones and Morgan and every one else this morning by drilling so well. Capt Hobson put us through the double-quick, nearly the whole of the drill hour, and we did admirably. Co^l Jones said he never saw as good drilling any where. We were out on battalion drill this afternoon, but did not stay long as dark and heavy clouds began to appear. Soon after we got back, we had quite a storm. It rained very hard indeed, so much that it rained through our tent and we had to go to ditching. After the rain the weather turned quite cool—

July 2, Tuesday

JHC: Very cool indeed, as cold as a November morning in Alabama. Every one has donned his overcoat, which is not at all uncomfortable. The 1st South Carolina Regiment passed here today, having been disbanded as they only enlisted for six months. Although it is so cold, still they draw the perspiration from a fellow on these drills, for we do nothing but double quick. Received another letter from Father this morning. His health is improving and he thinks of returning to the regiment this week. Battalion drill pretty rough this evening— Seve (our cook) was taken sick this evening and we are in a bad fix in the way of cooking as not one of us know any thing about it. The Company had a big dance to night and all in fine spirits. Still quite cool.

NOTE: In his reminiscences published many years later, Captain J. W. Williams estimated that perhaps as many as thirty slaves (whom he called "faithful servants") accompanied their masters at various times during the Greensboro Guards' Confederate service. The body servant's main task, according to Williams, was to anticipate his master's every want: foraging, carrying knapsacks, minding his effects, and cooking food. Few of these servants were purchased at the front, but rather were brought from home. See "The Faithful Body Servant," *Greensboro Record,* October 22, 1903.

July 3, Wednesday

JHC: Another quite cool morning—though not so cold as yesterday. Seve is quite sick this morning from the medicine I gave him last night— Heard from home this morning through a letter from Mr Owens. All well and the crops good. Nothing but the double quick step now a-days we are put regularly through. The weather has become quite warm and it makes a fellow sweat like a horse, but we nevertheless have to jog along. As warm this evening as any day we have yet had. Wrote a long letter home this afternoon and then thought I would take a short snooze, but the call of the drum soon aroused me from my anticipated pleasant dreams and away I had to trot over stumps, stones, ditches through briers &c for three hours. Our drill ground contains an abundance of the above articles. Our drill this afternoon was not so hard as usual. I think Co^l Rodes felt a little lazy himself as he allowed us to rest twice. Tonight about nine o'clock we were all sitting out in front of our tents laughing and talking, when suddenly we heard the report of a musket and then the usual cry of "turn out the guard." Then the long roll was beaten and such hustling about as was never seen. We snatched up our guns and accoutrements, ran out on the "color line", formed and fixed bayonets ready for any emergency. Our company was the first on the line and numbered seventy men, while this afternoon on drill we only had twenty-eight. The thoughts of a fight brought all hands out in double quick time.

July 9, Tuesday

JHC: Last night two more sentinels went ~~fell~~ asleep on their posts, and were discovered by the "grand round". One of them a member of the Cahaba Rifles, was stretched out upon the ground, wrapped in his blanket sound asleep, indeed so sound that his gun was taken from him, before he awoke. He however swore that he was not asleep. The other sentinel who was found asleep, was a member of the Talladega Company. This morning we went down again to attend to the breastworks and worked like horses. We have a bad place to work in— a bottom full of roots and stumps and we have ~~the~~ a longe~~str~~ portion to build ~~of~~ than any other Company. This evening I took a good long nap, and awoke to find a heavy cloud arising. We went to work, fixed our tent and awaited the coming of the rain, we had not long to wait, for soon it came in torrents. A very fine rain indeed. Our Co^l seems apprehensive of an early attack from the enemy. He has given orders to each Captain to detail men to be in readiness to strike tents on the first alarm. It is certain that the enemy are advancing upon us, and we know not at what moment we may be attacked, and wherever we are we will certainly have to retreat, for we have not our breastworks finished. This is a fine night for sleeping and I expect to take advantage of it.

July 10, Wednesday

JHC: A very fine morning. Heard the drums beating in every direction early this morning and thought the Yankees were coming, but found it was for reveille just at daylight. Had my hair trimmed this morning by 'Squire Griggs and had a small portion of my ear clipped off. On guard again this morning and free from the hard work on the breastworks. Squire Griggs is our Corporal today. Have always been fortunate in getting on the first or second relief. I say fortunate, for I am then off guard at meal times. Saw Co^l Seymour today for the first time. His regiment of Louisianians is in our brigade. I made note several days ago of the death of two members of the regiment. I am glad to correct the error, as Mr. Lee of the Pickensville Blues is not dead. Another of the Warrior Guards is about to die. I went in to see him today, and found him very low indeed with congestion. His face, neck and chest being almost black. Men have died in every Company in the regiment excepting ours. We have been very fortunate so far. We however have some very sick men. Mr. Bulger has been very sick at Culpepper Court House with Typhoid fever. We hear that he is improving. I hope we will not have a death in our Company during the whole campaign, but this we cannot expect. Another very heavy rain this afternoon and to night it still continues, and what is worse I have to stand guard in it.

July 11, Thursday

JHC: Am not well this morning. Have an acid stomach from eating too much supper last night. Last night was very dark indeed, a fine night for the enemy to approach our camp, for the woods being wet one could slip up very near a sentinel without making much noise. Then the rain drops falling from the trees made a noise which would have concealed the noise of footsteps. No one however came near my post. Dark and lonely were the moments I passed. Every one in Camp quiet and asleep sheltered from the rain. The sentinel alone was exposed as he walked his line with watchful eye, regardless of the pelting storm. The Gentleman belonging to the Warrior Guards died this morning between three and four o'clock, a Mr Liverman, quite a young man, and said to be a quiet and good soldier. He was buried today at eleven o'clock by the Warrior Guards and our Company. Had quite a time cleaning up my gun this morning, which rusted considerably last night. Had a little excitement in Camp this afternoon, in consequence of a little fight betweeen Seve our cook and another negro. Neither were hurt as I stopped them as soon as I saw them. We have just received orders to prepare three days rations, as we may have to move at any moment. The enemy advanced three miles yesterday to Chestnut Hill. The camp as usual on such occasions is in a state of bustle and confusion. The sick are being removed and the well are preparing their rations and packing their knapsacks. All our boys are anxious for an encounter with the enemy. Another rain this evening. Sam Dorroh and Alonzo Chapman are to go back with the sick as they have not yet entirely recovered from the measles. Thos Moore is also going back. The excitement still continues as news is being brought in every few minutes. Co^l Seibles (6th Ala) was here this evening as was also Genl Ewell. Our boys are in better spirits this evening than I have seen them for some time. They are in for fighting[.] Ours is the liveliest company in the regiment, always in for fun. Wall a member of our company who was left on the road sick arrived this evening and brings us the painful intelligence that Bulger is beyond recovery. Miller is also very low with Brain fever. We have orders to hold ourselves in readiness to move at a moments warning.

July 12, Friday

JHC: Father arrived this morning about 12 o'clock from Richmond. The drums beat the reveille this morning before day light, which caused every one to think it was the long roll, and such jumping, pitching tumbling and shuffling was never seen. Some got on pants of others a foot too short, others ran out without coats, and a good tale is told on Bob Jeffries, who it is said tried to put on Gilliam James pants for a coat. Bob however denies it. We confidently anticipate an attack very soon, and we are all ready at any time the "blue bellies" may come. Our wagons are standing in the encampment ready for the baggage. Father states the Bulger is improving some, but that Miller is very sick. The boys are all in great glee today, I suppose on account of our pay having come, but more particularly on account of some whiskey Father brought with him. He gave all hands a drink just before dinner which enlivened them considerably. I have been busy all day, except when drilling, making our bills against those for whom Father bought things in Richmond, such as paper, envelopes, pens & ink &c.

The boys care for nothing else scarcely but writing and receiving letters. Went on battalion drill this afternoon and had a time of it in our old stumpy field, fell down once and came near skinning my shins a second time by running over a stump. After drill Co¹ Rodes gave us a talk in reference to what we should do in case of an attack. He says that it is beyond a doubt that the Yankees are advancing upon us, and says further, that however superior in numbers they may be, he will not retreat without a fight and advises perfect calmness and composure and a strict obedience to orders. He appears to have great confidence in his own ability and in the courage of the regiment. Brother stands guard to day and night. A scouting party was sent off this evening to make observations. We are to keep three days rations on hand all the while until further orders.

July 13, Saturday

JHC: To day two months ago we were mustered into the service of the Confederate States. It appears more like six months than two. Was surprised this morning to be awakened by a heavy shower of rain, for when we retired last night, it was a perfectly clear and beautiful night. Continues to rain lightly, and will be a disagreeable day. We have had no drills today, on account of the officers having to attend to the paying off the regiment for our two months service. The boys, of course, are all in fine spirits, having plenty money[.] The privates received thirty-nine dollars and ninety-six cents, including twenty one dollars for clothing for first six months. I never saw such an amount of paying out and collecting, a good many collecting poker debts, some have not enough to pay out, while others refuse to pay at all. Silver is as scarce as "hen's teeth". I have seen several offer a five dollar bill for four and a half in silver, and were refused. Father has been busy all day, setting up his little accounts with the boys, for paper, envelopes &c bought in Richmond for them. He swears he will never take another memorandum for a man unless it is accompanied with the money. They take a quire of paper and package of envelopes and offer a five dollar bill to be changed, which would take all the change in the country. Wrote to Mother this morning. This afternoon another cloud came up, and we were abundantly supplied with its contents. Yesterday evening a party of about fifteen men from the regiment went out scouting under the command of Cap¹ Shelley and Lieu¹ F. A. Brown. To day some of them returned, others did not. About ten o'clock this morning as they were scouting the woods, they came within an hundred yards of a battalion of Yankees drilling. When the enemy saw them, they arose, leveled their muskets and commanded the scouts to halt. They endeavored to surround them, but off went the scouts at full speed, and prevented the accomplishment of their object. They ran across a road within forty yards of the enemy, but fortunately they were not fired upon, although their guns were leveled upon them all the while. Six of our scouts have not yet come in. There were two from our Company, B. C. Adams and Rob¹ Paulding. Adams got safely, after having to do some tall running. Paulding has not yet come in and fears are entertained of his being a prisoner. He is an excellent soldier, having served a time of eight months in the Mexican War. Should he be lost the company would sustain a severe loss. It is now ten o'clock and nothing has yet been heard from him.

NOTE: Robert Paulding was indeed taken prisoner.

July 14, Sunday

JHC: Quite cool this morning, and I feel finely, having taken an excellent cold bath. Formed the acquaintance to day of Mr Thomas Willingham, son of our friend and neighbor Mr Philip Willingham, a very clever and intelligent young man. He is a member of a Texas battalion, commanded by the Hon L. T. Wigfall. Also saw Ed Ramsey, a brother of Dr Ramsey of our Company. Paulding has not yet come in, and every one has come to the conclusion that he is a prisoner in the hands of the enemy. The whole subject of conversation is concerning him. It has cast a gloom over the whole company. Every one thought a great deal of him. He is said never to have been angry in his life. I have never seen him the least displeased since he has been in the Company. Always in fine spirits and every one loved to hear him laugh. About nine o'clock this morning, Slaughter one of Capt Shelley's men who was out on the scout came in and quite sick. He was sick at the time he ran from the Yankees, but evaded them and remained at a house last night on the road side. He reports that he heard firing soon after he got out of sight of the Yankees. None of the others heard them. He did not see Paulding at all. One of Capt Fowler's men is still out, Fiquet by name, also one of the Pickensville Blues by the name of Walker. The guide has not yet made his appearance, and the impression is that all four were taken prisoners, and what their fate is or will be we know not. We hope we may yet see them safely in camp and hear them tell of their escape from the clutches of Lincolns mercenaries. Only one of the men suspect the fidelity of the guide, all the others appearing to have perfect confidence in him, as he advised them to be careful or they would be surrounded. Another disagreeable day we had rain three times to day, and as Squire Griggs says they were all whales. Genl Ewell was here this evening and reviewed us on dress parade. He did not look very neat as I think he had on a dirty shirt.

JHC: Another song, written while on picket guard within four miles of the enemy's camp. Air Rob Ridley—

Oh! a Southern boy only wants his right,
    But the Yankees say we've got to fight
And will meet us with without compunction
    Just down here near Manassas Junction.

But just there we'll show them the sight,
    How Southern boys are trained to fight,

We'll scatter Old Abe's men to the wind,
  And make him his proclamation rescind.

Beauregard knew we wanted fun,
  So he marched us up to Bull Run,
But soon he found it would'nt do
  And then to Fairfax marched us through.

We started at seven with all our might,
  And marched the whole of Saturday night,
At Farrs Cross Roads as day was dawning
  We found ourselves last Sunday morning.

Though tired, sleepy, our strength well spent,
  Each man went-in and pitched his tent,
We then lay down and took a nap,
  Until the drum for dress parade did tap.

So we took our places on the color line,
  With faces washed and feeling fine,
After that we took our tea,
  And the way we slept, *O! Lordy*

On Monday came the bitter pill
  Of going through our accustomed drill,
The ground being broken and very rough,
  Our drilling duties are very tough.

The boys of Company "I" are "some,"
  And take their hardships as mere fun.
With Hobson in the lead and Dedman all right
  We'll show them that the Greensboro boys can fight.

July 15, Monday

JHC: A very pretty morning and quite cool. Father is unwell again this morning, having another attack in his feet. We all had quite a laugh last night at some of Squire Grigg's anecdotes. He told us of one concerning his father who once had a hat stolen from him. He went bare headed for six months, for he said his hat would have served that length of time. Went to church and every where else always bare head. Have cleaned and greased my gun, and now have it in fine order. Can look in the muzzle and see the bottom of the barrel. A gun is considered pretty clean when the bottom of the barrel can be seen, and very few have their guns in such condition in the regiment. This afternoon a company of cavalry was attached to our regiment. We now have a fine regiment and had we only a battery, we could whip any regiment the Yankees could bring against us. We were informed today, that a man had seen the guide who was with our scouts and that the Yankees had him and two others prisoners. We do not know which two they are, as three are missing. We hope the one still out may prove to be our friend and comrade Paulding. The Baltimore Sun, formerly a good democratic newspaper, and one of the best published in the South, has been frightened into the service of Lincoln, and comes down "hot and heavy" on the Rebels. Its last weeks issue contains a very graphic description of our camp, its strength, the fortifications &c. Gives the name of our Colonel, and states that he is a man of great military skill considering that he is a southern man. They think that we are strongly fortified and will be difficult to handle. They have a singular opinion of our leaders. They know that we will fight, but think we fight from courage alone and not skill. On dress parade this evening we did miserably. Could not march properly, nor could the officers understand the commands. Father is quite unwell this evening, so much so that he can scarcely place his feet to the ground. Have just had a good laugh at J. W. W. telling us of his courtship, his "popping the question", being discarded and laughed at. Says he turned his face from her, and popped the buggy wheel with his whip for about two hours. Says he was never so badly plagued in his life.

   NOTE: "J. W. W." is Jonathan W. Williams or Jno. W. Wynne.

July 16, Tuesday

   JHC: Father improving some. Slept in Lieut Dedman's tent last night to avoid hurting his feet, it being so crowded in our tent. A proposition was made last night by the Capt to use the twenty one dollars given us to get us a new uniform. They kept talking and arguing about it until I got sleepy and went to bed, leaving them to settle it the best they could. Do not think they came to any conclusion. On guard again today. Have a good post on the second relief, guarding the commissary tent, where should it rain I would be sheltered, and if hungry could eat, as there are twenty five barrels of crackers, and several hogsheads of sugar. Provisions Capt Webb tells us are getting scarce and we will have to take good care of all we get. Lieu^t Williams is officer of the guard today. There are some of the greatest fools in this regiment I ever saw, perfect green horns. It is amusing to hear them talk. Did not know Alabama supported such. Lieu^t Williams and myself have enjoyed ourselves finely laughing at their [. . .] A gentleman from Culpepper C.H. brought the painful intelligence of the death of our comrade in arms Bulger. He died Monday morning after a protracted illness of Typhoid fever. He is the only man we have lost since we have been in the army. He was a good soldier, and respected by all who knew him. To night between ten and twelve o'clock Couriers came in to Co^l Rodes, bringing orders from Beauregard to have every thing in readiness for an attack from the enemy, as they have flanked and gotten below us with a large force. Every thing for awhile was in a perfect stir, packing knapsacks and preparing rations. Every one got himself ready, and slept upon his arms. The guard has to remain awake all night. Went the "grand rounds" tonight with Capt Fowler, and came very near being shot by one of the sentinels. We walked up within ten feet of him before he saw us. When he did see us, he wheeled around and was the worst frightened man I ever saw. He cocked and brought his gun down and would have fired, had not Capt Fowler spoken as quickly as he did. I do not think the fellow will get over his fright in several days.

NOTE: "Captain Webb" is J. D. Webb Sr.

July 17, Wednesday

JHC: After all the hustle and stir last night, no yankees came, but on the contrary every thing went on as quietly as ever, and I believe more so, for every one kept as still as possible, listening for the expected attack. This morning we heard firing out toward the pickets and all around the country. About eight o'clock a couple of scouts came in at full speed, one having a yankee behind him captured by the pickets. The regiment was immediately put in order of battle and marched down to the breastwork. Tents were struck and the wagons loaded. Father who was unable to walk, mounted a wagon horse and went off with the baggage. Where we got to the breastworks Capt Shelley's Company was sent out as skirmishers, and soon we heard them open fire upon the enemy. The firing was kept up for about an hour. The balls whistling over our heads, I have often heard of balls whistling around a fellows head, but never knew what tune they played until this morning. They came thick and fast, some falling within a few feet of us. The pickets were driven in, but they came in orderly, displaying great coolness and bravery. They fired each three or four rounds. We remained at the breastworks about an hour and a half. The pickets killed some ten or fifteen of the enemy. We had only two men wounded, they very slightly. One a member of the Warrior Guards (Tarrant) shot through the leg. The other of Capt Shelley's company, having a portion of his ear shot away. They came upon us with a large force and tried to flank us, and would have succeeded had we not received orders from the commanding general to retreat. I think Co^l Rodes intended to give them a fight, but had to obey the orders to retreat. We left our breastworks with great reluctance, for there was all our work to be abandoned to the enemy without a fight. The pickets from our company who were attacked were Jim Locke, Wm Kennedy, George Nutting, John & Joe Wright. They all got safely into Camp. We left the breastworks and marched slowly and in order down the Centreville road. The day was intensely warm, but we had to march ahead to avoid being flanked, as the enemy were pressing forward with great rapidity. We marched eleven miles to Bull Run, where we met two Mississippi regiments, one South Carolina regiment and the Washington Artillery. Here I found Father, who was much rejoiced to see us safe and well. A good many broke down on the march. Brother broke down, but managed to get a ride behind some one and came on safely. I think one could have followed up our retreat and gathered at least two wagon loads of clothing, knapsacks &c, which the boys had thrown away. A good many have now no clothing at all, not even a blanket. We only remained at Bull Run about two hours, when we took up our line of march to a place called Union Mills, a distance of three miles. We arrived there shortly after sunset, stacked arms, made fires, and dried our selves, as we had to ford creeks on the march. Feel like I can do some sleeping tonight, as I did not have an opportunity last night.

NOTE: The Guards were engaged in skirmishes at Fairfax Court House. Reading in the Washington morning papers that Northern troops were advancing, General Beauregard reinforced his line at Bull Run. Davis moved his force from the Shenandoah Valley to Manassas, avoiding General Patterson's force sent to block him.

July 18, Thursday

JHC: Arose early this morning and broiled a piece of meat on the coals for breakfast. After eating, we were marched off about a half mile to a bridge across Bull Run where we were stationed along the banks of the creek and on the railroad. We had been here but a short time, when we heard the booming of artillery, in the direction from which we came yesterday. The firing was kept up all day, ceasing three times only for a few minutes. When we heard the connonading and occasional volleys of musketry, our company was placed in the bushes to watch for the approach of the enemy. We remained there all day. This afternoon Lieut Williams, who was left behind yesterday, came in and reported a great battle fought about three quarters of a mile from where we first went yesterday at a place called Mitchells Ford. The enemy eighteen thousand strong attacked our forces four thousand strong. The attack was made with both artillery and infantry. Our forces had the Washington Artillery from New Orleans. They first attacked the centre and endeavored to take our battery, but were repulsed with heavy loss. They then attacked the right wing, but were again repulsed. After this they collected themselves and made another attack on the left and were for the third time repulsed with even greater slaughter than before. They then retired from the field. When they attempted to storm the battery, they were allowed to march up to within a short distance of it when our infantry rose up and turned loose a volley into them which completely routed them. They ran in the utmost confusion. After going some distance they rallied, when Gen¹ Bonham gave the order to charge them, but before our troops could get near them they broke and ran like sheep before wolves. Report says that we lost sixteen killed and forty of fifty wounded. Their loss is estimated at from five hundred to a thousand killed and wounded. The Yankees made a bold stand for awhile, but could not contend against southern bayonets and the Washington Artillery. Received two letters today, one from Brother, the other from Aunt Ann. (Mrs. Cheney) All well at home and the crop good. He says there is [not?] a danger of Lincoln starving us out. To night we have every indication of a heavy rain, as we can hear the distant rumbling of the thunder and the clouds are flying overhead. We have to sleep in the bushes and but few of the men have blankets. Father sent me a blanket, but I could not find the man he sent it by, so have to do the best I can and take the rain if it comes.

NOTE: Cowin is describing the engagement at Blackburn's Ford and skirmishing at Mitchell's Ford.

July 19, Friday

JHC: Fortunately for us we had not much rain last night. Slept very soundly, three of us under one blanket. The trees kept off the heavy dew. Four or five of the boys came in this morning. They broke down on the road and were left behind. Brother came back from the Junction, where he went yesterday of account of being sick. He states that Father is very unwell, not being able to walk at all. He was quite uneasy all day yesterday as he thought we were in the fight. The enemy sent over a flag of truce this morning asking permission to bury their dead. They say that they lost fifteen hundred men. The correct list is however hard to get at. Our loss is thought to be between fifteen and thirty killed and forty or fifty wounded. Have not heard a gun today. The bearer of the flag of truce states that they had retired to Centreville and are throwing up breastworks, thinking that we are pursuing them. We are again placed in the bushes to prevent the enemy from crossing to our side of the creek. We have orders to charge them should they attempt a crossing. Co^l Rodes says he wants to give the Greensboro boys a chance at the enemy the first opportunity and he thinks this the best way to do it. The glorious news of the repulse of Patterson by Johns[t]on came in this afternoon. It is said that he has driven him beyond the Potomac, which we hope may be true. Whether it be true or not Johns[t]on has sent Beauregard four thousand men to reinforce this line. An attack is expected and all the sick have been removed from the Junction; Among those sent by Johns[t]on to Beauregard is Co^l Syd Moore's regiment. The Yankees have made no advance today. Guess they do not like southern balls and bayonets. At Winchester where the engagement took place between Johns[t]on and Patterson, Johns[t]on found he could not dislodge the enemy from their works, he gave the order to storm them. The South Carolina boys pitched in and ran over their works in short order, completely routing them, capturing their artillery and ammunition and fifty prisoners, who arrived at the Junction yesterday. Our provisions got pretty short today, but fortunately some were sent down to us, and we pitched in like a pack of hungry wolves. We have nothing but hard crackers and fat meat. Our cooking utensils consist of sticks sharpened at one end, upon which we put our meat and hold to the fire until done. It eats firstrate too especially when a fellow is hungry. We sleep again tonight under the trees and bushes.

NOTE: The "Junction" is Manassas Junction.

July 20, Saturday

JHC: Slept finely last night although it rained, of which however I was not aware until this morning. Brother was on guard last night and this morning is a little unwell. Hard at work this morning throwing up breastworks along the creek bank[.] Expecting an attack all the while and we are preparing for it. We do not expect to leave here without a fight. We have orders from Gen[l] Beauregard to prevent a crossing of the enemy at all and every hazard. He says our stand at Farrs Cross Roads was worth seventy five thousand dollars to our side, for it was a perfect ruse, the enemy thinking we had nothing to fall back upon, and was the cause of our victory. The weather is quite warm today, but we get along very well with our work, as we are divided into platoons and work alternately, so that it is comparatively easy upon us. We finished as we thought, about dinner time, and a good work it is, certainly bullet proof, as we have rock and railroad iron in it, we are now ready for the enemy. After finishing work we fell afoul of our fat meat and crackers and eat as none but hungry men do. Did not enjoy my dinner as much as I wished to, for some thief stole my tin cup, after I had strapped it nicely to my canteen and thought it all safe. I am sorry to know that there are rogues in our regiment. After dinner the boys all stretched themselves out upon the ground for a nap, but soon we heard them calling out for the men to fall in to go to work again. Some were already asleep and when the order came, they got lazily up rubbing their eyes and cursing the yankees and their luck. There is no use swearing about work for we have it to do, and the sooner we do it the better for us. We worked till night and made the works doubly as strong as they were before dinner. Do not think the Yankees could shoot a cannon ball through them now. The Yankees have been burying their dead all day. Nine hundred and fifty of them are missing, and a large number wounded. There are however so many reports in circulation, that it is hard to get at the truth of any thing. It is now reported that we will have to advance upon the enemy tomorrow. How true it is no one knows but the officers. I do not mean our officers, for they do not know any more than the privates, some of them not so much. Cap[t] Hobson is unwell today, and has been lying under the shade of a tree all day. It is amusing to see us cooking our meals down here on the creek, we however enjoy it as well as if we were in camp.

July 21, Sunday

JHC: Slept cold last night as I had only a single blanket whi[ch] was too small to sleep upon and cover with at the same time, besides the night was colder than usual. Arose quite early this morning and found we had orders to prepare to take up our line of march. We got breakfast as soon as possible, which occupied but little time as we had only to stick a little piece of meat on a stick, hold it over the fire a minute or two and breakfast was ready. Soon after eating we began to hear the booming of cannon, apparently about two or three miles off, which still continues it now being about 12 o'clock. There seems to be fighting at two points, on the extreme left and centre. We soon got ready and the regiment crossed the creek. We crossed and recrossed several times before we got upon the regular march. We however got straight after a while and had a forced march of eleven miles to the battle field. It was indeed a battle and a bloody one. We passed ~~on~~ in sight of one place where they were fighting but did not stop, as we were going to the assistance of the 4th Ala Reg[t], which we heard was being terribly cut up. On the march we met many wounded returning from the field. We marched on to avenge the blood of those who had fought so gallantly. We witnessed sights we had never seen before. The horrors of a battle field. As we marched in sight the cowardly villains were retreating, we could see their guns glittering among the bushes as they moved off. We heard that the 4th Ala was surrounded at one time by the overwhelming forces of the enemy, and cut up terribly. General Bee was badly wounded. Heard that Co[l] Jones was killed, Lieut Co[l] Law and Major Scott badly wounded. Syd May was in the fight but came off unhurt. It is said that the enemy came up with a Confederate flag, and our men thinking they were friends did not fire upon them, but as soon as they got within an hundred and fifty yards of our troops, turned loose both artillery and musketry, mowing them down like grass before a scythe. It was the bloodiest battle ever fought on the continent. We lost a great many in killed and wounded. Their loss was tremendous. The enemy were completely routed, losing fifty pieces of artillery, ten thousand stands of arms and a great many prisoners. The Virginians did excellent fighting. They charged their famous Shermans battery. The Cavalry pursued the enemy under the command of President Davis in person. The number of killed cannot yet be accurately ascertained. Both sides lost heavily. It is said that the enemy lost at the lowest calculation between four and five thousand in killed and wounded. To night we have orders to march back to our bivouack. Squire Griggs[,] Joe Grigg, and myself came to Manassas Junction to see Father, who is here with the baggage. We found him well, but very uneasy as he was confident that we were in the fight.

NOTE: General Ewell began marching his brigade, which included the Fifth Alabama, to the north side of Bull Run near the Stone Bridge, but the order was countermanded. They passed within sight of the Fourth Alabama, whose commander, General Barnard Bee, that day gave Thomas J. Jackson his nickname: Stonewall. They finally arrived back at camp about ten that evening, having marched twenty miles. Meanwhile the Federal forces were driven back in disarray. President Davis did not lead the cavalry but did arrive at the battlefield late in the day.

July 22, Monday

JHC: Arose this morning very tired and sore, scarcely able to walk at first but after breakfast felt better and walked around to see what was to be seen after yesterdays fight. I was witness to some awful scenes. Saw the wounded, shot in every portion of the body, head, neck, body, arms, hands, legs & feet. Some with their limbs taken completely off. Some have died since being brought here, others dying. Wherever I walked the same spectacle presented itself. Among them all I heard not a word of complaint and scarcely a groan. From what can be ascertained we lost in killed and wounded between fifteen hundred and two thousand. Went around to a large pen of prisoners. There were four or five hundred in the pen

I saw, and nearly all of them the lowest class of foreigners. This afternoon, a portion of the cavalry brought in seventy five more of the wretches. They were all marched off to the cars and sent to Richmond. As one squad of thirty passed our tent to the cars one fellow spoke to us, saying "Good bye boys I left home to go to Richmond and by ————I am going.["] We learn to day that the 4th Ala Reg[t] was not so badly cut up as was supposed. There have not been more than forty or fifty killed. Co[l] Jones was not killed, but shot through both legs. Gen[l] Bee died this morning. The Cavalry captured a large amount of baggage, ammunition &c. We got one very large gun from them which they familiarly called "Long Tom". We got also a very fine ambulance, in which the medical staff were conveyed about. They had every thing complete. I suppose it was the best equipped army that ever started on a campaign. Old Scott is a great fellow for having everything ready before he makes a move. The small arms captured were the finest minnie muskets, which will be of great service to the army, as we are in need of more arms. It has rained all day without ceasing, making it very disagreeable here, especially for those who have no tents, and a great many here have none. The tents of the 4th Ala were left at Winchester. Capts Porter King and Balls sleep with us tonight, making ten or twelve in the tent, but we can sleep very well, as we are not very particular how we sleep.

    NOTE: Modern estimates put Union losses at 481 killed, 1,011 wounded, and 1,216 missing; and Confederate losses at 387 killed, 1,582 wounded, and 12 missing.

    "Old Scott" is Winfield Scott.

July 23, Tuesday

    JHC: Clear and cool this morning. After breakfast got ready to take a tramp down to Union Mills, four miles, where the regiment is still stationed. So we left the sickening scenes of Manassas for our quiet and shady retreat. We found all the boys in good spirits, though they all got wet yesterday. We are all squatted down in groups under the trees and bushes along the creek bank and behind our breastworks. All around us are hills of the highest kind, in fact mountains. Our place of bivouack is in rather a damp place. When we got here we found the boys preparing to leave. We heard before we got here that Co[l] Rodes had sent after us, but such was not the case, we however thought so, and came all the way in quick time. Some of the men of the brigade began shooting off their guns, this morning, and our officers thought the Yankee's were upon us, so had us in the works in double quick time. There are some officers in our regiment who have not the common sense of a regular corn field negro. They know nothing of military affairs and I do not think they will ever learn. I get so mad some times that when I hear them try to command, that I almost wish myself out of the regiment, but I suppose it is the same case in every other regiment. We took our stand behind the breastwork for about an hour, then had to be marched out and halted in the hot sun on the railroad for about two hours more. We then took up our line of march for a camping ground about three quarters of a mile and in an elegant place. The brigade can check double its number of the enemy here, though I do not think we will ever have an opportunity to try it here, for I hear the Yankees did not stop running from Manassas until they got to Washington City. They ran through Alexandria without stopping, although the troops there were made to fire upon them to stop their flight, but it did no good, they kept on. I do not know whether they have stopped yet or not. We have four pieces of artillery with us, a portion of the celebrated Washington Artillery of New Orleans. Major Morgan informed me this morning that we had taken John Cochrane of New York, who with several other Congressmen had come down to see the "Rebels" whipped into subjection, by their "Grand Union Army". The others could not be caught as it is said they ran like deer through the woods. Even the Cavalry could not catch them, although they went at full speed and on good horses. The Cavalry made sad havoc with the retreating Yankees.

July 24, Wednesday

JHC: All our baggage and servants came last night, but too late to pitch tents. Some of the boys had to sleep out on the ground. I was fortunate enough to get a tent to sleep in, and it was quite cool before morning. This morning began our usual drills. Rodes I think has the drill-mania, for I think he had rather drill than eat a good dinner. I suppose however it is to our advantage. The boys grumble considerably. I suppose he intends us for regulars, and treats every one alike, and that is very cool. I understand that two of the Captains have handed in their resignations. They did not like such treatment as they get. Some of the captains would no more think of doing such a thing than attempt to fly. They are afraid of Rodes. The company is now in need of a uniform, but I do not know when we will get it. We do a great deal of talking, but little acting. Father came into camp this morning looking very well, his feet having gotten nearly well. Our baggage we found in a scattered condition, some entirely gone, father not being able to attend to it, on account of his feet. One of our tent poles we found missing, so 'Squire Griggs and myself went to work to make another. We got all our things together, pitched our tent and every thing looks like old times. Co¹ Rodes had us trotting around on battalion drill, this evening. Our drill ground is very small and hilly, but it makes little difference with Co¹ Rodes for I think he can drill a regiment on a piece of ground, that would puzzle many to drill a company. He seems to have "turned over a new leaf," as he says he intends to deal more strictly than ever. Oh! who would'nt be a soldier.

July 25, Thursday

JHC: Slept finely last night, as we had our tent fixed up better than we ever had it. Quite cool this morning. We have now come regularly down to our work, nearly all our cooking utensils were left at Farrs Cross Roads, and there are two or three messes actually cooking upon a spade. We have nothing now to eat but hard crackers and salt meat. My tongue and gums are very sore, and Father can scarcely eat at all. He has to use a solution of Chlorate Potash for his gums.

There is no flour at all at Manassas, so we have to use the crackers altogether, and they are hard almost as a rock. We got a Washington paper today, which corroborates the statement that the Yankees did actually run through Alexandria to Washington and that the regulars mistaking them for our men fired into them, quite a singular mistake, unless they thought we had killed and captured their entire army. The paper estimates their loss at six thousand, and acknowledges a complete rout. Co^l Syd Moore 11$^{\underline{th}}$ Ala Reg^t, was here to day, and looking well. His regiment is encamped on Bull Run, without tents and from all accounts, we will have no more after we leave here. Co^l Rodes received an order from the President or some one, cutting us down to one wagon to an hundred men. It is thought that we will march upon Alexandria soon. Two of our men brought in a couple of the Virginia militia, who had deserted from Manassas. There are a great many of them unwilling to take up arms against the United States, and desert every opportunity. They ought to be tried and hung. Had the hardest drill this evening we have had in some time. An order was read out this evening that we were to have but two drills daily, but when the officers went up to salute, Co^l Rodes told them that the usual drills would continue. To-night we had a first-rate supper, as we stumbled upon a piece of mutton and some corn meal, we soon made way with it. The boys are running all over the country hunting something to eat. They go sometimes four or five miles. We are all in a bad fix for something to eat.

July 26, Friday

JHC: Our fare has improved considerably, but at our own expense. Seve (our cook) went out yesterday evening and made the raise of a couple of chickens and an old gander, so that we had chicken for breakfast, to which we did full justice. Our gums all feel much better since having mutton yesterday and chicken this morning. Father and Brother are both unwell this morning, the latter quite so. A good many of the boys are on the sick list, though none of them seriously ill, drilling too hard. Co^l Rodes has issued an order to all the Orderly Sergeants to report to him in person all the absentees from drill, beginning with the officers. He seems to think that there are not so many sick as are absent. Tighter and tighter on us every day. The day has been intensely warm, and we had hot work drilling over the rocks and gullies. Battalion drill this evening awful and made doubly so to me, by my hurting myself. We were going at double quick, when I stepped upon a very rough rock, bruising my foot badly. My shoes being worn out, the rock had fair play. I am now nearly barefoot, and the next march will put me entirely so. Have however sent to Richmond for a pair of shoes, but know not when I will get them. I dislike very much to lie up in camp, while there are so many absent. I have not failed to answer to my name, at roll call since we left Richmond, and I was in hopes that I would never be absent at all. I may however be able to drill tomorrow

July 27, Saturday

JHC: Did not sleep very well last night, as I had to sleep with my head down hill, our encampment being on the side of a hill, besides our old gander which was tied near my head, kept up a noise nearly all night, and to cap all when the gander would cease Squire Griggs kept up an awful snoring, and upon the whole I had a rough night of it. This morning my foot was worse than yesterday, and I was compelled to report myself to the Surgeon to be excused from drill. Co^l Rodes had about forty men put under arrest to day, for being absent from duty yesterday. Some gave excuses and were released, others had not sufficient excuses to give and were kept in all day. This evening he sent word to them, that if they would not be guilty again he would excuse them. Some promised and went out, others and mostly from our Company sent him word that they would see him at the devil before they would promise him any thing. Whether he received the message in these words I know not, but certain it is, they are still under guard. Had but one drill today, that battalion drill this morning, which we never had before in the forenoon. Do not know what he means by it, and care but little, so he continues it. Have been in my tent all day reading newspapers, and got hold of a novel, the first I have read in a long time. Read the New York Tribune, and was much amused at its lies, about the war, what they have done, are doing and intend to do. Poor deluded devils they know not what they are doing. It was reported to Genl Ewell to night by Co^l Hunter that Genl Scott was dead. How true that statement may prove, remains to be seen, we can rely on nothing. If this news be true, it will be hailed with joy throughout the entire South. It is appears singular that the death of a man should be hailed with joy instead of grief by a nation too as civilized and chivalrous, but when we consider the man, an old and Southern born soldier, fighting against his mother state, and against those who led him triumphantly through Mexico, and placed him in the position he now occupies, and he fighting too with such fierceness, no sympathy could or will be extended. He has proven himself a traitor of the meanest stamp. His name will be a byword for the millions, and his former deeds of valor be doomed to the dark waves of oblivion. Even the North will call him a traitor, while the South will rejoice in his death. His name and fame will soon pass away and be numbered only among the things that were. So much for a report.

NOTE: Winfield Scott did not die until 1866.

July 28, Sunday

JHC: Reported myself well this morning and ready for duty. Company inspection, of arms and accountrements, which amounts to nothing, as very little attention is given to it. On general inspection it is not so, for Co^l Rodes inspects in person and is very particular about every thing, never passes over any thing and is always sure to reprimand a fellow, whenever there is any thing amiss. Some of the men still remain in the guard house still refusing to promise anything. Rodes told them this morning that they would tire of it before they got through.

Everything is very quiet in camp today. The heat is very oppressive and every one is in quarters lounging about, some reading, others writing while others still are playing cards. I have been reading a novel, Margaret Moncrieffe or the first love of Aaron Burr. Sunday is very little respected in Camp. There are a few who read the bible, but not because they are interested in its teachings or expected to profit by them, but for the simple reason that they promised the "folks at home" they would read it, and they are desirous of fulfilling the promise. Have heard no more news of the death of Old Scott and believe it all a hoax. A portion of our brigade left this morning, but know not its destination. It is reported that troops from the same state will be formed into brigades. The one which left was the 6th La Co^l Seymour. I am sorry it left on account of its fine music, as it had an excellent band. Syd and William May came over to see us this evening[.] Their regiment (4th Ala) is encamped near Co^l Moore's on the battle field. Will says he has a furlough to go home. He has an old Mare, which he says a fellow got off the battle field and gave him. Both will remain here tonight and are now sitting here in my tent telling some long yarns about their adventures up about Winchester & Martinsburg. It is very amusing to listen to them.

NOTE: Charles Burdett, *Margaret Moncrieffe, The First Love of Aaron Burr: A Romance of the Revolution* (New York: Derby and Jackson, 1860).

July 29, Monday

JHC: Father and Jack Wynne were both quite unwell last night, and slept but little. They are this morning better[.] There are a great many in the regiment sick, at least four hundred. We make but a poor turn out at this time. Four or five ~~boys~~ men from our Company have been discharged from the service on account of their health. They are Chas T. Briggs, James Lister, John Wheeler, J. W. Miller, & L. P. Wall. Father had an idea of applying for a discharge but Co^l Rodes told him he would prefer him to remain with the regiment, and that he would require no duty from him. He will send for a horse soon if he consents to remain. Co^l Rodes has discovered that he was in disfavor with the regiment or at least a portion of it. He is under the impression that our company is prejudiced against him. He did not drill the regiment today. L^{t}Co^l Jones drilled us this morning and Major Morgan this evening. The Major drills very well for a new hand, he never having drilled us before. Met with an old schoolmate today. Wm Fulton of Sumter Co. Ala. a member of Capt Vandegraf's company stationed at Manassas. Syd & Will May left this morning. The death of old Scott is all a humbug and we are sorry for it. Father received a letter from Aunt Ann today, stating that she had sent us a box of provisions. This evening the box came and with it a profusion of every "good thing". Hams, eggs, butter, preserves, biscuit, light bread and two bottles of good whiskey. We will now live elegantly for awhile and ask the Confederacy for nothing but to allow us to remain here until we get through with them.

NOTE: "James Lister" is James Lester.
"J. W. Miller" is William D. Miller.

July 30, Tuesday

JHC: Another hot day, intensely so on drill. It appears that Co^l Rodes has quit drilling us, as he was not out today. I suppose though he wishes the L^{t}Co^l & Major to learn. W. J. McDonald 3^d Ser^t applied for and received a discharge from the service. He has an affliction of the Lungs. He left this morning for Lynchburg, Va. where he will remain until he is able to go home. Genl Kerr and Lady arrived here this morning. The Genl is direct from Greensboro, bringing us letters and packages from home. I received one from Chas Whelan Jr stating that the crops are fine, the health of the country good, and the young ladies anxious for the return of the soldiers. Received several letters from Greensboro, but none directly from home. I learn that Robt Chadwick was married to Miss Mary Willingham on the 24$^{\underline{th}}$ ins^t. May peace, prosperity, and happiness attend them through life. A little excitement was raised in camp today, caused by two young fellows bunging each others eyes a little. Father was at the Junction today, and says he never saw so much plunder, as was taken from the Yankees. We captured more guns, than we started the campaign with. Says there is a little of everything. It was the best equipped army that ever started out. The boys have gotten a great many things from the battle field, such as canteens, haversacks &c. They have better ones than we. Their canteens are made of blacktin which keep the water cool longer than the common tin. Spent the afternoon writing letters and then trying to sleep, but the flies would not allow any such thing, and lastly though by no means least of the evenings work—drilling, as this last formed the larger part of the programme.

July 31, Wednesday

JHC: Messrs Paulding and Coleman from Union Town Ala arrived here last night. The former father of Robt Paulding who, was taken prisoner from our company, and the latter of A. G. Coleman. Felt quite unwell this morning, I suppose from eating too much last night. We have now so many "good things" that I eat too much. I however did not lie up, but went on with my duties and soon felt well. This has been decidedly the warmest day we have had. One could scarcely leave his tent, and in the tent was like an oven. We are fortunate enough to have Major Morgan to drill us. He rests us oftener than Co^l Rodes, and he drills very well. The men appearing to try to do better for him, as he does not break us down. When a man gets tired he becomes careless. Nothing very exciting or interesting has occurred today. Squire Griggs has been hard at work all the afternoon, leveling the tent floor, our heads having been before lower than our feet. Wrote a letter for Father this afternoon to Mr Tallman, Father being indisposed. Rained slightly this evening, just enough to break up battalion drill. After dress parade Major Morgan read us an address from Gen^{ls} Johns[t]on & Beauregard congratulating the soldiers on their success in repulsing the Yankees. The adjutant informed us that a couple wagon loads of handcuffs were taken from the enemy. A call was made upon all who had any, to deliver them up, as they wished to get them together, for what purpose I do not know. We feel of course under many obligations to the Yankees, for their bracelets, but as we are not fond of show we must decline wearing them, and if we can ever meet them, will return them and escort them to Richmond, where we have spacious apartments prepared for them. I should not be surprised if we had another visit soon, for Old Scott says he will draft every man north between the ages of twenty one and forty five years of age. I understand that eighteen thousand of Pattersons men have gone home, refusing to serve longer as their turn of service has expired. An appeal was made to them, but they heeded it not but struck a dog-trot for home.

NOTE: Robert Paulding was captured July 12.

August 1, Thursday

JHC: Rained pretty much all day, and if the old saying holds good, that "if it begins raining on the first of August it will rain forty days", we will certainly have a hard time of it. We have had a disagreeable day of it, having to stay in tent all day. I however amused my-self reading and writing. Received several letters from home, all well and the crops good. One of the letters was for Seve from his wife, answered. A change has been made in the Post Office department for the benefit of the soldiers. We can send our letters without prepaying by putting our name, regiment and company on the envelope, and those to whom the letters are addressed pay for them before delivery. None can send us a letter without prepayment. It is an excellent arrangement for the soldier, for it is very difficult to get silver. We have plenty money in notes but we cannot get the stamps for the notes. There has been no drilling at all today, only dress-parade this evening. No war news today. Heard the firing of cannon this morning in the direction of Falls Church. Know not the cause of it, unless we are capturing some more hand cuffs. Sent to Richmond a few days ago for a pair of shoes, by a Lieutenant in the regiment. Today they came, and no more fitted for the army than no shoes at all, low-quartered bad leather, in fact they were made for negro women for Sunday shoes. Had to take them in self defense. The time has now arrived when we begin to think of getting, or rather making some movement towards getting our winter clothing. So tonight after tattoo, it was proposed by the Captain, that we authorize Genl Kerr to go to Richmond, make a selection of goods, and have a suit made up for the company. The proposition was agreed to and a vote taken upon it, to which no one made objection except one man S.B.J. So Genl Kerr starts tomorrow morning for Richmond to see about it.

NOTE: "S.B.J." is Samuel B. Jackson.

August 2, Friday

JHC: We have one more clear weather, but awful hot. Very little air stirring making it disagreeably warm. Dr Hendon from Newbern and Mr Madison Jones from Greensboro arrived here today. They report fine crops in Ala. I understand that the C.S. Secretary of War has recommended five-hundred and sixty thousand troops in the field. Dr Hendon says that every body South wishes to come to the war, and that the road from Selma Ala to this place is crowded with soldiers coming on to the war. The whole South is aroused and intend to act as a unit. J. G. Harris of Greensboro is getting up a company for the war on our side of the river. Prof Brame is Captain of a company in Greensboro called the Dixie Guards. The ladies are giving concerts &c to raise money to buy clothing for the soldiers. There has been a concert in Greensboro by the young ladies of the Female Academy and one in Newbern. The planters about Greensboro say we shall never be in want of money, but that whenever we are in need of anything as clothing, we have only to let it be known. Hurrah! for Old Greene and the ladies. Received a letter from Aunt Ann today which was very interesting[.] Joe Grigg got a sick furlough tonight for fourteen days. Instead of going to a hospital, he will go home as his father's residence is only about thirty miles from Richmond.

NOTE: John Gideon Harris raised the Planters' Guards, Company I, Twentieth Alabama.

The Dixie Guards consisted of some thirty or forty Home Guards who desired to drill more frequently.

August 3, Saturday

JHC: Have been very unwell all day and have suffered a great deal, my digestive organs being disarranged. No better to night, and still suffering. Walton Glover of Forkland Ala arrived here last night. He came with the intention of joining the regiment. He does not know whether he will join this company vs the Warrior Guards. The Beacon came today, no news of any importance. Received a very interesting letter from Miss A.G.W. in which she expresses her sorrow at the death of Joe Grigg. I cannot tell how she ever heard such a thing. Such lying reports is a disgrace to our people. The Yankees lie enough without our pitching in too. It is reported at home that Joe Grigg & Gilliam James were killed on picket guard. Joe left here this evening for home having a furlough for 14 days. He was anxious to get home. Sam Dorroh and Alonzo Chapman came in from Culpepper Court House looking as fat and healthy as any two men I have seen in many days. They state that they have been enjoying themselves finely with the young ladies. They are done with flying around the ladies now

NOTE: "Miss A.G.W." is A. G. Willingham, nineteen-year-old governess for Thomas Hord Herndon's children.

August 4, Sunday

JHC: Feel but very little better this morning and slept but little last night. Answered Miss A.G.W.'s letter, wrote her a letter of twelve pages length. Saw several of my old acquaintances today. Steele formerly of Greensboro, a shoemaker. It is amusing to hear him talk. James Lee was also here. Dr. George Thornton from Forkland, an old friend and college mate. He came to join the regiment. I think both him and Glover will join the Warrior Guards, as there are several in that company from their immediate neighborhood. Glover is anxious to join our company, but cannot get a mess to suit him, as all the messes with whom he is acquainted are filled. A good breeze has been stirring all day, rendering it very pleasant. A good many of our boys have been visiting today. Our boys beat any for running about that I know of. They will go anywhere and at any time, just so they can get out of the sight of Co^l Rodes. This important personage returned to day from a visit to his wife, we did not know what had become of him. The first word he asked one of the boys whom he met, was if he had been drilling any since he left. Feel quite unwell tonight

August 5, Monday

JHC: Feel better this morning. Think I will be able to return to duty in a day or two, hope so at least, for there is no fun lying up here in camp all day. Moved our camp today upon a hill about two-hundred yards from the former ground. It is a more pleasant place than the former as we get every breeze that comes along, though it has been very warm up here today. Think we are here for some time, hope so any-how. Several of our boys were moved to the country today on account of sickness. J. D. Webb Jr is quite sick with Pneumonia. Lieut Dedman has the measles. There are several cases of them in the Company. Saw some Buckwheat to day growing, the first I ever saw. It resembles cotton very much. No drill today, on account of the move. Nothing important today in regard to the war, only we heard that the Yankees were fighting among themselves—a lie though.

August 6, Tuesday

JHC: Still feeling better this morning, but not able to enter upon any regular duty. We have been brought back to the first rudiments of drilling as we now have orders to drill in squads and without guns during the morning and to drill for three hours, the afternoon being devoted to battalion drill and dress-parade. Joe Grigg came back to day from the Junction, not being able to get off to any hospital, though since he has been here he has received a permit to go to one and will leave tomorrow. Father was at the Junction today and bought for the mess a set of knives and forks. All we need now is a set of tin plates. Report says that England and France will soon recognize us. No news today except that it is reported that the Yankees will bring down upon us, when they come again an hundred and fifty rifled cannon, so we will have another opportunity to get a fine lot of artillery. McClelland the Commander in Chief of the U.S. Army intends doing things on a grand scale. Rations are drawn now at the Junction for one hundred and four thousand men. It is reported that Capt Dawson, Magnolia Cadets, 4th Ala Reg^t will be tried for cowardice. Twenty new recruits came in tonight to the Cahaba Rifles.

NOTE: "McClelland" is George Brinton McClellan, who would not replace Scott as general in chief until November 1.

August 7, Wednesday

JHC: Still unwell, more so than yesterday. Getting tired lying up here in my tent. Co^l Rodes has given orders to have more drilling, so now we have company drill for an hour commencing at 8½ o'clock. Then the officers drill for an hour, then at eleven we drill again. We have gone back to our A-B-C's in drilling. It is entirely too warm to drill at eleven o'clock. The officers now complain as much of Rodes as the privates. The drill at eleven o'clock is worse than battalion drill. Do not know the object of so much drilling. In the battle the other day there was no necessity for the manual of arms nor any of the many movements we are put through. We all think Rodes is mad about something and is giving vent to his spleen upon the men. If so he is indeed a *brave* man. A member of Capt Hall's Company (A) died last night. The surgeon says his death was caused from the effects of whiskey. Dr A. H. Moore was taken suddenly very ill today, is better this evening. Joe Grigg went to the Junction today, but had to return not being able to get off. He has a hard time of it. Serg^t McDonald has not yet gone. The boys all have plenty whiskey to drink now, as Genl Kerr sent up some from Richmond. Wrote a long letter home to Mother this evening. The weather is oppressively warm, and a fellow has to stay in his tent all day, (except when drilling) and then he nearly sweats himself to death.

August 8, Thursday

JHC: Was amused this morning by the announcement that there were three letters for me. I jumped up, washed my face and pitched into the contents of the letters, one from Mother, one from brother and one from little Sallie W——, a very interesting trio of letters. All well at home. Crops good, and fruit of all kinds in abundance, watermelons, peaches, apples and pears. It almost made my mouth water to read of them. Suppose we will have fruit here soon, as I have seen some peaches nearly ripe. Have squandered the day in idleness, only answering one letter, that of brothers, which however was a long one. The cause of my idleness was indisposition. Tried to sleep, but it was so warm and the flies so bad that I did not succeed well. Another member of the regiment died today. Capt Dents Co. No war news today. Every thing very quiet in camp. Last night Capt Shelley received ten or twelve recruits. Three came to our Company. Am not personally acquainted with them, but think their names are Allen, Elliott and Wilson, from the neighborhood of Havana Ala. Rodes is putting the recruits through. Shelby Chadwick has joined our Company. Genl Kerr arrived to night, bringing a number of things for the boys, among them a pair of shoes for me.

NOTE: "Brother" is William S. ("Tood") Cowin.

"Allen" is W. H. Allen.

"Elliott" is probably William Elliott.

"Wilson" is James Ezra Wilson.

August 9, Friday

JHC: Feel pretty well this morning. Very warm indeed today, though this evening had a heavy rain. Wrote a long letter this morning to Mrs. Dorroh. Prince Napoleon was out this morning reviewing our troops with Gen^ls Johns[t]on & Beauregard. Some of our men saw him of course, for nothing is ever going the rounds without some of them know it. Do not know the object of his visit to

America at this time, unless it be to find out the true state of affairs, which it will not take him long todo. It is reported that Alexandria has been burned and evacuated by the Yankees, no credit is given to the report. No news today. All quiet in camp. No drill this evening on account of the rain. The sick are all getting better and returning to duty.

August 10, Saturday

JHC: Another very warm day indeed. The Surgeons complained to Rodes, of his drilling the men too much. They told him plainly that the weather was too warm and that if he persisted in drilling so much he would kill all his men. So he had but one drill and dress parade. Saw George Dent today, who has a transfer from the 3^d Ala to this regiment, his brother having a company in this. The 3^d is stationed at Norfolk[.] Wrote to Mother today. Beacon came, but contained but little news. Gid Harris has raised his company numbering I believe about eighty men. It goes in for the war. The Greensboro people are now fully aroused, except some few about there. Prince Napoleon has gone back to Washington City, having I suppose, visited the battle ground and seen where the "Grand Army" was routed. Jack Wynne and myself went bathing this evening, and I now feel elegant. The boys are all in fine spirits tonight, I suppose from the fact that they are not broken down by drilling. Raining a little tonight and very warm indeed.

August 11, Sunday

JHC: Did not sleep well last night, as I was taken sick during the night. Another warm day, though we had quite a refreshing shower this evening. Preaching today by the Rev Mr Porter. Did not hear the sermon, as I was unwell, but lay up in my tent all the morning reading the Beacon, which contained the speech of the Ohio Congressman Vallandigham. It was a good speech, showing forth the usurpations of power and the unconstitutional proceedings of Lincoln. We have had quite a dull day. A good many of the boys went into the country to see the sick, who are at different houses in the neighborhood. Heard cannonading this morning, but have not ascertained the cause of it. We will move from this place in a day or so, up towards our old camping ground. Do not think we will be ordered to retreat again without a fight. Rain continues though slowly and on account of it we had no dress-parade.

August 12, Monday

JHC: A very wet and disagreeable day, on account of which we had no drill. Returned to duty today, as I am tired of lying up in my tent. Father went to the Junction today and assisted in getting Joe Grigg off. He has been trying to get off for some time, but only succeeded today. While at the Junction Father found a box of provisions which Aunt Ann had sent us a week ago. When we opened it, all the bread was moulded and unfit for use. We had also a box of Chickens, about fifty, and the agent having nowhere to keep them, the soldiers stole every one. We grieve more for the Chickens than any thing else, for Chicken does go fine in the army. I can just imagine how they would have tasted with good hot biscuit and butter.

August 13, Tuesday

JHC: Still another wet and disagreeable day. Several heavy rains during the day, but in the intervals we were out drilling. We have now to go through the manual of arms, the wheelings, facings &c. This the most of us learned before we left home, but there are some who know no more about it, than when they left Camp Carson in Greensboro. The weather has been quite cool, which has stirred up the whole camp. Never saw the boys in such fine spirits. They have been frolicking and kicking up a noise all the evening. The funniest thing that happened during the evening was that while rearing around Fred Borden ran against Jim Ed. Webb's table which was set for supper, knocked it over, broke it and threw the crockery all over the ground. The frolicking broke up in a little row, which did not amount to any thing as one of the parties ran like a quarter-horse.

August 14, Wednesday

JHC: Very cool indeed this morning, so cool in fact that an overcoat is not at all uncomfortable. Our drill however soon drew the perspiration. We are kept busy at it. We amuse ourselves now pitching quoits. Sam Dorroh has Jaundice, and looks badly, though not confined. We have very few men in the Company sick at this time. Father was at the Junction today, and brought the glorious news of a fight at Leesburg, in which our forces captured fifteen hundred of the enemy, and killed three hundred. Two thousand of them crossed the Potomac, when our forces attacked and killed and captured nearly the whole command. This is only the report at the Junction, not official. The boys are again on a big spree wrestling, jumping &c. Dan Webster & Gid Westcott wrestled which resulted in Westcott getting a fall, though it was a pretty tight tussle.

August 15, Thursday

JHC: Another cool morning and a clear one. Our blankets wrapped closely around us are by no means uncomfortable at night, though it is warm during the day. The drills draw the perspiration from one. Father left here today for WoodStock to get him a horse. Expects to be absent until Sunday. Wm Fulton, a friend of ours came over to see us to day, but was taken sick and had to leave pretty soon. Mr Crawford from Eutaw Ala arrived here last night. Heard from the election in Greene County. Benners and Coleman are elected to the Legislature. Jack & Perrin getting but few votes. W. A. Sims & B. A. Carter came to camp this evening from Culpepper Court House, where they have been sick. The boys are not so lively tonight as usual, as we had drill this evening.

August 16, Friday

JHC: Another cold night and morning. Had to get up this morning and spread my overcoat upon me, besides pulling up the blankets. Detailed today to go to work upon a railroad bridge, which was burned the day of our retreat. There are several to be rebuilt and eighty men from our regiment detailed today. There were three of us. Wm Dufphey, Shelby Chadwick and myself, had to go about three miles. After getting there we had some pretty hard work to do, placing together the arches. The day has been wet and disagreeable and we had to take the rain all day. I was fortunate enough however not to have to go in the creek. I am however now wet through and with a sore throat. No roll-call tonight on account of the weather, so I shall soon wrap myself in sweet slumbers and bid adieu to the 16th of August.

August 17, Saturday

JHC: Dank, damp and disagreeable as usual for the past two or three days. Not much rain, but a cool unpleasant drizzle, just sufficient to keep a man indoors. A good day for chills, also a good one for drinking hot punches to those who are fond of the "creeter". An occasional cry can be heard from some of the boys "of who's got any whiskey,["] but they do not get the whiskey, as it has just all given out. A great gambling mania has seized upon the regiment and betting runs high. Several Chuck-luck banks have been started and the boys bet furiously. A few win while by far the majority lose. Raffling is also afloat, men can be seen going around with paper, pencil and an old watch, knife or pistol asking "who will take a chance at a fine watch, knife or pistol." Never having become interested in such things, and having an utter contempt for card playing, betting and such like, I have not been as yet seized with the mania and if I continue in the possession of my right mind never will. There are some who engage in it that surprises me. I thought they never engaged in such things. But a campaign like this is the best place in the world to find out what a man is. If a man has any fault it will soon show itself. Co^l Moore came over this evening to spend the night. His regiment is encamped at Bristol Station five or six miles south of the Junction. Although so wet muddy and disagreeable Rodes had us out on battalion drill and put us regularly through for an hour and a half.

NOTE: Chuck-a-luck is a game of chance involving three dice and a bank.

Co^l Moore is Sydenham Moore, colonel of the Eleventh Alabama.

August 18, Sunday

JHC: Again I have to note another day of rain and disagreeableness. Have been in my tent all day reading and writing, wrote a letter home, and since have been reading the bible and newspapers. To day reminds me of Sunday on the plantation at home. All have our clean clothes on, faces washed and hair combed just like the negroes. If we were only as well off as they I would be satisfied, for they have warm and dry houses to stay in, plenty to eat and good warm clothes, we of course have plenty to eat and wear, but not the houses. Saw the full and official returns from the election in Greene Co. Ala. Clarke is elected State Senator over Co^l A. C. Jones. Benners and Coleman over Jack & Perrin. Those at home do not appear to like the war men for offices, as they have voted against them all. They think the war men can be of more service where they are. Brother has been quite unwell all day, having had a chill yesterday and fever all night.

Looked for the return of Father today, but was disappointed. Undress parade this evening. Although it is Sunday men were working all day on the bridges. Had a long talk to night with Billy Tinker on the subject of religion and the war. He has become strictly religious, and says he feels safer than he ever did before. I believe he does as near right as he can. He talks a great deal on the subject, and says he is preparing himself for the worst. He has become very fond of drilling and makes a first rate soldier. Drills himself a great deal.

August 19, Monday

JHC: I begin to think I will have to note down the fair instead of raining days, for it appears as if we were not going to have any more fair weather. To day has been very disagreeable indeed, raining all day and very muddy in camp. Was appointed and entered upon my duties as a Corporal in the Company. We have now all our officers appointed. The non commissioned officers are 1ˢᵗSergᵗ Hill, 2ᵈBorden, 3ᵈWebb[,] 4ᵗʰJones, Corporals Westcott, Griggs, Britton and myself. Hope I may be able to discharge my duties properly. Father got back this afternoon and brought with him a fine horse. Sam Dorroh is again sick, and quite so this evening, having fever. He has not been entirely well since he was attacked with measles, and returned to duty too soon after he got back. We have now a good many sick, some quite so. Have just enjoyed the luxury of a good cigar and as there will be no roll call tonight and the rain still continues to pour down, I will now bid adieu to the cares of the world and wrap myself in sweet refreshing sleep.

NOTE: First sergeant is Thomas C. Hill.
Second sergeant is Joseph Borden.
Third sergeant is probably James D. Webb Jr.
Fourth sergeant is Edwin Pompey Jones.
Corporals are Gideon G. Westcott, James E. Griggs, William G. Britton, and John H. Cowin.

August 20, Tuesday

JHC: Was called up this morning about 3 o'clock to see Sam Dorroh who was quite sick. Remained with him until he was relieved. Quite cool this morning and for the first day in nearly two weeks that we have had no rain. Coˡ Jones had both his horses stolen from him last night, by a negro who had been waiting upon Coˡ Rodes. Major Morgan, Capᵗ Webb and Father went in search of them, but while they were out both horses came in, and Carter Adams caught the negro about three miles from here. The negro implicates some white man, who he said gave him two dollars, and after getting him off, threatened to kill him if he did not go with him. Nothing has been seen or heard of the white man. Coˡ Rodes has gotten very particular in regard to policing, and has had the police squad out half the day. He drilled our Company in person today, for the first time, and put us through. We did better than we ever did before, I suppose because we were scared. Received a letter from brother this evening, all well at home. I judged from his letter that he had fallen desperately in love with some fair damsel as he sighed for some lone spot to rest his wearied spirit. He wishes one of us had remained at home and he had gone to the wars. We think of moving from here on Thursday to Sangsters Cross Roads. Quite cool tonight and fine for sleeping. Sam Dorroh has gone to the country to recruit his health.

August 21, Wednesday

JHC: A fine morning indeed, cool and bracing. The sun came forth in all his splendor and all nature seemed alive once more. Good day for drilling. The Company turned out largely and drilled well. 'Squire Griggs has been appointed wagon Master of the regiment. He gets the pay of forty five dollars per month and a horse to ride. This is much better than his corporalship. Received a letter today from Joe Grigg, who is now at home and his health rapidly improving will return as soon as he is able. David Barnum came in camp today. He is the son of Dr Barnum formerly of Greensboro, but moving to Selma in 1852 died there. Mrs Barnum marrying again, now resides in Minesota. David has been in the Naval Academy at Annapolis Md. When the war broke out he came South and now desires to join our Company. This morning the order was read out for the first five companies to take up their line of march tomorrow morning for Sangsters Cross Roads. To night the recruits came in. L.T. Whelan, Jule and Ed Bayol, Wm Hafner, A.G.Ward[,] A C Waddell, Stans Gawecki, Wm Ellison, Henry Christian, Robt Chadwick & Sherron. Dr Blackford also came, but I do not know whether he intends joining the Company or not. Received a long letter from Chas Whelan Jr in which he mentions a good deal about the girls. Dr Sledge of Greensboro died very suddenly, on monday week last, of disease of the heart. A member of the Cahaba Rifles died today and was buried with military honors by several companies.

NOTE: "Dr Blackford" is Dr. William T. Blackford.

August 22, Thursday

JHC: Arose earlier this morning than usual. Father went to the Junction with Co^l Jones, who is going to North Carolina to recruit his health. His family is there. Dr Charles Hill arrived this morning. Five of the Companies left here this morning. The weather has been fine for marching, cool and cloudy all day have had but little rain. Am on guard today for the first time in the capacity of Corporal. It is much better than a privates lot, having to stand on post. 'Squire Griggs has entered upon his duties as wagon Master, and has gone with his wagons to move the first five Companies, will be back tonight to move the others tomorrow. We have every prospect for a heavy rain tonight. It is now raining. The lightnings flash, the thunder rolls and the darkness is awful, yet we are compelled to weather the storm, though the officer of the day has issued an order to take off the guard if it continues to rain. We are now in the guard tent, some playing cards, others snatching what little sleep they can.

August 23, Friday

JHC: To day we moved. Left our camp about 8 o'clock, and marched about six miles. The march was not at all fatiguing as we marched slowly along with the wagons. Arrived here (Sangsters X Roads) about half past one o'clock, took dinner and pitched our tents. Brought our plank floor along and fixed up nicely. The recruits stood the march finely, as the march was slow. The whole camp was thrown into a considerable state of excitement this evening, by the announcement that the enemy was advancing. A scouting party was immediately sent out, the long roll beaten and we were formed on the color line to await orders. We threw our knapsacks into the wagon, and took one long lingering look at our tent so nicely arranged, and resumed our places on the color line. We remained there until dark, when Co^l Rodes dismissed us with orders however to sleep upon our arms and with our accoutrements on. We are now preparing to take a little rest, but are expecting every minute to be called up and ordered to march. If we march it will be toward Fairfax Court House, which is only four or five miles distant. I am in hopes we will not be called up, for I am sleepy tonight, having been up on guard last night, and had a pretty rough time of it. All the sleeping I got was on a pile of corn and a bag of it for a pillow. This makes the second time I have had to march after being on guard the night before. Now for trying to sleep a little— Good night—

August 24, Saturday

JHC: Fortunately for the Yankees and arguably to us, we were not called up last night. Had we been, I should have felt like exterminating the whole Yankee race. Slept pretty well until this morning before day, when I awoke nearly frozen, having only a thin blanket over me. We have the largest dews here I ever saw almost like a rain. The recruits were out today drilling. Hobson put them regularly through. Received a letter from home this afternoon, stating that Mother was quite sick, so I feel quite uneasy. The rains have injured the cotton considerably, and there was a good deal of sickness in the neighborhood. Battalion drill this afternoon, a good deal double-quicking and no rest at all. To night a vote of thanks was given to Co^l A. C. Jones for the presentation to the Company of five hundred dollars

August 25, Sunday

JHC: Quite cool this morning, and before day had to have the blankets close up around me. Sunday has again come and once more the Company looks decently dressed in our red flannel shirts and kersey pants, sent by the citizens of Greensboro. They are very comfortable. Did nothing today but lie about the tent, wrote one letter and the balance of the day read newspapers, which are yet filled with accounts of the battle of Manassas. Russell has written a long letter to England giving a graphic description of the battle, the rout &c. Don't like his letter at all, believe he is a consummate scoundrel and ought to be sent back to England forthwith. Saw a list of the prisoners in Washington City. There are a good many from Alabama among them, Paulding, Walker & Fiquet of our regiment. The boys have been variously occupied today. Some writing, others reading, some in groups laughing and talking, and some playing cards. I think orders ought to be issued from head quarters prohibiting card playing on the Sabbath. It is a shame for men to be playing today, men too brought up by strictly religious parents. Yet they play every Sunday more than during the week.

August 26, Monday

JHC: Another cool morning. The nights are now getting longer and we have reveille before sunrise. Went to work directly after breakfast and put up an arbor in front of our tent, then made a table to eat upon. We now have the best fixed up tent in the company. We have a good plank floor, an arbor in front, a table to eat from and plenty to eat. Seve keeps our table pretty well furnished now with corn, tomatoes, onions and today we had a mess of cucumbers. We send him out every day to hunt us up something to eat and he always succeeds in getting either meat or vegetables. I think our company is now living better than any in the regiment, for we buy every thing we see. We find fruit very scarce here. I have only eaten a part of one watermelon and several peaches this season. The recruits are drilled pretty hard now, in order to prepare them for the next battle. They do not go yet on battalion drill. This afternoon our whole company turned out on drill in their new kersey pants and red flannel shirts, we looked well and drilled finely.

August 27, Tuesday

JHC: Co^l Rodes has given our camp the name of Camp Masked Battery. Why the name I do not know. If the Yankees hear of it, they will not be apt to molest us, for they have a perfect horror of masked batteries and Virginia Cavalry. Co^l Rodes drilled us this morning in the manuel. Our regiment now forms the right wing of the brigade. The 12$^{\underline{th}}$ Mississippi 6th Ala and 12$^{\underline{th}}$ Ala regiments being to our left, all within half mile. The 6$^{\underline{th}}$ is encamped on the farm of a gentleman whose large fine house was burned by the Yankees on their march down here. Every thing was laid waste, even the enclosure around his grave yard was torn down. We have three or four different camps to the regiment, the regular camp, one for an itch squad, one for a squad with the mumps, one for a squad having body lice on them, and another for the wives of Capt Pegues & Lieu^t Potts. No battalion drill this evening owing to rain. We went out for dress parade, but just as we were forming it began raining again, and we were dismissed. We left the field in double-quick time. To night the wind blows quite cool, but we are well fixed up.

NOTE: Ewell's brigade included the Fifth Alabama, Sixth Alabama, Twelfth Alabama, and Twelfth Mississippi infantry regiments as well as the King William (Virginia) Artillery.

August 28, Wednesday

JHC: On guard again today and a dark, damp and disagreeable one it is. We had orders this morning to prepare one days rations as it is thought we will have to move from here. Some think our regiment will be transferred to Longstreet. Dont much like the idea of leaving Genl Ewell, as he thinks a good deal of this regiment and the men are all well pleased with him. Dont know yet what is to be done. Had my sentinels singing out for me all the morning. Have the first relief, and all the boys from our company. Father was at the Junction today and brought out the mail and with it two letters for me, one from brother which gave us great relief as he states that Mother had recovered from her recent illness. The other letter from Mrs Dorroh and a very interesting one indeed. The cotton crop has been greatly injured by the great abundance of rain. Brother states that it has been raining for twenty one days. We have made a fine crop of corn. The health of the neighborhood not very good. After preparing our rations and getting everything ready, we learned that we did not have to move. The picket guards of the two armies have been skirmishing for several days near Falls Church. There is a large peach orchard up there and the peaches being ripe, they were fighting for them, the best men getting the peaches. To night the sentinels have been calling the Corporal nearly all the time and I have had to stand for them almost the whole of the two hours. Some of them get lonely and call the Corporal because they have nothing else to do.

August 29, Thursday

JHC: The sentinels last night kept me running nearly the whole of the time my relief was on. So I had a hard time of it, rained all night. We have a house for the guards, but it is so small that only about one relief can sleep at once. So there was but little sleeping done. Was much amused at some of the sentinels giving the countersign to the relief guard. It was Austerlitz and some of them never having heard the name got it mixed up and had it *oyster lips*. It is amusing to hear some of them converse with each other. We have had another miserable day. Rained all day and our streets look more like a hog pen than any thing else. There has not been a roll call today. Wrote a letter to brother. No mail came in today. The sun came out this afternoon and we thought we were to have fair weather, but it again clouded up and now looks as dark as ever.

August 30, Friday

JHC: Once more the sun has come forth in all his brilliancy, making all nature wear again the garb of gladness. Beautiful and bright is the morning, reminding me of the soft sunny days in Alabama. The drum and fife sound loud and clear as they summon us from our rest to enter upon the duties of another day. Although such a beautiful day, we have under foot an abundance of mud in camp. Have had quite a warm day, very warm today on drill. Lieut Dedman was out today for the first time since he was attacked with measles. Sam Dorroh and J.D. Webb Jr came in today from the country where they have been for some time sick. Dr Syd Webb, Wiley Croom and several others left camp today on account of sickness. We have one cause of mumps in our Company. (Crowell has them). Willie Borden has Typhoid Fever and at this time is quite sick[.] There has been several cases recently in camp. Major Morgan drilled the regiment this afternoon but did not do very well. He has not yet gotten the hang of it. Tomorrow is the day for general inspection. Gen[l] Ewell inspects his brigade. Our regiment comes first. We go out with guns, accoutrements, haversacks and canteens.

August 31, Saturday

JHC: General inspection day and a beautiful day it has been. No cloud in view to dim the brilliancy of the sun and a soft breeze gently fanning the heated and tired soldier, as he lugged his arms and accoutrements around the field for inspection. Genl Ewell was on the ground at half past seven o'clock, and looked better than I ever saw him. He was dressed in a grey suit and looked well. Our Company turned out largely and in their red shirts and kersey pants, looking and marching well. On some occasions we do remarkably well and on others remarkably bad. After inspection, for the gratification of Major Morgan we were taken out on battalion drill. We stumbled about over the field for an hour and then had holiday until dress parade. We had however in the mean while to police our quarters for inspection. So we flew around considerably, picked up all the trash, swept before our tents and arranged every thing neatly. Those who had not raised floors, went off, got rails and leaves and arranged every thing nicely, then awaited the inspection of Co^l Rodes, but he did not come. We have however cleaner quarters than usual. Got order to again prepare one days rations, as the enemy is reported to be advancing.

September 1, Sunday

JHC: The old month of August has glided away and will now be numbered among the things that were. The new month was ushered in smiling with beauty and grandeur, clear, cool and calm. Company inspection this morning. Received a letter from home today. All well. Serg^t Redis of the 12th Miss Reg^t dined with us today. Have been busy all day writing and setting up the mess account. Wrote to Mother, afterward had a regular settling up. I find it no little trouble to be chief of a mess, especially one that buys as much as we do. Alonzo Chapman is again unwell and unfit for duty. Dr Hendon was over today and reports all the sick doing well. He says he intends remaining with us as long as he is needed[.] He is acting nobly. He is an old man, and has left his family and all home comforts to come here to attend our sick. Received a bundle of papers from Greensboro, but no news in them of any importance. Heard today of the capture, by the Federals, of Forts Hatteras & Clark, in North Carolina. It is reported that they also took five hundred prisoners[.] At dress parade an order was read that we were to be fed on beef, five days rations of beef and two of salt meat. If they continue I think we will be learned to live on nothing, or only that we buy. We are now out of coffee and sugar and have had nothing but tough beef for three or four days, and from all appearances there is no prospect of a change soon. I suppose however this all happens in a fellows life time.

September 2, Monday

JHC: Awoke this morning trying to pull more cover upon me as I was quite cold. We are now having some cold mornings, and soon old winter will be upon us and with it will come that which we never before experienced. A winter in Virginia is severe enough, when one is in comfortable quarters, and we know not what suffering is in store for us if we remain in tents. I am in hopes we will soon go into winter quarters. Nothing new or important today. Gen¹ Ewell was here this evening and witnessed our drill. He appears to be rather a singular man, very unassuming. Saw him the other day sitting flat upon the ground holding his horse. Received a letter this evening from Cousin Sarah Langham. All well at home. The crops have fallen off greatly on account of the recent rains.

September 3, Tuesday

JHC: Last night about tattoo a balloon was discovered in the direction of Alexandria, supposed to be the Yankee Prof Lowe on a reconnoitering expedition. Trying to discover the forces out here, so that the Yankees will know how to come against us. Should like for him to get his balloon disarranged and land over here among some of our regiments. Dont think he would make another reconnaisance soon. Was quite sick all last night, and slept but little in consequence of it. Have suffered considerably today, but have been attending to my duties as usual, only had to leave ranks this morning on drill. On battalion drill this evening we had a considerable amount of double quicking to do. Co¹ Rodes carried the regiment through the firings, by company and files. I understood that there was a bet between Gen¹ Ewell and Co¹ Rodes. The General bets that we cannot form a square before he can get into it, he being three hundred yards distant on his horse. It was not tried this evening. Willie Borden is lying dangerously ill with Typhoid Fever. Coleman lost his servant this morning with it.

September 4, Wednesday

JHC: Still feel a little unwell, but not enough to keep me from duty. We drill now in the morning exclusively in the manuel, most in the loading and firing. Had Lee Whelan butchering beef today. Feed us on beef now altogether and frequently there can be seen men walking about, half bent with their hands upon their abdomens looking awful ugly. Have gotten up a brass band in the regiment, and they are practicing every day. They have as yet made but little progress, but will soon learn and we will have a fine band. Father received a letter from Aunt Ann, stating that she had sent us a box of provisions and a dozen and a half chickens. Have not received them yet. Co¹ Rodes has ordered that the Captains shall drill the regiment alternately, beginning on the right.

September 5, Thursday

JHC: It is often said "a fool for luck", which if true I flatter myself that I am not a fool, for if any one is unfortunate in this regiment, I am the one. Just so certain as I come on guard, it is certain to rain or we have to move next day. We have enjoyed fine weather for the past few days, but I was detailed last night to go on guard today, and before day it clouded up and rained very hard. Rained this morning all the while my relief was on. Sent a wagon yesterday down to the Junction for a box of provisions and some chickens there for us. This evening this wagon came back with the box that the chickens were in, but "nary" chicken, besides this a box of pies &c was torn open and half of them taken out. Who did all this we are unable to find out. There are some terrible scoundrels in the army, men who would steal a dime from a dead persons eye and then kick him because it was not a quarter. There are some of this kind in this regiment, though I am sorry to say it. Have had a pretty rough time of it today, which will continue through the night as it has rained all day. Was much amused tonight at one of the sentinels telling of his trip to Egypt. Did not sleep in the guard house as we are getting afraid to do so, on account of itch and lice. Lost two of my sentinels tonight and could not find them so had to get one man to attend to two posts. Will fix them the next time so that they will not get away.

September 6, Friday

JHC: Came to my tent this morning at four o'clock and slept 'till six, but it did not refresh me much. Went back to the guard tent and was relieved at eight. Then I slept 'till twelve which refreshed me considerably. Capt Hall drilled the battalion this morning. Did not drill with the Company as those who are on guard the night before are excused from the morning drill. Co^l Rodes put us through this evening. Double quick in abundance, which made us blow considerably. Brother is still unwell, but improving. Listened to some eloquent speeches tonight from the Hon J. L. M. Curry, Congressman from Ala, and from Major Morgan. Both good speeches[.] They made us feel as if we could whip all the Yankees that could be brought against us. Co^l Rodes also paid us a compliment.

September 7, Saturday

JHC: According to custom went around to the guard time with my relief to police the camp, but not finding the officer of the guard did not police. It is customary for the guard that comes off one day to police the camp the next, under the direction of the officer of the guard. Had a big time drilling today. Had Congressman Curry and McRae to witness the drill also Genl Ewell and Major Baily a Baltimore lady who ranks as Major in our army. Had a pretty rough time of it, double quicked half the time and in fact it was the toughest drill we have had in a long time. Hope no more "big folks" will come to see us drill. We however had no drill this afternoon. Our Company was out in the red suit. Have orders to prepare for the Springfield picket tomorrow nine miles distant

September 8, Sunday

JHC: Started from camp this morning at half past six and arrived at Springfield about half past ten o'clock. While on the road the post master landed me a letter from Miss A.G.W—— a long and interesting one. While on the road we passed a rail road watch house, and on the walls was all kinds of writing done by the Yankees on their "grand march" to Richmond. Caricatures of Jeff Davis hanging &c. We looked at every thing, and wondered if they were now in as good humor as then. When we arrived at Springfield we found that our scouts had captured three large fine looking Yankees, about a mile and a half from here. They were members of the 5th Maine. One of them a very talkative and sensible fellow. He conversed a good deal with our men, but was smart enough not to give any information of the movements of his army. He says that they are awaiting an attack from us. Just as we marched up to the station saw a regular fisticuff between two Mississippians. They knocked each other about awhile, but "nobody was hurt." Major Morgan is in command of the forces here. We have four Companies here, one from each regiment in the brigade. Am on guard today, and only two of us (Corporals) to the three reliefs. We are within six miles of Alexandria, and can go on a hill about a mile and a half from here and see the spires of the churches over there. The station here is occupied by a man whose son in law is a prisoner in Richmond. He was guide to the Yankees and was captured at the battle of Manassas. We can hear the drums of the Yankees very distinctly as they beat for dress parade and tattoo. Have made arrangements with the other Corporal to sit up the first half of the night and he the other. Lieut Williams is officer of the guard. He and I sit up 'till twelve o'clock, the Sergeant and Corporal the remainder.

September 9, Monday

JHC: Nothing of unusual occurrence. Heard one gun fire during the night, but some distance off. Do not think I slept an hour during the night, for after twelve o'clock when my turn came to sleep, the corporal would awake me every few minutes to ask some question, such as the time, or he would forget the countersign and come to me for it. I was considerably vexed, for I was tired and sleepy after the fatigues of the day. Took breakfast at the house of a lady near here, but got nothing extra. Could have cooked a better breakfast myself. Was very much surprised to find here this morning all the boys we left in camp. Co^l Rodes sent them down yesterday evening. They got here last night about ten o'clock. Jack Wynne, Lee Whelan and myself built us a house today of rails and bushes. After we thought it finished and all right, and were sitting under it resting and admiring it, we suddenly heard a noise over head and looking up found it falling in. We hustled out in double quick time and had scarcely time to get out before down came the roof and there was all our labor lost. We however went to work and rebuilt it, doubly as strong as before. Think it will now stand the storm. Alarm given today about twelve o'clock one of the sentinels ran in scared out of his wits. No cause for it could be ascertained by Major Morgan and Capt Hardaway, who went out to see about it. Did my own cooking today. Had bacon and fried corn for dinner. Made a failure in frying the corn. We did very well for supper as we only had meat to cook. Cold biscuit, fried meat and a cup of sour milk constituted our supper. Hope I will sleep better tonight than I did last night. Five of us occupy our house to night. Father and myself take one side, Jack & Lee the middle and Bob Jeffries the other. It is now about eight o'clock and we are all prepared for sleep, so out goes the light and here we go to the land of dreams.

September 10, Tuesday

JHC: Aroused three times last night by the firing of guns. Some of the pickets scared out of their wits cannot tell the difference between a hog and a man, the former of which they were firing at. Arose early this morning and got breakfast. Made an elegant cup of coffee, but had no sugar or cream to put in it. Improved on the corn this morning as it was fine and well cooked. No prisoners caught today. Dr Charles Hill is with us and was out on a scout with some of our boys this morning. There is a house about two miles distant from here, to which the Yankees are in the habit of coming, and where the three before alluded to were caught. They were there this morning seven strong, but left before our men got there. Capt Hall's Company arrived here this morning to relieve us. So we now prepare to leave for Camp. At Camp— Left Springfield about twelve o'clock and got here about five, some of the company did not get here until after dark. Our company is awful for scattering on a march, worse than any other in the regiment. Jack Wynne and myself came on together and made good time, only stopped twice for water. Some of the boys are pretty well broken down. Some I fear will be made sick by the march. Every thing looks natural in Camp. Took an elegant cold bath tonight and feel much refreshed. Will be all right in the by morning and ready for some of Rodes' drills.

September 11, Wednesday

JHC: Brother had a very severe chill this morning and has been quite sick all day. Has to night a high fever and complains a good deal. Mrs Sanborn arrived in camp today. She comes on as nurse to the sick. Had two ladies in my tent this evening, Mr[s.] Sanborn and Mrs. Fowler[.] They came in to see brother. It is awkward talking to ladies now, we have been from their society for so long. Capt Pegues drilled the battalion this morning and Capt Blount this evening. Both did very well. Several of the boys have been made sick by the march yesterday from Springfield. Glover and Dufphey are both sick. Have orders to again prepare one day's rations. Do not know what is in the wind. May leave tomorrow, but do not feel much like taking another march soon, but we are not generally consulted as to what we like or dislike, but only have to obey orders. Wrote a letter to mother in answer to one received this morning. All well at home. To night very blustering and warm with good prospects of rain before morning.

September 12, Thursday

JHC: A heavy rain last night, but clear and pleasant this morning. Brother much better, being free from fever. Sam Dorroh sick again, having had a chill this morning. He has never been entirely well since he had the measles and I fear he will not be able to stand the campaign. Glover still quite sick, also Britton and Dufphey and Robt Chadwick. Have not been well myself today, but hope to be all right by morning. A member of Capt Dents Company died this evening. The band was out on dress parade this evening and performed very well. They have improved very much, but will not commence performing regularly until next week. Heard today that there had been a little fight at Munsons Hill, but had no particulars.

September 13, Friday

JHC: Brother much better and entirely free from fever. Sam Dorroh quite unwell, having a fever all day. The other sick getting on very well. Norborne Jackson, Knight & Wiley Croom came in today from the country. Capt Webb also came in but looking badly. Mrs Chadwick came in camp this evening. Capt Fowler commenced drilling the battalion this morning but before proceeding very far we received orders to prepare to march to Springfield, as the enemy is reported advancing. So we were dismissed and prepared for the march, filled our haversacks, canteens and rolled up our blankets. We were in expectation of receiving marching orders every moment ~~did~~ but did not get them until about four o'clock. Co^l Rodes who was at the Junction on a court marshall, was telegraphed to, Father bearing the dispatch to Fairfax Station and making the quickest time I ever knew to be made on horseback. About four o'clock we were drawn up in line and marched off. We had proceeded about half a mile when we were stopped by a courier and told that the alarm was all a humbug. So we had to return to camp. Every company turned out largely and appeared anxious to go on. Co^l Rodes caught us on the road and was loudly cheered. We made something by the alarm for we got off two drills. Genl Beauregard will hereafter hold Fairfax Court House as head quarters. The band was out on dress parade this evening and did very well. Our Sergeant Major (Green) has resigned and John Martin of the Warrior Guards appointed in his stead. Green was a member of the Mobile Continentals and will return to the Company at Pensacola.

September 14, Saturday

JHC: Quite warm this morning on drill. Being under marching orders we had only one drill today. Had orders to day to march to Anandale with ten days provisions. We got all ready to march and then got orders to only hold ourselves in readiness. So here we are kept in suspense all the while and know not what we have to do or when we have to move. I am pretty certain we will have to move soon. Genl Beauregard is moving his head quarters to Fairfax. There is something in the wind but we poor devils are not in the secret and are left to conjecture, and many and various are the conjectures made. Every one has his own opinion about things. The sick are all getting on very well. Sam Dorroh has had some fever today, but tonight is perspiring and free from fever. Mrs Rodes, Mrs Martin and Mrs Kerr are now in camp. Every thing quiet in Camp tonight.

September 15, Sunday

JHC: Calm, quiet and beautiful. The sun shone forth in all his brilliancy, reminding me of my good old home in Alabama. I oftentimes thought of home today and contrasted a Sabbath at home with one here. How very different. But there is no use in giving way to such thoughts, for it will be many Sabbaths before I can enjoy one at home. Devoted the morning to writing a long letter to brother and reading newspapers. Read an account of a fight between Gen^{ls} Floyd and Rozencrantz of the Federal army. Only saw a northern account of, which acknowledges a loss of twenty killed and one hundred wounded. Our loss was not stated. Night put an end to the fight. The Yankees withdrew and Floyd crossed the river Gauly. Two regiments of our brigade moved up to Anandale today, and I learn were put digging entrenchments. Am glad we did not have to go for we have had our time digging.

NOTE: On September 10 at Carnifix Ferry along the Gauley River, Federal forces under William S. Rosecrans struck at Confederate forces under John B. Floyd; the confederates withdrew, helping to keep western Virginia in Union hands.

September 16, Monday

JHC: Sam Dorroh quite sick last night. Excused from duty today to attend on him. Wrote to his mother in regard to him. Fear he is going to have a serious attack but hope not. Heard the booming of artillery all the morning and a fight is reported going on at Clouds Mills about twelve miles from here. Have heard none of the particulars. No information concerning it has yet reached head quarters. Do not know why. Capt Fowler drilled the regiment this morning, but kept them out only a few minutes when he brought them to a halt, he was called upon for a speech. He made a short one and wound up by saying that he thought that these twelve o'clock drills were humbugs, and dismissed the Companies to their respective quarters. Have been with Sam Dorroh all day. He remains about the same, partly delirious all the afternoon. Have been reading all the afternoon the life of Franklin by Holly. Hear this evening that instead of a fight at Clouds Mills the Yankees were trying to drive our forces from Munsons Hill, they being on Arlington heights a distance of four miles. Bigger fools than I thought they were.

NOTE: O. L. Holley, *The Life of Benjamin Franklin* (Boston: J. Philbrick, 1856).

September 17, Tuesday

JHC: Sam Dorroh still quite sick, rested badly last night, has had however but little fever today. Mrs Kerr came in to see him, and bathed his head and hands which seemed to revive him very much. I think him now past danger and that he will be well soon, though there is no telling yet. Has been more cheerful today than usual and has a better pulse. Co^l Rodes had the prisoners out today at work. There are seven or eight of them and one from our company, whose name I of course forbear to mention. Capt Hobson drilled the regiment this morning and did very well, only on one occasion Capt Dents Company was thrown entirely out of the regiment. Last night the officer of the guard, the sergeant and corporal all went to sleep and caused one man to stand on post four hours instead of two. Co^l Rodes found it out and ordered them all to report themselves under arrest this morning. What disposition he will make of the case I do not know. Brother received a long letter from Aunt Ann this morning. She is very anxious to come down to see us, and is very much troubled about our losing the provisions she sent us. Received the Beacon to day. Nothing in it of very great interest, noticed a correspondence between the Rev Mr Hutchinson and Genl Kerr in reference to a box sent to the Company. Saw the Richmond Dispatch of yesterday. Not much war news. Wrote to Mrs Dorroh again tonight. Dr Ramsey and my self sit up with Sam tonight.

NOTE: The politically moderate *Richmond Dispatch* had the largest circulation of any Richmond paper.

September 18, Wednesday

JHC: Slept but little last night, as I was up several times with Sam Dorroh. He rested very well, sleeping most of the night. We put a large blister upon his abdomen last night which required our attention. This morning he is much better though very feable. Badenhausen of our Company has taken charge of the band. A good joke is now going on in our Company. Crowell who was acting sergeant a night or two since and giving to sleep together with the Lieutenant and Corporal and for it being placed under arrest in quarters, still continues under arrest, Co^l Rodes not knowing that he is only a private. He is perfectly satisfied, for he has no drilling to do, but walks about his quarters and has his own fun. Genl Ewell dined with the Co^l to day, and had on a clean shirt. Co^l Syd Moore & Co^l Forney are in Camp tonight. Co^l Moore is looking very well. Sam Dorroh received a long letter from John today to which I replied tonight. Am still devoting my leisure moment to the reading of the life of Franklin. I find it very interesting. Have read it before but by a different author. We have now most beautiful moon shine nights, almost as bright as day. Capt Shelley lost a member of his company yesterday. He was buried today. Capt Goode of the Monroe Guards is lying dangerous ill, not expected to live. Dr Ramsey and myself stay with Sam again tonight. He is much better.

September 19, Thursday

JHC: Sam Dorroh slept very well last night, awaking only twice and then to call for water. This morning he is much improved and looks better than I have seen him since he has been sick. Wrote to Mother this morning. Am having a very lonely time of it now. Never leave the tent only at meal times. Would much prefer drilling as far as pleasure is concerned, but as it is a duty I owe a friend, I will cheerfully continue with him until he recovers. Capt Shelley drilled the battalion this morning. I think this twelve o'clock battalion drill will soon cease, as I believe with Capt Fowler that it is an intense humbug. Two men members of the Warrior Guards are now under arrest for a most grave offense. They attempted an outrage upon an old negro woman, at the same time beating her husband and slightly bayoneting him. Capt Fowler has taken their uniform off and swears they shall never again come into his company. Squire Griggs was up at Springfield today, after forage, and saw Alexandria and the forts in front of it very plainly. One of Capt Goode's men shot himself to night through the foot. Not seriously hurt. Some say that it was not an accident. Sam has some fever tonight. Have been reading to night a Washington paper.

September 20, Friday

JHC: Was up several times last night with Sam, as he was very restless, rolling and tossing about nearly all night[.] So I slept but little and was up early this morning. 'Squire Griggs and Father went up to day beyond Springfield for provender. They were within three miles of Alexandria. Father says he could see the city and the two forts this side very plainly. The Yankee pickets were only three quarters of a mile from them and could be seen very distinctly. One of our men crept upon three of them sitting upon a log, and fired twice at them, but did no damage, although when he returned he stated that he had killed one and wounded another. He happened to be seen by our men, who were watching his movements with glasses. Nothing has transpired here to day of any importance in the war line. A number of Capt Blounts Company died today, also one of Capt Goode's men died. We have had for some time past very unsettled weather and with it a great deal of sickness. I am in hopes cold weather will soon set in, as I think it would be beneficial in point of health. Father received a letter from home today stating that Mother had again been quite sick but was then improving— Sam Dorroh very restless today and getting a little cross which I think a good sign. Lt Co^l A. C. Jones returned this afternoon after an absence of a month, looking very well though a little thin. He had quite a severe attack. Have just bathed Sam's feet and hope he will rest better tonight, as I feel like sleeping some myself. Wrote a letter to day to his father stating his condition. The weather very warm today but pleasant to night.

September 21, Saturday

JHC: Slept elegantly last night, as my patient did not call at all during the night, but rested finely himself. To day has been passed as usual, with few exceptions. The Beacon came today, but contained nothing new or interesting. It contained the obituary of Dr Sledge and also several marriages, though of persons I did not know. Father received a letter from brother. All well at home, we have some cotton packed. No news of any movement of either army. Think McClellan is fixing up to give us a hard fight next time. Genl Smith has taken command of the forces of Genl Johns[t]on while the latter has command of both the forces of Smith & Beauregard. Genl Ewell dined with the Co^l today. Rodes seems to be very popular as he has a great deal of company. Again it rains and very hard[.] It appears as if we would have a regular season of it, as it has set in just right. Sam has been doing very well all day and I greatly hope will have another good nights rest.

September 22, Sunday

JHC: About three more such nights as I spent last night would wind me up. It rained, it blew hurricanes, and the fly of the tent being torn kept such a flapping that it drove from my eyes all thoughts of sleep. It was enough to make a preacher swear. Sam was very restless and could not sleep. He was calling all night. So I do not think I slept an hour during the night. After it ceased raining the guards kept up as much noise as if they were at a negro wedding. I got vexed; would jump up, light the candle, attend to Sams wants, then try to fix the tent so that he could sleep, but just as I thought every thing all right, blew out the candle and laid down the prop would blow out and the flapping commence again. I finally let it alone and gave up all thoughts of sleep. I lay down and frequently the guards would break out in laughter like a lot of negroes at a corn shucking. All right thought I, I'll yet have my full share of sleep, and so I passed the night. It became very cool before morning and continues so. The regiment received orders this morning to march to Springfield to relieve the regiment there. They left about ten o'clock. I was unable to accompany them as Sam wished me to remain with him. They are to be gone four days. Sam still improving—no fever today. A good many of our company remained in camp on account of not feeling able to march so far. Some of them I think make it a point to get sick every time we have to march any distance. Father went to the Junction this morning and found a box sent him by Aunt Ann; on opening it found a large jug of whiskey, which I was sorry to see for there are some here rather too fond of it, and Father gives it away to any and every body. I was in hopes no more would be brought into camp. I have liked whiskey as well as any body, but I have found that a man can do better without than with it. So I have quit it. Wrote a letter this evening to Mr Dorroh in regard to Sam. We have had a beautiful day, and to night quite cool. In hopes the cool weather may continue as it will be of benefit to the sick.

September 23, Monday

JHC: A most beautiful morning, clear and cool, almost cold enough for frost. I spent another night of sleeplessness, but not so bad as the night before. Sam was again delirious last night and at one time got off his bed down on the floor without any covering at all. I was up three or four time as also was Dr Ramsey. This morning he has tympanitis and complained very much of pain. His pupils are very much dilated and upon the whole I do not think him as well as yesterday. He has however a good pulse and very little fever. It looks a little lonely here since the boys left, though there are at least one hundred here yet. Mrs. Rodes caught her dress on fire this morning, and it came very near resulting seriously, but Sims extinguished it, burning himself slightly. She was very badly frightened, though was not at all hurt. I heard this evening that a fight was expected at Springfield and that four companies from our regiment went out this morning, among these our company. Some of Capt Goode's men returned today on account of the mumps. They stated that we had captured about sixty of the enemy. How true it may prove remains to be seen. To day has worn the appearance of Sunday, very lonely[.] Sam has been quite sick today, but this evening is better and if I can get him to rest well tonight he will be much improved. There is however so much uncertainty about such fevers that it is very difficult to tell what will take place. To night is cool, calm and beautiful. The moon sheds her silvery light in all her loveliness and seems to invite sweet and refreshing sleep to all earths creatures.

JHC: Robt Lanier and myself sat up 'till one o'clock this morning with Sam and Dr Ramsey and brother the remainder of the night. He rested very well the latter portion of the night. He is in a very low condition and if a change is not soon brought about will die. The Guards were all on a spree last night and created considerable noise. There were only about as a third as many on as usual, but they made more noise than if there had been fifty. The sergeant of the guard was drunk and Co^l Jones found him out, whether he intends reporting him to Co^l Rodes or not I do not know. Had Rodes been here there would have been nothing of it. But "when the cat is gone, the mice will play." The longer a man lives the more he learns, and camp is the best place to study human nature I have ever seen. A man can so easily be found out. Every trait in his character will be drawn out on some occasion, whether it be good or bad. I find from observation that white men require watching as much so as negroes. I think there are many who ought have masters to watch over them at all times, and Co^l Rodes is just the man to be over them, for if any one could keep them straight he could. J.D.Webb Jr and S.B.Jackson returned from Springfield this evening on account of sickness. Webb tells me that our company is on picket within sight of the Yankee picket, and that some of our boys had been in conversation and swapping caps and knives with them. That appears to be too familiar on short acquaintance. Wm Willingham was quite sick to day with Cholera Morbus, is now better. Five of our men with thirty five others from the regiment went up to Springfield to day. Co^l Rodes having sent for forty. Sam still very low, but some better this evening. Have a slight headache this evening myself. There is some talk of our being ordered back to Ala, but I give no credit to the report, as I have heard the same before.

JHC: Dan Webster and myself sat up till one o clock and Dr Ramsey and brother the remainder of the night. This morning Sam is better, pulse good and skin soft and moist. He slept finely last, but on awaking was somewhat delirious, think though partly from the effects of an opiate. Another most beautiful morning, clear, calm and cool. A fire is very comfortable indeed, and every one has a large one before his tent, which looks more like camp life than ever. Dan Webster has been appointed Commissary, in place of Dr Farley resigned. He now ranks as and receives the pay of Captain. Poor Sam has been getting worse. This morning he appeared to be considerably revived, but soon a fever set in, which ran very high. From the moment the fever set in he began to sink, which continued throughout the day. I knew his case was hopeless. He sank more rapidly than any one I ever saw, and at eleven o'clock to night breathed his last. He died perfectly easy, and rational to the last. He prayed three times about an hour before he died, and knew every one about him until a few minutes before death. Thus died one of my best friends and messmates in the army, and nearest neighbor at home. May his soul have winged its way to heaven. How sad to behold the cold and lifeless corpse of one who but a few months since presented the embodiment of health. Strong, active and brave, cheerfully performing every duty imposed upon him. A warm and devoted friend, a bold and chivalrous soldier. In his death the company has sustained the loss of one of its best numbers. But he is gone from the scenes of earth to quietly rest among the dead. With an anxious attention have I watched by his bedside, and administered to his wants. Just before his death he grasped my hand with a warmth that indicated his gratitude and attachment for me. Deeply do I deplore his loss, but can only exclaim God's will be done. He giveth and he taketh away.

September 26, Thursday

JHC: Sent up to the Court House this morning to get a coffin for Sam. There were none made, so had to 'wait for one until this evening, and about six inches too long. We endeavored to get transportation for him home, but could not, and for no other reason than that he was a private. Capt Goode died last night at half past ten o'clock, just half an hour before Sam died. They have given his body transportation and an escort home. So this is the difference between an officer and a private in the army. I hope the day will soon arrive when we will all again be on an equality. Sam Dorroh was as good as any officer in the army, but simply because he volunteered his services as a private, no privilege is allowed him, not even a decent burial. Such injustice cannot surely go unpunished. We dug the grave this evening and will bury him tomorrow[.] He is worse disfigured than any one I ever saw. Gangrene of his bowels had taken place before death. A member of Capt Blounts Company died this evening, making three men in less than twenty four hours who have died.

September 27, Friday

JHC: Rained this morning, and quite a cold one. A member of Capt Shelley's Company died last night which is four deaths in two nights and a day. In this way we will all soon be gone. Disease will kill many more than the enemy. More men in the regiment have died recently than since we have been in the army. Our pickets had a skirmish yesterday at Springfield. Killed two Yankees, and one of Shelley's men slightly wounded in the leg. Major Morgan has sent for another horse, and Co^l Rodes for all the men able to march. A fight is anticipated soon. Through the kind consideration of Co^l Jones none of us were sent up today. Buried Sam today about twelve o'clock. We have now done every thing for him in our power. I sat by him and administered to his wants until he died, assisted in dressing and laying him out after death, assisted in placing him in his coffin, assisted in digging his grave, and assisted in burying him. He was buried with military honors. A very disagreeable day this has been, rain and this evening a regular gale, blowing down tents and arbors all over camp. Brother received a letter from home this evening. The family all well, some of the negroes sick with chills.

NOTE: Of the thirty-three Guards who died during the war, sixteen were killed and seventeen died from disease. A full breakdown is given in chapter 9 of *Guarding Greensboro: A Confederate Company in the Making of a Southern Community.*

September 28, Saturday

JHC: Had a considerable blow last night, but fortunately our tent stood the storm. Clear and cool this morning. The wind continues to blow. Rob[t] Hardaway came in this morning from the regiment, but knows nothing of its movements. Cap[t] Webb, 'Squire Griggs, NB Jones, Allen, Sheldon and Cap[t] Fowler also came in. Our forces have suddenly evacuated Munson & Mason hills—Springfield and all the points up there. No one can give any reason for such movement. Every thing is wrapt in mystery and we are left in utter obscurity as to the reasons. There are various surmises, but no one knows anything. Our regiment is now on the old Braddock road about six miles from here. Have been looking for its return all the morning. Father received a letter from Mr. Johnson, the overseer this morning. All well at home. Cotton crop not good but corn fine. Plenty hogs and beef cattle. The regiment came in about twelve o'clock[.] The boys all looked very much fatigued. They report having had an awful hard time. Marched nearly the whole of last night, through mud and water. They were also pretty hungry when they got here. They look very rough and dirty an indication of the hardships they have undergone. There is something in the wind which will no doubt develope itself soon

September 29, Sunday

JHC: Every thing reduced to quietude again and the regular routine of business gone through. Very cool this morning. Received a letter from Cha[s] Whelan Jr. No news of any importance from Greensboro. Mrs M[c]Faddin and Miss Alice Lipscomb died last week. A great Confederate victory in Missouri at Lexington. Gen[l] Price captured Co[l] Mulligan and thirty five hundred men under him. Answered the letter received this morning. Preaching today by Rev Mr Porter, attended and listened to a very good sermon. Took his text from the 17th Chapter of Matthew, which reads thus, What would you give in exchange for your soul. Good many in attendance. Took a long walk in the country this evening. Saw some very pretty young ladies and gathered some Chinquepins and grapes. First time I have been out of the lines since I have been in Virginia. Order read out on dress parade to have all extra baggage packed up and sent off tomorrow, as Co[l] Rodes says we will have to leave here soon. "How are you Joe?" is a great by word with the boys now. Every one who comes into camp receives the salute of How are you Joe, by half the regiment. Giving out cartridges and caps tonight. Expect a fight soon and we are liable to be ordered off at any time.

NOTE: On September 20, Federal Colonel James Mulligan surrendered to General Sterling Price's Missourians at Lexington, Missouri.

September 30, Monday

JHC: Another cool morning, but not so cool as yesterday. Regular routine of duty commenced again. This morning instead of the regular battalion drill, the companies were drilled in the skirmish drill. First time I ever drilled in it. It is a very pretty and important drill. All the companies appear to understand it pretty well. Received a letter from brother, all well at home. He writes me that a negro woman had attempted to poison Mrs Hardaway of Eutaw. It is said that she put pounded spiders in Congress water, which she was accustomed to drink. Fortunately she did not succeed. An English vessel has run the blockade at Savannah and landed sixty five hundred enfield rifles. President Davis came up from Richmond today. Has gone up to Fairfax Court House. A lot of hooks and scaling ladders have been brought up, in anticipation of fighting soon. W$^{\underline{m}}$ Willingham is quite sick this evening, having been delirious since twelve o'clock. I think he is frightened, Sam Dorroh having died only a few days ago, and they being intimate. Dr Hunter of the Cahaba Rifles has been appointed Surgeon of the regiment until Drs Venable and Park return. A great many are "down upon" Dr Park and express a wish that he may not return. The camp looks beautiful now at night. Every tent has a blazing fire in front of it.

NOTE: Congress Water was mineral water sold by the Congress and Empire Spring Company.

October 1, Tuesday

JHC: On guard today, and on the third relief, for the first time since I have been Corporal. The only objection to this relief is that we are on duty at meal times, and the day we come off have to stand over the usual time, waiting for the new guard. It appears that I am unfortunate in getting reliefs that are too fond of calling the Corporal. I was called three or four times the first two hours. The regiment received orders to march to Springfield to dislodge the enemy who had taken possession of it since we abandoned it. Co^l Rodes excused me from guard duty by putting another man in my place, so I went with the regiment. We started about three o'clock this evening. Met the 13th N.C. regiment coming back. We went as far as Burkes Station when we were halted and rested about half an hour. After resting, to our surprise we were faced about and ordered back. We got back to Camp about sunset without any incident worthy of note, only we had a march of eight miles for no purpose[.] We marched in quick time both going and returning. After we returned the officer of the guard wanted me to take my place on guard again, as the man who took my place refused to act after we had gotten back. I pretty soon let them know that they could not play such games on me.

October 2, Wednesday

JHC: Rain today and in consequence of it there was no morning drill. The men of Cap^{ts} Shelley and Dent had a regular hog killing this morning. They were out of provisions and with but little prospects of getting any soon, so they pitched into somebody's hogs. Killing eleven, and of the finest kind, some of them weighing over two hundred pounds. Rodes sent a guard out, but the men ran off and left a very large hog. The guards dragged it up to the guard house, and Co^l Rodes had it cut up and divided among the guards. Chapman being on guard we came in for a share of it, but it was so fat that we could not eat it.

I understand that Captains Shelley, Dent and Pegues have been placed under arrest for allowing their men to kill the hogs. Wrote to Mr Willingham to day concerning the condition of his son. He is very low indeed, delirious all the time. To night his pulse are at one hundred and fifty. He sleeps none at all, but is exceedingly restless. It is rumored in Camp that fifty thousand of our troops have crossed over into Maryland. Do not credit it. I fear it too good to be true. Our Camp fires became so disagreeable tonight that they smoked every one of us from the supper table. Every tent has a large pine fire before it, and they smoked awfully tonight. Nearly every one has red and watery eyes.

October 3, Thursday

JHC: They are beginning to wake us up pretty early now as the drum beats half hour before sun rise. A very pretty day but very warm, almost as hot as any we had during the summer. Some trouble was anticipated in Camp this morning in regard to the arrest of the three Captains but all went off smoothly, only several of the Companies refused to drill on account of it. Again we are called upon to mourn the death of another member of our Company. W^m. H. Willingham died this morning at half past ten o'clock of Typhoid-Pneumonia, after an illness of about two weeks. He had been delirious since Sunday and was not conscious of his approaching end. He bore his sufferings with much patience and quietly and without a struggle breathed his last. He is the last person upon whom one would have thought that death would fix his hold. He was one of the largest and healthiest men in the Company. But death makes no distinctions, but seizes upon all alike. His brain was very much affected. Even before he was taken down he appeared troubled and unhappy. He is now freed from all earthly troubles and I hope has found a resting place in heaven. His parents were telegraphed to immediately after his death. He will be buried tomorrow by the side of Sam Dorroh. Three and only three from our Company have died from the same neighborhood. All three our nearest neighbors—and within two miles. We have now a brigade sutler who has his tent about a quarter from our encampment. Went down to his establishment this evening and found it crowded with men eager to buy. Charges double price for every thing he sells, yet is busy all the while. I only got a package of envelopes of common brown paper, for which I paid twenty five cents. President Davis reviewed the troops today at Fairfax Court House. He left for Richmond this afternoon. Cannon booming and musketry rattling all the afternoon. The President told the troops that this was no time for speaking, but that Johns[t]on & Beauregard would soon speak from the thundering mouth of the cannon. Did not drill today.

October 4, Friday

JHC: Another very warm day. Our company did not drill this morning on account of having to dig the grave of our deceased fellow soldier Wm H. Wellingham. We buried him this afternoon at three o'clock. Capt Fowlers Company turned out with us. He was buried by the side of Sam Dorroh, where they will both rest from the labors and troubles of life. The death of these two fellow soldiers and friends has cast a gloom over the whole company, and the men all wear the look of sadness. We know not upon whom death may lay his icy fingers next as in both these cases, it may be upon those whom we least expect. We received orders this morning to pack up every thing but our tents and prepare to march as the enemy were reported as advancing. But we did not go. The enemy came upon our pickets this morning and I understand shot three of the Cavalry. They however did not come very far. We were on battalion this afternoon and had the music of the band to march by. They are beginning to play very well, and we will soon have very good music from them. We received orders this evening on dress parade to prepare three days rations to march to Burkes Station, about four miles up the railroad from Alexandria.

October 5, Saturday

JHC: Arose early this morning and began to prepare for our march. Started about nine o'clock, the weather [. . .] indeed and consequently our march was very fatiguing. We arrived at our destination about eleven o'clock. We are stationed on a high hill commanding a view of the country for a mile around. Our rear is covered by a skint of woods, through which we could easily retreat were we ordered so to do. We have been here all day without any incident worthy of note, except that the Company were amused at the expense of S—— who got a little under the weather from the inhibitation of too much red eye. He is very comic and as a sensible fellow, quotes large from Shakespeare. He soon however became boisterous, and the Captain came very near sending him back to camp under arrest. No news of the Yankees except that Dr Blackford tell us that there has been a skirmish at Munson's Hill, but we have not heard any of the particulars. We are all bivouacked in the woods, having made us shelters of bushes and rails. We are now preparing to go to rest, with our arms by our side ready for any emergency.

October 6, Sunday

JHC: Slept only tolerably well last night for Alonzo Chapman pulled all the cover off me and I got cold. I however buried myself under the bushes and caught an awful cold, in consequence of which I do not feel very well this morning. Father, Mr Hall (father to Capt Hall) and Dan Webster came to us this morning. Mr Hall is just from Greene Co. and states that the crops are tolerably good. Father brought the mail, I received a letter from Mrs Dorroh, dated Sep^t 28$\underline{th}$ in answer to one I wrote concerning Sam. She had not learned that he was dead. I could not avoid shedding tears while reading it. She appeared to know that he was dangerously ill and wrote to me to say to him to meet her in heaven, if no more on earth. Father and Dan Webster left before dinner for Camp, as they did not appear to like our place of encampment much. After dinner we were ordered to move up to the Station, from which we were about half mile. The whole regiment is now at the station encamped in the woods and an elegant place. We are camped where the Yankees camped when they were down here on their way to Richmond. Some of our boys occupy the same arbors. Some from our company went out this evening and killed a pig. Capt Hobson however paid for it and found out who were engaged in it.

October 7, Monday

JHC: Slept badly last night, caught an awful cold and feel very badly. Had for breakfast this morning some of the pigs the boys killed yesterday, as one of the fellows got scared and would not eat his share, but gave it to us. Our Company on picket today, about three miles from the station. We had a pretty warm march of it, we relieved Capt Fowlers Company. Lieut Williams has charge of the men besides my self, who occupy the advance posts. We are in the woods a mile or two from water or any habitation that we know of. Have heard the booming of artillery all the morning up towards Alexandria and the Potomac. Provisions are getting pretty scarce today, but fortunately for me through the kind consideration of brother I had a good dinner. He sent me a couple of chickens and a haversack of biscuits. A person unaccustomed to such a life as we now lead has no idea how such things make a fellow feel. We [are] away off in the woods, a mile from water with but little to eat and that poor tough beef and half done biscuit. Such things as a chicken and good biscuit make a fellows mouth water to think of them. This afternoon dark clouds began to appear threatening a heavy rain. Lieut Williams and myself having oil cloths fixed us up a kind of shelter, and were pretty secure from the rain. But very unexpectedly to us, we received orders to pack up and be ready to march as another regiment had arrived to relieve us. We left, after posting their pickets, about five o'clock and started for Camp. When we arrived at the ~~camp~~ Station we found the regiment had left us, so we put out after them. We had gone only about half mile when rain drops as big as the end my thumb began to fall, and soon it came in torrents. We were on the railroad and no place to stop at, so we were drenched to the skin very soon. We trudged along through mud and water up hill and down. Every little branch had become a small river. We nevertheless has some fun although under difficulties. As we were crossing a branch over which there was a rail, John Semple slipped off and down he went heels over head, gun accoutrements and all. He scrambled about for a while and finally got out swearing like a sailor. We arrived at Camp about eight o'clock, as wet as water could make us. The worst of the whole business was that when we got here expecting to find— every thing all night and day, we found our tent had over flown and every thing wet. I went into Westcotts tent, put on some dry clothes and felt finely. Our tent was too wet to sleep in, so we struck out each one to find another tent. I got a place with Robt Lanier in the next tent to mine.

October 8, Tuesday

JHC: As heavy a rain fell last night as I ever heard and it continued nearly all night. I slept only tolerably well, as the tent I was in leaked a little and drops of rain were occasionally falling upon my head all night. It was the first night that

I have slept in any one's tent but my own since I have been in the army. Our tent floor remained wet nearly all day and is still damp, but we will sleep upon it nevertheless. Rodes had us out drilling today, but no one paid any attention to the drill as every one was tired and felt badly from yesterday's trip, which was well calculated to make one feel badly, as it was the worst I was ever in. On battalion drill this afternoon we doubled quicked the largest portion of the time and I may say we were regularly put through. Capt Dent's Company was ordered off this evening to BullRun for some work, I know not what, I suppose however to build bridges as I understand some have been washed away. Our Camp looks lively tonight, as there is a big fire in front of every tent. The weather has become much cooler and I should not be surprised if we had some pretty severe weather soon. It is clear and cool tonight, presenting quite a contrast between this and last night, am in hopes I will get a good night's rest.

October 9, Wednesday

JHC: We were called up about half past three o'clock this morning by the long roll. Did not know what to make of it, nor do I yet, for we have not had any orders to move. After getting up and finding we had no orders to march I went back to bed. These false alarms are calculated to do injury, for our boys pay but little attention to an alarm now. We have had orders to be ready at a moments warning to march and have not done so for the last three weeks, so the boys are becoming careless and never make any preparation. Some of them often start off on a march with nothing at all in their haversacks. But I recon its all right, we are in the army anyhow. Had only one drill this morning. Quite cool this morning, and looked as if we would have a little snow, but it became warmer this afternoon. Seve (our cook) was taken sick this morning with a chill and has pneumonic symptoms. So we are now left without a cook unless we can hire one. Am in hopes he will soon recover, for when he gets sick we are in a bad fix. Co^l Rodes gave us a pretty severe drill this afternoon. Double-quicked us the better portion of the time. The Rev Mr Hutchinson from Greensboro arrived this evening. He came on to bring some boxes sent the company. He had to leave the boxes at the Junction as he could get them no further on account of there being so many before him.

October 10, Thursday

JHC: Arose quite early this morning, brought a bucket of water, made a fire and fed and watered Father's horse. Seve being sick brings about a considerable change in our mess, we have to do a little something for ourselves. Drilled twice this morning. Co^l Rodes drilled our company in the skirmish drill. It is a very pretty drill, but I do not like the loading and firing lying, though it is very necessary when we are actually engaged, but here on the damp and muddy ground it is not so very pleasant. Mr Hutchinson looks as natural as ever. He had quite a time getting the boxes on with him. Father received a letter from Dr Grigg and I received one from Miss A.G.W.——. Dr Grigg states that there is a great sickness in the neighborhood. He is kept busy all the while. The letter I received was a very short one, an expression of sorrow at the death of Sam Dorroh. She had not heard of the death of her brother. We did not drill this afternoon on account of the weather. Received orders tonight to march at three o'clock in the morning. Three regiments from our brigade, two from Early's, a battery and a cavalry company are all going together, where or for what no body knows. All we know is that we have orders to go and prepared with three days rations. The worst of the business is, we have not the provisions to carry.

October 11, Friday

JHC: We were aroused at half past two o'clock this morning[.] After getting up, eating breakfast, having every thing ready, and forming the Company, we received orders not to march until six. So I straightway went back to bed and slept 'till six. We started from Camp and instead of the whole brigade, only this regiment and two pieces of artillery went. Went to Pohic Church about twelve miles from Camp as a guard to sixty wagons for forage[.] When we got there the regiment divided, the right wing going with the wagons, the left on another road to prevent a surprise. We (in the left wing) went about three miles with one piece of artillery, the right wing having the other piece. We had a very good place to make a stand but saw no Yankees. This evening about five o'clock we heard a volley of musketry of about forty or fifty shots over toward the right wing. We were quickly formed, a party of skirmishers sent out and every thing kept in readiness to receive the enemy, but we saw nothing of them. We heard that the firing was by Shelley's Company, at party of Yankee Cavalry. They killed a fine horse, but did not get the rider. They took from the horse a fine saddle and bridle and an elegant Colts Navy repeater. The Yankees fired and ran but hurt no one at all. We are in a dangerous position tonight.

October 12, Saturday

JHC: Stirred us up this morning at three o'clock to leave. I was up from half past twelve on account of rain, which fell in abundance, giving us a good soaking. We did not get off until four. Had five creeks to ford, which gave us a good wetting. The weather was very cool indeed, so it was disagreeable marching. We however trudged along through the mud and water and met the right wing at Pohic Church, we remained there half an hour or more and while there Dan Webster issued out whiskey to the regiment. We set out for camp full of *spirits* and came very rapidly indeed. The whiskey got the upper hand of several and caused several quarrels and one fight[.] D.B. became very pugnacious and finally wound up by having to be brought to camp under arrest. He struck J.H. over the head with this gun and cut it slightly. We arrived here in camp about eleven o'clock and about as tired a set of men we were as has been seen in some time. This afternoon I took a short nap but was not much refreshed by it. Saw the Yankee saddle bridle and pistol that which were taken yesterday. The boys very quiet tonight and half of them asleep. Do not think it will require rocking to get me to sleep, as I feel very much fatigued.

NOTE: "D.B." is David Barnum.
"J.H." is probably J. C. N. Herran.

October 13, Sunday

JHC: Slept finely last night and until a later hour this morning than usual, as there was no roll call. Quite cool this morning has so continued throughout the day. Received a letter from brother. All well at home except some of the negroes who are sick with chills and fever. Father received a letter from Mr Palmer, who expected to come on to our company, but will not be able to leave Greensboro before the 20th as his resignation as postmaster has not been acknowledged. Wrote a letter to Aunt Ann in regard to having a couple of over coats made for brother and my self, as it appears that if we do not provide for ourselves, nobody else will. None of us have any winter clothing yet and but little prospects of getting any. We have to draw regular *bust head* whiskey now instead of coffee and I am sorry for it, for the boys drink all they give them and it sometimes turns a fellow a fool. Both Lieut Dedman & Christian have received their resignations and will leave for home in a day or two. There is considerable excitement in camp now in regard to the election of two lieutenants. Capt J. D. Webb and Father are candidates and Dr Ramsey and B. C. Adams their opponents. How the election will result is yet uncertain. Both Cap' Hobson and Lieut Williams are opposed to Webb and are doing every thing against him. I hope they will be defeated for Capt Webb is the best man in the army.

October 14, Monday

JHC: A crowd of us sat around our camp fire last night and amused ourselves telling stories. Laughed heartily at some of Crowell's stories of which he has an inexhaustible store. Scarcely any thing has been talked of for the past few days but the election of two lieutenants to fill the places of Dedman & Christian. It came off this morning. Capt Webb did not run on account of an appeal made to him by Co¹ Rodes not to do so, as there was no one else in the regiment who could fill his place. Father was unanimously elected second and Dr Ramsey third lieutenant. Every one seems to be perfectly satisfied with the election. Jas. L. Boardman and Joe Wright were appointed third and fourth Corporals. Westcott is assistant to Dan Webster in the Commissary department. Regimental inspection this morning. Father has an unlimited furlough to go in search of cloth for a uniform for the Company. Do not know when he will start. The boxes sent from Greensboro arrived this morning. More socks than any thing else. Mother sent twenty six pairs and three pairs of gloves. Heard the firing of Artillery this afternoon and understood that a fight was progressing at Vienna. Have heard none of the particulars. Mr Hutchinson took supper with us tonight and asked a blessing which sounded rather singular as we had heard none in so long.

October 15, Tuesday

JHC: Lieutenants Dedman and Christian, Mr Hutchinson and Father left this morning at four o'clock. The three former for home, Father for clothing for the

Company. He will first go to Richmond and if unable to procure the goods there, do not know where he will go. About half past four heard the long-roll over in the Sixth Ala. then in the Twelfth and then in ours. We were drawn up in line of battle, remained there about half an hour in the cold and then received orders to repair to our quarters to get breakfast. After breakfast, which was at the usual time instead of marching upon the enemy, who is reported at Pohic church, we received orders to police our quarters. Did not drill this morning. Have been quite unwell all day, but went out on drill this afternoon. We had the band out to march by. We are to be reviewed by Genl Van Dorn tomorrow. Co^l Rodes carried us through the movements in review, as one time the guides lost distance in wheeling and Co^l Rodes told us that such would not do and that the reviewing officer would play the devil with us. We all did pretty well this afternoon. To-night after supper while sitting about smoking and talking we very unexpectedly received orders to march. We packed up every thing, formed on the color line, stacked arms and returned to quarters, now in anticipation of marching orders every moment.

October 16, Wednesday

JHC: Our feelings tonight are entirely indescribable, tired, sleepy, and worn out, half sick and a little of every thing else conceivable. We were up all last night, struck tents about eleven o'clock and there we were in the cold without shelter, wagons packed and started off for Union Mills our old Camping ground. We bid adieu to Camp Masked Battery about daylight and took a retrograde movement instead of an advance upon Alexandria. It is useless to conjecture why the move, for we are utterly in the dark as far as regards a knowledge of it. All I know is, that we have moved and to Union Mills, encamped on a high hill opposite the old camp, occupying a very commanding position. Every thing around here looks very natural. Our old arbors still stand, and the good old spring of water still sends forth her icy cold drinks far better than the water at Camp Masked Battery. Saw Genl Van Dorn for the first time. Did not have time to take a good look at him. His most prominent feature is an enormous moustache. Himself and Aids are very fancifully uniformed. His appearance very unassuming. His head quarters are just in front of our encampment, and I will have a better opportunity of seeing him soon. Several of our boys lost their knapsacks, to day, by the wagon turning over and ~~losing~~ throwing every thing out. There were a great many things left, I believe, however we brought every thing we had worth bringing. The King William Artillery, Capt Carter—is planted on the same hill with us. Read the full account of the attack on Billy Wilson's Zouaves on Santa Rosa Island, by a party of our men under command of Genl Anderson. The cutthroats were completely routed and a good many killed. We lost ten or twelve killed and thirty odd wounded. The Zouaves ran for Fort Pickens. Their camp was completely destroyed. Billy Wilson happened to be at the Fort and escaped. Some prisoners were taken. This took place on Tuesday night, Oct 8th. It was in retaliation for their attack on the Judah (a vessel) at the Navy Yard some time since.

NOTE: The King William Artillery, commanded by Thomas H. Carter, was organized in King William County, Virginia.

In retaliation for the destruction of the Confederate privateer *Judah* on September 14, General Richard Heron Anderson led a thousand Confederate troops against Colonel William Wilson's Zouaves (Sixth New York Infantry) on Santa Rosa Island on the evening of October 8. After initial success, Federal forces in Fort Pickens forced the Confederates to withdraw.

October 17, Thursday

JHC: Do not think I moved last night, but slept like one dead. Think it was the best nights sleep I have had since I have been in the army. The only thing we missed was our plank floor. Do not know what we are to do without a floor, as there is no plank about here but what is taken, and all the boys got they had to pay fifty cents a plank for it. This morning moved our tents about fifty yards further to the right of the hill. The Artillery is now to our left as is also the 12th Miss Regiment, all on the same hill. The Sixth Ala is to the right of us on another hill across the run. All the troops are moving down from above and taking positions along Bull Run. A great many troops passed here today, having moved from about Fairfax Court House. Every thing has been in a stir today, moving tents and running around generally hunting plank &c. We have not been fortunate enough to get any yet. We have a better place for our tent than we have ever yet had. Heretofore we always happened to get in a gully, but this time our ground is level. Received orders this afternoon to get ready immediately to go on picket to Sangsters Station, three miles from Camp. Did so, and here we are, half of us without anything to eat. Fortunately I had the same provisions in my haversack that I brought from the old Camp. Arrived here after dark and relieved a North Carolina regiment.

October 18, Friday

JHC: Often have I heard and read of dark and stormy nights, of rain falling in torrents, and thunder rolling deep, of vivid flashes of lightning illuminating the night, the dismal howling of the wind and the groaning of the trees, but never experience one until last night. There were a good many shelters here, but they were all taken before I could get one, so I had to weather the storm. E.P. Jones and myself got us a bundle of straw and after hastily cooking our supper fixed ourselves for a—well not exactly for sleep—but for a good wetting. It continued to rain nearly all night. We however did not get as wet as we expected, having some oilcloths which kept us dry. Did not get up 'til late this morning as I did not get to sleep until late. After cooking breakfast beating up my coffee with the handle of my knife on my gun stock, we got ready to leave for Camp. We were relieved by the 20th Georgia regiment, got off about twelve o'clock and arrived at camp about half past one. Went to the creek, took a good bath and since have felt elegant. A great many troops have passed here to day. The 12th Miss and our regiment, are throwing up breastworks in front of the encampment. We are worked 'til ten o'clock at night. Saw a balloon this evening over toward Fairfax Court House. It only remained up a short time. An attack is expected soon. Dress parade this evening. Have been hauling up cross ties from the railroad to make a floor to our tent. Feel somewhat fatigued to night.

October 19, Saturday

JHC: Had us up this morning before day light policing our quarters. Think they are trying to overdo the things. If they continue in this way, we will all be worked to death before the Yankees come. A very cloudy and disagreeable morning, with little rain. Progressing finely with the breastwork, will finish it in a few days. Sent Seve out this morning to hunt up something to eat. He found six pounds of butter for which he paid forty cents per pound, and two dozen eggs for which he paid thirty seven and a half cents per dozen. We spend our months wages in a few days buying provisions. If we did not we would have a hard time of it as we get nothing but tough beef. Wrote a letter to Mother and ~~wrote~~ received one from brother Thomas, and one from John Dorroh. Brother informs me that there is a great deal of sickness in the neighborhood and that we had lost a negro girl about fourteen or fifteen years old. Gen[l] Van Dorn was out inspecting the breastwork this morning. We have not made our floor down yet, as we are awaiting the assistance of 'Squire Griggs, who desires to have a hand in it as he understands it better than we. There are a good many sick in Camp at present, and the Sergeant has a hard time to get men enough to fill out the details. Every thing still continues in a stir, hauling cross ties and building breastworks. Work 'till ten o'clock at night.

October 20, Sunday

JHC: Up again very early this morning, but not quite so early as yesterday, went to sleep again after roll call, and slept 'til breakfast. Sunday makes but little difference in the work of a soldier. Working all day and tonight on the breastworks. Have no time for drilling now. Heard today that the Yankees had burned Springfield and fled to their entrenchments the same day that we moved down here, but there are so many rumors afloat that one knows not what to believe. There are no Yankees this side of Fairfax Court House for our pickets extend two miles the other side. Begin to believe there will be no fight here, nor any where near here soon. Put our floor down at last, but it is not near so good as the one we had at Camp Masked Battery, better however than sleeping upon the ground. Cleaned & greased my gun today, it being the first opportunity since I have been here. Received a note from Father this evening who is at the Junction, to send his horse up, but did not send him, as I did not get the note until after supper. Am glad he has returned as I feel lonely now without him. Have not heard from brother yet, who left here for Richmond the day we came down here. I now prepare to take my first nights sleep upon cross ties. Expect they will be pretty hard at first.

October 21, Monday

JHC: Sent Seve down to the Junction after Father, who got here about twelve o'clock. He is in fine health and has arranged every thing satisfactorily concerning the uniform. Made a contract with the same man (Spence), who disappointed us before. He says he thinks he can make more out of him than any one else. Had quite an excitement in the Mississippi regiment this morning. One of their men, who had just been turned loose from the guard tent yesterday having been there for two months for stealing money, commenced his old trade of stealing another pocket book[.] He ran off and both the regimental guards were turned out after him. They formed a kind of horse shoe around him and himmed him in. I understand they intend whipping him, but I do not think they have the power to do it. Genl Beauregard was here at Van Dorns quarters this evening. Did not get a good look at him. Battalion drill this evening. On dress parade the Sergeant reported seventy five absent from our company, we had only nine files out. The most of our men are detailed on the work squad, and some are sick, more than we have ever yet had. Was very much surprised tonight to meet with Wm H. Chadwick. He is just from Texas and belongs to the 5th Texas regiment. They have not been armed yet.

October 22, Tuesday

JHC: Another as disagreeable day as we have seen for some time. Rain, mud and cold weather. Has been quite cool all day. The weather puts no stop to the work, for the boys have been hard at it all day. Some were detailed to go up the railroad to tear it up. A telegraph line is being established from here to Centreville, and there is some talk of building a railroad. I am in hopes we will not have it to build, for we are beginning to tire of such work. If however there is one to be built we are very apt to have a hand in it for such is our luck. Wrote a letter home this morning and sent some Confederate postage stamps as I expect small change is getting scarce every where. The stamps are similar to the United States postage stamps only they have Jeff Davis on them and are five cent stamps, and are of a different color. The thousand and one rumors about the probability of our being ordered back to Alabama this winter, are still going the rounds. I am only in hopes they may be true, for it would be much more pleasant there this winter than here. Do not expect much fun at either place, but we might accidentally have an opportunity of seeing our "home folks" and *sweet hearts,* which would be amazingly pleasant. Squire Griggs has been unwell all day, for the first time since he has been in the army.

October 23, Wednesday

JHC: Lee Whelan had a chill last night which made him quite sick. Squire Griggs remains about the same as last night. There was a fight last Monday at Leesburg between three of our regiments, 17th & 18th Mississippi and 8th Virginia, and four Yankee regiments. We achieved a glorious victory, took five hundred prisoners and five hundred are reported drowned trying to cross the

Potomac in their flight. The fight lasted six or seven hours. The loss in killed and wounded has not yet been ascertained, the prisoners being hurried off the same night, as there were some fears of another force coming against us. Loss of the enemy supposed to be considerable. Some of our men were at the Junction today and saw the prisoners. There were five hundred and twenty six privates, and three field officers besides the Company officers. Co^l Baker of Oregon was shot through the head and mortally wounded. He was the scoundrel who ran against Lane for the Senate. Capt Webb has been paying off the Regiment today. Our company has not yet been paid off, but will be tomorrow morning. An order was read out on dress parade this evening that we prepare to go on picket tomorrow morning to Sangsters Cross Roads, but tonight was countermanded. Suppose we are to go next day. Have been playing Eucre tonight, a very pretty game, but no game of cards ever did interest me. Very cold indeed tonight, and I think we will have frost by morning.

NOTE: Colonel Edwin Dickinson Baker was killed at the Battle of Balls Bluff on October 21, a humiliating defeat for the Union.

October 24, Thursday

JHC: Quite a cold morning, think it the coldest one we have had. Rather a disagreeable day on account of the cold wind. Blew very hard last night, so much so indeed that we had to put an extra rope to our tent to keep it from blowing down. Received our pay today for two months. Mine amounted to twenty three dollars and twenty three cents. The 5th North Carolina regiment went up to Sangsters today in our place. We will have to go tomorrow although we have had no orders as yet. Jack Wynne and Glover returned from Richmond today where they have been on sick furlough. Both look well. Received a letter from my old friend Gus Wynne, who is a member of the 4th Texas Regiment. I also received one from Miss A.G.W.————[.] 'Squire Griggs and Lee Whelan are both improving. The artillery moved to day to the hill opposite and in front of us. Commenced another breastwork over there as they say the one we have just finished will not answer. One hundred and thirty two more prisoners were brought in today from Leesburg. It is reported that the enemy are forty thousand strong at Anandale and advancing upon us.

October 25, Friday

JHC: A very heavy frost this morning, indeed as heavy one as I ever saw at this season of the year. Started from Camp this morning after breakfast and arrived here, Sangsters X Roads, about eleven o'clock. Three companies were detached for picket duty, Warrior Guards, Barbour Greys and our Company. We are in elegant quarters, being in a house and having a good cooking stove with all the appurtenances complete. There are only ten of us so well quartered and fortunately and singularly too I am one of them. The rest of the Company being about half mile back, are being on the outpost. We anticipate a good time, provided we are not disturbed by the Yankees, of whom there is but little danger.

We have three rooms and a kitchen, much better quartered than at Camp. Think we will remain here as long as we are on picket. There are good prospects of rain soon, but as we are well quartered we can let it rain, though I would prefer no rain, as we will have a muddy walk back to Camp. Nothing of interest has transpired here today. Before leaving Camp this morning there was a fight in Capt Dents company, which resulted in the knocking down of several and one man Dr Jenkins seriously hurt. He was struck upon the head with a stick which caused concussion of the brain.

October 26, Saturday

JHC: Talk about rats, we had a few around us last night. Lieut Ramsey and myself slept together or rather tried to sleep, but the rats had such a frolic, kicking over chairs, boxes, pans &c that we proposed standing guard over each other to prevent them taking us off. We however escaped, though I think they tried to take our guns and accoutrements off. I am sure they drilled with them all night as I found my gun misplaced this morning. This place certainly deserves the name of Rat Den, and I shall ever remember it as the Rat Den picket. Heard nothing, saw nothing, dreamed of nothing and swore at nothing but rats last night. Arose early this morning and got breakfast, then Dick Adams and myself took a stroll through the country. Went to the house of a Mrs Butts whose husband is in the Yankee Army. She has a very pretty and intelligent daughter, with whom we spent a very pleasant time. Provisions were sent us from Camp today. Heard that Co^l Rodes had been promoted to the rank of brigadier general. He is well worthy the promotion and will do credit to the office. We are getting on finely out here now and would prefer staying here to going to Camp. The only trouble we have is at night with the rats. Hope we will not be troubled with them tonight as we take our quarters up stairs in a good and comfortable room.

October 27, Sunday

JHC: Slept finely last night as we were not so much troubled with the rats. Have an attack of neuralgia this morning which gives me considerable pain and consequently am not feeling so well as usual. Up early this morning cooking breakfast and now all that is wanting is a book or news paper to read. Some wagons from the 12th Miss reg^t came here today and we got them to carry some things to camp for us. Carter & Dick Adams sent up an elegant stove and I a small three cornered cupboard. We are now left without any thing to cook in, but our servants brought our provisions ready cooked, so we are still doing well. Sorry to hear that the fight in Capt Dents company resulted so seriously. Dr Jenkins who was struck upon the head is reported to be dying. His skull was fractured by the blow. It all resulted I believe from the effects of whiskey, and that they now give us is mean enough to make a man steal his own pocket book. The report of Co^l Rodes being promoted is confirmed. Saw a very amusing incident this morning. Carter Adams caught a colt and mounted it without saddle or bridle. Coleman struck it, when off it went kicking and plunging until Carter was sprawled upon the ground. Saw the Beacon today. It contains a letter from Jule Bayol giving a description of his trip to Springfield and Anandale, on picket some time ago. I never enjoyed a picket before this, for we have certainly had a good time. We have had no rain, and have had a good house to sleep in, had plenty to eat and a clever crowd. Such trips are very few and far between. Has continued quite cool all day. Have not been over to see Miss Mollie Butts today, though would like to do so, as it is very seldom we get in ladies company. Nothing of importance has transpired today only I have suffered considerably from neuralgia. Feel some what relieved this evening.

October 28, Monday

JHC: Again slept finely last night and awoke this morning to find a heavy frost upon the ground and the weather quite cold. After breakfast prepared to leave for Camp. We were relieved by the 12th Ala Regt and left for Camp about twelve o'clock, and arrived here about three. Have suffered extreme pain all day in and above my right eye, and could scarcely see at all. Found the sick all improving, and the others hard at work on the entrenchments. The 6th Ala. has two or three breastworks, and some very good ones. They are much better fortified than we are, though we will soon be pretty well fixed if the enemy does not come down upon us before we finish. There was a letter received to day from Walker (Pickensville Blues) who was taken prisoner at Farrs Cross Roads. He states that the enemy will be down upon us on the third of November which is next Sunday. The letter was brought through by a spy. I did not see the letter consequently do not know all it contained. Dr Jenkins died this evening at four o'clock from the effects of the blow received. Ustick is the name of the man who inflicted the blow. What will be done with Ustick, for it no one appears to know. Court Marshalled though I presume.

October 29, Tuesday

JHC: Another tremendous frost this morning. We are beginning now to taste the bitters of a winter in Virginia. Our mess is pretty well supplied with every thing comfortable. A good tent, pretty good supply of blankets, plenty to eat, a good cup board and table, plates, knives, forks cups &c. There are a good many who are not so comfortably quartered. We all have pretty good tents and will have plenty blankets soon. It is reported that the enemy is twenty thousand strong at Burkes Station. The Northern press states that McClellan considers the fight at Leesburg a complete victory to Northern arms and expresses himself well satisfied with the result. How that can be is a mystery to me. We took nearly seven hundred prisoners, besides a great number killed and drowned[.] Their whole force was completely routed and put to flight. Yet they consider it a victory for them. "O tempora: O mores." It was reported today that there had been another fight there and that we had captured fifteen hundred more prisoners. This however needs confirmation. Wrote a letter to brother this evening, who is now at Woodstock, Va. Have suffered but little today from neuralgia, and sincerely hope it has entirely left me. Heard today that President Davis would be here tomorrow to dine with Gen¹ Van Dorn.

NOTE: "O tempora: O mores" translates as "Oh these times, Oh these ways" (Cicero).

October 30, Wednesday

JHC: Much warmer today than yesterday and some prospects for rain soon. Went down to the Sutlers store this morning, to make some purchases. There was at least an hundred men in and around the tent. Had to jam, push and squeeze my way in, and then got only some pins, ink, and tobacco for which I had to pay about three prices, but had to take them or do without. Heard today that Gen¹ Van Dorn expressed his opinion as to the probability of a fight here tomorrow. He may have some grounds for thinking so, but I have not been able to discover them. He has ordered all extra baggage to be sent off today, guns to be cleaned up, and ammunition all right so as to be ready for the anticipated attack. Have suffered some today from pain in my eye. The boys are still hammering and digging away on the entrenchments and building a bridge across the creek, but they are getting on slowly as they seem to take but little interest in it. If they do no better work than they are now doing, it will take them two weeks to finish either the bridge or entrenchments. Yet they have a large number from each regiment every day. Nothing new or interesting today. The boys all have a mania for pipe and ring making. They are made from the root of the ivy of which there is an abundance around here.

October 31, Thursday

JHC: Much cooler this morning than yesterday, as we had some frost. As far as I could see or learn the Yankees did not attack us today. I heard, on the contrary, that the fight was postponed for some future day, and that they were marching upon Fredricksburg. Am in hopes they will meet with the same reception that they have always met with at the hands of the Southern boys, at the point of the bayonet. If they did, I would be willing to swear that they would not take the place, for there never yet has been an instance in which they did not run from a charge bayonet. This afternoon we had dress parade at half past four o'clock in order to parade a flag before the regiment, which has been adopted as a battle flag, to prevent the Yankees stealing a march upon us, by hoisting the Confederate flag as they did at the battle of Manassas. Co¹ Rodes took his leave of us a Co¹ in a very interesting and feeling manner. He complimented us for our courtesy toward him also for our bearing up under the many and toilsome and as he termed them famous marches. At the conclusion of his remarks we cheered him lustily. He will endeavor to get us in his brigade as it is in contemplation to throw the troops of each state in the same brigades—

November 1, Friday

JHC: Capᵗ Dan Webster, Syd Webb, Ezra Wilson and Bob Chadwick returned last night from Richmond, where the three latter had been for several weeks on sick furlough. They are all looking finely. They are getting very strict now concerning the sick. The Sheriff of each County is authorized to arrest and send to camp every soldier who has not a pass and who is not sick. Serg^t Jones and myself took a stroll in the country this morning. Went to a Mr Butlers where some of our extra baggage is stored. We walked about three miles, and stopped at several houses. Saw only one young lady and she not very pretty, which is not at all uncommon in this country. Have heard the firing of artillery all day up toward Dumfries. Expect we were attacked there today. Co^l Jones tried his hand on battalion drill this evening. Did very well. Have not been very well today, but feel better tonight. We have not a great many sick in camp at this time and I am in hopes all will soon be well and ready to meet the enemy. Our breastworks not yet finished.

November 2, Saturday

JHC: I have often heard persons talk of and I have read of stormy nights, of rain falling in torrents and the wind blowing hurricanes, but last night was ahead of all that I ever heard or read of. It commenced raining before we went to bed and continued all night without ceasing. The wind blew terribly. I could hear men all night calling for assistance to keep their tents from blowing down. Three tents in our company blew down to the ground and tore to pieces, others were torn and let the rain through in perfect streams. Ours did not blow down but the fly was torn to pieces which caused the tent to leak a good deal, so we suffered with the rest. A great many were blown down in other companies. This morning it continued so that we could get no breakfast cooked until eleven o'clock. One or two more tents blew down this morning and were badly torn. A great many got nothing to eat at all until tonight at supper for it has rained all day. We had to keep in tents all day and do nothing but talk, sleep, play cards, smoke and chew tobacco. To night the rain has ceased and the weather quite cool. We had some hail today. Father is unwell and I fear his feet are going to hurt him again—

NOTE: On this day, Robert E. Rodes assumed command of Richard S. Ewell's brigade (which included the Fifth Alabama), reporting as the Third Brigade, First Division, District of the Potomac. The day before, George McClellan had succeeded Winfield Scott.

November 3, Sunday

JHC: We slept pretty comfortably last night and this morning found it clear, quite different from yesterday morning. It is however warm and I fear we will have more rain soon. The railroad bridge across Bull Run has washed away and the creek is all over the country, so there is another job of work for our regiment. Building railroad bridges and such things is our luck. Quite an accident occurred today on Bull Run. Two members of the 12$\underline{th}$ Mississippi regiment were drowned, one of them attempted to cross but the current being too strong carried him under and he was drowned. Another fell from the bridge and was drowned. The latter was said to be under the influence of liquor. Received a letter from Chas Whelan Jr. Learned that Mother was convalescent. Wrote to her and answered Charlie's letter. Mr Madison Jones leaves for home tomorrow. The report is in circulation now that half the army will be sent to the coast and the other half remain here. If that be the case we will be very apt to remain here. Genl Rodes has succeeded in getting our regiment in his brigade. What others he has I know not. He will be very apt to get us to remain here. He wants to win a name.

November 4, Monday

JHC: Was detailed this morning to go out in search of Whiskey that the country people were selling the soldiers, but did not go, as another detail was made from Genl Early's brigade. We got a sight of Genl Van Dorn and came back to our quarters. Dr Blackford went up and exhumed the bodies of Dorroh and Willingham and will start for home with them tomorrow. We pitched the coffins this evening to prevent their being offensive. He certainly deserves great credit for his exertions. Last night he walked three miles in the country after supper and this morning before day hired a wagon and horses and went for the bodies. He got them here before twelve o'clock and had them well pitched this evening. Received a letter from brother William. His health is improving. Also received one from home. Mother has recovered from her recent illness. Heard this evening that Seward, Cameron and Chase had resigned their seats in Lincoln's Cabinet, and that Pennsylvania had gone by fifteen thousand for peace. How true this is remains to be learned. Also heard that we would have a fight here in a few days. This does not look much like peace. Heard that the enemy was at Fairfax Court House. So I have heard a good deal.

November 5, Tuesday

JHC: Detailed again this morning for the same purpose as yesterday, but did not get off so easy, as we had to go this time. There are twenty five privates[,] four corporals, two sergeants and a lieutenant of us. I had a detail of eight men and took a stroll over and around the Sixth, Twelfth and Fifth Ala and the Twelfth Miss. regiments, with orders to report all offal, arrest all chuck-luck dealers, all men found beyond the limits of their encampment without a written permission; and to confiscate all whiskey and arrest the one who sold it to soldiers. No one was arrested by my squad nor no whiskey found. Our head quarters are at a barn opposite our encampment. The man in the 12th Miss regiment who stole the pocket book some time ago, is here under our charge. I understand he tried to desert but was taken up by a scout and brought back. He has a very bad countenance indeed. Major Ellis who once figured so largely in Greensboro and afterward left so mysteriously has been here under arrest for having a difficulty with an officer in the 12th Miss regiment, of which he is a member. I witnessed this morning one of the most solemn scenes I have been witness to since I have been in the army. It was the burial of one of the men who was drowned on Sunday last in Bull Run. The music which followed the corpse added great solemnity to the occasion. He was followed by an escort of soldiers who buried him with the usual military honors. Father received a letter from Mother which was a source of great pleasure to us to know that she had recovered from her recent illness; a great amount of sickness has prevailed in the neighborhood among both white and black, but happily very few fatal cases. The second relief was out this evening, but brought in about the same report that my squad did. Found no whiskey or chuck-luck dealers. To night we have to quarter in the barn. Happily we are near our encampment so that we are able to get our blankets and go to our meals. The papers of today's issue made no mention of the many rumors that were in circulation in Camp yesterday.

November 6, Wednesday

JHC: Rained last night but luckily we were in a dry place, so we did not get wet. Relieved by the 5th North Carolina regiment this morning. Nothing of any interest transpiring in Camp today. Every thing quiet. The Richmond papers made some mention of a row in Lincolns Cabinet, but did not credit the report. All a false rumor as the majority of things are we hear. Has cleared off and we have had a very pretty day of it, and tonight is quite cool. Think there will be frost before morning.

November 7, Thursday

JHC: Moved our place of encampment today, over on the same hill upon which the breastworks are erected. We have now an elegant place if they will only allow us to remain here, but I should not be surprised if they had us moving soon. They are reorganizing the army and having troops from the same state put together. Gen[l] Rodes is in command of our brigade[.] Do not know what other Ala regiments will be placed in the brigade. Some think the 4th Ala. Met with Lowndes Womack today, an old college mate. Worked very hard today in moving and tonight feel quite tired.

November 8, Friday

JHC: Detailed this morning to take a squad of men down to work on the bridge, on which we have been at work ever since we have been here and yet they have scarcely made a start toward building it. I never saw one built in the same manner as this is being built. It is very heavy work indeed and the men have to go in the creek which is enough to kill a man. Gen[l] Rodes came down today and had a barrel of whiskey sent us. Some of those who went in the creek got pretty full and were quite lively. Lieu[t] Goff closed the whiskey drinking pretty early this evening, so that my squad did not get a drink at all as they were at work some distance from the barrel. I guess it was better for them as it was of the meanest kind and I should dislike to see a friend of mine get drunk on such whiskey. We were dismissed this evening about four o'clock after having done a pretty good days work. Bought some apples to day for fifty cents a dozen and very inferior ones at that. Jim Gordon of the 11th Ala regt was over here today. He is looking finely. Quite cool tonight. Slept very cold last night, although had the same covering that we have always had. No news to day of importance.

November 9, Saturday

JHC: Introduced a new programme to the proceedings in camp. The orders now are to have dress parade at nine AM instead of evening. Then comes battalion drill. This morning we were called out for drill. Our company mustered fourteen men, the Warrior Guards eight and the Cahaba Rifles three. It was really amusing to see the lieutenant march out with his three men. The whole regiment only turned out one hundred and twenty men, all the others being on the work squad and on guard. We have now a brigade and regimental guard, besides a large number to work on the bridge. Genl Rodes told the men today that whoever refused to go into the water he would have him shot. I guess he was only trying to frighten them. We have had a very disagreeable day. Commenced raining about dinner time and continued 'til night. Very cold indeed and we have no wood. Heard that Lincoln's fleet had attacked some point off the coast of Georgia, but did not hear the result of it. On the coast is where the trouble will be, for I do not think we will have much fighting here, as the roads will be impassable to their artillery. To night am not very well but feel very sore and sick. Hope I will be all right by morning. Received a letter from brother William. He will be in camp Monday.

November 10, Sunday

JHC: Sunday has again rolled around, yet one scarcely knows it, for there is but little change in our life. We do not drill, but only have our guns and accoutrements inspected and go on dress parade. The men are sent off to work as on other days, guard duty the same. We have no preaching now as our Chaplain has left us. We sit around camp and talk, read and write letters. I have written three today, one to Mother one to Miss A.G.W—— and one for Seve to his wife. Nothing has occurred to day of interest. So I will have to close with one page. Expect to go to the Junction tomorrow as we are looking for brother.

November 11, Monday

JHC: Had roll call this morning for the first time in several days. Orders were read out the other day, that we should have roll call every morning at half past five o'clock and that a commissioned officer should be present at every roll call. Capt Hobson was out early this morning. It goes pretty hard with him, but he will do his duty. Cloudy and damp this morning but no rain. Went to the Junction in a wagon and of all the rough riding I ever had this beat all. The roads are in an awful condition and we had a poor driver and a young team of mules. They were sure to go in every mud hole in the road. After we got there we were disappointed in finding brother as he did not come. So we knocked around there awhile and bought a few things, among them a few quart of oysters for which we paid eighty cents. Father and I sat down on some plank and eat them. Had to buy a coffee pot to put them in, as the vender had no place to serve them up. They were first rate. Got some cheese for which we paid fifty cents per pound. Soda they sell at sixty cents per pound. Heard no news while there. Got back about two o clock pretty tired after the rough ride. Built a fire place this evening in front of the tent.

November 12, Tuesday

JHC: Another big frost and had to go out in it to roll call. No one can see the necessity for having it so early and every one goes back to bed afterward. Yet we have to go out. There are a great many things we have to do that we can see no necessity for, yet our officers can, or if they cannot, the orders are issued and we have to obey. The opinion of a private in the army is not worth the expression, yet some of them are far superior to those of the officers, for I have seen some in command who had not the good sound sense of a common corn field negro. Brother has not yet come and I am afraid he has again become unwell, but hope not. Battalion drill this morning and a poor affair it was, very few men out. Our scouts brought in three Yankees this evening taken at Accotink Creek. The Union men in Tennessee have burned the railroad bridge across the river, cutting off all supplies from that quarter. Brownlow swears he will rot in the public jails before he will take the oath of allegiance to the Confederate Government. I understand the fleet has taken Port Royal on the coast. It is said that black flags are floating all along the coast signifying the asking and giving of no quarter. No more prisoners there.

NOTE: Parson William Brownlow was charged with treason October 24 and his Knoxville *Whig* closed.

November 13, Wednesday

JHC: We have now passed through only half of our campaign. If the next six months be as arduous as the past, we will have had a memorable campaign, and such will be very apt to be the case, for we yet have the winter before us. Today we were out on drill and succeeded better than yesterday. Orders were read out this morning to the effect that there should be two drills daily, battalion drill in the fore and company drill in the afternoon. We however did not drill this evening. Father is on guard to day as junior lieutenant, we having now two lieutenants, three sergeants and three corporals and not so many guards as usual. This is an order from Gen¹ Rodes. Lieut Carter Randolph and Ben Borden were here today, members of Capt Tayloe's Cavalry Company, stationed between Centreville and Fairfax Court House. More prisoners were brought in today making five in all, and three horses, one Captain, a Lieutenant and a Sergeant. They say that McClellan will be down in a few days and whip us out. Understood to day that Mr Palmer was not coming on at all. Do not know when we will get our blankets and clothing now. To night twenty eight years ago Squire Griggs tells me we had the meteoric shower in 1833. Have heard the firing of cannon all day. Am unwell tonight and have taken some medicine. The Yankees have Port Royal.

NOTE: What was perhaps the most spectacular instance ever of the Leonids meteorite shower centered on Alabama during the evening November 12–13, 1833.

1862

March 23, Sunday

JST: Left Greensboro at 2 O'clk A.M. got to Selma. Went aboard the Senator & arrived in Montgomery at 12 M

NOTE: John S. Tucker's diary begins two weeks after enlisting, as he makes his way to join the Guards in winter camp, five miles east of Orange Court House, Virginia.

March 24, Monday

JST: Spent the day in Montgomery & had quite a dull time of it.

March 25, Tuesday

JST: Took the cars at 8 O'clk A.M. Got to Atlanta at night.

March 26, Wednesday

JST: Arrived in Augusta got Breakfast & took the cars for Weldon

March 27, Thursday

JST: Arrived in Weldon at 10 A.M. Met any quantity of troops. Could get nothing to eat & had to remain until night when we took a Box Car for Richmond

March 28, Friday

JST: Arrived in Petersburg at sun up. After passing a *very cold* sleepless night in an open Box Car—went through the city on foot & took the train for Richmond where we arrived at 11 O'clk A.M.

March 29, Saturday

JST: Spent a very unpleasant day in the city. Wrote home to Annie. Snowed sleated & rained all day

NOTE: Annie is Annie Nutting Tucker, John S. Tucker's wife and sister of Guards George and Edwin Nutting.

March 30, Sunday

JST: Still in Richmond. Took Box Cars at 4 O'clk & remained at depot until 8—spending the most unpleasant night since we left home

March 31, Monday

JST: On the RR all day with scarcely any thing to eat. Got to Orange C.H. in the night. Went to Epis Church & slept till morning.

April 1, Tuesday

JST: Got up cooked our breakfast & left for Camp 5 miles east of Orange. Arrived about 10 O'clk and met all the Boys

April 2, Wednesday

JST: Spent the day in camp. Went to the 6th Ala & saw a good many acquaintances

April 3, Thursday

JST: Got orders to strike tents & report at Orange C.H. Got there about 11 O'clk P.M. & camped on the side of a hill in an oak thicket on the east side of the Town & R.R. pleasant night

April 4, Friday

JST: Rec. orders to go back to camp. bundled up put out & got back about 3 O'clk P.M. Pitched tents drew rations & got a good nights sleep.

April 5, Saturday

JST: Got orders early this morning to *again* strike tents & report at Orange C.H. as soon as possible. Packed up put out & got there at 11 O'clk A.M. & took open cars at dark. traveled all night. Got no sleep at all

April 6, Sunday

JST: Got to Richmond at 12 O'clk & was treated very hospitably by the citizens who met us with cakes, Pres Bread, Meat & every thing good to eat. Passed through the City & took a Steamer at 3 O'clk P.M. & at 12 M got off & marched the remainder of the night with out any sleep for 2 nights.

April 7, Monday

RHA: Took up line of march for Lebanon Church, a very disagreeable one too. Stayed about 2 hrs. marched to Lees farm, Gen. Magruders Headqtrs. Commenced raining about 4 o'c & rained all night. Very disagreeable night, plenty rain, no sleep & a superabundance of cold, cough &c. Severe skirmishing going on. Heard a beautiful volley of musketry this evening. The rain still pours down. Poor boys, how long.

NOTE: Richard Henry Adams' diary begins as the Guards are moving toward Yorktown, where fifteen thousand Confederates are under siege by the Army of the Potomac. McClellan plans to drive his massive force up the Peninsula and capture Richmond. Finding at Yorktown what he mistakenly believed to be a huge army commanded by Major General John Bankhead Magruder, McClellan began a siege on April 5.

April 8, Tuesday

RHA: Still at our Bivouac. Rain, Rain, Rain. Skirmishes still going on. Everybody wet & mad. Cleared up about 12 o'c slightly. 4 o'c commenced again to rain. Much to everyone's delight we got ordered to go to our Right wing. Got off about 5½ o'c. Mud, slop, Rain, holes of water to farewell &c &c. On we went until dark very well—but when night had thrown her sable mantle it became one of the most disagreeable marches I ever experienced. Men falling and stumbling about in every direction. Rain pouring down all the time. Every drop seemed to make our blankets 10 lbs heavier. About 12 o'c we stopped at a camp right by the 5th La. where we went to work and made up a fire by the aid of a bench that I stole. Had a very disagreeable night's rest on the wet & cold ground. Companies scattered all about amongst the La. Regt where there were a great many extra sheds. The one we got was very wet and leaky.

April 9, Wednesday

RHA: After we got breakfast and were very hospitably treated by Co. A 5th La, to whom we will be under lasting obligations, we moved camp about ½ mi. in an old pine field. Nothing worth burning. In sight of the enemy. Our cannon every ½ hr during the day were shelling them at a house which they set on fire and left. Night and hard rain coming on. Gilliam James & myself went to the La. Regt & spent the night, being comfortably in a tent with a plenty of straw & the most hospitable set of men I ever saw who gave us *2 cups* of *coffee.*

April 10, Thursday

RHA: Having had *one more* good night's rest, we awoke in fine spirits this morning to see the sun shine forth but only now and then. Our La. friends set before us Coffee & warm bread, which being eaten, we made our way back to camp. Went out on the redoubts to witness our batteries shell the enemy in a house. Saw several of the Yanks. A part of our Regt. had a slight skirmish to day on picket—nobody hurt. Night found me on the damp ground trying to sleep.

April 11, Friday

RHA: The sun rose clear & bright. Seemed as a smiling old friend returning to its accustomed ground. The 5th Ala. seems to like the Peninsula better as this is the first fair day we have seen. A beautiful day, the sky one spotless blue, the wind blowing lightly, the King of Southern Rivers the James dotted with canvas, as streatched all along our Right. All seem to enliven our boys & make them more ready & willing to do their part in the great battle which we are on the Eve of fighting. Got orders about 2 o'c to report to Gen Rodes Headqtrs. Had a rather rapid & disagreeable march 13 mls. Reached our destination about 8 o'c. Stopped at the 11th Ala. on our way. Having reported to Gen. Rodes we stopped in a piece of woods which was soon dotted with numerous fires. We took a repose with the *consolation* of knowing we would be roused about 3 o'c which amounted to nothing.

April 12, Saturday

RHA: Having cooked our scanty meal, sat down & wrote a letter home. We started for Ft. Magruder ¾ ml. distant. Reached the place we were ordered to relieve a Co of 9th Ala. Regt in a ravine just below the fort. A very dirty place.

Have a beautiful view of the enemy but no "Skrimmaging" as the piney woods say. On guard 1st part of the night from 8 to 11 o.

JST: Got up & continued the march to Yorktown & camped on the field that Cornwallis surrendered on and closed the first "American Revolution" Plenty of Yankees in sight of us but no fighting going on. Fair pretty day. Feeling much better to day than yesterday.

April 13, Sunday

RHA: Slight skirmishing going on. Went into Yorktown to get something to eat, whi by the way was damn scarce. Succeeded however as I generally do in such places, to get a little. 32 loaves of bread. Relieved at dark. Went back to our former bivouac. Our stillness & quiet slumber was broken about 1½ o'c by immense firing of cannon, bursting of bombs over our camp. The enemy began to shell our camps. Nobody hurt. Using the *eloquent* & *stirring* words of the *immortal* Lincoln, all the boys got up & dressed but on I went with my sleep whi I greatly needed.

JST: In camp & doing nothing, the day most unlike Sunday. Some playing cards. Some washing clothes & others at various other things. Went in Town & looked all over it. A very dilapidated looking place. Most of the houses shelled burned or pulled down & camps in place. Fine day

April 14, Monday

RHA: Lying in camp doing nothing but all hands trying to see whi can tell the biggest lie. Many of them wonderful "yarns". Badenhausen & self went down to Yorktown. Ran the blockade & in other words got a big drink apiece. Saw our batteries fire at the enemies gunboats which was done by way of experiment. The gunboats were firing at the opposite shore where we have a cavalry picket. The patrol ran us back to camp. I just reached camp in time to get on a detail to work on breastworks. The party left about dark. Got to our destination & were put on second relief from 2 o'c until day break. So we slept until 12. Was in hopes that they would not find us but too sharp for us. W. Tunstall, Pick Moore & myself slept together & very little work we did. Laid down again & went to sleep but was pulled up by Col Seibles who was commanding the working. Fooled around until day break when we left for camp but found the Regt under arms at one of the breast works. We came to camp though & got breakfast.

On reaching camp on morning 15th Apr we went to work & got breakfast & made up our nap, after whi I went to camp of Jeff Davis Artillery. Came back & am now sitting on a log writing & now & then hear a cannon open & a bomb burst over on the enemy's line. Here's for another nap. Good night I must say though only 12 o'c. Took a refreshing nap, ate dinner & went down to the branch. Washed, put on clean cloths & feel like an animal that exists in large quantities *out* of the *army*, viz a *white man*. The first time I have had that good feeling since I left home. This is a very warm day. Our Regt started on picket about dark, I on post on 1st relief from 7 to 9 & from 1 to 3. Rather sleepy as I was up last night. Saw nothing of the enemy but several sky rockets they sent up. Some firing nobody hurt but a dog.

NOTE: The Jeff Davis Artillery was organized in Selma, Alabama, and during the Peninsula Campaign served under D. H. Hill.

April 15, Tuesday

JST: Still at Camp—weather fine. Detailed to cut out a Road & had to work awful hard. Finished returned to Camp & wrote to Annie

April 16, Wednesday

RHA: Awaking this morning about 6 o'c found our pickets and the enemies firing on each other & a balloon from their side whi is looking down upon us. Keeps out of range of our guns though. 7 o'c on post again. Balloon still up. A rascal just shot at us but his shot did not hold up. 8½ o'c cannon open to our Right rapidly. 4 or 5 guns on our side at once. Can see the enemies bombs burst high up in the air, but ours seem to strike & burst in their midst. 10½ o'c balloon just gone down. Heavy firing still on both sides. They sound beautifully. Now & then musketry heard on our side whi seem to be mocking to the much heavier report of our big guns but they, small as they are, are doing their proper execution I am confident, for they are in the hands of men who are fighting in a righteous cause, and men too that have brave hearts. On the firing goes. The enemies bombs still bursting high & short of aim. A grand sight a cannon battle. Just relieved by Carter & Lonnie who are sitting at our Rifle pit. 12 o'c firing still going on. Just then an old bomb came singing into our camp causing everyone to fall flat on his face. Fired from the boats. There goes a 32 pounder from Yorktown. There a shout from the crowd as the old bomb bursts among the boats, which tell its effect. A good many shots were exchanged in that quarter, the bombs of the enemy bursting high up & before they got to the fort. 2 o'c—All firing but an occasional shot from the enemy to our Right ceased. 3 o'c again cannon and musketry open heavier than ever. Beautiful. On it went, worse than at the battle of Manassas. Such heavy firing, both cannon & musketry, never was heard, lasting until 6 o'c when the musketry ceased. But we kept up the firing with cannon all night but not so rapid.

NOTE: "Carter" is Buck Carter Adams.

"Lonnie" is Alonzo Coleman.

On this day President Jefferson Davis approved an act requiring the conscription of white males between eighteen and thirty-five years of age.

April 17, Thursday

RHA: Every thing quiet this morning but an occasional shot from the enemies cannon. At the same place they got a position directly in front of us about 10 o'c & fired bombs into our redoubts—which were well directed several bursting in the fort to our left & in the fort at Yorktown. A 64 pounder directed from Fort Magruder ran them off. About 2 hrs. they came back again. Fired several more, one of which was well aimed at our big gun. Several bursted over us right in front

of the fort—which we were on picket. One of our shots aimed at a Cavalry Co
going across a field which fell amongst them scattering them in every direction.
Moved back at dark behind the fort as they supposed the enemy had gotten the
range during the day & would shell us & we were in danger both of our guns &
those of the yankees. Were sleeping quietly the moon shining brightly, all silent
but an occasional shot from our pickets—I dreaming of home & loved ones when
all at once I was awakened by immense firing where the fight came of yesterday.
It lasted 10 minutes very rapidly. We were all ordered under arms thinking they
w^ld attack us next but "nary time". Went to sleep again. About 1 hr. afterwards
was awoke by the same firing at the same place but shorter. Heard our men yell
as they drove the invading scoundrels back. God favors the Right.

April 18, Friday

JST: Got a good nights sleep & have been sleeping good part of to day. Weather
still clear & pleast. Wrote to Annie to day.

April 19, Saturday

RHA: Proceedings about the same—one old routine—working us like thunder. Very warm today. Saw Rich Christian. Moved back on Picket at dark. Commenced Raining as soon as we were posted. Never spent such a night in my life.
Many & many a time during the night I thought of home & home folk & the
month I had just spent there. Pondered over The Lone Rock by the Sea &c &c.
Went to sleep about day break. The Yankees made a second attempt to cut the
dam last night. Had a heavy fight for 10 min.

NOTE: "The Lone Rock by the Sea" was a popular song of the 1850s.

April 20, Sunday

RHA: Rain all day. Went over to 4th Ala. Everything on us wet. No sleep
hardly.

JST: Rained all night last night. All hands got wet—dident sleep but very little.
To day seems most unlike Sunday. Instead of resting from our labors & listening
to Church Bells, we hear nothing but the Roar of artillery & rattle of Musketry
& see nothing but large squads of men at almost every imaginable army work &
duty. Those not on duty or most of them amuse them selves by playing Poker,
singing vulgar songs, Cursing & swearing &c &c Rained all day

April 21, Monday

RHA: Drizling rain. Today is my 21st birthday. The most disagreeable birthday
I have ever spent. The yankees seem to be celebrating it by firing bombs into
our camp from their gun boats. Feel myself highly honored. The sun, my best
friend, seems to be ashamed of me & refuses to venture out & gaze upon me.
Would be most happy to see the old fellow. All hands lying low, from the bombs.
Relieved tonight by 2 Mis. Bat^n. Heavy rain until 9 o'c at night. No sleep until
late, wet as a rat, hungry as a wolf & poor as a church mouse. Thus passed my
21st birthday—1500 mls from home & sold for 2 years—poor critter. Oh Saul
why persecutest thou me, we all think but few read the holy book it's from. We are

getting pretty tired of Fort Magruder—pretty anxious to get back to our bivouac in the woods.

April 22 and 23, Tuesday and Wednesday

RHA: Lying in the reserve doing nothing but getting wet &c. 23$\underline{rd}$ rather clear & pleasant. I was on picket tonight. Very cool.

April 24, 25, 26, Thursday through Saturday

RHA: Still on picket. The enemy still firing on our batteries now & then & we returning their shots. We were relieved on the evening of the 25th & came back to our camp in the woods. Rather more comfortable than the open field where we had been for the last 10 or 12 days. Streatched some blankets somewhat in the shape of a tent & slept very comfortably, the 1$\underline{st}$ for a good while. Drizling rain all 26$\underline{th}$. Very disagreeable.

April 27, Sunday

RHA: The conscripted 5th Ala. Regt. today reorganized with the following elections. Capt. Pegues—Col. Capt. Hall—Lt. Col. Hobson, my Capt.—Maj. Jno. Williams—our Capt. Ramsey—1$\underline{st}$ Lt. Joe Borden the best old fellow that ever lived, 2$\underline{nd}$ Lt. & Wiley Tunstall another one of the boys—3rd Lt. Had an amusing time electing non commissioned officers. I aspired to nothing higher than "private in the rear ranks".

JST: To day the election of officers take place. Still cloudy but not raining this morning. Passed the Whiskey round & opened the polls. Election resulted— Pegues "Col", Hall "Lt Col", Hobson "Major" as field officers. For Company I "Greensboro Guards" J W Williams "Capt", Dr Ramsey "1st Lt", Joe Borden "2d Lt", W C Tunstall "3d Lt", E P Jones "O.S." This has been a big day in many of the Regiments in electing their field & company officers & a great many of the men got gloriously *tight*. Ordered from the woods back to Yorktown at dark—110 men in the Co & 60 odd on the sick list.

NOTE: The Fifth Alabama reorganized as follows:

Company A   Barbour Greys (formerly Company K)
Company B   Talladega Artillery (formerly Company E)
Company C   Monroe Guards (formerly Company D)
Company D   Greensboro Guards (formerly Company I)
Company E   Sumter Rifle Guard (formerly Company F)
Company F   Cahaba Rifles (formerly Company G)
Company G   Livingston Rifles (formerly Company B)
Company H   Pickensville Blues (formerly Company C)
Company I   Grove Hill Guards (formerly Company A)
Company K   Haymouth Guards (new).

The Warrior Guards disbanded; most joined either the Greensboro Guards or Fowler's artillery company.

April 28 and 29, Monday and Tuesday

RHA: Got the news this evening of the fall of New Orleans. Every one looks & seems to be quite desponding—but more ready & willing to do the important work called on them to do on the Peninsula. We must & shall retrieve the loss of the "Crescent City"—dear to us all & an important scene of action during the great Revolutionary. Why did our patriots not fight to the last behind the cotton bales like our veteran fathers. But our Gens know best & I feel satisfied that it was done for the best. One of Capt. Blackford's men badly wounded on picket. The silence & stillness of the days often broken by cannon both from our lines & that of the enemy, which has become very common. Relieved by 6$\underline{th}$ Ala. Regt. Came back to the woods. Witnessed from redoubt No. 5 a nice little skirmish between 15 of our & the enemies pickets. Felt very ticklish as I was anxious to go, which I could have done had I been at my post, but a run about baby, if I am 21. Got a letter from Cousin Caroline Lathrop which some enlivened my natural flow of spirits.

April 30, Wednesday

RHA: Playing a social game of cards, one of the company handed me a letter from Father, the 1$\underline{st}$ that I have received since I left home. Home sweet home. There must be something in dreams, for I dreamed I got a letter from home last night, amounting in words the same as the one I got. Rather disagreeable day, drizling rain. Played cards & told lies all day. 3 years camp life with nothing to do will ruin any man. Especially when he has to tell lies to keep up his spirits. Firing oftener today than usual.

May 1, Thursday

RHA: May must (if omens have any to do with it) be a month in whi there will be a great many battles, for as day broke, heavy firing on the picket lines opened, followed by numerous fires from the largest guns from Fort Magruder & whi awoke the dreaming soldiers from their quiet slumbers. We were certain the ball had opened. Many were anxious, others complaining of being *sick* (too old) &c. On guard today at a spring & by a breastwork used by our fathers in the Revolutionary, so I am now sitting on what I call sacred ground. Wonder if as many of the revolutionary soldiers used water out of it as they do now. If so, the sentinel, if any was more attentive than the present for I have not spoken to a man this morning. My post not by any means lonesome. Slept at the Commissary's tent—Carter acting Comy. Sergt. Awoke again by firing both of muskets & cannon 12 o'c at night.

May 2, Friday

RHA: A very interesting but tiresome & disagreeable day to me. Gen. Rodes' Brigade got orders for 3 day rations to be cooked. About 12 o'c the waggons got orders to go to Wms.burg with the Commissary stores, officers baggage &c. I being on guard, had to go along with them. That was left to me however, but thinking the Regt was coming on too, I went as I could have my luggage carried. Got about 2 mls. & never saw the like of waggons before. One continual streatch from there to Wms.burg—12 mls distant. Alex McCall & myself guarded the Commissary waggon which stuck fast in the mud about 10 o'c which we had to push out, with other assistance *of course*. On we went solemn & slow. I must say the latter term applies very well but there was not a great deal of solemnity on the occassion—popping whips, cursing horses & men *hollering* to make them pull. Got about 7 mls where a crowd of artillery was stuck. Went ahead where they had to cross a bridge & where there was tight pulling. Was very much amused at a company of Irish, who are the most amusing characters to me in the world. Seeing these m[. . .] on horse, whipping & shouting, a little incident occurred here which I will never forget between the Capt. of said co & a Dutchman, which again occurred 3 mls further on. Will not hand it down to posterity however as it would take up too much room in my little book which is getting scarce. Got to Wmsburg about 4 o'c P.M. Went 2 mls on Richmond road & haulted. We are now fully convinced that Yorktown is to be evacuated. Saw the ladies in Wmsburg which did my whole soul good. They seemed to be greatly distressed at our army pulling back & leaving them in the line of the enemy.

May 3, Saturday

RHA: Carter & myself went back to camp. Baggage guard did not suit me. I have a hankering for a more active life. Afraid the Regt will get in a little fracas & I not be in it. Will say nothing about the march—suffice to say I was well worn out by the time I got to camp & was worse when I heard the Regt was going right to the place I left tonight. Hard times coming thinks I. Well to begin, of all the marches that ever was heard of, that beat all. Marched from 9 o'c until 3 & only went 2 mls, there were so many troops on the roads. After day break we got along finely but the way my old knees ached was a caution to Davy Crockett Esq. But I stood it like a trooper.

NOTE: Having held off the Army of the Potomac, twice its size, for over a month, the Confederates began to evacuate Yorktown. The Union forces would discover the next day just how badly they had been fooled.

May 4, Sunday

RHA: Reached our waggons about 2 o'c. Was badly used up. Rested that night *rather* soundly. Was roused about 3 o'c at night expecting orders to move somewhere.

JST: Marched all night last night through the mud & got to Williamsburg at 12 O'clk M. a very nice though quite an old looking place. The country surrounding for miles being all cleared up rendered the view magnificently beautiful—the whole plain being covd. with Troops, artillery, cavalry, wagons, ambulances &c all moving in the same direction extending as far as the eye could see. In passing through Williamsb'g all the eligible places in the buildings were crowded with men, women & children all of whom wore a countenance of sadness & deep regret. They knew we were on the retreat and I could not help feeling sorry for a people who were burning with a feeling of humiliation at the prospect of their quiet firesides soon being visited by a set of "Yankee Marauders" & made desolate. We were marched out 2 ms north of the City where we camped for the night & had the pleasure of enjoying a good nights sleep, which all hands were much in need of.

May 5, Monday

RHA: A day that will never be forgotten by the 5th Ala & the troops that fell back from Wmsburg. As there was an engagement on hand, had a rapid & disagreeable march 4 mls. Went through Wmsburg cheered on by the noble ladies. Who could not help fighting when he had such ladies to cheer them on as we did and give such words of sympathy. On we padded through the slop, until we got on the outside of the place where we got in sight of the contested field. All were ready and thought the fate of war had gone in our favor—we were to fight. What a glorious feeling. Our Brigade being drawn up in line, were ordered to the left where a new fight was going on. We were marched rapidly there but ah, too late—like at Manassas. It was then 5 o'c and every one said no chance for us this evening. Now was the time for ones patriotism to be tried. Down came the rain in torrents & we could do nothing but take it. There we stayed all night until 3 o'c drawn up in line, taking the weather without a spark of fire. Then it was we thought of home. At 3 we got orders to move off—where to we knew not or cared not for I had rather be dead than alive cold and wet. I went knowing I had companions in the same fix. Of all the roads, that from there to Wmsburg beat all. Slop knee deep with mud in proportion. Never before or never after do I expect to see such a time. The road would not have been known had we not known exactly where we were, it was so badly used up by so many troops passing over. Left all the sick & wounded in Wmsburg. Took 350 prisoners all of which we passed on our way to the battlefield. Too tired to write.

JST: The advance of the Yankees attacked our rear guard yesterday & had a sharp skirmish in which we repulsed them taking 1 cannon 5 caisons & a number of prisoners. The attack was again renewed this morning with more energy & most of the army was ordered at day light to the scene of action a short distance south of Williamsburg. We left for the scene of action at 1 P.M. & double quicked it for 2 miles through mud & water. Were drawn up in line of Battle & held in reserve—the fight raged all day & rain poured down incessantly. We captured 9 cannon, a lot of Horses, over 300 prisoners & a stand of colours, besides killing many. Loss on our side very small until late in the evening when 2 Reg were ordered to charge a redoubt in an open field and were nearly annihilated. Dark came on & separated the Combatants each holding their own positions—all kinds of wounds could be seen as the men were brought in. The Reg had to stand in line of Battle in an open field nearly all night without fire & in a cold hard rain. I was detailed to assist in carrying off the wounded & at dark *flew up to Roost* in a Hen house but dident get a particle of sleep.

NOTE: Advancing Union soldiers met the retreating Confederates a little east of Williamsburg. By the evening the bluecoats had outflanked the gray, forcing them to continue retreating toward Richmond. The battle was costly: over twenty-two hundred casualties for the North and about seventeen hundred for the South.

May 6, Tuesday

RHA: At day break we were just ½ ml from Wmsburg. Marched all day with only one rest. Pretty tired—badly used up. Moorman missing. Afraid the yankees have got him. Stopped at James City. Left about sunset. The Col sent for the waggons & provisions. Douglas came with them & cooked up some biscuits. Glorious.

JST: Commenced retreating again this morning at 2 O'clk A.M. the troops nearly all broken down from fatigue, hunger & want of sleep. The Road for 5 miles was strewn with Blankets, Over coats, Clothing, Knap Sacks, Cooking Utensils, Sick Men &c. &c. Roads awfully muddy & wagons & artillery continually bogging down. The sick & wounded left in Williamsburg at the mercy of the Yankees. The march was continued 18 or 20 miles to a little place called "Ordinary" (quite an appropriate name) where we camped for the night. The men were so hungry that they ate corn, collard stalks, turnips, beets, or anything they could get hands on.

NOTE: "Douglas" is the servant of Richard H. Adams.

May 7, Wednesday

RHA: Started on our way about 9 o'c. Marched until 12 o'c when we haulted to cook provisions. Got orders about 5 o'c to move back. Went back 1 ml, about faced & came back. Stayed 1 hr. Went farther back in the woods. Had just finished our fires & ready to lay down for the night & rest when we were ordered to keep on. Marched 2 mls very *slow*. Came to Liberty Church as 12½ o'c P.M. where we are on

May 8, Thursday

RHA: I am now sitting by a branch. Just been talking with a yankee prisoner just brought in, who seems to be of the opinion that it is *rather hard* to be invading ones country. Our Co with Capts Renfroes & Riley went on picket. A courier was sent us about 3 o'c to come in but we did not get it. Were left by ourselves & would have been cut off had not Carter Randolph, who was on the Cavalry guard, come by. Told us that the enemy were advancing in large quantities & that our Brigade had gone. We went back to our old camp in a hurry & pushed on from there in a hurry until we caught our Brig 4 mls on the way. Marched all night until 3 o'c pretty rapid & badly used up when we haulted near Cousin Christiana Christian's house. Carter, Henry & John Christian & Coleman & myself stayed in her yard on the grass & got a good breakfast. Went back to where the boys were with a clean face.

May 9, Friday

RHA: Left about 11 o'c. Marched until 3 o'c with only one rest. Very fast & hot. Rather take it in the night as we did yesterday. Haulted Chicahominy River. Went in bathing in the evening. Good gracious what a feeling. So much like a white man after the best part of the soil of the Peninsula had been taken off my body.

May 10, 11, 12, Saturday through Monday

RHA: Still at Chicahominy River at our bivouac. A very disagreeable place. Bad water. Commenced drilling. 2 Battallion drills a day. Pretty hard for old soldiers like ourselves. Take a bath every day. Had a stag dance on the night of 11th. Enjoyed it finely. The boys all in such a fine flow of spirits. Jule Bayol our dancing master & prompter. After the dance was over Dr. Park & Ned Bayol gave us some delightful music. One piece (my favorite) The Lone Rock by the Sea, which brought back many pleasant recollections of a fair one. Felt like a subdued lion, in front of the music, for I had to face it. Spring has now covered the earth with a green mantle, which is very refreshing, but this once beautiful & happy country does not by any means present the same picture that it did formally. One is very much disenchanted that looks on it now. Sent Douglas to Richmond to get our trunks on 11th.

May 13 and 14, Tuesday and Wednesday

RHA: The anaversary (13th) of our enlistment in the service. Instead of being out & at home as we anticipated we are all conscripted. How unpatriotic it sounds. I am one (I am happy to say) that reenlisted. Jule Bayol & myself were detailed to go out in the country & get some meat for the Co. Came across a place where I scraped up acquaintance & connectionship & engaged milk for the season when many fellows that went before me had to leave crestfallen without it. Begin to think I have a "nack" for getting food. Douglas got back this (the 14th) with our trunks full of something good to eat. How I enjoyed it after eating hard crackers & salt meat. On guard tonight. Had a *delightful* time as it was raining. Began to feel natural, had not seen any rain for so long. Felt very *sentimental.*

May 15, Thursday

RHA: Still in camp at Chicahominy bridge. Got orders to leave about 10 o'c but did not leave until 3 o'c. Camped at a beautiful place about 4 mls from the bridge. We are now in old Charles City County, the land of my forefathers. Better pleased with this part than any other. There is a good deal of novelty & romance in the place. Got pretty damp but dried off by a fire & slept on the damp ground. We hope for a fight & better things. Found the march not very disagreeable or agreeable either. Short & tolerably sweet.

May 16, Friday

RHA: Left camp about 2 o'c. Marched over a very disagreeable road until 10 o'c at night. Haulted & the woods were soon dotted with soldiers, some asleep too tired to hold open their eyes. Others like our mess making "Flapjacks" for supper. This is a species of batter cakes, fried instead of baked. Ate a hearty meal, went to bed, slept finely & soundly —Amen—

May 17, Saturday

RHA: Marched 5 mls. Haulted in 4 mls of Richmond. Ate a big dinner out of our trunks & slept soundly.

May 18 and 19, Sunday and Monday

RHA: Moved again in 2 mls of Richmond. We are now in sight of the "seat of treason & rebellion" where we expect to die in our tracks fighting for it. I am now around the homes of my forefathers. Can fight like a devil as Badenhausen says. Sent Douglas back to Cousin Anna's with the cart. He brought us a letter from home which was directed to Care Christian & Lathrop. Gilliam James & myself run old Haden a good deal about his boy that we took when we were out on picket at Dascund Bridge. Rather strict orders about keeping us in camp. Have details to go for water. Took a bath in a mill pond & put on clean cloths. Shaved off clean & heard it was Sunday so I enjoyed my clean cloths. Slight rain on 19th. Capt. Blackford ate dinner with us. Had a bully dinner—tomatoes &c.

May 20, Tuesday

RHA: Still in camp near Richmond. Doing finely but kept very strict & drilled like the mischief. Weather beginning to be quite warm. 20th our Regt made a complete failure out on Battallion drill which amused the boys a good deal. The once proud & well drilled 5th Ala. with Rodes as Col has "played out". With Pegues as Col she has fallen, her proud mien is dragging in the dust. Her officers & men can no longer speak of her with the same pride of former days. Her reputation at Sangsters plus Rodes notoriety left us with our much beloved Rodes. He came up with every confidence in his old Regt which he said made him what he is, to drill & show her off to the rest of the Brigade. But after the failure he went off in disgust.

May 21, Wednesday

RHA: Did very well on Brigade drill this evening retrieving its lost character somewhat. Read today an order from that dog & degraded character, Butler in New Orleans in reference to the ladies of that place. Nothing more could be expected from such a low bred dog. Never seen decent society. This is the base brute that Lincoln has set at the head of the army to tyranize over the people of N. O. It makes the blood of every true Confederate soldier boil to think how the beloved ladies of our land are to be victimized by this villain who has no parallel in the history of villany & vice. We will all die in our tracks before the wreatch will be allowed to come farther than our line & see the ladies of Richmond who have so long stood by our sick couches, be treated as those noble women of N. Orleans.

NOTE: On May 15, Brigadier General Benjamin Butler of Massachusetts issued an order stating that the women of New Orleans who insulted the Union soldiers then occupying New Orleans would be treated as prostitutes—an order that outraged both North and South.

May 22 and 23, Thursday and Friday

RHA: On guard first day. Had a very easy time as I "hogged" the others on guard. Made the arrangement with them to stand all our guard at one time. They were all agreeable. I on the third relief—had decidedly the upper hand. Had a good sound sleep all night instead of walking a lonely post. But lost all the *sentiment* of the thing. A great time to *meditate* in *private* which is certainly a relief from the noisy camp. Not being that kind of a youth I did not regret it exceedingly. Rested the next day until Brigade Drill which was very tight. Some ladies came to see the famous 3rd Brigd drill. Did my heart good to look upon them. Had not refreshed my eyesight from the not by any means enchanting form of a soldier, for a long time, as everybody had left the country through which we passed, so there was little chance for my usual activities with the ladies, as was my custom in the army of the Potomac. Got a letter from Jean & Willie Selden, the first that I have gotten since I left "Home Sweet HOME".

May 24, Saturday

RHA: Firing heard today towards the left wing. Got orders to be in readiness to move at a moments warning. All ready & as willing to act. Rain nearly all day. Started with the patrol squad twice to Richmond but did not get off. Wrote to Jean.

May 25, Sunday

RHA: Today Sunday, while they are all sealed in church at home, our Brigade has marched out either to attack or meet the attack of the enemy. We have haulted & are all sitting on the wet ground. Wonder what is to come. Time & patience will show. Perhaps soon into battle & I may be soon cold with death—but God only knows. It turned out that we came on picket. The enemy reported us advancing though. Heard their drums & bugles & considerable talking at night when stillness reigned. Cannon opened to our left, several shots about sunset. Shooting perhaps at dogs who generally venture out about that time from their posts. Let them come when they will. We will stand up to the rack & give them a twist or two.

May 26, Monday

RHA: Still at our post on picket—our time not come yet to go out. Gilliam James & myself went out in the country to hunt something to eat. Found the country full of soldiers although we have strict orders to keep them in camp. They as well as ourselves can run the "blockade" so let them journey. Found it very difficult to find anything but came to a very nice place where there was no one but two old negro women. Both of us scraped up acquaintance with one of them. She knew some of both of our kinfolks. Promised to let us have some milk & bread tomorrow on account of old acquaintanceship. Went back satisfied & found 8 pies on our way back which we bought. Went back & made some "flapjacks" & dined. Commenced raining about 3 o'c. Got the news of a glorious victory won by Jackson. Also got orders to be ready to move tomorrow at 3 o'c which was early rising. Spent a terrible night—rained the whole night. Water running under me all night. Old Gilliam got mad & Haden nearly blew his eyes out trying to make up a fire & finally consoled himself by lighting a piece of candle to *look* for a *dry piece*. Very practeacle as he says.

May 27, Tuesday

RHA: Three o'c came & with it the Orderly Sergt to wake us up to start, agreeable to orders. Raining hard all the time. We certainly expected a forward movement but went back ½ ml where we stopped. About 9 o'c the rain stopped & Old Sol came out. 10 o'c the Brigade passed us but was soon turned back & we took our same position. That move hard to understand. Our blankets were as wet & heavy as they could be. Not very pleasant to carry. Slept soundly, making up for lost time, although the ground was wet, cold & damp. If this sort of a life, what sort of a ball will lay us low. Carter rather unwell.

May 28 and 29, Wednesday and Thursday

RHA: Relieved (28) & went back 1 ml to a very disagreeable place where the 12th Ala (who had just relieved us) left. I on guard. Awakening on 29th heard the pickets to the left of ours firing very rapidly. All the Regts of the Brigd were ordered under arms. All to no avail. No fight as yet although every night when I lay me down to sleep on my damp couch (mother earth) I expect to hear at the gray dawn of morn, the "cannons opening roar" & be double quicked several miles.

May 30, Friday

RHA: Very disagreeable day, heavy rain all night. Slept in puddles of water. Stretched blankets did no more good than a musquitoe bar as to keeping out the rain.

May 31, Saturday

RHA: Another wonderful & eventful day in the history of our country. Called from our wet & damp beds, we bucked on our armor to advance against the enemy. Now the time had come. Everyone knew from the noiseless movements of the soldiers who spoke in subdued tones as they prepared their repast. Soon on the march. Went about 2 mls, heard the first opening of cannon right in front of us. "Thank God we open the battle" said all our Brigade. Had a very disagreeable march through a thick wood. The Yankeys had cut the trees down & water was knee deep all over. Here our Regt was badly scattered. Could not find their way out, our Regt being let loose on the yankeys who was entrenched. Thick as hail the grape fell amongst the blood thirsty old 5th Ala. Chris Selden was wounded right by me. Soon all our Co. got together & we moved to Rt, grape pouring into us all the time. Saw the yankee encampments. Now the 12th Ala & 6th Ala was engaged & we soon after, behind the 6th. Only 3 companies of our Regt, Blackfords, Moseleys & the famous Greensboro Guards. Thick as hail fell the shot around us, more different tunes than were ever heard to them. Some burst as they struck, others a fluttering noise, & then the keen whistle of the minnie ball. Ordered back to the left. We charged the breastworks, got into them, took 10 pieces of artillery. The enemy were then drawn up in line to our left, but were driven back. How they flew when we charged. We got into the redoubt & stayed about ½ hr., all the time Carters battery playing beautifully on them & "committing a good many depredations" on their lines. A gallant leader, Capt. Carter. We were ordered out of the redoubt & carried through the yankey encampment—where we were drawn up in line & there it was I "fit & bled" in my country's cause. When the ball struck me I rolled over in the mud, but got up & staggered back a little to where Carter had placed Lonnie Coleman who was also wounded. We went back behind a pile of wood where we found Haden wounded. I cut loose a horse from the battery we had just taken from the yanks, took Haden up behind me & we made off the battle field. Of all the sights, that field beat all. Wounded & dying. Night coming on darkened the scene. The moon & stars abashed, refused to look upon such a heart rending scene.

"Thousands had sunk on the ground overpowered
The weary to sleep and the wounded to die."

Often I thought of those two lines as we were leaving the field that night. Rode on pretty rapidly. Our horse stuck in the mud & fell but I got him up & with the assistance of a *gentleman* I got again upon his back. Haden had limped to a caison & got up on it to mount again. We came straight on to Richmond & came to Mr. Wilkins where I now am (3rd June) a wounded man writing in bed, Haden lying opposite. I suffer a good deal of pain from my wound. I have to laugh, to run on with my foolishness, to keep from thinking about my leg. Haden says I keep his spirits up too by being in such a fine flow of spirits. God knows my old *game leg* hurts though got my wound fixed up about 10 o'c. The wounded men just poured in. Never do I expect & little do I want to see another battle field. The rumbling of baggage waggons & the occasional booming of a distant gun fired on the retreating foe alone disturbed the mournful stillness of such a horrible sight. I saw our noble Gen. Rodes when he was wounded. He has no fear. Gen. Johnston was also wounded badly I hear.

NOTE: At the Battle of Seven Pines where the brigade stormed Casey's redoubt, the Guards suffered serious casualties: two dead (the first Guards to die in combat) and at least seventeen wounded. Over half the troops of Rodes' brigade were either missing or dead. Total Union casualties during the two-day battle estimated at 790 killed, 3,594 wounded, and 647 missing; Confederates lost 980 killed, 4,794 wounded, and 405 missing.

Carter's battery is King William Artillery.

May 31 and June 1, Saturday and Sunday

JST: Had 2 days rations hard bred issued fixed up & moved off at 8 O'clk A.M. to attack the enemy—had to go through mud & water, the latter in many places waist deep. Creeks, Pond & branches—for about 5 miles. Engaged the enemy at 2 O'clk & had a desperate fight which lasted until dark. We drove them back one mile taking all their earth works a large number of canon, small arms, ammunition, camp equipage provisions &c &c—our loss very heavy. Most of our Boys exchanged their guns for better ones. Got canteens & many other little tricks from the Yankees. We slept on the field and on the attack was again renewed on our left & a desperate fight ensued lasting until about 12 O'clk & resulting in the repulse of the enemy with the loss of their camp equipage &c &c. We buried all of our dead this morning & at night marched back several miles over very muddy roads & camped for the night—all hands nearly broken down

June 2, Monday

JST: Remained in our camp all day to day sleeping resting & reorganizing for more desperate fighting—all hands writing home. Wrote to Annie.

June 3, Tuesday

JST: A fight expected to day & the whole army drawn up in a line of Battle where they remained until night without a fight. our whole army fell back yesterday about 2 miles this side of the Battlefield of Saturday & Sunday for the purpose of getting a better position & an other Big fight is hourly expected. Commenced at dark & Rained the entire night as hard as it could pour and our camp was in a complete float.

June 4, Wednesday

JST: Still Raining very hard this morning & every one of our bunks half leg deep in water[.] Blankets, Knapsacks, clothes and every thing we have as wet as water can make it. The country is generally very low & flat and rains oftener & more than any place I ever saw in my life. All quiet along our lines to day.

June 5, Thursday

JST: Still cloudy & raining. Brisk skirmishing, heavy cannonading and the Reg in line of Battle near all day but had no fight. Wrote to Annie again & sent some Yankee letters picked up on the Battle field.

June 6, Friday

JST: Still raining all quiet along the lines. sent Ed's Knapsack to him by Ellison but afterward learned he left for home yesterday morning.

NOTE: "Ed" is Edwin Nutting, Tucker's brother-in-law.

June 7, Saturday

JST: Rained nearly all day. Sharp skirmishing going on a good part of the day. Issued whiskey to the Reg & the Boys all got pretty lively.

June 8, Sunday

JST: Heavy cannonading near camp this morning. Went to church to day for first time in the army & listened to an excellent sermon. Introduction—Hymn "Show pity Lord O Lord forgive—Let a repenting *rebel* live." Text—2 ch & 3d verse of second Timothy, in which was drawn a striking contrast between the C. Soldier & the soldier of the Cross—delivered by the Rev. Mr. Hazen—a talented & nice speaker. He gave us much good advice, the most important of which was to abstain from the use of *Ardent Spirits* & profane *swearing*, two of the worst habits in an army—particularly the latter as an *oath* is always on the end of the tongue of at least three fourths. The former is not much indulged in as it is seldom issued—however we got a ration of it yesterday & all seemed to enjoy it finely— and I some times think that [if] it was occasionally issued in small quantities where we are in the rain mud & water it would be an advantage—particularly to health. Got a letter from Annie to day & answered the same, also wrote to Ma.

NOTE: "Show Pity, Lord, O Lord, Forgive" was written by Isaac Watts (1674–1748).

June 9, Monday

JST: Today is the first clear day we have had in some time. All quiet along the lines except occasional cannonading.

June 10, Tuesday

JST: Commenced raining last night and has continued unceasingly all day long. All housed up in our "Bunks" & every thing quite still & quiet on the line.

June 11, Wednesday

JST: Clear to day—nothing worth noticing whatever.

June 12, Thursday

JST: Another clear day has passed & our camp is drying off very much. Reg went out on picket this morning. I did not go & have been quite lonesome all day long—no signs of a fight.

June 13, Friday

JST: Clear & quite warm—camp is again dry. Beautiful weather for fighting but none going on except a little cannonading this morning out on the picket lines. Wrote to Bill Walter to day. Reg returned from picket—have passed a dull quiet day

June 14, Saturday

JST: Clear quite warm to day—in fact the heat in the middle of the day was offensive, all quiet & no indications of a fight soon. however it is hard to tell any thing about what is going to occur. Got a lot of Tents to day & are now getting pretty well fixed up.

June 15, Sunday

JST: The whole army was on the move to day & about 12 O'clk marched near a mile in the direction of the enemy where it remained until dark & returned to camp without a fight. At about 3 P.M. for one hour I don't think I ever felt warmer weather—then came up a very hard rain which lasted until night preventing any further military operations.

June 16, Monday

JST: The weather clear & pleasant. All quiet in camp & nothing of interest to note.

June 17, Tuesday

JST: Quite cold last night & there was almost frost this morning—clear, cool & pleasant day. Got the appointment of Com'y Sgt. which relieves me from all company duty, gives me a horse to ride & pays $7 a month more than a private. Delightful day. Heavy firing all the forenoon in the direction of City Point. Supposed to be between our Batteries & the Yankee Gun Boats. Caught a severe cold last night and have been very unwell all day.

June 18, Wednesday

JST: Weather continues clear & pleasant. Nothing has occurred to day worthy of note. Had several false alarms of the approach of the enemy & all the troops soon ordered in line of battle for a short time. Saw 2 Yanks brought in to day that were bagged on our picket lines. Wrote to Annie & read a letter from her.

June 19, Thursday

JST: Weather still fine. Affairs extremely quiet & dull along our lines— seemingly no indication of a fight. Wrote to Annie again to day.

June 20, Friday

JST: No news whatever—times quite dull—weather fine

June 21, Saturday

JST: Fair pleasant weather—a little warm in the middle of the day but a good breeze blowing all the time—the night being cool & delightful. Went to Richmond to day after a load of Bread.

June 22, Sunday

JST: To day has passed off very quietly—at this writing I am sitting on a Breast work beside the Williamsburg Turnpike, 3 miles from Richmond in a large though barren field, where I can see at a glance any quantity of Camps, Troops, Wagons to & fro—Artillery, Caissons, ambulances, Horses and all the appliances of our "grim visaged War" and in the distance far above the top of trees is plainly exhibited the Yankee Balloon taking a view of our position works and Capital. That some important movement is on foot is evident but what it is none except the leaders know. The day had been beautiful and pleasant beyond description & the weather all that could be desired since May 30th, but alas! its too far from *home* & the loved ones, to render the situation agreeable or pleasant to me under any circumstances.

NOTE: Before First Manassas an experienced balloonist named Thaddeus Lowe offered the Lincoln government his services in gathering intelligence on enemy troop positions. Lowe made many observations during the Peninsula Campaign until contracting malaria. Later support of his services depended heavily on the whims of his commanders.

June 23, Monday

JST: Pleasant day & nothing new to note—all quiet on the lines. Wrote to Annie by Sam Wright.

NOTE: Sam Wright had been discharged for disability caused by chronic diarrhea.

June 24, Tuesday

JST: Continues pleasant & dull. Had a hard summers rain late in the evening which effectually layed a disagreeable dust. Visited the 11th Ala to day & saw a good many of the Marengo Co boys.

NOTE: The Eleventh Alabama included two companies from Marengo County.

June 25, Wednesday

JST: Pleasant though quite cool with a stiff northern wind. Reg at work on Breast-works until 11 A.M. then called out & remained in line of Battle until dark—a heavy picket fight occurred in the evening in which our side sustained a pretty heavy loss—that of the enemy unknown. Went to Richmond to day after a load of bread.

NOTE: The opening of the Seven Days' battles. Rodes' brigade, now part of D. H. Hill's Third Division, Army of Northern Virginia, was assigned the Third Alabama and the Twenty-sixth Alabama to replace the Twelfth Mississippi. The brigade now included the Third, Fifth, Sixth, Twelfth, and Twenty-sixth Alabama infantry regiments, as well as the King William Artillery.

June 26, Thursday

JST: Our Reg was called up twice last night. The second time at 3 O'clk this morning when they were moved off about 6 miles to the Mechanicsville Turnpike where a hard battle has been going on since 4 P.M. until this writing (after sun down) with what result I know not, having been left in charge of Com'y stores—its quite likely our Reg and Brigade is engaged. Will join them in the morning & learn all the facts[.] The weather is beautiful & any quantity of fighting is anticipated tomorrow.

June 27, Friday

JST: Went to sleep last night with the roar of canon sounding in my ears & was woke up before day break this morning to pack up & move Com'y stores &c and the same sound was going on. I hastened to the scene of action & succeeded in finding the Reg at 11 A.M. & found they had not been engaged. I then returned to bring up the Com'y wagons & did not get with it again. Saw any quantity of wounded & dead men & all the paraphanalia of war—truly is war a horrid necessity. The weather is clear and pleasant & the roads very dusty.

NOTE: The Guards were engaged at the Battle of Gaines' Mill, where Lieutenant Ramsey was killed by artillery fire. The action also saw the Fifth Alabama's Colonel Pegues killed and the Guards' Major Hobson succeed him as regimental commander. Estimates place Union killed at 894, wounded at 3,107, and missing at 2,836; the Confederates lost 8,751 killed and wounded.

June 28, Saturday

JST: Got back to Maj Webster's camp last night & remained with him. This morning had the wagons loaded with provisions and returned to the Reg finding it late in evening—in going on I passed over several Battle Fields that were strongly contested & the sight of dead men & horses was appalling—lying in every direction & horribly thick. Southerners & Yankees all together. The fight was hardest yesterday evening & Geo Prior was badly wounded in making a charge. We have any quantity of goods & chattels captured from the enemy

June 29, Sunday

JST: Remained at the wagon yard to day & issued rations to the sick in camp & rested. Nearly worn out from riding night and day. The fight still goes on and the enemy continues to fall back as fast as they can.

June 30, Monday

JST: Got up this morning at day break. went to Richmond and then on to the Reg. & found all the boys well & in fine spirits all doing well & regaling over their Yankee trophies. Returned to camp at 11 P.M. tired enough having rode all day

July 1, Tuesday

JST: Went out on a *rifling* expedition to day with a 2 horse wagon & picked up any quantity of little necessary articles. Dident go to the Reg to day but heard heavy firing & hard fighting in the direction of the army. Result as yet unknown. Weather though dusty has been very fine since the fight was opened.

NOTE: The heavy firing and hard fighting that Tucker heard was the assault on Malvern Hill, the final battle of the Seven Days' campaign, where the Greensboro Guards suffered heavy casualties: in its aftermath, only seven were capable of continuing the fight. The Yankees withdrew to Harrison's Landing, which they would eventually evacuate. The final estimates for the campaign were 1,734 Union killed, 8,062 wounded, and 6,053 missing; the Confederates suffered 3,478 killed, 16,261 wounded, and 875 missing. Lee assigned D. H. Hill's division to Jackson's Second Corps.

July 2, Wednesday

JST: Commenced raining last night & still continues this morning. Went down to the Reg & found only 10 men in Company & they were worn out. Was on the battle field also & never saw such destruction before. Returned to Camp late at night & have caught the mumps.

July 3, Thursday

JST: Went to Richmond this morning. Came back to camp and remained all day quite unwell. weather fine.

July 4, Friday

JST: Got a good nights rest last night and rose early this morning feeling much better. Got breakfast & left for the Reg. 16 miles below and got to them about 1 P.M. found them all lazying round doing nothing except resting. No fighting going on to day but our forces are in pursuit of the Yankees. No national salutes have been fired by the Yankees as is their usual custom. Guess they are tired of listening to the roar of artillery for the last ten days. Got a letter from A & wrote to her.

July 5, Saturday

JST: Remained in camp to day & in the evening went to the battle field—all the dead were buried except a few Yanks—and the field did not present such a harrowing scene as when I was last there. Mr Jeffries remained in our camp last night & left for town this morning. Wrote to Annie & sent a bundle by him. The weather continues clear & pleasant & the roads are rapidly improving from the condition produced by the heavy rain on the 2d inst.

NOTE: Jeffries' departure was occasioned by his having lost a foot and leg following the Battle of Gaines' Mill.

July 6, Sunday

JST: Went down on the James River to day & was near City Point. When the Yankees got to the River they threw away guns, accoutrements & knapsacks in immense quantities. Not getting transportation as they no doubt expected and were doubtless broken down, they killed any quantity of hogs, sheep & cattle. The country is lovely beyond description—splendid large farms of clover, wheat & corn & many large magnificent residences & negro quarters giving evidence of much wealth. Picked up on the trip many little Yankee tricks. Got back to camp at 4 P.M. & partook of an excellent dinner—Chicken Pie—made of an old Muscovie & Blackberry Pie for desert. All things as still & quiet as the midnight hour

July 7, Monday

JST: The Reg was moved about 2 miles further on to day where they could get excellent water and get rid of the effluvia of dead horses & men. The new camp being an excellent location. Wrote to Annie to day

July 8, Tuesday

JST: Issued rations this morning & left for wagon yard near Richmond where I arrived last in the evening with a high fever which lasted nearly all night making me feel very badly. Had a hot dusty & disagreeable ride. Wrote a few lines to Ed

July 9, Wednesday

JST: Got up this morning feeling very unwell and had to keep my bed most of the day—one testicle swollen as large as a squash. The weather has been fine though quite dusty.

July 10, Thursday

JST: Remained at camp all day & improved a little. Commenced raining in the evening & continued through out the night.

July 11, Friday

JST: Still rained until 12 M. & I got a full benefit—being in it all. Reg came back last night a little nearer Richmond than their old position—all quiet & dull.

July 12, Saturday

JST: Clean cool & pleasant day. Nothing of importance to note—been sick all day. Rec'd a letter from Dr & one from Ma.

July 13, Sunday

JST: Fair day—all quiet in a military way. Went to Richmond for the purpose of getting a good dinner. Stopped at the American paid one dollar and got almost no dinner at all. Completely tuck in—returned to camp as sick as a horse.

July 14, Monday

JST: Pleasant weather. Everything dull. Quite unwell. Wrote to Ma & Dr B. Went out in the evening & gathered some Black & Huckleberries to make pies. Intend to have something good tomorrow.

July 15, Tuesday

JST: Warm day—Everything dull. Had Blackberry Pies for dinner. Eat a *whole one* & it almost cured me. Rained in the evening.

July 16, Wednesday

JST: Went to Richmond to day & had a very warm ride of it—Col Pegues died this morning & the Regt went in for the purpose of burying him but an extremely hard rain came up wetting the whole crowd and the services were postponed in consequence of it. I was fortunate enough to remain at camp.

July 17, Thursday

JST: Remained in quarters to day & was busy writing. An occasional breeze & showers though quite warm. Wrote to Annie and rec'd a letter from her though old data—also rec'd one from Bill Latter. All quiet in camp—& no apparent prospect of a move soon.

July 18, Friday

JST: Nothing to note to day of interest. Very warm. Wrote to Walter & Joe Atkins

July 19, Saturday

JST: Wagon went down below Seven Pines to a Yankee Hospital & got a fine lot of Ice. Had a lot of "Bust Head" commissary whiskey on hand & what a time we have had drinking Cocktails Mint Jewlips and Ice water though no one got the least *tight*. fine day though warm.

July 20, Sunday

JST: Spent the day in writing to Annie & enjoying the luxury of our fast melting ice. The day has been quite pleasant, though dull & lonesome. Capt Adams spent the day in Richmond & with the exception of some of the boys occasionally dropping in to get some *Ice*, I have been alone much to my gratification. Drilling for the day was dispensed with & many could be seen reading their Bibles while others were whiling away the time in sleeping & writing to the loved ones at home. What a reformation fighting brings about in a Regiment and what a change has come over the spirit of the dreams of the 5th Ala since the Battle of Seven Pines. Had a good dinner but its too far from home to relish it with any degree of satisfaction.

July 21, Monday

JST: Have had occasional showers—pleasant—Been busy making out returns all day[.] The roar of artillery has been sending forth its thunder peels all day, with short intervals, and for what purposes did not occur to me until dark when I could see numerous Sky Rockets going up in the City and other extensive demonstrations in fire works. I recollected that it was the anniversary of the "Battle of Manassas". The cars on the York River R.R. also came by our camp from the White House with a full display of fire works.

July 22, Tuesday

JST: Fine day—cool and pleasant. Nothing new to note. All quiet along the lines & no indications of an early movement. Drilling & reorganization goes briskly on. Health of the men are not good.

July 23, Wednesday

JST: Cloudy day with occasional showers. Everything is going on about as usual. Got a "Beacon" of the 18th inst. but it contained nothing new of any importance. Had a good dinner. Living finely nowadays. Busy making up the

Commissary returns. Tim is much better to day but is very imprudent in his diet. Hope he'll soon be well.

July 24, Thursday

JST: Weather fine. A little warm. Wrote to Annie nothing new to note. More than everything remains quiet.

July 25, Friday

JST: Pleasant day. All quiet. Good news from Morgan in Ky. Wrote to Ed in regard to the extension of his furlough. Busy making up returns. A tedious job sure.

July 26, Saturday

JST: All quiet to day & nothing new to note of interest. Came up a very hard rain in the evening.

July 27, Sunday

JST: Pleasant weather—cool & nice since the rain yesterday eve. Had a crowd to dine with us & had a very good dinner. Remained in camp all day, & took a good nap in the evening.

SP: Mama, Jamie, Mary, Lou, John & I went to Wesley Chapel and heard a sermon from Rev. Mr. Hutchinson. There were a good many persons at church considering the war times. Met Tom Moore from the Greensboro' Guards who is now at home on sick furlough. We all walked out this evening to the Cross roads, and saw a negro with a pair of young raccoons which he wanted to sell us at $5. But as we thought that a five dollar bill would be of decidedly more use than a pair of [. . .] coons in these times we declined taking them.

NOTE: Samuel Pickens started writing his diary at his plantation home, Umbria, west of Greensboro in Hollow Square (a precinct named for a hamlet). There he lived with his widowed mother, his brothers James (Jamie) and John, and his sisters Mary and Lou. The family was enormously wealthy, owning several plantations, such as the Canebrake and the Goodrum Place. In 1860 the matriarch of the family reported to census enumerators that she owned $209,600 in real estate and $250,000 in personal estate (mainly slaves).

The Greensboro Guards remained in camp on the Peninsula after the disastrous assault on Malvern Hill.

July 28, Monday

JST: All quiet & nothing to note. Weather quite pleasant.

SP: This is a clear bright and very warm day. Mr. Grigg called in this evening and sat a while with us. In an extract from a N.York paper of some date this month I noticed that some confiscated Sea island cotton had been sold there at from 68 to 75 cts. per pound. And short staple middling up lands at 41½ cts. with tendency upward. Afterwards a piece from a planter in Montgomery advising people not to sell cotton at the present prices offered in the markets in this state, said that in N. Y. it was 55 cts., in Liverpool 35 cts., at Columbus & Atlanta, Ga. at 20 cts and that before Christmas it would be 25 cts. It has not been over 16 cts in this state. In Greensboro' it has been selling at 12½ and some at 15 cts. pr. lb.

Speaking of high prices, while I was in Mobile—June—I knew Cotton cards to sell at $12. a pair; and the common price was $9 or $10. Bacon was 50 @ 60 cts. Sugar, Dark brown 25 cts. Light 30 cts. to 35 cts. Molasses 1\underline{^{25}}$ @ 1\underline{^{50}}$ per Gall. Corn $2. @ 2½ . Copperas 1\underline{^{25}}$. Bi Carb Soda 1\underline{^{50}}$ lb. & every thing in proportion. Capt. May bought a pair of thick soled, high quartered, sewed shoes—right nice ones and gave an even $20 bill. Good thick sewed boots from $25 to 30. I heard a man say that he knew a merchant in Richmond to ask a soldier $50 for a pair of boots.

July 29, Tuesday

JST: To day has passed off about as yesterday.

SP: This morning Jamie and I rode to Hollow Square where we met a good many of the neighbors discussing the news contained in the morning's paper. John Dorroh interested us with an account of his recent [trip] to visit to Miss. and La. He was in the neighborhood of Baton Rouge & had to [be] very cautious to keep out of the way of the Yankees. Was in hearing of them several times and would leave the road & ride into the woods till they passed by.

Ab. Evans, Wilkes Monette, John Dorroh, Mr. Sawyer, Jamie, Willy and I went fishing this evening to a lake in Hinds' creek swamp and we caught 150 Perch in 2½ hours.

Two soldiers from Tupelo, Miss. who had been in the battle of Shiloh have come in to spend the night with us. Their names are Dr. Night and Lieut Minor of Ky. The former had been wounded. They are members of "The Buckner Body Guards," a Cavalry Co. going on to East Tenn. to join Col. John H. Morgan.

July 30, Wednesday

JST: Nothing to note to day—dull & quiet weather fine. No prospect of a fight soon from appearances.

SP: In the paper recd. this morning we get a copy of the Confiscation and Emancipation bill, which passed the Yankee House July 11$\underline{^{th}}$, by a vote of 82 to 42, and the Senate, July 12th, by 27 to 13. Mary & I rode on horse-back to Hollow Square this evening.

July 31, Thursday

JST: Today is a type of yesterday

SP: Jamie and I got up about 5 O'clock this morning. He went to Hol. Sq. before breakfast and got the paper. After breakfast I started on horseback to the Canebrake Plantation. Stopped at the Goodrum Place and took dinner. The early corn in generally pretty good. The late corn very poor, except in the low, rich places in the Mead tract. The fodder on the high-thirsty land is almost all burnt up. There are about 40 acres of Pease which look flourishing and seem to stand the long & severe droughth better than any thing else. Cotton was planted only on such poor spots as would not bring corn and consequently is very small and looks badly. But Cotton is beneath notice this year & you never hear it spoken of or see it noticed in the news papers. Every one gave up Cotton and turned his attention to raising an abundant Grain Crop for home consumption and the support of our Armies, except a few avaricious men who continued to plant cotton thinking, I suppose, that so much corn would be made any how that it would be very cheap and they would buy from their more patriotic neighbors for little or nothing all that they might need and would have so much the more Cotton on Land when the Blockade should be raised. I then rode on to the Cane-brake plantation and got there an hour or two by sun. Peyton and I walked out to see the Colts. They are in fine order and looking beautiful. The three largest ones must be broke this Fall. The dark horse and blaze-face mare will make a nice pair for a double buggy.

August 1, Friday

JST: I have only the same to note to day as yesterday

SP: Today I rode with Mr. High over the plantation. The early corn is much better than I expected to see even in the Cane-brake after such a terrible drought. Good, large, heavy ears. Late corn will not make much except along the creek & in moist spots. They are getting on finely with fodder pulling, and will save a great deal. Commenced pulling at both places last Monday week—July 21$\underline{st}$. Mr. H. says he has the place planted as follows—as near as he can come at it—viz. Corn 850 to 900 acres: Cotton 60 acres: Pease and Potatoes on what remained that had not been in Wheat or Oats: and then the Clover field. With so much corn planted we will have a good deal to spare I suppose; but some people up in the sandy land will not make enough, although they planted largely in grain also. If the planters had not pursued the course they did, and put in Grain crops almost entirely, we would have been ruined: certainly so if the drought this Summer had been as severe through the South as it has been in this state—though in Ga., Fla. and Texas I hear they are making fine crops. We had a refreshing little shower after dinner but not enough to wet the ground a half an inch. Mr. H. says that he has not had a rain to do any good since the middle of May; now about 11 weeks. There was a nice shower of half an hour at Umbria also this evening. It had been 9½ weeks since there was any rain there except a sprinkle two or three times.

I saw about 10 bushels of Salt to-day made from the Smoke-house by leaching the dirt of the floor, and boiling the brine down. It is very dark and has the smell of bacon. It can be clarified tho' and made very nice & white. A good deal more can be made as the dirt is pretty salt[y] for 2½ or 3 feet deep. The military authorities called for ⅓ of the effective male force around in our neighborhood and below here to work on the R. Road from Demopolis to Meridian. So we sent 6 men from the Cane-brake and 3 from the Goodrum Place last Monday 28$\underline{th}$.

August 2, Saturday

JST: Had a heavy rain to day which cooled the air very much. Some artillery shooting down on the James—with which exception all is quiet on the lines & no indication of a fight soon

August 3, Sunday

JST: Went to the creek & had a splendid wash all over—had an excellent dinner & took a fine nap afterwards. Weather clear & pleasant.

August 4, Monday

JST: Reg. went on picket. I dident go. weather continues good though a little too warm in the middle of the day to be pleasant. Got a letter from Annie & answered it.

August 5, Tuesday

JST: Finished up all the returns this morning. Dined with Maj Webster & had a *splendid vegetable* dinner. Very warm. Heavy cannonading in the direction of Drewry's Bluff & a report that fighting is going on down at "Malvern Hill". Will go down to the Regt in the morning with provisions.

August 6, Wednesday

JST: Weather very warm. Division ordered down to Malvern Hill—did not go down.

August 7, Thursday

JST: Left for the Regt this morning at 2 A.M. A fight was expected but dident occur. Yankees "skedadelled" to their boats & we again occupied the hill. Troops left for camp & traveled until 11 P.M.—then bivouacked for the night.

August 8, Friday

JST: Returned to Camp. Weather very warm.

August 9, Saturday

JST: Awful hot day—all quiet & dull.

August 10, Sunday

JST: Wrote to Annie & Parks. Continues extremely warm. No news.

August 11, Monday

JST: To day is a repetition of yesterday.

August 12, Tuesday

JST: Went to Town. Very very hot day. Got marching orders.

August 13, Wednesday

JST: Weather continues quite warm. No news of interest. Wrote to Mrs. N.

NOTE: "Mrs. N." is Mrs. Louise Nutting, Tucker's mother-in-law.

August 14, Thursday

JST: Went to Richmond with [. . .] and left him at 2d Ala Hospital. No news at all. Weather very warm

August 15, Friday

JST: Got up at 3 A.M. & went down to the Reg^t. on Picket. 8 miles below camp, gave out rations and then went to a house, spent several hours in company with some nice Ladies, got a good dinner for $1 and then returned to camp. Weather cool & pleasant.

August 16, Saturday

JST: Went to Richmond and called to see Tun—found him doing finely. Came back to camp & whiled away the remainder of the day. Got a letter from Annie at dark & answered it immediately

and on

August 17, Sunday

JST: Went down to the Reg.ᵗ on picket again and got back to camp in time to partake of a good Dinner, then went to the Hospital in Town & found Tun pitching into the Cakes & Jelly which Davis W brought us from home. I pitched in & havent enjoyed any thing as much in a long while. Caught cold & feel quite unwell.

NOTE: "Tun" or "Tunie" is "Tun" Tucker, John S. Tucker's younger brother.

August 18, Monday

JST: Regᵗ returned from picket. Three day's rations issued with orders to be in readiness for a march. Weather continues quite pleasant.

August 19, Tuesday

JST: The whole division was stir[r]ed up 2 hours before day & took up the line of march at Sun up. Went through Town called on Tun and found him doing finely. Took the Brook Turnpike in the Northern suburbs of the Town & Bivouaced 8 miles from the City. Road was very dusty but we had a good time getting plenty of green corn, apples, peaches, melons, chickens, Eggs, Cider &c &c. on the way.

August 20, Wednesday

JST: Continued our march early this morning with nothing new to note & camped on the banks of the South Anna River, near Hanover C.H. Passed a lovely Country, abounding in every thing good to eat and with the exception of dust had a pleasant time. Got this Book & Contents from Annie, sent by Davis Williams.

SP: Went to Greensboro with Mr. E. Sawyer & purchased 3 yds. dark gray cloth N. lias goods. It is \$1$\frac{75}{}$ per yd. & have to pay in Wool at \$1$\frac{00}{}$ lb.

August 21, Thursday

JST: Got up early & wrote to Annie. Eat breakfast & then continued our journey 2 miles north of Hanover Juncᵗ when we struck camp & pitched tents for a temporary stay. Had a Hard rain in the evening.

August 22, Friday

JST: In camp lounging round doing nothing. Wrote to Tun at the 2$\underline{d}$ Ala Hospital.

August 23, Saturday

JST: In camp busily engaged doing the same thing I did yesterday. Went to the North Anna river in the evening and went in swimming, & had a glorious wash.

August 24, Sunday

JST: Had an awful hard rain last night & our tent was in a flat place & completely flooded.

Wrote to Annie went to the Junction drew provisions, came back, issued them out and slept nearly all the evening.

August 25, Monday

JST: Nothing of any importance to note to day. Got orders at 9 P.M. to cook 3 days rations preparatory to an early start in the morning and all hands went to work.

August 26, Tuesday

JST: Struck Tents, loaded wagons packed up & moved off at Sun up. Traveled all day nearly parall[el] with the Central RR crossing it every few miles and camped in an old Field 2 miles north of "Beaver Dam Station". Walked all day & was tired enough at night to sleep quite soundly. Weather—pleasant. Roads firm & free from dust.

NOTE: The Guards missed the battle at Second Manassas.

August 27, Wednesday

JST: Got up early this morning & continued our march but did not make much headway. Camped 20 miles from Orange CH

August 28, Thursday

JST: Continued the march this morning after some delay in getting off. Nothing of interest out of the usual routine of travel to note.

Stoped at several houses on the way & found the people hospitable & clever. Delightful weather.

August 29, Friday

JST: Continued on march again early this morning. Got to Orange C.H. at 12 M rested awhile & wrote to Annie while there. Went to Rapidan Station where we drew rations & camped for the night. Weather clear & good.

August 30, Saturday

JST: Took an early start Crossed the Rapidan River (the troops all wading across) and got to Culpeper C.H. at 2 P.M. Never have seen such destruction of property fences, farms, & every thing in my life. Rode over the Battle Field of Cedar Mountain & saw any quantity of dead Yankee feet & head sticking out of the ground: about half buried & causing the air to be filled with quite an unpleasant effluvia. The Town of Culpeper is much devastated but a pretty little place. Saw any quantity of sick and wounded Yankees in the place that Old Pope dident have time to get away. Traveled on 4 miles north of Town & camped on Mud Run.

NOTE: Cedar Mountain was costly. Union casualties (killed, wounded, and missing) amounted to nearly 2,400 of their 8,000 engaged; the Confederates lost about 1,350 of their 16,800.

August 31, Sunday

JST: Commenced raining this morning before day & continued all this forenoon. Took up our line of march at 12 A.M. & camped near the Rapahannock River. Gloomy day

September 1, Monday

JST: Commenced traveling again early. Went by Warrenton Springs & took a good look round. Hotel burned and the place literally torn to pieces. 5 miles farther on & we came to the little Village of Warrenton—decidedly the handsomest Town I've seen in Va. Came on through & got dinner at a private house and struck camp at Gainsville 8 miles from Manassas. The Country north of Culpeper C.H. is quite broken though rich & pretty notwithstanding the Yankees have nearly destroyed everything they could. The people rec'd us every where with demonstrations of gladness, particularly the Ladies. Had a very hard rain in the evening & got gloriously wet.

September 2, Tuesday

JST: Continued our Journey through a very pretty part of the County. Went all over the Battle Field and never saw as many dead Yankees on a field before. Was at the store house when the 4th Ala fought on the 21 July 1861 when Bartow fell and nearly all over the old Battle Field. Camped at dark 10 miles from Fairfax CH on the Winchester Turnpike.

September 3, Wednesday

JST: Cooked rations early & took up the line of march for Leesburg passing through a delightful Country & passg through the Town after dark[.] The moon shown brightly & the Ladies & citizens crowded through the side walks cheering us up & seemingly perfectly delighted to see us—which was duely appreciated judging from the deafening yells that went up from each reg[t]. as they filed by. Went out 2 miles & camped for the night.—

SP: After being up nearly all night, Jamie and I bid Mama and the children good-bye and took the stage before daylight at our gate & proceeded en route for Mobile. Stopped at Eutaw long enough to get breakfast and change horses. Paid 75 cts. for the meal & $4.00 apiece—stage fare to Gainesville from Umbria. Mrs. Dr. Crawford of Mobile, spending the summer in Greensboro', was a passenger as far as Col. Crawford's. There was another female passenger and two males— pretty rough old cases. One from Texas who made himself the hero of a good many yarns about Buffalo hunts, Indian fights &c. The other was the Uncle of Jones who murdered Herzfeld in Hollow Square, but seemed to be a plain, honest sort of a man; and told a number of amusing anecdotes & among them a good one of Judge 'Zeke Pickens. We traveled on slowly, hardly making 4 miles an hour, and got to Gainesville, after getting a fresh team in Clinton, about 1 O'clock P.M. We dined ($1.00 for the meal) and then sat about procuring a pass-port, as the place is now under martial law. We had some trouble in getting it, but finally hunted up Lieut. A. Wynne in the company from our side of the River, stationed in Gainesville to guard Government stores, and he went with us to the Provost Marshall's and gave us recommendations, whereupon we recd. a pass-port. I then went to Col. Rosser's Office, commander of the post.

We went on to the Rail R. depot, took the cars and started at 4 P.M. The distance to Gainesville Junction is 20 or 22 miles & the fare $2.00. Here we bought tickets to Mobile—$8.15 & after waiting 15 or 20 minutes for the train on the M. & Ohio road, got aboard & were soon rattling away. The train was very much crowded—a good many sick and wounded soldiers, and a dozen or so prisoners—so I did not get a seat until we reached Meridian where a good many got out. I then had a chance to sleep.

September 4, Thursday

JST: Remained in Camp near Leesburg all day. The Reg^{t} moved off & went to the Potomac.—

SP: Awoke this morning about sun rise & found our train had come to a halt a mile or two below Citronelle in consequence of the smash up of a freight train the evening before. It was carrying Molasses and Sugar and the waste was considerable. Sugar barrels with heads knocked out and Mol. barrels crushed and their contents running over the ground. There was a low place where the Molasses had collected making a little puddle. Jamie and I made our breakfast off the lunch we brought from home. We were kept there several hours—till a train came up from the city & took us down; so we did not get to Mobile till 1½ P.M. instead of 6 or 7 A.M. The Battle House was so full that we could not get one, but as it turned out we did not need it. They charge $1^{50} for Dinner now but we had not time to eat it. We went to Pickens & Green's office & met with Joe Pickens. Talked over our business—i.e. the chances of getting a Substitute for Jamie, & looked over the papers to see if there were any advertised: but found none. We knew then that our only chance was with Stookly who was the agent for hiring substitutes, and as a great many that he furnishes are said to desert, we concluded to come home & try to find one in Greene who would be reliable, although we would probably have to pay a good deal more. Went about trying to do a little shopping for Mama, but could not find any thing scarcely. No Longcloth—no check shirts. I saw some colored worsted over shirts at $10^{00} apiece. I bought a couple of Toothbrushes at $1^{50} each & they would not sell any more. Water melons $1^{50} @ $2^{00}, and when I was there in June they were as high as $2^{50}. Got a Passport and Jamie & I left at 5 P.M., & met with an old school mate— Aquila Hutton, of Capt. Wemyss' Co., Smith's Regt, who was going home on sick furlough.

NOTE: Under the first Conscription Act, passed by the Confederate Congress in April 1862, all healthy white males between the ages of eighteen and thirty-five were required to serve for three years. Those not exempted by occupation could hire a substitute, as James Pickens was seeking.

Colonel Robert Hardy Smith commanded the Thirty-sixth Alabama.

September 5, Friday

SP: We traveled slowly last night and are 5 or six hours behind time. Arrived at Gainesville about 1 P.M. & found the Stage at the Hotel door ready to start. There were 8 passengers inside and 7 on top. I was one of the outsiders & had full benefit of the hot sun; & whenever we got to a rough piece of road was on the lookout for an upset as the coach was so top-heavy. Got to Eutaw a little before dark and sent a note to Mama to send horses over for us the next morning. Jamie and I then went in the Hotel—washed, fixed up &c. and walked over to Mrs. Pickens'. From the time we left home Wed. morning until we got here, we ate only two regular meals, and slept only about two hours the night before starting, not much Wed. night & scarcely any Thurs. night; so upon the whole it was a tiresome & disagreeable trip.

September 5 and 6, Friday and Saturday

JST: Our Reg^t & Brigade crossed the Potomac just below the "Point of Rocks" early this morning & were the first troops to make tracks on the soil of Md. I left after dinner Crossed over to the Reg^t and then came back after the wagon train at Camp, riding all night & getting no sleep at all, and crossing back into Md Saturday Sep 6th at sun up feeling as sleepy & hungry as a man well could feel.

Took up the line of march for Frederick a distance of 15 m^s from the Potomac & camped in 4 m^s of the Town. I rode in Town & saw a very pretty place. Got dinner on the way side [. . .] and a very good one at that.

September 6, Saturday

SP: We spent a very pleasant evening & had a delightful nights' rest. After breakfast went up town and made enquiries for a suitable man: heard of a few whom we are to see. Were too busy to eat Dinner, and started home on horse-back about 4 P.M. Met the Sawyers, Mr. Jimmy Reynolds, Mary, Lou, Marky &c. riding out towards Hollow Square. The Sawyers & Mr. R. spent the evening with us. Many was very much disappointed & depressed in spirits at our failure to accomplish the object of our trip to Mobile. During the last two or three days we have been getting by Telegraph brief accounts of most glorious victories achieved by our forces in Virginia & Kentucky. On Thursday Aug. 28th 5 P.M. the Yankees attacked Taliaferro's (Jackson's Old Divis.), Ewell's & A.P. Hill's divisions near Groveton on the Warrenton turnpike & fought obstinately till night. Our loss estimated between 800 & 1000 killed & wounded & the Yankees' more than double that No. Genl Taliaferro was wounded slightly. Gen. Ewell severely in leg, which had to be amputated. Next day, Friday, August 29th they attacked us again but were repulsed with loss. It is stated that Pope admits his loss in this days fighting to be 8000 in killed & wounded. Baltimore papers say that their losses in the recent engagements up to Friday night amount to 17,000. then on Sat 30th the enemy, consisting of the armies of Pope, McClellan, Burnside and Hunter, met our army under the gallant Lee, & a desperate & decisive battle ensued. It began about 3 P.M. on the Warrenton Turnpike, Longstreet on the right & Jackson on the left, their line being in the form of a V, and was fought on almost the precise spot on which the former battle of Manassas Plains took place on the memorable 21st of July, 1861. The result was a great and glorious victory on our part—the rout and defeat of the enemy surpassing that of July 21st, 1861. The slaughter was immense, and the field for three miles was covered with the dead and wounded. Our artillery did unusual execution: it occupied commanding positions in the form of a half circle, somewhat, and as the Yankees advanced within the concavity poured upon them a destructive storm of iron. In a letter to Pres. Davis, Gen. Lee says we paroled 7,000 prisoners and captured about the same number of arms & 30 pieces of cannon. On last Tues. 2nd, the President sent a communication to Congress giving two dispatches from Genl. Lee. He compliments the Gen. & his army highly & says "from these dispatches it will be seen that God has again extended His shield over our patriotic army, and has blessed the cause of the Confederacy with a signal victory on the fields already memorable by the gallant achievement of our troups" &c. The first dispatch, 9 P.M. Aug. 29th says "So far this army has steadily advanced, & repulsed the frequent attacks of the enemy.—Many prisoners are captured, & I regret quantities of stores had to be destroyed for want of transportation." The 2nd Aug. 30th, 10 P.M. "This army achieved to-day, on the Plains of Manassas, a signal victory over the combined forces of McClellan & Pope—We mourn the loss of the gallant dead in every conflict, yet our gratitude to Almighty God for his mercies rises higher each day. To Him & to the valor of our troops a nation's gratitude is due."

September 7, Sunday

JST: Remained in camp to day Resting & cooking up rations for a further march. The weather for several days has been delightfully pleasant.

Wrote to Annie.

SP: On Sat. Aug 30.th, Gen Kirby Smith's army gained a victory, also, near Richmond Ky. The President has issued a proclamation setting apart Thurs. 18th inst. as "a day of prayer and thanksgiving to Almighty God for mercies vouchsafed to our people, & more especially for the triumph of our arms at Richmond and Manassas." To-day's paper says a Confed. force has occupied Winchester & captured 90 prisoners & a large amt. of stores & ammunition. It is also confirmed that Huntsville, Ala., has been evacuated by the Yankees. The Confed. War Steamer "Florida", Capt. Maffit—8 guns ran the blockade into Fort Morgan on night of the 4th inst. Had an exciting chase by the Yankee cruisers & lost 1 man Killed & 2 wounded. She was built in England. Mama, Jamie & Mary went to Church in Greensboro' to-day & heard a sermon from Bish. Wilmer.

September 8, Monday

JST: Still in camp & nothing new to note. Weather fine.

SP: Jamie & I rode on horse-back to-day up to Geo. Livingston's about 10 ms. on the Green Springs road. Dr. Sawyer, Mr. Reynolds & Miss Markie came & spent the evening. We had some interesting & pleasant games.

September 9, Tuesday

JST: To day is a repetition of yesterday
Wrote again to Annie.

SP: William went to Eutaw this morning very early to go on to Gainesville with Mr. Wm Hardaw[a]y. Mr. H. kindly offered to go over on business for us. John drove me to town this evening in the buggy.

September 10, Wednesday

JST: Got orders to march this morning 2 hour's before day hooked up & went about 2 miles & camped which took us all day owing to the immense number of troops that went in front of us. I spent the day in Frederick & got a splendid dinner—free of ch'g—talked with a good many ladies & got a lot of Yankee papers.

SP: Had quite a blow and a fine rain of ¾ of an hour's duration on last evening. Mr. Hardaw[a]y called by to let us know that his trip to GainesV. was not attended with much success. There were a few men there who probably might be hired at enormous rates ranging from $2,000 to $5,000. Did hear of a man who lately returned home, but can't give us an answer yet.

September 11, Thursday

JST: Commenced traveling this morning at day break & made very good headway—passed through Frederick about sun up & got to Middletown, a little one-horse *Union* place situated at the foot of a mountain at 12 M. went on 6 ms & camped amid hills & mountains had a hard rain just at night & got gloriously wet.

SP: The weather is very dry & hot. Jamie & I rode to the Goodrum Place, & after dinner went to Port Royal, where we are making brick. The yard is for Professor [. . .] house. A Mr. Doug. Patterson is employed to supervise until we get the hang of the [. . .] operations, and he will return & burn the kiln when we shall have made enough. We propose making a hundred thousand if the weather remains favorable. In this morning's paper [. . .] the following congratulatory orders from Gen. Bragg to [. . .] "Alabamians, your State is redeemed! Tennesseans, your [. . .] are almost restored without the firing of a gun & [. . .] Kentuckians, the first great blow has been struck for your freedom. Soldiers from the other States, we share the happiness of our more fortunate brothers, and will fight on with them rejoicing in the hope that a brighter future is in store for the fruitful fields, happy homes, fair daughters of our own [. . .] South." Yellow fever is said to be prevailing among the Yankee troups in New Orleans, but I am afraid it isn't hurting as bad as we would like it to be.

NOTE: Leaving Chattanooga, Braxton Bragg's army pushed Union forces under Don Carlos Buell out of central Tennessee and into Kentucky. Bragg was unsuccessful both in capturing Kentucky and in convincing Kentuckians to rally to the Confederate cause. His army would be forced back into Tennessee after the battle at Perryville, October 8.

September 12, Friday

JST: Took an early start this morning for Hagerstown but traveled very slow having quite a mountainous road to go over. Passed through Boonsborough early & found many warm Sympathisers in the place. Camped in 6 ms of Hagerstown. Expecting a fight and may remain here several days. Had another rain this morning—

SP: There is very little news in the paper this morning. It contains a highly interesting and realistic sketch of a very distinguished partisan chief, Col John Hunt Morgan. It is by the Chattanooga Correspondent of the Charleston Courier. I had the pleasure of seeing Col. M. a few minutes in Mobile last Spring. Jamie & I rode up to see Mr. John Daves on business this evening.

September 13, Saturday

JST: Remained in camp to day. Nothing to note of interest. Look for the Yankees every hour but to day has been extremely quiet.

SP: Glorious news. Our army is in Maryland. Three divisions crossed the Potomac on Friday & Sat., the 5th & 6th inst. The troops were in the highest spirits & at Edward's Ferry rushed into the River with cheers & there was an exciting race between the regiments to see which should be the first to get across. We may now look out for interesting news. The N. York "World" says "The Rebels could have afforded to pay ten millions of dollars for the results accomplished by the cavalry raid on Genl. Pope's headquarters at Catlett's Station on Friday night"—during the battles of Manassas. Mr. & Mrs. Sawyer, Dr. S. & Miss Markie spent the evening here.

NOTE: At Frederick, two Union soldiers discovered Lee's orders, and that evening McClellan's army was headed after the Rebels by way of the gaps at South Mountain.

September 14, Sunday

JST: Was ordered off early this morning back in the direction of Middletown, where a hard fight is going on 9 A.M.—Genl. Garland killed early this morning. The 5th Ala ordered to the scene of action early in the morning. In the evening a general engagement commenced which resulted most disastrously to our arms— Our Brigade "cut all to pieces" & many of our men taken prisoners—only 40 odd men to be found in the 5th at dark, at which time we commenced retreating leaving all our wounded in the enemy's hands—traveled all night long. The fight was at North Mountain 1½ miles east of Boonsboro from which I presume it will take its name. Never saw so many stragling in all my life.

SP: The weather is clear and beautiful. It is estimated that the Yankees lost in killed, wounded and prisoners on the 30th ult., 30,000 men. added to Friday's (29th) loss = 38,000; and in previous engagements, including the battle of Cedar Run, would bring the total loss of the enemy, since our forces first crossed the Rapidan, up to 50,000 men. A result almost unequaled in the history of modern campaigns. Four days after the battle Dr. Co[o]lidge Med. Inspector U.S.A. wrote Gen. Lee that there were still 3,000 wounded who had not recd. surgical assistance. At N. York Gold is quoted at 118⅞ and Cotton 58 cents for Middling. Jamie & I rode to Mr. Saddlers this evening to see Dr. Grigg. After sitting a while Jamie returned home, & Dr. G & I went to Mr. Borden's and spent a very pleasant evening. We found Mr. Robert Withers & Tom Moore there.

NOTE: While Lee consolidated his forces along Antietam Creek near Sharpsburg, the Guards were among a few companies in the Fifth Alabama ordered to hold South (not North) Mountain at Boonesboro Gap. McClellan's forces captured the company and brought them to Fort Delaware. The Guards were exchanged after some seven weeks. This episode is extensively recounted in *Guarding Greensboro.*

September 15, Monday

JST: The army was halted 1 mile from Sharpsburg & 3 from the Potomac, and forward in lines of Battle where they remained all day having a little fight in the evening. Rode all day try to get provisions for the men. Some of our men came in. Harpers Ferry captured.

SP: This is a damp & drizzly day. John drove me to town in the buggy. The rain continued to fall slowly nearly all day.

September 16, Tuesday

JST: Jackson's Forces came up early this morning and in the evening a furious fight commenced which lasted only a short time.

SP: We are now having the Equinoctial blows & rains, & the weather consequently is quite unpleasant. Genl. Lee's headquarters are at Frederick, Maryland. Our forces were enthusiastically welcomed. Confederate notes are freely recd.

September 17, Wednesday

JST: The fight was opened this morning at day brake & an awful canonading continued on boath sides until about 10 A.M. when it partially ceased & small arms took the place for a short time. The fight continued unceasingly & most furiously lasting the entire day & until 9 O'clk at night when all things quieted down except the rumbling of the ambulances, which were going all night. Great many wounded on our side but not many killed. Enemys loss not known as boath parties held about the same position as when the fight commenced.

SP: We were all up before daylight as Jamie was to take the stage for Mobile. The Stage came by crowded; so Jamie had to take a double buggy and a pair of mules with William to drive and started in the rain to Gainsville. They left at 6 A.M. &, as I afterwards learned, got there at 1 P.M.—7 hours. Just 3½ hours before the Stage. The distance is 32 miles. Mr. Jas. Simms is to assist Jamie with his business.

NOTE: While the Guards were in prison, the rest of Rodes' brigade defended Bloody Lane.

September 18, Thursday

JST: All quiet to day except picket skirmishing. The army engaged most of the day in burrying the dead. Wagons all crossed the Potomac into Va. Weather fine.

SP: In Congress they are still hammering away on the extension of the Conscript bill from 35 to 45 years of age, and the exemptions. This is the day set apart by the President for thanksgiving to Almighty God for the great blessings vouchsafed to our infant Republic; and I hope it will be strictly observed.

September 19, Friday

JST: The whole army fell back last night several miles on the Va side of the River. Rode nearly all night long.

SP: Genl. Loring's command entered the Kanawha Salines last Sat. 13ᵗʰ & took possession of the Salt Works, which were not much injured. Large quantities of Salt were on hand selling at 35 cts. per bushel. In the battles of Richmond, Ky. on the 30ᵗʰ Au. Genˡ. Kirby Smith after fatiguing marches & with less than half his forces fought three separate battles whipping the Federals badly & the last time getting possession of the town of Richmond. He took 3,000 prisoners,—wounding Gen. Bull Nelson the commander, & killing another,— about the same number of small arms, all their Cannon and transportation. He entered Lexington on the 1ˢᵗ in. and was recd. with the most enthusiastic joy. Morgan arrived on the 4ᵗʰ. Scott's Louisiana Cavalry took Frankfort on the 3ᵈ. Gen. K. Smith called for 20,000 stand of arms, & issued an address calling upon the Kentuckians to rally for the rescue of their State. Several regiments are being raised by Gen. A. Bufort. He also made a strong and beautiful appeal to the people of Kentucky.

September 20, Saturday

JST: Marched nearly all day. Stoped at Smithfield got supper & then traveled all night long.

SP: Yesterday evening Mr. Sawyer and I went and spent the evening at Mr. Saddler's. Gilliam James arrived during the evening from his father's. Mr. S. gave us some music on the Melodeon and we had a pleasant time. Thought Jamie might possibly finish his business & get back this evening, but he did not.

September 21, Sunday

JST: Camping Sunday Sep 21 5 miles north of Martinsburg at 10 A.M. all worn out & as sleepy as possible to be. Got breakfast & slept until evening then got up & wrote to Annie.

SP: Our forces under Genˡ Longstreet went up to Hagerstown; D. H. Hill with his division held "Boonsboro Gap", while Genˡ Lee planned the capture of Harper's Ferry & sent "Stonewall Jackson" to execute it, with the divisions of A. P. Hill & Lawton. On Sunday 14ᵗʰ, the Yankees in overwhelming force poured down upon Boonsboro' Gap & attempted to force a passage but Genˡ Hill was to hold it at all hazards & a desperate fight continued all day. The loss was considerable on both sides.

September 22, Monday

JST: Rested to day & cooked up rations[.] Will [. . .] leave to night or in the morning. Fine weather. The Boys got in from home. Got a short note from Annie.

September 23, Tuesday

JST: One more day passed quietly in Camp. Wrote to Annie.

September 24, Wednesday

JST: Had a nice shower of rain to day. In camp all day & every thing very quiet. Wrote to Ma.

September 25, Thursday

JST: Moved camp to day on the Baltimore & Ohio RR some 3 miles from the old one & nearer Martinsburg in a beautiful oak and hickory grove woods lot—a very nice place.

September 26, Friday

JST: Remained in camp all day. had a very big frost this morning. Weather fair. Under marching orders.

September 27, Saturday

JST: Moved off early this morning on the Winchester pike. Traveled all day & camped 10 miles from Winchester. Had a time giving out rations after dark.

September 28, Sunday

JST: Remained in camp to day. Got my Books & a letter from sister Frances. Weather fair

September 29, Monday

JST: Spent one more day in camp. Wrote to Annie and sister Fannie. Rec'd a letter from Ma.

September 30, Tuesday

JST: Remained in Camp all day doing nothing.

October 1, Wednesday

JST: Nothing new to note to day. Wrote to Ma & SHW.

October 2, Thursday

JST: Fine weather — every thing quiet. Wrote to Mr. S.

October 3, Friday

JST: dull, duller, dullest. nothing to note. Fine weather though quite dusty.

SP: In the Selma Reporter recd. this morning, "Personne", the eloquent correspondent of the Charleston Courier, gives an interesting account of the battle of Boonsboro' Gap, Md. which occurred on Sund. 14th Sept. It was a desperate fight in which we with 15,000 men under D. H. Hill held the Gap against 80,000 Yankees who used every exertion to force a passage. Hill was instructed to hold it by all means till he should hear that Jackson had taken Harper's Ferry. We learn from a letter recd. from Lt. Col. Hobson that in the Greensboro' Guards the loss was one killed, eleven taken prisoners (among whom was Joe Grigg & Capt. Williams—), and four of those wounded; three only of those who were in the fight escaped and two of them were wounded. Fortunately some of the men were on detached duty and a good many others at home on sick and wounded furloughs. The same correspondent gives also an account of the capture of Harper's Ferry with 11090 Privates and 425 Fed. Officers, 1500 small arms, 73 cannon and a large number of Wagons, harness &c. Lincoln's emancipation proclamation is out—declaring that the slaves in all the states which shall still be in rebellion on the first of Jan. 1863, shall be free; and promising to uphold and assist them in any measures that they might take to gain their freedom.

October 4, Saturday

JST: Reg. paid off. still remain in camp. all quiet.

SP: "Personne" gives also an account of the battle of Sharpsburg, Md. on Wednesday, Sept. 17$\underline{\text{th}}$. There was some fighting in the evening previous. Jackson, with Lawton (commandg. Ewell's Divis.), after capturing Harper's Ferry came up during the night and took position on the left of our forces. When it was known that Jackson had come up it inspired the army with the greatest confidence & enthusiasm. The fighting commenced at daylight, the Yankees having 200,000 men, it was thought, to our 70,000. There were 100 cannon on each side booming away at once. The battle raged all day but we held our own against the overwhelming odds. It was rather a drawn battle but inasmuch as they were attacking & we held them at bay, we had the advantage. The Yankees drew off during the night and did not renew the attack next day. Our forces then on the night of the 18th crossed over to the Va. side of the Potomac.

Jamie & I went to Greensboro' & made arrangements with Mr. Harry Johnson for Leather from his private tan-yard to make into shoes, for our Negroes. We let him have a Spinning Jenny valued at 225\underline{\text{00}}$ & he is to pay for it in Leather. Sole leather at $1.00 per lb., and Sides at an average of $5.00. It will not be enough but is all we can get. Mr. J. says he has been offered $4. per lb. for it. We are having a very warm spell of weather.

October 5, Sunday

JST: Dull day. had preaching by Mr Armstrong. dident attend.

SP: Attended preaching at Wesley Chapel & found a large congregation. Met Manny Wynne who is just from Va. He was wounded in the leg in the last battle of Manassas.

October 6, Monday

JST: Nearly every body gambling at Chuckaluck all day. More than a dozen banks going all the time besides various other games—Poker, Seven up, Euchre &c. Weather continues clear, coo[l] & dusty.

SP: Mr. and Mrs. Enoch spent the evening with us. The weather is clear, dry & beautiful—splendid for gathering Corn. We are having the most clear & beautifully bright moon-light nights that I have ever seen.

NOTE: The banks refer to faro banks, a gambling game.

October 7, Tuesday

JST: Still continue to have a quiet dull time. Wrote to Annie & sent her 80 $ by Mr. Melton.

SP: The morning's paper has an account of another battle at Corinth. Price attacked. A correspondent of the N. Y. Herald says in attempting to cross at

Shepherdstown their loss was terrible. A Penn. Regt. (118ᵗʰ) crossed with 1040 & lost at least 800. It was Jackson who entrapped them.

October 8, Wednesday

JST: packed up early this morning moved camp about 4 miles to "north mountain" on Wright farm. Good water & pretty nice place. Weather fine.

SP: I went to the Goodrum Place & found they were about half done pulling Corn. Lawless thinks we will make 6000 bushels and can spare 3000.

October 9, Thursday

JST: In camp—nothing to note.

SP: Lying in bed this morning about sun-rise Jamie & I saw three Squirrels skipping about in playful glee on the large old black oak that stands between our room, No. 1, and the office. They were busily engaged getting acorns for their morning's meal.

October 10, Friday

JST: dull and quiet day. Wrote to Annie. rained nearly all day—which only added to the monotony of the times.

October 11, Saturday

JST: Went to "Jordan Springs" to see DGW but he was gone. very nice place—got a drink of the mineral. Quite cold since the rain yesterday & last night.

NOTE: "DGW" is Davis G. Williams.

October 12, Sunday

JST: Wrote to Davis Williams and a P.S. to Annie. Cloudy and cold

October 13, Monday

JST: Damp cold & disagreeable day

October 14, Tuesday

JST: dull day—all quiet. nothing to note.

October 15, Wednesday

JST: The same as yesterday. dined in the country & had a good dinner.

SP: Dr. Grigg, Gilliam James & Mr. Enoch came in to day and sat some time. We read the papers and talked over all the war news, &c.

October 16, Thursday

JST: Had a hard rain to day. Got orders at night to be ready to march.

SP: Got up before day & went over & got in the buggy with Mr. Sawyer and went to the Goodrum Place to go turkey hunting. Lawless was away & did not get back till near dinner time. We went in the evening but did not find any turkeys.

October 17, Friday

JST: Packed up this morning at daybrake & remained so all day expecting to get off any minute but dident get off

October 18, Saturday

JST: Been on the que-vive for a start all day and in the evening the orders were countermanded. fair weather.

SP: Went over before day and got Mr. Enoch to go to the Goodrum Place turkey hunting. Crossed the river at Millwood & hunted thro' beautiful wood. In Sam Dufphey's field started a flock & killed only one all day.

NOTE: Millwood was the home of Dr. Robert W. Withers, along the Black Warrior River west of Greensboro.

October 19, Sunday

JST: Spent the day in camp—dull.

SP: Heard a good sermon at Wesley Chapel from Revd. Dr. Wadsworth. There was a good congregation.

October 20, Monday

JST: Dull, quiet. nothing to note.

SP: Jamie & I went down to see Manny Wynne this morning. The ladies were all out spending the day. 2 wagons from the northern part of the state passed loaded with Apple & Peach brandy at $15. per Gallon. It is getting scarce.

October 21, Tuesday

JST: Had a good rain last night. fair to day. Wrote to Ed & 2 letters to Annie

SP: I recd this morning a beautiful and highly-valued present from a young lady friend of mine. It was a fancy needle-case & pin-cushion combined, tastefully finished and almost too fine to be used.

NOTE: Such sewing kits were commonly called a "soldier's housewife."

October 22, Wednesday

JST: Turned very cold & the wind blew [. . .] extremely hard all last night & to day. Wrote 2 letters to [. . .] sent one by [. . .] other [. . .] to Ed

SP: Not much news in the paper this morning. A militia muster in town to-day.

October 23, Thursday

JST: Tun & Ed [. . .] to camp last evening. Wrote to [. . .] again [. . .] day [. . .]

SP: Mr. Chas. Stickney came to see about renting our land for another year. On the 15th inst. Cotton was worth 61 cts per lb. in N. Y.

October 24, Friday

JST: Spent the day in camp. fine weather but quite cold. Took supper in the Country

SP: Mama & Mrs. Sawyer went to visit Mrs. Charles. Jamie & I rode through the woods on the Lyle tract. Mr. Enoch came over & sat a while. No paper this morning.

October 25, Saturday

JST: Struck tents this morning at day brake and started off in the direction of Charlestown. Got to the RR in the evening & comc'd tearing up the track. Troops worked all night and destroyed the road within 3 miles of Harpers Ferry.

SP: Went to town on DiVernon, & met Cousin Israel & Pick & Tom Moore. also Capt. Jon. Williams, Jim Webb, Davis Williams &c. The three last were in the battle of "Boonsboro' Gap" & taken prisoners, except D. Williams who was wounded & escaped. Saw, also, Lt. Col. Hobson & Maj. Webster. I had worn a thin cass. coat, & in the evening it blew up cold & I started home just before night, & never had such a disagreeable ride in my life scarcely. There was a stiff, cold west wind blowing a cloud of dust in my face. It was the most sudden change I ever saw. My hands & feet were aching & I was chilled through & through. Met John near Mr. Saddler's with my overcoat & found it a great relief. Thermometer at 50° at bed-time.

October 26, Sunday

JST: Rained all last night & all day long. very cold & disagreeable. Moved about 3 miles west of Charlestown [. . .] went into camp.

SP: There is Ice this morning & the thermometer is at 44°. Mama & the children went to Wesley but it was cold there were not enough people to have a sermon. In the evening we all walked up the road & Marky joined the children.

October 27, Monday

JST: Cleared off this morning early & have had a fine day except being windy & cold.

SP: Still very cold. Pretty severe frost last night & Ice. Cotton, Potatoes &c. killed. We are having Ground pease dug to-day. Jamie & I rode to Hollow-Square & then returned & went through the woods where Mr. Stickney's negroes are getting timber for a Screw.

October 28, Tuesday

JST: Left camp early this morning & traveled about 15 ms. camping within 3 ms of Berryville at night. Got a good dinner at a house on the way-side.

SP: Jamie & I left home on horseback at 10:30 A.M. & went to the Goodrum Place to dinner. They are putting up a large Corn crib of hewn logs & will cover it with weight poles, as we have no nails. Then rode on to the Cane-brake where we arrived near dark. They have nearly completed a double crib of pine poles. It is a very nice job.

October 29, Wednesday

JST: Rested to day. Wrote to Annie & Mrs. N

SP: Digging a few potatoes. Those on the black land are not turning out well. Those over the creek are better. Caught up the blaze face sorrel mare and the dark brown horse, both five years old, and commenced breaking them. They at first plunged about considerably but they soon began to lead pretty well. They are getting on finely gathering Corn. All the old cribs are full and they are now throwing in the new ones. It will take about ten days more to finish. Fine chance of pumpkins but a good many are not ripe. Pea crop is very good.

October 30, Thursday

JST: Took up the line of march again this morning, passing through BerryVille & another little Town and camped at night on the banks of the Shenandoah. Weather fine.

SP: There are 140 hogs to kill. Some of them are very large, but most of them are rather small. There are 180 Shoats & pigs for next year. We saw the Saw-mill started this morning [. . .]

October 31, Friday

JST: Crossed the Shenandoah this morning early and it was amusing to see the boys pitch into the cold water & wade across. Took Tun over on horse back & Ed rode in a wagon. Crossed the Blue Ridge Mountain & passed through a little Town at the foot of the mountain called Paris. Saw one very pretty woman in the place. Camped at night near "Upperville" in Faquier County near the spurs of the mountain.

SP: Jamie & I started home and dined at the Goodrum Place [. . .] went on & got home at dark.

November 1, Saturday

JST: Remained in camp to day. Went to Upperville & took a look at the Town. Weather fair.

SP: I went to town to-day on DiVernon & found it quite warm riding in the sun. After a busy evening I returned home to supper.

November 2, Sunday

JST: Got orders early this morning to fall back & went near Paris & formed in line of battle to await the approach of the Yankees. Remained in this position until day-light Monday morning the 3$^{\underline{d}}$ and then recrossed the mountain taking the road to Front Royal which [. . .] along the banks of the Shenandoah at the foot of the mountain. Camping at night 6 ms from F Royal.

SP: Mama & Jamie went to church in Greensboro' today. Mr. Enoch Sawyer came over and sat with me some time. The weather is warm & the roads very dusty as we have had no rain for a long time. We all walked out this evening on the road.

November 3, Monday

SP: A great many persons are selling part of the whole of their last year's Cotton crop to the Government. Jas. H. Simms is the Agent in Greensboro'. He is giving 15 cts. for Middling. Mama & Mary and Cousin Icha went to town to [. . .] but he was not [. . .] Mr. Enoch and I rode to Mr. Saddler's and saw the Dr., Gilliam & Pick Moore[.] This evening I went to Mr. Kimbrough's, to ask his opinion of the no. of acres of land on our Umbria and Eubank tracts and what it ought to rent for. He says he thinks there are near 100 acres in the field North of the road and 35 or 40 in the South; anyhow 125 in both; and in the Eubank section at least 400 of tillable land—making in all over 500 acres—which ought to rent for $2. per acre, but considering the hard times now we ought to profit at $1.50, which he thought a very reasonable price.

November 4, Tuesday

JST: Traveled on to Front Royal where all were halted & cooked up 2 days rations expecting a fight. Wrote to Annie.

SP: Mr. Sawyer, Jamie and I went to the Goodrum Place today to weigh &

sample the cotton that was picked out to sell to the Government. Got [. . .] Lewis to come over and [. . .] it was very laborious work indeed, especially to the sampler, who was Mr. S. We sample it by cutting a hole in the bagging on one edge of the bale and pulling out a wad of cotton of the 2$\underline{nd}$ or 3$\underline{d}$ layer. The bale is to be marked on one end C.S.A. The 74 bales weighed 37,412 lbs. average 505½ lbs.

November 5, Wednesday

JST: Troops on the look out all day for a fight but were disappointed. Rode round through the Country & bought some chickens & turkeys.

SP: This being the day for my departure to join my Company "D", 5$\underline{th}$ Regt, Ala. Vols., in Virginia, I packed up my clothing & got everything ready. Went over and told all good-bye at Mrs. Sawyer's. After dinner with sorrowful heart bid an affectionate farewell to my dear Mother, Sisters and brothers. Mama and all were deeply affected at my leaving, and I was equally so at parting with the dear ones at home. Started about 3 P.M. accompanied by Jamie & Willy. We went thro' Greensboro' and as the road was very sandy and heavy, drove slowly and got to Newbern at 8½ P.M. We found Maj. Dan. Webster and Jack Wynne there. Took supper and soon after went to bed, but there was no sleep for me. I lay awake in a restless and excited state of mind thinking that I was leaving home now to be absent I knew not how long.

November 6, Thursday

JST: Skirmishing going on all day but couldent get up a regular fight. army fell back at dark to the west side of the River, evacuating Front Royal.

SP: We were roused up some time before day this morning & having no fire in the room found it very cold, for the weather had made a great change during the night. I had very little covering on my bed and passed a very disagreeable night & took cold. I am afraid Jamie & Willie will suffer from the bad accommodations we had at Newbern, and from the cold ride they will have home. After eating breakfast at 5 o'clock, we walked down to the Depot, where soon after I took leave of Jamie & Willie (& also William) and started at day light on the train to Selma. Gilliam James & Pick Moore were to have met us at N. & gone on with us, but failed to do so. I met with Mr. Hanson (Revd.) and Marschall, the artist, on the cars. At Selma we found the Str. Senator No. 2 going up the River & took passage on her. The river was very low and consequently we traveled slowly. The boat was crowded and all the berths taken, so our party with many others had to sleep on pallets (?) in the cabin.

November 7, Friday

JST: Dident sleep any at all last night. commenced Snowing early this morning & O! my how cold. Hills & mountains covered.

SP: I was unwell last night and felt chilly and afterwards had some fever. Arrived in Montgomery a little while after breakfast, and soon set about looking for vaccine matter to be revacinnated, as the Small Pox is in the Army at Winchester. We got our transportation to Richmond and at 4 P.M. left on the cars; I got a ticket for John as far as Augusta.

November 8, Saturday

JST: Ceased Snowing last night & cleared off to day. Rode round the country & got a good dinner.

SP: Passed thro' Atlanta at daylight this morning, and got to Augusta at 5 P.M. Supped at the Augusta House, and at 7 P.M. started on. We got off at Branchville & the Cars up from Charleston had not arrived: so after waiting a few minutes the train we got off started down and came in an ace of having a collision, but avoided it by reversing the engines.

November 9, Sunday

JST: Got orders this morning to be ready to move. Weather *very* cold. Left Camp at 10 AM & crossed at Strausburg

SP: Took an early breakfast at Nickerson's Hotel Columbia, S. C. We ate dinner out of the box of nice provisions that Mama put up for me. It contained a ham, a turkey, some chickens, biscuits, pickles and some nice Cake. So we enjoyed them very much & did ample justice. Passed Charlotte early in the evening.

November 10, Monday

JST: Took the Winchester Pike up to Middletown & camped. our Reg. going back to Front Royal to destroy the R.R. & do picket duty.

SP: Changed cars in Raleigh some time before day, and in Weldon about dinnertime. Arrived in Petersburg about 4 P.M. and put up at the Bollingbroke Hotel.

November 11, Tuesday

JST: Came from the Reg. this morning back to Middle Town & had a very cold ride.

SP: I wrote a letter to Mama this morning telling her of my safe arrival here, &c. Jack Wynne, Mr. Jones of Demopolis & I walked over the town. I purchased a rather small size silk handkerchief for which I paid $3.50. After dinner we took the evening train for Richmond, and got there after dark. J. Wynne's knap sack with every thing in it was stolen on the cars. His boy Carey had charge of it & went to sleep, when some one stole it. We got in a cab & drove up to Mrs. Barnes', thereby eluding the guard at the Depot who take charge of all soldiers and carry them to "The Soldiers' Home", an institution we preferred not passing through.

November 12, Wednesday

JST: Remained in camp to day. doing nothing. Weather fine.

November 13, Thursday

JST: Nothing of interest to note. Wrote to Annie Ma & Mr. S.

November 14, Friday

JST: Reg.^{t} came off of picket—dull day—still in Camp

November 15, Saturday

JST: In camp doing nothing—dull times

November 16, Sunday

JST: To day the same as yesterday.

November 17, Monday

JST: Maj W. got back yesterday. brot a letter from Annie. dull times.

November 18, Tuesday

JST: Rained all day. Got a letter by mail from Annie & wrote to her at night.

November 19, Wednesday

JST: Remained in Camp all day. nothing to note of interest

November 20, Thursday

JST: Still in Camp doing nothing. Got orders to march early in the morning.

SP: *Notes on our Marches*

On *Frid. Nov 21st* at litt. aft. light broke up Camp near Middletown in Valley of Va. and mchd thro Strasburg & on thro Woodstk & camped at least 20 ms. from where started. Stopped not ¾ hr. in all the day, nearly broke down &c. sore stiff. Cooked & next morn *Sat. 22nd* bef. Sun-rise went on pssd. thro' Edinburg, Mt. Jaxon &c. Sev. Rabbits caught by troops. At N. M. left valley turnpk and took East across the mountains. Came bout 20 ms. M^{c} caught Pheasant & had for supper. So stiff & sore hardly able to move.

November 21, Friday

JST: Took up the line of march this morning at sun up in the direction of Staunton. Camped near Woodstock at night and continued the march early on Saturday the 22 taking the Culpeper Pike at New Market & camping three miles east of the Town

November 23, Sunday

SP: Went on & crossed a mountain fr. top which we had beautif view of the valley one or 2 towns & country houses scatterd bout. Went [. . .] Was so sore & worn out accepted invitation fr. Maj. Webster to ride in wag.

November 24, Monday

SP: Had a hd mch of it over the [. . .] 10 or 12 ms. over the mount. Most windg & circuitous road ever saw. Could see a parallel road nearly on the side of the mount. Road lined with the white top wagons lookd very pretty & [. . .] the long winding line of troops up on the mount. with arms glisting in Sunlight.* Could hear the shouts of troups as they would gain the top. I was in the wagon & could enjoy the view fr. the top. some places where the stragglers cut across a few hundred yds. & cut off several miles went nearly 24 ms. (Crossg. the Shenandoah on a bridge made of puncheons &c hastily fixed up.)

(*Like Nap. cross the Alps. It was 10 or 12 ms. over the mount.)

November 25, Tuesday

SP: I marched again & we went thro Madison CH. & went about 20 ms. crossed the Rapids on a long Covered bridge. Small steam near. Large mill on it. Camp in 2 or 3 ms. of Gordonsvl. Just after making fire late in eve. a gang of Part. th. had been scared up & flew thro the encampment. lit in leaves & brush near us. They so much frightend they did n't fly & I caught 2 & some of my mess caught 4 others & John cooked them nicely for supper. We had one apiece & enjoyed them.

November 26, Wednesday

SP: Ellison [the] Sutler came up & got some of the Sugar, Coff., Candy & preserves from him. Remained in camp resting to-day. Saw a large fox Squirrel caught by troops. Cut tree against one he was on & jumped out & large crowd pursued till caught him.

November 27, Thursday

SP: This evening Col. Hobs. Lt. Jo. Borden, Gill. Jas., 4 others came in camp—just fr. home. They brot me 2 letters fr. Mary, one fr. Lou & one fr. Jamie. I was very glad to get them tho' the latest was written only a week aft. I left. Col. H. brot. me a pr. boots & left 'em in Richmond.

November 28, Friday

SP: This morng the Drum called us up bef. day to prepare for marching. Went on a mile or 2 on Gord. road & then turned off to left (east) & went thro plantations &c. passed thro Orange C.H. crowd of ladies on sidewlk waved large flag as we passed. Kept the plank road to Fredericksbg some distance & then turned off to go lower down. Mchd. bout 18 or 19 miles to-day.

November 29, Saturday

SP: Marched on not knowing where we were going but rather thinking it must be to Fred. I stand this mch. better than the first one fr. Middletown. Went 'bout 18 miles.

November 30, Sunday

SP: Mchd. on gradually to-day & passed about 4 m s. of Frederks. Stopped on a hill side in pretty woods of small timber early in evening & we heard that we wd. probly lie over a day or 2 to rest. Came 'bout 15 ms. today. I have been surprised at finding so mch wood land in the old state of Va. We have nearly always camped in pretty woods of generly smally sized trees of Hickory & oak. Convenient for making fires.

December 1, Monday

SP: We were disappointed in our expectations to stop & had to go on this morng. again. Going now towards Port royal on Rappa. Passing some very pretty open country, good large farms & woods more level than [. . .] & in the valley [. . .] make great deal wheat [. . .] with cedar trees on [. . .] limbs grew together [. . .] near Guinea Station [. . .] & Fred. R.R. We got acquainted with servants at night however & got us some Corn-bread, potatoes sweet & Irish.

December 2, Tuesday

SP: Happy to find that we are to rest here to-day. John got us a half Shanghai hen & some meal & 1 Doz. eggs for $1.00. Enjoyd the rest very much.

December 3, Wednesday

SP: Started again & mchd. bout 14 ms. further and camped very near the Rappahan. & about 5 ms. above Port Royal. Rations are very scant—Don't issue more than ⅔ our due & sometimes no salt. If it were not for what John gets by foraging we almost wd. starve. I was detailed with a squad & sent out as a patrol on the roads soon after stopped to pick up the men that had gone out foraging. We caught 25 or 30 & carried them up to Gen Rodes Hd. qrs. some time aft. dark [. . .] last that were caught was one fr. 6ᵗʰ Ala. Reg. I was sent to guard him [. . .] off but I tol him could [. . .] tie his shoe & put out thro bushes & I [. . .] holl. him to halt. fell und. thick tree I [. . .] but rolled on & got away—fol'd some time. Went back & found over-coat & hat & peck walnuts—bundld up & carrd to fire where we stationed & had nice time crackg & eating.

December 4, Thursday

SP: The Drum beat later this morng. as we are not to march. Had a poor brkfast of Little stewd beef & crackers mashed up & soaked in melted beef tallow for gravy. Wood is pretty scarce here & its hard to keep a good fire. I was nearly all day writing a letter to Mary that I commenced in Camp near Gordonsville. We drew arms & accoutrements for all who had n't them. So I'll have an addition to my load of baggage. 40 rounds; Cartridges are pretty heavy. Late in eveng found we had no supper & started John out to a house to try to get something. We sat round fire hungry & impatiently waited for John, finally pretty late he came in with a nicely cooked duck & a pitcher gravy & some warm corn bread. Never ate such a hearty supper in my life hardly. It was nice. Then went to bed.

December 5, Friday

SP: After brkfast it commencd raining & continued all day very cold & sleeted some. Most disagreeable day. we moved down under a fly with another mess to stay till the rainy weather is over. We are a day behind in rations but John manages to get plenty of Corn meal in the country @ 75¢ per Gall.

December 6, Saturday

SP: A little before dark yesterday eve it came snowing & fell pretty fast. Very cold & was still snowg when we went to sleep. This morng the ground was white & a hillside opp. our fly covd. with little pines & Cedars lookd beautiful. Trees were all bending under their snowy burthen & lookd very pretty—I spent a miserable night. All of us were crowded under a [. . .] & I was so wedged in tight I could not turn over & lay on one side all night. We lay on a [. . .] blanket—no leaves & the grd. cold and damp. My limbs got stiff & cramped & slept very little. Got up before day & stood by the fire. The snow hasn't melted any to day it was so cold. Up on the hill where had dress parade it was about 1½ in. thick.

December 7, Sunday

SP: Last night was the coldest night we have had. I rested badly & got up 2 or 3 hrs. bef. day & stood by fire. Had inspection arms today. Cold exercise but got thro quickly. The troops were paid off up to Nov. Had poor supper Corn bread & cold boil beef without any salt. rations are short ¾ lb. flour other day & 3 crackers. March one day on 1½ crackers.

December 8, Monday

SP: Last night very cold. Water in canteens froze in ten minutes after brot. & hanging near the fire[.] Rations are scarce & but for the meal, pork &c that John buys out don't know what we'd do. We got flour & beef & no salt last night—thro neglect of Commis. we have failed several times lately & biscuits made without grease or salt & boil beef without salt is poor fare. 5 cos. of the Reg. went on picket this morng ours was not among them tho—I went on guard this morng. The pioneers of this Div. have dug rifle pits near the Rap. river 3 or four miles from here & there is where picket is stationed. a few nights ago one of our batteries threw a few rounds at 1 or 2 of the Yank. small boats & drove them down lower. Ellison the Sutler came in last night & brot. bag cakes with him wh. we [. . .] brought up his wagons this morng & we got some nice cakes & Candy at [. . .] & sugar & coffee (Confed.)

December 9, Tuesday

SP: James Reynolds came over fr. the 3ᵈ Ala. & hunted me up. Glad to see him—he is looking well, talked of the pleasant times he spent at Mr. Sawyer & our house last Summer—he hated coming back very much. Some caught a Squirrel which I tried hard to get but didn't succeed. We moved Camp ¼ mile where more wood & plenty water convenient. Have a nice bunk—Tent cloth stretched one side on grd. & other up & straw under it, & big fire before it.

December 10, Wednesday

SP: I slept deligh. last night better than since left Middletown. First time had straw since then. Wrote a letter to [. . .] to-day & one note home & I've recd. [. . .] brought by Mr. Cowin &c. Drew Ba—[. . .] made nice biscuit out [. . .] heavy cannon firing [. . .] boats. Heard nice music fr. N.C. band to-night.

December 11, Thursday

SP: *Camp near Port Royal, Va.*

We were roused up before day this morning to go on picket. Soon as it was light good we went at a quick march over the hardest frozen road I ever saw & was cut up & very rough part of the way. It is a very cold morning. Marched 4 ms. to the Taylor place & then bout 2 ms. more down the River to where the picket is stationed. We were posted along the bank of the river & the Yankee cavalry pickets were on the opposite bank. We talked with them, askᵈ if they wanted the war to close &c. where Jackson was want to go to Richmd. 20000 crossing at Fred. they said. An hour or 2 bef. day I was roused & heard a heavy cannonading going on below Port Royal & a few big guns occasion. towards Fredericksbg. After we got down on picket firing bel. Pt. Royal ceased & heaviest sort was carried on at or above Fred. big siege pieces & fast & continuous. It was kept up the entire day. we were told to watch out for Gun boats & shoot thro port holes. About night the cannonadg stopped off. The night was so cold that we could not sleep much. I went on post at 2 & stood an hour. instruc. to look out for rockets, but none seen (at P.R.) a false alarm was given of rockets seen & all of Hills Div. was mchd. down to Taylor's farm bout 3 A.M.

Frid. They all returnd to Camp tho' soon after. Col. Hob. came down to Picket post bef. dn. and sat with us. Little aft. light he sent our Co. up to Taylor's farm. We expected to have to work on breastwks but did not & had good rest. Cary came out with havre sack full of Corn bread & little beef. In eve. walkd. around & looked at the remains of Taylor's house. it was 'bout 150 ft. long, brick. The walls all standg. yet. Very pretty front yard—laid out & planted with shrubbery—hedges &c. The Rap. river is just back of it. Magnif. farm. 6000 acres open land we were told. No divis. of fences at all. Land lay beautif. level or gently rolling. Most splendid place I've ever seen. covd. with thick growth of luxur. grass—& lots of rich clover that grows, waist high. Mr. T. is bout 25 years. old & is now priv. in Cavalry Co. & stayed all night with an old negro of his, the only one left, last night & was getting someth. to eat this morng—he was moving his hands to another plant. & they ran off robbed his house & burnt it & went to Yanks—60-odd hands one night. The place belonged to his grandfather Col. John T. of revolut. fame.*

While walkg. 'bout order came to leave & started just bef. night movd. back near camp & found the brigade & balance of our reg. with it had gone an hour & half & we followd on & had the worst march imagin. [P]erf. dark & roads rough cut up & frozen in places & muddy in parts. We had good deal double quick. Moon rose about 11:30 P.M. & then it was a little better. I never was so completely broke down in my life & had no idea that I could go as long as we did. Actually, when going slowly I would close my eyes & 'most go to sleep walking. We got to wh. the Div. was campd. bet. 2 & 3 Oclk

*The can. firing contin. all day again & 1 or 2 'Clk hear. & fastst. we had yet.

December 13, Saturday

SP: *Sat. morn.* 15 or 16 ms. fr. Tay's farm. Our mess warmd our feet at Cols. fire & spread our blankts. & slept soundly till sun up. Got up hungry as ate no supper & broild some fresh pork we had & ate all corn bread. Bet. 8 & 9 can. firg. commencd up towards Fredbg. & our divis. movd on. Went 2 or 3 ms. & lay under a hill where we could hear the fighting going on very plainly as it was not far off. Cannon princip. but sometimes volleys of musketry. After a while the Shot & shell came hissing & whistling over us, making all kinds of unpleasant sounds. Some shells burst bef. getting to us & some aft. passg. over. They would fall in a meadow below us & knock mud & tufts of grass up high as the trees. A piece of artillery about 200 yds. fr. us had a man & horse killd & another horse's leg broken. The wounded began to fall back to the hospital—some walking assisted & others in litters. Our brigade was order[ed] over on the right to meet an attack & had to pass thro' an open field. While doing so the shot shell & grape passed over & some very low. On getting to edge of woods we formed a line & loader. It seemed as if we were to charge right ahead but it turned out to be a feint—the real atta[c]k was on our left, so we turned & went back. Could see little white clouds of smoke appear away up in the air where shells burst & then enlarge & disappear. Coming back a man in the Co. ahead of us had his gun broken & bent in his hands. The ball must have passed thro' the ranks, bet. the files as no one was hurt. We went & lay down on the hill side again. Several squads of Yank. prisoners passd. by going to rear, all with blue overcoats. Some comg. back fr. fight told us, A. P. Hills forces had driven them back but they recd. reinf. & were advang. again. One brig. fought till they got out of ammun. they let yanx get close & then fired away with effect. We were in the eveng. carried into the woods & formed line & held as reserves. bet. sun down & dark Jackson sent order to Early to take commd. & make general advance. We started & soon got double quick & confused & were about 8 or ten deep & comps. mixed & scat.d. Came up another line of troops & halted in confus. & while trying to form a Yank battery open[ed] on us. It was very near us. We all lay down & shell, grape & canister whizzed just over our heads & cut bushes & saplings all about—a ball struck bet. Col. Hall & a man beside him. one man in the reg. was shot in shoulder & 1 with finger off (Sheldon)[.] 6$\underline{th}$ Ala. ran off some distance & lay down—made noise & Yank shot higher making much better for us. 15 wd. of 6$\underline{th}$ & 1 killed. Soon as it ceased we were orderd to about face march & we got of[f] silently some distance & formed & went back & campd—saw some poor fellows killed & some wounded coming off. Made fires & Col. Hob. gave me 2 bis. gave 1 to Ned B. & then we'd one apiece & broild rest of Pork on coal & ate our scant supper & went to bed. Had light brkf. & no din. It was a profiden. thing that none of our Co. was hit for were scattered & Shell & grape passed just over & thro' us.

NOTE: At Fredericksburg an estimated 1,284 Union soldiers were killed, 9,600 wounded, and 1,769 missing; the Confederates lost some 595 killed, 4,061 wounded, and 653 missing.

December 14, Sunday

SP: Moved at day light forwd. & formed the lines of battle as reserves. [. . .]

December 15, Monday

SP: [. . .] on our side & open [. . .] field to front [. . .] by Yanx [. . .] sort hill [. . .] on wh. they have Artil. Soon as day broke I read a let. recd. last night fr. dear Mama—first recd. Gave me much pleas. Our skirm. & Yank. adv. close to each other & some firing. Their lines advancd steady & in perf. order. Not far tho'. Saw flags truce, they want bury dead, not allowd. Dead lying both sides road & wd. most Yanx.

Course of day we saw a balloon ascend in the distance wh. looked like a white ball

Mon. 15$\underline{th}$ Continued. We remained all day in expectant of being attacked at anytime. The Yank lines were plainly to be seen & the pickets were pretty near each other. In the evening late a flag truce was brought over & exchange of dead & wounded made. We thought certain the big fight would come off in the morning. Were divided into 3 reliefs and 1 had to stay awake 3 hrs. each—I was on fr. 10 to 1 A.M. Slept very little before it & I scarcely got fixed after it when we had to tear up the R.R. & pile timbers & iron so as to afford some protection for batteries on our flank—as it was feared Yanks might enfilade us—A pretty hard shower rain fell before day & I got pretty wet & cold. After light I was one from our Co. sent out as skirmisher. As we went forward (it was dark foggy morning) the men began to say they believed Yanks had gone as none could be seen & when we got to line where skirmishers were placed found the Yanx really had gone & so silently that our skir. knew nothing of it. the most of skir. had gone forwd. plunderg. & soon men could be seen coming in every direct. over the field picking up things—I found our Lieut. in charge was not strict & no use of being there & I put out too. Got me a nice new minie musk. made at Bridesburg. U.S. 1862. —Threw away the old smooth bore I had. Got a hatchet and a butcher knife wh. gave to John for cookg—a little bot Ink—2 books & some bullets & grape Gil. got in woods—tried to get oil cloth but found no good one & a good new Yank canteen. Came on back & we were sent for[w]ard to stop plunderers & sat in ditch with high bank side road. Yanx threw good many shells over us one bust pretty near—Squads of Prisoners were coming back and a Brig. band & instruments were captured. Great many dead Yanx lying about all over the field & many dead horses.—*rubbish of every discription scattered over the field. Ditches full of boxes tin plates, cups, pans & pieces meat everywhere guns—cart. boxes, knapsax, tents plenty—If leave that much when go off in order what must it be like when routed. Their dead were lying just as we left—Did not pretend to bury. Gen. Lee rode along our lines & such cheering as they gave him. 12 or 1 o'clock we were ordered in & our Brig. marched off towards Port Royal & camped after going 5 or 6 miles, near Grace Church, Spotsylvania Co. John had been to Rich. with Ellison & came in just as going bed brot some nice apps. & cakes.

   *(Genl. T. R. R. Cobb killed & Massy Gregg suf. mort. wound.)

December 16, Tuesday

SP: Drew Minie Cartr. to fit my muskt. Got some Cake & Candy from Ellison & enjoyd the nice things very much after hard times we have seen of late.

December 17, Wednesday

SP: Moved Camp a little distance to where more wood & water. Fixed up comfort, bunk covd pine tops & straw in it. Went to branch & took wash all over. Let fr. Jamie. It was coldest ever had—Cold wind blowing—hung towel to dry few minutes & it froze.

December 18, Thursday

SP: Read letter from Jamie. We are having drills Co. in evening. Now Coldest spell weather ever felt. Can't keep comfort. Cold N. wind blowg. & at the fire one side is hot & other most freezing.—

December 19, Friday

SP: Commcd a letter to Mama but can scarcely write for cold. Recd. let. fr. Mary. Rations very scant. Often have beef without salt given out & biscuits without any grease—not even beef tallow & no salt.

December 20, Saturday

SP: Was on a work squad to-day & cut out roads thro the Regt. Contin. let. but did not finish it. It is a great treat to see News papers now. Occas. get hold Rich. Paper. It seems the bat. of Fred. was much more serious one than we first supposed. Some Yank papers admit loss of 15,000 to 20,000—& call it most disastr. defeat of the war—

December 21, Sunday

SP: We had inspec. of arms. & accont. as usual this morng—but so cold they were not partic & got thro' very quickly—Dress parade this eveng—.

December 22, Monday

SP: I at last finished letter to Mama & got it off. At dress parade had results of Court Mart. read out—held to try men who absent without leave when—see other side—their Cos. went into battle [. . .] tied to tree & placed a straggler [. . .] ride pole 4 ft fr ground 3 days intermis of 11 min. every hr. & others still to wear barrel several days with [. . .] in barrel head & arms thro' holes in side. Pretty tight.

December 23, Tuesday

SP: Our rations are outrageously short now. The Regt. com's scales are worn out & weigh incorrect & conseq. we lose by it. We got req. fr. Lt. Jones for 10 lbs of flour & got it by com. scales & weighd it by spring steelyards & it was only 6–4 lbs. lost in 10—& we are [. . .] nearly out. With scant rations & 2 servts to eat on what we draw for 4, in addition it don't begin to do us—& very diff. to forage too & get very little. Pork 50 ct. lb. & flour 20 c. & meal $1 Gall. at rate of 8$ bus. & not good meal either too fine—Yer-morn. had last of beef for brkfast. & that eveng (we eat only 2 meals a day now) dry bisc. without grease & no meat this morng—dry biscuits again but not enough & had to make out brkfst on parched corn. This eveng would have had no dinner at all until we drew rations, but John started out foraging & Mr. Jim Ed. Webb gave him a hand sak of flour & a beef shank—of which John made the richest soup I almost ever saw—it was splendid, first meal since yest. morn. & we ate a big meal & enjoyed it much.

December 24, Wednesday

SP: Christmas Eve & a dull pros. for to-morrow. We moved camp about a mile & ¼ to where there is plenty of wood. We may stay here a month or more if not called away by the Yanx—fixed up a nice fly with ends wh. we drew a few days ago—& put straw in bottom—very comfortable. Capt. Williams, Dav. Barn, Mat Jones, Chris, Webb &c came in this eveng. I recd no letters but a nice lined blank. & havelock Mama sent [. . .] Capt and have many I can carry.

December 25, Thursday

SP: Dull Christmas less like one than any ever saw—Ed., Pasteur & I are to spend it in the delightf. way of standing guard. A fiddle which has been introdu. into camp & which some one is jerking at is only thing that reminds of what Chr. formerly was—This is clear mild day & most pleas. weather we've had for good many Christmas—This eve. Ellison came & brot a little Christm. Never saw such crowd as collectd round him. Our mess got 12 Doz—Cakes (sugar) & some ginger bread, $2 candy, $5 sugar, bundle Confed. coffee, $2 pepper & lb. Butter. He was to bring us the materials for an Egg nog—but he sorely disappointed us in that—about the first Ch. ever spent without nog—

December 26, Friday

SP: Had best brkf. had since I've been in Regt. Hot biscuits, fresh, butter—fried tripe, [. . .] beef & bacon, genuine coff. & sug. Who wd have better—What contrast with one few morng back—Cake & Candy lasted long enough to keep us pretty well stuffed to-day again.

December 27, Saturday

SP: Dav. Barn. & Mat Jones have come into our mess & we now have very nice one. We have to go 1 mile to an old field to drill & have dress parade since came to present camp—very troublesome. Recd. letter long & inter. from Mary & inclosg one fr. Loutie—this eveng went to Dr. Tom Hill & got some turpentine to rub breast & a powder of morphine to make me sleep. Have severe pains in breast every night & can't sleep much—

December 28, Sunday

SP: Went on sick list this morng. Didn't sleep off effects of Morph. & got up to Roll call sick at stomach & feeling badly. Our Co. had to exchange their Enfield Musk. for Minie Muskts. I happend to have a Minie wh. got on bat. field so I was all right. We had to shoot off our guns & shot at head barrel 100 yds. Rodes bet an oyster sup. that no Co. in Regt. would hit blk. 4 Co. shot bef. us & hit barrel 10 times, Co. D hit it 9 times & the Blk once & won the oysters.

NOTE: According to Alan J. Pitts, who has looked closely at the armament of Rodes' brigade, nearly eighty thousand model 1853 Enfields (.577 caliber) began to arrive through the blockade during the spring and summer of 1862. During those same months, the Confederates captured a great number of Springfields (58 caliber), the "Minie Muskts" mentioned by Sam Pickens. The fact that both weapons had rifled barrels and shot minié balls suggests that the ordnance officer was trying to standardize weapons.

December 29, Monday

SP: I had to go on the sick list again this morning as I have severe pains in my breast. can't sleep any scarcely at night. Rub my breast at night with Turpentine. Dr. Hill Ass. Surg. says he has no cough remedies & nothing but the very coarsest & strongest remedies. Took the bad cold & brot. on pains on my breast I think by stripping & washing in the branch bout 2 wks. ago—on very cold day.

December 30, Tuesday

SP: There was a Brig. inspection of arms this morning preparatory to a review by Gen. Rodes to-morrow. Commencd a letter to Jamie this morning. Got some very inferior apples for $1. a dozen. There are some very nice ones at the wagon yard—5 for $1.20 cts. apiece.

December 31, Wednesday

SP: I have a miserable time of it every night. Sleep a little when first lie down & then the pains in breast come on & my rest for the night is over. Change position to try & get relief for few minutes—with difficulty—that I can turn over. We are so wedged in by the crowd that can't turn unless others do, too. Capt W^ms advised me to try & get in at some house in the neighborhood where would be comfort. & free from exposure. So started John out to find one. He came back late in the evening & had been to several but every one had houses crowded with refugees from Fredks. & couldn't take me.

1863

JHC: The new year came in clear-calm and very cold. The sun came forth in all his brilliancy yet it remained cold all day. Commenced the year with a good breakfast consisting of tripe brains coffee &c. At nine o'clock we were ordered out on squad drill, the non commissioned officers drilling the men. At eleven Company drill over at Genl Rodes' Hd qrs. Then at half past two Co^l Hobson took us out on battalion drill. Drilled about an hour, had dress parade and returned to quarters to eat beef molasses and biscuit not quite so good as the breakfast. To night it still continues very cold though quite calm.

SP: This is the opening of a new year—may it prove a prosperous and happy one! It is the third year of the war and I trust may be the last one. I started John out again this morning to look for a house in the neighborhood where they would take me in as a boarder, as I have been suffering for a week with bad cold & severe pains in my breast & feared an attack of Pneumonia. He returned in the evening, however, saying that every house was filled with the refugees from Fredericksburg & not one would take another boarder—that they found it difficult to feed those they had; in fact they had only two meals a day, as we do in Camp for the same reason. Tean Nutting swapped a puppy with one of the Commissaries for a small canteen full of molasses. It is the first I've seen since leaving Richmond, I could not resist the temptation to try some right away; so I put on a hoe-cake & as soon as it was done several of us ate it, & then parched some corn & ate that with the molasses—it went finely too.

January 2, Friday

JHC: Last night slept badly, our tent being on the side of a hill. I kept rolling down from under the cover and getting cold. This morning did not hear the drum beat reveille and would have lain there without calling the roll had not some one reminded me that the drum had beaten. I then jumped up and could not find my boots, hat, jacket or roll book &c. I had to go out in my stocking feet and shirt sleeves and call the roll without a book. When I got out the company had formed and was waiting for me. This morning was witness on a court marshall against J. C. McDiarmid for falling out of ranks and leaving the battle field at Fredericksburg. It was the first time I was ever before a court of any kind. Have not learned the decision of the court. Hope it will be nothing severe, though it is nothing but right that men should be punished who straggle at such times. Saw Gen¹ Jackson today for the second time. He was dressed in a neat Confederate uniform and looked much better than when I saw him before, as he then had on an old suit full of dust and dirt as he had just made one of his famous marches. This afternoon Major Blackford drilled the regiment. A battle has been fought in the mist and Gen¹ Bragg whipped Rosencrans. Captured 4000 prisoners, 31 pieces of artillery & 200 wagons and trains.

SP: Immediately after reveille the boys, having found out that Ellison, the Sutler, had come with a load of goods, hastened up to his wagons & brought a number of sugar cakes & ginger cakes which all hands pitched into, & I ate a good many before getting up. Our mess—now composed of Jack Wynne, Ed. Pasteur, W<u>m</u> Lenier, Tean Nutting, David Barnum, Matt Jones & myself invested $3. each in cakes principally & some apples. Had 26 doz. sugar cakes & a lot of ginger cake. All day long we were eating cakes & apples. A collection was taken up for the benefit of the Fredericksburg sufferers to day in our Division. I gave $5.00. Wherever collections have been made I understand the soldiers have given liberally. I finished & mailed a letter to Jamie this evening. I had another miserable time last night—pains in my breast & spine; so Capt. Williams got a permit from Dr. Hill for me to go to some house in the country. I got in Ellison's wagon going to Hanover C.H. & started about 4 P.M. We drove to Bowling Green, the Co. seat of Caroline Co. & stopped to get supper; but it was over & there was a crowd of soldiers there—so we could neither get any thing to eat nor lodging. We then drove on 5 or 6 miles & camped out on the side of the road. It was a cold & beautifully bright night. John collected some dry wood & we soon had a blazing fire. We made our supper off the cakes I have in my havre-sack.

NOTE: Cowin refers to the battle at Murfreesboro, Tennessee, which began on December 31. The next day, Lincoln issued the final Emancipation Proclamation.

January 3, Saturday

JHC: Last night Capt Williams promoted J. P. Moore and E. T. Pasteur to the rank of Corporal. We now only need a 3^d lieutenant to have our complement of commissioned and non commissioned officers. Saw last night the disapproval of a transfer by Genl D H Hill. It was quite amusing. It ran thus. "The 3^d Ala Regt stands proudly preiminent in applications for furloughs, discharges transfers &c &c &c &c &c &c &c. I regret to see that the 5$^{\underline{th}}$ Ala one of the very best fighting regiments in the service, and distinguished on every field, has sought to rival the 3^d in all manners forms and kinds of furloughs transfers &c &c &c. All disapproved. D H Hill Maj. Genl[."]Was up early this morning, called the roll, got up the sick list, made out my morning report, and came back ready for breakfast, but before I got back I was informed that my work squad had not reported to the Serg^t Major. I however soon had him, and thought everything was going on finely. But soon after breakfast I was politely informed by the Serg^t Major that I could consider myself under arrest and confine myself to my quarters, by order of J M Hall Co^l Commanding 5th Ala Regt. The cause of it was that while I had gone to make out my report the drum beat for the work squad to fall out, and my man coming up behindhand was told by Alex McCall that the squad had gone. So he put out, and did not find out the mistake until the ~~guard~~ squad was formed and ready to leave. He then came stalking up and I was put under arrest for it. And here I am in my tent having a good time as I have no duty to perform, but just lay here and read and write. I cannot say that I like it very much, but taking every thing into consideration the man who put me under arrest and the offence &c I do not care so much about it. Co^l Hall is so much afraid of Genl Rodes that he renders himself perfectly ridiculous and is a perfect byword to the regiment. He is laughed at by every man in the regiment. Wrote a letter to Co^l Harvey & sent him a muster roll of the Company. Genl Bragg has certainly repulsed Rosencrans. The loss on both sides was very heavy. It is reported that six iron clads had arrived at Charleston from England. Only a rumor.

SP: I slept rather cold last night—having only one double blanket. Got up & warmed at the fire several times, though, & then lay down again. We started an hour before day ~~and~~ when it was very cold and the ground hard frozen. Drove 5 or 6 miles and took breakfast with an old man named Reynolds, and a good breakfast it was too—to me who had not seen any thing but beef & biscuit for two months. Among other things they had a large dish of fried cabbage which I enjoyed very much. After finishing the meal & waiting for the horses to eat, we traveled on to Hanover C.H., 12 miles distant and arrived in time for dinner. The place consists of a Court-house, jail and a large hotel—framed building. The Depot is a half a mile off on the Central R. R. 18 miles above Richmond & as ms. below Hanover Junction, where the Fredericksburg & Central R. R. cross. There is a small hotel & 1 or 2 private houses at the Depot. I wrote a note to Gilliam James requesting him to send my letters down here.

January 4, Sunday

JHC: Was released this morning by Col Hall. After he was told the circumstances of the case, he said that he would not have placed me under arrest had he known them. It is my opinion that an officer should inquire into these things

before acting on a case. It was however doing very well, as I had no duty to perform, and was having a good time generally. Inspection this morning. The news
from Gen¹ Bragg's army still continues good. The Yankees have been repulsed
and driven off with heavy loss. There has been a large mass meeting held in New
York addressed by several very distinguished men advocating a settlement of
the difficulty and bringing about peace. To night I heard of a report that was in
circulation concerning me at Tallman's party in Greensboro. It originated from a
young lady who accused me of a breach of decency, but which I am glad to know
has no foundation in facts and is a base falsehood. We had a high time last night
laughing over it and something that Pick Moore & Gilliam James were guilty of
while at home. The report about me was rather a bad one to originate among the
girls, and it would only make it worse to try to remedy it.

SP: There is a large Episcopal Church near here but no service to-day. John
went to Richmond yesterday evening with Elliott & rode up a horse for Ellison
to-day. He brought me a box of Hebrew Plaster which I will try on my breast
& spine. Ellison got in to-day with his other wagon & says the Army has recd.
orders to build Winter huts & put chimneys to their tents &c. at the same place I
left it—our Regt. near Grace Church, Caroline Co. This is a very pleasant change
from Camp life, especially as I was unwell and suffering from exposure. I have
a comfortable room & good bed: and the fare here is excellent for these hard
times. I never ate so or enjoyed eating as much in my life. After living on beef &
biscuit & that scanty at times, I don't know when to stop eating the good fare
here. I heard some gentlemen speaking to-day of the destruction of property in
Fredericksburg while the Yankees were in possission of it. Every house in the
place was searched from garret to cellar & robbed of every thing worth carrying
away. One gentleman said he lost a great many handsome paintings & engravings;
besides a valuable clock, silver & china ware, bedding & every thing. Our soldiers
are now cooking in his two parlors & occupying the house. The people of that
city have truly been sufferers. The negroes in all the country around, as a general
thing, have gone off with the Yankees.

January 5, Monday

JHC: Was up very early this morning and had roll call before day light. We get
up by the drums of the Sixth Ala. as our drum is broken. Sent off six men from
our Company this morning on the work squad as a double duty for Saturday
mornings work. I think it was a price of injustice to punish innocent men for the
acts of others, but some of our officers never take such things into consideration
so they clear their own skirts. Had only one drill this morning and that Company
drill. Gen¹ Rodes ordered three drills daily and unless he countermanded the
order something will certainly happen, for our officers would drill us six times
were they ordered. We had a considerable battalion drill this afternoon. Major
Blackford drilled us. There were some ladies out to witness the drill and either
they or the bad drilling was the cause of our drilling so long. All the other

regiments had dress parade and left the field before we got through drilling. The news from west is not so good as it was. The dispatch read that the enemy had retired only a short distance and had returned and assumed their former positions.

SP: Quite a crowd stopped here last night—Soldiers going & sutlers going from & returning to the army—There are compar. few about to-day—8 or 10 ladies permanent boarders—some refugees fr. Fred. ~~We hear~~ Bragg has gained a vic. at Murfreesbr. Tenn. on 31$^{\underline{st}}$ ult. It is called by the papers "a worthy sequel to bat. of Fred. & the glorious campaign of 1862." He drove back their right wing several miles takg 4000 prisoners amg. them 3 or 4 Brig. Gens. 30 odd pieces cannon, many small arms—200 wagons, &c.

January 6, Tuesday

JHC: The papers today bring us the news of Genl Bragg's army falling back about thirty miles and the occupation of Murfreesboro by the enemy. The enemy acknowledge a loss of thirty thousand men killed and wounded and call it a drawn battle. I once had some hopes of Genl Bragg retreiving his fallen fortunes but now I am done with him, and do not think him capable of wielding a large army, but think he has no superior in the management of forts and shore batteries. Had only one drill today on account of the weather[.] Have had a cold and disagreeable rain all the afternoon, with good prospects of its continuance. Had a little excitement in camp this afternoon in the shape of a small fisticuff between B.A.C. and G.N. No damage done to either party as they were separated too soon. Have been in my tent nearly all day sewing and doing nothing generally. Vaccinated myself again this evening. Gilliam James quite sick today.

SP: Bragg fell back in perfect order, this morng—paper states, & bring. everything with him, & now occupies a strong position 30 miles. The Yanks admit loss of 30,000 but claim a victory. Public rather disappointed that he did n't whip Feds. badly & retake Nashville. It is very dull here to day—hardly any men about the house. Ellison & his partner came up fr. Rich. this evening with pretty large lot Sutlers stores. He had some apples nice—like Pippins wh. cost him 'bout $1.50 per Doz. He opened a box & told me to help myself. Ate 3 or 4 big ones & bot a doz. but he says he won't take pay. He loaded up his wagons to make early start in morn.

NOTE: "B.A.C." is Benjamin A. Carter.

"G.N." is George Nutting.

Estimated losses at Murfreesboro (or Stone's River) were 1,677 Union killed, 7,543 wounded, and 3,686 missing; the Confederates lost 1,294 killed, 7,945 wounded, and about 2,500 missing. A strategic victory for the Union, the battle lifted Union morale and put Rosecrans' army in a position to advance on Chattanooga.

January 7, Wednesday

JHC: Last night we had rain, sleet and a little snow, and this morning it is quite cold, though since day it has become fair and the sun shines out very pleasantly. The left wing of the regiment moved today, where there is more wood. Our wood is getting scarce and we will have to move soon or carry our wood a long distance. Company drill this morning. There is some little excitement in camp today in regard to furloughs, as I believe an order came to the effect that they would be granted to those who had never been home. Five or six from our Company have handed in their applications. I think they ought be granted to those who have not been home since the war broke out. Co^l Hall says he will not sign but four from a company. Battallion drill this afternoon by Maj Blackford. Did not drill much as we had inspection. Jim E. Webb and Capt Peyton were the inspectors. The evening was very cold indeed, and every one suffered considerably from it, as he had to stand there for an hour or more. We came back to quarters at a double quick in order to get warm.

SP: I had a doz. Eggs John had bought for me at $1.25 & as hadn't had Egg-nog this Christ. determd. to get up one & So Ellison last night brot. up plenty of Sugar & I got pint whisky for $3.50 & after sup. went in our room & beat it up. John helped about it & we beat the Eggs splend. Invit. our host Mr. Chisholm in to join us & sent glass to Mrs. C. I never enjoyd. anything as much in my life & drank more. Chis. said it was very nice but you could see he ate very little & was surpris. at being so thick—how we made it so? Virg. put milk in it & let white float on top—very dif from our way. Told him that was way made it in Ala. Hope they will show me how Virg. make it, soon. Ellison left this morng. bef. sun up. Very cold & got up lit. aft. day—lay awake 4 hrs. or more bef. day as couldn't sleep for pain in small back & breast. They are sending off the Conscripts from this Co & all others around I believe, to Camp Lee. As in Ala. there are many afflicted among them. Physical disability very common. I wrote a letter to Mary yester. eveng.

January 8, Thursday

JHC: A very cold morning indeed. Was up before day as I got so cold that I could not sleep. A very heavy detail was taken from the Company this morning, six men for guard and four for the working party. Saw Co^l Hall get wrathy this morning with several of the officers on account of drilling. After we had been drilling some time in the field near the regiment the Co^l came up and ordered us out to Rodes Hd.qrs. Capt Williams marched the Company up to the Sutlers tent, halted and gave the command to warm, and swore he would not go over unless Hall followed. So we kept standing there until he came up and ordered us out he taking the lead. We went over, drilled about ten minutes and came back to quarters, and all the other Companies followed. When we got back, he sent for Capt Williams and several of the officers and gave them a talk. The latest European news is very good for us, as it states that we are recognized by France. I believe as much of it as I please for I have heard such news too often, Though this is taken from the New York Herald. Have orders to prepare for picket tomorrow morning. Letters from home to night.

SP: This is the Annivers. of Bat. of N. Orleans. The Yanx have had some reverses on the water as well as on land recently. Off the coast of S or N. Car.

their splendid Iron clad vessel, The Monitor, sprung a leak & sunk with entire armament, ammunition & everything. Another is also said to be lost & Galena badly damaged. Cause by a severe gale. On Coast Texas our Gun boats captured the Harriet Lane, one of their fastest vessels, & another to avoid being captured was blown up by the crew, most of whom perished.

January 9, Friday

JHC: Was up this morning before day and had my work squad and morning report out before sunrise and then got ready for picket. An order was read on evening parade yesterday that regular schools should be established for the non-commissioned officers. Text books 1st volume of Hardees Tactics. I think it a very good idea, for if any attention is given it we will derive great benefit from it. Every non commissioned officer ought know how to command a company, and by these means will soon learn. If any is found not to improve he is to be reduced to ranks. So reads the order. We left Camp about nine o'clock and are only about two miles from Camp. We have only a tolerably good place for camping as it is between two hills and the ground is rolling. Only four of our mess came out today, the others being sick and on other duty. We have plenty wood and a fly to sleep under. The men have been catching squirrels all the morning. They have caught half dozin or more. The 6th & 26th Ala Reg's are on the outposts today. Think we will be the last to go out. Dress parade this evening and orders given to have two drills daily while here.

SP: The weather looks gloomy like it will snow or rain. I commencd a letter to Louty this evening.

NOTE: William Joseph Hardee's *Rifle and Light Infantry Tactics,* first published in 1855, was the standard work used during the Civil War; several editions were published in the Confederacy.

January 10, Saturday

JHC: Slept better last night than I have in some time owing to my having more cover. Alex McCall and I slept together. Capt Williams had to get up during the night and kindle up the fire. Had Skirmish drill this morning but only drilled about half an hour as it is [. . .] day. The boys are still after squirrels. If they ever show themselves they are as good as dead, for they climb any tree that the squirrels do run him out and kill him with sticks. Commenced raining today about eleven o'clock and continued all day and rendered every thing extremely disagreeable. Our fly leaked in several places but happily I had my oil-cloths with me and kept my blankets dry. We had sent us from camp today some cakes, eggs, candy, sausage and souse, which our mess had received since we left. They are now living well there. The things came from Gilliam James' Aunts. I am now acting surgeon of the regiment as Dr. Park is sick and Dr. Hill is at Camp. To night it continues to rain some and is quite cold.

SP: This has been a cold, rainy, disagreeabl. day. Part of the time it poured down hard. The Landlord has a bar here & there is a good deal of drinking done by his male boarders & every one that comes along the road stops & gets something to drink—50 cts. is the charge & at some places—as Bowl Green for instance $1.00—& still people drink more than ever I believe & care for it more, as liquor gets scarcer & dearer. I have seen soldiers give $1. just to take a few swallows of the raw stuff out of another's canteen. And they will give $10.00 a qt. for it freely about Camp. It is the same way about any thing to eat too. They are imposed upon shamefully by sutlers & soldiers them— (& hucksters generally) selves will by a barrel of cakes or apples & bring into Camp & retail at exorbitant rates—for inst. they ask 50 cts for a mean, tough, almost tasteless piece of ginger bread not near as large as what we used to get for 5 cts & $1 & $2 a dozen for trifling withered little apples. I heard a man say that he saw a barrel of Apples that cost in Rich. about $20. sold up at the army for $164—what swindling. Every thing is immensely high now. In Rich. Coffee is $5.50 lb. & Sulpher $1.00 to 110. Salt has been $2.50 lb. but I'm happy to hear has fallen to 40 cts. You cant [buy] a pr. Boots for less than $50. scarcely & good Cavalry boots run in fr. Maryland, fr. 75 to $90. The stores are said to be fuller than they ever were in Rich. with goods that they buy from Yankee land at low prices & still these exorbitant prices are demanded in Rich. Caval. horses are very high tho not as high as they were last Summer. They sold in Rich. at 5 & 6 hundred dollars. A man has 3 here now to fatten up that he says cost him $1700. There is no telling what things will come to if the war continues much longer—& the Gov cont. issue half mill. daily in Treas. notes.

January 11, Sunday

JHC: Had quite a rain last night after we went to bed but before day it became fair and we had a heavy frost. After day light however it again clouded up and now threatens rain or snow. We were out on inspection this morning. There were some young ladies out to witness the inspection, but it was too cold for them to remain long. Had an elegant breakfast this morning of sausages, Souse, Jowl, Chicken and biscuit. Several of the company came out this morning from Camp. Yesterday's paper states that Genl Magruder had captured the U.S. Steamer Harriet Layne, and that another was blown up to avoid being taken. Although the weather was so indicative of rain or snow we have had a dry day and the sun is now sinking clear while a few thin clouds fly high overhead. Did not have as good dinner as we did breakfast as we had not such a variety, as we only had Jowl, sausage, butter and biscuit. It was however good enough for me, as I am not hard to please provided I get enough. We were on dress parade this evening and heard a few unimportant orders.

SP: In comp. with Lt. White of Norflk. & Mr. Haynes of Rich. the young men who have been staying here, I walked to church this morng. The Ch. is Epis. denom. & situated a half a mile fr. this Hotel. There was a very good lady congrega. but very few men, of course. John came down fr. Camp to day & brot. me what I wanted more than any thing else in the world—viz—some letters fr. home. One fr. Mama, one fr. Jamie & 1 fr. Louty. It had been a long time since I had had any & was gettg quite uneasy. Mamas dated Dec. 10th a month comg—Jamie's Dec. 26th. They had not recd a letter fr. me in a very long time, altho' I have written regu. 1ce a week. Mails are certain badly managed. Finishd my letter to Louty & sent it off this evening—:

JHC: We have had a beautiful day, not a cloud to be seen and the sun shining most beautifully and pleasant. Though this morning it was very cold, Company drill this morning for an hour and a half and some young ladies to witness the drill. After drill wrote a letter home as they will not write to me. Cooked my own dinner today which was not so good as I have been accustomed to for the past few days. Battalion drill this afternoon and a tiresome one it was, as we drilled in marching by the front and flank all the while. We have come to the conclusion that we will not be sent on the outposts at all, and we are not at all sorry for it, for we are very well fixed up and do not care much about moving. The Sixth Ala has been out ever since we came home and refuses to be relieved. They have been trading extensively with the Yankees, they crossing the river and trading tobacco for coffee. They give one plug for a gallon of coffee. Have not seen a paper in several days, and in consequence of it have heard no news. There was to be speaking to night in honor of the secession of Ala but it failed.

SP: Went to Depot where Elli[o]t & John were loading sutlers wagons this morng. [B]ot. 4 Doz. sugar cakes—& drove his wagon up in wh. there was a barrel cakes with head knocked out just at my side—so I took toll by eating as many as I wanted. I walked all thro' the Old C.H. here. It is a very old building, put up in A.D. 1735–128 yrs. ago. The brick were brot. fr. Eng. with wh. it was built. It looks as well almost as ever I suppose. The great Pat. Henry who was born in this Co. & raised, has often spoken in it before the Old Rev. War. Henry Clay, also a native of this Co. no doubt has spoken in it too.

JHC: Did not sleep very well last night as there were five of us together which rather crowded things. Not as cold this morning as yesterday, and is cloudy and appears as if we were to have rain or snow. Skirmish drill this morning for an hour and a half and our mess had to go out on an empty stomach as our breakfast was not sent us until late. It was here however when we came off drill and we soon dispatched it, as the drill sharpened our already keen appetite. Read the paper today of yesterday's issue and found nothing of any importance except a little something about France and mediation, which amounts to nothing. Co^l Hall ordered today a detail from the different companies to go to Camp and build him a kitchen. Capt Renfrew refused to send any man and Capt Williams sent him word that he could not get any more men for such a purpose. There are three grown negroes there doing nothing, and wants men to build him a kitchen. Battalion drill this evening and we had a cold time of it out there.

SP: I spent to-day reading Gullivers Travels which I picked up in the house. There was a large crowd of soldiers here to supper. Genl Fitz. Lee's Brig. of Caval. have come down & campd. in Prince W^m Co. across the Pamunky. River—about 6 or 7 ms. fr. here.

January 14, Wednesday

JHC: At camp again and we are all glad of it, though we did pretty well while on picket. We found every thing as we left only provisions are more plentiful. We had no breakfast sent us this morning and consequently had to do without until we got here which was after twelve o'clock. Heard today that General D.H.Hill had resigned his commission on account of a spinal affection. Do not know who will now command the division, but think it will devolve upon Genl Ripley. A vote was taken today after returning to know whether the majority of the Company was in favor of moving our camp. It was agreed not to move, so we are here and without wood. We now have two Sutlers in the regiment and one of them has gotten half the regiment drunk today. On dress parade Capt Williams had to send two men from our Company to quarters, and Co^l Hall would not go through the regular form of a dress-parade. I saw one Captain so drunk that he could not stand still. There are some half dozen in our Company on a spree, all belonging to the same mess. After dress parade so much noise was created that the guards were turned out and some five or six were arrested and carried to the guard house. Our Captain was placed under arrest for resisting and insulting the officer of the day. Capt Renfro was arrested ~~yesterday~~ today for refusing to furnish men to build Co^l Hall a kitchen for his negroes. Capt Williams was not arrested, though he refused to detail men for the purpose[.] To night the guards are still walking around among the men to keep every thing quiet, and arrest all boisterous men.

SP: Genl Fitz. Lee, the nephew of Gen. R. E. Lee, took brkf. here this morng. but I got up late & saw him only at a distance as he rode off. I made another Egg nog last night & invited Mr. Chis. & his son up. Put milk in it & made like Va.ins do, very nice but not as good as our way.

NOTE: D. H. Hill had suffered from spinal problems since a cadet at West Point.

January 15, Thursday

JHC: To day has been more like a spring day than any thing else. A cool, strong wind has been blowing all day. Have been quite busy to day making out reports of the arms, accoutrements, Camp and Garrison Equipage and clothing on hand and needed by the Company. I never heard of as many reports as are now required to be made out. And when we have no reports to make out we are detailing men for guard duty and working squads. Today two details of three men each have been made from this Company to go on the work squad. Why they send a squad out at night I cannot tell. It is reported that the Yankees have cut out a road on the river in front of our working party. Genl Rodes is now in command of the division and Co^l Hall has been acting brigadier today. Genl Hill has gone to Richmond and it is thought will resign. Went out this afternoon to have battalion drill but the wind blew so strong that we could not hear the commands of the Colonel. So we had to return to quarters, and we were nothing loth to come back as we all felt lazy.

SP: The weather is as mild as Spring to-day & very windy. I walked out about a half a mile or ¾ to Mr. Winstons place, & back & found it quite warm. Commencd. letter to Mama this eveng.

January 16, Friday

JHC: Last night about ten o'clock it began to rain and continued until day light this morning. Six of us were under a fly. (The tent being occupied by Britton's Servant who is very sick with Typhoid Fever.) Our blankets all got perfectly saturated with the rain, and occasionally a large drop of water would fall in my face rendering all hopes of sleep vain. I could only lay there and amuse myself dodging from the drops of rain and wishing for day light to come. Capt Ferguson of Co. "G" is being court marshalled to day for cowardice at the battle of Malvern Hill. There are a good many witnesses against him, nearly his entire Company are bitterly opposed to him and wish him out of the Company. Britton's Servant John died today about half past twelve o'clock and was buried this afternoon. No coffin could be procured and he was buried as a soldier, wrapped in his blanket. The weather has become a great deal colder since morning, and every thing will soon be hard frozen. Our sharp shooters are now drilled twice daily in the skirmish drill and are excused from all other duty. We have four, B[a]rnum, Geddie, McDiarmid and McGehee. Brother is on the work detail to night.

SP: The weather has blown up quite cold again & this evening the temperature is very different from what it has been for a few days past.

January 17, Saturday

JHC: This morning Corp^l Pasteur, Hausman, Webb, Rowland and Westcott left for home on furlough. They were a happy set, and all went off in the highest spirits. No drilling to day as it is wash day. The men however are not doing much washing. Most of them are building houses, and a good many have them already put up and are staying in them. Our company is too lazy to put up houses and are remaining in tents, under fly's and bush arbors. To day is very cold indeed, and last night was awful, though nine of us slept under one fly and so close together that we could not turn over, still some of us came near freezing. Our tent we took down yesterday to give it an airing as Brittons servant died in it. The papers today contain very important Northern news. A proposition has been made in Illinois for a cessation of hostilities and a convention of all the states for the purpose of establishing peace. A speech was delivered by a Senator denouncing the administration of Lincoln & desiring peace, but restoring the union. Received a letter from home this evening.

SP: I finished my letter to Mama this morning & sent it by Mr. Chisholm to Richmond to be mailed there. I recd. this morng. three letters forward. from Camp—one from Mama, one from Mary and one from Louty. The latest date was Decr. 30th—Mary's.

January 18, Sunday

JHC: Another awful cold day, though the wind did not blow so disagreeably. Last night slept better than the night before, though it was pretty cold. The ice this morning was thick enough to bear the weight of a horse. Inspection this morning, which I think useless in such cold weather, for an hour to stand out there for nearly an hour in the cold and then the officers pay but little attention to the inspection. Two men were excused from a weeks guard duty for having clean guns. After inspection wrote a letter home to brother. I was once fond of writing letters and could find something to write about, but now I dislike it for the reason that I can find nothing to write about, an in consequence of it my letters are dull and uninteresting. I am so thoroughly disgusted with the war that I do not take the proper interest in anything. I just manage to do my duty and then take no interest in anything else. Every one, both officers and men are in the same state of mind. All the artillery has been ordered back here from the rear, which looks as if a fight was expected soon.

SP: I took a walk down the road to Ashland-wards. this morning & found it quite cold. This eveng the wind blows extremely cold.

January 19, Monday

JHC: Still very cold indeed. Every thing hard frozen. When we wash our faces every morning and dampen our hair, it freezes before we can wipe our faces which I think a pretty good sign of cold weather[.] The Court Marshall of Capt Ferguson for Cowardice is still going on. It seems to be a very important case, and many seem to think that he will be Cashiered, which is a considerable disgrace. Were I a commissioned officer I would prefer going into an hundred battles and being shot to acting the coward and hiding in the bushes as he is said to have done. This afternoon we were out on battalion drill under command of Capt Riley. I have seen the regiment drill badly, and pay no attentions; but this afternoon bangs all I have seen in some time. We had to drill in the mud which nearly broke us down and then half the time could not hear the commands, then the men did not give their attention at all, but got along in any way. Upon the whole it was a very poor affair and did not reflect much credit upon they who have been in the service two years.

SP: I thought I would have the pleasure of seeing the operation of getting Ice & housing it to-day but it is not quite thick enough. Most persons about here I believe have filled their Ice houses.

January 20, Tuesday

SP: A young Dr. Fountain—Brig. Surg. of Fitz. Lee's Brig—is to be married to a Miss Price of this neighbor. He with a good many of his officer friends had a dinner party here this eveng. Genl. F. Lee, Col. Rosser of 5th Va. Ca. were of the Party. They started down to the bride's father's after night in a rain & it was very dark. I was chilly all day to-day & was afraid was taking mumps (& felt badly)

January 21, Wednesday

SP: Still raining & very disagreeable. I feel better today than I did last night.

January 22, Thursday

SP: Last night Julian Chisholm, Lt. White, Mr. Hacock 2nd Va. Cav. & I had an Eggnog. It was well made & was excellent. We drank about 5 glasses apiece. The weather still rainy & disagreeable.

NOTE: Mud stopped the Army of the Potomac as it tried to cross the Rappahannock and attack the Confederates.

January 23, Friday

SP: Papers give an acct. this morng. of the sinking of the Fed. Gun boat Hatteras by the C.S. Str. Ala. 20 ms. from Galveston, Tex. The crew went down with her except an officer, 45 men who were picked up in a boat by the [. . .] Brooklyn. Another gloomy drizzley day.

NOTE: The CSS *Alabama* sunk the USS *Hatteras* on January 11.

January 24, Saturday

SP: A few days ago we'd information from Gen. Bragg that some of Wheeler's Cavalry had captured a gun boat & 5 Yank. Transports laden with provison on the Cumberland River, & in this morng's paper he says Wheeler's Cav. capturd. & destroyd another large transpt. of prov. & on 21$^{\underline{st}}$ 100 of Morgan's Cav. dashed into Murfreesboro' & brot. off 150 Prisoners & 30 wagons. Weather has not cleared up.

NOTE: On January 13 at the Harpeth Shoals along the Cumberland River, Joseph Wheeler's Confederate troops captured the federal gunboat *Sidell.*

January 25, Sunday

SP: Gloomy weather has at last given place to a sun-shiny day which is really cheering after the very disagreeable spell of weather we have had.

*(The Snow is 18 inches deep in Staunton.)

January 26, Monday

SP: In the paper this morn. an extrct. from N. Y. Herald says on 21$^{\underline{st}}$ inst. Middling Cotton was worth 75½ [to] 76½ cts. per lb. Gold 147⅝ . Exchange 163. John came up on the eveng. train from Richmond & brot. me 5 letters. He left Camp Sat. eveng. I never had such pleasure reading letters in my life scarcely. One was from Jamie, 3 from Mary, 1 from Willy & 1 from Louty. 3 of them were brot. on by Mr. Joe Grigg who arrived in Camp several days ago & 3 came by Mail— They afforded me the greatest pleasure. Mama inclosd. me $100. in Jamie's letter which I was very glad to get as it came in good time.

January 27, Tuesday

SP: Last night Julian, Hacock, & I made a big Egg nog. It was not as good as usual as we could get nothing but App. Brandy to put in it & it did n't taste well. Commencd. letter to Jamie this even'g.

January 28, Wednesday

SP: Recd. this a long & exceeding kind & interesting letter from Mama & 1 from Louty. Very sorry she could not help being very uneasy about me in spite of all the assurances I gave her that there was nothing serious the matter with me. It is unavoidable tho' with an affect. & anxious Mother. She urges me to get a furl. to go home to recuperate which I'd be most happy to do if it were necessary, but fortunately, I have gotten over my cold & pains in breast &c. & am able to return to camp.*

*Awoke this morng. finding it snowing beautif. & continued all day 'till bed time to-night

January 29, Thursday

SP: The mail was closed when finished my letter to Jamie yest. eve. so put post script to it to-day & mailed it this eve.—answering in it another let. recd. from Jamie this morng. It containd good deal of home news & conseq. very interestg. Am really in luck for receiving letters now & hope it will continue. This morng. it is perfectly bright & the snow looks beautiful coverg. the ground & tops of houses & sticking on the trees. It is 3 or 4 inches deep. (This is court day at old Hanover & grt. larg. crowd assembled here. Bar open in this hotel & conseq. grt. deal drinkg going on & some drunken men staggerg & lying about. Disgusting objects! greatest rage for drinkg now when liquor is extremely mean, rather scarce & exorbitantly high. Peopl[e] who used to care nothing for it now drink all can get. Have seen soldiers give $1. just to take swallow or two of raw stuff out Canteen of some fel. happend to have it.)

January 30, Friday

SP: The weather is moderating and the snow beginning to melt away. John went to Richmond this morng. to take a horse of Ellison's.

January 31, Saturday

SP: Julian Chisholm, Hacock & I sent to Rich. to-day for a gallon oysters—$5 selling at now & 2 Doz. Apples $3 doz. & to-night 11 or 12 'clock stewed them nicely (John officiating) & made a large bowl of hot app. toddy as I had determd. to return to Regt. Mond. morng. wanted to have something nice first. We 3 easily ate all the oysters which very nice & drank much of the ap. tod. as we wanted & it excellent. Set the bowl aside to take another glass or 2 in morng. after giving the servts waiting on us some.

February 1, Sunday

SP: We were provoked to find that the negroes had drunk up all our toddy so we were cut out of the pleasure of a glass before brkfast. I was also much vexed when I went to my room after brkf. & found the chambermaid wh. cleand up the room had gone into a havrsk. of little ginger cakes that John had brot. fr. Rich. & intend. to take with me to Regt., & stolen nearly all & nearly half of one of Apples. As I was going away so soon I did not make any fuss about it. I wrote a letter to Mary to-day answg. her 4 last, & telling I was going back to Regt. Monday.

February 2, Monday

SP: Got up very early this morng. packed my knapsak & paid my bill $50 mth. & 4 for John. Ate early brkf. & took leave of mine host & hostess who invited to come bk. if ever had the opportunity & sorry I was going &c. They are very kind folks he a very liberal man. Walked to Depot with Hacock & Julian, parted with them & John & I went up on train to H. Junc. wh. got off & waited for freight train wh. very long one & loaded with flour. Crowded in 1 with car with crowd of soldiers & went up to Guinea Depot on Frd. road. grt. concourse Soldiers about there & larger depot of Provisions several sutlers tents &c. After getting some Apples & warming, John & I marchd. of[f] to Regt.* where we got some time bef. sun set. I was very glad to get back to Camp & meet the boys whom was happy to see, especially Mr. Joe Grigg wh. had not seen in long time. I noticed the greatest change had taken place in the looks our Camp since I left. The woods wh. were quite thick had been cut down almost entirely & rough, odd looking cabins, huts & sheds had sprung up thick you could see all around the neighborhd. & many camps with their white tents were visible wh. form. could not be seen. Our mess had just built a chimney to our tent that day, & it looked much more comfort. It had not been carried up high enough & smoked when wind blew.

(*6 or 7 ms. distant).

February 3, Tuesday

SP: Woke up this morng. & found it had turned very cold & bleak & was snowing. The Regt. had to start out on Picket at 8 A.M. for 5 Dys. So we got brkfast & fixed up to go. When the Drum beat to take places in Ranx, Capt. Williams told me as just come fr. comfort. house, I had better not go on Picket as weather so bad & be such great change & exposure. So I very willing—stayed. It is a terrible day—wind blowing cold & biting. It snowed very fine & didn't continue long.

February 4, Wednesday

SP: Last night was a very cold one. Was so uncomf. that could not sleep altho on very thick blank. & covd with 4. Had rations cooked up & sent out to our mess mates on picket. Sup. they glad to get it as did n't take much with them.

February 5, Thursday

SP: Last night the weather was so cold that I couldn't keep warm & therefore slept very badly. It commencd. snowing this morng. early & it fell quite fast until ground covd. to depth of 2 or 3 ins. It was so cold to-night that we preferred sitting up by the fire until late, so D. Barn. & I having a novel "The Neighbors" in 2 vols. by Fred. Bremer, went up, by Ellison's to get some Candles but he had none; so we were disappointd, howev. sat up some time reading by firelight.

NOTE: Fredrika Bremer, *The Neighbors, A Story of Every-Day Life,* translated by Mary Howitt, second edition (London: Longman, Brown, Green, and Longmans, 1843).

February 6, Friday

SP: The Co. is still on Picket but the men in quarters have had a big time. They got a good deal Whisky & some got tight & several fights was the unpleasant result. It was a disagreeble & exciting day, on that acct. The Richmd Disptch. says last Tues. night was the coldest weather since '57. Therm. 8° below zero. It was terrible.

February 7, Saturday

SP: This is a pretty mild & pleasant day, it having cleared off. We had sufferd so much fr. the tent being open & chimney unfin. that I made many proposit. to work on it to-day, but they seemed indisposed to do so—finally D. Barn. & I set to work on it & got a negro to do dobbing for us, & compl. chimney & filled in back. Tho the firkin we put on chimney was too small for rest of it, & it smoked pretty badly. The music. in 6$\underline{th}$ Ala gave us some good perform. tonight. Kettle drum, bass & a fife, best drummer ever heard. Playd Devil's dream as fast as a fiddler & splendidly.

NOTE: "Devil's Dream" was a popular traditional fiddle tune.

February 8, Sunday

SP: The Regt came in about 12 O'clock & after getting something to eat & putting on clean clothes the men gathered in groups about on the hillside to sun themselves as it was a warm, sunny, delightful day. Such a pleasant change after the disagreeable weather we have had. Had no dress parade this eveng.

February 9, Monday

SP: Our mess have had a busy day of it. Mr. Joe swapped our fly off for a good bell tent & we moved down in the bottom where it is much warmer. We leveled off a place, stretch. the tent and ditched around it. Then brot. down the straw & all our baggage &c. & arranged them in the tent. It is very close & comfortable & much bet. situated than the other. Will have chimney to move down another day.

NOTE: "Mr. Joe" is Joe Grigg.

February 10, Tuesday

SP: Drill morng. & eveng. now—Co. Drill—I went to the branch to-day & took a nice wash & put on clean clothes. At midday the sun very warm. It is quite cold at night.

February 11, Wednesday

SP: The Richmd. papers to-day had extracts from Northern paps. stating that cotton had sold at 96¢ in N.Y. on the 3$\underline{d}$ inst., I think, a pretty round sum for a lb. of Cotton. If all the Cott. in South was owned by Govmt. & could be sold at that price it would pay off our War debt & more than. Mr. Joe, Matt. Jones & I walked over this eveng. to the sutler tent of 12$\underline{th}$ Ala. Regt. & got some apples. We bought a little sheet iron Yankee stove to-day for $10.00 & put it in our tent instead of building another chimney. Extracts fr. Northern papers quote Gold in N.Y. at 162½ . It is getting up high & hope it is good sign & will have its effect. I wrote letter to Willy to-day & had to wind it up very hurriedly in order to get it in evengs. mail.

February 13, Friday

SP: We are drilling every day now in Hardee's Tactics—the manual of arms. I think it much prettier than the old way. Got a letter fr. Jamie this eveng. containg. sad news—the sudden death of Simon (Little). Dr. Grigg performed a post mortem examination & was of opin. that was poisd. He was to have 'nother with Dr. Moore next day. I hope he did not meet his death in that foul way, but if so, the guilty perpetrator may be found out & receive his just punishment.

February 14, Saturday

SP: This being wash day for the soldiers we had no drilling but some fine games of "Bull-pen", "Cat" & "Stick-it-to-him". It reminded me more of School than any thing I've seen in a long time. The men pitched in like schoolboys & we enjoyed it exceedingly. The exercise was so beneficial & so pleasant on a mild bright & beautiful day after being kept housed up in our tents by wet & cold weather. We brot. up enough wood this eveng. to last till Monday or Tuesd. have to bring it from a hill side over the branch 2 or 3 hund. yds. off & it is right smart work. I had the happiness to receive a letter from Mama this eveng. of $3^{\underline{d}}$ inst. & one fr. Louty of $1^{\underline{st}}$. They contained much interestg. news, but nothing was said of the result of the investigation of Simon's sad death. I am anxious to hear it. Jamie promisd. to write me all about it & probably has done so but the letter miscarried and is still on the road.

February 15, Sunday

SP: Woke up this morng. findg. it raining. Mr. Joe was to go on guard but the weather was so bad Col. Hall dismissed them. We lay in the tent nearly all day, reading some & talkg. a good deal. About 3 O^{c}lock we sent up to Ellison's & got some Oysters. Mr. Joe & Jack Wynne assisted a little by David B. ate 2 qts. raw, & Matt. Jones & I ate 2 qts. stewed. They were fine & we made a hearty meal & enjoyd. it much. Walked up on the Drill ground late in the eveng. & lookd. on at a game of "Bull pen". We finishd. off the eveng. till bed time singing or rather trying to sing hymns.

February 16, Monday

SP: Matt Jones & I havg. to go on guard this morng. got up before the rest took a nice wash & commencd. makg. preparat. for brkfst. but after we had put on a cup to make coffee & sliced up some bacon to broil, the Drum for guard mounting beat & we had to go off without it. As good luck had it we were taken for Brig. guard & went over to Maj Websters tent. There happend to be no commiss. stores on hand & no guards had to be posted. Matt & I got permission to come over & get brkfst. & stay till eveng. There were games of Bull pen, cat, town-ball going on all day except at times for drillg. I took part in the eveng. & had a fine time. Matt. & I ate dinner about sundown & walkd over with Maj. Webster. We were to keep watch 2 hrs. each & M. & I came on at $2^{\underline{nd}}$ & $3^{\underline{d}}$ Relief. So we did n't get off till 1 A.M. when we returned to our tent & retired.

February 17, Tuesday

SP: This morng. when we awoke it was snowing fast & kept it up all day. If the snow had not melted as fast as did, it wd. have been a deep one: as it was at night when it ceased it was at least 4 inches. A grand game of snowball was kept up all day nearly. The N.C. Brig. campd. near us came over to whip us, & a no. fr. several of our Regts. turnd. out to meet them. Sevl. of the Regt. flags were borne on each side & it was a lively scene & was conducted a good deal like a real battle. Sometimes one side wd. give way & fall back, then rally, charge on their antagonists & drive them back in return. Frequently flags of truce wd. pass for exch. of Prisoners &c. Our Flag-staff was broken in ineffect. attempt to capture it, & a N.C. flag was taken, & staff of another brok. off & brot. away.

February 18, Wednesday

SP: I was detaild to work on roads & left directly after reveille. It was such a bad morng. & snow 4 in deep that after sloshing about in it to report. at Brig. & Div. Hd. Qrs. we were excused—& I got bk. just as our mess was about to pitch into brkfast. Stayed in tent mostly all [day] as it is so cold no drilling of course.

February 19, Thursday

SP: The snow is melting fast. The boys sit in tent & play cards most all the time. Commencd letter to Mama to-day. Crowell brot. me down a knife with spoon & fork in it. A most valu. thing in Camp—sent to me fr. Rich. by John.

February 20, Friday

SP: I was engaged nearly all day finishg my let. to Mama & just got it ready by time Hands. Chad. left with mail. I recd. a letter from Jamie Mary & Lou. this eveng. telling of the death of Col. Isaac Croom of Pneumonia on the 8th inst. & also that Old Charley, the useful, faithful old horse died of blind staggers. in the Carriage in front of Mrs. Stickney's when Mama & Jamie were going to Greensboro' on 9th inst. I was also very glad to hear that after the Post mort. exam. made by Drs. Grigg & Moore that their conclus. was that Simon's sudden death caused by congestion of heart or lungs.

February 21, Saturday

SP: Having no beef for brkfst & nothing but fat rancid bacon we sent up to Ellisons got a gallon of splendid oysters & stewed them nicely & had splend. brkfast—the only fault consisting in the fact that there were not near enough for 8 of us. We pay $10. now. This is washday again & no drilling. I went up & had nice time playing Town ball. Made 4 rounds. Mr. Joe excellent hand at ball playing.

NOTE: Town ball, a variant of the British game of rounders, was an antecedent to baseball.

February 22, Sunday

SP: To-day is Washingtons (annivers) birth day & the Yank- guns fired in celebrat. of it could be plainly heard. What a farce that those fanatical wretches should be celebrating the birth day & pretending to have admiration for the grt. & good Wash'g. It commend. Snowg. abt. bed time last night & this morng. was quite deep & still snowg. very fast—part of time the largest flakes I ever saw. Continued nearly all day & is about one foot deep the largest snow I've ever seen. where it drifted upon our tent it was near 3 ft. deep. There was some sport this morng. caused by Britton who wd. stand out & call to men that Capt. W^{ms} wanted to see them, & in going to his tent wd. fall in a hole 2 or 3 ft. deep level full of snow. Had good laugh on Joe Brown for falling in.

February 23, Monday

SP: The Regt. went on picket this morng. It is very cold & they must have had a hard march down to the River 4 or 5 ms. off thro' the snow. Capt. W$^{\underline{ms}}$ said one in each mess must stay to attend the cookg. & sendg rations to those on Picket so we got Pack Cards & cut for it. One cut King & all thought he wd. be 1 to stay, but I cut last & got Ace. I therefore remain at camp. Owing to bad weather a grt many went on sick book. Mr. [. . .] was unwell & stayed with me. Tean Nutting and D. Barn being on guard stayed also.

February 24, Tuesday

SP: I had biscuits cookd & sent over by [. . .] He says the men are [. . .] houses. We had a nice [. . .] Tean & I amused ourselves to-day [. . .] sparrows & caught 4 wh. we cookd & ate [. . .] delicious morsels. After supp. David Barn & I had long time to talk about books we had read &c. He has a [. . .] disposition & is very anxious to get a transfer to Navy, has grt fondness for sea, & [. . .] till he gets on it, to travel about [. . .] Ellison came in then & had been dr[ink]ing Eggnog, & gave the life & adventures of Murrell & Co. in toto till he put us all to sleep & exhausted subject & left abt. midnight.

NOTE: Before his arrest in 1834, John Murrell and his gang repeatedly stole slaves and resold them, sharing the profits with the slaves in return for their cooperation. His exploits became the subject of books and folklore.

February 25, Wednesday

SP: Slept very late morng. & got up & fixed biscuits [. . .] sugar & Coffee for boys on Picket & started [. . .] skillet full was left raw for us. I tried to [. . .] Coffee but the fire was so low that could not & [. . .] I ate a qt. raw oysters & some crackers for brkfast. I wrote a letter to Icha to-day & recd a very neat & pretty little valentine. Got qt. raw oysters for Supper for had nothing but dry biscuits. Am just beginning to eat them raw & [. . .] a good deal when very hungry tho' nothing like as good raw as cookd any way. Dav. Barn & I caught [. . .] birds in traps, dead fall yesterd. & Tean Nutting [. . .] morng. They are delightf morsels [. . .] going on Paul Lavender's tent tonight [. . .] Tom Ward, Jno. Christian, Dolf Ellison [. . .]

February 26, Thursday

SP: Night before last 2 cav. pickets deserted & came over to our regt. one from [. . .] from Ky. Last night I hear another came over to another Regt. Mr. Joe Grigg, Gilliam, P. Moore, Tean [. . .] had a 5 qt. oysters stew. [. . .] went round to Col. Hobson's tent where Ellison gave Eggnog (J. Grig[g], Gill & I went)[.] The whites fell & went to not. state & was last. put app. brandy in & then stirred in some Snow in the Yolk & it was elegant. Col. Hob. is very fond of it about as much so as I am. We sat & talkd till 12 Oclock—& came to tent & went to bed.

February 27, Friday

SP: Gil, Pick & Joe Gr. went over to dine with Maj. Adams. John came back from Rich. where he had been with Ellison for more th. week. He had goldwatch that he gave $200 (& chain)[.] This eveng. Braxton, M. Jones' boy got back from Amelia Co. where been to Mr. Jones & Mr. Grigg with barrel of eatables. Contained 2 hams, a Turkey, jole Sausage meat, Pease, Beans, Cabbage, bread,

I. Potatoes, Cake & bot Tom Catsup, &c. &c. (Butter). We were very glad to see them.

February 28, Saturday

SP: The boys came in from Picket to-day & we had a big game of Town ball, after wh. we had dinner & Co. Hobs. & Maj. Webster ate with us. had a first rate meal—Turkey, Sausage, fried eggs, Light bread & fresh butter. Every one ate heartily & enjoyed it very much. As were going to bed we sent up & got some Apples, very nice.

March 1, Sunday

SP: Maj. Webster & Adams came in & sat a while this morng. Jim Webb, Jeff Childress & D. Ellison dined with us—had large pot pease & jowl & hopn. John— brot. some wood & took walk in eveng—read in bible bef. going to bed.

March 2, Monday

SP: We all took down our tents to sun the ground wh. was very wet. All cleaned up guns & had quite busy day. In eveng. had inspect. & guns lookd very pretty. We don't get any papers now. A bridge bet. H.Q. & Rich. has been washed away*.

(*Sent illust. news to Jamie eveng. & Recd. letter from Mama)

March 3, Tuesday

SP: As we were eating brkfst. we were agreebly surprisd by seeing Tom Biscoe ride up with the Adjt. of his Regt. They came in & sat for several hours but could not stay to dinner. I was very glad to see Tom. He is lookg. well tho' Mr. Joe says has fallen off very much since left Umbria. His Div. is on its way to Hamiltons Xing. to take place of Hoods Div. Hope I'll see him often now as will be only 5 or 6 ms. off.

March 4, Wednesday

SP: To day is an. of Lincoldn't 2$\underline{nd}$ year in office. The old Congress went out yesterday & has given him all power of an emperor—a mil. Despot. Since he has been given men, money & power supp. will make a grand endeavor to crush us out yet. This eveng. Joe Bord. drilled us & had fine fun, men falling &. [. . .] Ed. Webb came eveng. fr. Ala. brot. me letter with $100. & bundl. shirt, sox Towels—he looks finely & enjoyd furlough very much

March 5, Thursday

SP: I wrote to Jamie to-day but did not get let mailed. There was a Yank. Balloon up on other side Rap river this eveng. It was white (very) in sun light. A man fr. Co "E" was buried this eveng. Was quite a solemn procession—guns reversed—firing 3 rounds.

March 6, Friday

SP: There being a Court Mar. in session to-day there was no drilling. Added to my letter to Jamie this morng. & mailed it. Bought a ½ gal. Molass. & it a treat as we had not had [. . .] any in so long a time.* D. Ellis. having recd. barl fresh Oysters invited Joe Grigg, Tean Nut. & myself to come up & eat Oys. sup. with him—So bout 10 clock P.M. we went up & Mr. J. carried his bottle Tomato

Catsup—Dolf. had a large pan of Stewed & with Catsup they were elegant. Joe ate some raw but I (& Tean) preferred the stewed. We made very hearty meal. So much so that I did not feel like going to bed, but walkd with Tean who was on guard to guard house & sat with him till next relief went on & then both came to our quarters & went to bed.

*(Recd a letter from Jamie & 1 fr. Mary this evening. in Van dorn cavalry fight in west recently 1000 of enemy killed & 2600 made prisoners. Our loss tho' was quite heavy also.)

NOTE: On December 20, Van Dorn captured the Union supply depot at Holly Springs, Mississippi.

March 7, Saturday

SP: Had Oysters for brkfast. Matt Jones & I went to brach to-day & took delightful bath in tubs, & donned a clean suit. I read part of Scotts' Lord of the Isles. It is a beautiful thing & extremely interesting. At night some one having Scott I commencd Mustang Gray—wh. is also very interesting.

NOTE: Sir Walter Scott's *Lord of the Isles* was first published in 1815.

Jeremiah Clemens, *Mustang Gray: A Romance* (Philadelphia: J.B. Lippincott, 1858). Clemens was an Alabamian.

March 8, Sunday

SP: Had Co. inspect. Arms this morng. The weather very mild & spring [. . .] rain.

March 9, Monday

SP: We drilled 2ce to-day. On dress parade were read out sentences of several men amg. them D. Barnum for violating 1 of articles in Army Regulat. by (wh. were Court Martiald) applying directly to Sec. of War for transfer from Army to Navy was Barnum's. Alex. McCall got a 30 da. furlough to go home to Ala. & was proudest fellow I ever saw. I wrote to Mary & gave him the letter to leave in Greensboro'.

March 10, Tuesday

SP: This being a drizzly-snowy-sleeting day we stayed close in tents. I finished "Lord of the Isles" & read good deal in Mustang Gray. Col. Hob. & Ch. Pegues came in & sat sometime to night.

March 11, Wednesday

SP: The Sun is again out this morng. & looks cheerful. So much more pleasant than yesterday. We had a game of Town Ball & I made 2 rounds & was caught out.

March 12, Thursday

SP: To-day I recd. letters from Mary, Will & Lou. They are very well pleased with teacher but Willy says very cross at times & calls him a fat cross Dutchman— he has many [. . .]

March 13, Friday

SP: I read Mustang Gray most of the day, & drilled some.

March 14, Saturday

SP: Very cold day but we had good game Town Ball read part of time. late in eveng had exciting game stick it to him. Played with Joe Grigg and rub. ball & it hurt when hit made it exciting. I got some good licks & gave some of the same sort.

March 15, Sunday

SP: Lt. Borden, Chas. Briggs, Joe G. & I walkd down to the Church in which Gen. Hill & [. . .] & Rodes now have for head-Quars. There was a grt. crowd there. The ch. full. We waited till near 12 bef. Minist. appearance, & several went out I sup. despairg of a sermon. so Joe & I secured seats tho much crowded. There were 3 or 4 ladies there. I shook hands with Genl Rodes who attended preach. [. . .] of striped and starred & gold-laced officers present. I met Col. Pickens of the 12th Ala. Regt., a distant relative. He is the same Sam! P. who stopped at Umbria some 12 years ago with 2 girls, his cousins. They were visiting their relations in Ala. He was then a small freckled faced boy. Grad. at the Military Institution in Charleston in '61. & recd. app. of 1st Lt. in Reg. army & went to Richmd. where was assignd to duty as Adjut. of 12th Ala. Regt. then in the city. Served in that capac. bout 10 ms. & was elected Major. Has since had 2 Cols. killed over him, the 2nd Col. Gayle in Battle of Boonsboro' where himself recd. severe wound in left arm, wh. cannot use well yet. So he is now Col. of his Regt. & is a very gallant fellow & an excellent officer. He is not as tall as I am, ruddy complex & Red hair, a (freckled a little) fine blue eye & a large nose (a characteristic of the Pickens). He seemed glad to see me & begged to be kindly remembd to Mama & all the children. In the eveng. it turned very cold & hailed thick & fast, & for a while the largest hail Ive ever seen in Winter, being as large as end of my finger. The grd. was completely covd. with it. At night it snowed a little—enough to cover ground. It was very cold night.

March 16, Monday

SP: This morng after getting up late & eating brkf. leisurely, to our grt. surprise an order for us to go on Picket immediately. We had just been congratul. ourselves upon not having to go on picket this bad weather & thought it would be several weeks before we'd have to go. We disliked idea very much. This time the order came unexpected. & after the sick book went round There was not one in Co. reported sick, whereas last time when order was recd night before 30 in our Co. went on sick list. I made John carry my blankets & we went bout 2 ms. from Camp, not far from Gordon's Place. Well fixed up by the way large residence on hill & a no of Double brick cabins for negroes. Stopped in thick woods where nice branch convenient. Immediately the axes were at work & trees felled on all sides. There was soon wood enough down to last Regt a fortnight almost. We had our tent & sent back for our little stove & were as comfort. then as in Winter Qrs.

March 17, Tuesday

SP: Got up pretty late this morng. as had no roll call at reveillè & went to branch & washed. After a while Carey came up with a havre sack of bread & butter for us. We made coffee, broiled some bacon & ate a very hearty meal. Joe, Jack[,] Lenier & I took a long walk hunting for broom grass to improve our bunks to-night. Could hear Yank. trains running on opp. side river & drums whi we supp. were theirs. We heard cannon firing during day & some very heavy that seemed some distance off. Paper to-day contains intell. of some success at Port Hudson, La. Some Yank vessels attempt. run past at night ($\underline{th}$) one iron clad got by much damaged, in ruined nearly & Pick & Gill. have found horses wh. got away night got bk. fr. Rich. with them & been hunt. ever since.

NOTE: Admiral Farragut's fleet passed Port Hudson on the Mississippi River on March 14.

March 18, Wednesday

SP: Last night after gone to bed Tood C. rode up with orders for Col. Hall saying the Yanks had crossed river. We expected nothing else than to have to be up & going before day, but 'greebly dispointed. Orders came round early, however, to cook all rations & be ready to march. Sent my big blanket to quarters by John & told take care knapsack. Wrote to Mama & ment. I thought we'd seen last of Wint. Qrs. &c. but in eveng. heard Gen. Stewart had sharp fight *cum* Yanx, whose force consisted of Caval & Artillery & driven them across river, Killing & Capturg. quite a No. We lost gallant young Maj. Pelham of Ala. commdg. Stewarts horse artillery & Maj. Puller of Va. in Cav. John brot us a bag of Cakes, some Potatoes & Cherry Pies—acceptable.

NOTE: "Tood C." is William S. ("Tood") Cowin.

John W. Puller and John Pelham were both killed at Kelly's Ford, March 17.

March 19, Thursday

SP: Mr. J. & I ate a very late brkfast & took Pains to get up a very good ones by warming bread frying meat & made a cup of very good coffee apiece part genuine. Jack & I slept cold last night so I sent to Camp for my big blanket again. It seems Yanx attempted exped. on grand scale but Steward *cum* Fitz Lee's Brig. whippd. & thwarted plans. So the fight will be deferred, & we'll be in W. Qurs. a while yet— Turned very cold this even. & snowed some. This month so far's been a tight one. Mr. J. says decidedy. most disagreeb. march he's ever seen, even in V$\underline{a}$.

NOTE: "Mr. J." is Joe Grigg.

March 20, Friday

SP: Still snowing so we lay in bed till ordered to get ready to return to Camp when hurriedly tied up blankets &c. & started that disgreeble walk thro' snow & found the place covd with snow. Waited till tent came & raked it away & stretchd tent. Gid. Westcott & Boardman & Sheldon got bak fr. furl. yest. & came over this eveng. Westc. gave me letter from Jamie containg $100. I recd 'nother by mail fr. Mama.

March 21, Saturday

SP: Terrible weather! Still snowg. lightly. We lay in bed very late. Carey warmed over what cold brd. there was & [. . .] & one or 2 others ate it up. Carey cleaned out rest of us were left with out anythi[n]g to eat. I got up tho & hunted up John & made him get us somethg. warm & fresh. Think it was bout 12 clk when we got thro brkfast.*

*Ed. Pasteur got back eveng. fr. his furlough & says he saw Mama Jamie & Mary at church in Greensboro' & th. Mama wished to send a box by him but he couldn't possibly bring it.

March 22, Sunday

SP: The snow melted very fast to day & in eveng. it had disappeared. I sup. this will be last snow of any consequ. hope so at least, for was never so tired of cold & disgreeble weather in my life. How different it is at home, where Jamie says in his letter fruit trees are in full bloom & putting out leaves. There corn is planted up—& both veget. & animal world is full of life.

March 23, Monday

SP: To day had drill in morng & policed our quarters in eveng. Phil Weaver came over to see me this eve. first time I've seen him since left Greene Springs. he belongs to Gulf City Guards, 3 Ala. Regt. I wrote to Lou. to day.

March 24, Tuesday

SP: Policd quarters again & cut up all stump, getting very purtie now that most time to leave them. heard of some fellow applying for Sandpaper to polish off what remain of stumps that couldnt be cut up. Eveng. Quars. condemmd. Off day & had be polic. over.

March 25, Wednesday

SP: J. arrg—arrvd. fr. furlg. Dress parade orders fr. Lee ready to send off all ext. baggage & be ready for active Camp 1$^{\underline{st}}$ Apl, also excel. address to soldiers regarding to observg. Thanksg. day Frid. 27. set by Pres. Davis.

March 26, Thursday

SP: Got note fr. Biscoe last eveng. had just heard fr. Umb. sent a reply to it by [. . .] this morng. Ready Lady-Lake. [. . .] balloon up today.

March 27, Friday

SP: Being thankgiv. day good many of us went to church night. heard from Rev. Mr. Hopkins most app. & good sermon. Text fr. Chronicles 14 Ch. 11$^{\underline{th}}$ vs. There large crowd, more than could get in Church. Minis. made excellent prayers & remarkd that in the midst of spell of inclement weather, we shd be blessed with such a delightf. bright & clear day for the occasion. Three or 4 ladies in ch. Comg. bk. we say Yank Balloon up. The man in it could no doubt see our large crowd soldiers returning fr. church [. . .] to see me. I was very glad indeed to see them. Mr. Joe sent to Maj. Webster's & got should-meat & some molass, as we were out of meat. We prevaild on them to stay to dinner & they enjoyd very much. They comp. of hard times & rough living &c. Tom says the Alabamians are treated much better than La-ians anyhow. They smokd. & sat 'while aft. din. & left. Crowd assembled on drill ground & we had a game stick-it-to-him!

NOTE: "Tom" is Thomas H. Biscoe.

March 28, Saturday

SP: Bad weather's commencd. again, raining so ha[r]d no roll call at Revillè & continued raing & drizzle most of day. Had 'nother game "hard-ball" in eveng late.

March 29, Sunday

SP: Recd. note fr. Col. Pickens of 12$\underline{th}$ Ala inviting me to spend day with him. Excused myself on grds. having promised to go with Mr. Joe & take dinner with Gilliam J. & Pick at Maj. Adam's Qrs. tho it was so cold & windy we didn't go. Hor. Burton & Jeff. Childress dined with us. Had dress parade for 1$\underline{st}$ time since Thurs. & wind blew & chilled me thro'—without overcoat. Got letter fr. Mama dated 17$\underline{th}$ inst stated Laws. Wood died of Pneum. on 15$\underline{th}$. We'd sold most our Corn at 1.25 & 1.50—& gov. agent pressed 600 bus. at $2.00. Takg meat also fr. those who have more than need.

March 30, Monday

SP: Clear & very cold morng. I am on guard to day. Jno. Christ. elected 3$\underline{d}$ Lt. 48 votes to Arrington's 7. Packed my big blanket in box ext. baggage to be sent to Richmd. May never hear of it again. Balloon up to day. Got letter fr. Louty with a nice little bouquet of early flowers.

March 31, Tuesday

SP: I had post no 1. near Guard house & got off at seven O'clk last eveng. & escaped a very severe nig[h]ts guard [. . .] it, commencd snowing in night & this morng. ground covd. 1 or 2 inches deep. It rained & melted snow off very rapidly.

April 1, Wednesday

SP: Altho the first of April it cold enough for winter. John went to Richmd. & carried [. . .] things to put in my valise. Lt. Jones & Matt Jones absent too on short leave absence. We have 2 Drills in morng. now & a battal drill in eveng—& with 1 o'clk roll call & Dress parade [. . .] up out very often.

NOTE: "Lt. Jones" is Edwin Pompey Jones.

April 2, Thursday

SP: Surg. Genl [. . .]ing, supp., health of army re[. . .] has issued orders to Commissar. to exert them selves to procure Pease potatoes &c. [. . .] pickles, crout, & dried fruit for Soldiers. They have neglected them very much—satisfied with [. . .] flour & Bacon alone. Surg. orderd detail be sent every morng. fr. every Co. to [. . .] vegetables—such as wild Onions, Lambs [. . .] Water crests &c &c. & the Commis [. . .] nets & catch fish. Plenty of shad in Rappah. now. By-way we had one for [. . .] fr. Sutler for $5.00—pretty high price! Commencd letter to Jamie to-day.

April 3, Friday

SP: Finishd. letter to Jamie & mailed it this eveng. On Battal. Drill Col. Hall, Hobson [. . .] horsebk & gave pretty tight drill. Col. Pickens brot. 12$\underline{th}$ out & drilled [. . .] not [. . .] than ½ as large as our Regt. but drills well. We had orders [. . .] to-morrow—but complaint was made to C Oneil commdg. Br[. . .] improved on & 'twas countermand

April 4, Saturday

SP: Grd frozen & [. . .] Ward & good many of our Co were in caf [. . .] Tean &c entertaind us with [. . .]

April 5, Sunday

SP: The ground covd. with snow again abt. 4 in. deep. Kept pretty close in tent all day. In eveng Lt. & Matt Jones returned & Ned. Bayol with them. he came in to our mess making the tenth man.

April 6, Monday

SP: We made a hearty brkfst. off a ham that E. Bayol brot. very nice, & as rather small ate nearly whole at the one meal.* (Got letter from Mary this eveng Sat. 4ᵗʰ).

*I lay down near eleven oclk. after hearing some very good music in Capt W's tent from Ed. Bayol on violin & Jim Lee on Flute, & roused bout 12 by Corp. to go on post. Fortunately found a good fire & sat by it most of time after guard rounds came round. Stood 4 hrs. pretty cold before got off, but kept up my fire. When my relief came I had forgotten countersign entirely & couldn't give it to him.

April 7, Tuesday

SP: Snow is still seen abt. on hill sides & places wh. sun couldn't get at it well. Drilled 2ce in morng. & in eveng. Bat. drill went thro loading & firing by Cos. by ranks & by files &c—tho' wind blew so chillingly Col. H. soon dismissed the Regt.

April 8, Wednesday

SP: Maj. Webster came over & sat a while with us & gave us an order for some meat wh. we were very glad to get as we entire without & would not draw more till tomorrow eveng. I am reading Vicar of Wakefield which is fine thing—so much of human nature in it.

NOTE: Oliver Goldsmith's *Vicar of Wakefield* was first published in 1766.

April 9, Thursday

SP: Clear pretty day but very cold for season. Bill L. was put under arrest to day for not saluting Hall who passd near his post, & I had to take his place. They are strict abt. guard duty & require to go by regulations. At the guard house a brother of the Col. Pickens called on me. He is the same one I saw in Ral. as he passed thro in Cav. of Hamptons Legion, & has been in it till recently when he was appointd by his brother Quar. Mast. of 12ᵗʰ Regt. Is abt. 26 yrs. old—2 or 3 older than Col. Both are youthful looking. He beggd me to be sociable with himself & brother. Got long & inter letter fr. Mama this eveng. & in it 1 fr. Lou.

April 10, Friday

SP: Hated havg to get up go to guard [. . .]. Joe Grigg went with fishing squad of Maj. Webs. to River to fish, seine &c. (Yest ate dried cherries ginger nuts &c for lunch[.]) Took a good wash at branch, warm & delightf. Quite warm on Battal. drill. some fellows got some snow in a hollow near by & very refreshg. D. Barnum & I knocked the ball some time in eveng—good exerc. & fine sport.

April 11, Saturday

SP: Policed Qrs. in morng. & then nothing more to do till Dress parade. Wash day—I was engaged off & on all day writing a letter to Mama. Recd. one fr. Mr.

High. saying all well at Canebrk. & getting on very well with planting. Upon Drill grd. this eveng. there were a good many running & jumping matches. W. Deloach is decidedly best jumper to his size that I've seen.

April 12, Sunday

SP: We had a very rigid inspection of arms this morng. John cleaned up my gun yest. eveng. but I feared it would-n't pass & workd. on it myself, & it got thro'. Tom Moore & Alex McCall came in to day. Tom has been away since June last. He brot. me a letter fr. Jamie containg. $100. & says he brot. a box on for me & left it at the station (Guinea's). It rained a little in evng.

April 13, Monday

SP: Alex M^{c}C. went to station & brot. up things amg. wh. was a small box for me. It was so diffic. to get any one to bring a box that Mama could n't send anything to eat, but only some clothing & pr. Boots for Biscoe, a nice p ^{r}. gloves for me 2 pckg. Envelopes, a pencil & some sealg wax for me, also a letter fr. Icha.

April 14, Tuesday

SP: Yank pickets taken way fr. Rd & thgt. they had commencd movg. but said they are back again this morng. Maj. Websters boy says his master has caught grt. many fish—200 & will bring 'em up to-day—all gammon suppose but hope it may prove true. Balloon up—& is very often now. Drank some dried apple cider at Ellisons last night $2 qt. pretty good. Just read Lady Lyons-Bulwer—& is a fine thing.

NOTE: Edward Bulwer Lytton's five-act play, *The Lady of Lyons,* was first performed at Covent Garden in 1838.

April 15, Wednesday

SP: Last night as we were going to bed Charley Hafner came fr. River & brot us a nice shad & string of Perch that Mr. Jas. sent, & this morng. we had a nice mess for brkfast. we drew also a day's ration fish—fresh herring—¼ lb. & had a mess for dinner & some left. Rainy nearly all day & kept closely in tent most day. Ed Bayol & Pasteur & I ate some ginger nuts & dried cherries at Ellisons for lunch.

April 16, Thursday

SP: Had the last of our fish for brkfast. The ground so wet we did not go to the fi[e]ld for Battal drill but had Co. Drill on our Camp dr. grd.

April 17, Friday

SP: I noticed some Peach trees blooming out to day for the first time—about 5 or 6 weeks later than they were at home in Ala. Tom Moore has gotten the position of Courier for Rodes & has bot. a very pretty little mare for 300.

April 18, Saturday

SP: I took a good wash at the branch to day with Pasteur & Bayol & found the water very pleasant. Wrote letter home to Mary to day but was prevented from finishing it by having a hard chill about tattoo, which lasted some time.

April 19, Sunday

SP: Had a miserable night of it after chill went off, a hot followed & lasted a long time. I took off my jacket & threw the cover off till I cooled off some. It seemed the longest night to me I had ever seen. This morng. Dr. Hill came around to see me & gave me a blue mass pill. Tom Biscoe (& a Capt. Wang) met some of our men at Grace Church & on learning that I was sick came over to see me & sat an hour or so. Gave Tom the 2 bundles Mama sent on to him & glad of the chance as I did n't know when I could carry them to him, as he is 6 or 7 ms. off & I would have been obliged to get (?) a pass from the Maj. Gen. & only for 12 hrs. & I'd have had to walk it at that.

April 20, Monday

SP: Walkd down to Dr. Hills & got dose Salts wh. took in Red pepper tea, & 12 Grs. Quinine which I made into 3 pills & took during the day. Rained nearly all day. Suppose Dear Mama who is so very careful with us & solicitous about us when sick could look in & see me lying wrapped in my blankts on the ground & the rain beating in tent door—& this my chill day too—wouldn't she be uneasy & think I would be sure to have the chill.

April 21, Tuesday

SP: I had the good fortune to miss my chill last night & feel much better today. (Got long letter from Mama to day. (Mon) Letter fr. Mary today) Reading crayon miscellany. Visit to Abbotsfd. & Newstead Abbey. This eveng. finished letter written in part to Mary on Sat. telling I'd missed chill & feeling well again.

April 22, Wednesday

SP: Went on duty this morng. almost incessant drilling thro' the day, which I am very tired of. John askd to go to Rich. again. I reluctantly consentd & gave pass; but told him it was to be his last trip. Sent by him for flower seed for Mary who's making flow. garden at home. Rit. Moore came to the Co. to-day & thinks of joining it.

April 23, Thursday

SP: This is a rainy, drizzly day so that there's no drilling[.] the camp somewhat excited in eveng. by order to be prepared to move at any minute. It was reported Yanks were crossg. river at P. Royal & also above about Fred. We put the servts. to cooking as about the only preparations necessary for our departure. (Went to bed early as rumord we'd start off 'bout 1 clk.) Had big goober parchg this evng, 10 qts—&7.50.

April 24, Friday

SP: Glad to wake up this morng. & find we had not been under disgreeble necessity to leave camp in such bad weather. Raind hard in night & kept on most all day. It seems the Yank demonstr. was 'bout 80 crossd night, P. Roy & stole 20 or 50 mules (Our mess had 6 doz. eggs scramb. brkf.—cost $12.00.) & recrossed as soon our forces approached. Finishd. Tour on Prairies. Irvg. speaks of the rough way of living he experienced on short tour of 1 mo. & primt. way of servg. up food, e.g. coffee in *tin* cups & *brown* sugar, &c&c Turk. venison & in wood tray! We never have any thing ½ as good on extra occasion & glad to get wheat (Confed) coffee in tin cups & without any sugar at all—that is those very fond of coff. tho I cant drink it without sug. Guard was relievd at 6 P.M. & new one put on for night as been rainy all day—of wh. I was one. Ben very windy & cold for season. Kept up a good fire in our little stove all day.

NOTE: Washington Irving's *A Tour on the Prairies* was first published in 1835.

April 25, Saturday

SP: On post fr 10 till 12 last night & found it very cold: wind high. went to bed & seemed it was no time be. corp. was waking Bill Lenier & me up to go on again betwn day & sun rise & stood till 8½ . Went to preachg at "Fair Oaks Church". (A party fr. Co. "D" went serenading & came back 3 or 4 o'clk. this morng.)

April 26, Sunday

SP: Had Reg. inspection which was very close one & lasted long time. Opend knapsacks & exhibited contents.

April 27, Monday

SP: I was on detail to gather wild onions & went 3 or 4 ms. (with Bob. Price fr. our Co.) down on River where the fields & covd. with them. We soon filled our havresacks & returned to Camp—& made hearty Brkfast on fresh shad & herrings. Exempt fr. drillg. & other duty rest of day. Lay down all the morng. & slept little. In eveng. wrote a letter home to Willie.

April 28, Tuesday

SP: Drilled once this morng. under Lt. Borden & then commencd drizzling & lasted all day. Kept pretty close in tent. Had a camp Rice pudding but 'twas rather poor excuse: not enough Sugar in it. Had orders to go on Picket next morng at 8½ .

April 29, Wednesday

SP: We were up pretty early this morng getting ready to go on Picket but instead of that we recd. information that the Yankees were crossing river & soon had orders to march towds Frdksbg. The roads were slippery & muddy & we had hot & tiresome mch. Passed Hamilton's crossing & went up in Piece Pines to edge of which we went to 13th Decr. last—day of Bat. Frdksbg. & formd in rear of 26th. & lay there all day. Yank. battery threw over occasional shells over at our batteries wh. we could hear whizzing & whirring thro' air & bursting.

April 30, Thursday

SP: We fixed up bunks just bef. dark as it threated rain & drizzled, stretchg blankts over poles. Very comfort. soft pine straw, but fr. excitement of the day & speculating on what the morrow would probably bring forth, I could sleep but very little. However, had sweet dream of being at home. Oh! that it could be soon realized. We were not allowed any fire last night & were routed before light & movd. forwd & to Right flank & had terrible mch. up muddy road—men fallg. & went in rifle pits, muddy & water in bottom. rained till I got wet to skin in places. Gen! Rodes aft. while moved us back in piece woods & made fires & warmed & dried clothes. Joe Grigg & Britton & others fishing squad came up broken down—havg. marchd bout 16 ms. They were provided with guns & accoutr. & J. Grigg (Carter & ———) slept & rested till evening & went to join Sharpshooters 1 of wh. he has been made recently. There was cannon firing kept up slowly all day—shells passing to right & left of our position whizzing by & bursting but none over us. We had a Whitworth gun on our right that threw shells over river amg. Yanks & made them scatter—their guns reachd right our brigade but not the Whitw. gun. Col Hall recd. orders to let troops remain in woods during night but send a guard to keep vigilant watch in the breastwks that we had occupied in morng.

May 1, Friday

SP: It was Bob Price & myself who were sent fr. our Co. as guards to brstwks last eveng. at dark. We were divid. to 3 reliefs & B & I stood 1st—fr. 8 till 11. Had fire in Ditch where a place was cut out for cannon. In eveng. Yanks. threw shell over it & 1 burst just in front of it & piece passd. very near Knowland's head & struck in bank wh. K. got & showed us. We could see our signal lights on eminences on our right & faraway to left—waving occasionally. Bob & I then spread our blankets & lay front of fire expecting to sleep 6 hrs—; but just after lying a little over 3 hrs. we were waked & all the guard orderd to join Regt. wh. we found in line of battle in edge of woods, & then ('bout 2½ or 3 A.M.) movd by left flank & marchd. up the river. Roads were very wet & slippery & bad for mchg. At Hamilton's Crossing we were detained some time by a continuous & & [*sic*] it seemed to me then an endless line of troops passing on up river by road into wh. we were then coming. There was the densest fog this morng I ever saw. We made very slow time during the morng. on acct. of the wagons in front stopping frequently. Passed many deserted camps wh. had been occup. during Winter by parts of our army. Halted between 11 & 12 near a house intended for hospital & rested, ate something & filled Canteens. I was very much exhausted & felt sick & faint fr. mching so hard thro' hot sun. Then fell in & loaded & Regts of Brig. moved on. As Col. Sam. B. Pickens of 12 Ala. passed we shook hands—& wished each other a safe passage thro' the impending battle. We then moved on down the road & came into the plank road leading fr. Culpeper C.H.? to Frdksbg. The cannon could be heard all the time firing slowly. Today for 1st time noticed trees budding & putting out new leaves. Stopped on Plank R. & piled up knap sacks & at same time our noble old Genl Robt. E. Lee passed followed by a troop of aids & couriers. He is a well set venerable looking man with white hair & beard. He passed so rapidly that I had not a good chance to see his countenance. Whether it was that he was not generally known by the troops or or [*sic*] our silent advance towds scene of action that caused it I dont know, but he passed in silence—no cheering. All who knew him was inspired with the utmost confidence & gazed attentively upon him. We then went on further & stopped little while [. . .] right flank in line of battle thro a very thick piece woods [. . .] confusion not possible to preserve any thing of a line in such a thick [. . .] & soon came to another road nearby [. . .] with plank—as hot as could be & nearly broken down. Went by left flank along the road, passed house where there were some of 12 Vᵃ who told us they had opened the fight on Wed. & there were some wounded men on litters in yard [. . .] Were orderd back a little distance & stopped—I then turned round & went still further up road [. . .] wounded & prisoners. In eveng. we made a large circuit thro' woods (Brig.) passg several lines of battle lying in woods & then stopped on brstwks at edge of woods—where we washed & lay down an hour or so & [. . .] mch. refreshed. Afterwds stacked arms & went bak for knap-sax—troops & artillery passing fast—men who went bak said saw 1000 troops moving. Jackson we began to see was about makg one of his favorite flank movements. We marchd on up Plank road till betwen. 9 & 10 & halted in field & orchrd. completely broke down. Had eaten very little but as had only a biscuit left & no prospect of getg. more concluded to keep it for Brkfst. Carey brot us biscuits Thurs. morng. at day light & we had a little smoked beef wh. we had lived on 2 days.

NOTE: In the Battle of Chancellorsville, General Lee split his army. While fifteen thousand men stayed behind to occupy Joe Hooker's Army of the Potomac, Stonewall Jackson's thirty thousand veterans marched west in a wide flanking movement, led on May 1 by the color company of the Fifth Alabama, the Greensboro Guards. Rodes' leadership of the flank attack earned him promotion to major general.

Hamilton's Crossing is on the Richmond, Fredericksburg, and Potomac Railroad about four miles southeast of Fredericksburg.

May 2, Saturday

SP: Put down blankets. Jack, Bill Lenier & I slept together *Sat 2ⁿᵈ* [. . .] had on the go 18 hrs. yesterday. Allowed to sleep later than expected after day light. went to branch & took good wash & made feel fresh. Resumed the march passing good many troops lying along the road. Stopped to rest a few min. & gave Matt. Jones ½ biscuit & ate the other & scrap meat & afterwds 2 or 3 little butter crackers—whole not more than 1 biscuit. We heard Commiss. wagons had been orderd up & hoped wd. overtake us but in this we were disappointed. We heard Yanks. cheering in their formal stiff way & some boys wished Jackson would come along that we might raise a cheer. In a little while the word was passed up lines to give way to left—& there came Glorious old Stonewall at a sweeping gallop—hat in hand on his sorrel horse followed by aids & couriers. All long line troops waved hats & cheered long & loud. I cant describe my feelings at thus seeing him suddenly for 1ˢᵗ time—but my breast swelled with emotions of pride & gratification, & all must have felt confident of success when we shd. meet enemy. Could only see he was a younger lookg man than I expected to see & not so stout but apparently well made—blk hair & beard & a little bald spot on back head that showed plainly after passing. But saw him again when we had passed enemy's right flank & were getting round in their rear—he gave some directions in remark. mild & cool manner as to where he wished our Divis. to go. His hair curls round edges of his military cap—regular features & very good looking & pleasant countenance.

(Sat. 2nd Cont) We moved on down Plank Road towds river I think then to the right & were in the rear of Yankees Right, & from being on Right of our lines—below Fredbg. on Thurs. we had moved to extreme Left-flanked Yankees & got in rear of Right of their lines. We formd line battle in woods as front line & lay down to rest (betwn 3 & 4 P.M.) while 2 other lines formed in rear of us to support us. When everything was ready about 6 P.M. wh. was so late that some began to think we might not make the attack till mornig, but we were ordered forwd & had very rough time getting thro' the thick woods. By & by we heard the sharp shooters firing & we started double quick—& most terrific volleys of musketry opened on our right & such was the excitement & the desire to be doing something too, that they commencd firing in our Co. & Regt. & as they were firing around me—altho' I could not see anything & still I thought the Yanks must be there & imagined I saw blue line on opposite hillside in pines & blazed away too. Capt. Williams immediately orderd firing to be stopped that there was nothing to shoot at, & I determd not to be guilty of such folly again & did not shoot unless I had a fair mark. We loaded & started in run yelling & soon saw the blue rascals running like turkeys & our men—shooting, cheering, & pursuing as fast as they could. When Yanks got behind hill or breastwk they would stop & shoot & minute or two—but as our men would come charging upon them they'd be off again. Saw a Y. shot down & as we approached, he jumped up & started again when he was again shot down. One fell standing by tree with but of gun up to signify he surrendered. Col. Hobson called to him to drop his gun & lie down or he'd be killed—he did so & Col. H. told him to go to rear. I soon got separated from entire Co. & looking round could not see one I knew but Col. Hob. & I kept with him—he was waving sword and gallantly leading the men on. Never saw such confusion in my life—men scattered & mixed up every way. It was a running fight & difficulty was to keep near enough to Y. to shoot them. They shot at us very little—only when they'd half a little behind breast wks. (redoubts) Our men from marching all day before & that day & having nothing to eat scarcely—were so much exhausted that great many were scattered along behind a long distance & some excited fellows were firing wildly over the heads of us who were ahead & really there seemed at times as great danger of being killed by our men as by Yks. & several times we'd stop & wait for them to get up in line with us. Some fired without takg. sight up in air & I notices ball strike grd. just in front of us. Some of our men were wounded by our own side. Grt. pity theres so much confusion & men get scattered so badly—several times men were stopped from firing into friends & I recollect joining in & screaming to them not to do it—several times I knockd up gun 1^{ce} of fellow in act of doing it. 1st redoubt we advanced on the artillery stuck out pretty well & threw grape & canister like hail—a good many of us in edge of pine thicket lay down a minute or 2 but on went our men & a shout told Yanks. were driven on. Parts of 3 Batteries were captured that eveng. Noticed a large N. Foundland dog—in agonies of death with a ball hole thro' him. Some of Y. officers on horsebk. rode along lines & tried to rally troops but all in vain. we drove them a mile & ½ or 2—till night closed in on the scene. At one time noticed flags of 2 Regts. close together & mass of men around & fired 1ce or 2ce into them. Passed on down slope & rose another & in edge of pines there was a horse standing. Hobson started to it—calling to some men to catch it for him & learned afterwds he was shot down before getting to it—he was struck in leg above the knee—fortun. only a flesh wound. I kept on & a wounded Yank. beckoned & called to me—shook canteen & offered water, wh. he drank—& askd name & Regt & said he would be ever mindful of me or somethg of sort—he was a Lieut, & said wanted to see a Surg. that imposs. & I passed on keeping as near Thomson with our Colors as could. He had become separated fr. Regt. or greater part of it. Finally fell in with Ed. Hutchinson & afterwds with Ch. Hafner & John Co[w]in & Jim Arrington. We kept together & went on till near dark when so exhausted we sat down in pines. Pretty soon Yanks. opened with battery & shelled woods, & threw grape everywhere. We could not go forwd or back without greatest risk & so lay close to ground. It was terrific cannonading—shell burst & grape cut trees all around & above us. When it ceased a squad of men came by with some Prisoners & we started on back to go over field & get some rations as were very hungry. I had one crack. that had taken fr. Yank. Havresak, going on & divided it with J. Arrington. As we went on men fr. various Regts. of diff. states were calling the name of Regt. trying to get together. Never saw such confus. & scattering. Occas. 1 or 2 & sometimes small squad of 5th Ala. fell in with us, & went on but did n't find any plunder or rations—the troops behind had swept them. Saw one fellow who. had 3 watches. finally we found out where Col. Oneil was collecting the Brigade & joined them. Everyone felt so grateful at coming out safely that he would shake each acquaintance warmly by hand & express delight at seeing him come out safely. 5 of our Co. were wounded—Matt Jones, Hausman, Youngblood Sr, S. Jackson & B. Price, also Col. Hobson. Stacked arms, made fires & ate supper wh. was taken fr. Yanks. the best had some time. Crackers, ham & Coffee. Yanks had 8 da. rations with them 5 in kn.sk. & 3 in Haver sk. It seems Rodes Brig. was halted late in eveng. & tried to collect & form it, but I with others had gotten separated way to right & kept on till dark—Met. Col. Pickens of 12th safe. All the boys had trophys fr. Bat. field & well supplied with oil cloths, Blankets, canteens & havresacks &c. Gave me 2 or 3 Yank. letters. Aft. sup. movd up road & to line brst wks, near Hospital. Good deal our artil going fowd. (Cannonading in front

& heavy volleys musketry bright pretty night. fightg kept up as men on guard said till 12 or 1 o'clk)

NOTE: While General Rodes commanded Hill's division, his brigade, commanded by Colonel Edward A. O'Neal, smashed the Union XI Corps.

May 3, Sunday

SP: Sprd. blankts & lay on edge entrenchmts with gun & accoutremts. ready to don at moments warng. didn't even pull off boots. Up pretty early & went to spri[n]g & washd. wh. refreshg. We were waiting for Cop. Hutchinson to come up with Provision wh. he soon did but bef. could give out enemy began to shell us pretty severely & all took to trench as it wd slacken some fellows wd go up & draw for 2 or 3 around him. Then moved front in piece pines & lay few minutes when orderd forwd.

NOTE: Rodes' brigade drove the enemy back about 300 yards to a little ridge in the southwest corner of the field around General Hooker's headquarters at the Chancellorsville Hotel. After halting briefly, the brigage overtook another well-entrenched ridge, where the Guards were caught in a deadly cross fire. Dr. Cowin was hit in his femoral artery and died. When the cross fire slackened, they charged another ridge and captured the redoubts above Chancellorsville. But the Guards had moved too far in advance of their lines and were surrounded. Rather than surrender to the enemy, George Nutting grabbed the colors and threw it into the woods as far as he could.

The Union suffered nearly 17,000 casualties and the Confederates 13,000. The Fifth Alabama lost 24 men killed and some 254 wounded or missing; of these 17 Greensboro Guards lay wounded, and perhaps as many as 4 had received fatal wounds. Fourteen Guards, including Sam Pickens, were sent to the Old Capitol prison in Washington—a brick building on First Street that had served as a temporary capitol after the War of 1812.

May 6, Wednesday

SP: Pr[i]soner of War—
Cliffburne Barracks
Washington City, D.C.
Care Col. C. M. Alexander.

Jno. Christian wrote home a list of Prisoners fr. our Co. Up pretty early this morning & out being counted & divided into squads of 50 & given charge of one our Sergts. to draw rations together. There are 5 rooms in our building & 10 cooks in each detailed fr. amg. Prisoners to do cooking & we go up by squads & as each man name is called he draws his 4 crak slice meat & cup coffee. There was grt. confusion this morng. as not know how much wd. take to feed us Rebels. 740 in no. Several politic. pris. too. Capt. W$^{\underline{ms}}$. Christ. & Jones brot in some light brd & meat for us. Went round to sutlers & got orang. app. & Pies. I'd 1.10 silver—only current funds. In evng. the officers all carried to another Qrs. sorry to part with them.

May 7, Thursday

SP: We are having very cold, rainy weather. Got 2 sh. Paper 2 Env. & stamp for 5 cts & wrote to Mama—Flg truce via Monroe—left unsealed, destination. 15 ambul. brot up evng. & carried of sik & wded. hospital. Bot some cheese cakes, orang & figs—enjoyd much. More countig off, takig names &c. Some low scoundrals have taken oath.

May 8, Friday

SP: For Brkf, crkers, small slice meat, mouthful frid Ir. Potato & cup coffee. Dinner Light brd. beans & rice boiled together. Supper Light brd. & Spoonful molasses & Coffee. Bef. Dinner went round trying buy tin cup & at house where Yanks eatg dinner 1 gave me cup & told pay what I wishd. Had scarcely any silver & gave him $1.00 Confed. lookd at it as curiosity & seemed surprised I offerd so much—& returnd it saying it wd. be useful to me when return home & no use to him & wd n't take it. He filled it with soup & gave me bread & seemed to be careful to see that no officer saw it. I thanked him & told him if he should ever be in South under same circumsts. I'd be glad to do him any favor. Offerd spoon. Another offerd me cup of soup & when declined gave to another prisoner. The soldiers disposed to treat us as well—much better than we wd. treat them in Richmd: but that is natural for we consider them invaders trying to subjug. & rob of everythg. we hold dear on earth. While many of them are only in army for a living & take no fightig in self defense on our own territory. Markd cup & will try take care of it. In Washington Chronicle saw some account of the recent battles. It is difficult to get a paper—news boys not allowed to bring in for sale to us, & when do get one a crowd gathers to hear read, & it passes from one to another till almost worn out. 5th La. fought em in [. . .] on Wed. & Col. [. . .] wounded & prisoner. On Thurs. Mahone fought at Charleston [. . .] 4 [. . .] Ely's ford [. . .] ending with Tues. 5$\underline{\text{th}}$ leaving on Wed and Thurs, 29 & 30, & say their loss kld wd. not exceed [. . .] Maj. Gen. B [. . .] and Brig. Gen Whipple killed at Chan. Our loss 15000 k. & wd. & 10000 Pris. [. . .] command 11 C [. . .] & Slocumb ? 12$\underline{\text{th}}$. Cav. Gen. Stones [. . .] circum [. . .] Lee's army—& tore R.R. at Han. Junc. & C.H. burned [. . .] 4 ms. Richmd. Cold, rain during [. . .]

May 9, Saturday

SP: Bright sunny morng looks beautiful. Trees are putting out pretty. Luxuriant patch Rye [. . .]ing in yard. [. . .] Barracks & long fine house & hear the owners are sympathisers. Saw 3 or 4 young ladies walking abt the grounds. Went to house on hill ½ mile fr. here pointed to us as 1 Jeff Davis used to [. . .] brkfst or supper seems I got [. . .] as here as might supposed or think [. . .] to do without it.

May 10, Sunday

SP: Were called out ready to [. . .] South or some other Prison [. . .] In eveng went to spring & took good wash. Some of coarse Irish Yank. women came about there with [. . .] older one advised us to take oath & be true to Stars & Stripes. She would starve us if had her way. This has been warm day & sat out in yard in shirt sleeves some time aft. night—very pleasant—till guards told us to go in.

May 11, Monday

SP: Ration getting scanty. 3 cks. scrap boil beet & coffee without sugar. beautif. Spg. morn. such as had in Ala. 6 or 7 wks ago. oak trees in tassel & trying to leaf—white Poplar & other forwd. trees are pretty well covd. in cloak of green. Accord. to report, no doubt of getting off for Dixie this morng—hope it prove so as we are all very tired of our confinement. Don't underst. why with Paroles in pocket we are kept confind under guard. Sure enough a strong guard came up fr. city & we were called out & then commencd slow & tedious operation of calling roll. This took at least 2 hrs. & all while we were kept out in hot sun. Guards formed in 2 lines & as each rebel's name called he marchd down betwn the lines. After getting every thing ready were mchd. off towds boat landing passing thro' Pa. Avenue past way by Willard Hotel, a large fine building. Crwd citizens along streets to see us, tho' officers would not allow any insults or remarks made by citizens. Good view of Capitol—magnif. edifice—lost cup—very fatiguing hot walk & finally reachd boat landing. Bot 2 Pies for 30 cts. Went on large boat—"State of Maine"—over 700 on board & were very much crowded. Started at 2 P.M. as passed Aquia Creek could see large smoke rising & 'twas said Yanks were burning all Depots & warehouses at the place to evacuate & fall back.

May 12, Tuesday

SP: I slept last night or rather tried to—in lower part used for sick & wounded— so very warm & close that slept very little. when got up felt as if been stewed very badly—went up washd & got top of boat. It was aft. sun up & we were lying at F. Monroe, a formidable looking place with low gray walls surmtd. with cannon & row Port holes below. Larg gun on sand bank on point our side fort— probly Sawyer gun. Rip raps to be seen opposite, on wh. is the Union Gun 380 lb. A no. of men of war & transpts lying around. gave us brkfast Coff & bread & such a crowd & rush of it I never saw—lay at wharf till 12 clk—put good many men on another boat & started. Could see Sewells Pt. on right of mouth Eliz. riv & just make out craney Island way toward left bank—& on farther past Newpts on our right—saw school porpoises 1st time rolling along showing [. . .] Passd scene of memorable naval engagement of Merimac with Yank vessel. Saw wreck of Cumberland & slight remnant of Congress. Came to a large man of war blockader & Iron clad gun boat we took for Galena (?) She had marks of a fight—iron battered & balls sticking in. hole thro [. . .] Higher up river passed ruins of Jamestown—nothg. but scatterd chimneys & remains of brick walls left to mark the site of first settlement made by white men in Va. Passd Berkley also where McClellan stopped after being. whipped in the 7 days fighting around Richmond. Got to City Point late in the evening & delighted to see Confed flag floating on top of hill. The whrf & sevral houses at the point had been burnt by the Yanks.

NOTE: Fort Monroe, commanding the entrance from the Chesapeake Bay into Hampton Roads and the mouth of the York River, remained a strategic foothold in Virginia for Union forces, who occupied it throughout the war.

May 13, Wednesday

SP: Remained aboard the boat till late this morng. when train cars came down & sick & wounded were to go up first & as most of our fellows were on sick list Tean Nuttg & I fell in with them & got to Petersburg about 12 o'clock. Just as we got in town severl cars ran off track & the one in which I was nearly turned over. It jumpd over cross ties in anything but easy manner but soon stopped & no body was hurt. Then marched thro' town up to Model farm where the Camp of Paroled Prisoners is 2 ms fr. Petersbg. Well of cold fine water & washed off finely & then bot some pies, cakes, Shad & bread & buttermilk—put up a tent & put plunder in it aft. which Sergt Wakefild & Sam Hood, Co. H.[,] Cruse C—Co. "E"[,] Sergt. Jones Co. "K" 2$^{\underline{nd}}$ N.C. Regt, Tean & myself got permission to go to canal or river near by to wash & got behind hill out sight guard & went down town—met———Godwin who treated us very kind, [. . .], offerd introduce to ladies who were very partial to Alabamians[.] Got iced mint Julep—the only thing of the kind that I've seen long time—it was splendid. Then went to Bollingbrook H. & got supper & to bowling saloon & playd. 10 pins till bed time when returnd to Hotel & went to bed. It really seemed strange to us who had been roughing it for some time in army to get in comforble house & nice bed.

Note: "Cruse C" is Cruse Coleman.

May 14, Thursday

SP: Took brkfast & went on street to see Yanks pass going fr. Rich. to City Pt. afoot—5000 in no & a dirty filthy low lived set—most all foreigners. I'm sure our prisoners preservd a bold front when in hands of Yanks mchig thro Washig. & lookd nothig like cattle that passd thro Petersbg. They walked us unnecessarily thro' Pa. Avenue & diff. streets just to exhibit & they now havg some it to do tho' not for same reason. Returned to the Camp & found givg out clothes & as was much in want of change under clothes tried to get some but none could be had as such crowd gatherd round place ahead of us. Commencd letter home to Mama but before writing much we were told to get ready to leave for Richmd. Glad to go as knew we could there find out bout our exchange & if possible get furlough home. Left Depot bout 4 P.M. in long train—our party in platform car & had very pleasant ride—passd Pickets Divis. bivoacked not far fr. Richmd. Great cheering by our troops & theirs. P. Hafner lost cap in hurrahing. Arrivd. Rich. sun down. We stard off up town trying to elude the guard, but Lt-in charge halted us & insisted upon our waiting & being shown to where the Prisoners we[r]e to be carried. We followd along & heard we were going to Camp Lee & as good luck had it we turned up Franklin Str. & going by Mrs. Barn's & Ring's V$^{\underline{a}}$. house where well acquainted, on getting to latter place ran in gate & into house where stood behind door till all passed & got rooms. We were Tean &

myself, Sergt. Wakefield & Sam Hood & Sergt. Cruse Coleman. Tean went over
to Mrs. Barn's & heard from Jno. Cowin was dead & that several several [*sic*]
of the boys are at hospital here wounded. Tean & I walkd down to Stoke's &
lookg over books saw Simms & Tom Ward registerd. They flankd guard also.
Tean, Cruse & I then went to Broad St. Theatre, the new & beautiful one lately
completed—handsomely finishd & rich & beautiful scenery. Only fault is that
seats are too crowded. They played the Jewess.

NOTE: *The Jewess* could refer to any of several dramas current in the mid-nineteenth century.

May 15, Friday

SP: After brkfst. Cruse went to Hospital & Tean & I went to Stokes, look
for Sims & Ward but they were out. We then went on to $3^{\underline{d}}$ Ala. Hospit. & saw
poor Britton who was severely wounded thro the lung—looks very pale & badly
but is doing as well as could be expected with such wound. also saw Ed. Bayol
with large grape shot wound in hip or rump but doing very well. Sam Jackson
with a toe nearly shot off—slight wound, & Bob Price with shot in leg—½ ball
in it yet but in fine spirits & doing well. Heard Sergt. Witherspoon was out at
Chimborazo Hospit. & Dick Simonds but as long way off we did not go to see
them. Then went by U.S. hotel (hospit.) & saw Col. Hobson. He was looking
very pale & thin & badly & was in the lowest spirits & told us he had frequent
& copious hemorages—bled like a hog—There was a lady with him ministerg to
his wants & comfort, & there were little delicacies on the table that had been sent
him by some kind ladies no doubt.* Tean & Joe Wright went to billiard playing
in earnest. After walking about town went to Mrs. Barnes & got dinner $2.00.
Sims & Ward had moved there as board at Stokes was too high. After dinner
went in my room in roof of Mrs. Rings to write Mama a detailed account of our
marching, fighting, stay in Yankeedom. Supper over went to Brd. St. Theatre
again where well entertained with a piece called "London assurance" a very good
thing.

*Frid. morn. telegraphed to Mama that I had arrived in Richmd. was very well & would write.

NOTE: Dion Boucicault's *London Assurance* was first performed in 1841.

May 16, Saturday

SP: Went down town this morning & took bath at Spottswood Hotel & had a
splendid wash & never enjoyed a thing more in my life for had washd & changed
clothes the night before leaving winter Qrs. (April 28$^{\underline{th}}$) for last time. Threw away
under shirt & put on a nice over shirt had taken out of D. Barnums trunk at Mrs.
Barnes—cotton drawers & socks instead of woolen pulled & a pr. cass pants
also David's. Then had hair shampood & trimmd & boots blacked & felt 1000
pr. ct. better. I attempted my first game billiards under Joe Wrights instruction.
was very awkwd about & scarcely ever made anything. In afternoon wrote on
my letter again but so warm & felt so little like writing that did n't finish it. Late
in evening we walked about Capitol Square which a place of resort for large no.
ladies, children, citizens & soldiers. It looks very pretty now that the trees are

getting in full leaf & grass green & luxuriant. Directly after eating supper went (Joe Wright & I slept too late to get brkfast at V$^{\underline{a}}$ house & went Oak hall saloon on Franklin St. & took ham & eggs—a pork steak & cup coffee & paid $4.50 apiece for the brkfast) again to Brd. St. Theatre & saw "Othello, the Moor of Venice["] played. It interested me very much as I'd never seen it before, but the actor (in char. of Othello) did not come up to my idea of the Moor of Venice. He was a small man & painted red more like an Indian. he is a good actor though (Harrison) & playd his part very well. Performce concluded with "Laughable farce of the inquisitive darkey." Ogden who is an excellent comedian & it was fine. Good luck to meet Gid Westcott who gave me $2.00 & I gave him order on first out flat.

May 17, Sunday

SP: Tean & I slept very late, got down after service had commencd at church. I went over to St. Pauls & heard a good sermon fr. Dr. Minnegerode. Large Congreg. Ch. crowded—Genl Lee was there & when came out had good look at him. Large heavy set man—very hearty & vigorous—blk eyes Gray hair & trimmed beard. Gen. Ewell & Ramseur also there. Took dinner at Mrs. Barnes & did ample justice as had no supper night before & no brkfast that morng. Went up to my room & finished at last my letter to Mama, over 11 pages in length; came down & found supper just ready & went in. It was such a miserable meal to pay $1.50 for that I determined to move over to Mrs. Barnes' as a regular boarder. She charges $5.00 a day but gives pretty fair table for these hard times. Joe Wright & I then walked down to the P.O. & mailed my letter, after wh. walked up to the Presbyterian Church near Square to hear the funeral sermon of Gen$^{\underline{l}}$ Stonewall Jackson preached but the house was already crammed & large crowd around outside, so as there was no possible chance to hear it I went again to St. Paul's.

NOTE: Sam Pickens describes a memorial service; Jackson's funeral was preached in Lexington.

May 18, Monday

SP: Tean & I got up early this morng. & move[d] over bag & baggage to Mrs. Barnes & settled with Mrs. Ring. After brkfst. walkd down to see Col. Hobson & found him a great deal better. he had had good night's rest & was in ~~fine~~ spirits' much better. A telegram was brot. in stating that his mother & brother were on the way to see him. We were delighted to see him doing so well for until a day or 2 before the surgeon attending him had very little hopes of his recovery. Dolph. Ellison came up to see him & went out with us. I tried another game Billiards & did better. I begin to understand enough about it to take interest in it & like it. It is beautiful game & a scientific one. John came in this eveng from Regt. & brot. my knapsack with clean clothes. Also four letters from home which I read with grt. interest. Lt. Borden had brot. me 2 a few days before.* Dolph treated us to ticket to Theatre & we saw "The Va. Cavalier" and were well entertained. Meet Cruse Coleman at Theatre every night.

*(Joe Wright & I got some Ice cream & Cake this evening—how nice & refreshing.)

NOTE: *The Virginia Cavalier* was a musical performed at the Richmond New Theater; one of its songs, "The Southern Soldier Boy," became one of the South's most popular tunes.

May 19, Tuesday

SP: The guard stopped us to-day but on showing our paroles were allowed to go on. Ever since we got to Petersburg we've been told that we were exchanged & wd be returned to Regt. in few days & no chance of furlough to go home in wh. we've been much disapp. as we were not included in exchge 6th inst. & heretofore exchges have taken place on 1^{ce} in 2 or 3 months. & yet our exchge is not published in news papers. Went to Spottswood & as rest boys shaving up & persuading me to do so too I concluded to try it for first time in my life & after cautioning barber had my side whiskers taken off. It felt rather funny to me who had never shaved before. It made me look & feel (or imag. I felt) cooler. Then took game billiards with Joe & afterwd walked down on Franklin & got me a very nice new hat. at manufactory in rear of Exchange Hotel ($15.00). Coming on back took a milk punch which was very palateable. Sat in Capitol Square till near dark looking at the ladies promenading & the little girls & children playing about on the grass or running along the walks & around the splendid statue of Washington. Again we went to the new theatre & saw an Indian play—"Metamora or the last of the Wampanoago." & "laughable farce of The Quiet family"—which the very opposite of its title & very amusing.

NOTE: Union and Confederate armies exchanged prisoners informally until an agreement in the summer of 1862 set up a system whereby prisoner exchanges were computed on the basis of rank and took place at certain specified locations, such as City Point, Virginia. Sometimes parolees were sent back to their own side on condition that they not take up arms until notified of an actual exchange. The system broke down as General Grant recognized that the system favored the Confederates, and Confederates worried that black Union soldiers might lead to a slave rebellion.

John Augustus Stone's *Metamora, or The Last of the Wampanoags* was first performed in 1829.

William E. Suter's *A Quiet Family: An Original Farce* was first published in the United States in 1857.

May 20, Wednesday

SP: Went to Spottswood saw Tean & Matt playing billiards a while, then walkd down Main got paper pens—& a tooth brush & fine comb: went up to Mrs. Barnes & read all my letters over & wrote a pretty long one to Jamie. I had my clothes washed—pants & Jacket too, & got a coat out of David's trunk. John took my old letters, woolen under clothes &c. to put in my valise at Mrs. Colquits'—she asked why I had not been to see her & says she knows how to make allowances for soldiers who had just returned from North as prisoners—& sent me a bundle nice sweet shrubs, wh. were very fragrant. Then mailed letter & went to see Col. Hobson, who had exhausted himself by talking & was not near as well as he had been. Miss. Sally Ann Swope was there with him & said she ought to have known me as Id oft. been with Mama to her house. I'm sure it must have been a long time ago for I have no recollection of it. I stayed but a moment & bid the Col. good-bye & wished him a speedy recovery. He told me he hoped I would always come out safely if had to go in any other battles. He is a noble souled, gallant man & I was very sorry to see him with such a serious wound & looking so feeble & pale. Went in Lt. Bordens room and found him looking right badly—he expects a furlough every day. Gave Rit Moore the bundle sweet shrubs & requested him to give them to Col. Hobson. Walked also to 3ᵈ Ala Hospit & saw boys then, all getting on well but Bob Price had been walking about & exposing himself & had chill & fever & caused leg to swell & pain him some. Returned to Mrs. Barnes & got Sims & Tom Ward, who were only ones of our boys there, & went to Pizzim's & ate Ice cream & cake. He had bunch green Bananas & some oranges & shaddock for largest shaddock he asked $5.00 apiece. Tonight as usual went to new theatre & saw "Dream at Sea" & "Alpine Maid". Had ballad "Rock me to sleep" by Miss Eliza Wren, & some fancy dancing by Miss Mary Partington. We were very well entertained.

NOTE: John Baldwin Buckstone's *The Dream at Sea: A Drama in Three Acts* was first published in London in 1835.

George Alexander Lee, *The Alpine Maid, or That Strain Proclaims My Lover Near: A Ballad* (New York: Hewitt, 1832).

May 21, Thursday

SP: Got up at 5 A.M. Ellison had got up (he Tean & I slept in same bed) & gone down town—& John could scarcely get us up. We were so sleepy having gone to bed after 12 o'clk. Sent John down to get me a havresack. Folded up D. Barnum's clothes & gave to negro woman to carry to Mrs. Barnes & put in trunk. We then went on to Depot & had some difficulty in getting in cars. Finally got ticket fr. fellow in side & went in 1 by 1 & handed out to another & so on till all got in. When we had gotten off conductor came round & latter was a good deal chagrined & fretted at finding how we had humbugged his sentinels & gotten in the train. On cars I was taken quite sick with nausea & diarrhea & for a time felt very sick. Got to Guinea's station about 10, having passed thro the very pretty village of Ashland on Fred. road above Junction. Had very hot walk out to Regt. bout 5 or 6 ms. was very glad to meet the boys. Davis Wᵐˢ & Chris Sheldon had returned. Davis brot. me fine lot writing paper from home. All said I was improved by trip north. How small the Cos. look compared with what they were 3 weeks ago & how reduced the Regt. in so short a time. Alex. MᶜCall 4ᵗʰ Sergt. in comd. of co. The camp is in nice place now—in thick piece woods. A letter was given me fr. Mama, dated 12ᵗʰ long & very interesting. She had been very uneasy about me but had seen telegram stating that I was among the prisoners captured & was very anxious to get a letter giving particulars, & extremely uneasy bout Biscoe also.

May 22, Friday

SP: As no official notification has yet reached here we will enter upon duty but have little more rest. Do dread idea of going to drilling again this hot & dusty weather. Oh! how heartily sick & tired I am of the war how happy I'd be to see it close. Gilliam was over to day & told me how to get letter to Biscoe, thro Corps Hd. Qrs. Recd. letter from Louty. Have a terrible cold & still affected with diarrhea. We are getting ½ lb. bacon now instead of [. . .] & it holds out very well.

May 23, Saturday

SP: Mr. Joe & I went over & saw Col. Pickens & met his brother Miles & cousin Rev. Pickens Smith. Joe soon left to see a fellow & I sat some time. We talked over the severl battles we had recently passed thro' & he told me of some hard fighting he had after I was taken Sund. He commd. part of 3 regts. They begged me to come over to morrow & eat fish dinner. I wrote to Tom Biscoe this evening & Mr. Joe took it up to Gen. Rodes Qrs. Mr. Joe has recd. appointmt. of courier for Rodes & went up to enter upon duties. he is [. . .] & a horse of Maj Websters Fixed up Johns likeness to go home by mail. Ed. Hutchinson & Bob. Chad. came in this evening & say they saw names of our officers registd on Bollingbrk Hotel, Petersbg—so they will be up in day or two.

May 24, Sunday

SP: The Revd. Mr. Hague of Richmond preached at 3ᵈ Ala. Regt. & it is said to have been an excellent sermon. I wish I had heard it but felt badly & lay in tent most of the day—not feeling like walking. The Brig. is going to try & engage his services to preach regularly. At dress parade order read out that we the paroled prisoners had been duly exchanged & would do duty. Very unpleasant news to us who wd. have been glad of little more holiday. Now have band fife, 2 kettle & 1 base drum. poor compared with what we heard in Yankeedom.

May 25, Monday

SP: Cloudy, cool & disagreeable day—hard to keep comfortable & would have found an overcoat most acceptable. Went to drilling again. much better ground than old place. Sat. paper filled with news that Vicksbg. had been closely invested & would almost certainly fall. Happy to see in Today's Yanks been repulsed 3 times & Johns[t]on getting reinforcemts—& trust it may yet hold out & stand. Its fall wd. be great calamity.

May 26, Tuesday

SP: Weather moderated & more pleasant. Lts. May & Watts came to-day & say our officers will be up tomorrow. No further intelligence fr. Vicksbg. Read Poem on Revlution of 61 & 62 by John H. Hewitt 1ˢᵗ Canto—thro' battles 'round Richmd. pretty good. Detailed to get guns & accoutremts & ammunition fr. Wagon yard. Guns in very bad order & we'll have a time cleaning them up to pass inspect.

NOTE: John Hill Hewitt, *War a Poem, with Copious Notes, Founded on the Revolution of 1861–62* (Richmond: West & Johnston, R. W. Gibbes, 1862).

May 27, Wednesday

SP: Capt. Williams, Lts Jones & Christian came in to-day. They were kept 10 or 12 days longer in Washgton than we were. They report our wounded boys in

Richmd getting on very well. Col Hobson still lookg very badly but as his mother & brother are with him he will cheer up & under their kind ministration will no doubt improve. I was very glad to hear from Cap. Williams that Tom Biscoe was a prisoner in Old Capitol with him. as I had written to him & recd. no reply was uneasy till then.

May 28, Thursday

SP: Cap W^ms drilled us this morng & had little easier time as he did not drill accordg. to the drum calls. The news fr. vicksbg show she is in critical situation I trust tho she successfully resist all attempts of the Yankees to capture it. I wrote a letter to Mary to-day. John sent $10 in it to his wife. I enclose a couple Yankee letters to Mary.

May 29, Friday

SP: We had a grand military display to day. Our Division was reviewed by Gen. Lee. The brig. were drawn out each formg line battle one behind other & Gen Lee would gallop down front & back in rear & so on thro' Longstreet, A. P. Hill, Rodes & others rode with him. He would stop in front of centre each Brig. & we'd present arms—flag bearers lowering flags, & Gen. Lee take off hat. After that, each brigade marched by the Genl. by Divis. (2 Cos.) except in new N. Car. Brig. Daniel's [(]lately came in place of Colquitts (Geo). wh. has gone to D.H. Hill in N.C.) in the Corps—in it were fully as large as our Divis. as they had never been in any battles. Had bands music at head each Brig. wh. played occasionally. Brass one in Iversons very good music. Rodes carried us thro it all as rehearsal before Gen. Lee came, so it was a most fatiguing day. It was abt. 2 ms fr. Camp in plain on road to Hamiltons Xing. Lasted fr. abt 10 A.M. till aft 5 P.M. & had a tiresome day of it—very dusty. Went to creek & took nice wash.

May 30, Saturday

SP: Lay up in tent resting fr. yesterdays labors—a Lt. Walter Garnett rel. or frd of Matt Jones came to see him & spent day with him. After dress parade went to creek & bathed. Strange I dont get any letters fr. home—only 2 since came bk to Regt & they immediately after.

May 31, Sunday

SP: Last night after going to bed & fixing for a nice nights rest. Orders came to rept. at head Qrs. We fixed up hurriedly & fell in & left about 11 O'clk & marched down to near Gordons house & got in line battle in road thro bushes. Iversons Brig. formed another line in front of us. It seems Yanks makg. demonstrats at Banksford & also some where below. very warm when got there but got cold & wrapped up in blankets & slept till after day—washed—ate cakes some had along & after while servts came with meat & biscuits. 11 or 12 we were ordered back to Camp & were very glad it was false alarm & to get back. Cooled off & slept till late dinner. At dress parade we took position on extreme left Regt as we are now Co "B". Left the Colors—which has been our position ever since I've been in Regt.

NOTE: The Guards remained officially Company D of the Fifth Alabama.

June 1, Monday

SP: This is the opening of Summer and a bright and beautiful day it is. After breakfast our Regiment went down to the river on picket at the same place we were usually station during the Winter. Our Co. & Co. "E" got into some barns on the bank of the river in a shady cool place. There has been a delightful breeze blowing all day. We lay about in the shade and slept for some time in the middle of the day and then went in swimming. It is the first time I've been in since June 1861 at New Market on the James river, when Jamie, Willie & I were at Dr. Harrison's school. The water was very pleasant indeed. A crowd went in again in the evening, while others of us tried our luck at fishing, but caught only a few small ones. Recd a letter from Jamie this evening that gave me much pleasure, for I had not heard from home in ten days. My telegram from Richmond of 15th ult. had reached home on morning of the 17th. The letters of Coln. Pickens & Mr. Joe Grigg had been recd.; but mine from Washington & the two from Richmond had not been. Jamie mentioned that some of the neighbors had cut wheat then (21st ult.).

NOTE: Dr. Gessner Harrison's School was located at Locust Grove, Albemarle County, Virginia.

June 2, Tuesday

SP: I slept delightfully & woke after sunup. This is a cool, fresh morning. There were men in swimming nearly all day, and others fishing. I went in in the evening. John brought down some peas for dinner & some cakes.

June 3, Wednesday

SP: I got up this morning at 4—daylight—to stand guard & found it uncommonly cold for the season. An over coat would have been very acceptable. It rained a while slowly. This evening Mr.Cowin, who had come on for John's remains, rode down to see us all & brought a no. of letters. I got a long & most affectionate one from Mama which afforded me sincere pleasure. I wrote to Lou telling her that we were under marching orders.

June 4, Thursday

SP: Last night we were relieved by troops of A. P. Hill's Division about 10 or 11 O'clock & returned to camp where rations had been cooked up. Filled our havresacks & got some cakes from Ellison & then lay down to take a little rest. At 2 A.M. we were called up & marched a little beyond Grace Church & lay on side of the road till breakfast time; when we resumed the march & near Guinea Station took a road to the right—the same one we traveled last Fall coming from the Valley. It was a very warm day & we were in a cloud of dust most of the time. We rested 10 mins. every hour, which is the rule now in marching. Passed through Spottsylvania C.H. & camped a mile beyond at 3½ P.M.—having come 4 ms. to Grace Church & 17 or 18 ms. = 21 or 22 since last night & without sleeping any scarcely. I was so much fatigued that I spread my blanket—threw myself upon it & slept till pretty late in the evening. My eyes, mouth, face &

hair were covered with dust, so I went with Joe Wright & Cruse Coleman to the branch & had a good wash. Cooked up one day's rations.*

*Recd. a letter from Willie this evening.

June 5, Friday

SP: We were on the road again this morning at 6 & during the morning got along finely as it was cloudy & there had been such a heavy dew that there was no dust; but by & by the sun shone out & it became very hot & dusty. In the evening were on the plank road for a short distance. I never was so tempted to fall out of ranks for I was almost as badly used up as I was coming from the valley. My legs pained all over & my feet were getting rubbed & sore—bathing, tho', helped considerably. Camped at 5 P.M., having come, as Tood Cowin—courier for O'Neal—told us, over 20 miles.

June 6, Saturday

SP: Started this morning about 5, but after coming 3 or 4 miles were halted as the enemy was making demonstrations at Fredericksburg, & bivouacked in a nice piece of woods in beautiful country with meadows of the richest clover & grass—while the Blue Ridge Mountains lifted themselves in bold relief to our left. We lay about & slept and had a good day's rest. It rained before night but we stretched our little Yankee tent & kept dry. John & Braxton being out of the way I made my first attempt at making biscuits, but by the time I had mixed & kneaded the dough well, John came & I resigned in his favor. Our mess being too large, Tean Nutting, David Barnum, Matt Jones & I withdrew & formed a separate one.

June 7, Sunday

SP: The drum for rising and getting ready beat at 3½ A.M. & we started a little after 4. At that time it was almost as cold as Winter, & was quite cool all day: fine weather for marching. This morning we waded the Rapidan. It was a little over knee deep & the current pretty swift. 10 ms. further on we passed through Culpeper C.H., a very old town in a poor, worn out country. French Strother, our first teacher was from this place. Marched about 2 miles further & camped in a pretty piece woods at 2½ P.M. Marched about 15 miles to-day. Last night we had a canteen of buttermilk & this morning one of sweet milk, which we enjoyed exceedingly.

June 8, Monday

SP: Yesterday evening I wrote to Icha & sent the letter by Jim Boardman's boy to-day. He is to give the letter to Mr. Cowin in Richmond. I enclosed my parole to Mama. We remained still to-day & enjoyed the rest very much. Had a slight attack of Diarrhoea & took Ginger & Paregoric. Walked over & sat some time with Joe Grigg at Gen. Rodes' Hd. Qrs. Saw there Gens. Ramseur and Daniels, of our Division.

June 9, Tuesday

SP: This is the anniversary of my birth day. I am 22 years of age to-day. Stewarts Cavalry was attacked by the enemy's cavalry this morning early & the fighting lasted nearly all day. Our cavalry were driven back several miles from the river but rallied & drove the Yankees back. About 10 O'clock this morning our Divis. was ordered forward to support the Cavalry & formed line of battle & expected to get into the fight all the evening, but did not. We heard the firing & could see the shells bursting. Late in the evening we came back a mile or so & camped in a piece of woods on the farm of John Minor Botts. He has a very nice residence & beautiful & extensive tract of open rolling land. The Cavalry fight today was, I suppose, the longest & hardest one of the war.

NOTE: Sam Pickens describes the Battle of Brandy Station, the largest cavalry battle of the war. Although the Confederates managed to avoid defeat, the Union cavalry held its own. Union casualties are estimated at 866, Confederate at 523— each side engaging about ten thousand troops.

Lee's army is about to march into the Shenandoah Valley and thence north into Pennsylvania.

June 10, Wednesday

SP: Remained still till evening, when two days rations were issued & ordered to be cooked up; but by the time we got our dough made up we were ordered off & gave up the rations to be hauled. Started at 4 P.M. & marched hard all the evening, making 10 or 12 miles. It was very hot & disagreeable. Judging from the direction, we conclude that we have taken up the line of march for the Valley. We sat up quite late expecting the Commissary wagon to come up. It did not, however, till away in the night some time & our Co.'s dough had been lost or thrown away.

June 11, Thursday

SP: Today we passed thro' some beautiful country—the richest clover pastures & grass—; & nice cool, shady residences. It makes a poor wearied broke down soldier think that if he could only stop there he would be perfectly happy— Passed thro' little town called Flint Hill, in which David Barnum got a canteen of milk, some hot corn bread & fresh butter, & John got another Canteen of Butter milk. We camped abt. ½ mile fr. town, quite early in the evening, & then made a hearty meal of the bread, butter & milk wh. of course we thought was the best thing we had ever tasted. A while after stopping we were much disappointed to find that our Brigade had stopped at the wrong place and had to get up—tie up our blankets, harness ourselves with accoutrements & drag on near a mile further. I was so completely broke down & my feet so sore & blistered that it was with difficulty I could get to the 2$\underline{nd}$ Camping ground. After lying down & resting a while Tean, Matt & I went to the branch & washed off & bathed our feet. The dust is almost intolerable & that together with the heat make the marching very severe. Walked over to the wagons & Mr. Tucker gave us some good hot biscuits & cold ham. Our Brig. marched in front of Divis. & our Reg. in front Brig. & as we were going left in front Co. "D" was at the head of Divis. We found it much easier marching too & had full benefit of the rests—10 min. every hour.

SP: To-day our Co. marched in the extreme rear of Divis—wagons & every thing, & was detached to act as rear guard. I saw Peachy Harrison on the road— he is in 2$\underline{nd}$ Va. Cavalry. Passing house I noticed a white guinea—it looked rather singular. This is the richest pasture country I ever saw—the greatest portion of the land is coverd with the most luxuriant clover & some meadows of Timothy & other grasses. We see also splendid fields of Wheat—a great deal of bearded wheat. Went thro' Front Royal this eveng. It is an old looking town—situated in the Valley & seems to be surrounded by mountains when you see it at a little distance. The people delighted to see us, & hoped we would be able to catch Milroy. His province extended only to the Shenandoah a mile above the town, but he frequently made raids on that side of river. One mile further on we forded the 2 branches of the Shenandoah. the bridges had been destroyed last year, I suppose during Gen. Jacksons operations in the Valley—the rivers were pretty wide but not more than knee deep. It was my good fortune to ride over both. Miles Pickens after crossing sent his horse back for me & I took Jack W. over behind me. I was very glad of the chance to ride for my feet were in very bad condition & it was caused principally by wading streams & getting my boots full of water & marching on in that plight. The skin of feet is made tender & shrivels & then rubs off or blisters. It is bad policy to march troops thro water without giving them time stop & take off shoes & socks. The two branches unite a few hundred yds below where we forded & there is where the RR. crossed. The bridge tho' was destroyed & track torn up last fall a short time before I joined our Regt., which assisted in the work. Noticed a fence built of the iron rails, wh. was certainly a strong & lasting one. Gen$\underline{l}$ Jenkins' Brig. mounted infantry, armed with Minie muskets, passed us after crossing the river. During the eveng. our Regt. & the 12$\underline{th}$ wh. had been in rear of wagon train as guard were ordered to go ahead & overtake Brig. so we had to cut across thro' the field & march pretty fast to get ahead the wagons. We passed one place on the left of & some little distance fr. the road wh. was the most inviting lookg-place to a tired & hungry soldier imaginable. A comfortable lookg house in a thick shady grove & on one side there was one of the richest meadows I have ever seen—covd with the most luxuriant hay grass of some kind, & along a stream running through it there were 2 rows of weeping willows—the largest by far and most flourishg I ever saw. They must swim in milk & butter all thro' this country. We crossed the mountains to day (Blue Ridge) at Chesters' Gap, abt. mid way between Flint Hill & Front Royal. It was a much easier crossing than the one we made in comg. from the valley last fall. It was 12 ms. fr. our Camp last night this side F. Hill to F. Royal & 1 to River; then we marched on at least 5 or 6 ms. further & campd. after dark in piece woods left of road, having come 18 or 19 ms. Drew dried beef &

crackers—took dose Paregoric as have not yet cured diarrhoea. I am completely broken down to night & my feet so sore & blistered that I can scarcely hobble along after sitting down a while.

June 13, Saturday

SP: Passed thro' the little town Millwood to day thro' which the citizens told us Yank. Cavalry had passed not an hour ahead of our Division. There were 2 glorious young ladies at a house on the bank of the stream as you enter the place, who worked like trojans bringing buckets of water to the paling for the soldiers. It was excellent water, too, cold as ice. We were a little excited to think of being so near the Yanks. We heard their infantry force was at Berryville & would there resist our advance. Got to within a mile or 1½ of the place about 1 or 2 P.M. & formed line battle & expected to have a hard charge to make as the Yanks. had excellent position on an elevated place & we would have been compelled to charge up a slant for near a mile, but we were much relieved to see our Brigade file into road & march by flank upon the town. The Yanks. had left. They had splendid redoubt—thick bank—planked up on inside. There were their tents all standing & left in the greatest hurry & confusion. Cooking utensils were on the fire with meat, beans &c cookg. There seemed to be three sep. encampments, but citizens told us there was 1 Regt. Infant. & 1 Cavalry. Formd again in line in edge of town as it was thought I suppose, that Yanks. might have fallen back to entrenchments on Charlestown Pike beyond town, & capped guns, but we moved off again by flank & as our Regt was passing 1 of the Camps Maj. Whiting detailed our Co. to guard it. We turned in & ran off all the Cavalry & stragglers that were plundering & Lt. Jones posted us around to keep them out. It was as much as we could do to keep men out; they'd slip in in spite of us. In this way we were kept so busy that we had but a poor chance to get anything ourselves. All however got plenty of coffee parched & grd. & some sugar Bakers' brd. & some got cakes & cider which was very nice. Some of the boys also got Lemons, a good many got boots & shoes, also clothing—Drawers, shirts, pants &c. A great many havresacks & canteens were found. I supplied myself with a good Havre sack, almost new & got a good lot of letter paper. After our troops had gone on & found the Yanks had gone off entirely, Daniels Brig. of N.C. came pouring back to the camp we were at & were soon all over it, so we who guarded it were kept so busy keeping out stragglers that we got very little before the N.C. poured in & then there was no chance. We guarded several tents to the last for Gen. Rodes, containing a great quantity sugar & coffee & barrels unopened. Officers mess chest &c &c. There was an abundance of good soap & some nice toilet soap. There were about 80 sick & some wounded Yanks left there. We took a good many commiss. stores that had to be destroyed for want transportation. The people were very glad to see us & have the enemy driven away & Yanks were comfortably fixed up & had no idea of being disturbed. Had martin boxes fixed up in their Camps. After resting about a couple of hours, we moved on, &

had the hardest rain to fall on us that I ever saw. The roads were flooded & water dashed along like a mill race. We were wet thro & thro. Camped in piece woods on right of road not far from house, about dark. Mchd. today———miles. Altho' it threatened rain our mess—Tean, Davy & Matt & myself were too completely used up to stretch our tent. They went to bed early & it commencd raing & soon had their blankets wet & water running under them; so I turned in with J. Wynne & 3 or 4 others who had some oil cloths stretched. We were all wet & very much crowded & water leaking in on us so that we slept very badly. Before the war I would have thought it would kill a man to lie all night in wet clothes, but soldiers can stand any thing.

June 14, Sunday

SP: This has been a long & eventful day. My feet were very sore & my boots & sox being soaked with water I could only manage to get my boots on without the sox. So I went to see Dr. Hill if there was any chance of my riding any; but he was over run with men who had sore feet & could not haul any, as ambulances were filled with fever cases. He gave me a pass to march out of rank tho' & I went to Commiss. wagons where Mr. Tucker was & made John make us some genuine Coffee & ate brkfst. Mr. Tucker[,] Jim Hardaway & I then went on ahead of Divis. & by so doing had a much easier time. The troops marched hard the latter part of the day & we had very little rest. Passed thro' the town Smithfield where the people were very glad to see us. A lady was standing before her door with a bucket of nice warm light bread sliced & buttered & pitcher buttermilk; as I passed by she gave me slice & poured milk in my cup. I enjoyed it very much & only wished for more. Troops cheered the Ladies who were waving handkerchiefs & we had a band playing too. I tried at several houses to buy milk & butter but could not. Cavalry had been ahead & got everything nearly—Tho at 2 houses they gave me milk in Canteen wh. Tucker[,] Hardaway & I drank. Saw a squad Prisoners that had been taken by Cavalry. There was skirmishing & fighting between our Cavalry & theirs all along the road the day before. Came thro Bunkershill & Darksville also. At Bunker Hill there had been a considerable fight. There was a brick house where Yanks had made port-holes & filled up part of windows with rocks & made a stubborn resistance. The house was marked & scaled up in great many places by Grape shot. The telegraph wires were cut down. It was late in eveng. when we got to within a mile or 2 of Martins bg. & formed lines of attack. Our Brig. was on right in rear of a battery that was having a duel with enemys batter in front a mile or more off. We could see the flash of their [. . .]

June 19, Friday

SP: This morning our Brigade waded the Potomac at Williamsport. Almost all the men were denuded of pants & drawers, & cut rather an odd figure. The river was about 200 yds. or probably wider. The water was just above the knees—swift & beautifully clear. 6 ms. further on we marched thro' Hargerstown to the air of the "Bonnie blue flag." We seemed to have a great many friends there, as the ladies all along the streets waved handkerchiefs & some Confederate flags. Our troops cheered loud & heartily. Hagerstown is quite a large place & in the central part there are some very nice streets. We marched 2 ms. further, on the Boonsboro' road & camped in piece of woods back of Funkstown at 2 P.M. A great many men went in bathing in a creek close by. David Barnum went over in F.town & got some excellent cherry pies. John brought up some Dutch bread—"preatzel" or some such name—rolled out round—the size of your finger & smaller—glazed over & pretty salt. It is the first I ever saw.

June 20, Saturday

SP: We were up pretty early this morning & got ready to leave, but the order was countermanded & we remained still. This creek upon which we are encamped is the celebrated Antietam on which the great battle of Sharpsburg was fought. The battle ground is about 3 or 4 miles from here. David Barnum got some nice light-bread & a currant pie in town to-day. There was a great deal of Whisky in circulation to-day. I saw and heard of a good many drunken men.

June 21, Sunday

SP: David & I got up pretty early & went a mile to a house & got 2 canteens of milk. We enjoyed for breakfast the rare treat of pure coffee with sugar & milk in it. We got some more milk in the evening & boiled some with coffee without any water & it made the richest & best coffee I ever drank. Hundred of soldiers went to Church in Hagerstown to-day. Those from our Co. went to the Catholic where Gens. Ewell & Rodes were. Heard a very good sermon on the importance of prayer—St. Matt. 15$\underline{th}$ Chap. 21 to 29$\underline{th}$ verse. After service a good many ladies & men went to the carriage & shock hands & conversed with the Gens. Most of the Catholics are secessionists. I wrote to Mama this evening & gave the letter to a sutler going to Richmond to-morrow.

June 22, Monday

SP: This morning marched back thro' Hagerstown & took the road to Chambersburg, Penn. Crossed the line at the town Middleburg, which is partly in Md. & Penn. A few miles further on we passed thro' Greencastle—9 ms. fr. Hagerstown, and camped 2 miles beyond off the road. We are taking all the horses & cattle that can be found, & have already got hundreds of horses & droves of beeves. I had as many cherries as I could eat this evening. There is a light colored cherry that is almost as large as our plums & very juicy: the finest I have ever seen. Wrote a letter to Jamie. We marched about 13 ms. to-day by 2 P.M.

June 23, Tuesday

SP: There is a large and splendid spring here. It breaks out of a rocky hill-side in a half a dozen places near together & forms a good large branch. The water is clear as crystal & cold as ice. Henry Childress and I went out about a mile to a house & got a bait of cherries. They were large, fine ones. Molasses was issued to us to-day & also a small quantity of sundries, such as cigars, smoking & chewing tobacco, a few envelopes, a blank book & a cake of Maple Sugar, which were found, I suppose, in some captured sutler's establishment. We saw this evening a copy of "The (Philadelphia) Press" in which was Gov. Curtin's proclamation calling out the Militia to repel the Rebel raid into the State.

June 24, Wednesday

SP: Left camp at 5 A.M. Passed thro' the village Marion & then thro' Chambersburg, which is quite a large place—6 or 8,000 inhabitants. The houses are mostly small, old & common looking & the population generally Dutch. It is 11 ms. from Greencastle to Chambersburg. We came on 1½ or 2 ms. & camped. By the time we stacked arms, the men went off by scores to the neighboring houses & brought back a great many hens, & milk, butter &c. David Barnum brought in a Canteen of milk, a cup of butter & a little *apple butter,* which was the first I ever saw & it was very nice. The people *gave* everything to the soldiers as they said our money would do them no good. We saw the finest kind of wheat all along the road, & some fields of Oats, rye & barley. Also the richest fields of Clover & hay grasses. This is a great country for small grain & stock. The bearded wheat is grown exclusively. There is very little corn planted. The barns up here are very large & almost as fine as the dwellings. Some are built entirely of stone & others of brick with glazed windows & green blinds though generally the first story only is of stone, which is used for stables, & the balance framed. They are situated very near the dwellings. Too near to be agreeable, I should think. (To-day 13 miles.)

June 25, Thursday

SP: We remained near Chambersburg to-day in order, as usual, to impress every thing found there necessary for the use of the army. I had a nice bath in a creek to-day. Saw the "Philadelphia Enquirer" of 22nd inst.; it was full of excited reports of the "Rebel invasion of Md. & Penn."!! & speculations about the plans & intentions of Gen. Lee.

June 26, Friday

SP: We had a very disagreeable march this morning to Shippensburg. It rained last night & nearly all day to-day. The road was very wet & sloppy. S——bg is a place of considerable *length,* being built along on each side of the road. It is a common looking place & is inhabited by common looking people—principally Dutch. I have not seen any nice, refined people since we have been in the State. After passing through the principal part of town we took a road to the right & went a mile on picket: that is the left wing of the Regt. We were quartered in a large barn where there was a plenty of straw with which we made very comfortable beds. There were a great many cherries & one large tree of black hearts which were the finest I ever tasted. A good many hens were about the barn but they soon disappeared. Some few were paid for by men who happened to have a little U.S. currency. David B. brought in 2 hens, some milk, butter & eggs. Matt Jones & I with Charley Briggs went to the wagon yard, a mile off through wheat & clover fields to have the hens cooked. Got an excellent dinner there of hot biscuits & butter, mackerel & molasses. When we got back to the barn we were wringing wet as high up as the wheat reached, thro' which we passed; but soon dried off by the fire. They issued whiskey & sugar to us, and Tean Nutting & I made a very nice *egg-nog* with milk in it. It was not beat as well as it ought to have been as we had to make it in our tin cups, but we enjoyed it hugely. John then came with the chicken stew & other nice things & we made a hearty supper.

June 27, Saturday

SP: We had a very hard march to-day. Left the Turnpike & came a muddy, clay road. Passed through the towns Leesburg, Centreville & several other smaller ones. In the edge of Carlisle our Brigade took the Baltimore Turnpike which formed an acute angle with the road we came [. . .] and went out a mile or more, then turned on another road & camped in a large orchard—about 2 miles from town. It was a mile from where we started to Shippensburg—then 20 ms. to Carlisle & 2 to camp = 23 ms. we marched to-day; & it was worse than 30 on a good dry road. I was completely broken down & my feet hurt me very much. a sign board in C. said 23 ms. to S. which if correct wd make our march 26 ms. We are now within 19 ms. of Harrisburg (i.e. fr. Car. to Har.) where a large force of Militia have been concentrated.

June 28, Sunday

SP: We remained still & had a good rest to-day. There is a large flour mill here run by water furnished by springs. The pond is 4 or 5 feet deep in places & yet the water is so beautifully clear that every thing on the bottom is seen as distinctly as if it were on the surface. There are large springs around the edges & some boil up in the bottom, & the water is so cold that it made my feet ache to keep them in it a few seconds. I had the pleasure of hearing from home to-day. Got a letter from Jamie & 2 from Lou. The latest was the 6th inst. I wrote to Mama this evening.

June 29, Monday

SP: We had marching orders to-day & fell in at 12 M., but the order was countermanded. Tean & Davy went foraging & were quite successful. We had an excellent dinner—Biscuits, butter, mutton, goose, molasses, apple-butter & milk—to which we did ample justice.

June 30, Tuesday

SP: To-day we marched through Papertown & crossed the mountains—South Mountain I believe—; then through Petersburg which is 14 miles from Carlisle. Here we left the Baltimore turnpike & took a road to the right (Gettysburg road) & marched on about 5 miles & camped at Heidelburg. It drizzled & showered frequently & the latter part of the road was muddy & slippery. Came 19 miles to-day.

July 1, Wednesday

SP: Left camp this morning at 6:30 A.M. & marched 7 miles on the Chambersburg road to Middletown, where we turned to the left on the Gettysburg road. As we approached the town we heard the cannonading & formed a line of battle about 2 miles off & advanced upon the Yankees. Our Regt. was on the left of the Brigade & as it moved forward it made a partial right wheel & thus kept us at a double quick march all the time; & as it was an excessively hot day & we were going through wheat fields & ploughed ground & over fences, it almost killed us. I was perfectly exhausted & never suffered so from heat & fatigue in my life. A good many fell out of ranks being completely broken down & some fainted. We halted & lay down for some time at a fence & witnessed an artillery duel between one of our batteries stationed about 150 yds. in front of us & a Yankee battery away to our left. 5 or 6 dead horses & 1 or 2 broken caissons or gun carriages were left by our battery when it moved off. Our Regt. then went forward, for the rest of the Brigade had gone on while we had been left to guard the space between our Brigade & Doles' which was on our left & prevent either from being flanked. We came up with the Brig., however, at a fence where it had halted and there our Company was sent forward to a barn to act as sharp-shooters. There were some N.C. sharp-shooters there who had shot away all their cartridge. W<u>m</u>. Stokes was wounded before getting to the barn, & Joe Brown while in it. We kept up pretty brisk firing at the Yankees, but it seemed as if we could do very little execution as they were so far off & behind a fence in the woods, though they made the bullets whistle over us. After the Brig. passed on we ran out of the barn & through an open field where the bullets were flying thick & went down on the left to a lane where the Regt. was. I never saw troops so scattered & in such confusion. We were under a heavy fire from the front & a cross fire from the left & pretty soon had to fall back to a fence where the Brig. was rallied by Col. O'Neal & Gen<u>l</u> Rodes. Paul Lavender was coming off wounded & asked Lt. Jones (in commd. of Co.) to let me help him. I got three of the ambulance corps of the 26<u>th</u> Regt. & a litter & had to carry Paul about a mile to get to a Surgeon. Mr. Mushat extracted the ball & after waiting in vain all the evening for an ambulance to take the wounded to the Hospital, I set out to find the H. & get ambulances, which I succeeded in doing after a long walk & a deal of difficulty. The scenes about the Hospital were the most horrible I ever beheld. There were the poor wounded men lying all over the yard, moaning & groaning, while in the barn the terrible work of amputating limbs was going on, and the pallid limbs lying around presented a most disagreeable sight. As soon as I could get 2 ambulances we set out & had to go a very roundabout way, so by time we got to the wounded it was some time after night & they had been put in a house & were so comfortable they did not want to be moved, so the ambulances were dismissed to return in the morning. In the mean time our troops had driven the Yankees and were in possession of the town of Gettysburg. When our Brig. was reformed it moved up & took position along the Rail-road to the right of town. Oh! what terrible work has been done to-day. The loss in our Brig. was very heavy—particularly in our Regt. I was much affected on learning that my warm friend & mess-mate Tean Nutting had been mortally wounded & died in a short time on the field. He was at his post with the colors. A nobler, more generous or braver boy never lived. He was a great favorite & will be much missed. Marched 14 ms. before getting in fight.

VET: Left H this morning, after march of 17 miles, were thrown in fight of Gettysburg. The loss of Co. D. as follows: Killed. Geo Nutting; wounded, Joe Wright, Joe Brown, P H. Lavender, and Stok[e]s; prisoners, Stokes, Butler, Knowlen, Lanier and Ray. We now occupy the town of Gettysburg and bivouacked near R R for the night.

JST: This is to me the sad[d]est day of the war. The troops marched to Gettysburg, where a terrible battle was fought in which poor Tunie was killed. Never shall I forget my feelings when I got to him & found him lifeless. How sudden & heart-rending the change—had parted with him only a few hours before in perfect health & fine spirits, never dreaming that it was the last & final interview. Thus ended the ~~noblest~~ life of one of the noblest & best boys in early youth that ever lived & brings vividly to memory the fact that in

"The midst of life we are in Death . . . ["]

NOTE: Rodes sent his men forward on this, his first test as division commander. The Fifth Alabama was on the left of O'Neal's brigade as it drove the Yankees through the town. The brigade then reformed and took its position northwest of town, where it remained until Rodes led his division against Cemetary Hill the evening of July 2. With the division significantly down in numbers, the soldiers did not attack but returned in darkness to sleep along one of Gettysburg's streets. On the morning of the third day, O'Neal's brigade again advanced against Federal positions on Culp's Hill while the Fifth Alabama, including the Greensboro Guards, stayed behind to hold Gettysburg, missing Pickett's charge. The fighting at Gettysburg is extensively covered in *Guarding Greensboro*.

July 2, Thursday

SP: The ambulances came this morning and conveyed the wounded to the Hospitals, & I, with Cruse Coleman returned to the Regiment. The town is full of the enemy's wounded & every large building has been made a hospital. David Barnum brought from town a havresack of candy, plenty of lemons & other nice things which were a great treat. It was pretty quiet during the morning while we were placing our artillery in position. Gilliam J. told us that 80 pieces were being massed on a hill to our right. After a while they opened all around & the cannonading was terrific: almost as rapid as musketry. Late in the evening our Divis. was moved forward in line of battle & as we advanced upon the hill where the Yankees had all their artillery & troops massed we expected to have to charge it, but it was then after dark & we lay a while in a wheat field & then went back in town. The loss in our Regt. in killed, wounded & missing is 226. The no. that left camp was 380; but a great many fell out of ranks, & Col. Hall thinks that not

many over 300 went into the fight—so our loss was very heavy, & nearly all killed
or wounded, for there are only———missing. In our Co. ("D") the loss is:—

Killed   —   George Nutting
Wounded —   P. H. Lavender—thigh.
                    J. L. Wright—shoulder.
                    J. M. Brown—foot.
                    W͟m Stokes—leg—& Prisoner.
                    W͟m A. Lenier—hand—& Prisoner.
Prisoners —   Jas. Burton.
                    J. T. Knowlan.
                    J. C. Ray

VET: Hard fighting on right by Longstreets corps, our corps lying still, enemy
hold heights in rear of town, heavy artillery duel to day. Move up to make a night
attack, but finally march back to town.

JST: Was present at the burial this morning & saw him as decently interred
as possible, fixed a head board & marked the plan of his burial. O! My what
an awful thought, that his final resting place is so far from his devoted Parents,
Bro'& Sister and in a Yankee Country.

(Direction—Buried one mile north of Gettysburg on the west side of the Pike
leading from Gettysburg to Middletown about ½ mile West of said Pike, near a
dark road at the foot and running parallel with a range of high hills right in front
of a large *Red Barn*-)

Fight continues all day but now I feel perfectly indifferent as to the Result. all
that was dear to me in this army is gone & I care not what the result is.

NOTE: The Guards were part of the advance on Culp's Hill late in the evening.

July 3, Friday

SP: We lay in line along one of the streets last night & this morning our Brigade
with the exception of our Regt. was sent down on the left with Johnson's Divis.
& participated in the fight. Our Regt. was attached to Doles' Brig. & stayed in
town during the morning—while our Co. was sent to the edge of town as sharpshooters. We built breast works and remained there till evening. An occasional
minnie ball whizzed over us & a shell passed through a stable or crib beside us
& exploded immediately after. The Regt. then moved up with Doles' Brig. & lay
in line of battle in a lane. There was no shade, & the heat of the sun was almost
insupportable. A heavy cannonading was kept up—a great many shells passing
over us—and some from our own batteries exploded over our line & killed men
in Doles', Ramseur's &, I think, Iversons Brigades. It was either very inferior
ammunition or great carelessness on the part of the gunners. Saw Tom Biscoe in
town to-day. His looks shewed plainly that he had seen hard service. His Brigade
(Hays') made a desperate charge upon *the Hill* last night & took a battery, but
were not supported & had to fall back. Tom is now in command of the 5͟th La.
Regt.

NOTE: An estimated 3,155 Union soldiers were killed at Gettysburg, 14,529 wounded, and 5,365 missing; Confederate losses are estimated at 3,903, 18,735, and 5,425. Casualties among the Guards included 3 missing (presumed captured) and 5 wounded (including two taken prisoner); George Nutting lay dead, the company's third color bearer killed in duty.

July 4, Saturday

SP: We were roused up about 12½ last night and moved back to a first rate position on elevated ground where after day light we built strong breast works. It rained during the day, & we put on tents & lay under them. There were a good many of the enemy's dead & dead horses lying back of our position which produced a most disagreeable smell.

VET: Ordered to fortify, awaiting an attack from enemy 12 o'clock at night. Commenced to retreat across South Mts. Chas Briggs missing.

JST: Fighting still Continues. Left Gettysburg this morning en route for Williamsport Md with the wagon train. Were intercepted on the mountain & lost a good many wagons—Yankees Captured Westcott & a great many others—& never saw such a running of wagons & [. . .] generally.

July 5, Sunday

SP: We evacuated our position between 12 & 1 this morning & marched off on the pike. The road was perfectly sloppy & so slippery that it was with the greatest difficulty that we could keep our feet. Came not more than 2 or 2½ ms. when we stopped on account of the road being blocked up by the wagon trains ahead, I suppose. Here we were drenched by a cold rain, but when it held up we made fires & made ourselves as comfortable as possible under the circumstances. Several hours after day light we continued the march through mud & water ankle deep in places. The wagon trains kept the road & a column of troops marched thro' the fields & woods on each side. Just on the other side of the little village Fairfield the Yankees (a small force which had followed us) commenced shooting our rear. Our troops & wagons crowded together in the little valley on this side & I was somewhat uneasy that the enemy might do us some damage; but some batteries were put in position & a Brigade, I think, formed in line of battle, & we proceeded onward till after dark when we bivouacked. Came about 10 ms. to-day.

VET: still on retreat. Enemy captured a portion of our train to day

July 6, Monday

SP: There was skirminshing in the rear this morning again. We were all scant of rations as our Brig. did not draw any last night, but we got some beef that was left on the bones by Ramseur's Brig. & broiled & ate it without salt & with very little bread. After going a mile or two we halted & stayed there till noon expecting to have to go back & whip the Yankees back from our rear but finally we got off & marched hard till after night. We crossed over a mountain where for the first time since leaving Gettysburg we had a firm & pretty good road. It was in this mountain that the enemy's cavalry with artillery cut into our wagon train & destroyed a few but an Infantry guard soon drove them off. Our Cavalry behaved disgracefully & ran like turkeys. We stopped after night near a barn where we made the most comfortable bunks we've ever had. Laid planks on sills & covered them over with straw; then spread blankets & had as nice a bed as could be desired. Our cooking detail with the wagons had only a half a day's rations to cook up, so we sent two or three men from our Co. to forage. They brought in flour only: Davy Barnum, though, came up with three hens. Marched about———miles to-day.

NOTE: The attack by Union cavalry was one of many skirmishes that substituted for Meade's main force, which stayed behind in Gettysburg.

July 7, Tuesday

SP: We were roused at 3 A.M. but did not start till after day light. Oh! how I hated to get up & leave our delightful bed. A mile from here we passed through Waynesboro'—a large town, & took a road to the left to Hagerstown 11 ms. distant. Went through another town—Lightersburg—& after a pretty hard march camped in a nice piece of woods a mile & a half from Hagerstown. There was a brass band on the side of the road near here playing "Dixie" & "Maryland" as we passed, & it had the effect of enlivening & cheering us up very much. I made & baked some elegant biscuits this evening. They had grease in them & were first rate. It was my first attempt & succeeded admirably. I wrote a letter to Mama telling her of my safety & good health—it being the first opportunity I had had since the battle of Gettysburg of writing home. Lt. Jones sent Col. Harvey a list of the casualties in the Co., to be published. We marched 11 ms. to-day.

July 14, Tuesday

SP: Late yesterday evening the troops left the breastworks quietly & commenced falling back, leaving one Regt. from each Brig. to fill the space occupied by the Brig. Our Regt. was one of the no. that remained. The Yankees soon found that most of our troops were gone & commenced a brisk skirmishing & on the left charged with a double line of skirmishers, & a line-of-battle; but Ramseur's sharpshooters fought splendidly & 3 or 4 pieces of artillery at the breastworks where we were, opened on them & they charged back again. About 8 or 9 O'clock the remaining Regts. fell back, while only our sharpshooters and a few Cavalry were left along the lines. We marched about two miles along behind the ridge on which are our fortifications, & where fires were left burning. What a splendid position we occupied! I think if the Yankees had attacked Gen! Lee he would have whipped them badly. We had very rough, muddy, & bad marching before reaching the pike, which was itself perfectly sloppy; & to make it still more disagreeable there was a light rain falling for a while. The road was so blocked up with troops that we did not get on very fast, & when we got to Williamsport we found it crowded with soldiers. Her[e] we had to *stand* & wait an hour or more, for there was no place to sit down as the streets were ankle deep with mud & water. Finally we moved on down towards the River, but every few yards the column would halt—so that we were just creeping along at a most fatiguing pace. We went to a ford several hundred yards higher up the river than where we crossed before—going up the aqueduct through water that smelt very offensively. As soon as we got near the river we knew the men were wading, by the yelling & hallooing that we heard. The Potomac being swollen, was very wide & was over waist deep. The water felt cool when we first entered it, but afterwards very pleasant. We waded two & two side by side, holding on to each other in order to resist the current better & be more steady. There were orders for the men to hang their cartridge-boxes around their necks, but a great many failed to do it & there was a considerable amount of ammunition damaged & destroyed by getting wet. Our clothes, blankets (partly) & havresacks all got wet, which increased our load & made it very disagreeable marching after crossing. The banks were muddy & on this side so steep & slippery that it was difficult to scuffle up it. We were very tired & confidently expected to stop directly after getting over the river, but on we went without stopping. Although the distance from Hagerstown was only about six miles, & we were on our feet from 8 or nine O'clock last night, it was day-break when we got across the Potomac. We passed by "Falling Water" where our Pontoon bridge spanned the river, on which Longstreet's & A. P. Hill's Corps were crossing & also the artillery & wagon trains. At 6 or 7 O'clock this morning we came to a halt. After being on our feet the whole night—marching on a sloppy pike, & stopped to rest only once (5 or 10 mins.) during the whole trip. Oh! it was a killing march. It beggars description. We waded into a little pond where we stopped and washed the mud off our pants, socks and shoes, then made fires and dried our clothes—after which we lay down and slept. At 11½ A.M., though we were called up & marched on 3 or 4 miles & camped in a nice piece of woods. As we had gotten our rations wet—what little we had—David Barnum & several others went out & killed two hogs. We broiled the meat at the fire & ate one for supper. I had the pleasure of hearing from home to-day by a letter from Jamie. Happy to hear Mama has, at last gotten rid of the Standenmeyers—having dismissed them. Our Mess was up till 10 or 11 O'clock P.M. cooking. Marched 8 or 9 miles from Williamsport.

VET: Once more in Dixie Thank God!

July 15, Wednesday

SP: We ate the other hog for breakfast this morning. Marched out in an open field at 8, & lay there in broiling sun 3 hrs. Then moved on to another piece of woods & waited till Longstreet's & A. P. Hill's Corps had passed, when we resumed our march and went to Martinsburg & camped in a grove to the right of the town. I was very tired altho' we had come only 4 or 5 miles to-day. John Warren & Bunk Butler were sent ahead for water with the canteens *early this morning* & filled them & waited on the roadside till we came up with them *late this evening.*

July 16, Thursday

SP: Started at 6 A.M. & marched 7 ms. to Darksville where we camped with the understanding that we would stay here some time. I have suffered a great deal with my feet, which are now very sore. After lying down & resting a long time I went out to an old field to pick Dewberries. I never saw the like—they were large & fine and there were hundreds of men scattered over the field gathering them. Tood Cowin being unwell, Matt Jones has taken his place as Courier & been started off with dispatches to Mt. Jackson. Sheb. Chadwick & Bill Hafner, who have been for some weeks at Martinsburg, rejoined the Co. this morning. I recd. a letter from Willy to-day & wrote a long one to Jamie. It seems a fixed fact that, after the various reports, & contradictions, Vicksburg *has at last fallen*!

July 17, Friday

SP: In addition to the sad news that Vicksbg is lost, it is rumored that Charleston has been taken; but of course no one credits it. It is merely a wild rumor that originated in the *fear* that that would be the case, since "Evils come not single spies, but in battalions,"; —and "One woe doth tread upon another heels, so fast they follow." John brought us some rations over from the Division Hd. Qrs. where he has been staying & assisting in the cooking for Maj. Adams & Mr. Tucker during the marching. Also some genuine coffee & sugar. Rained lightly most of the day. I have been lying up barefooted in order to let my feet cure up.

July 18, Saturday

SP: Nothing of interest going on to-day. Went to the branch & took good bath & put on clean clothes.

July 19, Sunday

SP: This is a very pleasant day. I heard an excellent sermon from Rev. Dr. Lacy. Text—Luke Chap. verse. It was very interesting & instructive. The M$^{\underline{c}}$Crarys who have been absent from the Co. for almost a year returned today. A nice fat mutton was given to the Co. as its rations of meat & we barbecued it whole for dinner. It was excellent, being seasoned nicely with vinegar & pepper.

July 20, Monday

SP: I was busily engaged from breakfast time till 2 P.M. cleaning my gun, which was the dirtiest I ever saw, for Brigade inspection by Major Whiting. Late this evening much to our surprise we recd. marching orders & went 5 miles towards Martinsburg. Our Regt. was on Picket & slept on our arms & had orders to keep on our accoutrements, but didn't do it.

July 21, Tuesday

SP: Marched on through town and halted. The Yankees—some three thousand said to be under Mulligan—had made their escape through the mountains, and we returned to our old Camp at Darksville. Marched 10 or 11 miles fast, although the day was very hot. Recd. letters from Jamie, Lou & Israel. They are having nice times at home—several Pic-nics & concerts—and plenty of fine fruit.

July 22, Wednesday

SP: We took up the line of march at 5 O'clock this morning for Culpeper C.H. with orders to camp in that neighborhood on the third night. It was a very hot day & we suffered much, though Mr. Joe Grigg walked & talked with me a long time, thus relieving the monotony of the march. Passed through Winchester which seems to have suffered considerably from the War, being occupied by the Yankees & our troops alternately. On the heights north of the town there is a strong earth Fort which was constructed, I think, by the Yankees during their possession of W. Marched on the Front Royal 2 ms. or more & camped at 1 O'clock P.M., having made between 17 & 18 miles. Capt. Williams who was taken sick & left us the 2$\underline{\text{nd}}$ day after leaving Grace Church, joined us near Winchester. He has been in the "Delevan" Hospital in Charlottesville where he has been well treated & had a nice time. There is a large tract of worn-out land near our Camp covered with Dewberries. I never saw them so abundant & so large & fine. The whole Brigade turned out and got as many as they wanted. I w'ld have enjoyed them more but picked them barefooted as my feet were sore & shoes hurt them. John came up in the evening & brought a havresack of hot biscuits and pan of nice fried Liver, Mutton & bacon, which were discussed with great interest by my hungry mess.

July 23, Thursday

SP: Capt. Williams is acting Major and has a horse to ride. Started at 6 A.M. & marched 17 ms. to Front Royal where we crossed the Shenandoah at the junction of the two branches on a Pontoon bridge. When we got there I was so completely worn out & my feet hurt so that I could scarcely get along, but did not stop as we expected to go into Camp very soon; but on arriving in town we heard that there was fighting then going on in the mountains on the Manassas Gap road about 4 ms. off. So our Division posted to the support of Wright's Ga. Brigade, which had been sent there on picket & were attacked by the Yankees. Our Brig. took its position in several different places & kept changing about, but was finally deployed as skirmishers, and our Regt. was on the left in the woods. Our Co. (the most of it) was sent up on the side of the mountain to watch the movements of the Yankees and prevent them from flanking us. From this position we had a good view of the fight. The Yankees were in strong force on the mountains fronting the Gap that we were in and brought down several lines of battle, but they were checked by Wright's Brig. which was deployed as skirmishers & by the sharpshooters of our Brig. The Yankees attempted several charges Huzzaing at the top of their voices, but did not come far, and when we opened on them with one or two small pieces of artillery they fell back. Their field officers behaved very well galloping in front of their lines & trying to lead the men on, but who on their part were not much inclined to follow. Some of the Color-bearers would run forward waving their flags & some of the men would run up on a line with them & fire off their guns, but the rest would be scattered on behind. There was very little execution done they were so far apart but occasionally we heard the cries of the wounded & saw the Yankees carrying off the field their dead or wounded. A few minnies whistled over where I was, on the mountain, & the right wing of our Regt. was slightly engaged & had one man killed in Co. "C".

NOTE: By stopping the Federal troops that had poured through Manassas Gap, Longstreet's and Hill's corps were able to escape into the safety of the Shenandoah Valley.

July 24, Friday

SP: Last night at 8 or 9 O'clock we quietly fell back to Front Royal & took the road up the Shenandoah river to cross the mountains at a different Gap, as Chester's Gap, through which Longstreet & A. P. Hill had passed, was now impracticable on account of the presence of the Yankees. Marched 3 miles from F. R. & stopped at half past 1 A.M., making 28 or 30 miles that we marched since leaving camp yesterday morning, and about 21 hours that we were up, & on the go most of the time. It was the hardest time we have ever had. I never suffered so in my life—was completely worn out & my feet hurt me so that I could scarcely get along. We were in an open field & slept till the Sun was several hours high, and consequently got up feeling as if we had been stewed—anything but refreshed. We then started & marched 10 ms. It was the hottest day I ever felt. & there was more straggling than I ever saw: which was unavoidable after the terribly hard march of yesterday & last night. Lt. Jones, Alex. McCall & most all of our Co. dropped out of ranks. I got behind the Rear Guard and took my time. I believe this is the only time since leaving Fredericksburg that I have ever been out of ranks when we stopped to Camp—the only time I've straggled. Took a good bath in a creek late this evening. Gilliam James brought me a havresack of biscuits & meat & a little honey, sent by John. Marched 10 ms. to-day.

July 25, Saturday

SP: We continued to march up the Shenandoah to-day. Davy Barnum caught an old horse that was wandering about camp this morning & fixed a sort of halter on him & got blankets from several of us to carry & use as a saddle just as he was mounted & starting off, a youth came up & claimed the horse; so Davy had to get down & take it afoot, as usual, which produced among the boys a hearty laugh at his expense. When within several miles of Luray we took a road to the left which crosses the Mountains at Thor[n]ton's Gap, and went about 3 ms., making about 11 ms. we marched to-day. The last 2 or 3 ms. were in an open lane where the sun shone down with an oppressive heat. Being very warm & wet with perspiration, I lay down at Camp to cool off & had a chill followed by fever.

July 26, Sunday

SP: I spent a very disagreeable night. It rained & as my mess have no tent I went in with Bunk Butler & Andrew Jackson, & being crowded & having fever & the tent leaking on us, it was disagreeable enough. John brought me some chicken & a Cucumber for breakfast & I enjoyed them very much. Capt. Williams ate with me. Heard an excellent sermon from Rev. Dr. Lacy—Text. Matt.

This evening an order came for all the sick & those unable to march to be sent around by another route in the empty wagons. I, with Dr. Witherspoon & Hausman of our Co. & also Lt. John Christian, got passes & went to the wagon train.

July 27, Monday

SP: Started at 6 yesterday evening and had a *very rough* ride. Went through Luray, a pretty large town, & turned to the left & traveled till 12 O'clock—having made 12 or 15 miles. This morning John C. & I walked on ahead & soon came into the New Market & Gordonsville Turnpike wh. we traveled last Fall, & wh. crosses the Mountains at Fisher's Gap. The Divis. train came around this way too, & when we got tired John & I got into Maj. Adams' wagon & rode & slept. J. & I got out on top the mountain & walked on all the rest of the day. There is a stream of cold—pure water that dashes down the side of the Mountain & crosses the road. Here we stopped & drank & washed our faces & hands. The road is very winding; so that by cutting across & going straight down the mountain a few hundred yards you cut off a mile or more in some places. The distance over the mountain is 14 ms., & I suppose we traveled about 20 in all to-day. John & I put in at an old lady's house out of a shower of rain & found Dr. Mushat there. We got supper which was a very good one at the 1st table, but I ate at the 2nd. & there was very little left. The wagons parked to-night not far from Criglersville—a small shabby village. I [was] really ashamed to be in a white persons house in the plight in which I was—my pants tattered & torn; but soldiers far from home & where they neither know, nor are known by any one, are sort of privileged characters, & expect to be looked upon with a great many allowances.

July 28, Tuesday

SP: Slept in Maj. Adams' tent & enjoyed a fine night's rest. Buck Adams came last night from Sperryville where he left the Division & says that it will camp several days in this neighborhood. Those sick enough to go to hospital went on to Gordonsville. Dr. Witherspoon, Hausman & I went of[f] the road & got dinner at a Capt. Thomas'. Stayed here till late in the evening on account of rain, & read the papers: then went out & got a great many fine blackberries & walked on to the wagon yard which has been moved to within 3 ms. of Madison C.H. We had hot ham & hominy for supper which was a great treat.

July 29, Wednesday

SP: Dr. Witherspoon & I walked on to M.C.H. & went all over the town this morning: after which we returned by a roundabout way & found our Divis. near the turnpike about 2 ms. fr. town. Got a great many berries & the first peaches I've seen at all fit to eat. Saw a few roasting ears in camp, but the grains were not half filled out.

July 30, Thursday

SP: It rained last night & as Davy, Matt & I had no tent we got wet. It was very late this morning before we could get a skillet to cook breakfast & had nothing but some mean biscuits at last. Got some green apples & peaches to-day that were very good.

July 31, Friday

SP: Got up early this morning & finished a letter to Mary. Took a good bath in Robinson *river* & changed clothes & on returning to camp was surprised to find the Regt. preparing to move. Papers to-day announce the death of Ho. W $^{\underline{m}}$. L. Yancey at his home near Montgomery, Ala.; & also the capture of Jno. H. Morgan (Gen.) in Ohio. We passed through Madison C.H. & went 4 ms. beyond, where we stopped for the night about 10 O'clock—making 6 miles.

NOTE: Yancey died July 28.

John Hunt Morgan surrendered at Salineville, Ohio, on July 26.

August 1, Saturday

SP: Took an early start & crossed the Rapidan on a covered bridge at Liberty Mills, 7½ ms. above Gordonsville. A half mile further on we left the pike & took the road to the left hand to Orange C.H. Being perfectly overcome with heat we stopped & rested in a piece of woods a short time, but soon started on. By the time we had gone a mile, however, the men were falling out so fast that we were marched out into the woods & took a good rest. We camped at 12½ P.M. in one mile of Orange C.H. having marched 15 ms. I think this is the hottest day I ever felt, & I was near fainting when we got to camp. Here we heard the whistle of the locomotive for the first time since leaving Culpeper on our way up to Md. & Pa., & it was responded to by a general shout of the soldiers. After lying down & taking a good rest, Davy, Matt & I went out & got a bait of fine large black berries. V $^{\underline{a}}$ abounds in black & dew berries & the largest I ever saw. They are a great treat to the soldiers &, as they make a change in diet, are beneficial to our health. We eat all the green apples we can get, too, & it is astonishing they don't make us sick. Wade R. Thomas transferred to our Co. from Co. "G".

August 2, Sunday

SP: This has been literally a day of rest with us. Almost every one after getting breakfast stretched out on his pallet to read the bible & the papers of yesterday which we were fortunate to get hold of, & then slept away a great portion of the day. Some few went out in the country & got dinner & vegetables, &c. John brought us a nice dinner of warm biscuits, bacon, snaps & Irish potatoes. It is reported that Gen. Stewart was whipped at Brandy Station yesterday.

August 3, Monday

SP: I am glad to find that instead of marching we will remain here again to-day. We have drawn a little sugar twice since we have been here. Got some little cakes from a sutler at $1. per Dozen that had scarcely any sugar in them. Wrote to Willie this evening. Got a pr. pants from the Quarter Master—price $10., I think.

August 4, Tuesday

SP: In the papers of yesterday there was an excellent & able address of the President to the soldiers of the Confederacy—calling upon all absentees to repair immediately to their respective commands, & granting pardon & amnesty to all absent without leave & under the charge of desertion (except those charged with having deserted twice), provided that they return to duty within 20 days from the publication of the address. He is confident of our final success, & says victory is within our grasp if every one will be at his post & do his duty. In a proclamation he appoints Friday, 21ˢᵗ Inst. a day of fasting, humiliation & prayer. I wrote to Mr. High this evening. We moved Camp—going through Orange C.H. to a nice piece of woods down the R.R. 2 ms. from town. Had the misfortune to lose my piece of tent. I lost one before, the night we waded the Potomac.

August 5, Wednesday

SP: Matt & I made a plate of corn battercakes for breakfast, which were elegant. Oh! if we could only have had some butter milk to drink with them. We have had meal issued for several days, & it is a pleasant change from flour. The Regt. moved 200 or 300 yds. to-day to be a little nearer water. The Florida has been playing havoc with Yankee merchantmen. She recently captured 4 within 60 ms. of New York. Edwd. Hutchinson returned from the Delevan Hospital at Charlottesville.

August 6, Thursday

SP: Henry Childress, Matt & I went to a house near by & got dinner. We had collards, beets, Irish potatoes, & big dish of fried apples, to all of which we did ample justice. Recd. a letter from Lou saying that all were well at home & that there are a great many travelers are on the road there—refugees from Mississippi.

August 7, Friday

SP: To-day seven years ago our family from Cousin Emma Hunt & Mr. Jno. Dix Weatherly, our private teacher, left home for a trip to the Vᵃ Springs. Commenced drilling to-day—Co. drill in morning & Battalion drill in evening. The Cars came up to-day & yesterday full inside & on top of soldiers. I am glad to see them coming. The army is growing stronger daily.

August 8, Saturday

SP: Put guard around the Brig. to-day, & I was on. Ellison came up with 2 loads of goods. We had rain this evening—making the fourth that it has rained in the same manner & the same time.

August 9, Sunday

SP: I stood 4 hours last night—from 8 to 12 P.M. Wrote a hurried letter to Lou. Matt & I took a good bath in the branch. John brought us over a first rate dinner—colards, Irish-potatoes, beets, cucumbers, etc. Recd. letter from Jamie, from which I am glad to learn that he has concluded to remain at home with Mama instead of going into the service.

August 10, Monday

SP: An order was read on Dress-parade yesterday evening that all men on detached service—as Commissary & Quarter Master's, Sergeants, clerks &c. must return to their Cos., & their places be filled by *disabled* soldiers. It is producing a good deal of fluttering amongst them, for don't relish the idea of giving up their easy berths & returning to the ranks. There are several from our Co.—Tucker, Jim Boardman, Jim D. Webb. Joe Grigg came over to see us to-day. We were mustered in to be paid off.

August 11, Tuesday

SP: Nothing of interest occurred in Camp to-day. Capt. Williams drilled the Battalion.

August 12, Wednesday

SP: *We were paid off to-day. As I was not with the Regt. last time it was paid, I recd. to-day 4 months' pay $44. & bounty $50. = $94.00. I had the pleasure of getting a long & affectionate letter from Mama.

*Tom F. Ward & Joe L. Wright promoted to 3 & 4$\underline{th}$ Corporals.

August 13, Thursday

SP: We are having excessively hot weather. In Richmond during the past 4 or 5 days the thermometer has stood at 98° in the shade. Matt Jones went foraging, but nothing but a peck of Irish-potatoes—for $2.50.

August 14, Friday

SP: A bold case of desertion took place in the 12$\underline{th}$ Ala. Regt. last night. Out of a Co. of 32 men 21 went off, with arms & accoutrements. Two squads went in pursuit of them with instructions to take them dead or alive if possible. Had a hard rain & wind storm this evening, that blew down some of the tents & wet every thing in them.

August 15, Saturday

SP: I wrote a letter to Icha yesterday to which I added a post script this morning & mailed it. Our Camp was put in order for Inspection. The tents of each Co. were put in a row. We policed quarters & cleaned up back of the Regt.

August 16, Sunday

SP: On guard to-day, Gen. Lee has introduced a system of furloughs—allowing 2 men out of every 100 for duty a furlough of 30 days, & on their return 1 from 100 will go. Six from our Regt. have drawn furloughs.

August 17, Monday

SP: Got some nice apples from Ellison: the first ripe ones I have seen. We had 2 water-melons @ $9. apiece, which are the first of that fruit I've seen this season. We had a great deal of policing to do this evening. Saw a copy of the "Southern Punch," recently gotten up in Richmond. It is quite funny.

NOTE: The first copy of *Southern Punch* (Richmond: Overall, Campbell, Hughes & Co.) had just been published two days before; the last edition came out February 13, 1865.

August 18, Tuesday

SP: We policed several hours this morning—cleaning up the woods & sweeping & burning leaves for a distance of 100 or 200 yards around the Regt. It is very dirty & disgusting work.

August 19, Wednesday

SP: Nothing of interest transpired in Camp to-day. I wrote to Lawless.

August 20, Thursday

SP: Capt. Williams' mess & Mat & I had a huge "Roly-Poly" or dried-Apple-bag-pudding for dinner, & it was delicious. Capt. W., Matt & I ate our first melon of the season to-night.

August 21, Friday

SP: *I finished & mailed a letter to Mama this morning. This being 'fast-day' five or six of our Co. got passes & went to Gen. Ewell's Hd. Qrs. where we heard a very excellent & encouraging sermon from Revd. Dr. Lacy. His text was 2nd Kings, 6th Chap., 16th vs. "For they that are with us are more than they that are with them." He exhorted us to have faith & be a better people. It was a very impressive service & I hope will do a great deal of good. Gens. Lee, Ewell, Rodes, Johnson, ½ dozen Brigadiers, scores of officers of lower grades & ten or 12 hundred soldiers composed the audience. And "last tho' not least" were some ladies—the wives & daughters of the officers. The newly married wife of Gen. Ewell—formerly Mrs. Brown of Tn—& her daughter were among the number. What a noble, venerable looking man is Gen. Lee. So easy & simple in his manners. After preaching, I saw him shaking hands & talking with little children. I returned to Rodes' Hd. Qrs. with Joe Grigg & spent the day with him, Gilliam & Pick. They have a good easy time of it—nothing to do but to ride around occasionally with orders. Joe drew a pr. of first rate English shoes, & let me have them. $8.75.

*Chris. C. Sheldon transferred to Co. "E", "Jeff. Davis Legion"—Cavalry.

NOTE: General Richard Stoddert Ewell married Mrs. Lizinka Campbell Brown in May 1863.

August 22, Saturday

SP: There was a large lot of clothing distributed to-day. Our Co. got 11 jackets, 18 pr. Pants. a no. of shirts & drawers & several prs. shoes & socks. The clothing was badly needed. I got a jacket & pr. pants. Matt & I had some elegant Apple-dumplings to-day. I recd. a long & interesting letter from Mary.

August 23, Sunday

SP: David Barnum with the squad who went to hunt deserters returned to-day. They caught 8 or 10, & had a right pleasant time. Davy had just recd. the appointment of acting master in the C.S. Navy & is making preparation to report in Richmond to-morrow. I recd. a long & highly interesting letter from Jamie & one from Louty. Capt. Williams, Sheb. Chadwick, Tom Ward, Peter Hagins, Henry Allen & I went to night preaching in the 6th Ala. Regt.

August 24, Monday

SP: Matt & I were invited to dine with Maj. Adams yesterday, but did not go. John brought over the best dinner I ever saw in Camp—okra, Gumbo, a variety of vegetables, fried chicken etc. Had Brigade drill this evening by Co. Hall. It is the first time I have ever been on one. Papers to-day state that Fort Sumter is almost battered down. The Yankee Gen.! Gillmore has thrown 12 shells into the city & demands the surrender of Sumter & Battery Wagner. Had a hard rain this evening that washed through the tent & wet our blankets.

August 25, Tuesday

SP: I finished a letter to Jamie that was commenced yesterday. Fifteen more shells have been thrown into Charleston no casualties resulted, however. Non-combatants are leaving the city very rapidly. Matt & I had apple-dumplings late to-night.

August 26, Wednesday

SP: Last night was quite cool & this morning, too; really fall-like. Capt. W^{ms}, Matt & I ate a water-melon this evening for which we gave $6. It was pretty good, but rather small for the price.

August 27, Thursday

SP: Brigade drill by Col. Battle. It is thought that he has been made our Brigadier. Our Brigade & Daniels' were reviewed this evening by Gen. Ewell, near his headquarters. He was dressed up much better than I ever saw him before. A Splendid sword & yellow sash & fancy saddle & bridle set him off to advantage. He is a good rider although he has a wooden leg. Gen. Rodes is a fine rider, too, & looked well on his splendid black—Maryland—horse. After our Brig. was reviewed we stacked arms & went up among the spectators to see Daniels' Brig. pass. There were several carriages full of ladies present & some young ladies on horseback. There was a Miss Ewell, niece of the Gen., who is said to be one of the most intelligent ladies in Va.; & a Miss Brown, his step daughter, who is quite pretty. There were some other very pretty ones whose names I did not learn. Judge Wm G. Jones came up to-day to see his son, Matt.

August 28, Friday

SP: Joe Grigg, came over & took dinner with us. Judge Jones dined with us, too. Joe & I went to Ellison's & ate a water-melon & some cakes, & cider. Capt. Williams, Matt & I ate another melon to-night that was the best I have seen.

August 29, Saturday

SP: On guard to-day. Just my luck to be on Sat. or Sund. & lose the holiday & not escape any drills by it.

August 30, Sunday

SP: Last night was very cool. Bill Sheldon & I made a fire on post which was alongside of the Co. & sat by it from 1 till 4 A.M. We cheated the 1st relief out of an hour, for they stood 5 hrs. Last night a large crowd of soldiers with the Brass band of Doles' Brig. serenaded Judge Jones & called for a speech. He was so taken by surprise that he made only a short address, in which he denied the report that there is a feeling in Ala. in favor of reconstruction & said that never before were the people more united & more determined to prosecute the war until our Independence shall be recognized by the enemy. He complimented this army very highly & says the whole country has the greatest confidence in it. We had a pretty little speech from Gen. Battle (former Col. of 3d Ala.) who has just recd. his commission as Brig. Gen. of our Brigade: & also one or two others. Matt left this morning with his father to spend 7 days in Amelia.

NOTE: Cullen A. Battle replaced Edward Asbury O'Neal as brigade commander due to the latter's poor performance at Gettysburg.

August 31, Monday

SP: Weather cool very. Lt. Jno. Christian got furlough of 30 days & will start for Ala. to-mor. morng. Sermon to night at 12th Ala.

September 1, Tuesday

SP: Begin. autumn & weather very cool & bracing. John came up fr. Richmd. this eveng. & brot. me 9 or 10$ worth fruit—but wh. was not much after all as its so exorbitantly high—4 canteloupes, some apps. Peaches & pears. Sent ½ to Maj. Adams. Cant. delightf—other fruit very inferior.

September 2, Wednesday

SP: There is a religious revival going on all thro'out the army, I believe, & the soldiers seem to take more interest in the preaching & prayer meetings held every night & on Sundays than usual. I had grt. pleasure of recvg. long & most interestg letter from Mama—1st Ive had fr home in 10 or 11 days. Extremely sorry to hear of death of Nela William in Choctaw Co. recently—Deaths of Gen. Dent, Lt. Bordens son & Mrs. Torberts child also mentioned in it. Country very sickly at home.

September 3, Thursday

SP: Paper states Price lately whipped the Yanx on White river (Ark.) & cap. 4 regts[.] Y. Price succeeded Lt. Gen. Holmes deceased, in Command. Mailed a letter to Mary this morng—10 pages note paper, rather long. Mr. Joe Elliot got to the Co. to-day.

NOTE: Theophilus Holmes did not die and Sterling Price did not succeed him until March 1864.

September 4, Friday

SP: Our Co were all very busily engaged to-day cleaning up our guns for Co. inspec. to-morrow. Those 5 of who have prettiest ones will be excused from guard duty & the balance of the Co made to do it all. Sumter & Wagner are holding out nobly; but Yanx are gradually approaching latter, working their way in ground like moles, & are now very near it.

September 5, Saturday

SP: Inspec. is over & the guns of abt ½ Co. were beautiful & passed—the others are to do all guard duty till theirs are as clean—wh all did that day[.] There were 10 deserters shot at Johnsons Divis. this eveng—some had to be shot several times.

September 6, Sunday

SP: I rode with Tom Moore this eveng. to a millpond 1 ½ ms. fr. Camp and witnessed for 1st time the process of baptising by immersion. Mr. Curry Color

Corp. wh. was ordained as Baptist minister today at Orange C.H. immersed 16 men.

September 7, Monday

SP: Went to Prayer Meeting this eveng. 6$\underline{th}$ Ala. These meetings are going on through the army & generally meeting with much success—many are professing religion & joining the church, not only in this army but in the Tennes. army also, I learn. Capt. W$\underline{ms}$ went up last night & joined the Epis. Ch. I think.

September 8, Tuesday

SP: On guard to day. Papers state Wagner evacuated & guns spiked. Recd letter fr. Mr. High—good deal sickness &c. Pickets Divis., Longstreets Corps, passed to-day going towds Gordonsville.

NOTE: After evacuation, Federal troops occupied Battery Wagner and Battery Gregg in Charleston Harbor on September 7.

September 9, Wednesday

SP: Heard wagons rattling along the road till 2 or 3 Oclk this morng. belong. to Longstreets Corps I suppose. Having come off guard this morn. I was not obliged to go to the review to-day, but was anxious to see it & also to see Tom Biscoe, & walked out there with Mr. Elliott, Bob Chadwick, Tom Ward & Henry Allen. It took place on large piece of open, undulating land east of Orange C.H. about 3 ms fr. Camp. Whole Corps present—drawn up by Divis. thus

Early's
Rodes
Johnsons

about ½ mile in leng. Grand sight. I would not have missed it for anything. Gens. Lee, Longstreet, Ewell & Hill; Early, Rodes, Johnson, Maj. Gen. Pendleton & innumberable Brig. Gens. also Gen. J.E.B. Stewart, Maj. Gen. Wilcox of Ala. Recd. letter from Mary.

September 10, Thursday

SP: Mailed letter to Willie that I wrote for John. Papers give account of night attack ½ past 1 A.M. yesterday morning on Sumter by Enemy & repulsed 3 stands Colors 4 barges, & 115 men captured. Battery Wagner wh. we evacuated two or 3 days ago garrisoned by 54 Regt. mass. negro troops.

September 11, Friday

SP: There was an inspec. of A.P. Hill's Corps to-day. Would like to have witnessed it but only 5 men allowed to go from Regt. & they had got passes ahead of me. I requested Matt J. to get list of Brigades in it & no. Regts. in each. As he was taking the list he was reported to Hill who had him arrested & after review saw him about it & told him & another, doing the same that they were indulging idle curiosity & must not do it. He took away their lists & dismissed them. We all had it as a good joke on Matt being arrested as a Spy.

September 12, Saturday

SP: Very warm day. Commencd letter to Mama but was too late for the mail & laid it aside. Mrs. Forsythe dined with Gen. Battle to-day at his tent.

September 13, Sunday

SP: I went by Rodes' & went on to Orange C.H. with Joe Grigg to Episcop. Church. Gen<u>l</u> Pendleton preached a sort of improvised sermon, as Bishop who was expected failed to come[.] Gen. Ewell was to have been confirmed. House crowded. Sat close to Gen. A.P. Hill. Smaller & more slender man than I thought. Determined looking man with keen, clear eye. Saw Maj. Gen. Heth & his wife: nice looking couple. When we returned to Rodes heard the Yankees were crossing in large force of Cavalry at several fords of Rapidan & orders were sent round to be in readiness to move. It was grt. surprise to everyone. began to think there would be no more fighting up here for some time. Attended preaching at 6 Ala. Regt. good sermon & had grt. many mourners & 10, I think, professed religion.

September 14, Monday

SP: Drum called us up at 3 this morning & got ready to march. Started at day light & marchd hard & fast about 15 or 16 ms. to Summerville Ford—Rapidan R. Excessively hot day & we rested only 3 times. Cannon firing & we expected to go right into a fight but were happy to find none of enemy a cross the river, & only Cav. & artil. to be seen on the other side. Artillery duel took place in wh. we lost 18 or 20 men killed & wounded. Gilliam's horse was grazed by piece shell under him. This eveng. a red fox was started & caught by the soldiers who managed to head him & run him around in a field & finally one knocked him over & caught him. 1<u>st</u> Red fox I recollect ever to have seen—'twas about the size of a common gray fox & was young, not near grown.

September 15, Tuesday

SP: There was some cannonading along the river to-day. We moved into woods & fixed up bunks as it was probable we would stay several days. Walked down towards the river where there is a very pretty & extensive view.

September 16, Wednesday

SP: Our Divis. was carried out to see a deserter executed: a member of 2<u>nd</u> N.C. Reg. Ramsur's Brig. A Chaplain prayed with him & then he was blindfolded—his hands tied behind his back, & kneeling was fastened to a stake. In a few moments more the command "fire" was given & ½ Dozen or more musket balls passed thro' his breast—killing him instantly. When we got back to Camp we heard of a daring little adventure that took place down at the ford (Summerville). 20 men volunteered & went over to burn & run out 100 or 200 Yankees—Killed one & captured 2. (guns &c) Wrote to Mama to-day, finished letter commenced on 12<u>th</u>. Heard excellent address to Brig. Chris. Associat. by Rev. Dr. Rosser, of V<u>a</u>.

September 17, Thursday

SP: Comm. Childress & Cunny James spent part of the day with our Co. to-day. Cunny has improved very much. He has a very pretty little horse & is delighted with Cavalry.

September 18, Friday

SP: It rained last night & till 9 or 10 Oclock this morning. A deserter came over last night & says there are 4 Corps opposite us & intended crossing this morning. Started 'bout 1 O'clk & marched down to Morton's ford where Doles was on Picket. Evening made advance as if to cross to-day. We were in a hard shower, that made road slippery & bad for marching. Formed in line battle & prepared to spend night there—built fires & dried off.

September 19, Saturday

SP: Last night we cooked some roasting ears for supper, & this morning great quantities of corn was brought in & eaten to-day, most of the men being out of rations. About 1 or 2 P.M. [we] were moved forward to the line on the ridge that we were to occupy in the event of a fight. Our Regt. rested in a perfect thicket. We went to work & built breastworks of fine logs that had been formerly cut down in clearing up the place & in an hour we had logs piled up of sufficient height & thickness. Then late in eveng. McDiarmid & Young Idom who had been out in the country & pressed a pick & shovel returned, & went to work & dug a trench & threw dirt up over logs & by 11 Oclock P.M. when we quit we had quite strong work—good defence. We have had another very warm spell but last night we had slight rain & weather changed very cool. Mat & I did not have tent up & blankets got wet & we were so cold we slept very badly. Had delightful dream of being at home last night. Thought Jamie was complaining of having to sleep on pallet made of comforts spread on the floor & told if he could only see the places we have to sleep on in army he would think that a splendid bed &c. New boots &c &c.

September 20, Sunday

SP: Instead of being waked up by the roar of Cannon &c. wh. we thought very probable—we found it a beautifully clear & delightful day, a quiet, serene, lovely Sabbath morning & everything quiet. It was so cold last night that I slept very little. We got the Beacon to-day containing some account of what is going on in Greene. Yesterday Mat recd. telegram fr. his father saying he had got appointmt of Cadet in C.S.A. for him & wanted him to go home. Deserter came over a day or 2 ago & stated the Yankee force across the river was heavy—4 Corps, & a spy of Gen. Lee's reported to have got in, states their force opposed to us as 7 Corps. Their corps are much smaller than ours.

September 21, Monday

SP: This morning there was a white frost on the ground & weather really wintry. Last night Matt & I took down tent & spread it & oilcloth on the ground before fire & covered with both blankets. We slept very comfortably & had much better nights rest than we have had since the change in weather. Worked on breast works again to-day—& strengthened it considerably. Works are complete all along the lines & we are well prepared for enemy should he cross here. Miles Pickens who has been home on furlough came to my tent with Cassius Smith this evening & we had a pleasant talk. A Frenchman of 3^d Ala. Regt. deserted yesterday & went to Yankees.*

*(To-day is the Autumnal Equinox.)

September 22, Tuesday

SP: Had pleasure of receiving this morning a very long & interesting letter from My dear Mama. Sorry to hear that she & Jamie had had severe spells of sickness but both had recovered their health again. There never was a more sickly season in our section before. At Umbria & both plantations great deal sickness among the negroes—scarcely enough well to attend to the sick. Hope they will soon have cool weather to put stop to bilious fever. Moved from breastworks into piece pines near by. I wrote letter to Jamie—pretty long one. There has been tolerably rapid cannonading this eveng above here. supposed to be Cavalry fight about Madison C.H. where we hear Stewart fought them yesterday. Just recd. cheering news fr. West—Bragg has defeated Rosencranz—capturing 2500 prisoners & 20 pieces cannon, & is pursuing him. Hope it may prove true.*

*Matt recd discharge fr. Sec. War & went over to Maj. Adams & will go to Richmd to morrow. He is ordered to report to Maj. Gen. Maury in Mobile.

NOTE: "Matt" is Matthew Jones.

September 23, Wednesday

SP: Took ramble hunting chincapins & grapes but found none. Got some good Peaches & apples fr. Sutler to-day. Cannon heard again this eveng. Our Regt goes on picket late in eveng.

September 24, Thursday

SP: Late yesterday evening our Regt. came down here (Morton's house) & after dark moved out near the river where we slept without fire—as support of the pickets. Never spent such a night in my life—was so cold that could not sleep & was cramped up. It seemed longest night I ever saw—Oh! it was *miserable* & I was very glad when we got up before day & moved back in rear of house where we soon had rousing fires & warmed up. I was on guard at 1 of old out houses. Paper of yesterday states the fight at Chicamauga Ga. progressing very favorably for us. They had been fighting terribly for 3 days, & Bragg had driven Rosencrans back captured 9 or 10,000 pris. about 70 Cannon, Our loss very heavy but enemys thought to be much heavier. Our loss in Gens partic. severe *Killed.* Brig. Gens. Preston Smith—Tenn. Wofford—Ga, Walthall—Miss. Helms—Ky, Deshler—Ala. & Maj. Richmond of Polks staff. *Wounded.* Maj. Gens. Hood—Tex, Preston—Ky, Cleburn—Ark. & Brig. Gens. Gregg, Renning Bunn, J. C. Brown, & Dan! Adams. = 5 Brig. Gens. killed & 3 Maj. Gens & 5 Brig. Gens wounded. Yank Gen. Little—kld. Ed. Hutch, Bill Kennedy & I went down to river & caught 3 little perch. very small stream & not leg deep. Were relieved & returned to Camp just before night.

NOTE: The Battle of Chickamauga, September 19–20, was a tactical, if bloody, victory for the Confederates, who forced the Union troops to withdraw to Chattanooga. Union killed and wounded estimated at 11,413, Confederate at 16,986.

September 25, Friday

SP: Papers to day contain very little additional particulars from Chicamauga—tho' Bragg was getting on finely & probability of capturing whole army as we had got between them & Chatt. I trust it may so result. Recd. a short letter fr. Mary.

September 26, Saturday

SP: News fr. Bragg falls short of what we have been getting. His last telegram stated 7000 Pris. of whom 2000 wd., 36 Cannon 15000 small arms, & 26 stands Colors. Wrote letter to Lou & recd one fr. Mary. Making Syrup & wine at home & having Brandy distill. at Stringfellows.

September 27, Sunday

SP: Heard 2 sermons today & 1 tonight. 2 fine ones fr. Rev. Mr.———of Ala. Sat little while with Col. Pickens who has had several chills.

September 28, Monday

SP: Just mailed letter to Lou this morng. Took good wash at branch & changd. clothes. Slept none scarcely last night.

September 29, Tuesday

SP: On picket again at M. Fd. I'm really losing grt. deal rest for its so cold that sleep very little at night & I cant sleep in day to make it up. Delightful day—very still & quiet down here. Wade T. swapped tobacco for nice little knife with Yank pickets & some boys have got coffee & late papers. I saw Wash. Chron. 27$^{\underline{th}}$ & there was Harpers Weekly, too. Returnd to Camp this eveng.

NOTE: "Wade T." is Wade Thomas.

September 30, Wednesday

SP: Everything going on as usual. Rept in Camp that Gen Lee has news too good [. . .]

October 1, Thursday

SP: Chas Hafner & Glover got here to-day. W. broke leg & been absent ever since last Feb. & Ch. wound. prisoner at Chan. May last. They had lots of news fr. Greene. Poor Joe Wright died there of Congestion chill on 16$^{\underline{th}}$. Ed. H. bro. Joe killed in bat. Chickmauga & Col. Lt. Inge. Tom Herndon wd. John Brown & Alf. Moore killed. Joe Brown has got to Richmd. in good spirits & walking bout on crutches. Jno. Chris. & Brit will be here in few days.

NOTE: "Ed. H." is E. T. Hutchinson, brother of Joseph Hutchinson and son of the Reverend J. J. Hutchinson.
"Brit." is William G. Britton.

October 2, Friday

SP: Today there is a change in the weather from the most beautiful spell of clear bracing weather I 'most ever saw. Rained most of the eveng. Chris Sheldon & Nor. Jackson spent day with this Co.

October 3, Saturday

SP: I am on guard to-day, & McCrary & Rinke. Regt went on Picket this eveng. We remained on guard round Brig. 3$^{\underline{d}}$ Ala. found out the good news T.

Watts wrote fr. Richmd. to Maj. of 3$^{\underline{d}}$ Recog. in 30 & Peace in 90 days. Wild rumor afloat in army.

October 4, Sunday

SP: Heard sermon fr. Dr. Rosser & went over & dined with Joe[,] Gill & Pick. Glover over there too. Sevl. Cannon fired to day at Yank forage trains over river. Did not know what it meant at first.

NOTE: "Gill" is Gilliam James.

"Pick" is James Pickens Moore.

October 5, Monday

SP: Reg. inspec orders came to be ready to move at min. notice—that enemy movg in heavy force on Earlys left. Som. ford. Wrote letter to Mary. Heard sermon this & last night. Weather again settled clear & cold.

October 6, Tuesday

SP: Got letter fr. Mary this morng. all well at home. Ben Sadler came. Drilled yest eve & 2ce to day[.] Cap. excus. 6 more fr guard, leaving only 10 to stand in Regt—strict

NOTE: Beginning October 9, the Guards, as part of the Fifth Alabama, skirmished with George Meade's Army of the Potomac in the Warrenton area. With nothing to show, Rodes' division returned to their old camp along the Rapidan near Raccoon Ford.

November 6, Friday

JST: Nothing to note since the 27th. In camp and quiet.

November 7, Saturday

JST: Yankees disturbed our quiet to day by shelling our Camps and crossing the river. Captured nearly all of the 30th N.C. Regt which was on picket at Kelleys Ford. Got orders & moved in train to Brandy Sta. where we stoped a short time, & then travelled all night long. Dident get to close my eyes.

November 8, Sunday

JST: Traveled on to day until we crossed the Rapidan River at Rapidan Sta.— then Camped until night when orders came to move down to Mo[r]tons Ford, which required nearly all night and makes two nights that I have had no sleep at all. Got to our old Camp just at day brake.

November 9, Monday

JST: Slept nearly all day to day. Got a horse and moved on it.

November 10, Tuesday

JST: All quiet. Very Cold. Had the first snow of the season to day.

November 11, Wednesday

JST: Some skirmishing to day. Several of our men wounded & one killed. Wrote to Annie.

November 12, Thursday

JST: Weather fine. Every thing dull & quiet.

November 13, Friday

JST: Every thing goes on as usual

November 26, Thursday

JST: Nothing to note since my last entry. Yankees reported crossing at Germanna Ford. Got orders to be ready to move.

NOTE: This marks the beginning of the Mine Run Campaign.

November 27, Friday

JST: Left Mortons Ford at 2 O'clk this morning & went to Willisville where every thing was halted & the army drawn up in line of battle. heavy skirmishing all day

November 28, Saturday

JST: Position of affairs still the same—throwing up earth works. Moved back on the plank Rd. with the wagon trains

November 29, Sunday

JST: Every thing still remains the same. Bad roads & bitter cold weather. Got a letter from Annie.

December 4, Friday

SP: A Mr. Smith of So.Ca.—neighbor of Col & Capt. Pickens—& who was at U. V$^{\underline{a}}$. when Jamie & I were there—came round distribut. tracts. He recognized me as I did him—& enquired after Jamie. Our Regt. went on Picket to-day—our Co. on post along river above Ford. There was a pretty smart fight up towds. Raccoon Fd. between some of our pickets who had crossed over & cavalry pickets of Yanks. A few shells thrown fr. our side. Most all Co. "D" got on a glorious tight to-day—on rum that they got at $20 a bottle. Some were very amusing.

December 5, Saturday

SP: There were 8 on my post & we had only 1 hr. each to stand at night. I was to stand last but day nearly came before they waked me & then all had to get up. Another little fight up river this morng. I took wash in river yest. eveng when there was stiff breeze blowing down river—it was *very cold* indeed. Were relieved & returned to Camp this eveng.

December 6, Sunday

SP: Recd very long & most interestg letter fr. Mama this morng. Glad to learn fr. it that Tom Biscoe was not taken prisoner. Charley & Tom have both been slightly wounded. Mama has bought buggy for $400. & engaged Carriage to be made by And. Johnson for $700. Wrote Tom a note & sent John with shoes, socks, package & a letter that came fr. Umbria for him. Weather is very cold.

December 7, Monday

SP: I am on guard to-day—2nd relief. Lt. Birney officer guard. John came back with very kind & grateful note fr. Lou. Commenced letter to Jamie but so cold that did not write much.

December 8, Tuesday

SP: Papers to-day give account of meeting of 3$^{\underline{d}}$—& last session of 1st Confed. Congress yesterday—Quorum in both houses. Pres. Miss. not ready—but will be ready to-day at 12M. Yankee Congress meets to-day also would that these 2 bodies could come to some terms leading to cessation hostilities & estab. of Peace! Finished letter to Jamie & mailed it to-night.

December 9, Wednesday

SP: I wrote a letter to Mama to send by John who went over to Maj. Adams this eveng. & will go on home with Dr. Adams to-morrow. Sent last of Cherry seed that I got at Papertown, Pa. fr. finest fruit I ever saw. Went down to see Miles Pickens & met the Col. there too. I find myself in very low spirits & home-sick at seeing John start home to spend Xmas there—when that inexpressible pleasure is denied me. Oh! what wd. I give to be as free to go there as John is!!

December 10, Thursday

SP: There is suspension of all duty to-day, as it has been appointed a day of fasting by Gov. Brown of Ga. & he wanted the Army, Navy & Confed. Congress to unite in it. An order requesting its observance was read on Dress parade last eveng. Read to-day Pres. Davis' message. It is a very lengthy document. He discussed fully the very unjust & unfriendly way the British Gov. has treated us, while professing neutrality she has done everything to favor North & injure the South.

December 11, Friday

SP: Bob Chadwk has been detailed to act recorder for Court Martial. It will be good thing as twill prob. hold all winter & exempt him fr. all duty with the Co. The members of the Co. who were in Gettysbg. fight voted a roll of honor to poor Tean Nutting, bout a week ago, who was killed in that fight July 1st.

December 12, Saturday

SP: Recd. letter fr. Louty—all well. She mentioned that Miss Annie Pearson was married to a Cap. Patton on 29th Ult. Clothing issued to-day. Troops are all very well supplied now. Ellison brot. up 2 or 3 loads to-day & as usual we invested in cakes & apples.

December 13, Sunday

SP: Had hard wind & some rain last night, but this morn is cleared off very prettily & is very mild—uncommonly so for the season. This is anniversary of battle of Fredksbg. wh. was 1st time I was ever under fire. Recd. a letter from Willie this morning. He says he has written to me 2 or 3 times since I wrote to him, but none of his letters have been recd. by me. I went on picket this eveng. We picket by detail from Brigade now instead of by Regts.

December 14, Monday

SP: Had right disagreeable time last night on guard as was on 3d Relief & went to post between 3 & 4 A.M. Very dark & road muddy; rained a little. Were relieved & came to Camp at 10.

December 15, Tuesday

SP: Jack Wynne, Hausman & I took a wash in creek, mountain run, this evening. Water very cold. Before war would never have thought of doing such a thing as bathing in creek in middle Decr. I found Capt. Miles Pickens a little sugar this morning—not much tho'.

December 16, Wednesday

SP: Jack is laid up to-day with fever—no doubt brot on by his exposure yesterday. nothing much going on. Rumor that our Brig. is going to swap with Clanton's Brig. & go to Pollard Ala.

December 17, Thursday

SP: Awoke this morning & found it raining, & continued all day long—the coldest rain I ever felt. Only way of keeping at all comfortable was to go to bed & cover up. Recd. letter from Jamie. Jack W. got letter saying Bill Ferrell was taken prisoner in battle Chattanooga & Jim Brown wounded—prob. mortally—2 of the Colemans wounded & 1 a prisoner also.

NOTE: "Jack W." is John Wynne.

December 18, Friday

SP: Recd. letter fr. Louty. Sorry to hear Mrs Sawyer, Sr. very ill. Peter Hagins & Young Idom left for home this morning on 30 days furlough.

December 19, Saturday

SP: I'm on Camp guard to-day. The weather is very cold. Cap. Furgusson, comdg. Regt. excused guard to night at 7 P.M. as weather is so severe. Been wanting to write home but bad weather & cold has prevented.

December 20, Sunday

SP: Got up at day light & put my relief on. On notice of ½ hour we got ready & started at 11 O'c we heard to go to Winter Qrs. but as we had orders to come off quietly so as not to be observed by Yanx. & as Lt. Hutchinson an aid de C. of Rodes said he did not know where we were going & strict orders to rear guard Co. "D" acting about straggling, we were very much of opinion that we were starting out on another flank movement. We marched very rapidly & as ground was hard frozen & very rough, it was fatiguing in extreme. Halted at place selected for our Brig. on plank road about a mile fr. Dr. Terrell's & 6 fr. Orange C.H. having come 12 or 14 miles. Got letter fr. Mary telling of death of poor old Mrs. Sawyer on 9th inst. at 1 O'clk at night & also that Capt. Wright was mortally wounded in battle of Chattanooga, both of wh. I was extremely sorry to hear. I took supper with Capt. Williams mess to night—rations being out at home.

December 21, Monday

SP: Went to work bright & early this morning getting timber for our Winter Cabins & before (late) brkfst had all the logs cut. Got pine logs large enough to split in two. Worked very hard all day & had logs all brot. up & started putting up house. Excessively cold weather—every thing hard frozen—even the timber.

December 22, Tuesday

SP: Worked like beavers all day to-day again & at 12 had house up entirely— then set to work getting board timber wh. had to toat up some distance, after night.

December 23, Wednesday

SP: Our forces considbly weakened to-day as Jack & Henry on guard & Bob gone to Court martial. However rest labored faithfully but could not accomplish much for want of frow. Timber very indifferent. Found ground cov (this morn) ered with snow good but soon stopped. Drew very good jacket to day—dark steel—mixed. Went over to Qr. master's & got fit—with Bill Sheldon. Made first fire in new fire place to dry it & by light of it I wrote a letter to Mary, wh. been anxious to do for a week past. Recd one fr. Louty.

December 24, Thursday

SP: Chinked & planked house & fixed chimney place while Carter—[. . .] went after more board timber. About 3 p.m. Jack & I took [. . .] leave & with Tom Ward went to Maj. Websters who had invited us over to Dine. He had an elegant dinner—baked turkey, ham & Cabbage & pototoes, genuine coffee & sugar &c. wh. we enjoyed exceedingly & did ample justice to. To-night Col. P. sent for me to drink eggnog with him & had very pleasant time indeed. I helped beat it & we succeeded in making it first rate. As theres nothing I like better of course I enjoyed it. Col. Goodgame, Maj. Proscow, Maj. Webster, Miles P & others present & spent most aggreeable evening. Returned to qrs. & found all handy wrapped in arms of Morpheus.

NOTE: "Col. P" is Samuel B. Pickens.

December 25, Friday

SP: Had all my Xmas on Xmas eve for worked hard to-day in order to complete house wh. did—including fixing bunks filld with straw &c ready to sleep in to night. We are first ones in Co to get in house too. Was invited to dine at Col. P's hd. qrs with Lt. Col. Maj. &c but as Sam & Miles were going to be absent at dinner party was Orange C.H. I declined doing so. Mess had Oysters for dinner tho wh. cost 18$ pr. gallon now.

December 26, Saturday

SP: Recd letter fr. Mat. Jones saying I could get place in signal corps in Maj Gen. Sam Jones command in West Va. & his father would secure it for me immediately if I'd accept it, &c getting transfer to his uncle too. Wrote letter to Jamie & went with Jack to carry it to Maj. Webster & sat & talked with him till (& Glover) 9 or 10 clk.

December 27, Sunday

SP: Maj. W.[,] Chas. Pegues, Pick M.[,] Jno. Tucker & Col Pickens left this morng on furlough home. Col P. going to Ala. also. Tood Cowin expected to be of party but disappointed. Capt. W. left yest. & will wait in Rich. for rest. Rained slowly all day. [. . .] of Flour, 2 or rice sug. & coffee & 5 of salt for 16 men, & John Warren lugged it all the way back a mile or more by ourselves. Recd. a letter fr. Louty—a dear little correspondent she writes so often. All well in the family. Genie U. going to be married to Dr. Seals in Choctaw. Mr Damar's son, poor boy died of consumption at Demopolis.

NOTE: James Pickens would marry Juliet Damer April 1, 1865.

December 28, Monday

SP: After being frozen for about 10 days the ground has at last been thawed by the rain of yest. & last night & is perfectly sloppy. Carter, Henry Childress & I took some timber over to the wagon yard, borrowed tools & made camp-stools. In crossing a branch the pole broke with me & down I went into water near 3 ft. deep & it was very cold. I dried off tho almost before going back to my house with exception of my socks.

December 29, Tuesday

SP: On guard to day. There's another order from Gen! Lee now—granting 4 men furloughs to every 100 present for duty & as our Rgt. nos. 400 we can furl. 16 at once. 8 are now gone home, so 8 more will leave now. The order in addition to this allows an extra furl. to every Co. that has 50 arms bearing men present. Cos. H. & [. . .] have that no:—so there will be 10 more furloughs fr. the Regt.

December 30, Wednesday

SP: Wrote to Dr. Grigg last night & was at it till about 2 this morng. & had to go relief on at 5 & stood at it till guard mounting—9 AM, so slept only bout 3 hrs. Made it by sleeping all evening—wh. is uncommon for me. Recd. a long & most interesting lettr fr. Mama. Find a bundle containing clothes for me & Tom Biscoe sent by Lt. J. Ed. Webb last spring was lost. 1st Ive heard of it. Lt. Pompey Jones who has been on road ever since 1st of month just got in to-night, with perfect cargo of boxes—I got box of Candy dried figs &c & hdkfs & bundle for Biscoe. Hausman box also. We will have some Xmas after all. Gen. Battle & Bill Kennedy who have been on furlough (six got back).

December 31, Thursday

SP: Sat up quite late last night to finish "No Name—Wilkie Collins["]—very singular novel & very interesting, plot very ingenious. Jack Huggins & Childress had night mare fr. eating so much last night & wondr all had not suffered in same way. Feasted to day on Candy Pound Cake figs &c. fr. home—Things that dont accord with every thing else about us as soldiers in least. Were mustered in for pay to-day. Meat rations suspended & in lieu drew 48 grs. coffee ½ spoonful sugar & some dried fruit. These extras not issued to the officers tho'. Counted the grs of coffee as the only way of dividing it—such small quantity. Its best little Confed. can do now but "There's a better time coming", tho' we trust. The last of the old year & a trying one it has been too—Thank God I am one of the fortunates who have been spared to see it close. May the new one bring with it brighter prospects of a speedy & glorious termination of this terrible war!

NOTE: *No Name*, by Wilkie Collins, was first published in 1862 in London and Philadelphia.

1864

January 1, Friday

SP: This is the birth day of another year—the 4th one of the War; & God grant that it may be the last. May the weather to-day which is bright & sunny—a pleasant change from the last ones of the past (old) year, be typical of a happy improvement in our national affairs. Wrote a long letter to Mat Jones. Jack & Harry been engaged all day in composing, revising, correcting & transcribing a letter to a young lady—& after all I believe are afraid to send it.

January 2, Saturday

SP: Recd this morng. a very long letter fr. Jamie—in wh. he expressed his intentions of coming on to this Co. & asking my advise in the matter. Very cold day—policed quarters, cutting up stumps & piling brush.

January 3, Sunday

SP: Joe Grigg came over & sat some time. His advice to Gilliam's & all my friends is to accept the signal place by all means, as I dislike leaving Co to go among strangers dont know what to do about it tho. Answered J's letter & recommended that he join Cavalry at Pollard Ala.

January 4, Monday

SP: Snowed lightly all day—nothing doing. Read some of "Persons I have met", N. P. Willis & "Royal Ape". Dramatic poem lately pub. poor thing & very vulgar.

NOTE: *People I Have Met; or, Pictures of Society and People of Mark, Drawn under a Thin Veil of Fiction* by Nathaniel Parker Willis was first published in 1849 in New York.

William Russell Smith, *The Royal Ape: A Dramatic Poem* (Richmond: West & Johnston, 1863). Smith was a prominent politician, lawyer, and writer from Greensboro and Tuscaloosa.

January 5, Tuesday

SP: Miles P. came & sat with us this morng. It took me nearly all day to sew stripes (Corp.) on my new Jacket. I made a nice job of it tho'.

January 6, Wednesday

SP: A dull, drowsy day & looks like its going to snow. Tried to read Aurora Floyd—but was too sleepy (to do much) & lazy.

NOTE: Mary Elizabeth Braddon, *Aurora Floyd; A Domestic Story; From "Temple Bar"* (Richmond: West, 1863).

January 7, Thursday

SP: The morning being bright & pretty I borrowed Miles Ps' horse & went round—got pass signed & struck out to hunt Tom Biscoe. Had good luck to overtake a man going down to Early's Divis. who knew the way. Had it not been for that Id had much trouble in finding Tom as his Brig. is in very out of way place. It clouded up & wind blew right in my face making it very cold indeed. Was much disappointed to find Tom away on C. Martial. He came in late tho, & I dined with him & started back just before night. The road being rather intricate & night dark—cold & snow falling—my ride back was most disagreeable & had to give reins to horse & trust his finding way back. Went on over to Miles' Qrs. & sat with him till bed time. Feet ached some time after getting there. Biscoe told me they've been getting meat only 1ce in 3 days & only enough for a meal then. Had for dinner light bread, Irish potatoes fried & seasoned with onions & pepper, & corn coffee without sugar—no meat at all. We filled up on apples after dinner tho. They are so far fr. RR is reason of such scant rations.

January 8, Friday

SP: The ground is wrapped in an immaculate sheet of snow, about 3 in. thick. this morng. Ch. Hafner, Ward, self & Webb—all Corps. for Co. "D" are on guard to-day. Relieved to-night. A sad scene was ended today in presence of Divis. wh. was drawn up to witness it—vis the execution of 12 deserters fr. Daniels' N.C. Brig. I on guard escaped seeing it. Must have been a grand but gloomy picture. They were shot 2$\underline{ce}$ before being killed. "All bloodless lay the untrodden snow" but twas soon stained with the life blood of these unfortu. men & became "Their winding sheet" & the 'sod beneath their feet, soldiers sepulchres'.

January 9, Saturday

SP: Our Brig. went on picket to Mortons Ford abt 10ms. early this morng. I was excused by Col Hall last evening, but so many men with bad shoes that Battle orderd all to go not "actually barefooted." However, I got permission to remain till Mond. as Tom B. is to spend day with me tomorrow. Wrote letter to Willie as Huggins & I left in house & good chance to write—there being no noisy crowd about us. Ed. Hutch & I went to Rodes' this eve & I supped & spent eveng with Joe G & couriers.

January 10, Sunday

SP: Hug.[,] Bob & I cooking all day getting up good dinner for Tom Bis. but unfor. for him he didn't come. Ed. Hutch dined with us. Had nice hoe cake & hopping John & peach pies. Went away over to Maj. Websters & drew 4 da. rations.

NOTE: "Bob" is Robert A. Chadwick.

January 11, Monday

SP: I concluded as Id have no duty to go down on Picket that I would not take the long & wearisome tramp down there. There's no use in it. Wrote to Mat Jones telling him I'd accept the place in Signal Corps, as all my friends here urge me to do so by all means. I'm most afraid to send the letter now, as I have no inclination to leave this old command, & would not be surprised if yet I decline going.

January 12, Tuesday

SP: It is very dull in camp now that the Brig. is on Picket. We go about from one house to another to get together & talk—to pass off time. I am reading Aurora Floyd too, which is interesting but I get along very slowly with it.

January 13, Wednesday

SP: Bob Chad. goes out to get a bed fellow—while Noah Huggins & I sleep together in my bunk & never get up till about 9 O'Clock & then make a fire & get breakfast. We feel more like white folks than ever before in army, as there's no drum to drag us up to answer to roll call at day light as is generally the case. Will Britton & Paul Lavender came to-day. Brit. look only tolerably well. Not 1 man in 100 would have ever recovered after being wound. as severely as he was: 'twas pronounced mortal by Dr. Hill & no one thought he could possibly recover. They represent people at home having gay time & not seeming to feel or care about the war at all. Altho' everything is so enormously dear they dress as fine & live as well as far as is possible as ever they did. The boys saw Gen. Jno. H. Morgan in Richmd. He is the city's guest & a perfect Lion. The highest honors & every attention are paid the distinguished hero & intrepid soldier, showing how much sympathy is felt for him for having been treated so harshly & ignominiously by the Yankees—having his head shaven &c, & then for his wonderful & hazardous escape. He says he is going to have a barber in every Regt. of his command & does not intend to die in debt to the Yankees.

January 14, Thursday

SP: Everything is perfectly dull & monotonous about camp, & we miss the boys very much. Bob. Chad, Noah Huggins & I had a big hopping-John for dinner, but unfortunately burnt it: however, it did n't seem to be any the less popular for that mishap.

January 15, Friday

SP: We don't get the mail here as it is carried on pickets before it is opened, & we never see a paper. Huggins made some of the best bread for supper I ever saw—meal & flour mixed with bacon grease & the cracklings in it. O! if we had only had some nice thick, rich buttermilk to have washed it down with—twould have been most excellent, or in Camp parlance "bully"!!

January 16, Saturday

SP: I wrote a letter to Mama, & Recd. one fr Jamie—a very lengthy & entertaining one—10½ pages large letter paper. brot. up fr. the River by Chris Hausman. The Regt. returned late in evening having had a most fatiguing & disagreeable march back; the roads having thawed & become very muddy. They say the Rapidan was frozen over thickly & there was skating going on by some La. soldiers who understood the art & had skates.

January 17, Sunday

SP: As Maj. Bryant is going home on furlough he had to pay us off to-day. There was some mistake in pay rolls wh. required several hours to rectify. Mean time Co "D" with detailed & extra duty men assembled there to draw their pay passed time very agreeably, talking, laughing, playing practical jokes, tusseling &c. Its as nice & jolly a crowd as you can find any where when the Co with its old members get together. Glover extended a general invitation to the boys to dine with him & seemed a little "got" by a whole crowd taking him at his word & going. He had an abundant table tho' & gave them all enough to eat. We drew clothing commutation money also & I got $130.13. 2 mos. wages past & commut. for clothes for 1 year ending Oct. 8$\underline{th}$ 1863. Dick Simons arrived in Camp this evening.

January 18, Monday

SP: Dull rainy weather. Rained most all day. Nothing transpired worthy of recording.

January 19, Tuesday

SP: Policed Qrs. raked up leaves, chips &c & carried them off. rained more last night & ground is now very sloppy & disagreeable for walking. It blew up a strong wind this eveng. & is turning very cold again.*

(*Finished Aurora Floyd by M. E. Braddon—a very interesting novel indeed. For the last 4 days we have had meat at only 2 meals & a very scanty allowance then. We draw a little sugar & Coffee occasionally & sometimes Lard.)

January 20, Wednesday

SP: Wrote a letter to Lou last night answering 4 fr. the darling little correspondent—all wh. have been recd. since I wrote to her. Had very cold & disagreeable work in shape of Policing Co. Qrs. to-day—burning brush, cutting up stumps &c

January 21, Thursday

SP: On guard to day. 2 Prisoners in G. house Co. A for refusing to cut up stumps, wh. is now the punishment for being absent fr. roll call. Antony Bayley's boy ran off to-day. He is believed to have stolen Mr. Elliotts watch a very good gold watch, for wh. he was offered 1250.$\underline{00}$ recently, & when they took him out to whip & make him give it up, he jerked loose & ran away.

January 22, Friday

SP: P. Hagins & Toney Idom got back fr. home last night looking very well. Peter & Tom Ward went to Orange C.H. to day after boxes of Provisions, but had not come up fr. Richmond.

January 23, Saturday

SP: Read a biography of Stonewall Jaxon to-day, by Chas. Hallock. Some slight inaccuracies are to be found in it but it's very interesting—as everything must be relating to that great, good, universally beloved hero.

NOTE: Charles Hallock, *A Complete Biographical Sketch of "Stonewall" Jackson, Giving a Full and Accurate Account of the Leading Events of His Military Career, His Dying Moments, and the Obsequies at Richmond and Lexington* (Augusta, Georgia: Steam Power-Press Chronicle and Sentinel, 1863).

January 24, Sunday

SP: Heard a sermon at Masonic lodge by Mr. Curry—on resurrection of the body—& reality of punishments fire brimstone &c hereafter—not figurative—metaphorical—as is belief of many & wh. belief is gaining ground nowadays he says. Passing 3^d Ala. saw man walking up & down in front of G. house with skillet on head—punishment for stealing one I suppose. Weather has become mild as Spring & very agreeable: but 'twill soon bring rain. Read on Dress parade an order thanks of Congress tendered to Gen. Lee & Offic & soldiers of his command for brilliant campaigns & successful defence of the Confed. Capitol. And a communication fr. General Lee saying a man in this Brig. sent him an anonamous letter with a slice of beef which he said was a days ration for 3 men and asking Gen. to keep it till it grew to the proper size. He had it inquired into & found that this brig. had been rationed more lately than any other in the army. Rations have been scanty in meat lines, from uncontrollable circumstances—Gen. Battle expressed deep mortification at its being in his Brig. It was evidently some poor dissatisfied fellow.

January 25, Monday

SP: by invitation I dined with Miles Pickens. He had got a box fr. home and had a splendid Peach pot-pie. Twas splendid. I missed hearing a speech fr. Gen. Battle to our Reg. this evening—on subject of reenlisting.*

*(Our Co. reenlisted for the war this evening. Sheb. Chadwick drew up the pledge in very pretty & appropriate language. Reenlisting has been commenced in the Tenn. army but we take the lead in this army. It will also have a good effect upon the army, the country generally & the enemy also, I hope.)

January 26, Tuesday

SP: We are having the most delightful weather, mild, geniel & Spring like. Peter Hagins went to Orange C.H. for the 3$^{\underline{d}}$ or 4$^{\underline{th}}$ time since his return—expecting a box of provisions up from Richmond, but it did not come.

January 27, Wednesday

SP: Rec'd a letter from Mary which was most acceptable, as I had not heard from home in some time.

January 28, Thursday

SP: Peter Hagins & I walked out to Orange & found it at least 7 ms. & very warm walking. Had my hair cut & shampooned, for which I paid $4. Charley Hafner & I took lunch at a restaurant & paid $3. a plate for stewed oysters, & not more than a dozen in a plate. Orange is crowded with soldiers, sutlers &c—every variety of human beings. After the arrival of the train, we returned to camp.

January 29, Friday

SP: I wrote to David Barnum in answer to a letter recd. from him some 2 months ago. He is on board the receiving-ship at Charleston, S.C. I then wrote to Mama—replying to a long letter from her that reached me this morning. Mama is very much troubled at Jamie's having to leave her: & Mary also, for she has made application to get into Mr. Sander's school in Tuscaloosa. Mama is unable to get a tutor & does not know what to do for Willie, Lou & Icha. Maj. Webster & Pick Moore got back this morning. I was really sorry to hear from Pick that Jamie is coming on with Capt. Williams. I am very well contented here myself, but do not wish to see Jamie come; for it is like breaking up our home, as Mama will be poorly able to spare him & says she can not remain at home without him. And then his constitution is delicate & I fear he will not be able to endure the rough & arduous service that we have out here. It would be much better for him to have joined a Cavalry Co. as it is a much easier & more pleasant branch of the service than Infantry. I have written him several letters advising him to do so, but he had not rec'd. them.

January 30, Saturday

SP: Tom Ward, Peter & Jack got their boxes of edibles & we have been feasting to-day. Jack gave us all a great treat to Cake & wine!!! How strange it sounds for soldiers in the Confederate Army to speak of having Cake & Wine! I rec'd. a very nice & most acceptable present of a bottle of delicious home made wine from Miss Bettie—which we opened to night & drank to her very good health. We have been feasting all day on everything rich & rare—Sausages & butter among the substantials, & pound cake, sponge cake & wine for dessert. How different from our usual dry, frugal scanty fare. A poor fellow from Ramseur's Brig. was executed for desertion to-day. He made the 5th one shot in this Divis. since I have been in it, & every one N. Carolinians.

January 31, Sunday

SP: Maj. Webster came over to see us this morning & is looking better than I ever saw him. He spoke of being at Capt. Williams' wedding & said that it was a very happy match. He gave me a little package in which was a beautiful & fancy Tobacco pouch—so fashionable with the young men now & worn swinging to a coat button—"a token of friendship" from Miss Mary Moore. So I have the credit of being a smoker at home. It almost tempts me to learn; but I'll find some better use for it. A very friendly note from Cousin Martha P. accompanied it, which I was much pleased to receive. Jack had a large, fat turkey for dinner, which was a great treat & highly appreciated. Recd. a letter from Willie. He speaks of going into the service next Spring or Summer, although he is only 15 years of age. Jack and I attended prayer meeting to-night.

February 1, Monday

SP: A meeting was held at the 12th Ala. Regt. to-day to which was sent a delegate from each Co. in the Brig. to represent the wishes of the men on the subject of reorganization. With the exception of two votes it was unanimously decided in favor of reorganizing; & a memorial to Congress was offered requesting that privilege in consideration of the valuable services rendered by this old Brigade. I was not in favor of it & believe that it will be very injurious to the Army, as some of the very best officers will be thrown out by it.

February 2, Tuesday

SP: I was on guard to-day & had the 1st Relief. Up to two or three days ago we had a week of the most delightful weather I ever experienced. It was clear & bright & as mild as May & made every one feel languid & lazy as he does when Spring comes on. Since then it has been cloudy & getting gradually cooler.

February 3, Wednesday

SP: Col. Hall recd. notice today that Jamie was mustered into this Co. on the 22nd ult. by Col. Boon at Eutaw. This evening after dark Jeff Childress was in our cabin picking the banjo & we were all having a nice time, when some of the boys came in & said that marching orders had come & we would have to leave tomorrow morning. It took us completely by surprise & put a sudden end to our sport, for there is nothing that would go so hard with us now scarcely as to have to quit our comfortable quarters & go to marching & lying in mid-winter. I went up to Col. Pickens' & met Miles there also. They had not heard of it & were as much surprised & troubled as I was. We talked it over for some time & as the order had not yet come to the Regts. we began to hope that it would be countermanded, but alas! the clatter of horse's feet reached our ears & a courier rode up with the order from Gen. Battle that commanders of Regts. must hold themselves in readiness to move at 6:30 next morning, & must carry cooking utensils & such things as would be needed in the field. That settled it & we dispersed to make preparations. Our mess went to cooking—& we hated having to move particularly bad on account of having a whole lot of butter, sausage meat, 2 large hams &c. that Peter brought on and which would have lasted us a month had we remained. However we determined to lug it along & boiled a ham cooked a quantity of bread and divided out the other ham, sausages &c and then went to bed.

February 4, Thursday

SP: The drums called us up before day light & I went over to Gen. Rodes' Hd. Qrs. & left my knap sack & a blanket with Gillam James. Started a little after light—Johnson's Brig. & our[s] under Gen. Rodes who is going with us. We halted at his Hd. Qrs. & 2 days' rations hard bread & bacon were issued. We then marched on to Orange C.H. 7 ms. & thence to Gordonsville 9 ms. further—making 16 ms. & it used us up completely. Most of the way from O. C.H. to G. was on the R.R. & the most disagreeable marching in the world. Took the cars late in the evening & had 'a time', for we were crowded 60 men in a box car, & half of Co. "D" were tight—blowing bugles, making speeches & several were very near having fights. Got to Hanover Junction about 12 o'clock or after & marched a mile or two on to a piney woods & bivouacked.

February 5, Friday

SP: Remained till late in the evening, when we marched 3 miles to the Winter Quarters that Picke[t]t's Divis. had occupied. We had thought that our destination was N.C. to reinforce Gen'l Pickett in his expedition against Newbern, but it seems we are only to take the place of his troops here. A thousand rumors are afloat, one of which is that 15000 negro troops are advancing on this point. There are not half enough houses for us & 12 men are assigned to each one.

February 6, Saturday

SP: It being thought we might remain here some time we went to work on the houses & repaired the chimneys. Got orders to-night to cook up rations & be ready to return to old camp.

February 7, Sunday

SP: Were roused up 2 hrs. before day to move. orders had come for us to go to Richmond. Had a most disagreeable march in the dark & thro' mud & water of 2 ms. to Taylorville on R.R. Here Gen. Battle recd. a dispatch stating that the enemy were pressing us on the Rapidan & also below Richmond & that he must hurry to the latter place. After considerable delay the Brig. at last got off on three very long trains. Had a good deal of amusement in passing thro' the city as the troops were in the highest spirits & jeered & taunted the men on the streets who ought to be in the Army, & who, even now that the city is threatened are dressed up & playing the dandy. The alarm bells have been ringing all the morning & the Militia has turned out. Went out 2 ms. on the W^{ms}brg. road & bivouacked in a nice pine grove.

February 8, Monday

SP: We learn from the papers this morning that a large force of the enemy crossed at Morton's Fd. on Sat. but were repulsed & pursued by Gen. Ed. Johnson's Div. The Yankees from the Peninsula crossed the Chickahominy & formed a line of battle but our artillery shelled them a little & they dispersed in direction of Williamsburg. So affairs are not near as serious as we supposed. I wrote a letter to Mama. Jack Wynne, Henry Childress & I with a no. of others went in to the Theatre to-night & saw "The Va. Cavaliers."

NOTE: Pickens apparently saw a dramatization of *The Cavaliers of Virginia, or The Recluse of Jamestown: An Historical Romance* (1834) by William Alexander Caruthers.

February 9, Tuesday

SP: A no. of us went in this morning to have some dentistry done but the dentist, Dr. Pleasants, would not commence on us till 4 P.M. I had one plug put in. Soldiers are charged $20 & others $30 & upwards. The gold used is now worth 1600^{\underline{00}}$ per oz. I made myself known to Dr. P. and he was very glad to see me & inquired particularly after Mama, with whom he said he was more charmed than with any lady he had ever met, & was very much attached to her. I had a chill & fever in the evening & felt so badly at the Theatre that I went to Mrs. Barnes & took a bed for the night.

February 10, Wednesday

SP: Felt so badly this morning that I could not go to Camp. Alfred Ward has just returned from home, where he has been ever since he got back from Yankeedom. He was wounded & taken prisoner at Chancellorsville. I saw in the papers the other day that the thanks of Congress had been tendered to Maj. Gen. Rodes & his Division. Gen. Lee had written a letter stating that the Divis. had been very successfully commanded by Gen. R. since his promotion for gallantry at Chancellorsville. He stated, also, that our Brig. was the first to reenlist in the Army of Northern Va.

February 11, Thursday

SP: Dr. Hill gave me a large dose of Blue Mass last night & Quinine pills which I have taken at intervals of 2 hrs. to-day. Missed the chill this evening.

February 12, Friday

SP: Got up this morning & went over to the parlor—feeling weak & badly though. John Christian & Alfred Ward are staying here, & also, some young ladies. Misses Barnes wrote to Mary to-day.

February 13, Saturday

SP: The soldiers have perfect freedom in the city now, as there are no guards on the streets—& this is the first time it has been the case since I have been in the army. Half the Brig. are in town all the time & the Theatre is crowded with them every night. Co. "D" lives in town & most of the members come in & have a dance with the ladies here at night. They are usually in *high spirits* too; & the girls have even accused some of having "the hives", which they use as a synonim for being inebriated. Was in the C.S. Senate a while this evening. They passed a bill giving ensigns the rank of 1$^{\underline{st}}$ Lieut; a good thing, for it is the post of honor & of the greatest danger. A bill was also passed giving officers rations & allowing them to purchase clothing from the Quarter Masters when there is a surplus on hand.

February 14, Sunday

SP: I went out to the Regt. this morning after paying Mrs. Barnes $10 a day for the time I stayed there. At the Spottswood Hotel board is $25 per day. I understood there were two men boarding there at $1 apiece paid in gold, which shows ~~that~~ how much our currency had *de*preciated & how much gold [h]as *ap*preciated in value. On the night of the 10<u>th</u> over a hundred Yankee officers escaped from the Libby prison through a tunnel which they had dug out. Amongst the no. was the notorious Col. Streight. A good many have been recaptured.

February 15, Monday

SP: It snowed this evening & turned very cold & disagreeable—so much so that I went in town to Mrs. Barnes' to spend the night. Went to the Iron Clad (negro) Minstrels, which was poor entertainment.

February 16, Tuesday

SP: Our Brig. took the cars & went to Hanover Junction, or rather to Pickett's old quarters. Orders recd. to-night to be ready to march up to old camp to-morrow as R.R. transportation can not be furnished us. Glad to get away from Richmond, as I got tired of it—lying out without any protection & only green pine to burn.*

*Recd. a letter from Mat Jones.

February 17, Wednesday

SP: Gilliam James sent me word last night that he had a horse for me to ride back; so I got up before light & walked to the Junction, 4 ms. Gen. Rodes & staff went up on the cars & Gilliam & Pick Moore, with 2 negroes were to carry the Gen's. horses up. After getting breakfast we started—I riding Dr. Mitchell's horse—but had proceeded a short distance only when Gilliam had the misfortune to meet with an accident which detained us some time. We discovered here that we had no money in the crowd, & returned to the Junction & got $100. from Capt. Preston. This has been the coldest day I think I ever felt: the ground was hard frozen & ice formed last night thick enough to bear the weight of our horses. It was so very cold that we suffered terribly, & had to walk & drive our horses a portion of the time, & also stop at houses & warm. We got a "snack" of ash cake & butter milk from an old negro at a station, for which we paid $5. Passed Beaver dam station & a little village called Green Bay, & stopped for the night at Mr. Pettus', having come 20 miles.

February 18, Thursday

SP: Mr. P. said he could not think of turning men off such a night as the last was, & gave us excellent accommodations. Had a splendid supper & breakfast—nice country fare, such as I have not seen since I've been in the army: & he charged us only $10 for everything. Passed near Frederick's Hall where all the artillery of Ewell's Corps is camped. To-day is another freezer & the citizens say they have not had such weather for years. The moisture from our noses froze on our moustache & icicles hung from the horses' noses. Pick & I put up at Louisa C.H., 21 or 22 from where we started this morning, while Gilliam & the negroes went on to M. W<u>m</u>. Overton's, G's uncle—12 ms. further on. We got very good fare, but had to pay $32 for ourselves & horses. A crowd of the quiet citizens were seated around the Inn stove talking over a fire that broke out last night in the building, when the whole town was again aroused & turned out on the street to see a pair of horses running away with a wagon. These two occurrences will be subjects of gossip with people of L. C.H. for some time to come.

February 19, Friday

SP: Pick & I started after 9 O'clock & rode to Gordonsville, 15 ms. by 1 P.M. where Gilliam soon joined us. We spent the last of the $100. here for some thing to eat & started for camp. Pick killed a partridge on the road with my Enfield musket. Gilliam undertook to carry us a near way of 11 ms. by Pender's Div. but we got on the wrong roads & I think we traveled 20 ms. Got to Maj. Adams' late in the evening about half frozen, & warmed up & ate supper. Then went on to Gen. Rodes' Hd. Qrs. & there learned that I had met with a loss in my absence; a tent had burnt up & in it my knap-sack, which I had left with Gilliam James; also a blanket of mine & all of Joe Grigg's clothes & other things. My bible, diaries, letters &c. were saved tho', & I did not regret the other things much. The Brig. had beaten us here although we came on horseback.

February 20, Saturday

SP: We are all very glad to get back to all houses & comfortable bunks. For the last three days the weather has been colder than I ever experienced, tho' it is moderating now. Some men in Brig. were near being frozen at night on the way up here. Some were roused with great difficulty & were speechless for some time. At Camp Lee, Richmond, some of the conscripts did die from the effects of the cold. James River was frozen over, which is a rare occurrence, I believe. Got a letter fr. Mary last night, dated the 7$\underline{th}$ telling of the death on the 5$\underline{th}$ of our kind & faithful old nurse, Mom Lindy. She will be much missed & regretted by us all.

February 21, Sunday

SP: On guard to-day. The Yankee papers admit that the object of their recent move was to surprise & capture Richmond & release their prisoners confined there. The demonstration on the Rapidan was a feint, while they made rapid march from Yorktown & got to Bottom's bridge—10 ms. from the city; but they found the ford blockaded or rather obstructed & were detained so long they had to give it up & go back. They say a deserter from them informed us of their plans & thus saved Richmond.

NOTE: On February 6 Union forces crossed the Rapidan at Morton's Ford and retreated during the night in the face of Confederate resistance.

February 22, Monday

SP: We find it very quiet & dull here now after being about Richmond. Weather becoming very pleasant again.

February 23, Tuesday

SP: Nothing occurred to-day worthy of being chronicled. Camp-life now "almost stagnates into ennui et tedium vitae."

NOTE: "Ennui et tedium vitae" means "the boredom and tedium of life."

February 24, Wednesday

SP: John Christian got back from Richmond this evening and bro't the cheering news that Sherman is retreating from Meridian, Miss., & Polk who had fallen back across the Bigby is in pursuit. The people throughout our part of the country must be much relieved.

NOTE: After a successful Meridian campaign, William Tecumseh Sherman's troops began withdrawing toward Vicksburg on February 20.

The "Bigby" is the Tombigbee River.

February 25, Thursday

SP: Maj. Webster & Joe Grigg, who have been down South of the James River collecting tithe meat, have returned with 12000 lbs. Dr. Hill started home on furlough this morning.

February 26, Friday

SP: Our meat rations have been very scant & we feel it most sensibly since all the ham, sausage meat & butter brought on by Peter Hagins have been disposed of. A ration now is ¼ lb. Bacon or ½ lb. salt beef, or ¾ lb. fresh beef. We draw two days' rations at once & eat all the meat the first day, generally, & live on dry corn bread the 2$\underline{nd}$. Sugar, Coffee & Molasses are also issued to us every few days. Jack, Tom Ward, Jim Webb & I, & also Young Idom & Sam Jackson went on guard to-night in order to relieve the men who stood to-day & let them cook & get ready to go on Picket in the morning. The Guard was taken off tho' at 9 P.M.

February 27, Saturday

SP: A letter was handed me last night after I had gone to bed which I find this morning to be from my dear & good correspondent—Louty. Its date is the 16$\underline{th}$ which is the last intelligence recd. from home since the 7$\underline{th}$. There's something wrong with the mails; for we have not had an Ala. mail of any consequence since our return from Richmond. The drum was beat before day & we got breakfast & started a little after sun up. Marched moderately & rested twice. The distance is at least 10 ms. & I got very much worried, for I had my "big blanket" along which is three times as heavy as a common one. We were posted at Raccoon's Ford but very soon the Picket was strengthened & our place taken by part of the 6$\underline{th}$ Ala. We then moved lower down the river, but there we stayed but a short while, for it seemed to be the rule in military affairs to do every thing of the sort in the most round-a-bout blundering manner, that will give the men the greatest amount of marching & the most trouble. So down the river we had to go, over the steepest hills, several miles to Morton's house. A non-commissioned officer was sent on the outpost, with Co. "C", while the remainder of the Co. were in reserve & were comfortably quartered in vacated negro cabins.

February 28, Sunday

SP: Tom Ward, Bunk Butler, & I walked thro' Mr. M's. yard this morning looking at the signs of the recent fight that occurred here. There are bullet marks on the house & most every tree in the yard is cut up by minnies. The plank fence, too, is right badly riddled, showing that there was hot fighting here. An old negro who was here at the time says two of our men & ten Yankees were killed about the yard. I met an old school-mate, Charley Pollard, now a Lieut. & Adjutant of the 61st Ala. Regt., which came to us at Richmond, in exchange for the 26th Ala. Recd. an interesting & lengthy letter from Jamie, dated Jan. 27th—month old. It is strange he said nothing of having enlisted. At 2 P.M. the balance of our Co. & Co. "A" went out on the river to relieve those who went on yesterday. Of our Co. there are 22 all told down here, & 17 left in camp.

NOTE: In the spring of 1864, Battle's brigade included the Third, Fifth, Sixth, Twelfth, and Sixty-first (replacing the Twenty-sixth) Alabama infantry regiments. The Sixty-first consisted of conscripted young and old men who, nonetheless, fought well.

February 29, Monday

SP: We have had a very quiet day of it. There was every appearance of rain but it has not come yet. This has been a most remarkably dry winter, &, with the exception of several severe spells, a mild one. So dry that we have been constantly apprehending active movements on the part of the Yankees. There are reports of a move being on foot now. We were relieved & returned to the houses this evening. It began to drizzle about night & it seems we are going to have some rain at last.

March 1, Tuesday

SP: Our Regt. was relieved by the 12th Ala. to-day & we went in reserve back of the breast works in the pines, & had a most disagreeable time, as it drizzled all day & after dark turned into sleeting & then snowed. We have only pine wood to burn too. We've had various reports of the Yankees having crossed the river above & below.

HB: Left home this morning, reached Selma in a rain. Left there at 1 P.M. on little Cherokee. Capt. W. and I slept under berth No. 6. Similar dreams of both.

NOTE: Henry Beck begins his diary.

March 2, Wednesday

SP: The weather is clear and bright to-day & affords a good opportunity for drying our blankets & overcoats. Peter Hagins came with the rations & said it is reported that a Corps of the enemy crossed away above here at Barnett's Ford, but were whipped by some of A. P. Hill's troops. Also, that a force of Cavalry are making a raid into our lines & have passed thro' Charlottesville & cut the Central R.R. I wrote to Mama this evening, which makes the 2nd or 3rd time since I've recd. a letter from her.

HB: Reached Montgomery about 12 o'clock, stopped at the Exchange, room no. 42, wrote to Brother and Al, took supper with Newman at Joe Pizallie's, went to theatre to Lady of Lyons, was introduced to Mrs. Hirsh, after theatre returned to the Exchange, found Captain W. in bed.

NOTE: Sam Pickens was reading *The Lady of Lyons* a year earlier in Virginia.

March 3, Thursday

SP: The artillery here got orders to be in readiness to receive the raiders, who have been whipped back by General Elzey at Richmond &, it is thought, will attempt to escape by one of these fords. We hear cannonading which is supposed to be target shooting at Kelly's Ford on the Rappahannock. There's no telling, tho, what or where it is.

HB: After breakfast got apples, wrote to Miss A.D. & sent them by R.B. Waller. Hurried to the depot and came near being left. Left Montgomery at 11 A.M. reached West Point at ½ past 6 P.M. Reached Atlanta at 3 P.M.

March 4, Friday

SP: This day has passed off quietly. Real March Weather very windy.

HB: Reached Augusta at 5 P.M., left at 7 P.M., reached Branchville at ½ past 12 A.M., Kingsville about 4 A.M.

March 5, Saturday

SP: Our Brig was relieved about 11 O'clock this morning but remained awaiting orders from Gen. Ewell; for there was a report that the Yanks were crossing at Germanna Ford. It turned out a false alarm tho, I suppose, as we were ordered to camp about 4 P.M. Made a fast march & got to quarters some time after night tired & hungry, & my clothes wet with perspiration altho' it was cold. Every one was out of rations to-day, but we managed to have a little for breakfast. We had coffee all the time on Picket & it helped out wonderfully.

HB: Reached Columbus at 8 A.M., missed connection, put up at the Nickerson Hotel in room no. 42, wrote to brother and Al. Left for Charlotte at 6 P.M. Gen. Ripley aboard the train.

March 6, Sunday

SP: Recd. a letter from Mama & one from Jamie last night. Tom Biscoe is at home on furlough. Jamie was going to remain & come on with Tom if Capt. Williams would consent. The past week has been one of excitement but things have relapsed into a state of quietude again. We missed a march by being on Picket—the rest of the Divis. went to Jack's shop near Madison C.H. Kilpatricks cavalry raid was a daring thing, but signally failed, & his destructive & barbarous programme was not enacted. Col. Dahlgren who was in command of one division of the raiders was whipped off from Richmond by some of the city troops, composed of Department Clerks &c. & in his flight was attacked at different points & eventually killed in King & Queen Co. On his person were found a copy of his plans, his address to his men, who were picked men &c. He was to release the Yankee prisoners on Belle Island (about 8000) sack & burn the City, for which purpose they had balls of oakum saturated with turpentine prepared. Also to burn the bridges over the James River; & to cap the climax, were to hang Jeff Davis & his cabinet. Had they been successful, Richmond would have suffered all the horrors imaginable. Heard a sermon to-night from Mr. Curry to-night.

HB: Reached Charlotte at 5 A.M. Stopped at Charlotte hotel. Capt. W. & I went to the Episcopal church. Left Charlotte at 6 P.M. Saw a Yankee who was killed for attempting to get away.

NOTE: On March 1, Hugh Judson Kilpatrick's cavalry got within a few miles of Richmond. Colonel Ulric Dahlgren's five hundred Union troops withdrew in the face of significant resistance. Dahlgren himself was killed the next day. Although not successful, the raid created a great deal of anxiety among Richmond residents.

March 7, Monday

SP: This is a mild, bright & beautiful day. Some of the raiders have been lodged in prison in Richmond & the papers are discussing the course that should be pursued with regard to them & are of the opinion that they ought not to be dealt with as prisoners-of-war, but as murderers & incendiaries.

HB: Reached Raleigh at 9 A.M., left at 11 A.M., reached Weldon at 7 P.M., Petersburg at 3 A.M., left Mrs. Gayle and family there.

March 8, Tuesday

SP: A slow rain fell during the fore part of the day, but the weather cleared up in the evening. Dick Simonds went before the board of Surgeons to-day and got a discharge from the service. Anchylosis of (right) arm & organic affection of the heart. Waddell & Young Idom, ambulance drivers, have been returned to this Co., & their places filled by disabled men. We'll have all the men we can get in the rank this Spring.

HB: Reached Richmond at 7 A.M., stopped at Mrs. Barnes'. Capt. W., Charley and myself took baths at the Ballard house, went to Antone's & got oysters, returned to Mrs. Barnes', repacked box, left $300.00 in gold with Mrs. Barnes, and wrote to brother and Capt. Curry, sent letters to office by Capt. W. Met Col. Hobson & Fred, Pick at the Spotswood. Col. Hobson & I went to Pizzani's, took ice cream, then went to look up Col. Fowler. On my return found Sims at Mrs. Barnes. Him and I went to the barbers at the Ballard, met with N. Jackson & Alex Sledge. N. Jackson went with us to Mrs. Barnes' where we found Col. Fowler. We returned about 10 o'clock.

NOTE: "Charley" is Charles L. Williams.

"Fred" is Fred Huggins.

"Pick" is James Pickens Moore.

According to the reminiscences of Captain J. W. Williams, Mrs. Barnes returned Beck's three hundred dollars in gold at the war's end (*Greensboro Record*, January 14, 1904).

More than one Greensborian bore the name Alexander Sledge.

March 9, Wednesday

SP: I dined with Miles Pickens & spent a very pleasant evening with him. Capt. Williams arrived this evening late with three recruits—his brother Chas. Williams,———Long &———Beck. He brought a lot of boxes also, filled with meat and clotheing, which comes in very well particularly the meat, for that important article of diet is uncomfortably scarce with us at present. He had 20 lbs sausages for Noah Huggins but lost it, & has given him a ham instead. Sims came also. Capt. W. & himself were both married at home; the former to Miss Carrie Avery & the latter to Miss Ann Briggs.

HB: Got up at ½ past 4 A.M., took the Central train at 6 for Gordonsville, reached there at ½ past 12 P.M., left for Orange C.H. at 1 P.M., reached there at about 3 P.M. Met James Boardman at the depot and marched to camp. Reached camp about 6 P.M., met all the boys, had, long talks, etc. Slept with Charley Williams that night.

March 10, Thursday

SP: We have had a good, old fashion, steady rain to-day, & we are all glad to see it; for it has been so very dry that we have been uneasy lest a move should take place. Got a letter from Lou last night, & wrote one to Mama to-day to send by Henry Childress.

HB: Passed off the day in talking and singing. Went up to Major Adam's quarters late in the evening, played whist with Boardman Tucker & Lavender, took supper there and stayed all night, slept with Lavender.

March 11, Friday

SP: A slow, drizzling rain still continues—just the sort to make the ground muddy, Henry Childress left this morning with brother Jeff, on 30 days' furlough; & Tom Ward & Bunk Butler got off on the evening train. Recd. last night, an epistle from David Barnum, C.S.N., & to-night one from Mary. She wrote to tell me that Dr. Sawyer would be in Richmond soon with Marky, who will be met at City Point by one of her uncles & taken to her relatives in Georgetown, & that I must be sure and go to Richmond to see her. Mary forgets that I am not a gentleman of leisure and master of my own time. It will be out of my power to get to R.

HB: John Tucker and I started to the Jeff Davis's Legion this morning, passed by Bordersville, our and the enemy's line of fortifications on Mine Run, from there to Spottsylvania C.H., thence by Massaponge church to the Legion, reached there just at dark, met with Syd Border, Emmett Jackson & Cunny James. I was mustered into Co. E, J.D.L. by Lieut. Doughdell, & approved by Maj. Lewis. Stayed with Border & Jackson that night.

March 12, Saturday

SP: I am to take charge of the Co. "sick book" for one week, commencing with this morning. No patients. I'm on guard to-day. Weather clear again. Yesterday Capt. Williams appointed Henry Allen 4th Corporal.

HB: After taking a cup of coffee, we started back to camp, reached there about dusk. Read the Beacon of the 4th inst. Thom. Ward having gone home, Jones & I slept together.

March 13, Sunday

SP: Gen'l Lee has issued an order suspending furloughs for the present. It is said that all the rolling stock on the Vª. R.Roads, & others also, has been 'pressed for transporting Gov. stores; but I believe that troops are to be moved, for Gen.

Longstreet has been up here & left Orange with Gen. Lee yesterday morning, for Richmond, I presume. Gen. Rosser's Brig. of Va. Cavalry passed down the plank road towards Fredericksburg yesterday & returned to-day. Heard a sermon from Mr. Curry.

HB: Sometime after breakfast walked up to Maj. Adams's, wrote to Miss J. C. Took dinner with Tucker Boardman & Lavender & Capt. C, then returned to camp.

March 14, Monday

SP: Night before last some of the split poles of which the sentinel walks are made, were burnt up, & upon investigation it was fixed upon my relief & turned out to be Taylor of Co. "H". I was ordered to see that he replaced the pieces & report him to his Co. commander to be made to cut up stumps as punishment— which I did accordingly. On the 19$\underline{th}$ ult. in New York Gold ran up to 170, & the market closed at 166⅜, which is higher than it has ever been.

HB: After breakfast wrote to Alfred Ward, read the company report, nothing unusual transpiring all day, unpacked box of Capt. Jordan from Mrs. Walton & found cakes, etc. in it, made proper use of it. After supper sang and had considerable tussle in the mess.

March 15, Tuesday

SP: I was favored with a very interesting letter from Jamie again last night. Mama has gotten her new carriage made by Johnson in Greensboro'. He acted the rascal in the matter, for after engaging to make the carriage for $700, he pretended when it was finished that some one else had a prior claim upon it & offered to pay him more for it; but said Mama should have it if she would give him 150 lbs. of lard in addition to the $700. They are taking advantage of Mama on all sides, & swindling her whenever they can. A very fine young filly of Jamie's was taken from the Canebrake by a lawless gang of Cavalry representing themselves to be impressing officers. Gen. Polk sent a detail in pursuit, but they will never be caught. I wrote to Louty this evening. Col. Hobson got to the Regt. to-day looking very well.

HB: After breakfast drilled in manuels, wrote to Brady. Col. Hobson reached here this evening, brought cake for Briggs. Tucker's application for exchange was returned for my consent, sent up again the same day, sang at Britton's house & retired for tonight.

NOTE: Henry Beck, in the Jeff Davis Legion (J.D.L.), and John S. Tucker, in Rodes' brigade, are making arrangements to exchange their positions.

March 16, Wednesday

SP: There are no incidents to-day worthy of record.
HB: Nothing of any importance transpired today.

March 17, Thursday

SP: An extract from a Northern paper states that it has leaked out that the official reports of the Yankee losses in several of the principal battles are as follows:—In killed, wounded, & prisoners at Chickahominy 30,000; 2$\underline{\text{nd}}$ Manassas 20,000; Fredericksburg 20,000; Chancellorsville 28,000; Gettysburg 25,000. Total loss in five battles 123,000.

HB: Went on brigade inspection this morning, wrote to S.H., Brother, Capt. Curry & J. E. Wilson.

JP: This is a gloomy morning to us, for it is this day that Tom & I have chosen to take our departure for Va. Mr. Enoch called over & spent an hour or two with us, after which he bade us good-bye & left as he was going to town. After dinner, of which neither Tom nor myself partook, we bade an affectionate adieu to Mama, Mary, Loutie & Icha & left in the carriage for Newbern. Willie accompanied us. We left Umbria at 2 h. 45 m. Stopped at Greensboro', where we arrived at 4 h. 45 m., to bid Miss I. good-bye. Had boots stretched as they hurt me very badly. Got to Newbern about 7½ o'clock. Took supper & all three (Tom, Willie & I) took one bed & went soon fast asleep. Had a bad headache on going to bed, which continued during the night.

NOTE: James Pickens begins his diary. He and his servant Willie will travel from Umbria, west of Greensboro, to Newbern, where they will catch a train to Selma. From Selma they will travel by boat to Montgomery. There they will go by train to West Point, Georgia; Columbia, South Carolina; Charlotte and Raleigh, North Carolina; and finally to Petersburg, Virginia.

"Tom" is Thomas H. Biscoe.

March 18, Friday

SP: The "Examiner" under the caption of Restaurant arithmetic, estimates that the profits made on *a pound* of Coffee at the restaurants in Richmond amount to $250.00. A. H. will make at least 50 cups, which are $5 apiece. This, it says, will be interesting as a part of history of the times.

HB: Received Beacon, read all the news. Tucker's exchange with me came back approved, so take effect 1st April. Went to the association breaking up of it and reorganizing.

JP: We awoke at about 5 o'clk this morn'g and proceeded to depot where, after expressing Sam's box & getting seats, we bade adieu to Willie & left Newbern for Selma, on train. Told William & Dread good-bye, also. They came with the jersey-wagon & our baggage. Got to Selma at 10 h. 15 m. Tom & I went immediately to Provost Marshal's to get passports for both of us & transport. for one, but we had to return twice afterwards in order to obtain them. John saw to our baggage at 'Florence Hotel'. Obtained our passes & transportation, finally; & then Tom & I went to Reporter office & left a year's subscription of $25. for the paper for D$\underline{\text{r}}$ Grigg. We then had a tiresome day of it, awaiting the arrival of a boat for Montg'y. Took dinner & yet no boat came. We walked several times to wharf to see if it had come. Took supper & were just going to make up our minds to take a room for night when 'twas reported the boat had come. We took our baggage to wh'f & after waiting on shore for about an hour for the boat it came & we took passage on it—the 'Virginia', and left Selma at 11 o'clock that night. Had to sleep on the *floor* of the boat, as the berths were full, & we could scarcely find room even there. Traveled all night; had a tolerably easy nap (Tom B. slept soundly by the way) and were roused the next day at about 5½ or 6 o'cl'k by the preparations of the servants for the breakfast.

NOTE: "John" is Samuel Pickens' servant.

March 19, Saturday

SP: Had the happiness to receive a most welcome letter from Mama last night. A Judge Mason of Tuskegee, Ala., at the Hd. qrs. of 3ᵈ Ala. Regt., this evening made a speech to the soldiers of this Brig. thanking them for the gallant services they had performed during the war & for the brilliant page they had authorized to be written in history. He said our prospects were very encouraging & that he believed that we would have peace before this time next year. That is a very general opinion now & I trust we may not be disappointed in it. He was very amusing at times & pleased the soldiers much. Gen. Battle being then called on made a brief address. I wrote a short letter to Jamie this morning & directed it to Richmond, care of Mrs. Barnes.

HB: After breakfast carried Tucker's paper to him. Charles Williams left for Staunton today. In the evening Judge Mason of Ala. & Gen. Battle spoke in front of Col. Forsyth's quarters. Attended association after supper, speeches by Chaplain Rutledge & Hutchinson.

JP: The sun rose clear, bright & beautifully this morn'g. After Tom & I had taken a good wash breakfast (for which there was a great rush made) came on, & a good one, (i.e. for the times) it was. We were a little hungry & broke our fast with a great deal of relish. It was 1½ o'clk P.M. when we got to Montg'y. We went to Exch. Hotel, & soon after took dinner. After dinner, Tom & I went into a room (large) which was formerly used as a reading-room, and wrote letters home; he to Mary, and I to Mama. After writing Tom began to read. I met Davy, Cous. Julia's servᵗ. who said that she expected me to go & visit her. So after a few preparations I went to her house about ¼ mile fr. hotel, by Episc. church, and waited a few minutes 'till cous. J. came. She I found had grown a little, had become a good deal stouter & seem'd to be in better health than when I last saw her. She sang a great many songs, such as "Virginia," "Rock me to Sleep," & others. I spent a half an hour or more very pleasantly there and then bade her good bye & returned to hotel, as 'twas not long before Tom, John & I had to leave on cars. We took our baggage & walked thro' a slight rain to depot, about a mile fr. hotel. Here we waited for at least 3 hours 'till the cars left. They were locked & we had to stand or walk about during all that time. At last we succeeded in procuring seats on the train & after buying John's ticket at about 8 o'clock P.M. we left Montg'y.

March 20, Sunday

SP: Gilliam, Pick and Tom Moore came over to the Co. to see us last night. Peter Hagins, Bob Chadwick and I took a walk down the plank-road toward Unionville church this evening.

HB: Shelby Chadwick and myself went to Boardman's & Lavender took dinner with them, spent the evening there. On returning met Dr. Witherspoon on his way to Richmond. Received letter of the 11th from brother. Horace Burton took supper & spent the evening with us.

JP: We traveled all night. Tom & I formed the acquaintance of a Lieut. of a Miss. company, who was going all the way to Richmond with us. He is a very clever & gentlemanly man indeed, & was also of a great deal of assistance to us in helping to get seats for himself & us. Arrivd at West Pt. about 6 o'clock A.M. Chang^d cars for Augusta at 4 o'clk P.M. arriving at latter place at 5 o'cl'k A.M.

March 21, Monday

SP: I rec'd a pretty lengthy epistle last evening from Dr. Temp. Sawyer, now in Richmond, & answered it to-day. Had batallion drill this evening.

HB: Wrote to Mrs. John Walton & answered brother's letter.

JP: Chang^d cars and arrivd. at Columbia at 6 o'clk P.M. We took supper, feeling very hungry. It consisted of hard biscuits & rye coffee. We had fire made in room No. 50, and wrote letters home; Tom to Mary and I to Mama. Had a good night's rest. Tom slept very well also. 'Twas clear to-night. The Lieut. with whom we were traveling was separated from us by taking a train for Charlotte Junction, instead of Columbia. Maj. Griswold, Prov. Marshal of Richmond, also went by the same train. For the supper which we had & which I mentioned above, and for a poor fire, we were charged $17.50 apiece = $35.

March 22, Tuesday

SP: I was on guard to-day, but it got very cold & began to snow in the afternoon, & the guard was taken off. Capt. Macafie, officer of the day, put Lieut. Smith of Co. "B" who was officer of the Guard, under arrest: & also Chas. Hafner, Sergt. Of the Guard, for not having a relief present when he came around. Col. Hall released them both though.

HB: Very cold this morning, commenced snowing about 12 A.M. Kept on all the evening.

JP: Tom & I arose quite early this morning (about 5½ or 6 o'clk.) some time before John who slept in No. 55, & quite comfortably. We dressed & without taking breakfast went to the depot about a mile fr. Hotel, & waited 'till train left. Found that the passenger train had left & that we would have only a freight train to travel on. Left at 7 o'clock. Had a snow-storm to-day, which lasted during the day. It is about five in. deep. Met two young men on train, with whom we became acquainted—a young Wilkinson & his friend a Mr. Kilpatrick. They were both Louisianians & of course were glad to form Tom's acquaintance. We got permission from the conductor of the train to build a fire in the midst of our car (a box car) as it was biting cold. So we put some moist sand on the floor & built a comfortable fire which warmed us considerably but almost suffocated us with its smoke. However we endured the smoke in order to keep warm. Traveled very slowly and arrivd at Chester So. Ca. at 6 P.M. instead of 1 o'clk, as we should have. This is rather a pretty little town, tho' we did not see much of it this even'g. Tom B., John & I slept by our fire in the car, keeping it made up all night.

March 23, Wednesday

SP: On getting up this morning we found the snow on the ground 15 inches deep. It was beautiful sight too, as the weather had cleared off & the sun was shining brightly. The soldiers had a grand frolic snow-balling and rabbit hunting. First, one wing of this Regt. fought the other; then the whole Regt. fought the 3ᵈ Ala.; then our Brigade and Daniels had it; and finally, in the evening, our Division fought a big snow battle with Ed Johnston's Divis. They were conducted a good deal like genuine battles—officers mounted commanded on each side & rode along the lines, led charges &c. Prisoners were taken & flags captured & some times an officer & his horse would be taken & carried to the rear. Gen Doles commanded the men from our Div.

HB: This morning the ground covered with a foot of snow. Our left wing attacked the right and had a pitched battle. Our brigade led by Capt. Smith A.I.G. attacked Gen'l. Daniel's Brigade. Ramson's then reenforced them and after two hours hard fighting, we drove them to their quarters, capturing many prisoners, horses & 1 stand of colours. At dinner information was received. that Gen. Johnston's division was going to give ours battle in the afternoon. Our division formed, and went to meet them, Col. Pickens leading our Brigade. We met them drawn up in line of battle, our sharp shooters were thrown out, and the battle soon became general. After several attacks we captured two stands of colours, worried them considerably, and fell back to our quarters towards evening.

JP: We were perfectly black with the smoke & cinders of the fire. Awoke with a bad headache, but it went off after a while. Went to hotel hard by and got a very good breakfast indeed—ham, eggs, biscuits, cakes, corn-bread, butter &c, &c. Felt very much refreshed after washing & eating. Left Chester this morn'g about 8 o'clk. Had a sort of accident yester e'en, by the cars running off track which detained us considerably. Traveled much better to-day. Arrivd at Charlotte this even'g at 1 o'cl'k. Went immediately into the train for Raleigh and procured comfortable seats. Our train was a long one, consisting of seven cars & coaches, I think. Waited 'till 6½ , sun-down, at which time the whistle blew, the locomotive began to puff and soon the train was winding its way 'on the wings of the wind'. The trains on this road I think travel faster than those on the Ga. & S.C. roads as the track is a much better one.

March 24, Thursday

SP: The snow is melting slowly away. There were to have tried the fight with Johnston's Divis. over to-day but did not.

HB: Snowballing all the morning. After dinner went up to Maj. Adams, wrote to Miss A.D., left letter with Paul to mail & returned back to camp.

JP: The train was crowded to overflowing this night. One could not move thro' the cars without stepping on some sleeping soldier. Traveled all night. Pass$^{\underline{d}}$ the "Shops" about 4½ or 5 o'clk this morn'g. Arrivd at Raleigh at 10½ o'clock. Put up at Phillip's hotel on the left hand side of the street leading fr. Capitol to St. Mary's. 'Twas too late for breakfast so we waited 'till dinner for something to eat, notwithstanding we were pretty hungry from traveling & could have taken a good snack. Dinner came on about 2 o'clock. Afterward, Tom & I walked over the town & visited the surroundings of St. Mary's & then came in again. The school looked very natural & reminded me of times gone by, when my dear mother & sisters & brother were staying there. Tom & I in the evening took an (mailed letter to Mama, writ. at Columb. and also one to xxxxxx) other walk with Wilkinson & a friend of his—Lieut.———in command of some Ga. Company. Had a long & pleasant walk. Went up Fayetteville St. as far as to the "Governor's Palace", where we turned & retraced our steps to hotel. On our arrival there I saw D$^{\underline{r}}$. Sanders. Left the office, went to our room & return'd to speak to the D$^{\underline{r}}$ but he had gone. Went down street in hopes of seeing him, but to no purpose. Bought at Pomroy's Book store a piece of music, "When this cruel war is over", for Mary, but did n't have a chance to mail it. Soon after our return, supper was announced & we ate of it heartily as we felt rather hungry. 'Twas a pretty good one, too. Had a good rest to-night.

NOTE: Several songs entitled "When This Cruel War Is Over" were published during the Civil War.

"xxxxxx" is Juliet Damer, whom James Pickens would marry April 1, 1865.

March 25, Friday

SP: It commenced raining this evening & will melt the last of the snow & leave the roads in an awful condition for going on picket to-morrow. I'm looking for Jamie every day.

HB: Nothing unusual transpiring today, hard rain all the evening. Briggs received April fool by mail.

JP: Altho' clear yesterday, it is cloudy to-day. We arose, dressed, ate breakfast about 6 o'clk & after getting our baggage together took omnibus for depot. Our fellow-travelers, Gen$^{\underline{l}}$ Humphreys, Maj. Griswold and others, had just arrivd fr. Charlotte the night before, & left with us to-day. Drizzled on our getting to depot. The train was too crowded for us to get aboard, but it went to the other depot where it took on another coach which afforded us ample room, (i.e. a seat for Tom & me) but for which I had to run ahead & encounter a good deal of bustle & confusion. We left the depot for Weldon about 7 o'clock. Traveled pretty well & got to Weld. at 2 or 3 o'cl'k P.M. Waited 'till 6, changed cars & left for Petersburg at 6 o'clock. Had a large crowd, and managed to get seats. (Today is Good Friday.) Tom B. became acquainted with a Surgeon or D$^{\underline{r}}$ whose name I did not learn. He, Tom & I during the night, had a good many songs, but I could do little at singing having a very bad cold & being very hoarse. By the time we were growing sleepy & felt like resting—tho' hard seats & having no room precluded the possibility of our doing so, we arriv$^{\underline{d}}$ at Petersburg. 'Twas about 12 o'clock when we got there. Had to walk from the depot where we arriv$^{\underline{d}}$, to the Richmond depot, at least a mile through the town. It was very dark & the streets were sloppy. Got to the depot where a great crowd were assembld to leave on train for Richm$^{\underline{d}}$. The cars were full. Recollected Miss Damer's friend, Miss Doherty, residing on Bollingbrook St.; but have to hurry on. Left Petersburg at 3 o'clock A.M. Sat. morn'g. Cars crowded.

March 26, Saturday

SP: Four Regts. of our Bri. 3$^{\underline{d}}$, 5$^{\underline{th}}$, 6$^{\underline{th}}$, & 12$^{\underline{th}}$ went on picket this morning. I was lucky enough to get excused from going, on account of having bad shoes, & am very glad of it, for I know they had a most disagreeable march & will have a bad week of it. Wrote a letter to Mary to-day—a pretty long one.

HB: Regiment went on picket this morning. Gov. Vance of N.C. spoke at Gen'l. Ramseur's headquarters this evening on the war. Gen'ls Lee, Stuart, Ewell, A.P. Hill, Rodes, Johnston, Brig. Gen'l Stewart, Ramseur, Daniel & Doles were present. Wrote to Brother by Boardman.

JP: Traveled very uncomfortably, not having seats even except our carpet bag & Tom's valise. Arrivd at Richmond at 8 o'clk A.M. Went to Mrs. Barnes' board'g house. Saw there Mr. (now D$^{\underline{r}}$) Witherspoon, Assis$^{\underline{t}}$ Surgeon of 11$^{\underline{th}}$ Ala., formerly of our Company. After getting breakfast Tom & I went to Barracks where he got me a pass to walk the city, & he then went to Gen$^{\underline{l}}$ Winder's where he got a pass, also. We then went to the house, Mrs. B's, where I pack^{d} up those articles which I did not intend taking to the army, such as my thick unmentionables & a few other things. Put them in Sam's valise in wh. I noticed some of his mementos of the Bat. of Fredericksb'g, consisting of some books, bullets, cartridges, &c. &c. We then took a walk over the city & return$^{\underline{d}}$ to dinner. Tom wrote home to-day. Mrs. Barnes gave me a letter fr. Sam, advising me to leave my extra baggage in his valise. I then took my boots down to———& Baker's where I succeeded in exch'g them for a better pair which fit me well; but had to pay $125. besides the boots ($140.), and had to borrow $100. fr. Tom to pay for them. Owe T. B. $103.50. Mailed Tom's letter & also the piece of music which I got in Raleigh the other day for Mary. Tom went to visit the Misses Pendleton. Stay$^{\underline{d}}$ until supper-time & return$^{\underline{d}}$ with a friend of his, Capt. ———, of 5th La. Reg$^{\underline{t}}$. After supper we went to bed, about 7 o'cl'k. John went to Theatre. Blew off very cold to-night.

NOTE: Zebulon Baird Vance supported the Confederacy only after fighting had commenced. In 1862 he was elected governor of North Carolina by a combination of former Unionists and Whigs. Vance repeatedly confronted President Jefferson Davis in defending North Carolina's interests, even urging the suspension of the draft. By 1864 he was advocating peace.

March 27, Sunday

SP: Joe Grigg came over and took dinner with me to-day. Late in the evening Jamie came to our door & spoke to me before I knew he was anywhere near here & so took me by surprise although I had been expecting him. He was looking very well but had a wretched cold & had changed but little since I saw him, except that his beard had grown a good deal. I was delighted to meet Jamie, but sorry to see him in the army, as I do not think he will be able to stand the service. He brought me a letter from Lou & one from Dr. Grigg. Col. Pickens & Col. Hobson came in to see Jamie to-night & sat a while.

HB: Capt. Wm. Britton & myself were asked to dine with Tucker & Lavender. Started up about 12, ate snow & sugar & cakes, after dinner games. Pickens came by from home & we returned to camp with him. Boardman left for home this morning.

JP: We arose at about 4½ o'clock & went to Barracks where Tom B. had a squad of men assigned to him (I was of the number) and went to depot, & aboard of cars. Left Richm^d at or about 6 o'clk. The day was misty, but the sun rising clear, the mist was dispensed & the day turned out a beautiful one indeed. Chang^d cars at Gordonsville about 22 ½ for Orange C.H., and arrivd. at the latter place at 3½ . Went to Hd. Qrs of the Sutler's clerk of Tom's Brigade (Hay's) & got some crackers & a cup of coffee apiece. We then took the plank road for Camp of 5th Ala. Reg^t, on foot. We walked pretty well, altho' the road hurt my feet considerably, as I had on my new pr. of boots. Came with Tom on road as far as the road to Raccoon ford where Tom left me. Met, just before getting to Tom's road and at the Comissary's Quarter's, Capt. Williams, Serg't Britton, Paul Lavender, & Mr. Beck, all of whom seem'd well & in good spirits. They, each in his turn, assisted me in carrying my carpet-bag, which relieved me of a little burthen. Met, also, & was glad to see Mr. Joe Grigg, who was riding on his way to Hd. Qurs. I believe. He looked quite well & reminded me of other days, when we were all at dear old Umbria, together. Hope similar days may soon arrive when the war shall have ended & we all shall have met at home again. 'Tis about 5 miles fr. Orange C.H. to the Road to Raccoon Fd. & about 1½ miles from said road to our Camp, "290". Arriv^d at Camp at about 6½ o'clk. Was glad to meet Sam, whom I found had not changed much, & who was not quite as large as Mr. Joe had represented him to be. He & others of our mess had finished supper & were engaged in reading when I came in. Sam did not expect me this even'g. John cooked a little supper for himself & me. Was a little hungry fr. my walk this even'g & enjoyed camp fare (bacon or pork & corn-bread) exceedingly.

To day is Easter Sunday[.] Is it possible that a year has fl[. . .] since we recognized the great one last Easter at home where all the ac[. . .]s were invited to attend? It is. A year has gone by with results which go to make up the history of a nation.

March 28, Monday

SP: I had a thousand questions to ask J. about home & we sat up pretty late last night talking. We went to-day to see a review of all the N. Carolina troops in this Corps by Gov. Vance of N.C. & heard an excellent speech from him. So Jamie had an opportunity very soon after getting to camp of witnessing a considerable military display & of seeing a number of our Generals—viz. Lieut Gen. Ewell, Maj. Gen. J. E. B. Stuart, Early, Johnston, Rodes, Fitz. Lee (Cav.) Brig. Gens. Ramseur, Kirkland, Geo. Stuart. Gov. Vance is a very young looking man, with long, black hair & is a very intersting speaker & knew exactly how to please the soldiers. He told a great many anecdotes by way of illustration & told them as well as any one I ever heard, convulsing his audience with laughter. His speech was very encouraging & he said if we could only "take the starch out" of old Grant as we had done for the seven preceding Yankee heroes who commanded their V^{a}. army, & hold our own till fall, he'd stake his head on it that we would have our Independence & peace. I sincerely hope he is right.

HB: Governor Vance reviewed all N.C. troops in the corps, after review spoke for two hours or more at Gen'l Ramseur's. Most of the generals present. No mail today.

JP: Slept, last night, in what is call'd a bunk, which consists of an upright piece inserted in the ground & nailed at the other end to the roof of the house. It (the piece) is placed far enough from one side of the house to allow for the length of a bed & far enough from the other side to allow for the width of a bed. Anoth[er] piece is nailed to this piece about four ft. from the ground (wh. forms the floor of our cabins) & on it are layed boards which are covered with straw, making a pretty good bed. The straw we cover with one blanket & use the others for covering. There are two bunks together; i.e. one upon or over another wh. is about a foot from the ground, and two sets to each cabin, capable of accommodating 8 persons. Our cabin is about 14 ft. x 12, is about 7 ft. high to the roof which has a slope of about 3 ft., making our cabin from the ground inside to the comb, about 10 ft. It is built of split pine logs, chinked & daubed (tho' pretty open in some places) has a large fire-place over wh. is a narrow board for a mantel-piece, & has a cup-board in the N.E. corner. The cabin is built East & West. The door is to the South, the chimney to the East, the gable to West & the back to the North & forms one of a row of——cabins, occupied by Co. D, of 5$^{\underline{th}}$ Reg. The other camps, forming the Reg^{t}. are ranged in rows parallel with this one, & all the Regts. form'g Battle's Brig. (3$^{\underline{rd}}$, 5$^{\underline{th}}$, 6$^{\underline{th}}$, 12$^{\underline{th}}$ & 26$^{\underline{th}}$) occupy a space of ground not quite a quarter of a mile square. Sam & I, & a good many others fr. the Co. & Reg^{t} went to hear Gov. Vance speak. He addressed the N.C. troops on subject of secession fr. Confed. & alliance with Yankees. The speech was attentively listened to by an interested crowd of several thousand soldiers fr. various portions of the army. There was a grand review of Ramseur's & part of another Brigade, just before the speaking. Gen$^{\underline{ls}}$ Rodes, Early, Ewell, Ramseur, Stewart, & others were present on the occasion. Return$^{\underline{d}}$ with Sam to our house, very much pleased with the events of the day. Saw Davis Williams, with whom we used to go to school at Mr. Tutwiler's. This even'g Capt. Pickens call$^{\underline{d}}$ to see Sam & me. Saw & was introduced to his brother, Col. Pickens (Sam), yester' even'g. He & Col. Hobson called on me for a few minutes. The day has been clear & pretty. Sam wrote to Mama.

March 29, Tuesday

SP: Last night I wrote to Mama to tell her Jamie had arrived here safely. Joe Grigg & Gilliam James were over here then to see Jamie. I have determined not to make application for a furlough now, but wait till Dr. Hill comes & try and get him to send Jamie before the Board of Examining Surgeons with a recommendation for a detail for some light duty. I had a talk with Capt. Williams on the subject & he told me he knew of no one who was more out of place in the Army than Jamie & would do all he could to have him detailed.

HB: Nothing of importance transpired today, heavy rain all day.

JP: The Reg.ᵗ (5ᵗʰ) are picketing to-day on the Rapidan, about 10 miles fr. this Camp. I think they will come off on Sat. next. There are only a few men in the Co., by reason of all being on picket, which renders it dull to some. Not having been here long, I find the few (ολιγος) to be preferable to the crowd (πολας). Sam wrote to Mama to-day telling her of my arrival at camp. Must write home soon myself. Having a bad cold I've not yet begun the duties of camp, such as standing guard, drilling answering at roll-call &c, &c. Would like to see Dᵣ Hill, Surg. of this Regt. in regard to my getting a detail to attend to Mama's business at home, or else a discharge fr. the service, as I do not think I will be at all able to stand the hard marching which will have to be taken during the coming Spring & summer campaigns. Wish Dᵣ G. could have had influence in getting me a disch'g. before I had join'd the army. I'm glad that I am with Sam, as I've not seen him for a long time, & would like to be with him if I'm to be in serv.; but do not think I'm able. Commenced a letter to Mary this evening, but owing to the rain had to defer finishing it 'till tomorrow. We generally retire about 9 o'clock, to bed.

NOTE: "Dr. G." is Dr. Grigg.

March 30, Wednesday

SP: Jamie wrote a long letter to Mama partly yesterday & finished & mailed it to-day. I added a postscript. Recd. a letter from Mary, in which she spoke of how much Jamie was missed & how sad they all had felt since he & Tom took their departure on the 17ᵗʰ inst. Mama had bought a pony from Mr. Burge @ $700 for Lou, but it did not prove as gentle as it was supposed to be, for it ran away with Tom B. & gave him a fall by the saddle's turning.

HB: Wrote to brother today. Col. Hobson took tea with us.

JP: Finished my letter to Mary this morning. It is very dirty & rumpled & is hardly fit to send—tho' such are the occurrences in Camp, I suppose, that it is hard to write decently. The rain almost prevented me fr. writing, last night. This morning it has ceased, but only for a short time I suppose. Wrote a letter for John to his wife Suckey, & mailed it with my letter to-day. Sam adds a post-script to my letter to Mary, writing to Mama in regard to his decision to await the application for a furlough until I find if I am able or not to do military duty. Would be glad if Sam could get a furlough to go home, as I know he is anxious to do so & Mama & the children would be delighted to see him. Hope he may be able to get one, even if it is decided that I am not able to stand the service. Our mess is composed of Mr. Carter, Peter Hagins, Noah Huggins, Hausman, Sam & myself. I think Henry Childress also belongs to it, but am not certain. Jack Wynne & R. Chadwick form another mess, but occupy bunks in our cabin. H. C. is at present on furlough at home, but is expected to return by 15th next month, I believe. Hope to hear from Mama & the children, soon.

NOTE: Two Burge families were planters in Hollow Square precinct, near the Pickens family.

March 31, Thursday

SP: Jamie brought me a carpet bag full of nice clothes and other things—a pr. pants & vest of very nice jeans, 2 nice knit shrts (under), socks, & a pr. gauntlets—a present from Miss Damar, also a large supply of paper & envelopes, lead pencils, stamps, tooth-brush, combs, handerchiefs, and in fact every thing in the world that I need—except a pr. shoes, & Jamie had a pr. boots, but left them as they were expecting me at home on furlough. He had a box in Richmond filled with every thing nice to eat, too, thanks to the dear folks at home who are ever watching for an opportunity to minister to our comfort & pleasure. J. brought me a knife also, for which he paid Stollenwerck $25. as an example of the high prices, demanded now-a-days. Jamie has a pr. boots bought in Richmond, for which he gave a pr. new ones (made in Greensboro' at $140.$\frac{00}{}$) & $125.$\frac{00}{}$ cash; thus making them cost 265\frac{00}{}$!! for a single pr. boots that you could get before the war for $10.—prodigious!!!

HB: Went to look at the prison at Division Provost headquarters, two men condemned to be shot. Received letter from brother of the 16th inst.

JP: The first Spring month will have expired when this day closes. How rapidly time passes! It has been two weeks exactly since I left Umbria and it has seemed to me an age since. Would that there were no war, that peace would be proclaimed & that Sam, Tom & I were all united at dear old home, sweet home, with our dear mother, sisters & brothers & those we love! Oh, what a happy & joyous day will that be, when we all meet again some day, when the bright-winged angel, Peace, shall smile upon our land & war with its horrors & calamities ~~may~~ be brought to a close! We must all look to God for a close of the war, as it is only by & thro' Him alone, that it will come. May He look in tender mercy upon our land, struggling against oppression & tyranny, & bid the wars of discord be calm & the winds of war to cease, & grant that soon peace & happiness may be restored to our county & we be joined to those most dear to us on earth. Oh, God! hear my poor prayer & grant the petition of Thy servant for Christ's sake.

April 1, Friday

SP: I wrote to Dr. Grigg answering the letter he sent me by Jamie, and request-ing him to send a certificate, as family physician, stating what he has known to have been the condition of Jamie's health—his belief of J's inability to discharge the duties of a soldier in the field, and recommending that he be detailed for some light duty. This I will show to Dr. Hill when he comes & try & get him to send Jamie before the medical examining board. Recd. an epistle from Lou, dated 20$\underline{\text{th}}$ inst.

HB: Became a member of Co. D today. Wrote to brother. Rain in the afternoon. No rations but cornbread today.

JP: To day is cloudy & we may expect more rain. If the bad weather impedes the enemy's movements 'tis well, yes well at all times. For whatever weather is sent to us is best for us. Hope no movement may take place at least until the first of next month. I expect the children are now engaged in the amusing sport of playing off April fools' upon the servants & others. It is usually their means of amusement on 1$\underline{\text{st}}$ Ap'l to spend it in this way & on the 14$\underline{\text{th}}$ Feb. to send valentines. There were several reports of cannon heard by us to-day in conjectured directions. Some supposed the Yankees were making some demonstration upon our lines & others that it was but an April fool. Others thought that it was taking place in the rear of the army, only as a trial of pieces or as a sport. Sam rec$\underline{\text{d}}$ a letter fr. Loutie to-day. I think Tom Moore called by for a short time this evening. He looks just as he used to, at the Greene Springs. Have seen a good many of Sam's & my acquaintances of other days—before the war.

April 2, Saturday

SP: It commenced snowing early this morning & fell in the largest flakes I ever saw, but the ground being very set, it melted away. I got up quite early & walked over to Gen. Rodes' to see Gilliam James, who is going to Richmond to-morrow, & get him to ship our box of provisions up. Jamie and I walked to 12$\underline{\text{th}}$ Ala. & sat & talked some time with Col. Pickens.

HB: Sleeting and raining all day. The regiment returned from picket today marching 10 miles in 1 hour and 15 minutes.

JP: It is cloudy & cold to-day & sleeted a little, I think. We generally have disagreeable weather, now; but it prevents an advance of the Yankees so I believe every one is satisfied. This morning Sam & I walked over & sat for an hour or two with Col. Pickens. He is a very clever gentlemanly young man & I'm very much pleased with him. It is cloudy to-day. Expect we will have more bad weather. This evening Sam walked over quite early to see Gilliam James who is going to Richmond on furlough for a few days, & get him to send our box, if it has arriv$\underline{\text{d}}$ at Richm$\underline{\text{d}}$. While at Col. P's tent was introduced to Rev. Mr. Moore, chap$\underline{\text{ln}}$ of 12$\underline{\text{th}}$ Reg$\underline{\text{t}}$. He was educated at a military academy at Charleston, & also Col. P. He seems to be a very gentlemanly young man of about 26 or 27 years of age. Would like very much to hear fr. home now & from Cara xxxxxx. Hope soon to have that pleasure, so I will hope and await the time with anxious solicitude. Well, camp life is very monotonous, but after one gets used to it it seems as a natural one for a soldier. One has, tho' to observe a great deal of punctuality in the various duties which devolve upon him on assuming the vocation of a soldier. Intended visiting Col. Hobson to-day but did not do so.

April 3, Sunday

SP: A very dull day. There was preaching in the Regt. but I did not attend as it was muddy walking & I was nearly barefooted. An order from Gen.———was read on Dress parade this evening with regard to furloughing men procuring recruits. Hereafter a furlough will be granted only in cases where the recruit is a *non*-conscript.

HB: Weather clear this morning, cold and windy. Heard of Ed. Nutting's anticipated marriage in the afternoon. John Christian and I went to Tucker's, got some meat and molasses up there, and returned home to supper. Answered to roll call for the first time at ———.

JP: There was preaching to-day in the Regt. but neither Sam nor I attended it. Quite dull in, to-day & very sloppy out. Oh, if this "cruel war" were at an end and all of us were at our dear homes, how happy would I, as well as thousands of others, be! What a day of rejoicing & of delight will the day bring when peace shall have been made. God grant that it may soon arrive. If Sam, Tom B., & I were now at home, 'twould be a day of great rejoicing to us all. For then we would see our dear mother, sisters brothers & those whom we love dearly. But, we must 'bide our time & await the coming of the day when we shall all meet again. There is generally an inspection of arms etc., every Sun. morn'g after breakfast, but do not think they had any to-day. Why they choose Sunday for this, is singular; as any other day would do as well, & the men could employ themselves in profitable reading on this day instead of allowing an interruption of their thoughts by a handling of & attention to arms. The Sabbath should be employed in religious reading & in serious & meditative contemplation of our selves & our actions, knowing, that of all these we must, at the last day, give a strict account to God our Judge & the Supreme Overlooker of our thoughts & actions

April 4, Monday

SP: I dressed up in my new clothes to-day, & walked with Jamie over to see Miles Pickens & sat several hours with him. Before we got back it was snowing, & continued to snow, sleet & rain the balance of the day.

HB: Snowing &. raining all day. Rec'd Beacon of 25th. Still raining hard, at night.

JP: Awoke to breakfast about 9 o'clock this morn'g. Sam, with the others, gets up to roll-call about 6 o'cl'k, but comes back to bed before breakfast. I have n't gone to the call yet as I have such a bad cold that I do not care to commence duties yet, if I can help it. Sam & I walked over to visit Capt. Miles Pickens this morn'g. after breakfast. His tent is at the wagon-yard, & is distant hardly a mile fr. our camp. The road or path thither is generally wet & sloppy. Found the Capt in his tent. He seems to be a very good-hearted & clever young man & I am very much pleased with him. Whilst we were visiting him it began to snow pretty fast & continued 'till we had reached our cabin again. In fact it continued to snow the greater part of even'g, but it didn't remain on ground as there had been a rain the night before. We have only two meals a day—breakfast from 8 to 9 in morn'g, & supper about 3 or 4 o'cl'k in even'g. There is not much drilling of the Co. now, owing to the bad state of the weather & the sloppy condition of the ground. Have not visited around much, since my arrival at Camp. Have visited Cap.[t] Williams once or twice. Must go & see Col. Hobson soon, as he has called several times to see us.

April 5, Tuesday

SP: The weather is still very disagreeable—drizzling & raining slowly. No drilling or any thing of the sort going on. We are all glad to see such weather as it will be apt to keep us in our houses till late in the season.

HB: Rainy and windy all day. Was on guard today for first time, slept in my quarters at night and returned to post for reveille.

JP: Awoke this morn'g while it was raining. It is a raw, damp & disagreeable day. It rained a little to-day, snowed, sleeted & hailed. Very changeable weather we are now having, but such suits the soldiers. 'Twould be very disagreeable to march & sleep out in such weather. Old man Elliott, formerly Ass.[t] Sutler of Reg.[t], came to-day from Orange Ct.H. with the news that the President of the Confederacy & Lincoln were arranging a treaty of Peace between the two hostile sections. This news was not credited at all, but each man hoped that it might possibly prove true in the end. As Peace will most certainly come, at last, not by the power of the sword, at the time, but through diplomacy, any news of this character is calculated to excite ones hopes that each day may bring forth a result so earnestly & devoutly to be prayed for as a cessation of hostilities & an adjustment of the discordant elements of the political world to Peace & happiness; not however with out the free & full recognition of every right & institution of the Confederacy & a restoration of all the territory which belongs to it as a separate and independent nation!

April 6, Wednesday

SP: Old Elliott came out from Orange C.H. yesterday with the report that negotiations for Peace were going on between the Federal & Confederate Governments! Of course it was not credited, but it made every one hope that there might be something in it. Nothing more has been heard from it to-day, however; sic transit all such pleasant rumors.

HB: Wrote a long letter to Al. Went to the association held by the 3rd Ala. conducted by Chaplain Rutledge.

JP: It is cloudy this morn'g, altho' the sun shines out occasionally. Suffered last night with a pain in chest—which I have not had before, I do not think. Would like to hear fr. home very much indeed. Hope that either Sam or I will get a letter or letters this even'g. We've not had a mail for several days past, the rail-roads having been out of fix. It became by 12 o'clock, a clear, bright & pretty day. Had a very good breakfast this morn'g—i.e. for camp—corn-bread & pork & coffee. This evening wrote a letter to Willie. This makes now the fourth letter wh. I have written home & have rec^d no answer. The mails are so irregular, tho', that I supposed that is the reason. The sun set clear & beautiful this even'g. 'Twas the prettiest western sky I've seen for a long time—the soft blue outlines of the mountains cast in bold relief against the clear & lucid sky, with a few golden-bound clouds floating over their tops, made a most beautiful scene. Sam, Hagins & I started at sun-set on plank road leading to Fredericksb'g and took a very pleasant walk out of about 1½ m. & return'd feeling much better. Sam got me a Dover's powder to-night for the pain in breast & cold with wh. I have been suffering. Had the pleasure of seeing the "Father of our Generals," & the noble leader of our armies, Genl R.E. Lee, who rode down the plank-road this even'g on horse-back & unattended by any of his staff or escort. He seemed to be a fine & venerable looking man & as one made to command armies.

VET: The regiment received 100 pairs of socks from "Ladies Aid Society," Lynchburg Va.

April 7, Thursday

SP: Jamie wrote home yesterday—to Willy; & recd. two letters this evening—one from Mary and the other from Lou.

HB: Dr. Hill & Cowin returned this evening, received brother's letter of the 24th ult. Dr. Hill informed us of Nutting's marriage.

JP: It is still clear & pretty this morning, tho' clouds in the sky seem to indicate more rain not far off. We have had very bad weather for the past few days & a change would be desirable. Maj. Webster called last even'g just before we went to walk, & spent a few minutes with me. We were introduced this morning to a brother of Mr. Carter of our mess. He belongs to 9th Ala., in Wilcox's Brigade. The weather continued good during the day. This evening there was a prayer meeting at the Chapel, which Sam, Jack & I, with others, attended. A few comments were made on the 1st Psalm, also, by Rev. Mr. Rutledge, chaplain of 3rd Regt. (Ala.) Before the meeting Sam & I attended by Hagins, went to walk on plank road in direction of Orange C.H. We met a very small little boy of about seven or eight years of age, who was on his way, alone to Genl Ewell's Head Quarters. He had been sent from Richmond by his mother, to an uncle of his who lived near said Head quarters. The little fellow was very small to be traveling such a distance by himself and excited our pity for & interest in him. We tried to prevail on him to stop at our camp for the night, but he insisted on going as far as he could by night. Dr Hollburg of 5th Al. Reg^t, who has been at home on furlough, came in this evn'g. He had a large crowd around him, hearing all the Alabama news. Had the pleasure, on coming fr. walking of receiving two letters, one fr. Mary & the other fr. Loutie. Dated Mar 25th & Mary's 27th & 28th ult. We were both glad to hear from home.

April 8, Friday

SP: This is the day set apart by the President as "a day of fasting humiliation & prayer" and I hope that the armies & people throughout the length & breadth of the Confederate States will humbly bow themselves before the Lord, the Supreme Disposer of all things, and earnestly invoke His blessings upon us, our Country and our Cause. I attended prayer meeting immediately after reveilé, heard a very good sermon from Mr. Rutledge, Chaplain of the 3ᵈ Ala. Regt. at 11 O'clock, & at 3 P.M. Mr. Curry, our chap. was to have preached, but was not prepared, so another prayer meeting was held. A number of us fasted all day till late in the evening. We have had a great deal of cloudy, wet weather of late, & to-day being mild, bright & beautiful it was highly appreciated & much enjoyed. Jack W., Jamie & I took a walk on the plank road this evening.

HB: Fast day today, wrote to brother & Fanny. Received first letter from Miss A. Attended the association tonight.

JP: The day tho' cloudy a little at first, proved to be mild & partially clear. This is the day set apart by the President as a day of fasting humiliation & prayer by the people of the Conf. States & the armies, to God, that He in much mercy may deliver us from further blood-shed & restore our land to peace & happiness. Would that all may join in the fasting & prayers, and give earnest supplication unto God to rescue us fr. the hand of our enemies & restore peace & happiness to our country. Took last night, a Dover's powder for my cold & was much re-lieved by it. Slept 'till 10 o'clk this morn'g. Mr. Joe came over this morning & he, Sam, Hausman, Huggins & others went to the chapel & heard a few prayers & some hymns from Rev. Mr. Rutledge, Chapl'n of 3ᵈ. He is a young man & seems to be very zealous & earnest in his labors. Sam, Jack W., Mr. Joe & I, fasted this day, but ate about 4 o'cl'k this evn'g, supper. Sam[,] Jack & I walked out on plank road on way to Martin's. Met on our return, R. Chadwick, Hagins & Chas. Hafner, who turned & came back with us. At 3 P.M. attended prayer meeting.

NOTE: "Fanny" is Francis Beck, Henry's sister.
"Mr. Joe" is Joe Grigg.

April 9, Saturday

SP: It has been raining nearly all day & I spent the time in writing a pretty long letter to Lou. Our house leaked so badly that the only dry place to be found was in the bunks, over which our oil-cloths were stretched against the roof. Our Ala. Beacon's came to-night, & contained the announcement of the marriage of an old school mate of Jamie's & mine, Gerard W. Creagh to Miss Emma May of Greensboro'.

HB: Heavy rains all day, wrote to Joe Elliott. John Christian and I went into a pledge not to swear, drink liquour or chew tobacco from this day on, under a forfeiture of Twenty two dollars, to be applied in case of either breaking the pledge, to buy supplies for the mess.

JP: It commenced raining this morning & continued the whole day. 'Twas a very dull day in Camp—no one being able to go out, or for a short time only. The rain will prevent a movement of the army. Sam wrote a long letter to Lou to-day. It rained so that he had to write on our bunk which was the only dry place in the cabin, being protected by an oil-cloth. The Beacon this morning came with the news that G. W. Creagh who used to go to school at Greene Spr'gs with Sam & me was recently married to Miss Emma May. It did not surprise me as I heard of his engagement in Dec. last when I was at the Canebrake. Commenced reading to-day, a little book called the "Destruction of Jerusalem"; being a description of this terrible fatality concerning this city as predicted long before by our Savior, & proves from this the divine origin of Christianity. It is a very interesting work & contains a brief narration of the horrors of the famine, pestilence & terrors attendant on the City of Jerusalem, during its severe & successful siege by Titus of the Roman Army who entirely laid it waste demolishing the temple & butchering the inhabitants.

NOTE: In 1864, Pickens could have read books titled *The Destruction of Jerusalem* written either by Josephus, Joseph Holford, or others.

April 10, Sunday

SP: I went on guard to-day, altho' my shoes are all to pieces nearly; consequently my feet have been wet all day, & I had a disagreeable time of it running around hunting up my relief. It rained during the evening but held up towards night, & the clouds in the West parted a little & aurora smiled out brightly for a few minutes & formed a beautiful rain-bow. While we were all looking at & admiring the rainbow, some of the men (Peter Hagins it was) said that those who believed in signs in the heavens could read in that a very encouraging omen typical of our revolution: for the Northern end of the bow was at first brighter than the Southern end but it finally grew dim and was first to disappear. Capt. Williams, Brig. officer of the day, by permission of Gen. Battle, dismissed the guard for the night—with the exception of two men from each relief who stayed at the guard-house to take charge of two prisoners there. I had the great pleasure of reading to-night a long & very interesting letter from my dear Mama, & must answer it in a few days.

HB: Fair in the morning, but soon turned into a heavy rain. Was taken sick today. Dr. Hill gave me order to go to hospital for treatment. At the request of Col. Hobson, we sang hymns. Wrote to brother today.

JP: It is clear to-day, altho' from the rain which we have lately had the ground is quite wet & sloppy. Altho' Sam has no shoes, yet he was detailed for guard this morn'g and went. He could easily have got an excuse, if he had wished; but would not do it. Would like to hear fr. Tom Biscoe occasionally, as to how he arriv^d at camp, how he is and &c, &c. I am very certain Tom was tired from his walk to Raccoon Fd, judging of his state by that of myself. I was very much fatigued, but would not have been so much so had my boots not rubbed the heels of my feet & made them so sore that to walk was a pain & a difficulty. I would gladly, however, take the same walk five times over in a day, if Sam, Tom & I were going home, the war had closed & peace with all its blessings & happiness had been restored to our land. Oh, may God look in pity upon our country and grant that the tide of war may be rolled from our land & our independence & peace be restored. It cleared off beautifully & the setting sun was most lovely. There was also a beautiful rain-bow. Sam rec^d a letter fr. Mama this even'g. Were glad to hear that she & all the children are well. It was dated 24th ult. & had miscarried.

April 11, Monday

SP: Jamie commenced doing duty to-day & has entered upon his first tour of Guard duty. He will find it quite fatiguing walking his post for two hours at a time. He wrote home to Willy to-day. Yesterday the sick & all who were unable to march were sent away & this evening on dress parade an order from Gen. Lee was read, which directed that commissaries shall keep on hand 7 days rations; that all extra baggage must be sent off by the 15th.; that Cols. of Regts. must inspect their men & see if they are properly provided with clothing—viz. a hat or cap, a coat, 1 pr. pants, 2 Shirts, 2 pr. drawers, 2 pr. socks & a good pr. shoes, also a blanket; & that all the baggage of a soldier must be carried upon his person: that transportation will be reduced to 3 wagons to the Regt. one for the Field & staff-Surgeon & Quarter Master, one for the Co. officers & one for cooking utensils. General officers are allowed only 60 lbs. of baggage, Field officers 50, & Co. officers 30. Gen. Lee is evidently preparing for active operations at an early day.

HB: Was on the sick list today. Went to see the 3rd Ala. Regt. hold dress parade, orders read to send extra baggage & sick to the rear, delivered Miss A. message to Horace Burton.

JP: Was detailed for guard to-day for first time. Answered to roll-call also for the first time. Had to go to guard-house before finishing breakfast, but returned with Sam, who has just come off guard, & finished breakfast with him. Return'd after brk'fst to gdh., & was soon put on post on the other side of 5th Regt—or the South-side. Stood two hrs. fr. 12 h. 45 m., came to cabin & wrote a letter to Mama wh. will go by this evening's mail. Ate a little lunch of bread & sorghum, with Sam, Hagins & Hausman, wh. was very palatable, after stand'g guard. Sam had gone to hear an address by Rev. Dr. Lacy, on the life &c of Genl T. J. Jackson, which he said was very interesting indeed. Would have like to have heard it, very much. Went to guard at 4 h. 30 m. & came off at 6½ o'clk. Went on again at 10 & came off at 12, at wh. time I lay down to rest a little, 'till next watch!

NOTE: In response to Lee's order to dispense with extra baggage, Sam Pickens sends his diary home on April 15 and does not make entries during the summer of 1864. Henry Beck and Sam's brother James, both not involved in the fighting, continue to keep theirs.

April 12, Tuesday

SP: No drill this morning. A lively game of Town ball is going on out in front of the Regt. The latest quotation of Gold in the North is 171. I heard a most eloquent & touching address, delivered yesterday at Ramseur's Brig. by Rev. Dr. Lacy. His subject was the distinguished & lamented Gen. T. J. Jackson. He sketched his character from boyhood to his untimely death & related many incidents illustrative of the greatness & the goodness of the distinguished hero. The Dr. enjoyed a long acquaintance of Gen. Jackson and was intimately associated with him during the last 6 or 8 mos. of his life, as Chaplain of his Corps, & was a member of the General's military family. Dr. L. is an able man & I think well qualified to write a biography of Gen J., which I hope he will do. The eyes of many a war-worn veteran were bathed in tears as he listed to the recital of the sudden & mournful termination of the brilliant career of the beloved chieftain who had so often led them to victory. I regret exceedingly that Jamie was prevented from hearing the address by being on guard.

HB: Major Joe Webb spent today with us, company inspection of accoutrements & clothing to be carried on march.

JP: Was awakened at 4 o'cl'k by the corp!, to go again. Having walked so steadily yesterday I was quite stiff & tired. Stood 'till 6 or 6½ o'clk when we were all relieved by the new guard. The sun rose very bright & beautiful this morn'g, but it clouded up after breakfast. May have more rain. An order was read out on dress-parade yesterday in regard to baggage, clothing, the sacks, &c. It seems they are preparing to march. To-day 3 years ago, (Ap'l 12$\underline{th}$ & 13$\underline{th}$ 1861) the Yankees fired on Ft. Sumter—the inauguration of the war of invasion of the South & its people. Read to-day an interesting sketch of the life of Randolph Fairfax, a noble youth of 20 years of age & a private in the Rockbridge artillery of the Stonewall Brigade, & latterly in a V$\underline{a}$ Reg$\underline{t}$ of Artil (Thompson Brown's) was killed in the battle of Fredericks'bg, in Dec. 1862. He was remarkable for his bright intellect, noble & generous qualities & above all for his strict moral & religious integrity of character. Full testimonials from all his officers, from his former tutor & also from Gen! Lee, as to the worthiness, bravery & christian attainments of said young man, were given in the sketch of his life. This is a pretty, clear day. The sun is shining beautifully. There was no drill this morning. The men on yesterday & to-day have been engaging in large & active games of town-ball. It is very interesting to witness these plays. Each one takes particular delight in it. Latest quotation of gold in North 171.

NOTE: Philip Slaughter, *A Sketch of the Life of Randolph Fairfax, A Private in the Ranks of the Rockbridge Artillery*, . . . (Richmond: Tyler, Allegre & McDaniel, 1864).

April 13, Wednesday

SP: We have Co. drill every morning & evening on the plank road; double quicked a good deal this evening, & it is a good way to prepare us for the active campaign which is about to open. Jamie recd. three letters this afternoon. The box of shoes brought on by Tood Cowin reached us this evening & Capt. Williams gave out shoes to those who were in need of them & the balance are to be sent back to Richmond—till they are needed. I drew a pr. of them. There were 33 prs. in the box for the Co. & 30 prs. for the Brigade. Chris. Sheldon is here on a visit to his brother & is looking finely.

HB: Brigade inspection by Gen. Battle, packed extra baggage to be sent to the rear company. Received box from G. today with a cake for mess No. 1000 & box with shoes. Capt. W. and I walked up to Maj. Adam's, met C.C. Sheldon, received letters from brother of 31st ult & S.H. of 4th inst.

JP: It is still clear to-day. The moon shines brightly at night. There are generally some clouds floating thro' the sky in the day, but by even'g they disappear and the sun generally sets clear & bright. Sam went last night & heard an interesting & touching address by Rev. Dr Lacy, at Ramseur's Brigade, on the life of the illustrious & lamented hero, Genl T. J. Jackson. Would have liked to have heard the address, very much, but being on guard was prevented from it. Hope Dr L. will write a Biog^y of Genl J., as it would be a means of affording interest to a great many who were denied the pleasure of his lecture on the life of one so intimately & affectionately connected with the cause of his country & his country men, as Genl Jackson most certainly was. Recd. three letters this even'g. One fr. Mama one from Mary & one fr. xxxxxx. Was exceedingly gratified to hear from them all and am glad that they are all well. How I wish we could be united again soon! No happiness for me could be greater. But it is all with God. May He soon grant that we may meet again. The box of shoes brt. by Tood Cowin came this even'g & were distributed to Co. by Capt Williams.

April 14, Thursday

SP: All hands were busily engaged to-day packing up extra baggage. I put my big blanket in Henry Beck's trunk which is to be left at Mrs. Barnes' in Richmond. Jamie & I packed up a Carpet bag with our surplus clothes &c., and will send it by John to Richmond to-morrow. These things also are to be left at Mrs. Barnes'. Gilliam James came over to-night & says he inquired at the So. Express office in Richmond for our box of good things from home, which Jamie & Biscoe expressed at Newbern, Ala. but it had not reached there. I fear we will never hear of it again. Tom Ward, Henry Childress and Bunk Butler were due here yesterday evening, but have not yet arrived. I will send off this Diary and 4 others—preceding—and hope John will deposit them safely in my valise & that they may not be lost. Jamie is finishing a letter to Mary to-night—by the poorest fire-light imaginable.

HB: Packed extra baggage for A, went to all the regiments in the brigade to witness dress parade. A man of the 3rd Ala. was marched down the line with a barrelled shirt on for absence without leave. Rec'd. letter from Mrs. H. T., Miss J.C. & Alfred. Went to prayer meeting tonight.

JP: All hands were engaged in packing up extra baggage which they are going to send to the rear. Gen.ᴸ Lee issued late orders restricting the men & officers to a limited means of transportation & to a change of garments & a good pr. shoes. Sam & I had his big blanket packed to be sent to Mrs. Barnes'. 'Twas packed in a box of Mr. Henry Beck's. Sam & I were engaged all this even'g after drill & dress parade, in packing up our carpet bag with extra clothing &c. which will be sent to Richmond by John to-morrow. These things we will have left at Mrs. Barnes also. Gilliam James returned fr. Richmd to-day. He inquired for but heard nothing of our box. So we conclude it is lost. Wrote a long letter to Mary and one also to xxxxxx this evening, in reply to theirs recd yesterday. Would we were at home to see instead of having to write from so great a distance to them. We went to bed to night about 12 or 12½ o'clock. Owls were hooting.

April 15, Friday

SP: John leaves this morning. Good-bye old Diary—Take care of yourself.

HB: Answered Mrs. Tucker's, Miss J.C. & brother's letters. Received answer from Joe Elliott. Went to association tonight.

JP: Sam & I walked over yesterday even'g to see Gilliam James & Pick Moore. Saw also Mr. Joe. G. was asleep, but came over & sat a few minutes last night with us. We then returned in time for our drill yesterday even'g.

This morning after he had got every thing ready, about 8 o'clock, John left for O.C.H., where he will take the cars for Richmond. Sam sent by him, besides our extra clothing, his letters, books, etc. and I, also, sent the few letters I had received whilst here & a small Diary which I had written, to Mrs. Barnes'. The day is clear and pretty & the weather pleasant. Am getting accustomed to camp life, soldiers' fare, &c., peu-a-peu. Sent by John this morn'g, a letter to Mary and one to xxxxxx. Will look anxiously for answers to them. This even'g Lieut. Jones drilled our Co., taking us down the plank-road about ¼ of a mile, in the direct. of Martin's, where we turned to the left into an old field, & drilled for a few minutes, then rested, talked & finally return.ᵈ in time for dress-parade. This last duty occupied only a few minutes; only one small order having to be read by the Adj.ᵗ. Chas Pegues, Adj.ᵗ, having gone away for a few days, Lieu.ᵗ Jno. Christian acted as Adj. He generally takes the place of Adj.ᵗ. Commenced reading, this even'g, before dark a book called "A Romance of a Poor Young Man", which I found quite interesting & pretty well written.

Tom Biscoe came to-day to visit Sam & me. We were drilling when he came, about 10 or 11. Capt Williams excused us from drill in order to see Tom. He is not looking quite as well as he did when he was at Umbria, altho' he looks quite well now. He wouldnt stay to dinner but left about 1 o'clock.

NOTE: *The Romance of a Poor Young Man, Translated from the French of Octave Feuillet* (Richmond: West & Johnston, Macfarlane & Fergusson, 1863).

April 16, Saturday

HB: Rain this morning, wrote to Alfred, gloomy weather all day.

JP: It rained to-day & is disagreeable & cold. Notwithstanding the bad weather, Sam was called for to post guard. He is now 1ˢᵗ Corpˡ of "Greensboro Guards". There was no roll-call to-day on account of the bad weather. Re. Dʳ. Lacy is announced to deliver a sermon to the Brigade, at the Camp of 3ʳᵈ Regᵗ. to-morrow, at 11 o'cl'k A.M. He is, I am told, an interesting and pleasant, as well as eloquent, speaker, & I've no doubt his address will be listened to by a large audience. Saw for a few minutes, yesterday evening, Cruse. Coleman, whom I have not seen since we were at camp of 5ᵗʰ Ala. when it was in vicinity of Richmᵈ in 1861. He is like a different person altogether. Has grown a great deal & improved wonderfully. Can hardly recognize in the well-grown, healthy & good-looking young man he is to-day, the small, puny & sickly little fellow he was at the Greene Spr'gs. in 1859. But tempus omnia mutat. The Co. had to do police duty this morn'g. Such as sweeping around Cabins & clean'g up. Sam, Jack W., & myself attended to-night a meeting of the "Association", at the Chapel.

NOTE: *Tempus omnia mutat* means "time changes everything."

April 17, Sunday

HB: Dr. Lacy preached in front of Col. Forsyth's quarters today for the brigade. Wrote to Miss I. Paul came to tell us goodbye. He leaves for Richmond tomorrow.

JP: The sun rose clear & pretty to-day, but after breakfast clouds began to rise in the sky & the day may not be clear after all. After breakfast, about 10½ o'clk, Sam, Jack Wynne, myself, our mess, & in fact most all the Co., repaired with stools to a Knoll, under some pines, just back of the Camp of 3ʳᵈ Ala., where, after taking our seats, a large concourse of soldiers was assembled. Dʳ Lacy, with other Chaplains soon made his appearance, and after having the audience move closer around him in order that he might be more distinctly heard, opened the exercises by a hymn. He then took his text, from 1ˢᵗ Chron., XXVIII Chap., 9ᵗʰ verse (latter part). "If thou seek the Lord, he will be found of thee; but if thou forsake him, he will cast thee off forever." His sermon was plain, eloquent and very interesting indeed, and was listened to by a large & attentive audience of several hundred men. Could listen to such a sermon if it were to be preached all day. It clouded up whilst we were at preaching, drizzled a little & turned pretty cold. We took, each of us, a little snack, & afterwards, some went to sleep. It sleeted a little. Dʳ L. gave out that there would be preaching at Camp of 61ˢᵗ Regᵗ. at 4 o'clk, P.M. to-day, by Rev. Mr. Brown. Mr. Sam. Jackson, his bro. Andrew, & I, proceeded to Camp of 61ˢᵗ at about 3 h. 15 m. Went to a tent of an acquaintance of A. Jackson's, where we remained till near time for preaching. (By this time, Sam, R. Chadwick, Jack Wynne & C. Briggs had come.) We then took our seats, made for the occasion of holding worship, on pine poles raised on others, running in front of the minister's stand & parallel with it. Mr. B. soon after came & took his text (after the singing of a hymn,) from St. John, XIV Chap., latter clause of 2ⁿᵈ verse; "I go to prepare a place for you." He preached a very good sermon, tho' not as interesting or as fine a one as Dʳ L.'s this morn'g. Charles Briggs &

another young man joined the Presbyterian Church. Saw after preaching was over, Capt. Miles Pickens, who return^d to his Camp. Sam, Jack, R. Chadwick, C. Briggs & myself then returned to Camp, and Sam & I prepared supper, for which we were pretty well prepared; being rather hungry. Just as we had finished supper, John came in f. Richm^d. He carried & left the things we sent by him, & got one Diary—all he could get: but did not bring our box of provisions, wh. I think is lost. Sam, Jack W., myself & others of our Co., attended prayer-meeting, to-night, & heard a sermon by Rev. Mr. Rutledge. Text, Daniel, Chap. VI, verse 10th. The chapel, which is not a large one, was very full indeed. Mr. R. seemed to preach better to-night than he did before. The sermon was a pretty good one. It clear^d off this even'g beautifully & the weather is very pleasant—very much like our October weather. The stars are bright & beautiful to-night. We sat up talking 'till about 12 o'cl'k, when we retired.

April 18, Monday

HB: Held a mass meeting of the brigade, at which resolutions of thanks were drafted to thank the people of Ala. for the contribution made up for this brigade.

JP: The weather is still clear & beautiful & the atmosphere, cool & delightful. A few light, fleecy clouds are floating in the blue azure sky, & the face of nature seems smiling to receive its new coat of verdure & loveliness. It can scarcely be imagined that discord reigns with men when so much loveliness prevails in the natural world. God grant that it may soon cease & that ere long the sky of the political world may soon be as clear as the blue expanse which is spread above us, & that peace, offspring of Heaven, may soon smile upon our land! Was detailed again this morning for guard, for the second time. Had to repair to guard-house, where the reliefs were formed & given to Corporals to post. After this, return'd & took breakfast at Cabin. I'm on the same relief that I had on last Mon. (3rd) & have, also, the same post (No. 2.) Sam was appointed on a Committee of the Brigade, to draft resolutions of thanks to the citizens of Ala., for their liberal donations to this Brigade, of shoes, clothing and other necessaries. Mr. Sheb. Chadwick informed Sam of his appointment. Went on post at 12 & came off at 2 o'cl'k, when Sam, myself & others went to Camp 3rd Reg^t where there is to be a mass meeting at 3 o'cl'k & where the proceedings of the committee will take place. A crowd soon gathered around, & after awhile Genl Battle rose and moved an organization of the meeting by appointing Col. Hall as Presid^t., and the various Adj^ts to act as Secretaries; the other Regimental officers, as Vice-Presidents. The Resolutions then were ready by Col. Forsyth, and a short speech was made to the assembly by Genl Battle. Went on guard at 6, again, & came off at 8 o'cl'k. Slept 'till 12 when I went again. Good news came to-night. Gold in N.Y., 179! continuing to rise. Genl Forrest has taken Ft. Pillow, wh. refused to surrender. Great slaughter of garrison.

VET: Meeting of Brigade in order to adopt resolutions relative to the clothing, shoes, etc., sent us from Ala. God bless the dear women, they never forget us.

NOTE: Nathan Bedford Forrest's cavalry attacked Fort Pillow, Tennessee, on April 12, killing twice as many black Union soldiers as white. The resulting "Fort Pillow Massacre" enraged Northern opinion and spurred black soldiers to redouble their efforts.

April 19, Tuesday

HB: Nothing of importance took place today. Rec'd. letter from Brother of the 9th.

JP: The night last, was clear & beautiful, the moon was as bright as daylight & the stars shone beautifully. Went for the last time on guard at 12, came off at 2 this morn'g and slept 'till 6. Then stood until 8 or 8½ , when the new guard was form$^{\underline{d}}$ and we were relieved. Was quite tired after my fatigue last night, so after eating breakfast—corn-bread and coffee—and reading, went to bed and took a rest—not much sleep tho'—'till about 3 o'cl'k P.M. Dress-parade came off at 11; but no orders being read 'twas dismiss$^{\underline{d}}$ sooner than usual. This evening Sam wrote a letter to Mama. The Reg$^{\underline{t}}$ goes on picket again to-morrow morn'g at sun-rise. It is predicted by some that 'twill not return to these Quarters; tho' I hope that is a mistake, as it is quite cold again—was like winter on guard, last night—and will be very disagreeable to sleep out of doors. Sam rec$^{\underline{d}}$ last night two letters, one from Mama & the other from Loutie—both dated 7$^{\underline{th}}$ inst. The news came this evening, confirming, in part, the news from Ft. Pillow. The butchery must have been great. Reported that 600 out of 700 men were killed. The men to-night were engaged in cooking up what rations they had, & making other preparations for going on picket to-morrow. Rec$^{\underline{d}}$ a "Beacon" this even'g, of date 8$^{\underline{th}}$ inst. It contains no local news. There is in it a very good letter to the Editor fr. Mr. S. Chadwick. Sam & I made our preparations & then went to bed.

April 20, Wednesday

HB: Brigade went on picket this morning. Wrote to Brother & Alfred, telling him of my dream. Briggs & I are all left here from the mess, made deadfalls to catch sparrows. H. Childress & Butler returned today, received letter from brother of the 6th by Butler.

JP: Were roused this morning about 6 o'clock by reveillé. Had roll-call & afterwards we got breakfast. We were then ordered into line (the 5$^{\underline{th}}$ Reg$^{\underline{t}}$) and set out for picket duty near the Rapidan. Capt. Williams is in command of Regt., & Col. Hall of the Brig. pro tem. Col. Pickens is field-officer of the day. Marched about 4 miles & halted for a few minutes to rest. The 61$^{\underline{st}}$ Regt. was in our front. Then we marched about 2 ms. & rested again, & again after march'ng 2 ms. more. After this we took up our line of march & came to camp of the reserve Regt., where we thought we had to stay 'till to-morrow; but we had hardly rested good & began to cook dinner & fix for the night when we rec$^{\underline{d}}$ orders from Gen$^{\underline{l}}$ Ramseur to relieve his Brigade this even'g. So we again began our march & after going about a mile, got to camp. A relief was soon sent out on post, Gen$^{\underline{l}}$ R.'s were brought in & his Brig. moved off to camp of reserve. It was about 6½ or 7 o'cl'k when we left Quarters & about 12 or 1 when we began to camp on a hill-side about 150 yds. from Rapidan R. Our tent (?) consists of a pole across some forks on wh. are rested (one end on ground & the other on the pole) other poles in which is layed brush. We then spread pine tops on the ground underneath & make our beds on it. The weather wh. to-day was threatening, changed this even'g, & it is now clearing off. The wind too is blowing & the atmosphere quite cool. Sam, R. Chadwick & I walked over to the River, saw the beautiful valley over there, the green fields & mountains (Blue ridge) in the distance. Also saw the Yankee videttes, on their horses going fr. post to post, also their pickets, & heard the music from their camps about 1 or 2 ms. fr. here (on the river.)

April 21, Thursday

HB: Went on duty with Maj. Webster today, and returned to camp in the evening.

JP: This morning is clear & beautiful, & the weather pleasant. The sun rose bright, altho' Sam, Chadwick & I slept 'till 9 o'cl'k. This last was the first night that I have ever slept on a blanket on the ground & I was as comfortable as in our bunk at the Quarters. Was very tired & sore after our march yesterday & Sam, also, but slept it off last night. Sam & I prepared a very good breakfast to-day, of bacon, & warmed corn-bread, & coffee with sugar. It was very palatable indeed. Sam, Jack & I went out hunting onions this even'g for supper. Passed several of our out-posts at wh. were Hutchinson, Lieut. Christian & others. Succeeded in getting a few for a mess, but with a great deal of trouble. The view of the valley over the river, from our works & cannon-pits, & of the mountains in the distance, was beautiful. They could be seen to greater advantage to-day as it was clear. There is not a cloud in the sky. Met Capt. Williams on our return to camps. Heard on our arrival that Genl Hoke in N.C. attacked some Yankee fortifications, captured a Bri. Genl, 1,600 men & twenty-five pieces of artillery! Glorious news for us! The God of battles is with us & is sending victory to our arms. Alex. McCall came fr. Quarters to-day. Brings news that Henry Childress has arriv^d, that he says our box is in Richmd. So Sam wrote to Hagins telling him to send a letter who S. wrote to Ellison to send the box to the former who will take charge of it for us. Sam & I, Jack & others to-night went to Youngblood's fire, about 8 or 10 steps fr. our brush tent, and heard a few songs by S. Chadwick, Lieut. Jones, Britton & others. The singing was very good indeed. After it was over, we went to bed. This morn'g there was a sham battle in the Yankee's encampment. Heavy volleys of musketry & roaring of artillery was plainly heard for several hours. The music from their drums can be distinctly heard.

April 22, Friday

HB: Returned to Maj. Webster's in the morning, no business on hand all day, staid all night the first time wrote to brother.

JP: Last night was beautiful. The moon shone as brightly, softly & its light was almost heavenly. Oh, how I thought of such nights at home, with the dear inmates of Umbria! and wished we were there with those whom we love most dearly! Rose & I ate breakfast about 8 o'clk to-day. Jack W. had finished. Was detailed for post duty this morn'g at breakfast, but Jacob Youngblood took my place until I had finished. My post is No. 13, & opposite to it across the river, is (what used to be) a pretty mansion, two storied, with Venetian blinds & gently sloping roof. The color of house is a yellowish brick dust. The house has pretty fields laid off around it. But now the war has driven its inhabitants away, & every house there seems to be deserted. Away in the rear of the houses may be seen Yankee videttes galloping their posts ever & anon, while at long distances may be seen their pickets, on foot. Pony Mt. is oppos. my post a little obliquely to right. I said no one inhabited the house just over river opposite my post; but there is an old man & his family, by the name of Nawle, who occupies it. Sergt. M⊆Call, M⊆Dairmed, Stevenson, W᎙. Sheldon & myself are on Post No. 13. Wearied the day out 'till this even'g, when I wrote a letter to Mama, and commenced one to Gayle Dorroh, also. It looks very much like rain this even'g, but hope 'twill not, as I've to stand post at 12 o'cl'k to night on the river bank. M⊆C. put up a tent under wh. he, Sheldon & I reclined. S. & I went to sleep for a short time. Awoke at 12 and went on post. Found on the one next to mine Mr. Trawick. M⊆D. then relieved me at 2 o'clock, when I return'd to tent for the rest of the night. It cleared off cold to-night.

April 23, Saturday

HB: Went to Division headquarters with Maj. Webster, returned by the 5th. & spent all the evening in sleeping. Thom. Ward returned today. Him & Briggs came to see me.

JP: The morning is clear, bright & pretty. Didn't awake this morning 'till about 9 o'cl'k. The sun shone brightly around, illuminating the face of nature with his genial rays. The wind sweeps by over the top of the bluff in swift & strong gusts. Finished my letter to Gayle this morning & added a post-script to the one to Mama, giving her the further details of Gen! Hoke's victory in N.C. It is reported that he captured 2,500 men instead of 1,600, as first reported, destroyed two gun-boats & a steamboat, & brought off a large quantity of meat & other provisions. Six or eight cavalry men of ours went across the river this morn'g foraging at the house opposite my post; they were evidently observed by the Yankee videttes who went off & returned soon after with a cavalry force of twenty or twenty-five men, when ours left & recrossed the River. We were relieved to-day & left the river, marching about a mile or a mile & a half & camping in a little vale on side of road near some old barns. The 61ˢᵗ Reg. took our places. Saw Henry Childress, this morn'g, who came out on picket yesterday—having just arriv⁴ from home. Ate supper this even'g just about sun-down. The day is clear & beautiful & weather cool tho' it was as hot in sun as summer once. Heard last night while on post on the river bank, the cry of the "whip-poor-will", the first time I've heard it this season. It is a different note from that made by the bird of the same species in Ala.; ours making the distinct sound, "chuck-will's widow."

April 24, Sunday

HB: Today is my twenty-fifth birthday. Nothing of importance transpired today.

JP: Sam, Hausman & I after supper last even'g sat around fire & heard a few songs by Lieut. Jones, Britton & others. We then spread our blankets on the grass by Capt. Williams' tent, & having the blue, star bedecked canopy of heaven for our covering, lay down to rest. Awoke about 8 o'clk this morning, having had a very good night's rest indeed. 'Twas the first night which I've ever spent in the open air asleep. Had breakfast after rising. Sam & I went to a spring about two hundred yards from Camp, where we refreshed ourselves by a wash. At 11 o'clock we attended preaching which was held in open air on hillside above our camp; services by Rev. Mr. Curry. Text, Galatians, IV Chap. 4$\underline{\text{th}}$ & 5$\underline{\text{th}}$ verses. The sermon was only an ordinary one. After service was over a letter from Gayle Dorroh was handed me. 'Twas written at the Univ. It seems that fatal disease, the meningitis, has not left the Corps yet. Another young man died of it, lately. (Commenced the Bible this morning.) His letter (G's) was very interesting. A dispatch was rec$\underline{\text{d}}$ soon after our return from preaching that the Yankees in force, are crossing at Germanna Fd., and an order was given to the soldiers of the Regt. to hold themselves in readiness & prepare to move at a moment's warning. 'Tis clouding up & looks a little like 'twill rain soon. The sun is as warm as summer. Finished yesterday a little book like this one that I'm writing in (a part of my diary) & gave it to Sam to keep for me. The pencil which I commenced using soon before leaving home is almost gone, being only about an inch long. Rec'd yesterday a little biographical sketch of Admiral Coligny, & to-day one of Rev. Edward Bickersteth. A party of us this even'g, walked up on a neighboring hill, on which were planted several field-pieces. There were several artillery-men there, who gave us a slight insight into the nature & use of the different kinds of artillery & ammunition in use by our armies, which was quite interesting. We then (Sam, H. Allen & I) walked to Raccoon Fd., & observed the breast-works of ours on the river, which are impregnable to assault. We then returnd to Camp or Bivouack & prepar$\underline{\text{d}}$ for sleep. Slept in a tent of the Youngblood's & others, & we were glad of it, as it happen$\underline{\text{d}}$ for it rained quite heavily during the night 'till near daylight. Our rest was very comfortable notwithstanding.

NOTE: The sketch of Admiral Coligny, the Huguenot whose assassination sparked the Saint Bartholomew's Day Massacre, was probably the one in Edward Shepherd Creasy's *Unsuccessful Great Men*, from Bentley's *Miscellany*, volume 31 (London?: 1852).

John Lang Bickersteth, *Memoir of John Lang Bickersteth: Late of Rugby School* (Philadelphia: American Sunday-School Union, 1850).

April 25, Monday

HB: Nothing at all transpired today.

JP: Altho' it rained very hard last night it cleared off this morn'g after breakfast, & the sky is now as clear as a bell, with the exception of a few clouds floating thro' its azure depths. We have n't moved yet, altho' some think it probable that we may soon be off. The mail came to-day, but unfortunately, no letter came for us. However, we cannot expect letters to come too often. Sam & I walked to the spring, which is about a quarter of a mile from Camp, just over the hill & due west of it. Got our canteens full of water for breakfast & washed. Ate about 9. Yester' even'g, on our return from the hill west of us, where the artillery was planted, a crowd of us took our seats on the grass, around Capt. Reid, who read to us Long's speech in the Yankee Congress. 'Tis full of interest, & shows with how much more freedom the acts of the Abolition administration are now criticized by their people than they were formerly. If there were in the North to-day a party of men with the same opinions & sentiments of Long, & who had the boldness to assert & the power to maintain those opinions & sentiments, we would, unquestionably, have peace to-morrow. May such a party spring up & soon bring about a consummation of our difficulties which shall secure to us a recognition, in toto, of all the rights, privileges, institutions & principles for which we have been contending for three years, with a full acknowledgement of our freedom & independence; and may this be done without farther warfare & strife. God grant that such consummation of our affairs may soon be realized by us, and that ere long we may be united together with those we love at home, in peace & happiness & prosperity! The Co. assembled on the hill-side above our tents, & engaged in jumping, hopping & throwing a cannon ball over the head, 'till a late hour this even'g. Then we went to Capt. Williams' tent & heard some good singing by our usual vocalists, Mr. S. Chadwick, Lieut. Jones, Britton & others after which we spread our blankets under our tent & went to sleep. P. Hagins came to-night before bed-time with rations for the Co. Our commissariat was rather scant before that, our supper having been only warmed bread & coffee. Could the dear ones at home peep in & see how we fare & manage, sometimes, 'twould make them smile. Sam & I manufactured a very respectable pair of suspenders for himself this even'g, out of an old pair of drawers; he making one & I the other. It drizzled a little this even'g but did not rain.

April 26, Tuesday

HB: Nothing at all transpired today.

JP: Had a very good night's rest. Hagins left for W. Quarters early this morn'g. The day is clear, bright & rather cooler than yesterday. Sam, Hausman & I went to Spring about 8 o'clk, got water, washed & returned to breakfast. The mail came to-day, but no letters for us. Well, we shall hope on and anxiously expect some. Hope soon to hear from xxxxxx, from whom I have not heard for a long time. Oh, how happy we would be, if peace had returned to bless our land and we were on our way to our homes & dear ones! How ardently do I hope that soon God, in mercy will cause the tide of war to roll from our land & restore peace &

happiness to it again. This evening about 1 o'clock, Col. Hobson came to where we are bivouacked, from Camp at Winter Qrs. We went to Capt. Williams' tent where he was. He says it is reported that Averell is preparing to make another raid down the Valley of Va. No other news. Thinks it probable that we will return to Winter Qrs. to-morrow. Our relief——passed by our Bivouack Camps this even'g going on picket. A party of us this evening, went up on the opposite hill from our Camp, armed with bayonets & hunted ground rats, which are a little smaller than the common rat, & which abound in the ground around our Camp. Growing tired of this, Sam, Henry Childress, Butler & I got some horse-shoes & pitched them as quoits 'till we were prevented by darkness. Henry & I only won a game or two to Sam & Butler's four or five. Hausman went on an onion detail* for our mess & returned with some which we ate at dinner as we eat eschallots at home. The wild onion grows in great abundance in low places near streams of water, & form one of the chief vegetables which a soldier enjoys in the Spring. They are *very* strong in odor, however, which is an objection to them. We rec$^{\underline{d}}$ an order to be ready to march back to Quarters in the morning at 8 o'clk. Night is clear & beautiful, & quite cool. Vegetation is much more tardy here than in Ala. The grass is just beginning to spring up & look green in the fields; the young leaves are at last making their appearance on the trees & a few briers here & there, have put forth their green coating. After a few songs from our usual singers, Sam & I retired to rest—about 9 o'clock.

*He bought some salt also, from a sutler, hard by—$1 pound.

April 27, Wednesday

HB: Maj. Webster & I went to Orange C.H. I was to go to Richmond, but failing to get the proper papers had to return. On the way stopped at Gen. Lee's headquarters. On reaching campground the brigade returned from picket. Boardman returned today.

JP: Were roused this morning about 7 o'clock by the noise & clamor of hungry mouths, & active preparations for breakfast. Sam, Hausman & I ate, & then fixed up for marching. We then took a game or two of quoits. It is a clear & beautiful day & during the mornings & even'gs turns quite cool, but in the middle of the day the sun shines with summer heat. Presently the command, "Fall in!" was given & soon our Brigade was winding its way back again to our Winter Quarters. Left Bivouack at 8 o'clk; marched leisurely along, halting three times as before on our way, & reached Camp about 12½. Was very much fatigued on getting back, and Sam suffered badly with sore feet. John who had been sick during our absence, is again quite well. Saw Huggins, Hagins, the Jacksons, & the others whom we left behind, & was introduced to Mr. Thos. Ward, who returned the other day fr. home having been there on furlough. We enjoyed a good dinner this even'g, of pease, rice, bacon & cornbread, which was relished after coming off picket. Made a clean toilette before dinner, which improved my feelings very much & tended to diminish the fatigue from which I was suffering. Had the great gratification & inexpressible pleasure of receiving a long & highly interesting & affectionate letter from my dear Mama this evening. All at home are well, tho' Mama said that she had been sick. Mama speaks as tho' she is troubled in having her business seen after & I know she is so. Would to God I could return to help her & lend the little assistance to her which I am capable of! I trust that I may soon be with her again to relieve her of the annoyances & inconveniences to which she is subject on account of her business. I'm only awaiting the reception of a certificate from D.ʳ Grigg in regard to my health & general physical ability, to make an application, thro' D.ʳ Hill, for a detail. I humbly trust in God that I may succeed in obtaining one, on my dear Mother's account.

April 28, Thursday

HB: Rec'd. letter from brother by Boardman, answered today. The execution of three men from the 4th N.C. Regt. took place today, for desertion. I returned to my command until further orders.

JP: Were roused, by the usual reveillé, this morn'g, to roll-call. The day is clear & pretty. Sam & I stole back to bed & got a few more moments' repose before the announcement that breakfast was ready. Sam shaved yesterday, making a great change in his looks, indeed. He took off his goatee, & left an imperial, side-whiskers & moustache. If Mama were to see him now, she would of course know Sam, but would observe a great change in his looks. At 1 o'clock to day our Brigade was called upon to witness a very disagreeable & heart-rending spectacle,—viz:—the execution of three deserters from the———N.C. Reg.ᵗ At the above hr., we were ordered to "fall in!" and took up the line of march for the scene of the event. It was about a mile & a half from our camp down the plank-road & in the direction of our way to picket, in a field. There were present about ten regiments, which I suppose must have been all, or a greater part of Gen.ˡ Rodes' Division. They were drawn up, on three sides around the place of execution. By-&-bye, two ambulances, with a file of soldiers on each side & a guard in front & rear might be seen, making a slow approach up to the spot. Then a band went in front & played the "dead march," to the scene. The three unfortunate men are in the ambulances. They are lead out, their hands bound behind their backs, to three stakes—a guard armed, all the while; they kneel in prayer, with a minister, for a few minutes, ere their spirits are wafted into eternity; they seem calm & composed, & kneel, each to a stake, & have their eyes bound by an officer. Finally, he retires about ten steps off & gives to a guard of about 20 men, with loaded pieces, the clear commands, "Ready!", "Aim!" "Fire!" and in a few seconds more the souls of these unfortunate men are launched, from healthy friends, a smiling earth, on which they might otherwise spent profitable lives, to an unknown eternity, & into the presence of their maker! Sad & heart-sickening scene! I felt the moment after the volley was fired, an indescribable & mixed sensation of sickness & horror at the sight. (Gen.ˡ Rodes & staff, Gen.ˡ Ramseur & staff, & other officers were present.) We then marched back to our Quarters, where we remained until about 3 o'clk, when we marched over about two and a half or three ms. to a field, on the plank road & about north from here, where we had Brigade drill for an hour & a half & return$\underline{d}$ to supper. Rec$\underline{d}$ a "Beacon" from Mama this even'g. Sam had a disagreeable time again with his feet, to-day. The shoes that he got from those that Tood Cowin brought on, hurt his feet very badly being made out of hard & stiff leather. M$\underline{c}$Call, Hafner, Henry C., Jack, Sam & myself sat by fire talking 'till late to-night after which we retired to bed.

April 29, Friday

HB: Wrote to Fanny. Brigade drill by Genl. Battle.

JP: We were roused this morn'g by reveillé, for the usual roll-call. The sun was just peeping over the eastern hills, gilding with his rays the trees, houses, fields & surrounding mountains. All nature is fresh with the fragrance of approaching Spring, & the trees & shrubs are beginning to put on their green mantles & the birds are tuning their merry lays to welcome her presence: Would to God that no cruel war were raging in our land & that man, too, would cease from strife with his fellow-man, & learning a lesson from the little birds, praise his maker in songs of thanksgiving, for sending spring-time & harvest upon the earth again! God grant that ere many days have passed, we may welcome the return of peace & praise His holy name in crowning our arms with signal triumph, securing independence & nationality to our country & immunity & safety from the hands of our foes, to our country! God speed the coming of that most happy day, when we shall be united again with those whom we love in happiness & peace! The chief amusement in Camp, now, is quoits; almost every one taking a turn in throwing them. At 9 or 9½ o'clk this morning we took our places in ranks & marched to the old field over the hills north of camp, where we had another Brigade drill. Several very pretty movements were executed which were creditable as well to the men as the officers in command. Once in forming a line-of-battle we charged up to the colors & guides at a full run & with loud cheering. The boys said it was exactly in a manner similar to this that they charged & captured all the batteries of the Yankees that we have taken. Was very glad when the drill was over, as I was very much fatigued indeed.

April 30, Saturday

HB: Major Adams returned this evening. Britton, Briggs, Sheb Chadwick, McCall, John Christian & myself sang hymns at our cabin after supper.

JP: Awoke, Sam & I, at the usual hour this morn'g. 'Twas very cool indeed, as all the nights & mornings are now. The day is clear and pretty. Would that we had sweet & lasting Peace in our country and that we were united with those whom we love, at home again! Hagins being unwell to-day, Hausman & I got the rations for the Co. Two days' allowance was given out. This is the last day of April—the second Spring month. Soon Summer will be upon us, in all its loveliness & the air will be fraught with the fragrance of sweet flowers & the notes & warblings of the winged songsters of the forest. Naught will disturb the peace & joy of Nature in her loveliness, but the grim visage & hollow, reverberating notes of horrid war. Oh God spare us we beseech Thee, from further slaughter & speak "Peace!" to our distracted country. Sam wrote a letter this evening to Mary. Intended writing to Mama myself, but did not. Jack W. & I walked over to wagon-yard where I got a pair of shoes (No. 8) for John, & Jack a pair of pants for himself. It clouded up & rained or drizzled a little while there & on our return. Mr. Joe G. called over to see us, this evening a little after "candle light," & gave us some papers with the news. Gold in N.Y. is very fluctuating, borne up on the current by the recent disasters to the Yankees, in La., Tenn., & N.C. It was at 184, at the last quotation. The northern papers admit the result of Bank's Red R. expedition as a perfect failure, & acknowledge their defeat also, in N.C., by Genl Hoke. Plymouth in that state, has been recaptured by our forces. I've suffer^d for several nights passed with severe attacks of heartburn, & had it to such a degree to-night that I could not sleep for several hrs. after going to bed. Sam & I & several others sat up talking 'till late to-night.

May 1, Sunday

HB: Attended preaching by Chaplain Rutledge. After services John Christian & I went to Maj. Websters, got the cake I sent for to Richmond which John & I ate on the road. After dinner John C., James D. Webb & myself walked up the plank road. On our return about dusk, conversation stopped, for sometime, when the stillness was broken by someone's proposing to state our different thoughts, which we did. We were all building air castles. Attended preaching again tonight.

JP: We awoke at reveillé this morning a little after sun-rise. It was clear, but clouded after breakfast, I think. Went on the sick-book, to-day & then at surgeon's call of bugle, I went to Dr Hill's tent & saw him in relation to the heartburn from which I had been suffering. He only advised me to eat supper at an earlier hour of an evening. Mr. Joe came by this morning & he, Jack W., Henry C., Sam & myself went to preaching. Heard a short but interesting sermon by Mr. Rutledge of 3rd Reg.^t. Text was taken from Exodus, Chap VIII, 1st clause of 10th verse; "And he said, To-morrow." There was an inspection of arms, before preaching; but I was not obliged to attend. The congregation to-day was quite a large one. After preaching Mr. J. return^d to Co. but went back to his Camp soon after. Mr. R. announced to the congregation that Mr. Curry would preach to-night. Read two small tracts to-day—one "An Address to Chaplains & Missionaries," by Rev. B. W. McDonnald, D.D. & Chapl'n of 26th Al. Reg.^t; a very good little book; also a tract called, "Pitching the tent toward Sodom", also interesting. This evening, R. Chadwick, Hutchinson, H. Childress, Sam & myself took a walk on pl'k rd in direct. of Or. C.H. Met Mr. Joe who walked a short distance with us, when meeting some friends he took a horse which one of them offered him & rode to his Camp. We walked a few hundred yds farther & then returned. The mail came during our absence, but no letters for us. 'Tis reported this even'g that

Gen! Hoke has begun an attack on Newbern N.C., which, it is thought, he will take. Sat 'till roll-call with a party in conversation, before Capt. Williams' tent. After that, Jack W.[,] Sam & myself Henry C. & others, went & heard a minister whom Mr. R. brought up to preach. His text was from the Acts of the Apostles, Chap. XVI, 30th verse, "Sirs, what must I do to be saved?" The sermon was an earnest one, but was not a good one. It drizzled a little while we were there. The preaching was behind the Chapel, out in the open air. A wagon with rations of fish (herrings & shad) came to-night & these scarce articles were issued as extra rations to the soldiers. Sam & I retired rather earlier to-night—than usually.

NOTE: A revival movement in the Army of Northern Virginia apparently began in Jackson's corps during the spring of 1863, peaking that winter, and continuing to the end of the war.

B. McDonnald, *Address to Chaplains and Missionaries* (Petersburg, Virginia: Printed at the Register Office, 1863).

Theodore Dwight Weld, *Pitching the Tent toward Sodom* (Petersburg, Virginia: Evangelical Tract Society, 1863).

May 2, Monday

HB: Reveille beat at day break, news having been received of the whole yankee army being in motion, received orders to cook breakfast, and be ready to march at a moment's warning. All quiet during the day. Late in the evening, we had a very severe gale.

JP: This morning is cloudy & cold. After breakfast Sam went on guard. Capt. M. Pickens called to see us a few minutes this morning. Sam was absent at guard-house, but came to see the Capt. It is reported that Grant has been reinforced by Burnside, with 25,000 men (of which number 8,000 are negroes) & that his artillery is in motion. We rec<u>d</u> orders to hold ourselves in readiness to leave at a moment's warning, & also to cook up our two days' rations. This looks as if some movement is near at hand. There is to be a Baptizing near Gen! Battle's Hd. Qrs., at 10 'clok to-day. Several from the Co. have gone to witness it. Wrote a letter to Mama this evening, but did not finish it in time to send it by this evening's mail. While Sam was on duty this even'g, we had quite a severe wind, almost a hurricane—before which the dust was carried like a dense cloud. The guard was dismissed on acct. of the bad weather & Sam came to our cabin. He got in just in time to escape a shower of rain which followed the wind. The night is very dark & stormy, but the western horizon was perfectly clear at bed-time. We sat by the fire talking to-night 'till late & then retired. Lieut. Christian, Davis Williams, Sam & others of our mess were talking over the events of some of last year's battles, wh. were very interesting.

May 3, Tuesday

HB: Nothing of importance transpiring during the day. At night we received orders to be ready to march at daybreak.

JP: We were roused by reveillé this morn'g at sun-rise. The day commences fair bright & cool. The weather is very much like winter—quite a change from yesterday. No orders having been yet rec$^{\underline{d}}$ for us to leave, 'tis thought we will remain here for some time still. Sam was roused quite early this morning to repair on duty again until the formation of a new guard at 7½ or 8 o'cl'k. He was relieved about this time & came off. Sam went to see D$^{\underline{r}}$ Hill for me to-day in regard to my getting detailed for some light duty. Have not heard the result of the interview. Our long-expected box came to hand this morn'g about 11 or 12 o'cl'k. Almost all its contents were ruined. But the pepper, sage, catsup, ham, candy & some of the cake, were all pretty good—the three first articles being as good as ever. We gave a sort of treat of the articles to our mess. 'Twas pretty good, but would have been splendid had our box come when Tom & I came on. Sam went this even'g soon after the box arriv$^{\underline{d}}$, with the Reg$^{\underline{t}}$ brigade on a drill of the latter, in the old field used for that purpose. We went again this even'g to Dr Hill who thought I could get a detail & told me how to proceed about it. He is quite a gentleman in every sense of the term, is affable, pleasant & well-educated man. I was very much pleas$^{\underline{d}}$ with him. Capt. Belcher came & had a short confab with him. Was acquainted with D$^{\underline{r}}$. Mushat this morn'g (or yesterday morn'g, rather.)

May 4, Wednesday

HB: Reveille beat before day, everybody getting ready to leave. We took up the line of March about sun up, marched to Raccoon ford, thence about five miles in a northeasterly direction. The wagon train ordered back to take the road to [. . .] church. Thence we went some three miles up the pike, when we received orders to move back again. Gen'l Johnston advanced, & found no enemy. Our train then went across Mine Run to Locust Grove where we camped for the night, issued rations, and went to bed about two in the morning.

JP: Orders rec$^{\underline{d}}$ yesterday even'g for us to get ready by morning at daylight (to-day) to leave Winter Qrs., not to come back again. So we were up at about 3 or 3½ o'cl'k this morn'g, & after eating a breakfast of some of our ham broiled & corn-bread, got ready & left about 6½ or 7 on plank-road for Raccoon Fd. We marched leisurely along & reach^{d} latter place about 11 o'clk. We rested there or rather on side of road thither, in a grass-plot for about an hour or more, awaiting orders. 'Tis said the Yankees are this side of the River, and marching down in direct. of mine-run about six or seven miles fr. the grass field where we rested. We rc$^{\underline{d}}$ orders to move to the former place (mine-run) & set out. Was very tired & exceedingly sore; so much so that I could scarcely move. Jogged along, however, & managed by hard & fatiguing marching, to keep up with the troops. Do not believe that I'm capable of enduring the toils and hardships of summer marching. After getting to mine run, or near there, we halted & bivouacked for the night in a grove of trees, to the right of the road by which we came. Was very glad to stop & get a rest as I was almost exhausted. Sam suffered very much with sore feet. They were quite blistered, when Jim Webb, he & I went to a branch near by our camp & washed our feet, putting on clean socks. We felt very much relieved after doing this. We were supplied with rations to-night, & those detailed to cook them made such a noise & bustle all the night that Sam & I got very little sleep. We spread our blankets for a bed under a tree—having one for a bed & others for covering.

McD: Left winter quarters five miles east of Orange, C. H. according to orders received on the night of the 3rd. Went in the direction of Morton's ford, supposing that we were only going to a new camp. On getting near the ford we were informed that the Yankee army was in motion and were crossing the Rapidan river at Ely's ford some distance below. We accordingly continued our march down the river to meet the Yankees. Camped for the night near Locust Grove and sent a detachment out on picket. Got two days rations.

NOTE: Joel Calvin McDiarmid begins his diary.

May 5, Thursday

HB: Rec'd. letter from brother. Got up at day break, the enemy reported in our front. Sharp shooters were thrown out, and our train ordered to the rear. We went about 8 miles, when we halted in an old field in a mile & one half of where we started from. Continual firing going on in the direction of Locust Grove, with heavy cannonading for some two or three hours. Battle's brigade was engaged. None of our Greensb. boys hurt.

JP: Were roused up quite early this morn'g at about 4 o'clk. Rec^d a letter from Loutie just as I had risen from sleep. 'Twas too dark to read it, so I delayed doing so 'till day-light. We were very glad indeed to hear from our dear mother, sisters & brothers and are glad to know that all are well at home. We ate breakfast about 6 o'cl'k; a very good one, of some of our sausages & corn-bread. Left about 9 or 10 o'cl'k—marched slowly along, halting every two or three miles. The enemy are reported just in front of us. A battle is expected momentarily. We marched 'till about 1 or 2 o'clk P.M., when we got in position under fire, & in support of Jones' Brigade which was driven back. Genl Jones was killed. After his Brig. was repulsed, our Brig. took its position, but some of our men retreated & with them I returned, being almost exhausted. Went to Lieut. Gorff's provost guard & remained there 'till about 3 or 4 o'clk, at wh. time we had repulsed the enemy at all points, captured a large number of prisoners & were building breast-works. Found our Co, & was very much relieved and thankful to find Sam there & safe. He had narrowly escaped tho', a ball striking his canteen & cutting it. Whilst I was at breast-wks. enemy charged them once or twice but were repulsed by our sharp-shooters who drove them back in confusion. We lay close to breast-wks & had orders not to fire 'till enemy had approached in good shot of us. There was terrific musketry firing on our right, for several hours after this charge took place. Sam got a permit for me signed by Capt. Williams & Col. Hall, to leave & got to the hospital, as I was very unwell. Sam gave me a portfolio (a very nice & convenient one) which he got fr. the battle-field. I feel thankful to God that He protected Sam from this day's dangers & has brought him safely through them. May He continue to guard & protect him & deliver him from all dangers in peace & prosperity & happiness. After getting some sugar, coffee & beef from Sam & Huggins I left for hospital, but couldn't pass the guard. Remained here (at guard) for about 2 hrs., met Mr. Joe Grigg who went to ordnance train, but soon return^{d} & invited me to stay with him to-night, which I was glad to do. We then went to Genl Rodes' Hd. Qrs. about 200 yds (in direct. of front) from the guard & were soon asleep & bivouacking.

McD: Was up early this morning and in motion. Marched down the turnpike about three miles, heard brisk skirmishing in our front. Formed line of battle across the road. Was in the 2nd line. The Yankees attacked the front line. We moved up at the same time. The front line gave way and part of our line retreated in confusion. A third line came in time to recover all the ground lost and then drove the enemy beyond their former position causing them to abandon two pieces of cannon. In the evening we regulated our line on the top of a ridge and threw up breast works and awaited an attack.

VET: Fell in at 4 o'clock, sent out sharpshooters, formed line of battle, moved forward and engaged enemy at 12 M. Ewell's corps facing Grant's whole army. Fight till night. Baily, Farrier, Bridges and Elias wounded; Ward, Martin, and Youngblood wounded and captured.

NOTE: The Battle of the Wilderness began for the Guards by continuing their march eastward along the old turnpike between Orange Court House and Fredericksburg. Early in the afternoon, Ewell spread his three brigades (which included Battle's) one behind the other along a ridge on either side of the turnpike. In the confusion of battle, the panic-stricken Confederates retreated. The Fifth Alabama troops regrouped and finally reached the same ridge they had earlier fled, where they put up breastworks that repelled Yankee advances. By day's end, four Guards (Bayley, Farrier, Bridges, and Elias) were wounded and three more (Ward, Martin, and John L. Youngblood) both wounded and captured.

May 6, Friday

HB: Firing commenced before sun up this morning, the battle soon became general, particularly on the right and left flanks. Our brigade was not engaged up to twelve o'clock, when the firing ceased. Telegraphed to Col. Harvey [that] Hausman wounded in the evening.

JP: Arose about 4 o'clk or 5 this morn'g. There was, soon afterwards, a heavy attack made on our line by Yankees. Our artillery replied briskly. Ate a hasty breakfast of a mouthful or two of fish & crackers & a cup of coffee. Got a signature to my permit from Major Whiting, to pass guard & set out for hospital getting here about or before sun-rise. Saw Dr Hill & got him to sign my permit also. He was surprised that I had attempted to engage yesterday with the troops in battle & advised me not to return but remain with him. The hospital consists of a large number of tents raised under a grove of trees on a hill & is about 2½ miles from our line of breast-works. There was a large number of Yankee prisoners which we captured yesterday, which passed to the rear whilst I was at the provost guard's last even'g. Also a quantity of wounded men, both of ours & the Yankees—mutilated & shot in almost every imaginable manner. The sight was shocking to behold. There was a considerable number of wounded at the hospital to-day when I got there, & ambulances were constantly arriving with them. Amputation is going on & there are several who have died of their wounds & been buried near by the hospital. Oh the horrors of war! no one knows until he sees for himself how much suffering & distress there is in battle. Would to God the strife were over & that peace again blessed our land! But God knows best when to stop the hand of war & He will do it in His own good time. There was heavy firing all this evening, both of musketry & artillery. It is said our works are now lined with artillery. Lost a strap which Sam gave me to keep for him, this morn'g at Mr. Joe's camp. Was very sorry indeed to lose it. Spread a piece of tent which Sam gave me to keep for him, on ground for a bed & covered with my blanket to-night. Went to bed at about 9 h. 45 m.

McD: Nothing but sharp shooting in our front but considerable fighting on both sides of us. The enemy defeated.

NOTE: While the Fifth Alabama lay safely behind its breastworks, the Federals launched a massive attack a few miles south in another attempt to turn the Confederates' right wing and place the Union army between Lee's men and Richmond. When A. P. Hill's corps collapsed and ran to the rear, General Lee attempted to rally his troops personally. Longstreet arrived with fresh men, who counterattacked and drove the Federals from the field.

May 7, Saturday

HB: Gave out rations & started to the front with the train. Staid about 1½ miles in rear of line of battle until late in the evening when we carried the train forward. I went up to the breastworks to Co. D, staid with the boys a while & returned to the train, which was ordered to move forward, brought it up immediately in rear of Gen. Daniel's brigade. Carried order to Gen. Battle to get a cooking detail, was under fire, while a hot skirmish took place. Rec'd. the cooking detail & carried them to the wagon train, where the rations were issued them to be cooked, staid with them all night when on.

JP: Awoke at 8 o'clk, I expect this mor'g. Being kindly invited by Dr Hill to partake of breakfast with him, I did so. Had a good appetite as my only fare yesterday was crackers. Dr H. also loaned me a basin with which I took a good wash. Felt much refreshed. Thought it would rain to-day, as 'twas quite warm, but the day is clear & bright, with the exception of a few clouds. The Yankee prisoners think that this battle will close the war. Hausman came in to hospital yesterday even'g. He was wounded about 1 o'clk, in the shoulder. The wound altho' not a serious one is quite bad & seems as if 'twould be very painful. But all seems to me thus. It is clear still to-day, altho' looking much like it would rain. Our Brigade was not attacked to-day or if 'twas very lightly. Would like exceedingly much to write to Mama to-day, but as I have no paper must defer doing so. Report says the Yankees have been badly repulsed along our whole line. That Buckner is on our right wing which has been reinforced by 15,000 fresh troops. We were ordered this evening by Dr Whitehill (who rec^d his orders from Gen![Rodes) to pack up every thing & be in readiness to move, as it is supposed our Brigade is going to change position further to the right. We left about 11 or 11½ P.M. to-night, going back the way we came last Thurs., via Locust Grove hospital thence by plank road & up it again near our lines, in rear of Gen![Longstreet. Marched all the night 'till about 3½ o'cl'k, when we camped or bivouacked in a field on left of plank road. We must have traveled six or eight miles. I was nearly exhausted & had it been in the heat of the day instead of at night, would have given out. Our ambulances & medical wagons make a long train. Hausman left to-day for Orange C.H.

McD: Still in same position. The enemy fell back from our front. Ordered to move at dark. Kept in motion all night but moved only four miles to the right.

VET: Enemy fell back during night, moved to right and took A P Hill's position.

NOTE: Union casualties for the three days are estimated at 17,666. Confederate losses are less certain, but the Fifth Alabama counted 5 killed, 28 wounded, and 48 missing.

May 8, Sunday

HB: At daybreak I carried the rations to the troops & sent the train to the rear. Our boys left the entrenchments of yesterday & moved about a mile to the right. Our whole army moved by the right flank in the direction of old Spottsylvania C.H. Our division reached there late in the evening, went into battle immediately. The engagement lasted about half an hour. In this Col. Hobson, Ed. Hutchinson & Charley Briggs were wounded. Bunk Buttler missing. Our train in the meantime moving in the direction of Beaver Dam camped all night in a clover field. Saw the Yankee Brig. Genl. Wadsworth at Gen. Wilcox's hospital about to expire from a wound received in the head.

JP: Left bivouac after eating a frugal breakfast of crackers, not a handful scarcely, we were again on move. Went about a mile & ½ or 2 ms. into a field, spread our blankets the drivers took out their teams to graze & we thought our hospital would be established & that we would get a rest, but Maj. Whiting came ordering the train to move in direct. of Fredericksb'g. It is thought the Yankees are trying to flank us on the right. Gen![Rodes' Div. has been ordered for to night—& we will encamp in his rear. D![Hill told me when I got tired to ride on one of ambulances; and after I had walked five or six miles in the heat of the day & under the glare of a meridian sun, I was glad to do so. Got in an ambul. that John Jackson had been driving, & he walked. Before getting into it we passed a cool & refreshing tree with thick foliage & under its branches lay down & cooled off. 'Twas a delightful rest. Heard as we went along heavy roaring of our artillery. The battle has raged since Thurs. and is still going on, notwiths. 'tis Sunday the day of rest, the Lord's holy day! 'Tis thought the Yankees will press us very heavily to-day as they generally try their whole strength on Sundays. We marched all day—it was as hot as summer in mid-day—& stopped at a church & grave-yard, until our Div. passed by. Gen![Rodes with his couriers also awaited the Div'n. In about an hour it came up. The men seemed very tired. I saw my dear brother,

Sam—(God continue to bless & protect him) but only for a few minutes. He seemed to be very tired indeed. I trust in God he may come out of the battle safely! I must write to Mama, my dear mother, to-day, if possible. Our train fell in behind the troops & continued their march 'till about 4 o'clk or after, having gone to-day at least ten miles, or more, & put up hospitals in a field to right of road. I rode to-day 'till within about 2 ms. of our resting-place, when I had to get out for a broken down soldier. Poor men—some of them fainted on their way & seem<u>d</u> almost exhausted. There was a heavy battle this evening & our Brigade was deeply engaged. The battle was very hot. Ed. Hutchinson & Charley Briggs were wounded—the former not badly in head & latter not enough to leave the Comp<u>y</u>. Jack W. brought Ed. H. from field to hospital. Col. Hobson is shot thro' thigh. Charley Pegues slightly grazed in neck. Maj. Prosko, of 12<u>th</u> Ala. badly wounded in shoulder, I think. My dear brother is reported safe. Would to God this cruel strife would end! Was so tired when I got here that I threw myself down upon my piece of tent & fell asleep. Awoke to find all hands building tents for & bringing the wounded to them. Helped build tents & did not go to sleep 'till about 2 or 2½ o'clk. Talked for some time with Ed. Hutchinson & Jack Wynne. Slept very soundly as I was quite fatigued.

McD: Began to march this morning at eight o'clock in the direction of Spottsylvania C. H. Being a very warm day, had a very hard march. Late in the afternoon we had a brisk little fight with the Yanks near Spottsylvania C. H. Drove them back a short distance; night came on and we lay on the battle field till morning.

NOTE: In the battle at Spotsylvania Court House, May 8–21, four of the five regiments in Battle's brigade would lose their colonels to wounds.

May 9, Monday

HB: Rec'd order from Gen. Ewell to issue rations, started off as soon as I got something to eat, traveled fifteen miles, when we halted near Spottsvy. C.H. Issued to the troops, after dark & after eating some, went to sleep. Saw Col. H. & Hutchinson at the hospital. Our boys were not engaged today. Rec'd letter from Ezra Wilson enclosed in one of Charley Briggs'.

JP: The day is clear & pretty. Hoped it would rain slightly in order that the dust might be laid & the atmosphere become more cool & pleasant. The roar of cannon is still to be heard. The only remnant of my accoutrements is my ram-rod, one which I got from a Yankee gun & put in my gun. The rest of the things were partly left on purpose & partly lost by me. My cartridge-box was lost at our former hospital, & I left my gun last evening on my way thither. I also have my waist-belt & cap-box. Oh, what a terrible scene it is to behold the wounded & dying; & to hear their cries how distressing! I have seen enough of battle. I would like never to see as much again as has presented itself to my view only in the past few days. John came up to our train this morning. Sam sent him with another blanket for me, which I am glad of, as the nights have been a little cool of late. Sam was quite well this morn'g when John left. Wrote to Mama to-day, telling her of our safety. I know her anxiety now & have been very desirous of writing to her, but we have been constantly on the move & I did not have an opportunity. God grant that soon I may be united with my dear Mama, sisters & brothers, and that it may not be long ere peace shall be proclaimed & that my dear brother be restored to them also! Oh how happy I should be if I were now at our dear home with my dear mother, sisters, brothers & her whom I love! Oh what great joy & happiness 'twould be for me! John got me a good supper this even'g. I had my meal cooked into bread this morn'g & managed tolerably well for breakfast. The Yankees have been again repulsed with great loss to-day. Went to bed about 9 o'clk to-night.

McD: Throwing up breast works all day. Continued quiet in our front except sharp shooting. Heavy fighting on our left in the evening.

May 10, Tuesday

HB: Our train moved off soon this morning in the rear of our division, occasional firing heard. About 10 o'clock heavy cannonading commenced and it grew to be a terrible fire all day, & lasted until about 9 o'clock at night.

JP: It is clear this morning, tho' from every appearance last night one would have supposed it would have rained before this. The night was not as cool as usual. Have not sent my letter yet—but hope to do so soon. Would be glad to hear how Tom. Biscoe is & whether he has been wounded or not. I do sincerely trust he is safe. John brought me my breakfast this morning; a very good one indeed—corn bread, biscuits & fried ham. Have not felt well for some time past. I would be glad if I could go to some place & remain & not have to take these long marches which we take every day or two. The only place at which I would prefer to be now, is Home, Sweet home. When shall we see home again? I trust in God soon. We recd. orders this morn'g to pack & move; left about 12 or 1 o'clock & about 2 or 3 P.M. pitched tents in a pine grove about two or three miles from where we were this morning. There was another battle fought this even'g, & Col. Hall was brought in badly wounded in arm. Col. Pickens also was wounded—slightly in shoulder. Have not seen them yet. Was sorry to hear Col. H. was seriously wounded. It is reported the enemy made eleven charges upon our breast-works to-day & were signally repulsed every time. Daniel's & Doles' N.C. Brigades, however, were driven from our breast-works, & several pieces of our artillery were captured by enemy; but our Brigade charged upon them & re-captured the breast-works & the artillery. The fighting to-day has been very heavy. Heard from dear Sam to-day, that he is well & safe. God be praised! It began to drizzle to-night, but did not rain & soon cleared off again. John helped me put up two pieces of a tent as a sort of protection, in case of rain. He then got me a good supper—for Camp—corn-bread & meat. Capt. Belcher has been sick & with the ambul. train for several days past. 'Tis reported that Tom. Ward, Tom. Martin & one of the Youngbloods (the elder) are missing, from our Co^y. Do not feel very well to-night.

McD: Unusually quiet till late in the evening. The enemy made a heavy charge on part of our line occupied by Genl Dole's Brigade and took the works. Our Brigade being in reserve was ordered to charge the enemy out of the works which they beautifully did, killing and capturing a great many. Col. Hall had his arm shot off.

NOTE: That evening twelve Union regiments with fixed bayonets charged the Mule Shoe, a half-mile long protrusion along the Confederate line about three hundred yards from the Greensboro Guards. The Guards ran forward to stop the attack without forming into lines, engaging in brutal and relentless hand-to-hand combat. After twenty minutes the Yankees retreated.

May 11, Wednesday

HB: About 9 A.M. our train was ordered to the C.H. where it remained all day. Went over to the hospital, found Capt. Williams there bruised on shoulder & leg. Col. Hall's arm was amputated this morning. Telegraphed to Col. Harvey the casualties in Co. D. Drew rations this evening. Carried them to the front, got a detail from Gen. Battle to go out to the road after them. Waited for the detail at Gen. Ewell's H-d Qrs., when Joe Grigg brought me an order from Gen. Rodes countermanding the order to issue, & ordered the rations back. Saw all our boys, they telling me of the noble charge they made the evening before, driving the Yankees out of Dole's and Ramseur's breast-works. Started back with my train, on reaching the C.H. found out that our Division train had been ordered across Pamunkey river. Had the wagons unloaded, and loaded them with cooking utensils. Left the C.H. in a drenching rain, about midnight and at 3 A.M. found our division train parked near the roadside. Jim Holmes and I kept together, he losing his shoes in the mire. Reported to Maj. Webster & Adams & went to sleep.

JP: Clear this morn'g, altho it looked very much like raining last night. Hagins called by this morn'g for a few minutes. Col. Hall's arm (right) was amputated this morn'g, just below shoulder. What a loss to him. He seem^{d} to suffer very little—tho' he was partly under the influence of chloroform. Capt. Williams came into the camp this morn'g, having been struck I think, but only stunned by a ball. Chas. Hafner also came in. He is sick & tired down. Saw Col. Pickens & Capt P. this morn'g. Col. P. is doing very well. Davis Williams & Maj. Webster & Mr. Glover also stopped at Col. Hobson's tent to see him. The day is clear & warm, summer weather. Thermometer must be 60° or 65° now. Col. Hobson, Col. Lightfoot & Maj. Prosko are all under one tent & mine is just above it. The papers were rec^{d} in hos. camp this morn'g, with the latest news from our field & our other armies. From all accounts, the several days' battles here have resulted in terrible defeat to the enemy & great destruction of his forces. It mentions (the paper—Examiner) the generals on both sides who have been killed & those taken prisoners by us from enemy. Our arms in the Peninsula, in N.C. & in other parts were alluded to, & all seem to indicate a signal triumph over our enemies. To God all our success is due. May we adore & magnify His holy name & ever give Him the praise for all our success, & not rely upon our own strength or on ourselves for a speedy, just & an honorable & a lasting peace to result to us (with Independence & happiness). God grant that soon this strife may cease & that peace, glorious peace may soon shine forth upon our land & bless us, for Christ's sake! It commenced to rain to-night at bed-time. Chas. Hafner slept under my piece of tent, & another man also, W$^{\underline{m}}$ Hafner also came in this even'g. I'm very anxious to hear from our dear mother, sisters & brothers. God grant they are well! Had a good deal of lightning & thunder this even'g which has cooled the atmosphere considerably, rendering it much better for the wounded. Got some pills from D$^{\underline{r}}$ Hill this even'g, as I feel very unwell.

McD: Very quiet all day. Took a new position on the line a few hundred yards to the left.

May 12, Thursday

HB: Woke up at daybreak & found the whole line in front to be engaged. Up to 11 A.M., the time of this entry, it was the heaviest firing on both sides, that had taken place during this contest. The battle was raging all day. The slaughter is said to be the severest of this war. Lieut. Jones was struck with a ball on the thigh. Stephenson shot in the head. Firing up to 12 o'clock at night. Tremendous rain all day.

JP: Awoke early this morn'g. 'Twas raining. Soon after the heavy roar of cannon & sharp musketry told that the fighting had been resumed. 'Tis the hottest we have had yet. Lieut. Hutchinson was killed. He died soon after being brought to the hospital. Was surprised to hear this, as he was very lively & cheerful only yesterday even'g. He was a very brave & gallant officer. Chas. Briggs was struck by a piece of shell & came to hospital this morn'g. John got me some breakfast. Tood Cowin saw Sam this morning & says he was then safe. As the enemy's shells fell close around the hospital, those who were able were advised by D$^{\underline{r}}$ Hill to go to wagon-yard, about 1½ miles distant. Davis Williams & I set out, had a very muddy walk & got to wagon-yard about 12 or 1 o'clk, having taken a very round-about way. It rained a good deal before we got here. Saw Capt. Pickens here who invited me to his fly-tent for the night. Also had dinner soon after of which I partook. Gen$^{\underline{l}}$ Daniels was wounded & it is said is dying. Few casualties in our Brig. or Co., except slight wounds. Capt. P. is very kind to me indeed. He is a very clever, gentlemanly young man. 'Tis said that Col. Swanson is the only Col. in Brig. who has not been wounded in this battle & that all the others have been. It is cloudy this even'g & I think 'twill rain to-night. John was coming over to w. yard, but have not yet seen him. Slept to-night in Capt. P.'s wagon, as his brother, the Col. this even'g, came over on horse-back from hospital & will sleep with him. According as I thought we had rain to-night. There is brisk fighting going on & it was kept up till about 8½ or 9 o'clk. Would like to hear from my dear brother, now. God grant to him safety & a speedy deliverance from all dangers & a restoration of us to our dear Mama, sisters, brothers & her whom

I love most dearly! We've not heard a word from home now for a long time but it is no doubt owing to the distracted state of affairs on acct. of this fight.

McD: At day light this morning made a heavy assault on our right and took a position of our works, capturing Genl Johnson and several thousand of his men. They also captured sixteen pieces of Artillery. Both sides massed all their forces at this point and a furious fight continued all day, the Yankees gaining no advantage but that gained in the morning. This was the most terrific fight of the war. During the night our forces took a new position a few hundred yards in the rear.

Vet: Moved to right at double quick to assist Gordon, then back to center, lay under heavy fire for some time supporting a battery. Stevenson and Youngblood wounded; Lt Hutchinson of Rodes staff killed.

Note: The Yankees attacked the Mule Shoe again, this time some distance to the west at the notorious Bloody Angle. This action came perilously close to breaking Lee's line, netted the Union some four thousand prisoners, and forced the Confederates to retreat to a more defensible line.

May 13, Friday

HB: Everything seems to be quiet this morning with exception of a few shells being thrown by the enemy. Neither of the two armies are moving today. Went by our hospital to see our wounded, dressed Col. Hobson's wound & returned to the train in company of Pompie Jones. Maj. Lewis & Lieut. Comd. Childress staid with us all night.

JP: The day is overcast with dark & threatening clouds & it is drizzling ever & anon. Think we will have more rain very soon. Was awake quite early this morning, feeling quite unwell. Would God I had never been guilty of so foolish an act as joining the service, a thing for which I'm no more capable than the most inefficient! But, perhaps 'tis all for the best. "Experience is the mother of wisdom". I will know better how to act another time. Oh God grant to me, an unworthy petitioner, Thy guidance & direction of my actions, and help me in all my difficulties, for Thy Son Jesus Christ's sake! Oh Lord grant that I may soon be restored to my dear mother, sisters & brothers to guard, help & protect them, & that it may not be long in peace & happi[ne]ss shall have been spread abroad through our land by Thy Almighty power, speaking peace to a distracted nation & bidding the clouds of war roll away from our country's sky! Oh grant we beseech Thee O Lord these our poor petitions for Christ's sake!

Was ordered over to the hospital this morn'g, with all those men who had not been detailed to wagon yd. Set out over a very wet & sloppy road with two or three others & after a very disagreeable & tiresome walk got to the hospital. Saw Col. Hobson, Maj. Proskow, Col. Hall & others off in ambulances to D̲r̲ Black's hospital. They will be sent thence to Guinea station where they will take the Richmond train & be off for their respective homes—having got furloughs. Col. Hall, of course, will not return as he is now out of the service forever. Col. H. seemed very cheerful & lively in the prospect of being able to visit his home in

Alabama. I wish we were all going with him. All who were able to walk being ordered fr. hospital to wagon-yd, I got a certificate of health from Dʳ Hill & went to Dʳ Black's hosp. where I was joined by R. Chadwick & Chas. Hafner. We were after some detention, passed to wagon yd, where Maj. Webster recᵈ me kindly & gave me a very nice warm dinner. Rice, nice hot biscuits, ham (broiled) & coffee with sugar. We are to be sent with the wounded, to Richmond to hospital there. Drew our rations at the wagon-yd & after arranging our things in a wagon by which means we are to ride to Guinea station, on the Fredericksb'g road, our party, consisting of Capᵗ Williams, his brother Charles, C. Hafner, R. Chadwick, Ed. Hutchinson & myself left for said station about 6 o'clk P.M. Our train of wagons is a long one, there being fifty or more, I think. They will carry the sick & wounded to the station & return with Commissary supplies. We travel very slowly, indeed. Saw Henry Allen at wagon-yd, who gave me a letter to mail for him. Got $100. from Maj. Webster this evening. The night is bad for traveling, being drizzly & the roads quite sloppy. We were very much crowded & cramped in our wagon, & no wonder, for seven of us were jammed in there something like a crowd of spoons when they are packed away in a drawer. This sort of arrangement is, what the soldiers call, "spooning"—a very familiar term with them.

McD: All very quiet today. Our Brigade ordered to the rear to rest.

Vet: Marched through bloody angle gathering up dead, wounded arms, etc.

May 14, Saturday

HB: Everything quiet in front this morning, went by our hospital, saw Col. Hobson & Hall as they were about to leave, told them good-bye, and started to the field where Lieut. J.J. Hutchinson was buried. Helped take him out of the grave put him in a box and reburied him. Issued rations this evening, carried them to the front. Saw all of our boys who were on the second line today. Had a considerable fight on our right this evening, whipped the enemy pretty severely & took a good many prisoners and three stands of colours.

JP: Did not rest well last night, owing partly to the rough roads over which we traveled & partly to feeling unwell. It is still cloudy. We *at last* got to Guinea station about 6 o'clk or, maybe sooner. Put up under a wood-shed. The cars we expect every minute 'tho it is uncertain when they will come. Ate a scanty meal of crackers & fried bacon. Also a cup of coffee which Capt. Williams offered me. The sun beginning to shine a little. Took a wash this morn'g after breakfast, & afterwards read in Bible. I try to read my Bible every day, but sometimes I am prevented by having to move or other unavoidable circumstances. I pray God to have mercy upon me & to strengthen me in faith & grace, that I may improve in spiritual strength & be accounted worthy to be united with his holy Church on earth for Christ's sake! We waited at the station 'till about 1 or 1½ o'clk when the train from Richmond arrived. Had a very good shower, soon after it came. Dʳ Hill finally got us passage on a freight-car (Have I to try a freight car again? It seems so) and after a good deal of delay, we left for Richmond. Had a miserable time of it on the train & part of the time was quite sick. We traveled with a crowd of wounded—men wounded in almost every conceivable manner. Rained from time to time during our travel. Capt. Williams, his brother Charles, Ed. Hutchinson, R. Chadwick, Chas. Hafner & myself compose our crowd.

McD: Ordered again to the front. Threw up works under heavy shelling. In the 2nd line of works, all quiet except shelling.

May 15, Sunday

HB: All quiet this morning, an occasional shell thrown by the enemy. Gen. Lee had an order read out on the line stating he had received official information of Steel's surrender to Price, also a congratulatory order to the troops under his command for the various successes gained over the enemy in our front as well as at Richmond. The enemy reported to have left in front of our left & moved to our right. Heavy rain yet.

JP: Arrived at Richmd this morn'g about 4 or 4½ o'cl'k. Were carried to the distributing Hospital where we rested 'till about 5 or 6 o'clk when we were brought over to Howard Grove Hospital, where we have been ever since. We got a tolerable breakfast, corn-bread fried meat & cakes (rye I expect)[.] The hospital is situated on a commanding hill about 1 mile fr. the city, under large oaks & pines. It is laid off into wards, which are each about 100 ft. long by 30 or 40 ft. wide & are nicely white-washed. It seems to be a nicely kept hospital indeed. The beds are arranged along the sides of the wards and are clean & well clothed. In all respects it is a treat to get off from hard marching & rough treatment such as soldiers meet with in the army, to some place where they can take a little rest for some time. Would that it were our privilege to visit our dear homes & that I could go to old Umbria & see its dear inmates our dear mother, sisters & brothers! God grant that soon we may be united together for Christ's sake, in peace & happiness.

It rained this evening quite hard for a short time. Would like to hear from my dear brother, Sam, now. God grant he is safe! They have breakfast here at hospital, at 7 o'clk A.M., Dinner at 1 P.M. and supper at 7 P.M. The fare is only tolerably good—tho' better than we get in the army. We all went, after breakfast this morn'g, to the bathing-house near here and took each of us, a good bath after which I felt very much better than I did before. Oh that we had peace & happiness again in our land instead of this cruel war, and that we were all assembled together at home to enjoy the society of those dearer than all on earth to us! God grant that soon this cruel strive may end & that we may again be blessed with those enjoyments, of the value & merits of which we were before so insensible! I earnestly trust that that time is not far distant, but that it may soon arrive and that God may ere long bless our land as it once used to be! Then will peans of praise & gratitude from a thousand tongues arise up to Him & the prayers & thanksgivings of a free independent & delivered people besiege the throne of the Heavenly Grace! Retired to bed about 9 o'clk to-night.

McD: In the same position as yesterday.

NOTE: In fact, Steele did not surrender to Price following an unsuccessful Camden expedition in the West.

May 16, Monday

HB: Thick fog hanging over us this morning, everything quiet in front so far, the sun came out today the first time in nearly a week, had sharp cannonading in our front, which was caused by the 2nd and 6th Yankee corps's advancing & attempting to charge our lines. Our artillery getting the proper range, threw shells among them pretty brisk, and caused them to run. Their officers couldn't rally them any more. Gen. Lee had a congratulatory order read out, stating the success of Gen. Beauregard around Richmond[.] Capt. Preston returned today. No mail again today.

JP: The morning is clear & bright. I thank my heavenly Father that He has vouchsafed to me his protection & guidance through the past night & that He has brought me to see the light of another beautiful spring morning. I trust in Him to grant protection also to my dear mother, my brother who is now engaged in battling against our enemies, & to my dear sisters, brothers, to her who is dear & precious to me & to all my friends & relations, wherever they may be; & grant Oh heavenly Father that soon we may all meet again in joy & peace & happiness! God grant this! The patients in hospital are all doing well to-day. The D^r makes two visits a day to the ward. Ours is Div. 1st Ward, 'O', Howard Grove Hospital. We got a pretty good breakfast this morning. Chas. Williams left hospital this morn'g going to officer's hosp. I believe & will thence go to Charlottesville. Two dispatches*, in the form of extras, were brought around for sale this even'g, containing glorious news from Genl Breckinridge in the Shenandoah Valley & from Genl Beauregard, on the Peninsula, or the South-side R.R., I think. The former is as follows:—

"New Market, May 15th '64, 7 P.M. To Genl S. Cooper,

This morn'g, two miles above New M'Kt, my command met the enemy under Genl Sigel, advancing up the Valley & defeated him with heavy loss. The action has just closed at Shenandoah river. The enemy fled across the North fork of the Shenandoah, burning the bridge behind them.

John C. Breckinridge
Major Genl Commanding."

The latter is as follows:—"A general engagement is in progress on the South-side. We have captured the 27th Massachusetts regiment, 840 men. Brig. Genl Heckman & staff were also captured. The prisoners have arrived in this city (Richmond I expect.) Beauregard is in command & our force is believed to be equal numbers to the enemy. The attack was made by us, and commenced about five o'clock." Altho' cloudy a little this morn'g, it is fair this even'g & the sun is shining prettily. The papers state that our line on the Rapidan remains as it was when we left. Grant has withdrawn his right wing some distance from our line & now his line runs N.W. & S.E. Capt. Belcher called around this even'g to see us. He kindly offered to take any $5. notes that the members of our Co. might have & exchange them for small notes. He got $50. from Co. "D." Took a short walk this even'g & did not observe 'till then that I was quite weak. Took a pile this evening—again. Have not seen Capt. Williams since we arrived at the Hospital. On Sat. I asked him to write to, or see Dr Cabell in regard to my getting detailed to the Hospital at Charlottesville. I would be glad to get there. Must write to Mama or send my dispatch to her. I asked the D^r to send the dispatch for me but he has no doubt forgot it as he has not asked me for it. Must write to Sam also. Oh that he may be preserved from all danger & that soon we may be reunited with my dear mother, sisters & brothers & with her who is dear to me my ever dear Juliet! God grant that time may soon arrive. How much joy & happiness will it not bring! Sent a letter to Juliet to be mailed to-day. Retired to bed at 9 o'clk to-night. God grant to us the protection of his Spirit this night, that we may all be preserved from harm & kept through His mercy for Christ Jesus' sake, Amen.

*These were printed on the same paper & the extra cost 50¢

McD: We occupy the front today. The enemy are withdrawing from our front. Our Division went in front a mile or two but did not make an attack. Rained very hard this morning.

NOTE: Pickens is referring to the battles of New Market and Drewry's Bluff.

May 17, Tuesday

JP: Awoke at 6 o'clk this morn'g. The day is clear & pretty. Hope we may have good weather now. I can scarcely realize that almost the whole month of may has passed & that only one more month will elapse ere it will have been a year since our school at Umbria was broken up. How time flies! Would that I could be sensible of its rapid flight & improve each moment! This morn'g after the D^r came around, Chadwick, Hodges, Sims, & I think Hafner, got applications for transfer to the Danville Hospital. This will suit Chadwick as he has relations there he says & will no doubt have a much better time than if he were here. The only two now from Co. "D", in this ward (or the Hospital) are Ed. Hutchinson & myself. I would be glad to get a transfer to Charlottesville. The Enquirer was rec^d by several here, but it contained no news. Only a summary of our late successes—in the Valley of the Shenandoah, on the Peninsula & a dispatch from Genl Lee as to the position of his & the enemy's lines on the Rapidan. From all phases in which it can be viewed our cause is progressing favorably and a glorious future with peace, independence, nationality & happiness in our land is awaiting us. God guard us against a show or spirit of certainty, but that we may calmly await the operation of His hand in these our affairs of trial & of danger. We had a very hard shower this even'g just before dinner & afterwards again about 2 o'clk. My dispatch to Mama has not gone to the telegraph office yet. I must either send it or carry it myself, as it will never go. Got a quire of paper for $3. from a sort of peddler to-day. Wrote a letter to Mama to-day, which will not be mailed 'till to-morrow I expect. I'm growing tired of the hospital & would be very glad to get to Charlottesville, or a furlough to go home. Oh, if this war were at an end, peace declared & we were all united together again! How happy I should be!

McD: Expected to be attacked. The enemy began to advance but was repulsed with Artillery. Late in the morning we went in front our works to feel the enemies position. Found them entrenched. Fell back to our position.

May 18, Wednesday

JP: Awoke about six o'clock this morning. Breakfast we get at 7. Do not feel very well to-day. Had several doses to take last night—once every two hours, which interrupted my sleep very much. Capt. Belcher called again to-day & brought the money which the Co. put in his hands to get changed. He only had $10. in change, $5. of which I took myself, as I gave him that amount the other day. I gave the remaining $45. to Hutchinson, after he came in. He had gone down town for a short time. We had quite a hazy rain to-day about dinner time. It has cooled the atmosphere very much indeed. The papers to-day contained not much news. Grant has changed the left of his line somewhat having retired it back on a little stream some distance farther from us. It seems he does not intend fighting again 'till he recieves reinforcements. Wrote a long letter to my dear brother, Sam, this evening, but as I did not finish it 'till night 'twill not be sent until to-morrow. Would that I could hear from him. Am very anxious about him, indeed. Our fare here at Hospital is rather limited that which two gets not being more than enough for one person. Moreover it is very coarse for sick & wounded men; but it does as well as can be expected, in times of such scarcity & speculation. No luxuries such as eggs, chickens, butter &c, can now be had without one laying out his fortune for one meal. We must all await the glorious time which I trust is not far distant in the future, when peace shall again enliven our land & invigorate its now deadened resources. When we shall all again meet to gether in joy and happiness at home with those who are dearer to us than all on earth! Lord hear our humble cries to Thee & speak peace to our land for the Redeemer's sake! All generally go to sleep at 9 o'clk & every thing at that time is very quiet. There is a patient here who is very low & not expected to live. (Mills—is his name.) He has pneumonia or has had it & suffers very much.

McD: Advanced our sharp shooters this morning and found that the enemy had withdrawn from our left flank. Followed him to an entrenched position but did not attack him.

VET: Heavy fighting on right.

May 19, Thursday

HB: Everything perfectly quiet this morning. Pompie, Glover, Woodruff & myself went out to graze our horses, about two miles from our camp. We stopped in a grove, where we found splendid grass. Met with four young ladies who lived at the house close by, asked us, if we couldn't shingle their hair for them. We returned to camp about 1 P.M. when we learned that our corps had advanced on the enemy. About 4 P.M. we heard heavy musketry & some cannonading, indicating that the strife had commenced. The object of this move was, to capture a wagon train, which was reported to be moving towards Fredricksburg. Portion of our corps succeeded in capturing forty wagons, but couldn't bring them off. Wm. Hafner was wounded in finger in this engagement. No mail again.

JP: Awoke before six o'clk this morning. The day is partly clear & partly cloudy. Got a Dispatch this morning, also an Examiner & Whig, but gave the latter to Duncan over on the other side of this ward. He bought & gave me a Sentinel yesterday. The best news in them is that Banks has unconditionally surrendered to Gen! Kirby Smith. This, tho', does not seem to be credited by the papers. Also that Grant made a movement our right the other day & was handsomely repulsed. It is stated that Gen! Johnston has certainly defeated the late attack made upon him in Georgia. The man who was so sick on yesterday died last night. From all appearances, we will have another shower to-day. 'Tis quite cloudy. We had quite a hard rain about 1 o'clock to-day. Have not felt well this morning. I would I could go to dear old Umbria & be with my dear mother, sisters & brothers! Oh, how glad I will be to see & be with them again! I do not know why I attempted to become used to the life & duties of a soldier as I am utterly unable physically, to perform its requisitions. God grant that I may succeed getting back home to my dear ones there! I would not leave them again if I were not compelled. If I had had some one to have helped me, I might have been detailed & been now at home. The Army I find, is no place for any one who is unable to meet its requirements, & these can only be perform$^{\underline{d}}$ by one physically strong, healthy & of robust & good constitution. Few of these qualities do I possess. Am naturally delicate & owing to sickness which I have had, my constitution has been so impaired that the labors of the army would soon wear me out. Have been in bed all day, and on getting up this evening was quite weak. would like to go down town to dispatch to Mama as I know she is now uneasy.

McD: Remained quiet till late in the evening. Moved round the enemies right flank and made heavy attack on his wagon train. Got in possession of several wagons but could not hold them. We had a severe fight but did not accomplish much. After dark we retired to our works. Very heavy rain this morning.

NOTE: This engagement marked the end of the battle at Spotsylvania. Grant began moving the Army of the Potomac again on May 21 south toward Guiney's Station and then toward the North Anna River.

May 20, Friday

HB: Everything perfectly quiet this morning, not a gun fired in our front all day. Carried rations to the front this evening, saw all of our boys, heard of Geddie's being missing. No mail again today.

JP: A bright & pretty morning it is, and our heavenly Father has again brought us to see its light. How thankful should we all be to Him for vouchsafing protection & guidance to us & for bestowing mercies & blessings upon us continually. Oh, Father make us grateful to Thee for all the mercies & bounties of the Providence which we continually recieve and may we never forget Thy praise & worship but ever give unto Thee prayers & thanksgivings for all that Thou bestowest upon us! 'Tis a little cloudy & may rain again. The crops down in Ala. are no doubt very flourishing now such as corn &c, &c. & gardens I expect are filled with nice & grateful vegetables—the chief part of my living when at home in summer. Would I were there now. At this time last year we were at school, at home & were having a pleasant time; i.e. in being with our dear mother, sisters & brothers. Now what a change! Away off in Virginia, & in a hospital, where no kind & soothing ministrations to my wants can be made by a fond mother or sister & where their benign influence is not felt presiding over my bed! I trust tho' that soon I may be permitted to return to that home & be again united with the dear ones there in joy & peace. The papers this morn'g contain news of the defeat of Averell, by Gen.̣ Morgan in S.W. Va., also a dispatch from Gen.̣ Lee stating that the attack by Grant on 18$\underline{^{th}}$ on Ewell's line were easily repulsed. Our loss was very slight. The enemy also cannonaded a portion of Hill's lines under Genl. Early. The enemy on the south-side remain as they were a day or two ago: viz:—behind their entrenchments & under cover of their gun-boats. Got an Enquirer to-day—25¢; also ½ quire of note (Confed.) paper 1\underline{^{50}}$, and a pack'ge of envelopes $1. Sent my dispatch to Mama by Ed. Hutchinson, who is going down town & who will give it to Capt. Williams or Chas. Pegues, to be sent. Have had no rain to-day. Would like to have some books to read, as I find it very fatiguing to be here without something to read. Ed. Hutchinson returned from town this even'g—too late for supper. He sent my dispatch—It cost 5\underline{^{10}}$. Wrote to Mary & to Juliet to-night. Went to bed to-night after 11 o'clock, in conseq. of writing. The night is clear.

McD: Remained quiet in our works all day.

NOTE: General Lee is referring to the futile charge against Ewell's troops at Spotsylvania.

May 21, Saturday

HB: Rec'd orders to move, our train got into motion about 10 A.M. moved on the road parallel with the telegraph road. Passed through Mount Pleasant. About 10 P.M. we camped near Market. Field's Division had an engagement with the enemy this evening.

JP: Arose at about 6 o'clk this morn'g. Day clear & beautiful, tho' twas misty at first. Got an "Enquirer" 25¢, which had little news. All quiet in Gen.̣ Lee's army, since 18$\underline{^{th}}$. Several got applications from the D.̣ in charge of our ward, for furloughs. They are to go before the Med. Board on Mon. To-day after breakfast, but rather not far from dinner-time I went the bath-house & took a good wash, and put on clean hosp. clothes; after doing which felt a great deal better. Our fare is very slim indeed; we get each only half what we could enjoy. 'Tis provoking to get an insufficiency—however, we must not complain. This even'g after dinner, Hutchinson, Conrad, another gentleman & myself walked down to town. H. & I went & sat for an hour or two with Capt. Williams & his brother Chas. They took supper whilst we were there. Afterwards we walked down to Post-office & I mailed my two letters. Would like to receive some now—They would be very acceptable indeed. Have had no word from home for several weeks. After leaving office, we went to the public Square & sat under the shade of the trees for sometime. The shade is beautiful & very thick. I was struck with the contrast in the appearance of the Square in March, when the trees were leafless & everything was bleak & now in May when the trees are covered with their thick green coating of leaves. We sat by the fountain & watched the playing of the waters some minutes, sporting children running over the walks & adding liveliness to the spot. Here & there too, might be seen groups of men (Congressmen, I suppose) engaged in conversation, whilst the noise & bustle of the streets reminded one that he was in a city & not in the free & open country enjoying nature's beauties & scenes. How often whilst sitting there did I call to mind those happy days of the past when we were all enjoying peace & happiness with our dear mother, sisters & brothers in this place! No desolating war had then invaded the peace & quiet of domestic tranquility & social serenity. After sitting here for an hour or two we walked with Capt. W. as far as his abode & then came back to hospital. Got on my way hither—a pen-holder for which I paid $1. got a pen with it, also. Our supper to-night consisted of dry light-bread & a little milk. Fare diminishing, gradually. The night is clear & pretty. Would be glad to hear from home now—from the dear inmates of Umbria, & from dear Juliet. Hope soon to have that pleasure, tho'.

McD: Began to move early this morning. Went through fields and woods and came in to a road that lead to Fredericksburg. Kept that road till we came to a place called "Mud Tavern" then filed off to the right and went in the direction of Hanover Junct. Arrived at the Junct. at 2 o'clock and went into camp. Very warm.

NOTE: James Pickens was sitting in Richmond's Capitol Square. The square's prominent equestrian monument of Washington was displayed on the Confederate seal.

May 22, Sunday

HB: Soon this morning we took up the line of march again, waded the North Anna about 1 P.M. Yankee raiders having burnt the bridge and the mill on the river caused us to have to wade it. We struck the C. R.R. about a mile below Beaver Dam. Kept on parallel with the R.R. until we got within two miles of Hanover junction, where we camped for the night.

JP: The [day] commenced clear & warm. We have not had rain for a day or two past & consequently the weather has become quite warm—almost summer heat. This morning after breakfast, went to bath house & washed my face & hands, then read in Bible. At 11 o'clock Hutchinson & I went to Chapel &

heard a sermon by an old gentleman (may-be the Chaplain.) 'Twas a very plain exhortion. The text was from Revelations, XXI Chap., & 25$\underline{th}$ verse—"And the gates of it shall not be shut at all by day: for there shall be no night—there." The congregation was pretty large. The Chapel is a building of an equal size with the wards & is about 50 yds. from the wards. After preaching we met, at the office, W$\underline{m}$ Hafner, & Mr. Long of our Co. They left the Co. day before yesterday morn'g; at the time they were all safe tho' very tired indeed. Sam they said was well except that he was, like the others very much exhausted. Dinner came on soon afterwards. Clouded up this evening & threatened to rain; but blew off with a slight drizzle without raining. The atmosphere is a little cooler. Hutchinson & Hafner went to town this even'g. To-night, Rinaldi, Duncan, Lewis, a friend of his & myself, walked up town & went to Methodist church, where we heard a very interesting & instructive sermon; I presume by Rev. D$\underline{r}$ Doggett. The text was taken from XIII Chap. of Jeremiah, & 15$\underline{th}$, 16$\underline{th}$ & 17$\underline{th}$ verses. Was very much pleased indeed with the minister—he had a very clear, sonorous voice & preached very well. The church is a very neat one indeed; large, imit. of fresco work, large pews, and a chandelier (gas) in the centre of the ceiling, which imparted a light to the room of a brilliancy almost equal to that of day. There was also very good organ & choir music. After service, when we came out 'twas cool & pleasant owing to the small rain we had to-day. The moon was just rising over the tops of the houses & we had a very pleasant walk back to Hospital. Found all asleep when we came in—one or two tho' awoke as we entered. 'Twas 11 o'clk I think when we went to bed to-night.

May 23, Monday

HB: After eating breakfast I rode up the road about a mile, where I found our brigade encamped near the R.R., went to the company, staid with them about two hours, when they got marching orders. They were ordered nearly on the banks of the Little river. I wrote to brother today. Mail came in today, the first in 20 days. No letter for me. Issued rations this evening, carried them to the troops, found the boys hard at work, digging breastworks. Returned to our train about 11 P.M. went to bed. Between 12 & 1 A.M. order came for our train to move immediately. Got up rolled up blankets & started off crossed the little river & found our Div. Supply train on the banks of the river. Found Maj. Adams there. Major Webster & I laid down under a weeping willow, slept at Boardman's feet until daybreak. Heavy musketry firing before day in direction of Beaver dam. Took breakfast with Maj. Adams. About 12 A.M. Maj. Webster, Capt. Preston, Cowin & myself went to the South Anna to bathe, found a splendid place to graze our horses. Occasional cannonading in direction of Caroline Co. Met the celebrated Dozwell running from the Yankees with his fine colts. Ed. Shakelford. & Bud Chadwick came to see us, former just from home.

JP: The day is clear & pretty; very pleasant, too. Let us be thankful to God for having brought us to see another beautiful spring morning & give him thanks &

be grateful to him for all the mercies & blessings with which He favors us. Our acknowledgements to Him for these should be constant, as they continually flow to us. This morning bought the "Whig", "Enquirer", & "Sentinel," (price of the three, 75¢.) They contained little news from the different armies, except that the brave hearts composing them are as confident of success & in good spirits as ever; & that our generals prove as wily as those of the Yankee armies. To God we must look & in Him must we trust for triumph in the end—knowing that all success & victory cometh from Him. I was quite fatigued last night after returning from town & slept 'till late this morning, in consequence. Our breakfast to-day was a piece of broiled ham & a piece of light bread; also a little milk. We are not apt to suffer with dyspepsia while we stay here, as our fare is hardly rich enough for that. After dinner this evening Ed. Hutchinson & W^m. Hafner went down to the city. Soon after they left I followed. Our dinner to-day was more plentiful than it usually is. We had ham, rice, greens, pickle & bread; a little more of them, too than we are wont to recieve. Bought a pocket-glass for which I paid $8., a piece of soap for $2. & 12 little cakes for $2. (a perfect humbug, having only a taste of sugar in them.) Also got ¼ lb. candy (not fresh) for $3⁵⁰. Got also Mrs. Adams' last novel—Macaria—or Altars of Sacrifice. Judging it by her former work Beulah suppose it must be an entertaining novel. After walking streets & remaining for sometime at West & Johnson's book store, went to store adjoining the Spottswood [Hotel], where I bought glass & soap. Then, or rather at P.O., I met Hutchinson, Capt. Williams & Hafner, who walked up to the Square. I went to Spottswood & washed my face & hands, which cooled me very much. I started back to hospital, but concluded to go by Public Square. So I turn'd off & had quite a tiresome walk up a steep hill which brought me almost opposite the Med. College. Walked down street & came into Main, then into Square. We stayed here 'till about 5½ & then return'd to hospital. 'Tis as warm as summer to-day. By the way the med. College building is a very neat structure, (stone of a dark yellowish color) & is large & finely built. We got back in good time for supper this evening. Feel languid & tired after taking the walk to town & back. The night is partially clear. 'Tis so warm that will no doubt rain soon.

McD: At eleven o'clock today we were ordered to meet the enemy. Went about three miles from the Junct. and threw up works but was not attacked.

NOTE: Augusta J. Evans, *Macaria, or Altars of Sacrifice* (Richmond: West & Johnston, Evans & Cogswell, 1864).

May 24, Tuesday

HB: Staid about the train nearly all day. Issued rations to the troops, saw all our boys. Large mail but none for me.

JP: Another clear & pretty day. Indications too, of its being very warm. The mid-days are of summer heat almost. It seems that it is prematurely warm for this climate. Capt. Williams will not leave, as he intended doing, to-day. Was put on full-diet this morn'g, so at dinner I'll have to go to the table. Have been on half diet heretofore & been receiving my meals at the ward. Have seen no paper to-day: tho it is reported Gen.[l] Lee has fallen back to Hanover Junction & that he had a fight with the enemy on South Anna R. this or yesterday morn'g. We shall probably know more in regard to movements of the armies & the other news from them, in the morning. Hope to recieve some letters from home soon. Oh, how glad I would be to hear from my dear mother, sisters & brothers & from my dear brother at the front! God guard & bless them all by His holy Spirit! Went to town this even'g in hopes of seeing Capt. Williams, but as he was not in I sat a few minutes with Mr. Ellison (I was at his Ala. Soldiers' Home) 'till Chas. Pegues came fr. his room & he & I walked up on the Public Square. Heard that Mr. P. Lavender has arrived from Greensboro' Ala., but he was not at Mr. Ellison's when I was there. Would like to see him very much & hear the news from home & thereabouts. After we left Pub. Sq. Chas. Pegues went to visit Capt. Belcher & I returned to Hospital. How very glad I would be to hear from home, now & from Sam. It has been almost, yes almost a month since I have heard from home & the latest news which I have had from Sam was from Mr. Long, who left him on morn'g of the 20th. Sam, he said, looked tired & broken-down. I hope he will come to this place & recuperate & remain here until entirely recovered. Oh, if he could come & get comfortably situated how glad I would be, as I know Sam is exhausted, having gone through so much hard work & laborious fatigue lately. I have been contemplating asking Judge Lyon's assistance in getting a detail or an exemption, but do not know how to get an introduction to him. To do this was partly the reason of my visiting town to-day. I did not succeed, tho I hope to be able to do so soon. I pray God that I may succeed in my endeavor & that soon I may be with my dear mother to be a help & assistance to her, & also be united with my dear sisters, brothers & with dear xxxxxx.

McD: Was moving long before day light this morning. Moved to the left and took a new position near the Junct. and worked on breast works hard all day. Heavy skirmishing in front.

May 25, Wednesday

HB: Went to Maj. Adam's after breakfast & returned to our train. After dinner went back drew rations, commenced giving half pound of meat today, carried rations to the front, cooking immediately in rear of the troops. They were at the junction holding breastworks. After getting through learned our train had moved. Maj. Webster, Glover & myself followed, waded the South Anna, got lost it being so dark, we couldn't find the road. Finally went across a field to the nearest lights & after a lengthy inquiry found our train. Being past midnight we retired. Got a letter from brother tonight.

JP: This is a clear & pretty morn'g, but is so warm that I think 'twill rain before long. We have now, or rather we have lately had pleasant summer showers which have tended greatly to cool the atmosphere & make it more pleasant. The weather in the middle part of the day is as warm almost as our July weather in Ala. Went, after breakfast this morn'g, again to the city to Capt. Williams room at Mr. Ellison's (Ala. Soldiers' Home.) He showed me a list of casualties in Hays' La. Brig., and amongst them, I was pained & shocked to see that of Tom. Biscoe whom it reported killed on 12th inst. The name was spelt "Capt. Thos. H. Briscoe" (with an 'r') from which I sincerely hope that it may prove to be another person. God grant that Tom, who was lately in such good health & spirits & in the enjoyment of life & hopes of the future, God grant that he is yet living & that he may survive the issues of this struggle for our independence, & be united to us afterwards unharmed, in peace & happiness, is my sincere prayer.

I saw Mr Lavender, to-day, who went with me to House of Rep's. & gave me an introduction to Judge Lyon, at the door of the House. He (Judge L.) is a venerable, white-headed gentleman & is a much older man than I had expected to find him. He is a very fine looking man indeed, with high intellectual forehead, dark eyes, medium height & well formed. He was quite busy having to attend the discussion of a very important bill; but told me to visit him at Judge Jones' on 6th St. between Main & Franklin this evening at any time between the hours of 4 & 7 o'clock. I return'd then to Ellison's & then Capt. W., Chas. P. & myself walked up on Sq. I then left them going in quest of Judge L. Congress had adjourned for the day, so I had to go to Judge Jones'. After a few minutes, waiting at the door Judge Lyon asked me in & I told him of my request. He was very kind & promised to do all in his power to help me, either to get a detail or exemption for me & offered to do anything else for me in his power. He inquired after Mama & said he was well acquainted with father & used often to visit at our house when Sam & I were small. I was very much pleased indeed with the Judge. 'Twas 5 o'clock when I went to Judge J.'s & they had just commenced dinner. They are somewhat like us at Umbria in that respect. Was quite hungry at Capitol to-day & got a flap-jack—made of dried apples stewed, in pastry—for $1. Got also before going to Judge J.'s a loaf of bread, $1.25, and four little ginger cakes, or rather sorghum syrup cakes, I presume for 75¢. On returning to Hosp. got one boiled sweet potatoe for which I paid $1.50. Got also an Examiner—price 15¢, at the office of that paper. There came up a thunder storm while I was at Judge L.'s & a rain soon afterwards. Got a little sprinkled before arriving at Hos. Had a piece of corn-bread, a small piece of bakers' bread & a little unsweetened rye-coffee, on getting in. The enemy made a light attack on our lines this morn'g—near Hanover Junction, but were repulsed. There is probability of a heavy battle soon to take place between Sherman & Genl Johnston, near Atlanta, for that place. God grant that the attempts of the Yankees may prove abortive & that they may be repulsed.

McD: Remained quiet in works all day. Very hard rain. Skirmishing heavy.

May 26, Thursday

HB: After breakfast finished a letter I had commenced yesterday to brother, expect to send it by Cummings who will start home tomorrow. Before I got entirely through, an order came to move again, went about a mile. Capt. Preston & I went to a clover field to graze our horses. Went to the front with rations this evening, more rain, got back to our quarters about midnight.

JP: This morn'g, after the rain & thunder-storm last night, it is clear & cooler. The sun peeps ever & anon thro' the fleeting clouds, sprinkling his golden rays through the green leaves & over the grassy ground making beautiful shades of that color which are very picturesque. The scene of that part of the city on the hill, grassy & endulating, which is viewed from the hospital, is very pretty & those shades cast by the sun over the scene adds to its picturesqueness. Wrote to Dr Hill for a certificate of my physical capacity, last night, also to Dr Cabell on same subject; also wrote to Loutie & to xxxxxx. Sat up 'till 1 o'clock or after last night. Capt. Williams & Paul Lavender came over to Hosp. this morn'g to see us, & I was glad to hear from the Cap. that Sam had arrived at Ellison's last night & was now there; but was sorry to hear that he is quite sick. He says also that Sam is very much fatigued & worsted. I hope he will come over here. When Capt. W. & P.L. returned I went with them and was glad to see on entering the former's room, my dear brother safe. Sam is really much thinner than when I last saw him & looks very badly. However I trust that he will be able to get a furlough & recuperate at home. How glad I would be on his account, & I know Mama & the children would be delighted beyond measure to see him. Oh, that he may get a furlough & if I succeed in getting detailed & we could both go home with Judge Lyon how rejoiced I would be. Sam gave me an account of the various hardships & fatigues that he had lately endured & I think it must have required super-human capacity to have withstood all the toil & exposure that he has lately passed through. I took dinner with him in Capt. W.'s room, & afterwards went to office mailed my letter to Dr Hill & the one to Lou & xxxxxx. Did not mail Dr Cabell's, as no mail goes to Charlottesville now. Did not inquire for our letters as I suppose I could not have got them. Sam, John & I then left to go to Hosp. at Howard Grove, tho' 'twas rain'g. We stopped & Sam reported at Seabrook's Hosp. & we then went on. Sam reported at office here & was assigned to a tent (No. 8) in 1st Div. Wish he could have got in Ward O, my ward, as it would be more pleasant than the tent. The rain ceased after we got here. Sam & I talked for a long time to-night, together & then went to bed about 10 o'clk. On our way up from town this even'g, bought a doz. little molasses cakes—price $2. Loaned Louis $2. which he never return'd. Got an Enquirer to-day—25¢.

McD: Skirmishing heavier than usual today. Orders to be ready to move.

VET: Enemy recross river.

May 27, Friday

HB: From the peals of cannon heard soon this morning, it seams that an engagement is at hand, shall go to the front during the day, to learn what is going on. About 9 A.M. received orders to move again. The whole army is in motion. We took up the line of march, went by Ashland, a beautiful little place. Gen. Lee sitting in his ambulance looking over his maps. About 5 P.M. stopped in a clover field, as we supposed for the night, when to our astonishment we took up the line of march again. Drew rations about midnight, traveled all night, and rested our troops just at daybreak. They were ready to move then, and consequently had to issue in haste. When we got through Maj. Webster, Capt. McCombs, Glover & I hunted up our division train, which we found [. . .]

JP: Awoke about 6 o'clk this morn'g, got up & dressed, after which went to Sam's tent, but he was asleep. I know he must be very tired after all the late fatigue he has had and that he must need rest. I'm on the half-diet again, to-day, so I get my meals at my bed as usual. The day is clear, bright & beautiful but warm as summer at 12 o'clk. Have been making attempts to get Sam transferred to our ward but have not been successful. There is to be a vacncy in it to-morrow, tho' and I hope then to be able to get Sam there. The D[r] who attends on him says he is perfectly willing for the transfer. Got a Dispatch & Examiner this morn'g. No news from the various seats of war, at present. A battle is imminent in Ga. From Gen[l] Lee, nothing comes save that the two armies confront each other at Hanover Junction, or in that neighborhood. There was some skirmishing going on yesterday. John came up from town this morning with the clothes which he washed for Sam last night. He brought letters for Mr. Long & others, but none for us. Sam looks better to-day than he did yesterday, tho' he is quite weak & confined to his bed. Oh, if the war were over & we at Umbria to recuperate (as in 1858, when we left the Greene Sprg's & went home with measles) how rejoiced would we not be! and how pleasant the recuperation would be! surrounded by a dear kind & attentive mother, & our dear sisters & brothers! The day wore away still clear & pretty. Sam & I talked 'till late to-night, of home, its inmates, its joys & comforts & retired about 10½ o'clock, to rest.

McD: Began marching at 6 o'clock today. Went in the direction of Mechanicsville. Very hard days march. Stoped at sun down.

May 28, Saturday

HB: On the road to Richmond parked near the yellow tavern. On reaching there took a nap & then got up to eat some. About 11 A.M. took up the line of march again, moved within three miles of Richmond, and took the Mechanicsville road. Passed over some of the prettiest country I ever saw. About 10 P.M. halted & parked for the night in 1½ miles of Mechanicsville.

JP: The morning is clear & pretty. Felt quite unwell to-day & did not rise until after breakfast & after the D[r] had made his visit. Tried again this morning to get Sam transferred to Ward "O," but failed again, being referred from one D[r] to another & finding none who knew how the exchange was to be made except the Surg. in attendance on Sam, who said I must get my Surg. to write an application to have Sam transferred to that ward & it would be done. Took a good bath to-day—cold—& put on a fresh suit of hosp. clothes—feeling much better after having done so. Then went to Sam's tent & sat until dinner, with him. Sam has improved considerably since his arrival here (Richmd) on last Wed. night tho' he is still weak & enervated by the fatigue & hardships which he has lately undergone. Could not get a paper to-day as I was asleep when the news-boys were here. Do not think there is much news of interest from either of the two armies.—Genl Lee's or Genl Johnston's. Genl J. is master of the situation in the Army of No. Ga., as Genl Lee is in that of N^o. Va. To-night I wrote a letter of eight pages in length to Mama. I would give any amount to hear from Mama & the children now. It has been so long since we have had one letter from home. Oh how glad we will be when a letter or letters from there come! It would fill us with delight. I also wrote a letter for John to his wife—Suckey, of four pages. John has been put on duty in Ward "L", every night since he has been here & must be very tired during the day as he sits up all night. 'Twas after 11 o'clk when I went to bed to-night. Sam fell asleep some time before I had finished John's letter & had read in Bible.

McD: Began to march at day light. Stoped near Mechanicsville about 11 o'clock today.

May 29, Sunday

HB: Everything comparatively quiet this morning, walked round the fortifications, several large guns mounted, and still improving the works. Drew rations this morning. Capt. Preston & I went to the front with them, was very much in hopes that we would be able to get through cooking by dark, as I hadn't slept any scarcely in 10 nights. When within a mile of our lines, our train was turned back by Gen. Rodes from the fact that the enemy was reported advancing, moved ½ mile to the rear, waited until dark and then carried our train up, got the cooking detail from Gen. Battle, guided them to the train. Saw all our boys, Capt. Williams having returned from R. Gave Jones a little bottle of brandy, which the boys enjoyed very much in my presence. Capt. Preston & I started back, reached our camp about 2 A.M.

JP: It rained last night & before daylight to-day cleared off cool & pleasant. A blanket would have felt very comfortable. We should feel thankful to God, our Father in heaven for having guarded us during the past night & brought us to see another beautiful spring Sabbath. Took breakfast at my bed as usual, this morn'g. Sam has not been transferred to Ward "O" yet, but I hope soon that he will be as I am certain he would find it more convenient & pleasant than the tent. Slept soundly for only four hours last night—from 11 till 3 o'clk. Heard the bell strike from 3 to 7 this morn'g when I awoke for the day. Sam continues to improve; I wish he had some delicacies, such as chickens, eggs, butter etc., which are so scarce that they have become to be regarded as luxuries. Went to town near 11 o'clk, to St Paul's church & heard a very interesting & fine sermon from Dr Minnegerode. His text was from 1st Epis. of St. Peter, IV Chap. 5th Verse. His language was plain & direct & his manner earnest & impressive. Could listen to one of his sermons with interest & pleasure were it protracted for hours in length. The church, both below & above, was filled with an attentive audience. The choir was a very good one & the music solemly grand. The whole service I think very impressive & beautiful. 'Twas 1 o'clk when I came out of church & consequently when I arrived at Hosp. found that I had missed my dinner; but did not care. However Keeley—the servant who stays at the ward, got me some soup & corn-bread, wh. I found very good. This morning Dr Hill stopped at the Spring near here (Ward "O",) spoke to me, asked after Sam, & told me he rec^d my letter & that he mailed me a certificate & directed it to the Hosp. I am afraid I will not get it tho', as mail matter is received very irregularly here indeed. I trust I will get it however & that Judge Lyon may be able to get me a detail. The old man who preached last Sund. at the Chapel brought us a copy of the "The Soldier's Visitor"—a very interesting Presbyterian paper published in this city. It had some very entertaining matter in it. Sam & I were awake 'till late to-night.

McD: Remained quiet until 4 o'clock p.m. then moved a few hundred yards, got position and began [to] throw up works. Skirmishing begins in our front but is at a good distance.

NOTE: *The Soldier's Visitor* began publication in 1863.

May 30, Monday

HB: Heavy cannonading heard on our right for about two hours this morning, wrote to brother today. Glover having rested yesterday carried, rations to the front himself. I am resting today, expect to go to the city in the morning if nothing happens. Our division attacked the Yankees about 1 P.M. some 3 miles the other side of Mechanicsville, charged two lines of battle, and repulsed then handsomely, none of Co. D. were hurt. The fight lasted until some time after night.

JP: This is still a clear & pretty day. The weather is very pleasant at night & in the morning, but grows warm in the middle of the day—& I think is fully as warm as our summer weather in Ala. Inquired at office for letters for Sam & me to-day but there was none. How glad Sam & I would be to get some letters from our dear mother, sisters & brothers as it has been age it seems since we have heard from them, But I hope 'twill not be long ere we recieve a whole quantity of them. Sam was awake & waiting for breakfast to-day when I went up to see him. How I wish he could get a furlough and that he & I could visit our dear home & be united once more with those most dear to us there! This even'g about 4 o'clk went to Baggage-room, got my boots & a clean shirt which I took to Sam's tent & put on & then went down town to the P.O., & inquired for letters for us, but did not get any. Then I thought of going to see Judge Lyon but concluded after-wards not to do so. I then met Maj. Webster who was on his horse at Gov.'s house (i.e. on that side facing street) talking to Ed. H., W. Hafner, Mr. Elliot & another man. I then went to office again inquired at army delivery for letters &, getting none, I returned to Hosp. Got Sam two loaves of good baker's bread ($2.) Could not get him any butter. Ellison's clerk said he had none this even'g but would have to-morrow some that he expected from Petersburg—fresh & good. It sells fr. $15. to $18 lb. Got back this evening too late for supper, but managed to "fill up" by eating some dry bread, part of a biscuit & a small piece of toast which Sam had left. Read a part of "Macaria" to Sam to give him an idea of the style of the book which I think he liked very much. The book as far as I have read in it is very interesting—tho' it is somewhat different from Miss Evans' other novel—Beulah. Intend sending it home when I finish it. The time passes off much more pleasantly to me, since Sam arrived. Before he came I generally laid down & tried to take a nap in the evening (which I would *sometimes* accomplish by dint of hard persuasion) or read. I now spend the greater part of my time in his tent. The walk from town this even'g was very hot.

McD: Remained quiet till after 12 o'clock. We were ordered to move to the right. We met the enemy and had a very hot little fight. After night fell back to the woods in our rear and remained till morning. This was the battle of Bethesda Church.

NOTE: Augusta J. Evans, *Beulah* (New York: G. W. Dillingham Co., 1857).

May 31, Tuesday

HB: Went to the city this morning, attended, to some business, staid there about three hours and returned with Wm. Carver. Had an elegant [. . .] there, which I enjoyed very much. Heavy cannonading on our left all the forenoon. Drew rations, carried them to the front after dark, saw our boys, who were about to move to the left. Carried detail out, and returned to camp, reached there about midnight.

JP: The weather is still clear & beautiful, tho' summer-like, as regard heat, in the middle of the day, or from nine o'clock in the morning until 6 in the even'g. Wrote a letter on day before yesterday for a man in Sam's tent by name of Johnston, to his wife. Have been troubled with a bad cough for the past few days which is very disagreeable indeed. This evening Sam is much better; he is improving a great deal & looks a great deal better than he did the day he arrived here. Went this evening down town inquired at P.O., & failing to get a letter for us or Dr Hill's certificate, went to see Judge Lyon. He seemed glad to see me & made further promises of giving me all the assistance he could & told me that he had no doubt I would be able to get a detail, thro' Judge Campbell, whom he said had been no doubt a friend of father's & the family & who would aid me further. He informed me that Congress had postponed adjournment to the 7th inst. & advised me to write again to Dr Hill for another certificate. Had quite a warm walk there. Judge L. also hoped I would be able to get a detail & leave with him. We got no paper to-day & consequently did not know what the news was. Think tho' that the armies are quiet. Sam & I generally sit up in his tent talking 'till about 10 or 10½ o'clock & then go to bed. The nights are very pleasant but the days are quite warm, that is, in the middle of the day. I trust in a merciful God to hasten the return of peace & joy, happiness and security to our country, and that soon our nation may fall down before the Lord in humility & thank Him & praise His holy name for all His loving kindnesses & tender mercies which have been ever of old. Oh Lord hear our prayers & speak peace to our land for Christ's sake.

McD: Threw breast works all day. The day passed off tolerable quiet. After dark we were ordered to move again. Moved back to the position occupied before the last battle.

June 1, Wednesday

HB: Very heavy firing on the line this morning, both artillery & musketry. More entries for today slipped my memory.

McD: Remained quiet in our position all day. Considerable sharp shooting and some cannonading and heavy fighting on our right flank.

NOTE: The battle at Cold Harbor began.

June 2, Thursday

HB: Occasional firing this morning. Started to the front with rations, when passed Mechanicsville heard heavy musketry & cannonading in front of our division, halted my train near the hospital, shells were flying in close proximity about me. The firing lasted until after 9 P.M. About 11 P.M. Maj. Adams returned from the front with orders to carry our train up to the entrenchments, that our boys left in the afternoon. All the detail of the division was there except mine. Waited until after 1 o'clock, & started to the brigade on my horse, not knowing the exact position they occupied, and it being so very dark, made it impossible for me to find my way through the thick woods. I went back left my horse with the train & took it [on] foot, walked about three miles, went over two lines of works that our boys drove the yankees out of during the afternoon, and finally found them hard at work throwing up earth works. Gen. Battle forgot to send out detail and I waited to get it & conducted them to the train. Day had broke when I got there. Jim Webb in trying to find the regiment, came across our train, found me & staid with the cooking party until they returned to the front.

JP: Sent John, this morning after breakfast, with a note to Dr Hill requesting the latter to send me another certificate, as the former one I have never recd. Dislike very much to have to do this as it will seem like encroaching on the D^r's kindness; however, as he promised me that he would help me & I cannot do anything without a certificate from him (and probably little with it, as the officials are so strict) I am certain or hope, he will not refuse me. The day commences clear & beautiful. At breakfast time to-day I called at Sam's tent to see him. Trust Sam may be enabled to get a furlough & go home if I go, that we may go together. Oh how happy I would be! Went to the P.O. here to-day in anticipation of getting some letters & after waiting with a great deal of patience (?) 'till the letters had been alphabetically & slowly called out, was repaid for all trouble a hundred thousand times—inexpressibly—and the list finally went on down to the letter

"P" came & I was glad to hear Sam's name & mine called several times. I rec<u>d</u> one letter from Mama & one from D<u>r</u> Hill—containing his certificate of my health &c. Mama's letter was long & as all hers are, very interesting indeed. It containd news of the health of all at Umbria & also of Bishop Wilmer's sermon on 15<u>th</u> ult. at the Prairie church & the confirmation of Mr. & Mrs. Bayol, Mrs. Bayol, Jr. Miss Annie Withers, Mrs. Grigg & a colored man. Oh what joy & gratification does it not afford us to hear the pleasure of the indirect but at the same time the nearest & sweetest communion with those from whom we are so far separated & whose society we cannot enjoy, being debarred that happiness! All were well at home & seemed in health & spirits. Mama had been sick & Loutie also, but were both well when she wrote. I would, with her, this war were over & that she could come to Va. & spend the hot months July Aug. & Sep. at the Sulphur Spr'gs, as they would be of great benefit to her. Was sorry to hear of the death of poor old Mr. Dorroh, who died on the night of the 8<u>th</u> ult. John & Gayle did not reach their horse to see him before his death. He was very feeble & all anticipated his departure at any time. Went to see Judge Lyon this even'g & found him at Judge Jones'. Gave him Dr. Hill's certificate & was told by him that he would get Judge Campbell to make a recommendation for a detail upon it to-night. He is quite kind & exceedingly obliging. Hope he will succeed in getting me a detail. John returned this evening with another letter of certif. from D<u>r</u> Hill, tho' I now have use only for the first one.

McD: Remained quiet untill late in the evening. We were then ordered to shove directly forward across our works. Found that the enemy had withdrawn all but his skirmishers. Drove the skirmishers back and followed them up till we came on their main forces. We had a severe fight for a few hours. Found the enemy behind works. Our brigade (Battle) charged the works and occupied them the length of the entire Brigade. No other troops got possession of the works except our Brigade. Fell back at night a few hundred yards and threw up works. Heavy rain all the evening and nearly all night.

VET: Battle Brigade support SS. Sharp fight, drove enemy. Wynne, Childress, and Sellers wounded.

NOTE: "SS" stands for Sharp Shooters.

June 3, Friday

HB: I returned to our camp, just as they commenced eating breakfast, took a wash and something to eat and started off to Richmond in company with Maj. Webster & Capt. Preston, attended to some business, telegraphed home about Henry Childress being wounded, ate some ice cream and strawberries, the first I had seen this season, enjoyed them very much. I started back to camp, overtook Rev. Mr. Hutchinson at the Howard grove where he stopped to see Ed. I went in, saw Ed Hutchinson, Jim Pickens & Wm. Long. Mr. Hutchinson, Dr. Harmond & Wm. Elliason started to the front. I rode along side of them. The conversation came up about Lieut. James Hutchinson. The old gentleman was under the impression that he was still buried without a case. When I told him that I saw his son James put into a box myself & helped bury him, tears of grief & joy were mingled at the idea that he will be able to get his son's remains home sometime or other. The old gentleman took me by the hand, thanked me kindly and with a current of tears streaming down his face, he assured me again and again of his gratitude for an act, which I didn't consider more than what one soldier owes another, particularly as noble & daring soldier as James J. Hutchinison was. In spite of myself, I couldn't keep from showing that I shared in his bereavement. I rode with him, until I got opposite my camp where I turned off and he proceeded with his journey. Gen. Longstreet's & Hill's corps engaged the enemy all day on our extreme right, the yankees charging our lines as many as ten times, but were handsomely repulsed every time. The battle lasted until two hours after dark. Mr. Dunlap of Gainesville & Alf Glover staid with us tonight. Col. Fowler passed by on his way to the front.

McD: Fighting begins early this morning. Most awful cannonading nearly all day. A Battery was stationed in the center of our regt. It suffered severely 28 men were killed or wounded out of forty four. At night we were ordered back to old positions.

NOTE: Grant ordered fifty thousand Union soldiers to assault the Confederate line at dawn. In a remarkably short time, the Union lost seven thousand men killed and wounded. Some five thousand Union soldiers had been lost the previous two days. Cold Harbor could be called the last of Lee's victories.

June 4, Saturday

HB: The contest seems to be renewed this morning from the firing nearly all along the line, turned out to be not much however. Mr. Hutchinson came by our camp & I rode to the front with in. Left him at Gen. Rodes' hd-qrs., & I went to issue rations, returned at 12 M. Neglected to make entries for want of time during the day & rest at night. Remember of calling on Col. Hobson at Genl. Anderson's.

McD: Remained quiet in our works. Collected arms etc. Heavy rain today.

VET: Ewell corps in reserve, quiet along line.

June 5, Sunday

McD: Was ordered to move early this morning. Our corps under command of Gen Early moved to the right and went in front of our works a mile or two. Skirmished a while with the enemy about Cold Harbor about sun down. Came back near Mechanicsville and bivouaced in rear of our works.

June 6, Monday

McD: Remained quiet all day. Ordered to be ready to move but did not move.

June 7, Tuesday

HB: Returned from the front about day break this morning after following the troops to a late hour last night, where they had been evidently to give the enemy battle, but Mr. Yank refused, passed through the lines the enemy occupied witnessed the wholesale destruction of everything in the neighborhood, even to bible cushions at Bethesda church, one house close by perfectly riddled with shells. After eating some, Capt. Preston & I had to go to the city after bread. We both understood our ability to stand up under the influence of our gallops, and consequently left the city pretty lively. Returned to camp about 1 P.M., laid down to take a nap when I was woke by Maj. Webster, who told me I had to take charge of the issuing rations to division hospital. Got ready & started down, found hospital immediately in rear of our boys, who were in the woods on the Mechanicsville turnpike resting. Being tired. & weary, I laid down under the wagon & went to sleep.

McD: Still in camp but under orders.

June 8, Wednesday

HB: We are still resting today, spend most of the day with the boys & returned to my wagon in the evening to issue rations. Received orders to be ready to move by dawn tomorrow.

McD: Remained quiet till late in the evening. we then received orders to move and moved to the right. Stoped near Gains' Mills about dark. We were then a mile or two in rear of works.

June 9, Thursday

HB: Kept in readiness to move all the morning, but up to 12 o'clock no sign of moving yet, was at last very agreeably surprised with a letter from Miss J—— about 5 P.M. received orders to move immediately. Everything was ready in a few moments, started off, and halted at Dr. Gaines' house near Gaines mill after dark. The troops are laying in front in sight. Our division had orders to go to Petersburg this morning, the order was countermanded however before we started.

McD: We were quiet today; in a warm place; an open field.

June 10, Friday

HB: Went over to see the boys this morning they still being in the same place resting in a hot open field. Rec'd the Beacon of the 3rd inst. during the day, containing my letter to brother of the 13th May from Spottsyva. C.H. Thought I had warned brother often enough not to show my letters to anyone, intend to write him a letter and give him a severe blow up, about acting against my will, in regard to my correspondence. The boys tried to tease me by calling me a regular correspondent of the Beacon. Tried to answer Miss J's letter, but failed twice, don't expect to attempt it again today. Everything quiet today except an occasional shell thrown by our artillery at the yankees, who are trying to fortify. The distance between the two lines is about 200 yards, too close even to throw out sharpshooters. Had the honor of showing President Davis Gen. Lee's hd.qrs about dusk.

McD: Remained quiet all day. Heard sermon delivered by Rev. D. Witherspoon

June 11, Saturday

HB: Everything still quiet this morning, this makes the fifth day our division is enjoying the rest, which we so much need. Received letter from Alfred today. Expect to answer tomorrow, if nothing happens. Moved our camp from the orchard back of Dr. Gaines' house to the top of the hill across the mill, a camp that the yankees occupied in 1862.

JP: Another day has been permitted to dawn upon us & again are we brought in renewed obligation to God our heavenly Father for permitting us, thro' great mercy & providential care, to see its light. Oh Lord make us sensible of the many blessings with which Thou continually crownest upon us & of all the comforts & necessaries of life; but above all of our being permitted to humble ourselves before Thee & in contrition to implore Thee to pardon our sins & turn us from the paths of sin & error into the ways of eternal life, that so being regenerated by Thy holy spirit we may become fit to receive Thy holy Confirmation & be admitted into Thy church, remain steadfast in it as long as we live & be ready & prepared when Thou shalt send for us, to die, and grant these my poor prayers for Christ's sake, Amen. Sam & I sleep very comfortably in Tent upon our little couch—tho' I expect no doubt he is very much crowded. The nights are quite cool at present and it is very comfortable to have a bed-fellow as two sleep warmer than one alone. Went this morn'g to see Judge Lyon but found him busily engaged in the debates of Congress; so had to wait 'till he had finished. Did not succeed in getting my papers. Am to meet the Judge on Mon., Deo volente. After seeing him I got Sam 1 qt. Cherries $4. also spunge cake $4. and a slice ginger-cake for $1.

McD: Quiet today. Can hear sharp shooting on the lines.

June 12, Sunday

HB: Went up to our headquarters this morning after my clothes, after I returned, wrote to Miss J was interrupted by Mr. Hutchinson, who came by and told me of his adventures with the yankees in Spottsylvania City, had some dinner prepared for him, after which he left. I resumed my writing again & finished just as Jones & Britt returned from the hospital. They stopped but a short while & went to camp. I laid down sometime after dark and was about asleep, when we received orders to get ready to move immediately, got up our train moved out met the troops on a road leading to Mechanicsville.

JP: This is the Lord's day. May we spend it in reverential contemplation, in devotional reading & may we improve each hour of it in a manner befitting Christians & those desiring to lead upright & pious lives. God help us is my sincere prayer. Dr Pleasants called to see us this morning about 9 o'clock & after sitting 'till about 10, he[,] H. Allen & I walked over to town & went to Dr Moore's (Presbyterian) Church. Heard a very plain, earnest, instructive & learned sermon. Text, Duet. Chap. 3rd, verses 25th & 26th. The day is cool for June weather. The spell of weather which we are now having is very cool indeed.

Blankets at night are indispensable. Sam & I have been occupying the same narrow bed together for the past week. It is rather narrow for both of us but we make out very well, indeed. Oh if we could only go home we could live this way for weeks.

McD: Heard two Sermons today, one by Rev. Dr. Rosser and one by Dr. Brown. Two or three shells came nearly into our camps.

June 13, Monday

HB: Marched all night, reached Mechanicsville after day break, went to the right of Richmond crossed the Central & Fredricksburg R.R. and it was then only, that we had an idea of where we were going to. Thought we were going up the valley. We halted about 3 P.M., rested after marching 25 miles since we started, staid 3 miles this side of ground squirrel church, orders to move at sunrise.

JP: Another day has been granted to us by our heavenly Father. Lord keep us from sin this day—for Christ's sake. Got 2 pieces pie for $2., glass milk 50¢, Cake $1. = $3.50, to-day. To-day clear & pretty—tho' clouds are not wholly wanting in the sky. Was to have met Judge L. at 10 to-day but did not see him 'till 3 o'clk. Went to the Office to see for my paper but it had not been rec$^{\underline{d}}$. Judge C., told me to meet him at his office to-morrow at 10 o'clock. Saw Capt. Wright whom it was thought had been killed at the bat. Chickamauga; he looks very well indeed. Promised if he had time to visit Sam & myself at the Hospital. Oh that we could now hear from our dear Mama, Mary, Loutie, Millie & Icha, those most dear to us, and from my dear xxxxxx! Hope soon to be with them all again, no more to be parted whilst life lasts. Oh God grant that my wish & desire to meet them soon may be gratified & also that Sam may get a furlough & we both be united with our dear ones at home in joy & peace & happiness! Oh, what joy & pleasure a reunion with them all would be to us. Nothing more dear or precious for us.

McD: Began to move this morning before daylight. Went in sight of Richmond. Many were conjecturing as to our destination. Many were of the opinion that we were going to the south side of the James river. When we arrived at the Telegraph Road, we started in the opposite direction from Richmond. Marched very hard all day, a warm and dusty march. Camped beyond Hanover Junct. late in the evening.

VET: Ewell's corps left Richmond in command of Early, marched 25 miles in direction of Louisa C H.

NOTE: Lee was unaware of the threat posed by Grant's move toward the James River and ordered Jubal Early's corps into the Valley. As part of that corps, the Greensboro Guards set out about two in the morning.

June 14, Tuesday

HB: Return to my quarters today there being no hospital on a march. Marched with the troops having no horse to ride today. While resting finished letter to Miss J . . . in the wagon, mailed it at Mount Pelia P.O. Hanover Co. some two miles this side the South Anna. Struck the Louisa Cty. line marched until 6 P.M. & halted for tonight, much to my relief, being almost broken down.

JP: Awoke before six or soon after 5 o'clock this morning. Am to meet Judge Campbell, at 10 this morn'g. I sometimes manage to get a ticket from Mr. Long (Ward-master now, of Ward O, vice Ames—resigned or removed) & sometimes I fail to do so. After breakfast we were glad to see Capt. Wright who called & gave us a long account of his capture during the battle of Chickamauga & of his escape & adventures in the north & of his eventual return to the Confederacy about two weeks, or may-be not as long, ago. This recital was very interesting indeed. Sam found Capt. W— a good deal changed. He looks very differently from the little delicate & tender man he used to be at the Greene Springs—having thickened a good deal & become more healthy than he then was. He is the same clever, talkative gentleman he ever was. We were glad to see him, it having been reported he was dead. Went to Judge C.'s & got paper from Surg. Genl. Then waited 'till Cong. adjn'd & Judge L., Sam & I then went to Judge Campbells. Found that Med. Board had disapp^d my being detailed, so could not get one from Judge C. Was much disappt^d. Bade Judge L. good-bye, thanking him for his kind endeavors to help me. Sam, John & I then return^d to Hos. Saw at Capitol to-day Robt Poore who was a school-mate of ours at Dr Harrison's.

McD: Began to move again at day light. Made another hard days march. Camped near Louisa Court House.

June 15, Wednesday

HB: Last night was the first since this move, that I got anything like rest, laid down about midnight, and slept in the wagon with Shelby. Got up a little after day, got a cup of coffee from Young Idom which I relished very much. Phil May going to our wagon train, had a horse to lead, I rode him, cut across the road from the Louisa to the old mountain road, passed by Brooks mill, where we got something to eat, milch & ice, etc, the first thing of that kind I ate in a long time. On overtaking the wagons, Keeler & I rode ahead, called at Mr. Wright's house about ½ mile off the road, and got an elegant dinner. Got in sight of the Blue Ridge during the day. Got in rear of the train & caught up after it stopped at Poindexter's store. After eating some, retired well worn out.

JP: Awoke at 5 o'clock this morn'g having had a good night's rest after the great disappointment of yesterday. The mornings are very cool & the nights almost as cool as our October weather. Got hash & corn-bread for breakfast & unsweetened rye coffee. The morn'g is clear & pretty. Oh if it had been granted me to have left for dear home yesterday & soon to have been united with dear mother, sisters & brothers again, how differently should I now feel! But, I will not despond, but feel that God has ordered this, & that it is for the best. I will continue to look forward to the happy times when we shall all be reunited in joy peace & happiness. God grant it may soon arrive. Sam went before the Board this morn'g at 10 o'clock. Do not know if he has obtained a furlough or not.

This morning Charley & Taco Wilborn called to see us & sat for an hour or two with us. They told us of Tom's death & Charley showed us an obituary on it, which was prepared by Adj. Seymour of Tom's Regt., & which will be published in to-morrow's Examiner. He also told us that he had written several times to Mama in regard to the matter, but had recd. no answer to his letters. These are two clever, gentlemanly well-educated & pleasant youth's & we were very much pleased with them. Sam recᵈ a long letter—tho' quite a sad one from Mama in which was also one from Mary. They contained the sad news of our dear Tom's death. Oh, how sad! to think that in the prime of life, in good health & of late so hopeful & happy, to have been cut down in the midst of all his hopes & expectations! But 'twas the Lord's will, & He doeth all things well! Mama mentioned that all are well. God be praised!

McD: Passed through the little town of Louisa in the morning, and took a road leading to Charlottsville. Made a hard days march.

NOTE: As the Guards marched through Virginia, the Army of the Potomac attacked Petersburg. Grant's failure to take it resulted in a siege that lasted the rest of the war.

"Shelby" is Shelby Chadwick.

June 16, Thursday

HB: Took up the march again, left the mountain road & got into the Charlottesville road, where we met up with the troops, stopped to see the boys and then returned with the coming wagons to our train, which was camped beyond Charlottesville, passed through after night, wrote a hurried letter to brother.

McD: Began to move at day light this morning. Kept the road to Charlottsville and camped within five miles of it. Drew shoes etc.

June 17, Friday

HB: Started off with the wagons this morning, traveled until about 1 P.M. passed through North garden, a lovely spot through these mountains. Our division took an early start this morning, marched through Charlottesville & took the same road that our train was going marched in rear of the train and went down the R.R. to North garden depot. Maj. Webster sent for me to meet him at the depot. I cut across to the R.R. passed by Dr. Long's & waited for him at the depot. When he came, asked me to ride his horse through, he taking the train with the troops to Lynchburg. Capt. Preston & I rode off & joined our train which we found parked near Coversville.

McD: Began to march at day light and went through Charlottsville early in the morning. The merchants gave us plenty tobacco. Continued our march down the Rail Road in the direction of Linchburg. The day was very warm. Camped late in the evening at North Garden.

VET: Marched and camped at North Garden. Where are we going to any how is the cry.

June 18, Saturday

HB: Capt. P. & I started off this morning. After long attempting we finally got ahead of our train, crossed Rockfish river, from there through a little place called

Lovingston. Capt. Priest overtook us & we all concluded to hunt some dinner, started out and finally got to Mrs. Baker's off from the road, where we rested and got dinner. On getting into the road again had to pass all the train again, crossed the Tye river & stopped all night with the corps ordinance train. Got some milch and some [. . .] at the house on the hill.

McD: Got on the cars about ten o'clock today. Went to Linchburg and camped about a mile west of town. Drew three crackers and a small piece of bacon. The town was in considerable excitement. The Yankees [commanded by] Hunter were within two miles of the place.

NOTE: After unsuccessful attacks against a strong Confederate force at Lynchburg, Union General David Hunter withdrew northward. This second Union defeat, following New Market on May 15, left the lower Valley open for Early's troops to march northward into Maryland and then southward to Washington.

June 19, Sunday

HB: Got up at day this morning fed my horse & started on my way to Lynchburg again. Passed through New Glasgow before sun up. Passed through Amherst C.H. & stopped some 8 miles from Lynchburg where we got some milch & bread, reached Lynchburg about 11 A.M. met Maj. Webster and others at the Piedmont House. Our quarters being established in the depot back of the Orange house, went round there & found all of our supplies there. Boardman & I walked about town for some purpose—went back to the depot & after eating some laid down.

McD: Was up at two o'clock this morning. Moved to a position where we expected to make an attack at day light. Waited till day light but found that the enemy had gone. Started in pursuit: to the new London Road and expected to find them there but was mistaken. We could see their destruction on the road side. They killed stock and burned fences, plundered houses etc. Marched rapidly all day and arrived at Liberty late in the evening. Had a skirmish with the Yanks in the Mountain Pass. Camped for the night near Liberty.

June 20, Monday

HB: Got up at 2 o'clock this morning to start off to the brigade which was supposed to be about Liberty 27 miles from here. Maj. Webster ordered me to stay with the supplies, until Maj. Adams' train came up. In the meantime carried Jack Wynne's boy, who was very sick, to Mrs. Rogers' on Church Street. Left Lynchburg about 10 A.M. took the Salem turnpike, rode a little yankee mule that Maj. Adams lent me, my teams giving out I had my mule hitched to the wagon in place of one broken down, had to stop about 4 P.M. to graze, had some dinner cooked & got ready to start off again. Passed through New London, met with old man Burton & passed right through, parked about 10 P.M. on bank of Big Otter river.

McD: Began to move early this morning, the enemy still retreating and we still in pursuit. A very "hard day." Nothing to eat. Caught up with the Yanks in the evening in another mountain pass. Had a skirmish. Camped for the night on the side of the mountain. Got a small ration of bacon but no bread.

June 21, Tuesday

HB: Started this morning about day break, drove until about 12 M., stopped to rest and eat, passed through Liberty in Bedford Co., a right handsome little town. At 4 P.M. took up the march again, traveled. until 11 P.M. when I halted the train for the night at Buford's gap.

McD: Began to move early this morning. Still in pursuit of the Yanks. Was ordered to make a forward march in order to cut them off from a gap in the mountains. The day was very warm and many of the men gave out, being overcome with heat and hunger. Arrived at the gap rather late but made the Yanks abandon several wagons and eleven pieces of Artillery. They set fire to some ordnance wagons that had barrels of powder in them, which exploded while some of their men were passing, killing six or eight men. We saw their mangled forms lying on the roadside. Some of them had their legs and arms torn off and thrown fifty yards from their bodies. Went back a mile or two and went into camp.

June 22, Wednesday

HB: At daybreak started my train to overtake the troops, got into Roanoke county today. About 1 P.M. caught up with our corps train, where the Salem turnpike and the Fincastle roads fork. The yankees having succeeded in getting out at the gap they made for, the pursuit was discontinued today & the troops got a days rest. I had a good night's rest camped on Tinker river.

McD: Rested all day and washed. Drew rations which we quickly devoured. Many of the boys went foraging but could not get much except cherries.

June 23, Thursday

HB: Started off with our wagon train this morning, rode about 4 miles, when we got into the Buchanan turnpike, where the troops were passing. I left the train & overtook my brigade, marched with Company D all day. We counted the number of ladies, who came out to see us pass & they were 159. Went into camp about 5 P.M.

McD: Began to move at day light this morning. Going towards Buchanan. Passed Botetourt Springs. Saw a host of beautiful ladies. Did not pursue the Yanks today. Marched twenty one miles and camped at 4 o'clock.

June 24, Friday

HB: Took up the line of march at 3 o'clock this morning, rode in a wagon portion of the forenoon, crossed the James river at Buchanan in Buckingham County, marched along with the train the balance of the day until about 6 P.M. when we camped in 6 miles of Lovington. Was in hopes we'd cross Cedar Creek at the natural bridge, but our division took the left hand road when in two miles of it, & Gordon's & Ramseur's divisions kept straight ahead, so my desire to see the wonder of the world was killed by this move of ours. Saw Gen. Breckinridge for the first time today. The heat was oppressive all day. Killed the first beeves this evening, carried some liver to Co. D, returned about midnight very much fatigued.

McD: Began to march before day. Passed through Buchanan early in the morning. Took the turnpike to Lexington. Marched twenty miles.

June 25, Saturday

HB: Took up line of march this morning at ½ past 3 o'clock when in 3 miles of Lexington, rested over an hour to let Gordon's and Ramseur's divisions get into the road ahead of us. Was requested by all of Co. D. to write a letter to all the families of G. saying how & where they were started & marched with Co. D this morning. In passing through Lexington our corps performed a solemn ceremony which seemed to be deeply felt by every man. On entering the town we passed through the graveyard by the grave of the lamented Stonewall Jackson who only 14 months ago was the commander of our present corps. We marched in two ranks with arms reversed, the bands playing solemn marches. His grave was covered with flowers & at the head of it hung the stars & bars on a pole erected by the ladies of Lexington. In passing by every eye was turned on the grave, and tears were seen flow in a great many instances. It was certainly a sad sight. In passing through the town, we were greeted by hundreds of beautiful ladies, who waited on us in the way of serving us refreshments of different kinds. Of the Military institute nothing but the ruins are left, the yankees having burned it down also Gov. Letcher's fine mansion, marched 7 miles beyond L. & camped.

McD: Started before day light. Went through Lexington about noon. Passed around Gen'l Jacksons grave at reverse arms. Our bands and drums played a funeral dirge. The ladies of Lexington kept the General's grave covered with fresh flowers. The people of Lexington manifested great kindness towards us. The Ladies crowded the streets and gave us ice water and some eatables. The day was extremely warm. Marched twenty three miles.

NOTE: On May 15 at New Market, cadets from the Virginia Military Institute joined Breckinridge's forces to defeat a Union force under Franz Sigel. Union forces under David Hunter burned the institute on June 11. It was to stop Hunter that Lee detached Early to the Valley.

June 26, Sunday

HB: Took up line of march at 3 A.M., passed through Brownsburg this morning, the weather extremely hot, towards evening some appearance of rain, but turned clear again. We were in expectation of resting tomorrow, as such was the order, but were sadly disappointed by the order received this evening to be ready to move at 4 A.M. Received letter from brother today of the [. . .] inst, camped at Middlebrook a little town 10 miles from Staunton.

McD: Began to march at three o'clock going in the direction of Staunton. The day very warm. Marched twenty miles.

June 27, Monday

HB: Took up line of march this morning at past 4 o'clock, marched 8 miles & camped about 2 miles this side of Staunton. On arriving there, wrote a letter to brother, we rested all day. Our transportation has been reduced considerably today, everybody is busy getting up their clothes. From present aspects, it appears as though we were going to Pa.

McD: Began to march at 4 o'clock. Marched ten miles and stoped about noon near Staunton. Selected a good camp as if we expected to remain some time.

June 28, Tuesday

HB: Packed up our clothes that we intend to take along, received orders to move at 4 P.M. & camp on little river 7 miles the other side of Staunton. At 4 P.M. took up line of march & reached camp near little river about 7 P.M. I had a yankee suit on today, in passing through Staunton everybody took me to be a yankee. Wrote to Alfred today.

McD: Remained quiet till one o'clock. We then got rations etc. and began to move. Went through Staunton and took the Winchester Pike. Camped five miles north of Staunton.

June 29, Wednesday

HB: Took up line of march at ½ past 4 A.M., passed through Mount Sidney about 10 miles from Staunton, crossed river, camped in the evening after marching about 19 miles, at a little place called Kieseltown. Rec'd letter from Miss A. tonight.

McD: Started at four o'clock. Left the Pike near Mt. Sidney. Took the Keezltown road, passed Xkees and marched in the direction of New Market. Camped after marching twenty miles.

NOTE: "Xkees" is Cross Keys.

June 30, Thursday

HB: Having staid with Maj. Adams last night, I did'nt start with the troops this morning, but followed his train. About 1 P.M. we got into the Winchester turnpike again, and marched until we reached New-Market, where we camped for the night, troops marched 20 miles today by 4 P.M. Wrote a long letter to Miss A. to Mr. Meigs. From this day on Lee belongs to Miss A & I.

McD: Began to march at 4 o'clock this morning. Came back into the Pike and went as far as New Market where we camped.

July 1, Friday

HB: Took up line of march this morning at ¼ to 4 o'clock, crossed the Shenandoah & passed through Mount Jackson. Passed through Woodstock this evening, met with old man Heller from H. who promised to give me a portrait of my father's, sat with him about 2 hours and started off to overtake my command, which I found encamped near the town, after marching 22 miles today.

McD: On the march this morning at three o'clock. Went through Mt. Jackson, Edenburgh, and camped near Woodstock.

July 2, Saturday

HB: Took up line of march this morning at ½ past 3 o'clock, passed through Strassburg, Middletown & Newtown, the latter place we camped at about 5 P.M. after marching about 22 miles. The ladies in all these towns are complaining of the depredation of the yankees.

McD: Marched at three o'clock this morning. Passed through Strasburg, Middletown and camped near New Town.

July 3, Sunday

HB: Took up line of march at ½ past 3 A.M., passed through Winchester about 10 A.M., amid greeting and cheering from the ladies. After passing the town some 3 miles we took the right hand road towards Smithfield, where we camped for the night, after marching 22 miles. Skirmishing at Leestown today with the yankees.

McD: Moving at four o'clock this morning. Went through Winchester and received many kind tokens from the citizens, especially the ladies. Heard that the Yankee cavalry had been there the day before. Rested a few minutes in town. Left the Pike five miles below Winchester and went in the direction of Harper's Ferry. Camped near Smithfield for the night.

July 4, Monday

HB: Passed through Smithfield this morning, thence through Charlestown, where we met with a warm reception by the ladies particularly. About 4 miles from Charlestown skirmishing with pickets commenced. Our division in course of the day drove the enemy off from Bolivar heights. The yankees kept up a continual shelling from the mountains, where they had some hundred pound parrots planted. About dark our brigade was ordered to go to Bolivar town to see what stores there were left. They reached the town at dusk & commenced plundering, found any quantity of quartermaster & [. . .] stores, which the yankees in their hasty retreat from there could not destroy. The yankees had made great preparations for a 4th July celebration. Our boys destroyed their fun however by giving them a little skirmish. They had all the citizens in the neighborhood invited to participate of their delicacies. Our boys found any quantity of eatables &c. delicacies such as brandy, whiskey, candy, ice cream, cakes, etc. They all came out next morning with filled haversacks, besides a quantity of shoes and clothing. The yankees left Harper's ferry tonight a mile from Bolivar town. Our train was some 3 miles in the rear.

McD: Began to move at day light. Passed through Smithfield early in the morning. Passed through Charlestown and went direct to Harpers Ferry. When we were within three miles of Harper's Ferry we met with some Yankee cavalry. Our sharp shooters were ordered out, and soon drove them back across the river. The enemy had some heavy guns on the opposite side of the river on the Maryland Heights that continued to shell us all day. We marched in ravines sheltering ourselves as much as possible. We continued till night in a deep ravine near town. We after night went in town and got a large quantity of bread etc. We had possession of quite a rich camp. Got many shelter tents etc.

NOTE: Beck's use of "parrots" refers to the Parrot rifles, the plentiful and inexpensive Union artillery developed by Robert Parrot.

July 5, Tuesday

HB: Our brigade returned from Bolivar town this morning, camped about 5 miles from Maryland heights. Carried our train to the front with rations, but the troops refused to take any, being well supplied with Yankee rations. Our division rested in a piece of woods all day. At dusk our division sent about 100 wagons to bring off the stores from Harpers Ferry, returned about 1 A.M. well loaded.

McD: Left town at day light this morning and marched from town two or three miles and went into a piece of woods to cook and rest. Was shelled considerably going out.

July 6, Wednesday

HB: Took up line of march this morning at 4 o'clock for Shepardstown. Between 10 & 11 A.M. our division crossed the Potomac and in half an hour after we were on Maryland soil, marched thence to Sharpsburg, where we camped for the day, reaching the place about 1 P.M. Sharpsburg seems to be a perfect union nest, the citizens are greatly troubled & more scared. About dark moved across the creek. Enjoyed a glass of ale today, which was captured at Harpers Ferry town.

McD: Ordered to move early this morning. Crossed the Potomac near Shepardstown and camped near Sharpsburg. The boys went bathing in Antietam Creek.

July 7, Thursday

HB: Had orders to move at ¼ to 4 o'clock this morning, didn't leave until about 6 A.M. however, took the Harpers Ferry road over the mountain. Heavy cannonading heard in that direction. Left the Harper's Ferry road & went by Brownsburg, where the Yankees appeared to be, staid there this afternoon, issued the rations captured at Harper's Ferry, camped there all night.

McD: Began to march early this morning. Stoped about noon at Auroraville. The front of our troops were skirmishing with the enemy cavalry. We formed line of battle near Auroraville and remained all day. Got plenty of very nice cherries and some of the boys sacked a store and got plenty brandy etc. We drew mollasses and dried fruit from the commisary. Had a very heavy rain.

VET: March through Robersville and Frederick City, s[u]pported Gordon Division in fight at Monoccasy Bridge on 10.

July 8, Friday

HB: Took up line of march this morning at ¼ to 4 o'clock A.M. after laying in a drenching rain for two hours last night reached Fredrick City about 10 A.M. A good many people showed their sympathies for us, privately however, at the suburbs of the city our whole force formed a line of battle, in front of the enemy. Heavy skirmishing between our cavalry and the Yankees. Our sharp shooters engaged the enemy all the evening on Monocacy river, drove several lines of battle back with the loss of a great many killed & wounded. Our brigade was first on the Baltimore pike, but afterwards moved on the Georgetown turnpike.

McD: Began to move early this morning. Went across South Mountain and took the road to Frederick City. Camped for the night near Jefferson. Had a heavy rain in the evening.

July 9, Saturday

McD: Began to march early this morning as usual. Got to Frederick City about ten o'clock. Found that the enemy had just evacuated the place and had taken position on the railroad about three miles from town. We formed line of battle across the Baltimore Pike and sent out our sharp shooters who kept skirmishing all the while. Gen'l Gordon attacked the enemy in his position on the R.R. and on the Washington Pike. He soon routed them and cut them off from the Washington Pike. Our sharp shooters advanced and drove the enemy across the Manockasee river. That night marched several miles on the Washington Pike.

NOTE: Six thousand Union troops slowed Early's ten thousand at the Monocacy River southeast of Frederick. The day's delay allowed the Union to mount a better defense of Washington.

July 10, Sunday

HB: After getting through with the cooking squad, which was after sun up, moved across the river, where our train was encamped, everything was ready to move, saw the effects of yesterday's fight, in Yankee killed and wounded, which were lying thick all around us. Took up line of march & marched in 19 miles of Washington City tonight.

McD: Crossed the river early this morning and began a rapid march toward Washington. The citizens seem very glad to see us. Camped near Rockville. Very tired and hungry. Got some fine cherries.

July 11, Monday

HB: Took up line of march at 4 A.M., marched very rapid all day, had an awful hard time today, driving cattle in the dust. Passed through Rockville, found a good many sympathizers of ours. Citizens along the road assured us of capturing the city. Our troops passed by the residence of Frank P. Blair, found any quantity of things, which he was bound to leave in his hasty departure from home. Our boys made use of everything portable. The Yankees commenced shelling us pretty severe which lasted all the evening. We camped in 6 miles of the city, our boys skirmishing all the evening.

McD: Up and going again this morning. A very warm day. Everyone seemed very anxious to keep up that he may be among the first to go into the city. Went within four miles of the city without being interrupted. When within a mile or so of the outer forts we filed off into the woods and were rested. While there we got a considerable shelling. Our reg't (5th Ala) was sent out late in the evening to support the sharp shooters who were then skirmishing with the enemy in their forts. The sharp shooters kept up a little firing all night.

VET: Came in sight of city, citizens leave home and rush into city. 5th Ala on picket near Fort Stevens, shelled all morning.

NOTE: Fort Stevens, the northernmost of Washington's defenses, was lightly defended and would have fallen had Early been able to assault it with fresh troops.

July 12, Tuesday

HB: Everybody was expecting to hear of an early attack this morning, but were disappointed, occasional shelling during the day but not much damage done. About dusk we took up the line of march for Rockville, our object in this expedition no doubt was accomplished, by withdrawing Grant from Richmond, marched all night.

McD: We expected to charge the enemy early this morning but we were disappointed. The enemy had reinforced largely during the night. We retired about sun up to a ravine a few hundred yards in the rear of the skirmish line. The boys began to plunder deserted houses. One house (a Mr. Kings) was an elegant mansion with a costly furnished parlor. The safes and cellars were well filled and equally well plundered. We feasted on wines, preserves, and liquors of different kinds. Late in the evening the enemy made an advance and we had to fight hard till night. After dark we began to fall back. We continued to march all night. Many of the boys went to sleep marching along.

VET: Heavy skirmishing all day. Enemy advanced late in evening driving in our SS. The 5th Alabama deployed and sharp fight ensued lasting some two hours. Will McCrary wounded. After dark fell in and started back to Dixie.

July 13, Wednesday

HB: Continued to march until 3 P.M. when we parked near Darnville long enough to feed. Took up line of march again at sundown.

McD: This morning came and found us in motion and quite a weary and sleepy set. After going about eighteen or twenty miles we stoped for an hour or two and lay down and slept a few hours. We were up and going again before night. Marched all night.

NOTE: "Darnville" is Darnestown.

July 14, Thursday

HB: Marched all night, passed through Poolsville, halted near the river long enough to feed. About 8 A.M. took up line of march again, crossed the river at Edward's Ferry. Halted some four miles from the river, where we camped all day. The enemy threw a few shells over at us about dusk from the Maryland heights.

McD: As we marched all last night morning came on us while on the march continued to march till nine o'clock. Rested a few hours and began to march again. Crossed the Potomac without any preparations. Found it to be about waist deep and very swift. The enemy was reported pursuing us closely. We crossed the river near Leesburg. Camped about two miles from the river.

July 15, Friday

HB: This morning we are still encamped and expect to stay all day. Our camp is on Swan's farm near Big Spring, between Leesburg and the Potomac. The enemy's cavalry reported crossing the river this evening, our cavalry had a slight skirmish with them, but were repulsed. Commenced letter to brother, expect to finish some other time. Everything quiet this evening.

McD: Have not moved today. Rest is sweet to us.

July 16, Saturday

HB: Took up line of march at ½ past 6 A.M. passed through Leesburg, marched with the troops until 12 o'clock, when Thom Moore & I rode off from the road to get dinner. We succeeded in getting a nice dinner at Mr. Birdsong's. About the time we started to catch up with the troops again, discovered considerable shelling about the pike. We changed our course and cut through the country to Snickersville gap. Some Yankee cavalry made a dash on our train, coming out of the Harper's ferry road, turned some 30 of our wagons out, most of which were recaptured however. They burnt a few & carried off 5 or 6. We captured 2 pcs. artillery from them & ran them out of [. . .] After everything was quiet, continued to march on & camped on top of the mountain near the Shenandoah tonight.

McD: Left camp this morning at 7 o'clock. Went through Leesburg and took the road leading to Winchester. About three o'clock the Yanks made an attack on our wagon train and captured about thirty. We about faced and soon repulsed them capturing two pieces of Artillery and some prisoners, also recapturing most of our wagons. Marched on top of the Blue Ridge and camped in the gap (Snickers)

NOTE: Early's troops were now back in the Shenandoah Valley.

July 17, Sunday

HB: Took up line of march at 6 A.M., crossed the Shenandoah, continued on the Winchester pike about 2 miles, when we turned to the right & took the Charleston road, marched about 8 miles today & went into camp near Mr. Allen's, expect to stay two or three days.

McD: Left camp at 7 o'clock this morning. Crossed the Shenandoah River at Snickers ferry. Went up the river in the direction of Charlestown. Selected a good camp after marching eight miles or so. Expected to remain some time.

July 18, Monday

HB: Our division still enjoying the much needed rest this morning, finished letter to brother this morning, giving him a few items of our trip into Maryland, etc. At 1 P.M. received orders to be ready to move at a moment's warning. Between 2 & 3 P.M. we moved off our train towards Berryville & the troops towards the river. Soon after we left the troops, heavy cannonading & musketry was heard on the river, warning us, that an engagement was at hand, which really proved to be true. Our division engaged the enemy, who was crossing the river at the time, the engagement lasted until after dark, drove the enemy across the river, but sustained a heavy loss. Co. D. lost in wounded John Christian and Britton, missing Pompey Jones & Rinkey. I staid with the train, which parked near Berryville all night.

McD: Everything is going on quietly this morning and the boys are all or a good many of them are out foraging. A nice rich country and milk etc. are plenty. About noon we hear cannonading near Snickers Ferry. It continues to grow fierce late in the evening. It caused all the boys to return to camp. About 4 o'clock orders to move immediately. Took the nearest way to where they were cannonading. The most of Hunters' force had crossed the river. It was now our business to drive them back. Very few minutes were required to get into the fight. It was quite a fierce little contest which lasted till dark. We made the Yankees take water and get back on the side of the river from whence they came. Posted our sharp shooters on the bank of the river and retired a mile [or] so to the rear to camp.

July 19, Tuesday

HB: Rec'd letter from brother of the 4th inst. this morning. John C. & Britton came by our train on their way to Winchester. Went to the front this morning with Maj. Webster, received no orders about rations, returned to our train near Berryville. Soon after returning got orders to carry rations to the front, started there & on reaching there, was ordered back to report at a church on the Charlestown & Newtown road, traveled all night, got through issuing about daybreak.

McD: Very quiet this morning. The Yanks were satisfied with their thrashing. Ordered on picket in the evening. Went up the river two [or] three miles. Ordered to march at ten o'clock at night. Went in the direction of Berryville.

July 20, Wednesday

HB: Moved off at sundown, traveled all day & got to Newtown in the evening passed through White Post. Our division on reaching Newtown was ordered to Winchester to assist Ramseur's division, which was slightly defeated there this evening. Rec'd letter from Brother by Jess Cummings of the 24th June.

McD: Continued the march begun last night. Passed Berryville before daylight. Stoped about day light to get rations and rest. Did not stop more than three hours. Began to march in the direction of New Town. Heard very heavy cannonading in the direction of Winchester. Reached the pike at New Town about sun down and turned towards Winchester. Was very tired but had to make a rapid march. The Yanks had thrashed Ramseur's Division and we were ordered to his support. We did not get to Winchester before we met his men retreating. We all turned back and came as far as New Town where we went into camp at ten o'clock, being very sleepy and tired.

July 21, Thursday

HB: Expected to stay here all day, but was disappointed by being ordered to Middletown about 9 A.M. went beyond Strassbourg, awaiting orders. In the evening was ordered to carry rations up, found the brigade near the mill 4 miles from Middletown, returned to our train, which I reached about midnight, wrote to Miss J. and brother.

McD: Began to march early this morning. Going towards Middletown and went as far as Cedar Creek. Passed Strasburg and went to Fishers Hill. Went out to the back road and went into camp.

July 22, Friday

HB: Started to Woodstock this morning, called on Mr. Heller for the purpose of getting my father's portrait, he informed me that he left it at Lorenzoville at Mr. Miller's house, where he used to live. I rode out, about 4 miles from Woodstock found the house & got the portrait to my greatest delight, started back to our train which I found where I left it in the morning.

McD: Things go quiet in our front but there was some skirmishing near Strasburg.

July 23, Saturday

HB: Our army is lying still today, the Yankees reported having fallen back, went back on the pike to have clothes washed, when I returned found our train had moved to where the troops were near Piper's mills, expect to make a forward move in the morning, wrote to Brother & Joe Elliott.

McD: Maneuvered a little but heard no signs of any Yanks. Ordered to cook three days rations and be ready to move.

July 24, Sunday

HB: Our division took up line of march about sun up in the direction of Winchester. I went back with Keller to get my clothes, overtook the train about 1 P.M. parked in a field, awaiting the result of a skirmish going on at the time near Kernstown, which resulted in the complete route of the Yankees, running them through Winchester. After everything was quiet moved on again about 5 miles this side of Winchester. Met with Alleck McCall on the road, just from the hospital.

McD: Began to move at day light this morning. Going in the direction of Winchester. Met with no opposition until we got near Kernstown. All the other troops were in front of us and were skirmishing with the Yanks when we came up. We formed in line on the right of the Pike and sent our sharp shooters forward. We followed and soon came in sight of the Yanks. They were retreating. We made a charge through some fields to overtake them. We run till we were completely broken down, but could not overtake them. We continued in line of battle for more than eight miles. We caused the Yanks to abandon and burn nearly all of their wagon trains. We stoped at dark five miles below Winchester after having marched 28 miles.

NOTE: This second battle at Kernstown routed the Union forces and sent them fleeing back to Bunker Hill, West Virginia.

July 25, Monday

HB: Had a very heavy rain this morning, making things look much better, rested during the rain, issued rations, moved off at 3 P.M., marched to Bunker Hill, reached there about 11 P.M.

McD: We found it raining very hard. Staid in camp till 3 o'clock. We then went up to Bunker's Hill and camped.

July 26, Tuesday

HB: Took up line of march at daybreak this morning, reached Martinsburg about 11 A.M., went into camp about 3 miles from town.

McD: Began to march at day light this morning. Went through Darkesville and on to Martinsburg. The Yankee cavalry had just left Martinsburg a few minutes before we got there. Went out about a mile from town and went into camp. Sent out a detail to tear up the Baltimore and Ohio R.R. Worked all night. A splendid road and hard to tear up.

July 27, Wednesday

HB: Went to town this morning with Maj. Webster, spent nearly all day & returned to camp in the evening.

McD: Remained in camp all day.

July 28, Thursday

HB: Remained quiet in camp all day, received orders to move at daybreak. Gen. Battle returned tonight.

McD: Quiet today. Preaching by Mr. Curry. Orders to be ready to move at day light.

July 29, Friday

HB: Moved off soon after daybreak this morning, marched to the Potomac opposite Williamsport, where we camped for the day & night.

McD: Began to march at day light. Arrived at the Potomac near Williamsport and went into camp. Sharp shooters and one Brigade went over the river. Some captures were made such as whisky, mollasses, soda, pepper, matches, tobacco, etc.

July 30, Saturday

HB: Fell back from in front of Williamsport this morning. Maj. Webster, Thom. Moore, some 4 or 5 others & myself left the brigade & went across on the mountain side to hunt cattle, passed through Hedgesville. While lying on the roadside a young lady accompanied by a servant rode up & asked Tom & myself to ride with her to the next house. We of course went, but not being able to find the house returned & had a good time on the side of the mountain, where we left them. Tom & I rode off then to overtake our party, but did not succeed, so we hunted our brigade, which we found encamped near Martinsburg, the same ground we camped on before.

McD: Began to move at day light and returned to our old camp near Martinsburg.

July 31, Sunday

HB: Left camp at daybreak this morning, marched until about 12 o'clock, & took up camp at Bunker Hill. The heat is oppressive today.

McD: Moving at day light. Went back to Bunkers Hill. A very warm day.

August 1, Monday

HB: We are still lying still today, hope we may spend the balance of the summer here. Nothing of any importance whatever transpired today, all anxiety is felt about the western army.

McD: Still at camp at Bunkers Hill.

August 2, Tuesday

HB: Everything still as yesterday, heard about Gid Westcott, through Lieut. Doss, wrote a letter to him, which I expect to leave at Winchester to be mailed after our army falls back, have felt rather unwell for the last two days.

McD: Still at camp at Bunkers Hill. Rain.

August 3, Wednesday

HB: Everything still quiet, received orders to be ready to move at daybreak tomorrow morning. Heard the glorious defeat of the enemy at Petersburg on the 30th ult. at the attempt of springing the mines. News from Ga. still anxiously looked for. Nothing of any note transpired today except of hearing an excellent sermon by Dr. Lacy at our Hd. Qrs.

McD: Still at camp at Bunkers Hill. Inspection.

August 4, Thursday

HB: Took up line of march at daybreak this morning, passed through Martinburg & camped near Falling Waters.

McD: Left camp at daylight this morning. Went as far as Falling Waters on the Potomac and camped.

August 5, Friday

HB: Continued our march at 4 A.M., crossed the Potomac at Williamsport, Md. passed through & went about 5 miles on the Boonsboro road, which we reached about 12 M., where we camped for the balance of the day & night.

McD: On the march at sun rise. Crossed the Potomac at Williamsport and went towards Sharpsburg. Camped near Funkstown.

August 6, Saturday

HB: We were considerably disappointed this morning by receiving orders for a retrograde movement. We all expected to go to Pa., but instead we marched to Williamsport recrossed the Potomac and camped near Falling Waters, Gen. Battle making his Hd.-Qrs. at Falling Waters church, wherein we slept at night on account of it threatening to rain. The heat today was immense.

McD: Found it raining this morning. Orders to march at a moments notice. Began to march at noon. Came back to Williamsport and crossed the river back into Virginia. Camped again at Falling Waters. Heavy rain.

August 7, Sunday

HB: Took up line of march at ½ past 5 A.M. marched to our old camp at Bunker Hill where we camped for the day & night.

McD: Began to march again this morning. Came back to Bunkers Hill.

August 8, Monday

HB: We are lying quiet in camp today, some rumors about us expecting to move on account of the enemy being reported crossing at Shepardstown, but nothing unusual took place & we retired at night.

McD: Remained at Bunkers Hill all day.

August 9, Tuesday

HB: Remained quiet in camp all day, although we were expecting to get orders to move every moment.

McD: Remained at Bunkers Hill all day.

August 10, Wednesday

HB: Marching orders were received last night to move at daybreak this morning, moved off & marched 8 miles, camped near the same place we once camped before. About dark our train was ordered to 1 mile beyond Winchester.

McD: Left camp at sun rise. Marched within four miles of Winchester and went into camp about noon. Some of the boys were captured near camp while out foraging.

August 11, Thursday

HB: The army moved back, evacuated Winchester today, the army moving on the pike & the wagon train on the back road, halted at some church close to a spring. About sundown received orders to carry rations to the troops, started off on the back road crossed the middle road & got into the pike at Newtown, our division was camped two miles from Newtown towards Middletown. On reaching Genl. Rode's Hd.-Qrs. learned that our brigade was on picket on the Cedarville road two miles beyond or rather to the left of Middletown, reached the troops about daybreak, but was not allowed to issue, travelled all night, about 16 miles from where we started in the evening.

McD: Began to march this morning before day. Went to Winchester and formed line of battle. Remained an hour or two and took the Pike toward Strasburg. Formed line of battle several times during the day. Got to Middletown about dark and had to go three or four miles east of town on picket. Very tired.

August 12, Friday

HB: Started off with my wagons, got a detail & was ordered to have rations cooked at Middletown. About the time I was making preparations for it, Maj. Whiting ordered me to take the wagons back towards Strassbourg. Waited there until our brigade passed, followed it to the back road where we went into camp close to Piper's mills, the same place we camped once before. Issued rations and got orders to move out again, on account of the enemy appearing in front, managed to get nearly through cooking before we moved. Camped on the pike 5 miles from Strassbourg tonight, where we arrived about 11 P.M.

McD: Left our picket post at nine o'clock and came back to the Pike in rear of army. Went through Strasburg and went to the back road. It has been extremely warm today. Orders to be ready to move at any moment.

August 13, Saturday

HB: I was somewhat disappointed today, everybody firmly believed that we'd have a battle today, but it turned out different. Everything perfectly quiet, except some occasional cannonading on our right, believed to be portion of Longstreet's corps, which is reported coming up here.

McD: Formed line of battle on the back road. Was ordered to throw up some little work out of rails etc.

August 14, Sunday

HB: Capt. Preston, Mackey, Dodge, Caldwell, Harkins & myself started off on a beef expedition this morning, went up the pike from Strassbourg, until we passed Edenburg, when we took the right hand which brought us out into the back road at Cabin Hill. After we got into the backroad made enquires about night lodging. After several miles ride, Harkins, Dodge & myself found accommodation at a very nice house, Mr. Lonas's where we found two elegant young ladies. Enjoyed a night's rest in a splendid bed.

McD: Still in our position on the back road. Are looking for the Yanks all day.

August 15, Monday

HB: After breakfast we started off to get with the rest of our company, found them about three miles up the road, turned round & went back the way we went this morning, went by Mr. Lonas's house where we got 5 heads of cattle. Miss Kate performed on the accordion for us, travelled backwards & forwards until dark. Staid at Mr. Heller's tonight.

McD: Still in the same position as yesterday. Rain this evening.

August 16, Tuesday

HB: Went up the backroad this morning about 5 miles took the right hand road, which leads to Arkley Springs, passed by the springs & staid at a mill two miles from there.

McD: Still in position on the back road.

August 17, Wednesday

HB: Crossed the mountain today at Brock's gap & got into the western part of Rockingham County. I was left with what cattle we had near the gap, the balance of the party going on towards Staunton.

McD: Orders to move. Began to march at nine o'clock. Went through Strasburg and started in the direction of Winchester. The Yanks had retreated and had set fire to all the barns and mills. Some of the troops caught up with the Yankees near Winchester and captured several hundred prisoners and some cannon. Camped near Winchester.

August 18, Thursday

HB: Occupied my time in reading & sleeping pretty much all day, it being rainy & cloudy.

McD: Marched through Winchester and camped near town. Heavy rain nearly all day.

August 19, Friday

HB: Rode down the Shenandoah this morning to have my horse shod, returned & read all day, it being too rainy to go anywhere.

McD: Left camp at sun rise and went to Bunkers Hill. Rain again today.

August 20, Saturday

HB: Capt. Preston & party returned today with a drove of cattle. We went on to Cabin Hill & stayed at Coffman's tonight.

McD: Rained a little all day. Some Yankee scouts came into our picket and created some excitement and we were ordered in line for a while.

August 21, Sunday

HB: Hurried on this morning to get to the army, which we heard had reoccupied Winchester. Went to opposite Strassbourg where our line of battle had been established, staid at Piper's tonight, with whom I left my horse, on account of being unable to travel.

McD: Left camp early this morning and went in the direction of Charlestown. Met with the Yankee picket at Smithfield. Drove them back on their main force at Charlestown. Sent out a heavy skirmish line and drove in the Yankee skirmishers. Continued to skirmish all day. Our reg't on the skirmish line all night.

NOTE: Early's troops failed to defeat Sheridan's, and the latter retreated to near Harpers Ferry, thus opening the Valley once again. After a few days of demonstrations, Early would split his forces to threaten yet again Maryland and Pennsylvania.

August 22, Monday

HB: Went in two miles of Winchester, slept in a field, saw the effects of the last Yankee raid, in the shape of burnt barns, wheat and hay stacks and all sorts of depredations. We found it very difficult to get anything to eat tonight, the Yankees having carried off every cow, etc. they could get hold of, managed to get some bread & milch by paying one gold dollar for it.

McD: Early this morning our whole skirmish line was moved forward. We drove enemy through Charlestown and into their fortifications near Harpers Ferry. Went into camp near Charlestown about noon. Kept strong skirmishers in front. Rain.

August 23, Tuesday

HB: Passed through Winchester this morning, thence to Berryville 10 miles distance, reached Charlstown about sundown, found the brigade in a mile of town, felt very much relieved at getting back to camp, found letters from Miss A. & Joe K. Elliott.

McD: Brisk skirmishing is kept up on the whole line. We are camped in line of battle so that we can fall in at any moment.

August 24, Wednesday

HB: Wrote to brother & J.K.E. sent by Waddell, who started home on furlough today. Went down to the Brigade to see Co. D, found Britton returned, went back to our quarters & found Wilson there.

McD: Still near Charlestown. The Yankee cavalry made a dash on the left of our skirmish line and drove them back and came on some of the boys that were in a corn field getting green corn. The boys did some good running and few were captured.

August 25, Thursday

HB: Marching orders were received last night & we took up the line at daybreak from Charlstown across toward Shepardstown, five miles from latter place we had a considerable skirmish with Yankee Cavalry. Lieut. Arrington was severely wounded, carried him to Mr. Hinkle's house on the railroad. I staid with him all night. J.D.W. came to relieve me, met with Miss Hattie Warner who enquired about Ed. Bayol, Aleck McCall & H. Childress, the first staid with her at Shepardstown while wounded. Misses Betty & Jessie Hinckle are beautiful young ladies & devote all their time to Lieut. Arrington.

McD: Left our camp at day light and went in the direction of Shepherdstown. About eleven o'clock we came on the Yankee cavalry near Leetown. Had a heavy skirmish with them and drove them back across the Potomac at Shepherdstown. Stoped to camp between Sheperdstown and the river, but did not remain. We moved back after dark two or three miles from the river. Went to sleep about 12 o'clock M.

NOTE: "J.D.W." is James D. Webb Jr.

August 26, Friday

HB: Sat up with Lieut. A. all night, after getting breakfast, started to the brigade which was two miles beyond Shepardstown, met Dr. Mitchell on the way, he concluded to move Lieut. A. today to Winchester. The ladies were extremely sorry to hear of it, returned to camp with Dr. M. Soon after arriving there rec'd orders to move back towards Leetown. On the way back stopped to assist Lieut A. in the ambulance, saw him off. The parting of Lieut. A. with the ladies was very affecting, the latter being very sorry at his leaving them, Misses Betty and Jessie crying. Encamped near Leetown tonight.

August 27, Saturday

HB: Left Leetown this morning, marched to Bunker Hill & camped close to our old encampment.

August 28, Sunday

HB: Today we were enjoying a much needed rest day, until towards evening, when orders were received to be ready to move in a moments warning, the enemy's cavalry was advancing in strong force on the Smithfield road, we didn't move however. Rec'd a very interesting letter from Miss J.

August 29, Monday

HB: Moved out close to the pike this morning, preparatory to a battle or retreat. Our division was in line of battle near Darksville. The enemy's cavalry advanced on the Smithfield road. Ramseur's division fought them & drove them back, they burnt several dwellings at Smithfield. Wrote to Miss A———. After everything was quiet moved back to our old camp. Today is set for the Chicago Convention to meet, much good to our distracted country is hoped to be the result of it.

NOTE: The Democratic National Convention convened that day in Chicago. The National Union Convention, representing Republicans and some war Democrats, had already convened June 7 in Baltimore.

August 30, Tuesday

HB: Rec'd orders before daybreak to hold ourselves in readiness to move at sunrise. Everything was under marching orders, until 10 A.M. when we were ordered back to camp, the enemy evidently having made no demonstration as was expected. Wrote to Miss J——.

August 31, Wednesday

HB: Our division moved out this morning, while our train was ordered to stay in camp & be in readiness to move at any time. The troops went two miles beyond Martinsburg, drove the enemy's cavalry before them. Nobody hurt in our Brigade. At night the troops returned to camp, brought the news that McClellan was nominated President by the Chicago convention. Wrote to Brother & Fanny today.

September 1, Thursday

HB: Everything quiet in camp today. Wm. Lanier returned to the Co. today, brought me letter from Joe Elliott. The brigade was paid off today. I received my first pay up to the 1st. of July.

September 2, Friday

HB: This morning we took leave of Bunker Hill once more, & marched in the direction of Winchester. When in 6 miles of the place, Vaughn's brigade of cavalry had a perfect stampede, running immediately through our division. The Yanks had attacked them & after fighting them for some time, took a running start, in which they couldn't be checked. Our Brigade was in rear today & the 5th Regt. rear guard of all the army. The 5th regt. attempted to stop our cavalry by cheering them but it was of no avail, & they turned in to abuse them by calling them cowards, etc. The Yanks captured all the cavalry train & some cattle, the latter were recaptured however by our Brigade sharpshooters & turned over to our Brigade. Our division on being informed of the enemy's advance was formed in line of battle & marched against the advancing column, drove them back to Bunker Hill.

September 3, Saturday

HB: Our division having fallen back some three miles last night, we marched back in the direction of Bunker Hill. When we got in sight our division formed in line of battle. It was not long before our cavalry came in falling back in front of the enemy. The Yankees came on, threw a few shells towards us. Our sharp shooters were sent out & the Yanks withdrew. Noah Huggins was wounded in the foot, while on the skirmish line. Dr. Whitfield had his arm broken by a shell. About dusk we fell back & camped near an old Quaker church, our Hd-qrs. were in the church. Heavy firing heard in the direction of Berryville.

NOTE: With a larger force, Sheridan began pressing Early's dwindling Confederates southward.

September 4, Sunday

HB: Moved from the Martinsburg pike to the Berryville pike went in 2½ miles of the place where we camped for the night. Our brigade made a circuit around portion of the Yankee army, got in sight of the wagon train but didn't attack it. The firing heard in the direction of B. was a severe engagement between Anderson & the Yanks, in which the latter were repulsed.

September 5, Monday

HB: Left the Berryville pike & went back towards Bunker Hill. While on our way there the heaviest rain that I ever saw fall, fell this evening, during which our Div. was engaging the enemy, who was attempting to get in our rear. Heard through Northern papers of the fall of Atlanta, camped in same church of night before.

NOTE: Confederate forces evacuated Atlanta on September 1.

September 6, Tuesday

HB: Soon this morning had to start off to draw rations & find the Brigade, which we couldn't last night on account of the rain, which continued during the night & all day, we camped on the Martbg pike opposite the large orchard.

September 7, Wednesday

HB: Everything quiet this morning, still in camp in the same place. There was some picket firing in our front, we got ready to move, but the Yanks were driven back & we remained in our old position. Rec'd papers containing the fall of Atlanta today.

September 8, Thursday

HB: Everything still quiet this day. Altho the sun came out bright this morning, it turned into clouds again & rained all the evening. No news of importance.

September 9, Friday

HB: Everything still quiet in our front today, some skirmishing on the right. The Yanks burnt three mills near Brucetown this morning, the smoke could be seen distinctly from our camp.

September 10, Saturday

HB: Altho the sun came out bright this morning, it was but few minutes before it turned into clouds & we had a severe rain. Having rec'd orders last night to move this morning, we marched off in the rain towards Bunker Hill. About 4 miles this side, our cavalry met the enemy, skirmishing commenced, our forces driving them before them, our infantry supporting them, altho not having to fire a gun. Drove them beyond Darksville. Our troops returned to the camp we first occupied when at this place. Had a tremendous rain during the night.

September 11, Sunday

HB: Continued rain this morning, orders to move again, moved back to where we came from the day before, went into camp again. Saw a G. Beacon this evening the first in two months. Large mail rec'd this evening still no news from brother.

September 12, Monday

HB: Remained quiet in camp today. Weather very unpleasant, cold wind mixed with rain.

September 13, Tuesday

HB: Heavy cannonading was heard soon this morning on our right and in Gordon [and] Anderson's front. We soon thereafter received orders to get under arms and be ready to move at a moment's warning. We didn't move however until about 1 P.M. when our division marched back on the pike and formed line of battle at the Stephenson house. The enemy was repulsed by other troops & we went back to our old camp. Took dinner with Maj. Adams today, had a splendid dinner. Had [. . .]

September 14, Wednesday

HB: Everything quiet today, the fair weather of yesterday has changed into rain again, which makes everything look disagreeable.

September 15, Thursday

HB: Everything still quiet today, weather still unsettled, cold & windy this morning had a considerable shower this evening, during which I drove up to Genl. Early's Hd.-Qrs. with papers for Maj. [. . .]

September 16, Friday

HB: Sky rockets were seen to be sent up by the enemy at a late hour last night. About midnight Pick Moore brought orders around for everything to be ready to move at daybreak, in consequence of it. Dawn came and everything seemed to be quiet, were quiet in camp all day. At night we all sat around Genl. Battle's fire, with [. . .] telling anecdotes. Wrote to John Christian today. Rec'd letter from Brother today.

September 17, Saturday

HB: Having received orders yesterday to move at 2 P.M. today, with two days cooked rations in haversacks, I issued an additional days rations this morning. At the stated time the army moved off in the direction of Bunker H. The expedition is a secret one, nobody but general officers are aware of the destination. Different conjectures were made by men as to where the expedition would lead to. I having felt unwell for the last four days concluded to stay behind with the train, which was ordered to remain in camp. About 9 P.M., about the time I was about to retire, received orders for our train to report at Div. Hd.-Qrs. Moved off &c. camped in rear of Stephenson house.

September 18, Sunday

HB: Laid quiet all day, while the troops were gone, wrote to Brother & Fanny today. Our Div. returned tonight, having gone to Bunker Hill only, while Gordon's

Div. went to Martinsburg, orders were received for the train to [. . .] the troops, after midnight. Keller & I staid until next morning however.

September 19, Monday

HB: Went to Maj. Adam's to draw rations, carried them on to the Brigade, met Gordon's Div. going to where there was considerable skirmishing going on at the time, to the right of Winchester. On reaching the Brigade found them getting ready to move, snatched a piece of bread & meat, which I devoured hastily & moved off with the troops. The troops formed line of battle at the Stephenson house. Genl. Rodes dispatched me to Maj. Tanner with orders to move his train to the right of Winchester. According to orders the train moved off. I staid with it, we halted in those fields close to W. In the meantime the skirmishing of this morning turned into a severe battle. It was not long after the battle began to rage, that the disagreeable news of Genl. Rode's death reached us. Everybody seemed to be thunderstruck on hearing of this awful catastrophe & everybody seemed to think for a time that all was lost. I started to W. to learn some of the circumstances. On riding through Main Street, heard some one call me in an ambulance, stopped to see who it was, and to my sorrow found Britton & Kitt Clarke in there, the former shot through the right arm, which was broken. I rode off to find our brigade hospital, when I returned found out, that they had already started to the corps hospital, overtook the ambulance and went on with it. Assisted B. & C. out of the ambulance and saw them placed under a tent fly. Staid with them for some time, the surgeons not having had time to examine his wounds, I concluded to go to the Brig. Hospital to learn something of Co. D. On my way there, stopped at the house, where Genl. Rodes' remains were lying in state, went in and took a last farewell glance at our beloved general, whose loss can never be repaired. A great many ladies were around his body with tears in their eyes, which caused a tear to drop from my own, in spite of all exertions to the contrary. While this was going on I heard a rush on the street at the same time, some ladies came in exclaiming 'The Yankees were right in town'. Maj. Adams & I rushed out into the street. I got on my horse, witnessed the grandest stampede I ever saw in my life. The cause of this was, our cavalry on our extreme left gave away in front of half of their number of Yankees & came charging through the town. The Yankees reached the edge of town, but were held in check by some two or three hundred [. . .] C.S. & others connected with the wagon trains. In the meantime there was a gap left open for the Yankee infantry to get in rear of ours. A panic seized the troops at once & they gave away on our left, which was followed by the entire army, and from which it was impossible to rally them for several miles. Everything had gone on finely up to before this stampede drove the enemy some distance. Our Div. drove three lines of battle, but with the others had to give up their previous success. We left all of our severely wounded & dead in the hands of the enemy. The number of the enemy's killed is said to exceed anything ever witnessed, altho our loss is severe also, mainly in wounded however. Britton was left at W. Everything moved back & after traveling all night, suffering from hunger & cold, I found myself at Strassbourg next morning.

NOTE: The third battle at Winchester started in the morning with the Confederates pushing back the Union army led by Philip Sheridan. But late in the afternoon, the Union struck back and Early was forced to retreat. Estimated Union casualties, 5,018; Confederate, 3,921.

September 20, Tuesday

HB: At Strassb. I learned that our train was on Fisher's hill, repaired there & found it. Took some breakfast & went to the troops, which have taken a position a little to the right of where we were before in the line of breastworks, issued rations to them & which took me nearly all day & when night came on it found me weary & sleepy. Wm. Long, Haffner, Willingham & Hausman returned today.

September 21, Wednesday

HB: Skirmishing commenced on our line soon this morning, our train was ordered off & moved to the same place where we were, when here last time. Sent a dispatch to Col. Harvey by Keeler today, giving casualties in Co. D. The troops laid quiet all day. I went over to the Pipers after my horse, met our train going to the troops in the evening, turned round & staid on the line of battle all night.

September 22, Thursday

HB: Was ordered back to the general train by daybreak, with orders to be ready to move at any time. We were quiet pretty well all day except some skirmishing on the line. Wrote to Mr. Britton. At 5 P.M. when I was about to start to the Brigade with rations, met the whole army running back, a similar stampede to that of Winchester. The Yankees flanked us by the mountain & got in our rear, which caused our cavalry to give away & cause confusion among the troops, when everybody put out the best way they could. We made a hasty retreat to Mt. Jackson, after traveling all night. Our loss here in men was not severe, we lost some 10 or 20 pcs. of artillery however.

NOTE: Early's forces were badly beaten at Fisher's Hill, posting 1,235 casualties (including a thousand missing) to Sheridan's 528.

September 23, Friday

HB: The troops formed a line of battle just beyond Mt. Jackson this morning, the Yankees not pushing very hard, we kept up the line all day & night. Rec'd. orders to be ready to move at daybreak.

September 24, Saturday

HB: The troops fell back before day this morning on this side of Mt. Jackson where they formed a line again. About 10 A.M. we commenced falling back. About 5 miles this side of New Market we took the Kesseltown road, where we camped at about 7 P.M.

September 25, Sunday

HB: At 1 A.M. orders came to move. I started ahead with my cattle after passing through K. took the Port Republic road, crossed the Shenandoah at F.R.

& started for Brown's gap, where we camped at the foot of the mountain. Wrote a few lines to Brother today. Briggs & Hutchinson returned today.

September 26, Monday

HB: The Yankees followed us close to the mountain. Skirmishing was going on pretty much all day, in which the enemy's right wing was driven across the river. Kershaws Division came up today, while coming up the river the Yankees attacked their wagon train but were easily repulsed without losing anything. The troops came back to the old camp again.

McD: Was ordered out and formed line of battle. The sharp shooters fought a little. We all returned to camp at night.

September 27, Tuesday

HB: The troops started out again this morning, it was not long before skirmishing commenced, the Yankees were driven back across the river. Col. Hobson returned today looking well. Near sundown we moved out of the gap & stopped near Weyers cave.

McD: Was ordered out this morning and crossed the Shenandoah river and had a sharp skirmish with the Yankee cavalry. Drove them back several miles. Camp near the river near Port Republic.

September 28, Wednesday

HB: Had orders to be ready to move at sunrise, didn't move until near 10 A.M. Previous to moving I visited Weyers cave, which is a sight worthy of notice. The guide who conducted us thither explained everything. When I came out the army was in motion, making its way toward Waynesborough, we traveled & dragged about all night, when about 4 A.M. we joined the troops about three miles from. W.

McD: Left our camp this morning tolerable early and maneuvered about nearly all day without doing anything or going any where. About night we started in the direction of Waynesboro. Marched nearly all night and got near town.

September 29, Thursday

HB: Laid quiet in camp this morning, couldn't move, on account of the troops having to cook rations. About 3 P.M. we changed camp to near Waynesborough.

McD: Slept for several hours this morning. Moved about ten o'clock across a field to a camping place.

September 30, Friday

HB: Everything quiet in camp today, can't learn anything of the enemy's movements. Had orders to be ready to move at sunrise in the morning, did not move however. Spent a good portion of the day with Co. D.

McD: Remained in camp all day. Rained a while today.

October 1, Saturday

HB: Orders came to move this morning at sunrise, did not move however until about 8½ A.M. We marched from W. to Mount Sidney during a severe rain, passed through New Hope. We camped near Mt. S.

McD: Began to move early this morning. Rained all day. Had a very hard march. Road very muddy. Camped Mt. Sidney on the Pike. The enemy reported retreating.

October 2, Sunday

HB: Although under marching orders, we laid quiet in camp all day, the sun shines bright today. We hear conflicting rumors about an engagement around Petersburg.

McD: Still in camp but under orders. Remained quiet all day. Drew shoes.

October 3, Monday

HB: Everything still quiet & in same camp, weather cloudy this morning, turned into a severe rain during the evening. Wrote to Brother & J.K.E. today.

McD: Still quiet in camp. Some rain.

NOTE: "J.K.E." is Joseph Knox Elliott.

October 4, Tuesday

HB: Nothing of any interest transpired on our lines today, we had a good many rumors afloat as regards the battle fought around Petersburg & Richmond, nothing reliable could be heard. Received letter from brother, sister & Fanny, answered immediately, and sent brother an overcoat by Cowin's boy Wm.

McD: Still quiet in camp. Clear today

October 5, Wednesday

HB: Everything still quiet with us. Lieut. Shorter returned today with Richmond papers, giving an account of the late battles around Petersburg & R. Col. Hobson dined with us today.

McD: Still quiet in camp. Cloudy.

October 6, Thursday

HB: About 10 A.M. received orders to move at once, went through Mt. Sidney, thence to Mt. Crawford & camped just this side Harrisonburg tonight. Today was an awful one to me, had a severe attack of cholic, which caused me to suffer a good deal during the day. The Yanks left H. this morning only, burning & devastating barns & mills on their route.

McD: Began to march at eleven o'clock today. Marched very hard. Followed after the Yanks who were retreating and burning barns, mills, hay, etc. Camped near Harrisonburg after having marched eighteen miles.

October 7, Friday

HB: I don't feel entirely relieved from the effects of yesterday's attack. About ½ past 7 A.M. we took up line of march. I followed the troops to Harrisonb. where I hunted up Mrs. Heller from H. & also Lovenbach & Bro. I found them & on making myself known, I was heartily welcome, found the children grown up and by the bye among the number three beautiful young ladies. I spent some 3 or 4 hours with them, during which Mrs. H. brought to my memory things which were long forgotten. I had to take leave of them however, in spite of all entreaties to the contrary. Mrs. H. put me up a little bottle of elegant brandy, which relieved me very much. I overtook Wilson, who rode with me slowly, until we overtook the army, which we found encamped near New Market.

McD: Left camp at six o'clock this morning. Went as far as New Market and went into camp. The Yanks burnt every thing as they went.

October 8, Saturday

HB: Today we are resting, nothing of importance transpired today. I am still under the weather. Co. D. being close to our quarters, I spent a good portion of the day with them.

McD: Remained quiet in camp all day. Had cold day, snow and sleet.

October 9, Sunday

HB: Today has much of a wintry appearance, the weather very cold and towards evening we had sleet. Cannonading was heard soon this morning down the pike, which turned out to be cavalry fighting. About 4 P.M. while everything was apparently quiet, the bugles sounded to fall in at once. The troops fell in and marched down the pike. Our cavalry had shown another of their stampedes, the Yanks running them from Woodstock to New Market, a distance of 20 miles. Lomax's cavalry lost 11 pcs. artillery, several wagons and ambulances. The Inftry. returned after night, the Yanks not daring to come any further.

McD: Still snowing this morning. The Yankee cavalry made a move which called us out of camp in the evening. We did not meet them. Returned to camp after dark.

October 10, Monday

HB: Pleasant weather, still cold but clear. Our cavalry turned round and from all accounts is driving the Yanks in return today. Haven't heard anything from [. . .] I sold my two horses today. Wrote a letter to Brother which I expect to send by Thom Moore, who will start home in the morning.

McD: All goes on quietly today.

October 11, Tuesday

HB: Still quiet in camp, nothing new whatever, received orders this evening to move at sunrise in the morning in consequence of which I had to look out for a horse having sold my two. Went up to Maj. Adams' and bought Lucy.

McD: Our reg't sent on picket today. Received orders to be ready to move at sun rise in the morning.

October 12, Wednesday

HB: Moved off [. . .] at sunrise & marched to near Woodstock, where we camped about 2 P.M. I rode with the troops.

McD: Marched according to orders rec'd last night. Camped near Woodstock.

October 13, Thursday

HB: Took up the line of march again at [. . .] moved off with the troops [. . .] called on Mr. Heller & spent about two hours at his house. Continued my ride until I found the train parked on Fishers-Hill. The troops had gone on beyond Strassburg, where skirmishing was going on at the time. Portion of Kershaw's

Div. went on & met the Yanks near Cedar creek where a fight took place, in which the Yanks were driven some distance. About dark the troops were ordered back & we camped on the line of entrenchments on Fishers-Hill near where we were before.

McD: Began to move at sun rise this morning. Went to Fishers Hill and rested a while. Heard cannonading near Cedar Creek. Marched over there and formed line of battle. Kershaw drove the Yanks across the creek. We came back to Fishers Hill.

October 14, Friday

HB: The troops on our left our Div. included moved some distance to the front, where a new line had been established. The enemy didn't show any disposition to give us battle & our troops went into camp at the same old place after dark.

McD: Went a mile or so in front of our works and formed line of battle where we remained all day. Returned to our camp at dark.

October 15, Saturday

HB: About 10 A.M. the same move as yesterday took place. About sundown troops returned to the same camp. Made the same move today we did yesterday. Had some rain today.

October 16, Sunday

HB: Apparently everything quiet today, no prospect for a move, in consequence of which I took out my writing materials to let my friends hear from me. I wrote letter to Mrs. Hutchinson, Brady, Alfred & Ezra. During the evening received orders to move at daybreak. Had a splendid vegetable dinner today.

McD: Remained in camp all day. Had preaching.

NOTE: "Ezra" probably refers to James Ezra Wilson, a fellow Knight of Pythias.

October 17, Monday

HB: Precisely at daybreak the troops moved off in the same direction of that on former occasions. The wagons were ordered to remain until further orders. About 8 A.M. Felix Wilson & myself rode out to the front, found the troops in line of battle, but apparently no move of any sort going on. Staid out sometime & returned to camp. Roper's cavalry & Grimes' brigade made a dash at the enemy's pickets last night, surrounded and captured forty [. . .] and two horses. About 3 P.M. the troops all returned to camp, with orders to cook two days rations, making having on hand three days. I judge that we'll move in the morning by the foregoing order. After night went up to Co. D where we sang until a late hour in the night.

McD: Left camp at day light and went to the front and formed line of battle and staid till after 12 o'clock. Then returned to camp.

October 18, Tuesday

HB: We were still quiet in camp all day, expecting to get orders to move all day, nothing of importance took place however, until 5 P.M. when we received orders to get ready to move at ½ past 5 P.M. with orders for the men to leave their canteens behind & not speak above a whisper on the march, of course we knew, that some secret expedition was on move and everybody eager to know what it would result in. We were not kept in suspense long. Precisely at 30 minutes past five P.M. Genl. Gordon in command of his, Genl. Pegram's & our divisions marched off. The wagon train was ordered to join the general train & to be ready to move at daybreak. I went back with the train. The troops marched down the pike and then went over to the mountain on the right of the pike. We marched over a narrow path on the brink of the mountain on the side of the river. The path was so narrow that the troops had to march in single file. We reached the Yankee pickets just before daybreak.

McD: Remained quiet in camp till sun down. We then began to move. Was ordered to leave everything we had in camp except our haversacks. Received strict orders about plundering on the battlefield etc. Marched down to the Shenandoah river and crossed over next to the mountains. Moved noiselessly in single file around and over the mountain craggs. All night was spent in this way.

October 19, Wednesday

HB: About an hour before dawn our troops crossed the river, wading it, which made it extremely cold, the night itself was an extremely cold one. The Yankee pickets were changed about the same time our division in junction with other troops charged their camps on their flank & rear. While this was going on, Genl. Early in command of Kershaw's and Wharton's divisions charged them in front just on the other side of Cedar creek. The surprise was complete & had the desired effect. The Yankees were driven, and routed out of their camps & good many killed & wounded in their bunks, not having had time to get up. They ran in great confusion, leaving everything in the way of baggage & camp equippage behind them. Artillery variously estimated from 22 to 40 pcs. were captured & turned on the enemy, ambulances, wagons forges medical wagons & things too numerous to mention here were captured & the Yankees driven, losing a great many killed & wounded & prisoners. About sun up Wilson, Catchett & myself rode down to the front passed over the camps & looked at the artillery etc. captured, passed on further to the front, met Sheb, and Briggs, the latter slightly wounded in arm, sat with them for sometime, then rode on still further front, where I met with Col. Forsyth & others, staid sometime & then returned to B & Sh. They went to the front & I to the hospital, where I expected to find Genl. Battle who was slightly wounded on the knee, but he had left & gone to the rear, saw Henry Allen & Charlie Hafner both wounded, staid with them some time. Rumors came in about our army falling back. I looked across Cedar creek, and in a few moments saw army coming back in considerable confusion. I got on my horse to go to the rear, not to add any to the stampede, if such a thing should occur, and it was well I did so, the entire army came running off, caused by Perry's brigade giving away & allowing the Yanks to flank us. Genl. Early in spite of all he could do with the assistance of other officers could not rally the men. They came on, passed through Strassburg & made for Fishers-Hill. Genl. Early was there again to rally them, but it was of no avail, the men were routed & nothing in the world could stop them. Between Strassburg & the stone bridge the Yankee cavalry clashed up & cut a good deal of our train off. They captured a good many wagons, ambulances & artillery besides some of the artillery we captured from them in the morning. A great many of our men dispersed to the mountains. Our army kept on the retreat all night, Yankee cavalry following us up. I went on with our train. In passing through Woodstock stopped at Heller's to warm where I also got supper. I reached Mt. Jackson about daybreak. Such are the fortunes of war, after having gained one of the most signal victories ever recorded in the morning, defeat & disaster was our lot in the evening.

McD: Crossed the river at day light this morning and attacked a Yankee picket post on the bank of the river. We captured the picket. Last night was very cold and frosty and waiding the river was a "bitter pill." We came out of the river nearly frozen and were anxious to be moving and even fighting. We gained by our nights march the rear of the enemies left flank. We formed line of battle soon after crossing and moved forward. We soon engaged the enemy near their camp. By sun up we had entire possession of their camp. Gen'l Battle was wounded early in the morning. The last command that he was heard to give was to "move steadily forward and sweep every thing before you. Close in on the coons and then cut their fur." We continued to drive the Yankees for several hours, capturing many prisoners, cannons, wagons, ambulances, and other military stores. But unfortunately we were halted and remained motionless for several hours. During our inactivity the Yanks massed their shattered forces on our left flank and made an attack. Some of ours behaved badly and ran away from their posts. A general stampede began. The worst ever known to us. Gen'l Ramseur was mortally wounded about the beginning of the stampede. He had been in command of our division since the death of Gen'l Rodes. The retreat could not be conducted in any order and the men left the road and fled in disorder to the mountains. The Yanks captured nearly all of our Artillery and many wagons, etc. Dark came on in time for us to save some things that would have been captured in day light. Thus a brilliant victory was turned into a mortifying disaster. Some one was in fault. But it is not becoming to say who was wrong. After dark some few rallied at Fishers Hill. They did not tarry long there but started for the next standpoint, New Market.

NOTE: The Guards' Lieutenant Colonel Edwin L. Hobson assumed leadership of the brigade after Battle was wounded at Cedar Creek, the battle that ended any threat from Jubal Early's army. About thirty Greensboro Guards entered the battle under command of a sergeant. At least three died from their wounds: James D. Webb Jr., William A. Lanier, and Charles W. Hafner.

October 20, Thursday

HB: We reached New Market about 12 M. where the troops caught up with us, went in the same camp we occupied before. Co. D. came in four in number, most of them wounded or missing. Henry Allen, Chas. Hafner, James Webb, W.T. Idom, McDiarmid, Briggs & Farrier all wounded. Wm. Long, Jack Wynne, Waddell, Hagins, McDiarmid & Andrew Jackson all missing, some of the latter will come up yet, I hope.

McD: Having marched all night is reasonable to suppose that morning found us on the march. Arrived at New Market late in the evening. Worn out *completely*. What few got to New Market went into camp at our old camping ground.

October 21, Friday

HB: Rec'd orders to be ready to move at daybreak, which was done however, to be ready in case the enemy should endeavor to continue his pursuit, but such was not the case & we were quiet. Wm. Long came in this morning, returned from the mountain. Wrote to Mrs. Allen in regard to Henry.

McD: Got up this morning somewhat refreshed. Expected the Yanks to come on after us but they did not. Remained in camp all day.

October 22, Saturday

HB: Everything quiet in camp today, heard that our cavalry drove the Yanks back to Fishers-Hill today.

McD: Remained quiet all day. Inspection.

October 23, Sunday

HB: Nothing stirring at all today.

McD: Remained quiet all day. Cold

October 24, Monday

HB: Everything still quiet, wrote a long letter to brother today.

McD: Remained quiet all day. Cold

October 25, Tuesday

McD: Remained quiet all day. Cold

October 26, Wednesday

McD: Remained quiet all day. Cold

October 27, Thursday

McD: Remained quiet all day. Rain

October 28, Friday

HB: Nothing of the least importance transpired in several days. Wrote to brother, J.K.E. & Dr. Witherspoon today.

McD: Remained quiet all day. Rain

October 29, Saturday

HB: Everything still shows an unusual quiet on our as well as the enemy's side, can't find anything worth recording. I expected to go to Harrisonburg today, but had to decline on account of not getting passport.

McD: Remained quiet all day. Clear

October 30, Sunday

HB: Everything still quiet, received a letter from brother at last.

McD: Remained quiet all day. Clear

October 31, Monday

HB: Went to Harrisonburg today, to see my friends, called on the Misses Heller, was introduced to Miss Wise. Had the pleasure of seeing Miss W. home, whence I called at Judge Woodson's house to see Henry Allen. Called on Miss Wise during the evening. Staid at Mrs. Heller's tonight, had some splendid musick by the young ladies of the house, also Misses———with whom I was made acquainted.

McD: Remained quiet all day. Clear

November 1, Tuesday

HB: Had a very pleasant time last night & also this morning but about 10 A.M. had to take leave from my kind friends to return to duty. Left Harrisonburg about 11 A.M. & returned to my command. I was much chagrined at not staying longer at H. after I learned that I hadn't been missed. I found our Div. in mourning for Gens. Rodes & Ramseur. In the evening dress parade was held by each brigade & the resolutions of a committee of officers read out, also a letter from Genl. Early about the same affair. Dirges by the bands were plaid with muffled drums in honor of the two commanders of our division. The affair was a very solemn one.

McD: Had the funeral of Gens Rodes and Ramseur today. Everything seems to be in mourning for these noble men.

November 2, Wednesday

HB: We had a cold rain this morning, wrote to Mr. Snyder.

McD: Remained quiet in camp all day. Sleet.

November 3, Thursday

HB: The weather still disagreeable, wrote to brother today. Received letter from Mrs. Britton this evening.

McD: Remained quiet in camp all day. Sleet.

November 4, Friday

HB: Everything quiet, weather clear *but cold.*

McD: Remained quiet in camp all day. Sleet.

November 5, Saturday

HB: Changed camp today to about 2½ miles this side of New-Market, where it is expected we'll stay for some time. Maj. Adams sent for me to go on some business for him, started to Staunton, but turned back & waited until in the morning.

McD: Moved camp to be more convenient to wood and water. Had snow.

November 6, Sunday

HB: Left camp at sunrise this morning for Staunton, stopped a few minutes at Harrisonburg, but didn't see the young ladies, they having gone to church. Capt. Preston was with me but turned off at Mt. Crawford. Reached Staunton at dark, stopped at the American Hotel, Maj. Bryan & I occupying one room.

McD: Remained quiet in camp. Very cold.

November 7, Monday

HB: Met Boardman & Cowin in town after breakfast, staid in town all day waiting on Maj. Tate, who didn't get to the office until late in the evening. After seeing him we rode out to camp, where our train was parked. Boardman & I slept under a hay wagon. Got acquainted with Mr. Witz. Moritez Heller was also in town today.

McD: Remained quiet in camp. Rain all day.

November 8, Tuesday

HB: Left Staunton this morning in search of wheat, went up the Middlebrook road, & turned off in the direction of Middle river, met with but little success in the way of getting any grain, staid with Mr. McCutchan near Summerdean, all night.

McD: Remained quiet in camp. Rain all day.

November 9, Wednesday

HB: Returned to Staunton today, staid in camp tonight, Boardman, Wilkins & myself sleeping in a wagon.

McD: Remained quiet in camp. Got orders to be ready to march at sun rise in the morning.

November 10, Thursday

HB: After waiting at Staunton until 11 A.M. I went with two wagons to Waynesboro after flour, camped in 3 miles of W. about dusk.

McD: Left camp this morning according to orders. Took the Pike in the direction of Winchester. Made a hard march and camped near Woodstock.

NOTE: Early was moving his greatly reduced force northward from New Market toward Sheridan, but with little effect.

November 11, Friday

HB: Proceeded on to W. saw my wagons loaded & started them to camp. Went to Stewart's mill, where I expected to find Boardman, but found Lumsden in his place, staid at the mill.

McD: We left camp early this morning. Found that the Yanks had left Strasburg. Followed them to New Town where we found them in heavy force. Camped near New Town.

November 12, Saturday

Samuel Pickens
Co. "D," 5th Ala. Regt.
Battle's Brigade,
Rodes' (old) Divis.
Early's Corps.
Valley of Va.

SP: We were up & had breakfast before light. Mr. Hagins came with some clothing & shoes for Peter. Gave William some money & sent by him some to the other servants—& before sun up Tom Moore & I, with John, Pittman, Bill

(Cowin) & Martin (Long) were rattling along on our return to old Virginia. Had the pleasure of renewing my acquaintance with two old school mates, Misses Laura & Mary May, on the cars: met, also, Mr. Dick Adams & Mr. Webster. Put up at Gee's Hotel. After getting our transportation, we met with Mrs. Wiley & a younger sister, Miss Bayol, and accompanied them in a very interesting & pleasant visit to the Foundry, where they were manufacturing shot, shell and cannon of the largest calibre; also rail-road (stringer) iron. Sent by Mrs. W. the following pieces of music home—viz—"Home, sweet home with brilliant variations"; "Drummer boy of Shiloh"—to Mary; "I'm going to my (Dixie) Southern home"—to Louty; "What are the wild waves saying"—to ———. Saw Rit. Moore—Lt. of ordnance, who is on duty at the Arsenal. Took passage on Steamer, and started after night.

HB: Left Stewart's mill this morning for Staunton, which place I reached about 1 P.M. After attending to my business called on Mr. Witz, with whom I staid all night.

McD: Formed line of battle and sent out our sharp shooters who skirmished with the Yank all day. Retired and came back to Fisher Hill after night. The enemies cavalry attempted to make a charge on us as we [were] withdrawing but was repulsed by our sharp shooters.

NOTE: Gee's Hotel was in Selma, Alabama.

J. H. Slack and Henry R. Bishop, *Home Sweet Home with Brilliant Variations* (Macon and Savannah, Georgia: John C. Schreiner & Son, 1861).

Will S. Hays, *The Drummer Boy of Shiloh* (various Southern locations and publishers, 1863).

Will S. Hays, *My Sunny Southern Home!* (various Southern locations and publishers, 1863).

Stephen Glover, J. E. Carpenter, and Charles Dickens, *What Are the Wild Waves Saying?* (New Orleans: Blackmar & Co., 1863).

November 13, Sunday

SP: Arrived in Montgomery about 10 A.M.—too late for train, & therefore will have to lie over 24 hours. Stopping at Exchange Hotel—board $30. per day. I wrote a letter to Mama this evening.

HB: Staid at Staunton until after dinner when I concluded to go to New Hope to visit the [. . .] Reached there in the evening, was extremely pleased with the meeting with old acquaintances & schoolmates, staid all night.

McD: Left Fishers Hill early this morning and started back in the direction of New Market. Had snow today, which made marching very hard and disagreeable. Camped near Edenburgh.

November 14, Monday

SP: Left this morning at 8 or 9 O'clock & arrived at Columbus a little before dark. The train was very much crowded, but Tom Moore went into the ladies' car with two ladies & secured seats for himself & me; however, we soon gave them up to some other ladies who came in, & had to stand up nearly all night.

HB: Expected to return to St. again this morning, but my friends insisted on my staying another day. During the day I rode out to Coiner's mill to see Capt. Preston, after which I returned to New-Hope, staid again all night.

McD: Left camp at sun rise this morning and got back to our old camp near New Market about four o'clock.

November 15, Tuesday

SP: Came through "Fort Valley" & "Butler" and arrived at Macon at 3 A.M. There was a tremendous crowd, but we got seats in the servants' car, & slept several hours. Met with a very clever fellow named Vinson & shared our breakfast with him. Tom, I & the servants live entirely on our baskets of edibles brought from home, & live well too, for we have everything that's nice & an abundant supply. Changed cars at Millen & got good seats. Met with young Adams of Miss. who was at the University, Va. in 1859 & '60; he is now a Lieut. in Forrest's Cavalry. Saw a lot of Yankee prisoners that are to be sent to Savannah for exchange. They were by far the most filthy, miserable, wretched set of human beings I've ever seen. Got to Augusta about 5 P.M. & went to Augusta House. The Planters' Hotel, we found out, is the one most patronized & is the best. We pay $10 for a bed.

HB: About 10 A.M. we started back to Staunton, staid there all night.

McD: Remained quiet in camp all day. Cold.

November 16, Wednesday

SP: Left at 6 A.M. on the worst crowded train I ever saw. It had been taken possession of by a no. of our prisoners now being exchanged at Savannah. We regret that we did not lie over to-day. At Branchville we made a rush, got into a car thro' the window & secured good seats. Reached Columbia at 7 P.M. & stopped at Nickerson's Hotel, where we got good beds.

HB: Went to Stewart's mill, where I staid all night in company with Capt. Preston and Lumsden.

McD: Remained quiet in camp all day. Cold

November 17, Thursday

SP: Took our departure at 6:30 A.M. in the ladies' car. Passed through Chester & Winnsboro', S.C. & in the former place got something to eat from the throng of negro women who came around the train with "snacks" for sale. Changed cars at Charlotte, N.C. at 5:30 P.M. & on

HB: Lumsden & I went to Middlebrook, where we staid all night, with a wagon.

McD: Remained quiet in camp all day. Rain

November 18, Friday

SP: at 3 A.M. were at Greensboro', N.C. Here the train being crowded we were forced to lie over & found lodging at Brittain's Hotel.

HB: After breakfast we proceeded to Mr. Wm. Dunlap's, where we expected to find Capt. P.A. Boardman, but they had gone, leaving instructions for us. We had a very nice time with Miss Mollie Dunlap, who sang for us. Lumsden went to Baylor's mill & I to Staunton, which I reached in the evening, pretty well drenched by a hard rain. Staid at the Hotel tonight.

McD: Remained quiet in camp all day. Rain

November 19, Saturday

SP: [. . .] got to Danv. about 8–40 m. Raining & very disagreeby cold. Mail car [. . .] mexican 24 [. . .] Rich. abt 10 P.M. behind time. Ala. 8 H. [. . .] gry. alt cakes.

HB: Returned to Mr. Dunlap's today, where I staid all night. Had a splendid time in the evening in the parlor with Miss Mollie D. & Mrs. Gibson.

McD: Remained quiet in camp all day. Heavy snow.

November 20, Sunday

SP: rain all day—wash. S[. . .] Batt. [. . .]

HB: Kept the Sabbath today, didn't do anything whatever. Capt. P. & B. returned this evening. Lumsden & I staid with Mr. McCutchan tonight.

McD: Remained quiet in camp all day. Snow.

November 21, Monday

SP: still rain wrote to Mama [. . .] likeness 45. Music [. . .] Mrs. Barnes. Theater [. . .] Ch. Whelan. finis [. . .] let. leave photog [. . .] Brown

HB: Business called me once more to Staunton, whither I proceeded this morning in a most drenching rain, which kept up all day. As soon as my business was complete I returned to Mr. D's where Boardman, Lumsden & I staid all night.

McD: Remained quiet in camp all day. Rain.

November 22, Tuesday

SP: 4 A.M. by Bar. left 7. cold—snow at sta[. . .] Amer. Hotel [. . .] well kept for times—polite servts. ground frozen. Mountains covd snow coldest night ever saw

HB: Snow on the ground this morning, which is freezing fast.

McD: Had a heavy snow last night. Was ordered out at day light to meet some Yankee cavalry that was coming up the Valley. Met them at Rudes Hill. Formed line of battle and sent our sharp shooters to meet them. Our cavalry and sharp shooters drove them back. We had a disagreeable time standing in the snow all day. Returned to camp at night.

November 23, Wednesday

SP: Rept. P. Mars men kept Camp—2 days rations. Went to Camp. Sent servts & baggage in Com. wagons to army. Miles P. [. . .] let. to Mary but too cold to write [. . .]

HB: Left Mr. Dunlap's this morning & moved to Baylor's mill, weather extremely cold. Mr. Dunlap asked us to come back & stay all night with him, which invitation we accepted. Boardman & I went up & Lumsden came in from Lexington. Passed the evening off very pleasantly, in conversation, music & playing cards. Miss Mollie & I were partners.

McD: Remained in camp all day. Very cold

November 24, Thursday

SP: Still very cold. Sherm. [. . .] prob. [. . .] Milledg[. . .] & mchg for Savan. night 2 days rations finished [letter] to Mary

HB: After breakfast we took leave & returned to the mill. I went over to Bowman's mill to load some wagons, returned to Baylor's mill. Boardman & I called on the Misses [. . .] this evening. Slept in the mill tonight.

McD: Remained in camp all day. Very cold.

November 25, Friday

SP: [. . .] Started 8 A.M. Passed 8 ms. [. . .]

HB: Went up to McCutchen's with Boardman. On our return met Capt. Preston, we all went to Bowman's mill to stay all night.

McD: Remained in camp all day. Very cold.

November 26, Saturday

HB: Capt. Preston & I started off in search of wheat, travelled all day until night in a severe rain. Staid at Capt. McBride's near Brownsburg.

McD: Remained in camp all day. Rain.

November 27, Sunday

SP: Arrived at Camp near N.M. at dark this evening. Stopped with J. G. Gill, Buck &c—& came with J. W. & M^cC over to Co. Glad to see all the boys & found them looking very well. Surprised to see so many in the Co.—28—expected to find only 7 or 8—but several of the detailed men have been returned to the Co. J. G. & G. J. & P. M. have gotten into cavalry.

HB: Went to Lexington today, where we staid all night at the Lexington House.

McD: Remained in camp all day. Clear cold.

NOTE: The Guards were encamped near New Market.
"J. W." is John Wynne.
"McC" is William H. McCrary.
"J. G." is Joe Grigg.
"G. J." is Gilliam James.
"P. M." is James Pickens Moore.

November 28, Monday

SP: Went to see Col. Hobson who is now in Com. of Brig. & delivered some letters. Also Maj. Webster, Walton Glover &c. Brig. Gen Grimes, N.C. commands our Divis. In last battle 19th Oct. Ch. Hafner was dangerously wounded and is supposed to be dead: Jim Webb lost a leg above the knee & left in enemy's hands. Henry Allen wounded in thigh & gone home.

HB: After attending to some business we left Lexington in the direction of Buffallo creek, we went up the creek and staid at Patten's mill tonight.

McD: Remained in camp all day. Pleasant.

November 29, Tuesday

HB: After riding about some in the morning, Capt. P. concluded best to send for some wagons for which purpose I started to near Middlebrook, where

Boardman was hauling wheat. After visiting until a late hour in the night stopped near Newport, for the night.

McD: Remained in camp all day. Pleasant.

November 30, Wednesday

HB: After conferring with Boardman, went to Bowman's mill where I staid all night.

McD: Remained in camp all day. Pleasant.

December 1, Thursday

HB: Went to Staunton this morning, after transacting some business went to New Hope, where I staid all night.

McD: Remained in camp all day. Pleasant.

December 2, Friday

HB: After taking dinner with my friend, [. . .], I started for Harrisonburg, which place I reached near sunset, staid with Mrs. Heller, where I enjoyed the evening most agreeably.

McD: Remained in camp all day. Rained.

December 3, Saturday

SP: Wrote a letter to Mama this eveng & gave it to a member of 6$\underline{\text{th}}$ Ala, who has been retired & will start home in the morning. I hope he will succeed in getting thro' for I know how anxious Mama is to hear from me; as she probably recd. my letter from Montg., but my subsequent ones written from Richmond & Staunton have not gotten thro, I presume.

HB: Upon my friends insisting I staid until after dinner, after which I started to camp, reached there after dark.

McD: Remained in camp all day. Pleasant.

December 4, Sunday

SP: Went to the branch running from Spr. & took a very pleasant bath this morning & on returning went to hear Mr. Lacy who preached to our Brigade & as usual gave us an excellent sermon, on the subject of the "Prodigal son returning to his father." In the afternoon Mr. Curry preached. The news from Ga. to-night is much more favorable than last night—& encourages us to hope that Sherman will yet be brought to grief.

McD: Remained in camp all day. Cold.

December 4 and 5, Sunday and Monday

HB: Staid in camp these two days.

December 5, Monday

SP: Put on my shoe, tho my foot is not entirely well & commenced doing duty to-day. Had Co. drill in morning. Battal drill in afternoon omitted order to make our reports of all men wounded since 4$\underline{\text{th}}$ May '64. No. in our Co.———in Regt.———more than in any other R. in Brig. On dress parade Sheb. C. now acting Adjt—officiated. Notice of Co. J. M. Hall's retirement was read out. The weather is much colder to-day—having changed last night & without rain.

McD: Remained in camp all day. Cold.

December 6, Tuesday

SP: We were up pretty late sitting at musicians quarters listening to some singing. There was one very singular & rather pretty piece called "The Swiss Warbler" wh. is in imatation of a hand organ & resembles the music of that instrument very much. Young Idom, the elder, sick & stricken with a sprained ankle, were sent to Lacy Springs to Dr. Black's Hosp. yesterday. I had charge of 2 sentinels this even'g who guarded [. . .] Cummings Co. & Bill Nusum Co. "F" who have been sentenced to 10 days' fatigue duty for having been caught out foraging a few nights since & who are policing Regt. grounds now. Heard little before sundown that Tood Cowin is going to start home on sick furlough tomorrow morning & most all of our Co. took advantage of the opportunity to write home. I wrote hasty letter to Jamie. News to-night is of a very pleasant character—viz—that things are going on as well as we could expect in Ga—Examiner thinks Sherm. will have to fight several general engagements in attempting to reach the coast—wh. if he succeeds in doing will be attended with loss of greater portion of his army;—& even hopes that he will be forced to surrender. God grant this may be verified. Hood & Thomas & Schofield fought a severe battle on 30th Nov. at Franklin, Mid. Tenn. of wh. as yet we have only Yankee accounts. Altho, they claim a victory they admit that they at dark retreated all night, not halting till within fortifications of Nashville. From wh. Ex. concludes the boot was on the other leg—the victory was ours.

HB: I prepared to go up the valley again. After receiving instructions started off in company with Maj. Webster & Heller. We rode together to Harrisonburg, they turned off towards Dayton & I staid at H. all night. Should I stay here another day, I intend to make my thoughts known to Miss L.

McD: Remained in camp all day. Cold.

NOTE: "Miss L" is Lucy Heller.

December 7, Wednesday

SP: Pegram's & Gordon's Divis. moved this morng—either to go nearer Staunton for purpose of going into W. quarters or else they are off for Richmd or Tenn. Very little news in papers to-night.

HB: My intention was to leave Harrisonburg this morning, but the object I had in view was one of so much importance to me that I was easily persuaded to remain until after dinner. Had the pleasure of Miss L's company all the morning, during which time I considered the subject well. The more I concentrated my thoughts, the more I thought the attempt worth trying, to which end I made up my mind. After dinner had the pleasure of Miss L's company to Mrs. Wise's & Mr. Lovenbach's. On our return I again expected to leave but not having accomplished my object I concluded to stay. In the course of the evening I made my proposition, and during the most interesting conversation, we were interrupted by the arrival of Mr. & Mrs. H. much to my sorrow. After the family had retired I took up the all absorbing topic again in writing this time, on account of Miss F's presence. After several questions on both sides, I received an answer in the affirmative. With what joy my heart received it, is beyond my power to describe. I felt that I was entering upon a new life, from which I could foresee nothing but happiness. After this interesting interview was ended, I retired, but only to wake & dream. It must have been near two o'clock before I went to sleep, only to dream again of the one whom I have learned to love so devotedly, also of the tobacco bag received in the morning.

McD: Remained in camp all day. Cold.

NOTE: In 1870, Henry Beck and his wife, Lucy, age twenty-two, were living in Greensboro with three children.

December 8, Thursday

SP: Got excused from drilling as my heel is not well yet & my shoe hurts it. Had Brig. inspection by Capt. Smith & Lt. Partridge this morning. Last night we had some very good singing in our Co. as is very frequently the case—Sheb C, Charles Briggs, Alex McC & one or 2 others—sometimes assisted by visitors fr. other companies sit around and while away the evening hours quite pleasantly.

HB: On coming out of my room this morning, the first object I beheld was my own dear L——. The thought of parting with her this morning was an awful one, nevertheless I determined to stand it manfully. As the time drew nearer my heart became heavier. After some pleasant discourse in the parlor, I rose to take leave of the family and then of my dear L——. I shall ever remember the last look I took at her at the window up stairs, after getting on my horse. I started off at last & thought it was very cold, in the morning, I never felt it, until I reached Mt. Crawford, so occupied was my mind with that dear object at the window. At Mt. C. I stopped at Jonas Keller's house to warm after which I continued my ride. Passed through New-Hope, stopped a few minutes at Lowner's, and then started to Coiner's mill, in search of Mahoner, whom I found at Parson Kenely's, where I staid all night.

McD: Remained in camp all day. Cold.

December 9, Friday

SP: This has been one of the coldest days of the season—ground hard frozen. Those who drilled complained bitterly. The poor fellows on guard must suffer terribly, for very few are properly clad by this climate & season.

HB: After breakfast I rode with Mahoner to Mr. Herran's, where I disposed of my business, after which I started to Staunton where I staid all night with Isaac Witz.

McD: Remained in camp all day. Snow 8 inches.

December 10, Saturday

SP: We had a pretty heavy snow storm that lasted nearly all night & this morning its about 6 in. depth & where it drifted against our tents is 2 ft. deep. We got up late, having lay in bed at least 12 hours. Waddell who went off with the forage wagons up about Lexington, sent us 20 lbs. flour wh. is most acceptable as rations are scant with us now—1 lb. flour & 1 of beef—bone included.

HB: The ground is covered with snow this morning, on acct. of which I delayed my journey. Took it on myself to write to L—— in hopes of hearing from her soon. Received letters from Mrs. Allen, Brady & Fanny enclosed in a bundle from home. John Smith & Capt. Ehart arrived this evening. All three of us staid with Witz.

McD: Remained in camp all day. Snowing

NOTE: Colonel Charles Forsyth of the Third Alabama was reinstated as brigade commander; the division was now commanded by General Bryan Grimes.

December 11, Sunday

SP: It is so excessively cold, roll calls, police, guard duty "et id omne genus" are dispensed with. Weather is too severe to live away from the fire. We have a most unpleasant & indeed I may say painful task in cutting & bringing up wood—for we have to shoulder & carry it 3 or 400 yds. thro' snow. The "on dit" in Camp now is that Gen. Lee has been fighting at Richmd. since Wednes. morng. Some of the men say they have heard the cannonading, & citizens in vicinity affirm that at times they could count the guns. It must be very heavy artillery wh. they are using as R. is distant fr. here on an air line of 140 or 150 miles. This evening after it became warm enough for us to make out to write I indited a letter to Willie: & also a few lines to Mama & enclosed some seed of good winter apples wh. we've [. . .] after eating apples [. . .] This great apple country [. . .] & we were getting some very nice ones brot into Camp by the soldiers—but as they kept increasing price to 4 or 5$ per dozen Col. Hobson issued orders prohibiting any being sold in camp for more than 2$. This has driven out good ones & given place to little trifling ones.

HB: Left Staunton about 10 A.M. suffered a good deal from cold. Met Lumsden at Steel's mill where I staid all night.

McD: Remained in camp all day. Very cold.

December 12, Monday

SP: Bill Shelden accompanied by servants Perry & Dave started home on furlough this morning & took our letters. Still cold as arctic Regions & snow shows no disposition to melt. Recd. a mail this morng—first from R. in 4 or 5 days & first fr. Ala. 2 weeks. I had pleasure of receiving fr. home first letters since leaving there—a most dear affectionate & valued letter, fr. my beloved mother & other of a like character fr. Jamie, Mary & Loutie. Col. S.B.P. got to our house on 3 or 4 days after my departure & all were greatly pleased with him & enjoyed his visit. He said if I had been at home he would have had my furlough extended. How sorry I am that I did not meet him, that I might have prolonged my happy, blissful visit at home. Col. spent a week at Umbria. Papers were of Wed. 7$\underline{th}$ so we could hear nothing of the rumored battle Thurs.

HB: After breakfast Lumsden rode down to Baylor's mill with me. We stopped at Mr. Dunlap's on the way saw Miss Mollie. In the evening we returned to Steele's mill. After supper all three of us rode to Middlebrook to a party at Dr. McChesney's, had a tolerable good time only. Staid at Mr. Steele's at Middlebrook tonight.

McD: Remained in camp all day. Cold.

NOTE: "S.B.P." is Colonel Samuel B. Pickens.

December 13, Tuesday

SP: Last night was a terribly cold one & as we have not a sufficient quanity of blankets, Peter & I were too uncomfortable to sleep much. We lay in bed tho' 11 or 12 hrs. A deserter fr. Grimes N.C. Brig. was executed to-day in presence of our whole Divis. wh. was as usual drawn up in form of 3 sides hollow sq. in a large field of snow. As I had witnessed this unpleasant scene several times, & preferred not to see it, I went off with Carter to grind some axes (& Spud) in order to avoid it. Ragsdale who exch. with Joe G. & wh. has been absent without leave & considered deserter, returned to-day. He had appealed in person to Pres. Davis—& shown that being at the time dismounted he had no other alternative left & was thus forced to come to Supt. & get permission to be transfer Cav. with consent of officers here. This will not affect Joe's swap at all.

HB: After a late breakfast we left M. for up the country, stopped at the mill a while to warm after which L & I rode to Lexington where we staid all night at the Lexington House.

McD: Remained in camp all day. Cold.

NOTE: "Peter" is Peter Hagins.
"Carter" is Benjamin A. Carter.

December 14, Wednesday

SP: Recd. orders last night to cook & be reach to march at 8 this morng. Up before day & started at appointed time. Snow beat down on pike & frozen & marching was very good till late when it became very sloppy & marched fast, making about 3 ms. hr. & camped at 5 P.M. in neighborhood of Mt. Crawford; having come about 23 miles. I was completely used up by march & my feet & legs very sore. Scraped off the snow & built hot hickory fire. Cooked flour & beef & hogs head that Waddell brought to us.

HB: Left Lexington this morning for Buchanan, when near the place, met Capt. Preston & Boardman returning with all the wagons empty. On learning the cause I concluded to go to Potter's mill, where we all staid all night.

McD: Left camp at eight o'clock this morning and went up the Pike in the direction of Staunton. We found it very hard marching through the snow but marched 23 miles. Camped near Mt. Crawford. Had to rake snow off the ground to get a place to lie down. Awful cold sleeping.

NOTE: Early's army was leaving the Valley.

December 15, Thursday

SP: Were up till after 12 cooking & then lay down, but as we were sleeping on oil cloths & ground so cold we slept but short time & woke so cold we could not sleep any more & got up a little after 4. Oh! it was miserable night & really torturing to be unable to sleep when we were so wearied after hard days march. Got pass & rode in ambulance, for I could not get shoe on, my feet were so sore. Cap. Nicholson of 12$^{\underline{th}}$ Ala. rode with me—a very pleasant gentleman. Passed thro' Mt. Crawford & Mt. Sydney—Cap. N. suggestion I put my glove in heel of my shoe so as to walk without hurting me—& got out making room for some of the many poor sorefooted fellows who were trying to ride. This was one time when we could not tell where we were going. Great deal surmise. Some said we were going to Tenn. others to Ga. but we afraid we would be sent to trenches at R. & Petersbg. Late this eveng. halted & after some delay went in woods in mile of S. i.e. our Brig. & Grimes, while Cook[e']s & Cox's were taking cars. Looked like mountain of snow, but fires sprung up as if by magic & soon dotted hill side over. After drying our feet & lolling about, we marched into town at 12½ A.M. *Frid. 16$^{\underline{th}}$* but found could not get off & returned to Camp. However, Jack W., J. Warren, M$^{\underline{c}}$Diarmid, W. Long & I stayed & slept on porch of Jail, very comfortable & up early & got good brkfast at restaurant [. . .] 12 apiece. Got off on train at 11 A.M. terribly crowded—60 men in a box car. Men got whiskey along road & several of Cos. A & B were drunk & very disgusting & noisy. Lt. T. made speech. Maj. B. heard fr. decis. of Court Marshal & is [. . .] He is very popular with the Regt. & is deeply sympathised with.

HB: After attending to my business, Boardman & myself went to Lexington, where we remained, all the evening & night.

McD: Left camp at sun rise and got to Staunton late in the evening. Stoped in the road near town for several hours. The weather was very cold and came near freezing. Left the road about dark and went into a little skirt of woods and built some little fires. About midnight we were roused up and marched down in town. Remained in town several hours nearly freezing. We were to take the cars but they were not ready for us. Went back to our fires about daylight.

December 16, Friday

HB: After breakfast all three of us started towards Staunton. About 4 miles from L. met Johny with orders to leave, our Div. having gone to Richmond, on account of which Boardman & I rode to Staunton tonight. Met Maj. Webster there.

McD: Went into town again about sun rise. Waited several hours and got on the cars and were off for Richmond. Got to Gordonsville about dark.

December 17, Saturday

SP: After a most uncomfortable nights travel, we arrived in Richmond about 2 hrs. before day this morning. Marched to Mayo's bridge & there found that our Brig. would have to march all the way down to the vicinity of Petsbg—whereas the other 3 Brigs of our Divis. had been sent by R.R. I had very sore feet & got pass with Chas. Briggs, also, to go down by the train wh. was to carry down the baggage &c soon after we were joined at P. Depot by majority of the Co.—viz— Alex McCall, McDiarmid, Jno. Warren, Jno. Carberry, Bayley & Clifton. Went to Ala. Sol. Home & got brkfst. met Col. Fowler, Chas. Whelan, P. Lavender &c. —Were little too late for 9 o'clk train & had to wait for 3 P.M. train. Went to Mrs. Barnes' & got a blanket—pr. old shoes to wear, socks & left my new hat in my trunk there & walked about town awhile. Pres. Davis is said to be very ill. I wrote a letter at the Depot to Loutie & meantime the rest of the boys up town got pretty tight on mean apple brandy & brot a canteen or 2 full with them. Had some difficulty in getting on train, but met with Capt. Smith, Brig. Inspector who assisted us—Alex M. though had quarrel with Conductor about getting in Coach, but we had to get on top, as C. insisted there was no room inside. Alex, McD, Warren & Carberry were very much intoxicated & very amusing during the 3 hrs. run, but kept me very uneasy for fear some would fall off. Got off at Dunlaps Station & walked out to where the Brig was camped 1½ ms.

HB: I had made up my mind on hearing of our Div. leaving the valley, to visit Harrisonburg once more, finished my business this morning & left St. about 12 N. reached H. about dusk, found my dear Lucy as interesting as ever. In the course of the evening I got her to accept the engagement ring I had made for her.

McD: Arrived in Richmond before day this morning and marched through the city and halted on Mayo's Bridge across the James and remained there till after day light. We then marched on the Telegraph Turnpike leading to Petersburg. Marched to Swift Run about three miles from Petersburg.

December 18, Sunday

SP: We had heard so many terrible accounts of a life in the trenches that we had a dread & horror of having to leave the valley & come down into them—& from being sent during such a hard spell of weather—& marched rapidly thro the snow, we were confident Gen. Lee was apprehending an attack & that our destination was the trenches, but we are much relieved to-day by hearing that we (our Corps) now commanded by Maj. Gen Gordon temporarily are to remain in reserve & build winter quarters immediately. How much better than we expected! Ed Hutch. brot a box of edibles from R. this morng & treated the Co. to some nice biscuits & cakes.

HB: During the forenoon, I experienced the pleasure of loving one, who I have reason to believe reciprocates my love. Lucy & I had the parlour to ourselves all the morning. The time rolled away so rapidly to me, that I was astonished to hear of dinner being announced. After dinner I had a severe task to perform, telling my dear one *good bye*. It was with much pain that I did so. The family all left the parlour to give us an opportunity of parting, which I made proper use of. After taking leave of them all, I mounted my horse to leave for Staunton, which place I reached long after night. On my way there, my thoughts were occupied with my darling only, so much so that I didn't notice the darkness of the night at all. More than once did I take a glance at the miniature I received from her, which only put me the more in mind of the real one. I staid with Witz tonight.

McD: Remained quiet all day. The weather is not so cold as it was in the Valley.

December 19, Monday

SP: Sheb. Chadwick has written a petition to Pres. Davis praying him to reinstate Maj. Eugene Blackford—which was signed by most all officers & much of the Regt. It is a very pretty thing & very complimentary to the Maj. I hope it will succeed for I believe there was much prejudice in the Ct. Martial which convicted him & witnesses interested parties. This eveng our Brig. moved ½ mile into woods (piney) where we are to build & some of the officers laid off the ground. The 2 battal's will be in parallel lines about 100 yds apart. Recd letter from Col. P. who had just reached home after "circuitous & tedious journey of nearly 2 weeks" from Ala. He spent six days with Mama at Umbria wh he says "were really happy days." Wrote with his left hand & did admirably—the wound in right not being well yet.

HB: Staid at Staunton all day anxiously expecting my wagons, which didn't arrive, however until late in the evening. I was greatly troubled at the idea of not having staid at H. until this evening. Late in the evening I directed a letter to Lucy dear. Staid with Witz again.

McD: Moved a few hundred yards and began to build Winter Quarters. We are some three miles in the rear of the main line.

NOTE: "Col. P" is Samuel B. Pickens.

December 20, Tuesday

SP: The mess I am with now consists of P. H., Y. Id., McD., B.A.C., J.H.W., Carberry & Waddell but latter now absent on detail. Having an axe pitched in bright & early bring up poles some of which we cut yesterday evening, for our house, & by late brkfast had enough for body. After getting ½ of them notched & put up—we had pleasure (?) of learning that mistake had been made in laying off ground & we'd have to move. And upon another measurement our Co. was thrown 60 yds further to left—& it took us balance of even'g to tear down what we had built & remove those logs to the new place assigned us. I have recd 2 letters fr. Ala. = 2nd time I've had any fr. home since I left. They were from Jamie & Lou dated 3 and 4th ult. Elias Lewis wounded on 10th May & been keeping shop in Richmond—was returned to-night to our Co. under guard. Cannonading going on regularly down on lines during the day.

HB: Capt. Preston, Johny & myself started off for Richmond this morning. On crossing the mountain I took a farewell look at the valley, particularly in the direction of H. Besides thinking of the one I love most, my mind wasn't concentrated upon any other subject. We staid in two miles of the mountain tonight at Mr. Ludlow's house.

McD: Worked hard all day cutting logs etc. Heard heavy cannonading on the front lines.

NOTE: "P. H." is Peter Hagins.
"Y Id." is William Young Idom.
"McD" is Joel McDiarmid.
"B. A. C." is Benjamin A. Carter.
"J. H. W." is John H. Warren.

December 21, Wednesday

SP: We had rain last night which continued till late this morning & prevented our working. As soon as it held up however we "pitched in" & put up the body of our house. very cold—Icicles hanging about on trees etc.—Drizzled most all day & weather very disagreeable indeed.

HB: The first thing I noticed this morning on getting up was a considerable snow on the ground. We never left until about 11 A.M. & rode to Charlottsville, where we staid at the Central Hotel all night.

McD: Most of us have the bodies of cabins up. Sleeting all day.

December 22, Thursday

SP: Rations are rather scant now for men with as good appetites as we have. We are entitled to 1 lb. flour or crackers—1 of beef & a little of coffee & sugar* but it passes through so many hands being carried around & weighed so often, that it falls short when we get it. For breakfast yest. morning we had simply a biscuit & cup of coffee & to day after waiting in vain for rations to be issued till 12 M. baked some meal we had bot & boiled some peas without a particle of grease or meat of any kind & breakfasted. We enjoyed it too, having with it plenty of what is said to be the very "best sauce"—"hunger"—one of the few things cheap & easily obtained in Confed: tho' I must say a little bacon grease would have suited my taste better, tho' not the "best sauce"—After hard days work & getting supper about ready & while I was making down my bed little before dark we were startled by beating of long roll & orders to get ready to move—& in a few minutes were off—bound we knew not whither. Marched rapidly without halting, 8 ms. up telegraph road towds. Richmond. Much speculation as to our destination—(& bivouaced at 10 P.M.) Some say we are going to N. side James—while many think that we are going back to Valley.

(*sometimes peace & rice)

HB: Saw Simms in town this morning, after procuring forage for the teams, continued our journey for about 8 miles, where we camped in an old house.

McD: Cold day. Worked till late in the evening. Was ordered to move. Went back towards Richmond. Marched about eight miles and halted. Went into camp by the roadside.

December 23, Friday

SP: Last night was very cold & windy, but we had large fires & slept very well. We remained here all day—nothing of interest occurring. We are near Howlett's

Station & about midway between R. & Petersbg. Peter Hagins & I having been much annoyed for some nights past by [lice]—the detestable plague of camp life—went to the branch this evening—washed and put on clean clothes altho the weather extremely severe—ground frozen & we were nearly so when we got through.

HB: Continued our journey this morning to Wilmington [. . .] City, staid at the hotel all night.

McD: Still on the roadside in camp. Very disagreeable place. The weather cold and windy.

December 24, Saturday

SP: Our Div. train, ambulances, butchers, & beeves etc. fr. Valley reached us to-day. Left here little before dark & marched back to new Winter Qrs. by 8½ P.M. & a most agreeable march it was too, for all wanted to get back here. We moved at night to avoid being seen from Butler's tower.

McD: Remained quiet till late in the evening. We then marched back to our quarters.

December 24 and 25, Saturday and Sunday

HB: Continued our journey, not letting Christmas interfere with us.

December 25, Sunday

SP: Christmas day & quite a pretty one. Very cold in the morning, but moderated towards evening. All quiet along the lines. At home this is a season of festivity, but with us poor rebels in the army it is almost ex necessitate a fast day. Rations are more scant than usual. For breakfast we had one or 2 "hard tacks" a scrap of bacon & a cup of coffee. For dinner we had to wait to draw rations & had a good, hearty meal about dark of biscuits, beef, sugar & coffee & rice.

McD: Being Christmas and Sunday, we did no work today.

December 26, Monday

SP: Rained most all last night & misting rain today. great deal artillery firing on the line. Young I. rived the boards* about 450, good, light, wide, pine boards & Carter assisted by Carberry & P. Hagin covered the house—while McD., J. Warren & I filled in the back & [. . .] of the fire place, which was no light job. I then finished a letter to Mama—which I commenced on 24ᵗʰ.

(*House 16 × 18 ft. ordered to have them all 14 × 16.)

HB: Arrived at Richmond about 1 P.M., attended to some private business, visited the theatre & staid with Joe Elliott tonight.

McD: Worked all day. Some rain. Heavy cannonading on the line.

December 27, Tuesday

SP: Weather being moderate & favorable for such work, we built our chimney & chinked & doubed the house—thus completing all the outside work. ours is first house finished in Co. & among the 1ˢᵗ in the Regt.

HB: Went out to have an ambro type taken for my dear L. but did not succeed on account of the cloudy weather. About 11 A.M. left the city for the army, which I found encamped on Swift creek four miles north of Petersburg.

McD: Still at work making a chimney.

December 28, Wednesday

SP: Fixed up bunks to-day for accommodation of 8 men—moved our plunder in & took formal possession of what I hope will be our quarters for the Winter at least. "Major" Geddie who has been missing since the battle of 19th May last at Spotsylvania C.H. & fr. whom we had never been able to hear from—surprised us all very much by making his appearance here last night. He is an excellent & meritorious soldier & all were glad to see him return. He was among the number of sick & wounded recently exchanged at Savannah. J. W. has left us—he & G. have gone in with Clifton & Farrier next door to us. Raining to night & how snug & comfortable to be in cabin, with bunks & hear rain on roof.

HB: Went round to Co. D to see the boys, heard nothing from none as yet, nor had a letter reached me from the valley.

McD: Still at work making bunks.

December 29, Thursday

SP: Weather cloudy all day & snowed some. Towards evening it turned considerably colder. Priv.———Wesson fr. Jeff. D.L. who exchanged with G. James reported to our Co. to-day, for duty.

HB: Laid up quiet in camp today, no letter for me yet.

McD: House completed. Had a little snow.

December 30, Friday

SP: I am on guard to-day in charge of 2nd relief. This is the first guard we've had at this place & it dissolved upon us to establish guard lines & quarters & clean them out. Spent dull & uninteresting day as usual on such occasions, sitting around a little smoky, green pine fire. Lt. Fleming, Co. "I" is of. Guard & also acting officer of day. Carter put up mantlepiece in cabin wh. will be great convenience. The guard was taken off to-night a little after dark—to my infinite satisfaction.

HB: Today I was fortunate enough to get two letters from my dear Lucy, answered them this evening.

McD: Resting from our labors today.

December 31, Saturday

SP: It snowed sufficiently this afternoon to cover the ground & weather very raw & disagreeable. With this day ends another year—4th one of the war & a very eventful & bloody one. Waddell came from R. & gave mess nice lunch—turkey biscuits & cakes—more Xmas than we've seen all together. I had my 3d Xmas however, this year in Oct. & Nov. when at home with dear M. sist. & bro.

HB: Nothing of note to record today.

McD: Resting from our labors today.

1865

January 1, Sunday

SP: A very cold day, ground hard frozen. Quiet prevails along lines of 2 confronting armies—sun bright & beautiful day opens the new year. B. A. Carter started to-day to N.C. on detail with forage wagons, to be gone some time.

HB: With the beginning of the year, I find nothing worthy of note to record. Everything perfectly quiet all day. At night I visited Jack Drakeford, staid there until midnight, he giving me a description of his courtship which was really pleasant.

McD: All quiet in quarters. Some snow on the ground. Every thing appears quiet on the front line.

January 2, Monday

SP: I am on guard again to-day. There are so few noncommissioned officers now present in the Regt. that it comes around too often. Col. Hobson let us have about 200 ft. rough edge plank—with wh. we made a very nice floor to our cabin. So now it is more like a house & more comfortable than any we have ever occupied in army. Have also a lot of stools, & to-night we borrowed an auger & put up shelves, gun racks, & pegs for hanging Haversacks, canteens etc. on. We have now every thing to our notion in the way of comforts & conveniences & will be perfectly satisfied if we are permitted to remain in them during the winter.

HB: Maj. Webster, Gilliam James & myself called on Maj. Adams this evening, had a splendid time until midnight, after which we retired.

McD: Remained quiet in camp. Very cold.

SP: Commenced policing & cleaning up this morn. each Co. in front of its quarters. For about 2 hrs. this morng there was heavy & rapid shelling on the lines. So much so that we were right uneasy lest we might be called out. It is hard to get accustomed to it, for in Valley it was most always signal for a move & probably a fight. Interesting accounts in Richmond papers of yesterday & to day of repulse at Wilmington of Beast Butler & Admiral Porters grand expedition against that city—on grand scale but failed to take Ft. Fisher & withdrew. Carberry went to Pg. & got 20 or 30 lbs meal at $1.15 per lb. Snowed this evening quite heavily, but ceased before bedtime—being about an inch deep.

HB: Not anything transpired today at all worth of note.

McD: Remained quiet in camp. Snow.

SP: Our portion of Sol. N.Y. dinner given by people of V$^{\underline{a}}$ to Gen. Lee's army, was recd. last night & we had it for brk. this morning. It consisted of loaf bread, beef, mutton, pork, venison, Turkey & chicken. When divided out it—the meats particularly—there was very little for each man, but it was a stupendous undertaking to prepare a dinner for a large army & will be recd. as a testimonial for the gratitude of the noble old Dominion to the army which has for 4 long years been battling with our Northern foes on her soil. John returned from Richmond to-day with some of the other baggage of our Co. = blankets, overcoats—woolen underclothes &c—& brot my mess a little oven, Dutch pot & axe—things much needed—also my wax taper wh. Mary & all the children made for me the morning of day I left home, soap, red pepper etc—wh. have increased our comforts greatly. I got worsted drawers & under shirts & my big lined blanket that Mama sent me the winter of 1862—invaluable. Peter H. got N.C.O. coat too, so we'll now sleep warm. Weather clear & very cold.

HB: Maj. Webster sent up his application for furlough today, advised me to do likewise, which I intend to do tomorrow.

McD: Remained quiet in camp. Very cold.

NOTE: "N.C.O. coat" is noncommissioned officer's coat.

SP: An aff. letter fr. dear Mama of 8th Dec. & one also from my dear sister, Mary of 11$^{\underline{th}}$ came to hand yesterday, & to-day one fr. Louty of 20$^{\underline{th}}$. I was truly glad to get them for I had pleasure of receg. very few letters fr. home since my return on furlough owing to Shermans passage fr. Atlanta to Savannah, Ga. & destroying our R. Roads in that section. They had likewise been without letters fr. me.—for Louty said Mama had just got my letter written fr. R. Nov. 21$^{\underline{st}}$.

HB: Had an application for furlough made out today but haven't sent it up yet.

McD: Remained quiet in camp. Very cold.

January 6, Friday

SP: Alex McCall and I sat up last night very late writing—Indeed, it was 1 O'clock this morng before we went to bed. My wax taper is so nice to read or write by these long nights. We policed in front of our Co. this evening—clearing up brush & undergrowth.

HB: Nothing of importance took place today.

McD: Remained quiet in camp. Rain.

January 7, Saturday

SP: Nothing of Interest transpired in Camp to-day—save the return to Co. of "Old man Long" whom we left sick in Stanton. To-night tho' whilst I was sitting writing to Co. Pickens & after most of the boys had gone to bed, Joe Grigg came in with some bad news for us—which has disconcerted us all no little—viz—that our Brig. to start at 8 A.M. to-morrow & take its position in the trenches—to relieve some other troops—so I've put aside my letter & must retire & try to get good night's rest.

HB: Everything quiet this morning. About 10 P.M. after having retired, we received orders to move at 8 A.M. next day. Had to get up issue two days rations. The thought of having to leave comfortable quarters after having gone to the trouble of putting them up, was terrible, a military necessity however.

McD: Remained quiet in camp. Rain.

January 8, Sunday

SP: Peter was called up in night & drew 2 days rations flour & bacon & he[,] Y. Idom & John staid up cooking nearly all night. We were all up little after day light—ate brkfast & got everything ready—& about 9 O'clk we started. Came round about way to avoid being seen from Butler's Tower = 5 or 6 miles & relieved Kemper's old Brig. Vᵃ. now ———. We could hardly believe this was front line, as the men were going about free & easy—everything quiet—no shelling no sharp-shooting, even. But the Yankee lines are 2½ ms. distant along here—& the Virginians say they never have shelled any & there has been no picket-firing except when Yank put negro pickets on & then our boys opened on them & kept it up till they were taken away next day. It was very cold—ground frozen, but it seemed they never would get us in quarters & after getting in we had to move several times, till just before night we got cabins and considered ourselves permanently fixed—brot. up a pile of wood—cut it up and stored it away inside, made fire, got supplies & were ready to go to bed, when lo! it seems some of 6ᵗʰ Ala. want more room & here came Capts. Green & Woodard— comdg. respective 6 & 5ᵗʰ Regts. & turn most all our Co. out our houses & we had to hunt places anywhere we could find them in Regt. for the night. This sort of doings is very vexatious. Woodard is a poor excuse for Regt. Commander & has no business with it. Peter and I crowded into a little hut with Alex McC & Hutch—wh. was just large enough for 2.

HB: The brigade moved out this morning relieved Terry's brigade of Genl.

Pickett's Div. in the trenches on the line. I went down with them, to learn their position, returned to our quarters in the evening.

McD: Left our quarters and went to the front and relieved a Brigade of Pickets' Division. Our position here is about half way between the James river and Petersburg. We find picket duty very heavy. One third of the men are kept on the out post. Our lines at this point is about two miles from the enemies works.

January 9, Monday

SP: Waddell, McD. & all the men left at camp on account of bad shoes. Were sent down here this morning. This is 1st rate position—breastworks about 20 ft. thick at base and 15 at top—ditch in front with pointed stakes sticking out fr. works to prevent an enemy from climbing over—then at distance of 50 yds in front an abattis (c. d. fr.) of pine sapplings tops to front & limbs sharpened—so Yankees would have a lively time in attempting to take the works. (everything combined) The cabins are generally small & roughly made—a row built on edge of trenches & dug down to the same depth, 2½ to 3 ft. below surface—with door opening to trench. Then other cabins are stuck about indiscriminately in rear of this row—but very near & all crowded together. As general thing they have bunks & accommodations for 4 men. All hands were turned out & moved again this even'g a hundred or so yds. to right. I, with Ed. Hutch, Farrier, Geddie & Lewis were detailed this even'g and went on picket. The p. line is ¾ of a mile fr. our works & Y. p. lines 50 to 150 yds fr. ours. Our posts are fr 25 to 50 yds apart & each 1 in charge of a noncommis-officer with 4 men. Our instructions are to keep 1 man with loaded gun walking post & on lookout during day & 2 at night & if a man sees another deserting to enemy & succeeds in shooting him he will get a 30 day furlough. The Yanks seem very peacably inclined & are always anxious to trade Coffee or anything they have for tobacco, but it has to be done slily—as both parties have strict orders forbidding all intercourse with each other. One of them wanted to exchange papers this even'g but we had none of ours with us.

HB: Went on the line late this evening to get a report, received a letter from Henry Allen, staid on the line all night.

McD: All quiet along the lines. Very cold.

NOTE: "C. d. fr." is "chemin de frise."

January 10, Tuesday

SP: We were relieved and returned to Camp about 3 this evening after having spent a wretched time. This is a tour of picket duty long to be remembered. I sat up last night till 12 O'clock & it commenced raining as I went to bed, but my squad was in a bomb proof pit wh. we thought water proof also, & as there was a good bed of leaves—expected to be all right—but were roused by water leaking on us some time before day, tho stood it till light & then crawled out and started little fire. Our blankets & clothes were wet & rained steadily till nearly time to be relieved. T'was a hard day & one we wished to pass off quickly—Just such a time as makes one disgusted with the soldiers life & everything connected with the Army. What a comfort it was to get back to my cabin—washed my feet & shoes in puddle in trenches in front of my door and put on pr. clean socks I happened to have & dried my clothes by the fire. Now if I were at home in similar condition Mama would be very solicitous about my health & have me to put on dry clothes immediately, rub my neck & head with spirits & take a toddy. O how different! Quandin Yankeedoodledom, will you continue to wage this wicked war upon us & necessitate our spending our lives in this manner!!

HB: Returned to our quarters this morning during a most drenching rain. It had rained severe all night & this morning the whole country is a solid sheet of water. Maj. Webster went to the lines during the day & on his return, brought me a letter from the idol of my heart, which I read with a good deal of interest, particularly after having dreamt about her last night a good portion of the night was taken up by me in thinking about the letter I received.

McD: All quiet along the lines. Very hard rain.

January 11, Wednesday

SP: Weather has cleared up & is cooler today. P.[,] Y.[,] M^{c}D.[,] C. & I went out split up a good quanity of wood. Needless to mention I am very well to-day & no manner of exposure seems to affect us out here (fortunately)

HB: I attended to finishing our office today, which was completed this evening. After supper I commenced a letter to my dear Lucy, but did not finish on account of being disturbed by company.

McD: All quiet along the lines. Pleasant today.

NOTE: "P." is Paul Lavender.
"Y." is Young Idom.
"McD." is Joel McDiarmaid.
"C." is Benjamin A. Carter.

January 12, Thursday

SP: Finished my letter to Col. P. & wrote one also to Jamie latter of wh. I sent by Waddell to Camp Rodes to Maj. Webster who sent us word that he would start home on furlough to-morrow. Had pleasure of recving long letter of 12 pp. fr. Jamie just as I was concluding mine to him. Date 30$^{\underline{th}}$ ult. all well. Mr. Cole has set in as overseer at Goodrumplace on 16$^{\underline{th}}$ Dec. & was getting on very well restoring it from the dilapidated condition to which Lowless bad management had reduced it. I was detailed with Briggs, Carberry, Clifton & Farrier & Lewis to go on picket, but as I had not finished my letters M^{c}D took my place & I remained till we drew rations & cooked supper, when I carried rations down & relieved McDiarmid.

HB: Took up the letter I left unfinished last night, also answered Miss F's note, sent letter off this evening. Started up my application for furlough today, in hopes of getting to visit home for a short time.

McD: All quiet along the lines. Pleasant today.

January 13, Friday

SP: Last night was a beautifully clear, still moonlight night and intensely cold. I slept from 9 till 1 & was up balance of night. It was 6½ before it was broad day light. A bell said to be on Yankee gun-boat strikes every ½ hour & the Y. sentinels pass the hours "eight O'clock, nine O'clk" &c. all along their picket line. Our boys very often take it up and pass it along our lines too. We are in the fork of James & Appomattox rivers & not more than 1½ or 2 miles from each. Butler's tower is in full view of us, & indeed looks like it might be knocked down by a long range gun, a Whitworth for instance. Ch. Briggs went down early & traded tobacco for coffee & case knife. Saw a late copy of Balt. American. In speaking of Richmd papers saying we would offer ourselves to England or France, rather than be subjugated by Yanx. It says those powers know the immense strength & resources of the U.S. & know too that receiving us under their protection would be a gross insult & casus belli & warns them against such a dangerous step. We were relieved this evening & returned to quarters.

McD: All quiet along the lines. Cold.

January 14, Saturday

SP: All quiet & nothing transpired today worthy of note. Am sorry to learn that a man from the 6th & 1 from 61st Regt. deserted last night. Was in hopes there would be none so vile in our Brig. Yesterday an order recd. fr. Gen. Lee allows 4 furloughs to the 100 men to be given to the most meritorious soldiers— who passed thro' the last campaign. There were six to our Regt. & each Co. selected a man—& Capt. Riley decided what ones of the 10 should have the furloughs—as follows—Co. A. Priv. Park, B. Sergt. McCall, C. Sergt. Finkley, D. Sergt. Alex. McC., H. Corpl Ball, K. Sergt. Brightman. Our Co. voted it to Alex. who immediately started up his application & is delighted at the prospect of going home again.

McD: All quiet along the lines. Windy and cold

January 15, Sunday

SP: Were relieved this morning by Grimes' Brig. & marched in high glee back to Camp Rodes, but on reaching it were ordered to cut no more standing timber & heard that our Divis. was under marching orders—which filled us with disappointment & gloom. Later in the day it turned out that the order in reference to the timber was on account of the land being owned by orphans & guardians were unwilling to have it cut; therefore it is said 5th & 6 Regts. will have to move about 1 mile & build other houses—of course we are much troubled & vexed at thought of having all this work & trouble over & are violently opposed to the move. No rations were issued yesterday even'g & this morn'g we had no breakfst—but John had picked up some meal somewhere & had something to eat for my mess soon after reaching camp. The rest of the boys tho had to wait till rations were issued—wh. was just before night & it is first they have eaten since yesterday evening & with a few it is the 1st since yesterday morning. Meal, flour, bacon & sorghum issued. 1$^{\underline{st}}$ sorgum this Winter. Paul Lavender was here to-day. His business is to have his certificate of disability renewed.

McD: Relieved this morning by a Brigade from our won Division. Got back to our quarters in the afternoon.

January 16, Monday

SP: On guard today. They are putting it to me rather heavy—as I am only non-commissioned officer in Co. doing duty. J. W. scalded his foot & did not go on picket nor is yet doing duty. An unusually large lot of clothing, blankets, & shoes issued to-day. I drew pr. drawers & no. 1 pr. English shoes for John. Happy to hear to-day that we will not have to move. Regt. all day hard at work policing—burning brush & had dense cloud of smoke wh. suffocated us almost.

HB: Not the least thing of any importance or interest has transpired for several days, wrote to Mr. Witz today.

McD: Had a general policing today.

January 17, Tuesday

SP: I had a very disagreeable time in hunting up the men & posting reliefs last night as it was like Chimerian darkness until moon rose, & I stumbled over logs & stumps & once fell in a mortor hole & got my foot wet. Corporals stood 4 hrs. each; & I had charge of 1$^{\underline{st}}$ & 2$^{\underline{nd}}$ reliefs & was up till 1 O'clk this morning. Billy Dick Witherspoon now Asst. Surg. 11 Ala. called by to see us to-day. Joe Grigg sent me over some nice pastry wh. he recd. fr. home. My mess cut, split, & piled in front of our cabin a fine lot of wood. We want to lay in a supply now that it can be had as we are prohibited from cutting down any more trees. Another Confederate reverse! Ft. Fisher, N.C. has been captured by Yankees on 15$^{\underline{th}}$ Sund. This is indeed a gloomy hour with our Confederacy. Trust that the tide of war will soon turn, & I still confidently believe that a merciful God will bless us with ultimate success. "The darkest hour procedes the dawn". God grant that dawn soon appear on the horizon of our political sky now thickly overcast with murky & portentous clouds.

HB: Except the hopes of getting my furlough appr. nothing seems cheerful to me today.

McD: More policing today. A little snow.

NOTE: "Chimerian" is an alternative spelling of "chimerical."

Fort Fisher was the Confederacy's last important port.

January 18, Wednesday

SP: This morning we filled up our fire place with mud to a level with the floor & smoothed it off nicely—wh. will be a great improvement on it. We then went to policing & after working hard raking up & burning leaves & trash, we were again thrown into a peck of troubles again on the subject of moving—B. Adams rode by & told me our work was all for nothing—that he had order fr. Gen. Lee for 5 & 6 Regts. to move on acct. of being in such a swamp. Now isn't such doings as this enough to provoke a saint. Some of the boys remarked that had

Job lived in these times his patience would have been overtaxed. Old Henry S. Foot was arrested at Fredksbg few days since on his way to Washington City—as he affirms to make peace. The air for some days past has been filled with rumors, & some of them been mentioned in news papers; viz, that Frank P. Blair now in Richmd & has come to offer terms of peace—one version is that Engld. & France are on [. . .] that we can get better terms fr. Yankees than any one else— etc. & that Gen. Singleton is also in Richmd on a peace mission—Stuff!! [. . .] are also rumored that Tredegar Iron Works & other Government property are being removed fr. Richmd preparatory for its evacuation. Maj. Webster started home to-day.

HB: Maj. Webster left here today for Richmond on his way home.

McD: More policing today. Clear.

January 19, Thursday

SP: The excitement about moving has blown over to day, as it is said army inspector has been to see our Camp & thinks that it will not be necessary to move. But Phoenix-like another takes its place to-night—for it is now reported that our Brig. is to be sent to Wilmington, N.C. We don't believe it tho'. In fact we don't believe anything we hear now, but still such reports trouble us a good deal for bad news much oftener than good comes true, his temporibus. Regt. inspection by Capt. Pickett. A. A. J. Waddell brings in another very pleasant peace rumor to night wh. came fr. Richmd. by a "reliable" gentleman.

HB: I made calculations of getting an answer to my letter of the 12th. inst. Although I was not disappointed in getting a letter from H. it was by far the one expected, a short endorsement by L—— on the back of [. . .] letter, showed that my letter hadn't been received at the time of writing.

McD: More policing today. Cold and cloudy.

NOTE: "H." is Harrisonburg, Virginia, where Beck's fiancée lives.

January 20, Friday

SP: Alex McCall started home on furlough (30 days) before day. I was up till 1 o'clk this morng. writing a long letter to Mary to send by him. I've been on detail for fatigue duty most all day—building a crib at Maj. Bryant's quarters. Dined with Glover, Beck & Tom Moore. Newspapers say Hood has been relieved at his own request of command of Army Tenn. which is now commanded by Dick Taylor—brother-in-law of Pres. Davis. Resolutions introduced to expel Foot from Congress—being considered unworthy of a seat in it, but were referred to Committee of elections.

HB: I looked for two important documents today. A letter from H. & the return of my furlough. While I was disappointed in the latter, I was rejoiced in the former. I shall await the return of my furlough before answering it, being particularly anxious to deliver an answer myself, previous to leaving for home.

McD: More policing today. Cold and cloudy.

January 21, Saturday

SP: It has been steadily raining the entire day & we are almost inundated. This morning the trees were coated over with ice & hung with icicles. One more rumor of a move, wh. I trust is last we'll ever hear—i.e. that we will be sent to Dutch Gap to-morrow & we were all rendered truly uneasy by Sergts. call after night, but it proved to be for purpose of making detail to work on P. & Boydton plank road.

HB: Today was the most disagreeable day we have had in sometime, a heavy cold rain poured down from morning until late at night. I was rather uneasy all day not knowing whether my furlough will come appd. or not. About the time I thought, papers had come down from Div. Hd. Qrs. I went over to Col. Forsyth's and to my joy found my furlough there all right.

McD: Rained all day and froze as fast as it fell.

January 22, Sunday

SP: This has been a cloudy damp, disagreeable day & very wet under foot. I was on guard as Sergt. but we were relieved at dark. Went over with Tom Moore, by invitation & dined with Joe Grigg. He had recd. a box of edibles from Amelia & gave an elegant turkey dinner & followed by rice, pease &c. decidedly the nicest green tomatoe pickles I've ever tasted (dessert—sorghum). Such a dinner as a poor soldier in these hard times rarely has the good fortune to meet with. Carberry has been quite unwell & under Dr. Marshal's treatment since [. . .]

HB: Made preparations to leave in the morning, which occupied all my time today.

McD: Rained a little today. Disagreeable.

January 23, Monday

SP: To-day again has been a very gloomy, drizzly and disagreeable one: so much so that every one has kept closely within doors. I had not had a letter from home for eleven days till to-day when my spirits were cheered by the reception of a nice little epistle from my dear little sister Loutie. It was not dated. She says Jamie & Mary were confirmed on Sunday. An unusually heavy cannonade has been going on to-night, and just this minute musketry opened—followed immediately by the sounding of our bugle, and now the drums throughout the Brigade are vigorously rattling the "long roll". Terrible! terrible!

HB: Left camp this morning for Richmond, spent today in the city, attended to my business previous to leaving for H.

McD: Rained a little today. Disagreeable. Cannonading begins on the line after dark. Later in the night it became more severe and small arms began. The bugle sounded and we were ordered out. The road was awful muddy and the night very dark and we had quite a rough time marching. We found the mud nearly waist deep in some places. We went a mile or two in the direction of the cannonading. The alarm began to subside and halted. Found out that nothing serious was the matter and returned to camp.

January 24, Tuesday

SP: After all had gone to bed but me and whilst writing in my diary last night at 9 O'clock, the alarm mentioned above occurred; and all hands hastily set to work rolling up our blankets, gathering haversacks, canteens, etc., got under arms & marched out. Our Brig. & all the Division except the Brig on picket went out on the Pike & halted. We had been quite uneasy on account of the unusually brisk firing, the flashes from which we saw distinctly, but deemed it almost impossible for any move to be made, as it was so dark a night & the whole country flooded with water. So imagine our disappointment when the "long roll" beat. Of all the miserable times we have had in the army I never anticipated a more miserable one than on setting out last night; for it was as dark as Egypt, the roads a perfect quagmire & the weather cold; but thank God after waiting a short time—the firing having abated considerably—we recd the order "counter march by file left" & returned to Camp. The troops demonstrated their delight by yelling lustily, and we cheerfully retraced our steps, about 1¼ ms. thro' deep mud & ponds of water 100 yards long in places, little minding it—so happy were we to get back to our warm firesides & comfortable bunks. It seems Grimes just called out our Divis. to be in readiness & on going to Gen. Pickett's Hd. Qrs near Chester Station, learned that the cannonade was from our gunboats which had run down the James. Ed Hutchinson being unwell, I took his place & worked on the record of this Company which we are making out to send to Col. Fowler. F. P. Blair is back in Richmond & has submitted terms of peace offered by the Yankee Government. "The Examiner" thinks it augurs well for us to see the nervous desire manifested by them to have the war ended. God grant this be the beginning of negotiations from which a speedy & honorable peace result! Oh! how glorious! how happy 'twould be!

HB: Left R. this morning for Staunton. About ten miles from R. the coach I was in ran off the track, didn't hurt anybody however, reached Staunton this evening.

McD: Remained quiet in camp. Pleasant.

January 25, Wednesday

SP: Last night & today the weather has been freezing & clear as a bell. Some ditching about our quarters done yesterday has done much good, as it has drained off all the standing water. Our Gun-boats broke through the Yankee obstructions & went down as far as Varina, meeting with little opposition: they have returned, however, without effecting any thing. Gold is tumbling in Richmond: from being at $70 or $80 for one a few days ago, and indeed none for sale at any price it is now at $35. Rumors abound now: to-day it is said an armistice of three months has been agreed upon—a man direct from Richmond saw it on the bulletins boards. (?)

HB: Left Staunton this morning for H. Took them all by surprise. Had a most elegant time with my darling Lucy.

McD: Remained quiet in camp. Cold.

January 26, Thursday

SP: Nothing of interest going on in Camp to-day. Charley Pegues, Adj. is back again. He still limps from the wound recd. at Fisher's Hill. I had the extreme pleasure of reading to-day a most welcome and affectionate letter of 14 pages from my dear Mama, which afforded me heartfelt pleasure. It was dated 5th inst.

HB: Spent the morning very pleasantly. Had a conversation with Mrs. H. in regard to what had taken place between L. & myself, received a satisfactory reply. After eating a splendid dinner prepared to leave again. Took an affectionate farewell of them all, particularly my darling Lue & left for Staunton. Although my stay was a very short one, it certainly was a very agreeable one. Reached Staunton about 7 P.M.

McD: Remained quiet in camp. Very cold.

January 27, Friday

SP: Trawick left yesterday morning on 40 days furlough for the Itch. Gilliam James started home this morning. The weather is intensely cold—the ink froze on my pen just now.

HB: Left Staunton this morning for Richmond, which place I reached about ½ past 7 P.M. Called on Col. Fowler, wrote a hurried letter to my darling Lucy, after which I retired for the night.

McD: Remained quiet in camp. Very cold.

January 28, Saturday

SP: Our Regt. started at 8 O'clock this morning & came with Dole's Brig. on picket at the same place we were before. Dole's Brig. is so small now that our Regt. & a N.C. Regt. 45th from Grimes Brig. had to come with it. I am in charge of a picket post with six men—viz Louis Elias, Farrier, Geddie, Sellers, & Warren of our Co., and Fen of Co. A. The N. Carolinians had three deserters from their Brig. (Cox's) and had very strict instructions for the Picket, which the Georgia Capt. commanding the detail that relieved them, tried to carry out with us.

HB: Had a good deal of business to attend to this morning, which kept me pretty busy running about. About 11 A.M. took the train for Danville.

McD: Our reg't was sent on picket today with Doles Brigade. Went to the part of the line we were on before. Very cold today.

January 29, Sunday

SP: I was up all night with the exception of a nap of two or three hours about the middle of the night. This is as cold a spell of weather as I ever saw. Eight or nine Tar-heels deserted last night—a whole picket post consisting of a recently elected Lieut. & seven or eight men of his Co. We were not relieved till 4 O'clock this evening—making our tour of duty about 30 hours long.

HB: Arrived at Danville after daybreak this morning, six hours behind time. Had to lay over all day. Wrote a few lines to my darling again, also to Mr. Witz.

McD: Our duty the same as before when here.

SP: We had some news in the papers this morning that is very aggreeable—viz. that Vice-President Stephens, Senator R. M. T. Hunter and Asst. Sec. of War, Judge Campbell have gone as Commissioners to Washington City to confer with the Yankee Government on the subject of Peace. We can't help entertaining some hope although there is really little grounds for hope of any acceptable terms from the Yankees after the successes they have recently met with, unless there is some truth in the report that England & France are threatening recognition and intervention which the "Examiner" says is not true. God grant they meet with success, & this lamentable strife cease!

HB: Left Danville at ½ past 1 o'clock this morning, rode in a box car to Greensboro, N.C. which place I reached about ½ past 7 A.M. Wrote a few hurried lines to my darling again. Met Maj. Miller & Catchett at G. Left G. about 10 A.M. for Charlotte. Reached Columbus, where I had to lay over all night again.

McD: Still on picket. Quiet on the lines. Clear.

SP: All the men from my house being on picket this morning save Wesson & me, it fell upon us to get up & make fire and cook breakfast. The cooking was easily done, as we had only some corn bread and meal coffee. Ate all our meat for supper last night. Our Division is under marching orders & it is said is going to Wilmington. Nous verrons. I went on picket again this evening with Elias, Farrier, Geddie & Warren. I'm in charge of the two posts on the left of our Regt.

McD: Still on picket. Quiet on the lines. Clear.

SP: I did not sleep a wink last night. We had the tightest instructions I've ever known, and the utmost vigilance was enjoined upon us. The Yankees are supposed to be making a movement and we want to discover what it is, & to see if any change takes place in our front. I had to post & relieve the videttes and report to the Officer commanding this portion of the line, Capt. Woodard, how things are going on at 11 P.M. & 1 & 3 A.M. This is very much like a Spring day & as mild as May. The sunshine & the atmosphere reminds us of that delicious season, and also the blue birds & others of the feathered tribe which are chirping, twittering & carroling merrily; but *una hirunds non facit vernum* and, probably, very soon we have some very severe weather.

McD: Still on picket. Quiet on the lines. Clear.

SP: Col. Winston of the N.C. Regt. with his Regt. and a detail from (Doles') Cooks' Brig. & our Regt. made an attempt to capture the Yankee picket posts on the right of our line & on the right as far as the Appomattox River, last night, but it proved a complete failure. At the first fire of a yankee vidette, Winston's own Regt. broke and ran—which threw every thing into confusion, and the project was abandoned. A few of the Yankees were captured but all escaped but two or three. To cover the movement our pickets were made to fire & we had to get up and get under arms at the breastworks. All was quiet before daylight, though, & the pickets in our front were on good terms again, talking the thing over, & swapping papers, knives, tobacco, etc. W$\underline{m}$ Sims and Robt. Price, both of whom have been on detached duty & absent from the Co. for nearly two years, have been returned and are at Camp Rodes.

McD: An attempt was made last night to capture the Yankee picket. Only a post or two was captured. The men became frightened and ran off, failing to do their duty. The excitement kept up till day light this morning. The project proved a complete failure.

February 3, Friday

SP: The weather is cold & cloudy to-day & it is sleeting. I am to go on picket at 3 P.M. and I fear we shall have a disagreeable tour of it.

McD: All quiet on the lines today. Some rain.

February 4, Saturday

SP: It drizzled & sleeted some last night but none to hurt and cleared off just before day; so we fared much better than we anticipated. I finished reading to-day an old volume of letters of Robt. Burns to his friends, brother poets, publishers, etc. and also some of his poems. The boys were trading with the Yankees again, but could get only papers as there was a very poor set of Yanks on post to-day. The "Phunny Phellow" had some very amusing comic pictures illustrative of the times in which Abe Lincoln, Jeff Davis, Gen. Lee, Phil Sheridan &c figured extensively. We were relieved at the usual time this evening. The balance of our Brig came down this morning & relieved the Ga. Brig; but our Regt. will have to remain another week—an arrangement we don't like at all for the duty is heavy. We are up 3^d night.

HB: Left Columbus this morning, reached Montgy at 3 P.M., took passage on the Southern Republic to Selma, reached there on the morning of

McD: All quiet on the lines today. Pleasant.

NOTE: The New York *Phunny Phellow* (1859–1876) was a lighthearted journal that included cartoons by Thomas Nast.

February 5, Sunday

SP: This day passed along very quietly, nothing of interest occurring on our portion of the lines.

HB: No train going towards home today, hired a mule & started off, staid at Mrs. King's near Hamburg all night.

McD: All quiet on the lines today. Pleasant.

February 6, Monday

SP: The morning papers give an account of the proceedings of our Peace Commissioners. It seems they were allowed to go only as far as Fortress Monroe and not permitted to leave the vessel on which they were passengers. Here Lincoln, accompanied by Seward, met them and laid down his ultimatum; which was that Peace was attainable only on the basis of our downright submission, reunion, total abolition of slavery, etc. Of course he was promptly informed that such terms could not be considered or discussed, and the conference soon ended.

HB: Continued my journey home, reached there about 3 P.M. to the astonishment of all.

McD: All quiet on the lines today. Pleasant.

February 7, Tuesday

SP: 4 P.M. Messrs. Idom, Long, Hutch & I have just been relieved from a wretched tour of picket duty. About 4 O'Clock this morning it began to snow and sleet and then turned to a cold rain which has not yet ceased. The water froze on our guns, hats, overcoats &c. We are truly glad to get back to our shanties at the breastworks to dry our clothing & to get something to eat. We have in anticipation too, a sound and refreshing night's rest. I've just received another batch of *letters* from *the loved ones* at *home*—ministers of comfort to the poor absent soldiers. One was from Mary, two from Willie, one from Loutie and one from dear little Icha! in propria persona; I think this is his first letter and it is surprising to see how well he has written it. Mama has written to engage a house in Tuscaloosa where she intends to put the children at school. How I wish I could be there to assist her in moving. I trust that she will be pleasantly situated.

HB: Went up town to see my friends, found all glad to see me. Maj. Webster came to town, staid all night with me, called on Misses A. & I. this evening.

McD: All quiet on the lines today. Had snow today. Late in the evening some fighting took place on the right.

February 8, Wednesday

SP: The "Enquirer" contains an account of a large and enthusiastic mass-meeting held yesterday at the African Church in Richmond. Pres. Davis made an excellent and encouraging address. He was surprised at the impudence and audacity manifested on the part of our enemies, and says if we will only be true to ourselves and do our duty in the future as well as we have done in the past, that before the Summer solstice they themselves will be sending commissioners to ask terms of us. Mr. Stephens, I think, & others followed in spirited & patriotic addresses. Since it is settled that the Yankees spurn the thought of an honorable peace with us, a spirit of determination and a great reaction is taking place, which I sincerely hope will spread like magic over our land. Henry Childress, Bill Sheldon & McCrary, who are just from home, came down to-day. They are looking better than I ever saw them before—fat, hearty & *clean,* as every one does now on returning from home. Capt. Williams & Lt. Christian came with them to Richmond, & the latter will be at Camp to-morrow. The Captain's health is so very bad that he has resigned & will immediately return home. I am very sorry for him. On Monday evening last & Tues. morning a pretty heavy fight occurred away down on our right, at Hatcher's Run, in consequence of the enemy extending his lines to the left. Brig. Genl. John Pegram of Richmond was killed.

HB: Called on Miss Jordan a few minutes this morning, walked about town all day, spent the evening with Miss Jordan.

McD: Some little fighting today. Quiet in our front.

February 9, Thursday

SP: I wrote a letter to Lou, which I began yesterday, but being interrupted had to lay it aside till to-day. These boys just from home give a deplorable account of the sentiments of the people in Ala. & also in Georgia & So. Ca. Every body whipped & despairing of our cause:—wanting peace on any terms, reunion, submission—anything. How shameful! I hope it is only a temporary fit of despondency caused by the disastrous campaign of Hood, the bold & well nigh unopposed march of Sherman, and the utter demoralization of our (Hood's) army down there, and that the words of cheer from our noble President and the spirit of renewed determination showing itself in the people of this noble old state, & in this army, will arouse a similar spirit throughout our whole country. As the Athenian orator said—"It is with the Gods to *give* success, but with mortals to *deserve* it."

HB: Aleck McCall came to town today. Miss Liza Simms is to marry tonight, was invited, but owing to a bad cold. I have declined going out.

McD: Quiet on the lines today. Clear and cold.

February 10, Friday

SP: Our Brig. passed a series of very patriotic resolutions to-day, declaring that we would never lay down our arms till our independence is gained, etc. etc.

McD: Quiet on the lines today. Clear and cold.

February 11, Saturday

SP: We expected to be relieved this morning by another Brig. but it has been deferred. I had a literary love-feast on letters from home, to-day—one from Mama, one from Jamie, two from Mary & one from Lou. I was perfectly delighted, & took a long time in reading them over. Wrote a very hasty letter to Mama just before night by Capt. Pickett, who was just starting to Ala. Sherman has again out the R.R. 28 miles N.W. from Branchville, So. Carolina.

McD: Quiet on the lines today. Clear and cold.

February 12, Sunday

SP: The weather is very cold & windy a perfect gale blowing constantly. I am sorry we have had some desertions from our Brig. this past week. Three men left the 6th Ala. a few nights since, & one from the 61st went last night.

McD: Quiet on the lines today. Clear and cold.

February 13, Monday

SP: More deserters: 3 or 4 scoundrels from the 12th Ala. went over last night. Our Brig. returned to Camp Rodes this morning, having been relieved by Grimes'

Brig. Yesterday was said to be the coldest day of the season in Richmond; & the weather is still intensely cold.

McD: Relieved today and returned to our winter quarters. We were kept on picket for more than two weeks. Our division was sent on the right and there was no one to relieve us.

February 14, Tuesday

SP: Lt. Christian is putting up a tent on a body of logs—this will make the 5ᵗʰ building in our Co. There were a good many orders read out on dress-parade this evening. We are to have 4 roll calls daily:—viz.—reveille—12 O'clock retreat & tattoo. We are to drill too, each battalion as a Company.

McD: Quiet in our quarters at old camp. Very cold.

February 15, Wednesday

SP: Lot M. Wilder came in to-day from the Hospital, where he spends most of his time. We had to cut our ditches larger & had a tough job of it, as the ground is frozen hard as adamant & had to be worked with the pick & axe, as if it had been rock or marble.

McD: Quiet in our quarters at old camp. Rain all day.

February 16, Thursday

SP: Maj. Whiting—Divis. Inspector—has threatened to report our Regt. for having neglected policing—so Capt. Riley has had us hard at work most all day enlarging the ditches in front and rear of our houses. Orders to "be ready to move at moment's warning" were recd. in the afternoon, but it did not stop our work. We are positively forbid[den] the use of any more wood on the tract of land & now have to *toat* all we use nearly a ¼ of a mile. I am tired—completely broke down by the work I've done to-day in the way of policing & getting wood. The "Enquirer" to-day has a long & able speech made by Mr. Dejarnette of Va. in support of resolutions introduced by him on the subject of the "Monroe Doctrine" & an alliance offensive & defensive between the United States & Confederate States on that basis. It was made pending the conference between our Commissioners & the Yankees' recently in Hampton Roads. Carberry & MᶜDiarmid went off on detail before day. They are to work on road or on breastworks down on the right of our lines.

McD: Quiet in our quarters at old camp. Rain. Some thunder.

February 17, Friday

SP: Mr.————Lyles from the 43ᵈ Ala. who exchanged with Mr. Speed, reported to our Co. to-day. We made a good swap for L. is a stout ablebodied man. I am on guard to day and am acting Lt. & officer of the guard, as so few Comm. Officers are present that a Lieut. can not be had every day. We are excused from duty to-night—thanks to a little shower that came on about dark. The bill for consolidating Regts. Battalions etc. has at last passed. A meeting of the officers was held in our Regt. yesterday evening to find out their views on the subject of taking negroes into the army, & if they thought the negroes would be most effective in separate organizations or mixed in with ours as recruits. Commanders of Companies then went around to learn the opinion of the men: & I think it was generally believed that negroes would do better service thrown in with the whites, but they did not like the idea; however, anything rather than subjugation by the Yankees, & they are willing to submit to any measures deemed necessary to prevent it.

McD: Quiet in our quarters at old camp. Rain and sleet.

NOTE: The subject of arming slaves was broached as early as August 1863 in Greensboro and raged throughout the plantation region of Alabama in 1864 and early 1865, a subject covered in *Guarding Greensboro*. Following support by Robert E. Lee, the Confederate Congress finally approved the use of slaves as soldiers and the measure became law on March 13.

February 18, Saturday

SP: I wrote a letter to Icha last night in answer to the one received from him a few days ago, & sent it by Jim Eustis, who left for Ala this morning. Had more work to do to-day—ditching between the houses. Bad news from So. Car. Columbia has been evacuated by our forces. About 10 O'clock to-night a volley of musketry was fired down on Gen! Pickett's line & skirmishing afterwards which made us all very uneasy, as we were expecting every minute to get marching orders.

McD: Quiet in our quarters at old camp. Clear and warm.

February 19, Sunday

SP: This is a bright mild & delightful day—such a one as we used to hail with joy, as the welcome herald of approaching Spring. But now how different is it! for we can't enjoy pleasant weather, knowing that it will, in all probability, bring on active movements & bloody collisions between the confronting armies. Mr. Curry preached a sermon to-day for the first time in the new Chapel. His text was from———. He also organized a Bible class which I intend to join. He preached again to-night—text from Psalms.

McD: Quiet in our quarters at old camp. Clear and warm.

February 20, Monday

SP: The "Examiner" has the official report of Gen. Jos. E. Johnston of the operations of the Tenn. Army while under his command; from Decr. 1863 at Dalton, Ga. to July 18th near Atlanta. It is a good document and confirms every one in this opinion that the removal of Gen. J. was a most unfortunate affair & injurious to our cause.

McD: Quiet in our quarters at old camp. Clear and warm.

February 21, Tuesday

SP: Maj. Blackford who has been reinstated, arrived in Camp to-night & as soon as it was known the majority of the Regt. turned out & cheered him heartily. Charleston was evacuated last Tuesday & Columbia was occupied by Sherman on Friday, last. I trust to the Lord that his successful career will soon be brought to a close.

McD: Quiet in our quarters at old camp. Cool today.

February 22, Wednesday

SP: Two hours before day we got orders to cook one day's rations & be ready to move. Col. Pickens returned from home yesterday & I went over to see him this morning. He is in fine health but the wound in his hand is still running & he will never have the use of it. He takes command of the Brig. to-day. After policing nearly all day which has been the case with us for the past week, we recd. orders about sundown to cook 2 days' rations & be prepared to abandon our Camp permanently to-morrow morning at 5½ o'clock. "Twas ever thus" in the army! and we've been looking for it ever since we have been here.

McD: Quiet in our quarters at old camp. Cloudy.

February 23, Thursday

SP: We were all up an hour & a half before day—got breakfast & everything ready, & just at dawn moved off. Marched down near Petersburg—turned more to right and crossed the Appomattox on a Pontoon-bridge 1½ miles from P. Then kept along the South-Side R.R. to Southerland's station where we camped in a very nice piece of oak woods.* The roads were very bad & we had twice as much baggage as we can well get along with, & being our first march it went hard with us. I suffered terribly, but managed to keep up. Passed Gen. Lee's Hd-qrs.—south of the Appomattox. Left John at Camp Rodes with the surplus blankets, clothing, etc. of my mess. Out of the 27 men present with the Co. (& our comm. officer), there remained in Camp Lt. Christian; 5 men sick—viz. Briggs, Carberry, Clifton, Hutchinson, Sellers, & 1 man to guard the baggage—McCrary; 1 man on work detail—McDiarmid; 1 man gone to Richmond on 2 days' pass—Waddell; marched out in the Co. 19 men—viz. Sergt. Wynne, comd'g Co., Corpl. Pickens, Bayley, Childress*, Farrier, Geddie, Hagins acting Regt. Commissary Sergt., Idom, Sr., Long, Lyles, Price, Sheldon, Sims, Warren, Wesson, Wilder, Youngblood, J. B., Youngblood, J. L., *Elias? Louis.

*Marched about 15 miles to-day.

McD: Got orders to be ready to move at a moments notice. Left camp at day light. Moved to the right of line and stoped near Sutherland station on the S.S. R.R. Had rain all day. The roads are quite muddy and marching is very disagreeable. Camp at Sutherland station late in the evening.

February 24, Friday

SP: It rained all night & has turned colder. Every one is entirely in the dark in regard to this move, our destination etc. Some think we will remain somewhere down here on the extreme right, while others think we are bound for N. Carolina to meet Sherman. Nous verrons.

McD: Still in camp at Sutherland station. Wet and disagreeable weather.

February 25, Saturday

SP: I was detailed & had charge of six men last night to guard 4 wagons loaded with officers' baggage, cooking utensils, forage, etc. Had a good deal of trouble finding the wagons & getting wood to make a fire as we were detailed after night. The "on dit" now is that arrangements are being made for the evacuation of Petersburg. That all ordnance stores are being removed, and that the tobacco & other things have been piled for burning. That this is done in order to straighten our lines, which will now run from Drewry's Bluff straight down in this direction. It is said also, that Sherman has reached Charlotte, N.C.

McD: Quiet in camp. Still raining.

February 26, Sunday

SP: It rained all day yesterday & most all last night. It is rumored this morning that our Corps is to be sent to South-Western Virginia. To-day were issued rations of flour, bacon, salt, *sugar, coffee* and *whiskey*—quite a treat; not the whiskey particularly, but flour instead of meal, & the sugar & coffee. The whiskey made a great many lively & in high spirits, and some got drunk and were noisy. Several men of our Brigade in the act of stealing corn or meal from a mill last night were set upon by a party of citizens & had to jump into the Mill pond to make their escape. One of Co. "B" Johnson was shot in the face with small shot.

McD: Quiet in camp. Still raining. Under orders.

February 27, Monday

SP: Last night 37 men deserted the 45th N.C. Regt. & at 10 O'clock this morning the drums were beat for roll-call, & at the same time Lieut. with a squad started in pursuit. Some men supposed to be from this Brig. charged the Depot last night to get some boxes of provisions belonging to some N. Carolinians who were guarding them, & when this fact was reported to Genl. Grimes together with the desertion of the "tar-heels", he was much excited & troubled & said to Maj. Peyton "What shall I do! *my* men are all deserting & the Alabamians are stealing every thing!" Our Brig. moved about a mile to a nice Camping ground where there is plenty of good oak wood & water convenient. The Camp was laid off in regular order—by Divisions (2 Cos.), perpendicular to the Color line, & we made pretty comfortable bunks—log pens filled with leaves & covered over with our little tents.

McD: We left our camp and moved a short distance and formed a regular camp. Clear.

February 28, Tuesday

SP: Wilmington has been evacuated & was occupied by the Yankees on 22nd. Gen. Wade Hampton burnt his handsome residence in Columbia when our forces fell back from there. We had a rumor last night that Sherman had been badly defeated, his wagon train & 8000 prisoners captured. This is only an example of the many wild & truthless rumors that we hear any time.

McD: Rain today. Quiet in camp. Drew rations of brandy. Quite a jolly time in camp.

March 1, Wednesday

SP: I sat till bed time with Col. Pickens & Lt. Geo. Dunlap of 3rd Ala. now acting A. A. Gen. We had some pretty songs by Lt. D. & a hot whiskey punch, which was very nice indeed. The weather cloudy & right cold. March is not coming in as much "like a lion" as it sometimes does. I wrote hurriedly to Jamie to night & gave the letter to a paroled prisoner going to Ala. Had to write by the light of our Camp fire—seated on the ground—a very uncomfortable way.

McD: Still quiet in camp. Cloudy but not raining. Warm

March 2, Thursday

SP: It has rained the livelong day, & the coldest rain I ever felt, it seems to me. Meal, bacon, sugar, coffee, smoking & chewing tobacco were issued to-day. We are getting Coffee & sugar pretty regularly since leaving W. Quarters, & it does help out wonderfully.

McD: Still quiet in camp. Very hard rain today.

March 3, Friday

SP: Jack Wynne, Sims, Price, Henry Childress, Mr. Idom & others sat us late at my fire last night talking over the war & the battles we have been in, the marches we have taken etc., & on dispersing to go to bed unanimously expressed the wish that the war was over & we were all talking these things over at *Home.* Whiskey was issued again to-day. Col. Hobson requires Commanders of Cos. to see each man drink his ration in his presence; & if a man gives his whiskey to a friend the Co. Commander takes charge of it & will not allow the recipient to take a second drink under an hour from the time of the first. This order was issued in consequence of so many men in the Regt. & throughout Brig. getting tight last Sunday.

McD: Still quiet in camp. Raining still.

March 4, Saturday

SP: This is a grand gala day in Washington City. Old Abe with much pomp & parade is being reinaugurated President of the United States (?) & enters upon his 2$\underline{nd}$ term of four years. During the forepart of the day it rained steadily, so that guard was not mounted till 2 or 3 P.M. I am on in charge of 2$\underline{nd}$ relief, which consists of 15 men, now that we have Brigade guard. Bad news comes to us from the Valley. It is said that Sheridan has captured Staunton & Charlottesville & is marching on Lynchburg. Also that Gen. Early was killed.

McD: Still quiet in camp. Raining still.

March 5, Sunday

SP: They are very strict with the guard duty now, & have it done according to—not Hoyle, but Hardee. I had to stay all night at the Guard fire, & consequently got no sleep. We had a sermon from Mr. Curry to-day. Lieut. Christian & Ed Hutchinson have come in & bring some War news: viz. that Hampton has whipped Kilpatrick & captured 8000 prisoners & that Sherman is in full retreat for Charleston! I trust it prove true! Gen. Early was not killed, but himself & staff captured.* The papers are not permitted to publish any war news.

*Early was not captured—"saved himself by flight." His staff & 1250 men were taken prisoner. No. cannon & wagons lost.

McD: Still quiet in camp. Clear and pleasant.

March 6, Monday

SP: Last night was very cold & there was an uncommonly heavy frost. To-day is beautifully clear & bright. We have pulled down all of our tents & put our blankets out to dry. We've also policed Camp—swept up the leaves & set fire to the piles, & have been almost smoked out of quarters. They will burn & smoke all day & night at least.

McD: Still quiet in camp. Clear and pleasant.

March 7, Tuesday

SP: No events worthy of record transpired in Camp to-day.

McD: Still quiet in camp. Clear and pleasant.

March 8, Wednesday

SP: Last night a band of 2 violins, 2 flutes, a banjo, triangle & bones gotten up amongst the drummers & mail carriers, gave a benefit to Brigade Hd-qrs. A large crowd was attracted by the music—which was pretty good. The weather for several days past has been so dry & pleasant that every one is expecting Gen. Grant to make an advance. We can't enjoy pleasant weather now-a-days.

McD: Still quiet in camp. Rain.

March 9, Thursday

SP: An order from Gen. Grimes assuming permanent command of this Division was read at dress parade. It was a first rate thing & was very complimentary Gen. Rodes, Gen. Battle & this Brigade. We had our first lesson to-day in tactics. John Christian has been selected to instruct & drill all the noncommissioned-officers in our Regiment. A few days ago—on the 5th I think—Sims was lanced Corporal & I Sergt.

McD: Still quiet in camp. Rain.

March 10, Friday

SP: This is the day appointed by the President as one "of fasting, humiliation & prayer with thanksgiving". Gen. Lee has ordered all duty as far as possible to be suspended & requests that all chaplains hold religious services & that all unite in a proper observance of the day. A cold rain lasting most all day tho' has prevented public worship.

McD: Still quiet in camp. Sleet and rain.

March 11, Saturday

SP: I wrote Willie on the 9th inst. but have not met with any one going to Ala. by whom to send the letter. I've been reading tactics to-day & also "Macaria". M—— is a very interesting novel; the characters tho', I think, are over-drawn. I read "Heaven & Earth" the other day, which has been torn out of a copy of Byron: Would that I had his entire works. Gen Bragg has gained a victory over a force of Yankees at Kinston N.C. which was moving on Goldsboro' from Newbern. He captured 1500 prisoners & 6 pieces of artillery.

McD: Still quiet in camp. Cool today.

NOTE: Sam's brother Jamie was reading Evans' *Macaria* a year before.

Lord Byron, *Heaven and Earth* (1821).

March 12, Sunday

SP: We were much surprised by getting orders to move 2 hours before day, and started before light. Marched on the R.R. from Sutherland's Station towards Petersburg. After going some six miles, the order, I suppose, was countermanded & we about faced & returned to Camp. I was detailed to take charge of 3 prisoners at Guard fire, & in the evening when Brigade guard was put on, I took charge of 1$\underline{st}$ relief. 'Twas Sims' time—Jack Wynne's mistake.

Marched from Suth[er]land's Station, on R.R. towards Petersburg 6 ms. and back—Weighed our baggage & found Mr. Idom's load was 67 lbs, M$\underline{c}$Diarmid's 47 lbs & mine 36 lbs!!

McD: Got orders to move this morning at day light. Got ready and began to march in the direction of Petersburg. Went up the Rail Road some eight or ten miles. Halted and faced about and returned to our old camp. Got orders to cook a days rations as soon as we returned. Still under orders.

NOTE: The paragraph beginning "Marched from Suth . . ." was written on the last page of Sam's previous journal. This along with loose scraps of paper suggest that he wrote drafts of his diary when paper and time allowed.

March 13, Monday

SP: At 12 or 1 P.M. we struck tents & marched. Proceeded over R.R. to within 6 miles of P. & turned off to the left to avoid being seen from Grant's observatories: afterwards got on R.R. again & kept it as far as Appomattox, when we turned off on road & went within a mile of town, then zig-zagged 2 or 3 miles it seemed to me & found ourselves entering the suburbs on Boydtown plank road. Passed near the "Model farm", & about 10 o'clock reached the lines at Jerusalem plank road & relieved Bushrod Johnson's Division. we came about———miles, & as most of the way was on the R.R. it completely broke us down; I suffered terribly. It was after a good deal of delay that we got our position in the trenches & then one third of the men were required to be up on guard.

McD: Remained in camp till 12 o'clock. We then fell in and started up the Rail Road again. Left the railroad and marched under cover of the woods. Got up to Petersburg after dark. Marched round about for several hours and came at last to the Breast Works. Relieved a Brigade or portion of one of Johnson's Division. Considerable sharp shooting on the line.

March 14, Tuesday

SP: I got very little sleep last night, but how sweet that was. The country around here is very open & level—sandy land; and the scenery is very picturesque. The land is dug up in every direction as far as we can see: there is our line of work, the Yankee line, the two intermediate picket lines—fortified—& then every hill top & elevated place is crowned with artillery. The duty is heavy here: one third of the men (left) are required to be up in the works during the night, & ¼ of them are out on the picket line. After dark we moved some distance to the left. It is dangerous to raise your head above the works after dark for the pickets keep up a constant firing all night & the minnies are whizzing over making every kind of sound imaginable—sometimes like a bird flying—a dog howling—a cat squalling, meat frying, etc. etc. Had a good joke on Sheb. Chadwick for stooping & dodging while passing the tent where a fellow was frying meat—thinking it was a Minnie.

McD: We find ourselves stationed in the Ditches about two miles from Petersburg. We find the duty very severe. More than one third of the men are kept on picket and they are not allowed to sleep neither day or night. One third of the men in the ditches are kept with accoutrements on and their guns near them. The pickets keep up a constant [. . .] all night but are friendly in the day time. Would keep up a constant traffic if permitted. Moved a few yards to the right after night.

March 15, Wednesday

SP: The weather has been cloudy & very windy to-day. Moved some 200 yards to the left after night—but 'twas a long time before we got settled as we kept getting too far to the left & vice versa. We were completely worn out by it, & one poor fellow, W$^{\underline{m}}$ Rayford of Co. G was shot through the head & killed.

McD: Remained quiet till after dark. Then moved a few hundred yards to the left. Had a man killed in the woods by a ball from the picket line.

March 16, Thursday

SP: It rained most all of last night. I had the 2$^{\underline{nd}}$ relief of ⅓ of the men, & was up from 11:30 P.M. till 2:30 this morning. We moved back about 20 yds. to the right to-day. The wind blew very hard & it rained occasionally. Late in the afternoon we *again had to move* to the left several hundred yards. It seems we will never get settled!

McD: Had rain today. All is quiet on the lines.

March 17, Friday

SP: There was a hard blow & heavy rain last night. Weather clear & cool today. It took my mess two turns apiece to bring all of our plunder from where we last moved—we had picked up so many little conveniences such as jugs, bottles, tin cans, tub, etc.

McD: Still quiet on the lines. Very windy.

March 18, Saturday

SP: We have a very good position on the lines now (our Co.) and are well protected by the breast works, traverses etc. In making their bunks, huts &c

the soldiers have dug up the ground along the works any & *every* way: having no care for order, regularity or looks, but entirely for safety & security from Yankee missiles. After sun down one of the mortar batteries near us opened on the Yankee lines & they replied. The shelling lasted about 1½ hours & was a very pretty sight indeed. We could see the burning fuses flying through the air like meteors, and sometimes we would send 5 shells up together. Mortar shells have the appearance of moving very slowly. Our guns beat the Yankees' badly.

McD: Remained quiet till late in the evening. Shelling began from mortars which lasted several hours. But little damage.

March 19, Sunday

SP: This has been a lovely day—one of the prettiest we have had this year. Had preaching by Mr. Brooks, brother-in-law of Mr. Long.

McD: Very quiet on the line today. Quite a beautiful day.

March 20, Monday

SP: I am on picket to-day—also Charlie Briggs, Henry Childress & others. At the point where our Co. pickets the lines run within 40 or 50 yds. of each other & it looks strange to see foes so near each other, & at the same time so free and easy—walking about or sitting up on the works. Altho' we have orders forbidding all communication, still whenever the men get an opportunity they will talk and trade with the Doodles. For a piece of tobacco you can get from the Yanks a "jack knife", pipe, pocket book, looking glass or anything of the kind they happen to have. H.C. exchanged papers & got a late Herald, & in it were rolled some circulars offering inducements to our men to desert. They call us "Johnnies". Our batteries kept up a slow fire to-day trying to burn a large white house over to the left of us on which the Yankees have a signal station, but they did not succeed. From 5 P.M. till night the firing on both sides was quite spirited. We could easily see the mortar shells, which look like india rubber balls.

McD: Some shelling today.

March 21, Tuesday

SP: We had a slow rain lasting from 11 O'clock till night & then set in raining very hard. I feel completely used up after sitting up all last night on picket & going half-bent along the line visiting the posts under my charge. *Tues. 21ˢᵗ.* Yesterday I had the happiness of receiving a letter from my dear Mama. It was brought through by Lieut. J. Ed. Webb, & was dated Febr. 28ᵗʰ, and was the first news I've had from home since 21ˢᵗ Jan. They've been writing by mail, but none of the letters have reached me. Ed bro't the news of Miss Bettie Wynne's marriage to Maj. Webster, Robt. Waller to a Miss Vaughan of Tuscaloosa. Mama enclosed $500 in my letter which is very acceptable as we have not been paid off since last Novr. Lewis Elias or Elias Lewis deserted to the Yankees on picket last night. He is no loss as he was of no account.

McD: Hard rain today. Quiet on the line.

March 22, Wednesday

SP: The wind blew a perfect gale to-day making it almost impossible to keep our tents up. I hope the Yankee fleets are catching it. The Non-Commissioned Officers of our Regt. were examined to-day by a board composed Co. Hill of the 61$\underline{st}$, Capt. Ross of the 12$\underline{th}$, & Capt. Riley of the 5$\underline{th}$. Jack Wynne says they gave him a rigid examination & he is right uneasy lest they pitch him.

McD: Very windy today. Quiet on the line.

March 23, Thursday

SP: I am on picket again to-day. It gets me every third day. A very high wind has prevailed all day, which blew up such a dust & smoke that at times you could not see any distance scarcely. There has been such a smoke down on the right that some suppose it was made by the Yankees to cover a movement of troops.

McD: Very windy today. Quiet on the line.

March 24, Friday

SP: Hard wind blew hard all first part of day. Cloudy & cold this evening. [. . .] much used up after my tour picket, tho' I can't sleep much in day time. Shelling is an every day business here.

McD: Very windy today. Quiet on the line.

March 25, Saturday

SP: Last night S. Shooters our Brig. order out dark etc. at 1 A.M. Brig order up with arms & accoutrements & 1 blanket leaving everything else in Camp & immediately marched. 9 guns & 8 mortar, 3 brass brot off. returned at 10 o'clock.

McD: Was ordered out at 2 o'clock this morning. Not allowed to take anything but one blanket. Moved about a mile to the left and made an attack on a fort in the Yankee line. Captured the fort with about six hundred prisoners. We held the fort for several hours but the Yankees concentrated their Artillery on us and made it necessary for us to withdraw from the fort. Lost some prisoners ourselves. We fell back and went to our same position.

NOTE: Confederate forces under Major General John Gordon succeeded in capturing Fort Stedman but were then driven back.

March 26, Sunday

SP: On Picket to-day. Got permission fr. Lt. Flowers to go up to quarters & wrote a letter to my dear sister Mary telling her of battle, &c. & my safety & good health. Sent it over by Waddell, who came over to see us, to Mr. [. . .] our chaplain who is staying at the wagon & who will start to Ala. to-morrow & carry our letters through.

McD: Quiet in the Ditches today. Rain.

March 27, Monday

SP: Very cool morning—white frost. We are required all hands to get up & get under arms at 4½ [. . .], but since fight we've got up at 3 in case of emergency. A ⅓ or more of the men are on our Picket line, then a guard kept on parapet day and night & ⅓ men in works are made to wear accoutrements during the day &

sleep in them near [. . .] at night. Thus the duty is very hard, but we are willing to do it if we are allowed to remain & hold this line & have no marching to do. Whilst very drowsy about that hour, etc. I was roused by Willie & Farris having a fight on picket.

McD: Quiet in the Ditches today. Clear

March 28, Tuesday

SP: This being most mild still & by far most pleasant day we have had in a coon's age—I took advantage of it & wrote a letter to my dear little Loutie as I'd heard of opportunity of sending it—& also answered Chas. Williams' kind note recd. some days since. Col. Pickens sent for me to-night & made me a kind & flattering offer of ———. I am afraid I am not competent to fill it, as I told him & besides did not like to go to another Regt. & accept a place which some of its members might expect. Told him however, I'd think about it. just after dark time for picket firing to begin, heard sudden volley—& very heavy firing last a minute or 2 wh. all thought must have been an attack, but learned afterwards it was caused by our men opening on several deserters from 12$\underline{th}$ Ala. who went over. Don't see how they survived the fire. Considerable shelling over our Brigade to-day.

McD: Considerable shelling today.

March 29, Wednesday

SP: On Picket to-day with Bob Price, Bill Sheldon, Clifton, Farrier, Liles & Sellers. I sent my letter to Loutie by Sergt. Marvin Co. K. who started home on retired papers this morng. Mailed my letter to Chas. Wilborn. Spent sometime in writing up my diary to-day as I had gotten behind hand in it—owing to the unusually disagreeable weather we've had—cold, rainy, or windy—with brief intermissions ever since I've been here in trenches.

McD: Very quiet today. Pleasant day. Had some excitement about dark. The pickets began to fire more rapidly than usual. Fell in with guns in our hands.

NOTE: With twice the manpower, Grant's Army of the Potomac moved against Lee's Army of Northern Virginia in this, the opening of the Appomattox campaign.

March 30, Thursday

SP: Last night about 10 Oclk all of a sudden a tremendous shelling broke out on our left about river & immediately heavy volley of musketry which ran down picket line & was taken up by us & Yanks in our front in hot style for a few seconds & subsided. We were very much startled & thought at first Yanks were making general attack. The shelling on left wh. was from mortars continued 1½ or 2 hrs. & was a grand sight—far surpassing any pyrotechnics I've ever beheld. Sometimes 15 or 20 blazing shells would be in air at once—crossing each other & some constantly exploding had the appearance of a grand [. . .] of lightning bugs & fireflies (a swarm of) 2 large mortars near us made some beautiful shots. It rained most all night & till late to-day. our picket posts are very uncomfortable, little raised up huts & as ours leaked we spent a very disagreeable

& wearisome night. These nights spent on picket, where are constantly on watch & not permitted to close an eye during the 10 hours of darkness, fr. 7 P.M. till 5 A.M. seem longer than any I ever saw any how. Picked up 2¾ lbs. lead in few minutes this morning artil. [. . .] tossing up in blankets.

McD: Quiet in the front today. Heard cannonading on the right. Had rain.

March 31, Friday

SP: Rained till 10 or 11 O'clk. then cleared off & became windy which dried the ground very fast. Could hear cannonading on right most all day yesterday & some this morning. Cold, wet, nasty weather for fighting. Sheridan's cavalry & his [. . .] those that we are fighting on right trying to get possession of S.S. R.R. They were at Dinwiddie C.H. Wed. 2 days ago. We saw the column passing in rear Yankee works some days since. Grant claims to have killed, wounded & captured 2,700 of our men in fight last Sat. morning: more men than we carried in!! Dried, compressed, desicated cabbage issued to us to-day—It makes pretty good soup or stew.

McD: Quiet in front all day.

NOTE: "S.S. R.R." is the South Side Railroad.

April 1, Saturday

SP: On picket with same squad fr. our Co. we had Wed. Some excitement in Regt. occasioned by one of 6ᵗʰ Ala. coming over & getting into a fight with Johnson Co. "A", effects of bust head, tangle foot whiskey issued this morng. Yanks threw 3 shells at our pickets coming down this morning one of wh. passed thro' ranks of 61ˢᵗ Ala, but strange to say no damage was done. This is retaliation for our artillery shelling theirs a little for last day or 2. Accounts in papers of fighting down on right since Tues. last state we repulsed advances of Yankees on Boydton P.R. & towds SS. RR. with severe loss to them in some of the charges. We captured 5 or 600 prisoners, but results not positively known. Grant, Meade & Sheridan said to have been on field with 4,000 men. I trust we'll be able to whip them. Sherman at Goldsboro halting to rest, clothe & shoe his army. Very sorry to see death of Jno. M. Daniels late editor, Examiner whose funeral took place in Richmd last evening. He was a gifted, far seeing man & a most able editor. We had to move 100 yds or so to left & regret very much as we leave a very good & safe position to go to unsafe & miserable one. Went up & got dinner, Dodgers Cabbage, soup & stewed fruit—& brot down some wood & water, bread & coffee for us on picket to-night.

McD: Pleasant day. Quiet in front. Some fighting on the right. After night shelling began on our left and came up the line till we were in the midst of it. Continued all night.

NOTE: "Boydton P.R. & towds SS. RR." stands for "Boydton Plank Road & towards South Side Railroad."

April 2, Sunday

SP: "Who can tell what a day bring forth?" How little did I think yesterday that to-day I should be a prisoner of war in hands of the Yankees. About 11 O'clock P.M.

McD: When the first streaks of gray was appearing in the east Yanks made a heavy charge on our works in front of our Brigade and carried the works with apparent ease. The men were posted at the distance of ten paces apart in the works and could offer but feeble resistance to the dense colums of Yanks that was opposing us. Our brave little Regiment continued till the last but was finally overpowered. We killed more than double our numbers before we were forced to surrender. The most of our regiment was captured. I found one hundred and fifteen in the rear where I was carried. Was captured about sun rise and then carried to the Hd. Qrs. of the 9th Corps where we remained the ballance of the day and all night. The enemy was fighting very hard on the right and had captured the works down there.

NOTE: Before five in the morning, Union troops had advanced along the Petersburg lines and taken the Confederate defenders, including the Greensboro Guards. By midafternoon the remaining Confederate troops were ordered to evacuate Petersburg, retreat through Richmond, and meet the rest of the Army of Northern Virginia at Amelia Courthouse. The government left that evening and Union troops occupied both Petersburg and Richmond the next day. Pickens and the other Greensboro Guards were being held at Point Lookout, Maryland, a federal prison on low land seventy miles southeast of Washington where the Potomac River flowed into the Chesapeake.

April 3, Monday

McD: Started early this morning to march to City Point. Distance eight miles. Arrived at City Point about ten o'clock. Got aboard the steamer John Brooks. Shoved off from the shore where we remained till after dark. Twelve hundred prisoners was on this Boat. After dark we began to go down the river. Passed quite a host of transports and ships of war. Drew rations after night, being the first we had gotten since captured.

April 4, Tuesday

SP: Landed 2 or 3 P.M. Divided into Cos. about 100 each—names taken searched & marched into the enclosure = ———— acres plankfence 15 ft. high. Took tents, oilcloths & all blankets ex. 1 I hid my knife in one sock & my pocket spoon in other, old letters in shirt pockets & Portfolio down my back. $300 Ala money sewed in lining pants—& 40 Confed. in lining hat. So nothing taken from us. One of Co. H [. . .] gave up 10 gold pieces = which he'll never see again.

McD: Some time last night we stoped in the lower part of the river. Started off this morning early. Passed Fortress Monroe about eight o'clock. Arrived at Point Lookout Md at three o'clock in the evening. Had our names registered and was introduced to the prison pen by dark.

April 5, Wednesday

SP: Aroused by ½ min. guns firing salute in honor of capture Richmd & 13000 men & some say capture of Lee & Staff & also of Jeff Davis. Rumor that 20000 men refused to follow Gen. Lee out Richmd—that our scattered & Yanks picking the men up in woods—Lynchburg burnt by Thomas. Of course we dont believe things are ½ so bad as they represent them. God forbid it! Yankees say war as good as over. Sherman promises to disband army in 3 mos. We'll never hear any thing reliable while in prison. Large squad who took oath & sent to Wash'ton sent back. Put up tents 60 in Co. F, 4$\underline{th}$ Div. Sheb, Sergt. Comdg., Sims, sick sergt. A Yank corpl. has comd of each Div = 1000 to 12000 men. Mid day drew ½ loaf bread & small mackeral—raw & no fire, no wood to be had in Camp. So hungry ate it raw & some bacon we had left. Captured Sund. morng. this 2$\underline{nd}$ time had anything to eat. Laboring under all disadvantages we treat prisoners better than that. Met Mr. Alf. Glover—brother to Walton & Terry, Sims found brother Frank too fr. Johnson's army. Some men are very comfortably fixed in frame houses made of cracker boxes & dont wish to be exchanged. Some carrying on pie making—ring making etc. & living well. Great deal trade & traffic in small way going on. Some peddling Coffee, bread, crackers, fish, clothing—wood anything [. . .] to make yank little money. Pumps always crowded. miserable water—mineral, sweet, chalybeate.

NOTE: "Chalybeate" means impregnated or flavored with iron.

McD: *What I Saw and Heard at Point Lookout*

It was late in the evening when I was introduced to prison camp. Denominated the "Bull Pen." It is an enclosure of about twenty acres. It is enclosed by a wall of planks set upright. The planks are about twelve feet long. On the outer side of the wall is a platform four feet from the top of the wall upon which the sentinel walks. I was somewhat disappointed in the appearance of the camp. I expected to find more accomodations for the prisoners. Some old prisoners who have been in prison for years seem to be comfortably situated. They had made for themselves small houses out of Cracker-Boxes and are living in ease. Our first night we saw nothing for us but the cold damp ground. The next day we got some small tents about large enough to accomodate four men but it was our lot to be cramed in six to ten in a tent. The weather we find tolerable cool and many of the boys are without blankets. We are not allowed any wood to make fires and we have quite a chilly time. We were quite hungry when we came into prison and we were anxious for "grub" time to come. It came at last and when it was issued each man was entitled to a small mackerel and half loaf of bread. We thought it would do for one meal as we thought it was intended for no more. But the fact was it was a whole day's rations. Every day we drew a half loaf bread and a fish or a small bit of pork or beef. We got our meat in the morning, bread about ten o'clock and something called soup about noon. When I got to prison I found in camp about six or more thousand prisoners. The most of them were old prisoners, Many of them had refused to be exchanged. Fresh arrivals of prisoners came in every day untill the pen was *full*. The number of prisoners continued to increase till we had about twenty six thousand or more. It looked awful bad to see so many of our men captured when we knew they were needed so badly in Dixie.

We could hear much that was going on and many things that seemed untrue. We did not feel any great uneasiness till we heard of the surrender of Genl Lee. This we doubted till the last. A salute of two hundred guns were fired in honor of the great Yankee victory. A large sheet of paper containing the correspondence and condition of surrender of Genl Lee. This seemed official and we no longer doubted that Genl Lee had surrendered. It was a gloomy thought to me, but many seemed to enjoy it. I then gave up all for lost and the cause of which I had suffered so much and so long I gave up in despair. My first impulse was that I would never go home again. But after two or three days reflection I concluded that I could bear any thing that my brave comrades had to endure. I can go home or any where else with a good conscience knowing that I have done my duty. My next thought was to know when I should be liberated and upon what terms. We all thought that we would be liberated on parole for some time but it was not long before we gave that up in despair.

In the meantime a card from the commander of the fort was placed on the "Bulletin Board" in camp asking all who would take the oath of Allegiance to the U.S. to report at the clerks office and register their names. Thousands went and registered but none were liberated. The Yankee officials at last told us that it was the only condition upon which any prisoner would be released, that those who refused to take the oath would be retained in prison or be banished. All the men from Battle's Ala Brigade held a meeting and concluded to take the oath. When the day for the whole camp to register came we all registered to take it. Very few, in fact none but foreigners, refused to take the oath under the circumstances. We had heard that the whole Confederate forces had surrendered and we were left without anyone to represent us and every one concluded to act for himself. Every evening we have quite a variety of rumors generally called "grape vine telegraph." Each rumor is in relation to our being released. An order came at last for all who had registered to take the oath before the fall of Richmond to report. This gave encouragement to the whole camp and all were looking for a general call to be made, but we find ourselves again mistaken. We are next to wait for an amnesty proclamation from the President of the U.S. and an order under that proclamation from the Secretary of War for our release.

Time passes slowly and wearily and many are anxiously waiting for the happy moment to come when we shall leave this awful place for our once happy homes. Thousands of different kinds of trades and employments and trafficks are going on daily in camp. Rings and tooth picks are manufactured by many and some elegant looking articles in that line are produced. Manufacturing is not confined to these two articles alone, but almost every thing that material can be obtained for is made here. Prison life has developed mechanical tallent that would have otherwise been lost. All kinds of gaming is carried on here and thousands assemble round the gaming tables. The stakes are various, such as *"greenbacks,"* "Confederate *scrip,"* tobacco, rings, and almost any article owned by the prisoners. The trade is always brisk. Regular shops are kept where tobacco, pies, bread, meat, cakes, beer, and any thing that is to be obtained by the prisoners is for sale. In addition to these there are thousands of regular traders walking through the camps and sitting in most public places with their different articles. The trade is not confined to purchases made but exchanges are made to suit both parties. Almost any hour of the day you can hear someone who is walking the streets, Cry out, "Here's your good coffee for your bread, meat, tobacco, or Green back," or "here is your bread for tobacco," or "here is your soup for your 'Chaw' tobacco." Tobacco seems to be a very *good* curency. It is counted by chews. When any article of little value is offered for sale, the question is soon asked how many "chaws" will you take for it. An order has at last reached the Point and the sick are being released. The work goes on slowly. But it now begins in the camps and five or six hundred take the oath and are released every day.

April 6, Thursday

SP: This seemed to me another very long day as we were in constant hope & expectation during morning of drawing something—but disappointed—never so hungry in my life—almost desperate—felt like revolting. Sheb. sold 25 [. . .] all he had for 50 cts. & took our tent out & treated to pie very nice, delicious— finally late in eveng. got cup soup *(bean)* & 5 or 6 small crackers—wh. seemed best thing in world, we were so completely famished. This is all rations we've drawn to-day. Sheb, Sims, & McDiarmid wrote letters to-day to acquaintances or friends north in hopes of getting few greenbacks to alleviate our condition. Never felt want of money so keenly in my life—never knew the value of it. A little money would do one more benefit here than any place I've ever seen in my life. Slept well last night for first time since Frid. night last. Mosby is said captured transpt ascendg Potomac loaded with rebs.

April 7, Friday

SP: For breakfst we drew a piece of ½ boiled bacon & were expected to have enough crackers left fr. yesterday for brkfst, but very few men had any at all.

About 11 or 12 M. ½ loaf bread, some vinegar & soap issued in eveng, for dinner got cup soup—poor stuff not near so good as yesterday. They are improving tho' not near as much like starvation as heretofore. Carberry stuck up his sign today "Hair cutting & tailorings", but has had no custom[ers] as yet. Rumor that we are to be paroled. Gen. Lee fallen below Dan R. Some Reb. I suppose put on bulletin board Lee captured most 2 Y. Corps utterly defeated them recaptured R. etc. & Johns[t]on whipped Sherman. Sheridan killed. [. . .] Rained in eveng. 600 men said applied for oath. Order issued yest. offering it again. Things not so bad as supposed.

April 8, Saturday

SP: We are getting very tired of this prison life—it is miserable. Never have enough to eat & when that case it makes one restless. It is cold & bleak too, stiff breeze blowing fr. bay. Haven't been comfortable since I've been here. We are terribly worried too by vermin—confeds, gray-backs—lice—yes lice as big as grains wheat and as thick as blackberries & annoy us exceedingly. Haven't been able to have any washing done & 'twill be impossible to get rid of them unless we have clothes boiled & have change. Grant claims 500 pieces cannon captured— all siege pieces & mortars & estimating Gen. Lee's casualties at 40,000.

April 9, Sunday

SP: Inspection of Camp by Maj. A. G. Brady comdt, & Capt. Barnes attended by posse of orderlies, couriers, etc. formed in open order faced to center & Inspectors &c rode thro ranks. Many of us were in hopes of drawing blankets & clothing. Only 2 of 6 in tent have blankets & 2 old things borrowed by Bob Price—happen to have 2 old tents to sleep in. Drew ½ loaf bread & mackerel yest. eveng. for to-day, also got cup soup to-day. Another day brings forth another battalion of rumors—Heard sentinel say they had Gen. Lee so situated that he would be compelled to fight or surrender. 800 men said to have applied to Gen. Hoffman for oath & 3000 gone out more going.

April 10, Monday

SP: Horror of horrors—200 guns fired here this morng. to celebrate surrender of Gen. Lee & army at Burkesv. Sheridan in front with 18000 cav. & Grant pressing rear. Later—all paroled for 3 yrs. officers allowed to carry out side arms & mounted off. their homes. Grand jubilee bands playing Yank doodle & Hail Col. cheering huzzas &c. all off. said to be drunk on strength of it. *Con. Mon 10th.* Lord have mercy on us! How little we expected this! Can it be possible! Rumor this eveng that Virginians will be immediately sent off & that Baltic & Atlantic sent for to carry Alabamians to Mobile next.

April 11, Tuesday

SP: 200 more guns fired at noon for capitulation of Gen. Johnston's army. "One woe doth tred upon another's heels so fast they follow". We can't realize the truth of the astounding events that are transpiring so rapidly—crowding up on us: & we cant believe it either. Weather drizzling & ground very muddy.

Terry came in late in eveng & says another dispatch recd contradicting report of Johnstons surrender.

April 12, Wednesday

SP: Off. report of Grant & correspondence between himself & Gen. Lee on bulletin board relating to Lees surrender at Appomatox Church Sund. 9ᵗʰ Off. gave their parole & Co. & Regt. off. those of their command not to take up arms against the U.S. until properly exchanged. Off. allowed to retain side arms & private horses & baggage, & all to be permitted to go home. Said to-day Johnston fighting like thunder. 1700 men went out & registered for oath yesterday & to be imm. sent away. Much speculation as to our going home & many seem willing to swallow oath & go. I'll wait for parole of course. Had codfish boiled for brkfst but I could not eat mouthful, disgusting. Great deal chuckaluck & Bob Price always at it—gets brkfst & off till night. 1000 Confed. money = 1.50 green backs. Bob gave us nice treat of bread & cheese other eveng & this eveng another of crackers & cheese—1st we've seen good in several years. (Today—4 yrs. ago Beauregard opened on Fort Sumter inauguration of this long bloody & calamitous war.[)] Oh! can it be possible that after all sacrifices made—immolation of so many noble heroes it is not to end in our favor—that we are to lose our independence & be in subjection to the Yankees! God forbid! Tho the end not be attained in the manner we boastingly flattered ourselves it would—viz—our conquering a peace—still if it is thy will, O Lord, deliver us out of the hands of our too powerful enemies & bless us with Independence & Peace!

NOTE: Reportedly Ed Hutchinson was the only Greensboro Guard at Appommatox Court House. Others on detailed service may have witnessed the surrender.

April 13, Thursday

SP: 4th anniversary of fall of Sumter. Some heavy guns fired on gun boats last night & to-day on strength of it we had report that Jeff Davis had surrendered himself & Confed. government. 15 or 20 Johnnies we are told have gone out as clerks to write out paroles. A lot prisoners (new) brot in this eveng—captured on 3ᵈ & carried with Yank army near Burksv. & thence marched back to city—point. Some doubt now Lee's surrender—rumor that he is fighting in 15 mi. Richmd. Bah. Rained last night & drizzled all morning, but cleared towds noon.

April 14, Friday

SP: Last weather quite cold—almost frosted took down tent & sunned ground, blankets etc. & sun became so very hot in middle of day that it was very uncomfortable lying out—this evening getting cold again. About 5,000 more rebs landed at the Point today & large lot brot in. Including those in Parole Camp & Hospital there must be 20,000 men here. I walked out on street in front Cook house—the grand thoroughfare late in eveng & never saw so many rebs crowded together in my life scarcely, & picked up some news Grant & Lee gone to Washington. Va. convention has met & carried state back into Union, & to morrow morning they are going to begin to parole & send Va. soldiers off. Yankees down on Gov.

Billy Smith & want him hung. Beast Butler has made bitter speech in which he holds Jeff. Davis responsible for the rebellion & for all the harsh treatment to their prisoners etc. & says hang him. Men came in say they were captured near high bridge near Farmville & Gen. Lee crossed it and burnt it. Ewells Corps (including Custis Lee's Div.) surrendered there. Army terribly worn out with constant marching & want of food. Gen. Lee making for F. to ration his troops. Brady gone to W. supposed to make arrangements for paroling us. Corp. Squint says papers for parole of 10,000 have been made out.

April 15, Saturday

SP: The flags have been at half-mast all day & we first heard it was for the death of Abe Lincoln, who was assassinated in Theatre last night in Washington city. We were all right uneasy too, lest the Yankees might retaliate on us—as it was said the assassin was thought to be a rebel soldier who had taken the oath. We afterwds were told by Corpl. Squint that twas a mistake about Abe L. & twas Maj. Gen. Baker died—who used to be commandant of this post. In evening, however, news was confirmed that L. being shot by Edwin Booth, tragedian Hamp Thomas—said to have been killed—has turned up a prisoner here—says Lt. Christian captured in fight near Farmville, & Bill Sheldon severely wounded in Shoulder. Sund. eveng (2$\underline{nd}$) in rear of our works near Petersburg. Army fell back that night. Col. Pickens had gone out ahead to get his horse in the country & Col. Hobson was then in command of Brig.

April 16, Sunday

SP: We have it all this morng. Lincoln was killed & his son Bob[,] Seward had his throat cut & speechless (his son and servt. also wounded in his house)—& Andy Johnson's house broke into & attempt made upon his life but failed. Old Squint says the North is aroused & great excitement & indignation prevails: & that whole country will now take up arms & put down Rebellion which might have been done 3 yrs. ago with great saving of life & treasure. 4 P.M. Latest grape is that Maj. Brady has returned from Washington with parole for 22,000 men—wh. is no. prisoners on "The Point". *Sund. 16$\underline{th}$* (Contin.) 5 clerks said to have certainly gone out to assist in paroling & they will begin with Virginians in the morng. "On dit" Andy Johnson & Beast Butler are suspected of being the instigations of Abe Lincoln's murder & that the former has fled fr. Washington & latter been imprisoned. Glover, Sheb, & I walked around late this eveng & found a large crowd of Johnnies on "Broadway" & about Bulletin board, eager to catch some new rumor. Frank Sims & Terry were around this even'g. Yanks have no news fr. Joe Johnston: but say now that Lee acted in bad faith & while surrendering portion of his force, sent the balance (including cavalry) to reinforce Johnston. Our mess is in bad streak of luck & has sustained loss for this place—viz—H. Childress went up with a detail yesterday eveng for Bread & some one stole 3 loaves—so when it was divided out our mess got no bread—not a crumb, & it was to last till dinner time Mond. & to continue the chapter of accidents—for "sorrows come not single spies but in Battalions" when our Co. went up to get soup this eveng about 15 flankers went in with us, & when Sims, Sick Sergt. went to draw the rations of Sick & absent he found there was only 1 coming to the Co.—while 2 of our mess remained in tent—so we had to divide our soup & had but scrap of bread apiece to eat with it. We thought it hard enough to get along when we got our full rations, but now we account it good luck if we don't starve—Dusk P.M. We were so hungry Bob Price has just bought 2 small loaves wh. we devoured with some raw mackerel. I do hope we'll soon be situated that when we are very hungry we can sit down & eat just as much as we want. I eat a plate full of Molasses & a whole loaf of bread right now.

April 17, Monday

SP: This is a clear bright day, but very cold. The crowding, quarreling, squirming & fighting around the Pumps is now broken up, & each Co. is furnished a barrel wh. is filled up early in morning & set out for use of Co. Each Co. has another for a different purpose & an unfortunate mistake was made in our 2 barrels, by a member of the Co. this morning, wh. I fear is likely to occur at any time. Flag still at ½ mast & ½ hour guns fired all day—I suppose Mr. L. internment takes place today—He did not live to enjoy the success which it seems is crowning the efforts of the U.S. under [his] administration has been putting forth against us during the past 4 years. Madam Rumor is less busy to-day than usual & we hear very little from her. It is said L. assassin was J. Wilkes Booth, an Englishman—not Edwin—& that he has not been caught. Mosby refuses to surrender—does not recognize Gen. Lee as including his band—& says he will fight as long as he has a man left. Yanks say they'll hang him. The 17th of——— & the weather is cold enough for Jan. Glover remarked that it was 1st rate weather for killing meat.

April 18, Tuesday

SP: The pleasant rumor of our speedy exchange was in circulation to-day again & Glover was in hopes of getting out as clerk. Several card players were around hunting up Bob Price for a game just after breakfast & he played a short time in our tent—7 up at 5 cts. & 25 cts. a game. He beat the 1st one out of 50 cts. wh. broke him & quit 5 cts. ahead of 2nd. After Bob gets breakfast we rarely ever see anything more of him till "taps". He spends his time at Poker, 7 up & chuckaluck: & always keeps a few Greenbacks on hand, but never gets far ahead of the game. Weather has moderated very much & is quite pleasant to-day. In strolling about Camp for exercise I passed down "Cracker-box row" wh. is the most business street—& was surprised to see how many trades were being carried on by enterprising Rebs—tho laboring under many disadvantages; for instance there were several shops where men were busily engaged making guttapercha rings & putting sets of pearl or of gold or silver, etc. They have glass windows & work tables sitting under it. Then "Boots & shoe shops"—Then fan factories, where they carve very fancy & ingenious fans out of a solid piece of white pine. Then the horse hair vest chains—very neat. At almost every house there was something for sale—bread—molasses, meal, pies, hoecakes, Cod-fish, mackerel, tobacco, etc. 20,785 men in this pen. 26,000 total. *Tues. 18ᵗʰ.* (contin) Some have boards with tobacco cut up in chews for sale. I was amused with some of the signs of which the following are examples—Dream last night & thought to-night.

April 19, Wednesday

SP: No details were allowed to go out to-day, as they say this is a day of fasting humiliation & pra others say that it is because Mr. Lincoln's funeral (services) takes place. Guns were fired fr. 1½ till 2½ P.M. Rumored too that Johns[t]on has surrendered his army on 17ᵗʰ—& Mobile has fallen. Yanks said to be in possession of Mobile, Montgomery & Selma. Also that negroes attempted insurrection in Charleston & tried to kill every male white under 14 yrs, but Yanks put it down. Beach lined yest. & today with men washing clothes & great many were in bathing too. Rice soup last 2 days.

April 20, Thursday

SP: This has been a quiet day—few rumors—except that paroling has certainly commenced at Hospital—one Co. H. our Regt. was paroled to-day, so says one of same Co.—who was out there to-day. Mobile did not surrender, but was carried by assault after a stubborn fight in which Yankee loss was very heavy. Alabamians contested every inch of ground! Hurrah for the Alabamians! Brig. of Negroes were brot.' here yesterday & Yank Corpl. says they are to guard us. These whites—relieved—are to be sent to Washington to be disbanded—others say they are to guard paroled prisoners on way to Dixie. 5 P.M. The fickle breeze has veered & brings bad news—Capt. Barnes Asst. Prov. Mars. who was in here riding around told a man that none of us would be paroled till rebellion was crushed, & Glover just came in with long face to say our bread rations were to be reduced fr. ½ to ⅓ loaf—because too much money in here & want to make men spend it—in purchasing bread fr. sutlers outside.

April 21, Friday

SP: One of the myriad of reports we hear has proven true—negro soldiers were posted on guard on the walls outside this camp to-day—the first cuffeys I ever saw under arms & accoutrements. It is indeed a novel sight to see a buck negro Corps. carry his sable relief around. They are blackest negroes I ever saw—don't look like our negroes. It is humiliating to think of being under such a guard—but really they are about as respectable as Yankees. Yank. papers state that Joe Johnston is in full retreat & pursued by Sherman—that the latter has taken Salisbury with immense quantities of Quarter M. & ordnance stores.

April 22, Saturday

SP: We were awoke this morning at dawn by firing of big guns—15 rounds fired in rapid succession & then ½ hour guns fired all day—on dit for the burial of Mr. Lincoln in Illinois. Had cod-fish for brkfst. of wh. I made out to eat a little, tho' mighty against the grain—'Twas nicely prepared with irish potatoes & black pepper by Sam Lynch—a good cook & an excellent servant. Sheb., Briggs & I went to Bay this eveng. My 1ˢᵗ bath in salt-water. Enjoyed luxury of putting on clean shirt & drawers—wh. I've not had since about 2 weeks previous to my capture. (Glover, Sims, Sheb. Henry & I took a shave to-day—I took my side-whiskers off.) Glover saw account in Y. paper of big fight at Marion, Ala. Roddy commanded, fought 5 hrs. & was whipped. Yanks took Selma & destroyed foundry & all Gov'mt building etc. & then took Montgomery.

NOTE: Pickens is referring to Wilson's raid through Alabama. Although Forrest's troops came through Marion, east of Greensboro, no battle occurred there.

April 23, Sunday

SP: Had usual weekly inspection this morning about 10 O'clock. The day passed off quietly & almost destitute of rumors—something remarkable. Weather quite wintry—cold wind blowing which kept us pretty close in tents & wrapped in blankets.

April 24, Monday

SP: Clear bright day & still cold in morning & evening, but sun hot at mid-day—unhealthy. Published in Washington papers that 22,000 pris. at Pt. Lookout had signed resolutions condemnatory of assassination of Lincoln & sympathising with his family & the U.S. generally. We saw nothing of such resolutions. "On dit" that there are 30 days' rations here & that there are orders that no more be brot here, *"ergo"* we are to be paroled & sent *home* within that time. Yanks say Johnston has surrendered to Sherman—but as twas on basis of peace negotiations—Sherman has been relieved fr. command & U.S. refuse to recognize terms. They say J. gave Thomas severe drubbing—he was flanking & trying to cut him off. Death occurred in our Div. last night—man taken sick in evening & died in night. We've had several like cases—& one man fell dead in street few days ago: one fainted & fell near our tent today. Delicious rumors received to-day—Yank Corp. & a Reb. made bet of 10$.d to-day that before Sat. night next, 5000 men would be paroled fr. this place. I'd rather see it than hear tell of it.

April 25, Tuesday

SP: Sims recd. a letter fr. daughter of Mr. Otto Williams of Williamsport containing $1 wh. small sum she says she sent only because of the risk & uncertainty of its reaching him:—& said she would be happy to send more. Yanks will not give prisoners money, but a "book" on Sutler—with whom he can trade to amt. of funds recd. Sims immediately invested 40 cents in to-bacco & [. . .] I could not participate in the chewing & smoking, yet it did me good to see the other boys enjoying it so much. They have suffered for Tobacco at time since they have been prisoners, & occasionally reduced to necessity of taking quid out & laying it by for a 2ⁿᵈ chewing—& of drying an old chew & smoking it. I deem myself fortunate in not using "the weed". This being a remarkably clear day & the Bay perfectly calm, we could distinctly see the trees on the other side—the eastern shore of Maryland & of Va. An old sailor & some young men who live over there say that the Chesapeake is 30 miles in width here. This is the first time I've ever been able to see across it. There are several Schooners passing this evening. Some sail vessels are almost always to be seen & sometimes Steamers & Gun-boats. Murry Rudolph brot in this evening fr. Hospital the straightest tale we've had yet—that Brady said in few days we would all be out of here & we all agree that if this don't prove true we'll never listen to another report. Chas. Briggs & I walked the street some time previous to going to bed—talking over our capture—the condition of affairs—rumors of Johnston's retreat—Jeff Davis' flight to trans-Mississippi, speculating on possibility of his offering that Department to French protection, etc., etc.

April 26, Wednesday

SP: We are having very delightful weather now, but shut up in this pen on a desert point can see no sign of Spring. A man in Co next us was paroled & taken out to-day, by having a friend to go his security in sum of 7,000$ wh. is now the condition of release. Glover dined with us—we get plenty meat, soup, & to-day got a loaf of bread extra. With vinegar & black pepper soup goes very well. Since I've been here I've finished Macaria & read—Pollards "8 months' observations in the North"—Marryaths "Pirate" & "3 cutters". Morgan has reorganized his school & Glover is an asst. professor—he has class of Greek, Latin, Geometry, Trigonometry etc.—but most of scholars are in primary Departments. Read N.Y. Herald of 24$\underline{\text{th}}$. accts. of Johnston's & Sherman's armistice & articles—wh. U.S. Gov. refuse to ratify & removed Sherman & sent Grant to resume hostilities.

NOTE: Edward Alfred Pollard, *Observations in the North: Eight Months in Prison and on Parole* (Richmond: E.W. Ayres, 1865).

Frederick Marryat, *The Pirate, and the Three Cutters* (London: H.G. Bohn, 1861).

April 27, Thursday

SP: Only incidents worthy of note to-day are the cases of summary punishment administered to two fellows for stealing. One who stole a little piece of Tobacco was bucked down by the one from whom it was taken & his friends—a Yankee Sergt. who came by had him released & would have bucked the other but he made his escape. The other fellow stole a man's rations of bread & was taken by the crowd & dipped head foremost into 1 of the barrels of filth sitting in the street—very severe & loathsome punishment. But he deserved it for stealing rations from a fellow prisoner—when rations are so scant that a man can't live comfortably on them.

April 28, Friday

SP: Sheb. Chadwick recd. to-day from his young lady friend in Martinsbo. Va. a package of books—magazines & light novels—but they are very acceptable to us & will help to pass off time. I read "The light Dragoons"—a tale of the Mexican War, & quite interesting.

April 29, Saturday

SP: Read today, "The Iron Cross or the Countess of Errol by Sylvanus Cobb," also right interesting. Of course I should consider it a loss of time to read them if I could get any solid reading—but "situated as we are & indeed I say circumstances" we are glad of any reading matter. I have a wretched cold & cough which are giving me a great deal of trouble. Had a wild rumor here to the effect that Sherman had sold his army to the Confederacy for a million & a half $.

NOTE: Sylvanus Cobb, *The Iron Cross, or The Countess of Errol: A Tale of High and Low Life, published along with The Convent Bride by E. Almy, and A Winter in the Sierra Nevadas by Frederick Stanhope* (New York: Samuel French, 1859?).

April 30, Sunday

SP: I had a bad night & am quite unwell to-day. Lay in bed greater portion of the day & ate nothing till evening—Lost all appetite wh. is conclusive evidence of bad health at this place. Inspection today—a mere matter of form, for no deficiences of clothing, shoes, etc. are supplied. Reported officially announced that Johnston has surrendered his army & all territory south & west as far as Chattahoochee river. Grape this evening is that we will certainly be sent home immediately. Order fr. War Dept. to clear this post as quickly as possible, but all must 1ˢᵗ take oath first—all who refuse to swallow it will be sent to other prisons & held as hostages—for deeds of guerrillas etc.

May 1, Monday

SP: We had rain night before last, & again last night it poured down very hard for a while[.] Weather very cool for this season. Men have been going out by fours all day for several days past, but seem to be impatient of that slow method & to-day whole Companies are getting their Sergts. in charge to register their names & sending the rolls over to Brady. I and all of our Co. are determined to wait till things develop themselves further; for while we believe we will have to swear allegiance to U.S. Gov. before we'll be released, yet no orders or conditions have yet been published to us—& I believe Yankees prefer all to go on & take it as they have been doing & then they will publish to the World that they took oath *voluntarily*—going to prove that the poor deluded, ignorant creatures were duped, misguided & forced into this war & are only glad of opportunity to return to *Galorious* Union & moreover we wish to see a *form* of the oath wh. is to be administered.

May 2, Tuesday

SP: A small meeting of Alabamians convened at our tent to-day & appointed Sheb. Chadwick, Sims, & Glover as Committee of 3 to see Gen. Barnes & learn if Confederate forces had all surrendered & if we would all be required to take the oath before released—& also to get a form of that oath. They therefore addressed a note to Genl. Barnes asking an interview at earliest moment that would suit his convenience. This evening notices are posted on Bulletin Board & other public places for "all persons—enlisted men—citizens & blocade-runners who wished to be released on taking the oath of allegiance to the U.S. to assemble at the gate at 8 O'clock to morrow morning."

May 3, Wednesday

SP: Above order countermanded & Yank Corpls. of each Divis. has order to form their Cos. in alphabetical order at 8 A.M. & march up to head of streets near Cook houses where clerks seated at tables registered the name—rank with place & date of capture, residence & occupation. It seems they take it for granted that all are going to take oath & they were right for every one being now convinced that our cause is irretrievably lost & that it is an evil that can't be avoided, went up & registered—including our Co, "D" & our friends who have been much averse to it, & wished to have interview with Gen. Barnes at least before acting. 3 or 4 Clerks in each Divis. have been busily engaged all day enrolling names.

May 4, Thursday

SP: One month to-day since we landed at this Point, & we have been thinking all the time we'd be out in a short time. 49 men who did not register yesterday did so to-day, & there are only two left in Camp who refuse to take oath on grounds that they were never U.S. citizens & do not intend to be. 125 bbls. of flour are daily consumed at this place. I'm getting over my cough & cold. I've suffered much with it & could get nothing but a weak decoction of liquorice root. How many nice & pleasant remedies I've thought of wh. My dear Mama would have used on me, had I been at home—sweet old home under her gentle, attention, & affectionate nursing.

May 5, Friday

SP: The anniversary of battle of Wilderness. Yes to-day 1 year ago we were passing thro' the dreadful ordeal of battle.* Rained last night & this morning—& ground has been very muddy. Saw Washington Chronicle of day before yesterday wh. reports surrender of Kirby Smith. Abe Lincoln was to have been finally interred at Springfield, Ill, on 4th. N.Y. is said to have surpassed herself in the grandeur & ma[g]nificence of the celebrations—processions etc—during the passage of the President's remains thro that city. The school has suspended operations in Morgan's House Cook H. No 9 & it is now occupied by a No. of clerks employed in making duplicates of the rolls of prisoners—which are to be sent to Washington, & we are of course all in fine spirits at prospect of soon getting out of this miserable pen & returning to our homes but oh! under what totally different circumstances fr. what we hoped & believed we would. Killed 1st musquito of the season this eveng & heard bull bats flying over.

(*Jamie participated in the battle also, & we were both mercifully shielded from danger tho' many a poor fellow fell killed or wounded near us.)

May 6, Saturday

SP: I've read in past day or 2 "The black Cruiser or the scourge of the seas" by——— & "The Maniac's secret or———["] by Sylvanus Cobb. Corn meal & raw mackerel were issued to us to-day—& nothing to cook in no wood—tho' there are no cooking utensils except frying pans & few camp kettles in here & no wood except in small quantities for sale—Perfectly inexcusable in Yankees who have every facility for having our cooking done. The men had to pick up little splinters along beach & began cutting on plank fence & braces outside etc. & thus worried negro sentinels till one shot at a fellow this evening. Sam Lynch [. . .] did our cooking. Maj. Brady said to have started to W. city with rolls clear, mild & pleasant weather. Issue of meal sent price of wood up 3 or 400 per cent—fluctuated worse than gold market in Wall Street.

NOTE: Captain Whitehead, *The Scourge of the Seas, or The Outlaw's Bride* (New York: George Munro & Co., 1864).

Sylvanus Cobb, *The Maniac's Secret, or The Privateer of Massachusetts Bay, A Story of the Revolution* (New York: S. French, 1859?).

May 7, Sunday

SP: Today gives lie to report of yesterday as is usually the case here—relative to Brady's going to W. city—for he was in here this morning. Usual inspection at 10 A.M. The blocade runners with their baggage were ordered out this morning & a large concourse were assembled at the Gate to see them go out. This circumstance tends to increase our hopes of getting out—indeed Yankee sentinels assure us that as soon as the rolls return from Washington—wh. will be in a day or 2—that they will begin to send us off. nous verrons. Glover was taken quite sick last night & was taken to the Hospital this morning. I hope he won't be sick long. Barber & Frank Sims were around this evening.

May 8, Monday

SP: *A.M. Warmer to-day than it has been this year—indeed very uncomfortable in the sun—I saw the 1st butterfly of the season. This evening an angry cloud blew up with thunder & lightning—& it rained very hard for a little while.

*March & fight 1 year ago to-day.

May 9, Tuesday

SP: Several fights occurred today & attracted large crowds to see them out. When a fellow gets into a fight here he has to fight it out to the bitter end, for the spectators instead of parting men encourage them in fighting. Sims is sick to day. Had a slight chill. He gave up sick sergeantcy a few days since to Henry Childress—as he was a little tired of the trouble of drawing & issuing soup, coffee, & medicines every day.

May 10, Wednesday

SP: Sims is getting on very well—Glover returned from the Hospital but is still looking badly—They gave him *no medicine* at all. Why is it? There is certainly no scarcity with the Yankees. A yell raised at soup time at Bulletin board spread all over Camp & we soon learned it was in consequence of an order being stuck up for all who had made application to take the oath prior to Apl. 3^{d} to report at Gate—They 1200 & odd in No. went out, registered & came back. They again went out at 5 P.M. to take final a departure as was supposed, but they returned about night. Brady addressed the crowd at gate about so many trying to "flank" out under that plea, & said all caught would be put in irons: that there was a special order for release of these men & that we would *all* (the rest) be detained but few days longer. 12 mos. ago to-day we were in a fight at Spottsylvania C.H.

May 11, Thursday

SP: Sheb, Sims & I wrote brief letters home to-day wh. we gave in charge of one of the Alabamians who was in squad, yesterday, & who expect (to leave at any minute.) (are ordered to be in readiness.) A pretty severe fight occurred in a tent opposite ours—one man was cut severely & Yank Corpls. with pistols flourishing around cursed & kicked the other & put hand cuffs on him—which he wore balance of the day.

May 12, Friday

SP: This is anniversary of terrible battle in the Horse Shoe at Spottsylvania a bloody day never to be forgotten by those who participated in the fray. Rained hard last night & Bob Price had a miserable time as he lay against edge of the tent & it leaked on him. Excitement gotten up just as we came fr. soup by order on board for "All who applied to take oath prior to fall of Richmond & whose names begin with A & B will report at gate immediately." This was misunderstood to [. . .] who registered before fall of R. & in addition all others whose names begin with A & B. So Chas. Briggs & Bayley rolled up their blankets—took their haversacks &c.—received our messages for home & bid us good bye. It was not long tho' before we had a good laugh at them for coming back disappointed. Had misfortune to have all our mackerel stolen out of tub inside our tent—many others were sufferers also—for tub was ½ full. A very light breakfast has been the result. Sergt. Philips—Co. "G"—next door met with same misfortune. Our sticks for carrying the barrels were stolen before it was "cleverly" dark this eve.

May 13, Saturday

SP: Finished Jacob Faithful (Capt. Marryatts)[.] It is a good thing with much of "human natur" in it. A call was made to day for men of above class whose names begin with the letters of alphabet from C. to L. inclusive. Brady came in "pen" this evening & said as there were not enough to make a boat load he wanted 100 more—whereupon a rush was made for the gate & the men were glad enough to get out—tho' they had none of their effects—not even their blankets & haversacks. Had some very good songs before retiring by our mess—assisted by F. Sims, Barber & *Burnstein* on the *base*.

Note: Frederick Marryat, *Jacob Faithful* (Philadelphia: E. L. Carey & A. Hart, 1834, and many other editions).

May 14, Sunday

SP: All prisoners of above class whose names begin with letters fr. M through-out alphabet are called out to-day. Heard a sermon at Cook-house No. 9. The weather is unseasonably cool. Capt. Barnes while inspecting remarked that we would not be crowded in here next Sunday & Brady told somebody that to-morrow would be a great day with us here—fr. which many take great comfort.

May 15, Monday

SP: The 30 days of mourning have expired. The flags are once more at full mast. Prisoners who made application in writing for oath [prior] to fall of Richmond went out to day. A large no. went out with latter class who came in here with us—among them was Jim Barber 43ᵈ Ala. Sims & Glover heard of it & went to try & get away too, but found they were required to take a solemn oath that what they said was true & of course abandoned their purpose. Bob Price's luck has changed!! After an unbroken chain of misfortunes in card playing since a few days after arriving here, he at last has met with success. He won 1000$ in Confederate money before brkfst—& came in this evening 2.50 or 3.00$ in Green backs. He treated me to cake & beer & gave the rest of mess some tobacco—also gave each of us a guttapercha button to have a ring made. Finished a little novel entitled "The Volunteer"—["]Maid of Monterey."

NOTE: Ned Buntline, *The Volunteer, or The Maid of Monterey. A Tale of the Mexican War* (Boston: F. Gleason, 1847).

May 16, Tuesday

SP: Our hopes have departed [it] is now said that there are no orders for release of any [mo]re of us. We are afraid we have to lie up in [this] miserable pen for some time & crowded together. [. . .] are there would be a great deal of sickness when [. . .] hot weather sets in in earnest.

May 17, Wednesday

SP: There are [rum]ors in the Camp to-day to the effect that Kirby Smith re[fuse]d to surrender & is determined to fight it out: That he de[nou]nced Gen. Lee & all east of Miss. as traitors, & called upon [the] soldiers to stand to their colors but a little longer & they would [re]ceive foreign aid. Also that Jeff. Davis has been caught in [Geor]gia, disguised in his wife's clothing & is on his way under [gu]ard to Washington City.

NOTE: Davis was captured May 10.

May 18, Thursday

SP: It is said that the women in New York City & other places have requested Andy Johnson to hold prisoners for a year & that it should not cost the Government anything—for they would furnish rations. Suppose they want to [. . .] themselves on the rebels for causing the absence of their [husb]ands & lovers—& the death of not a few of them. Yesterday [& to-day] have been so warm that we went in bathing. Had a [pl]easant time swimming about together. We are trying [to teach] Sheb. Chadwick to swim.

May 19, Friday

SP: Reports relating to [. . .] have again sprung up. "Reliable men heard Bra[. . ."] some men in here to-day that we would certainly be turn [. . .] in a very few days: & men on detail out side say the rolls [which] were sent to

Washington have returned—with orders for sending [. . .] Frank & W$^{\underline{m}}$ Sims, Briggs, Childress, Sheb, Glover, & I went in [swim]ming this evening & had nice time riding the waves. Went [. . .] to the piles where the water is deep & beautifully clear. Sheb. [. . .] learned to swim & of course is very proud of it.

May 20, Saturday

SP: [M]ore talk of our getting out, but nothing doing towards it—I fear "its all talk & no cider." P.M. Glover has news this eveng from Morgan (parson) that he was told by Catholic priest who came here from Washington that the blank oaths were brot. on same boat—& that stereotype plates with which to stamp Brady's name & moreover that B's clerk's are at work now stamping them.

May 21, Sunday

SP: Things are rocking [. . .] in the usual monotonous way. A Catholic priest [held] mass & confession early this morning & preached later in the day—I did not hear him. Rained last night & drizzled to day. Some are very sanguine of getting out to-morrow.

May 22, Monday

SP: I neglected noting that Sheb. Chadwick was made Sergt. Maj. of Divis. & Sims took his place as Sergt. of this Co.* Henry Childress has got tired of his office of Sick Sergt. & gets Young Idom to bring rations for sick, detailed, & absent. Rained hard last night. All our mackerel wh. had been nicely soaked & dried were stolen out of tent & we were a mad set when we discovered it this morning. Brady told some men to-day that he had recd. no orders for sending us away, but was expecting them every day & advised them not to write home for money, clothes, etc.

(*About 1 week ago.)

May 23, Tuesday

SP: To day the grand review of the army of the U.S. takes place in Washington City—& will [. . .] 2 days. The waves were running uncommonly high this afternoon when we went in bathing & an incident occurred which came very nearly having a tragical conclu[sion.] A little Louisianian named ———, a member of the [Wash]ington artillery went in with us & came very near being drowned—he could not swim well & ventured out [as far] as he could wade & then attempted to swim over [. . .] place to a bar further out. The waves began to bre[ak on] his face, strangling him, & he let down in water over [his] head, became terribly alarmed & began to drown. I was [near]est to him & went to help him out—at same time holl[ered] to the others to come. I had been swimming & was tired & knew the difficulty & the danger attending an al[. . .] to save a drowning man—instantly all [. . .] I've heard of drowning men seizing hold of & drow[ning men] who were trying to save them—flashed thro my mind [. . .] sunk twice, was swallowing water very fast & wo[uld] have gone down to rise no more—when I cau[ght him] & tried to swim & pull him along—just as I had

[. . .] tho' he grasped me & climbed up on me & sunk [. . .] alarmed me as I thought he might cause us bot[h to] drown, & I threw him off—rose & caught him by [. . .] began swimming again—when Fullerton of Co. H. 5[$\underline{\text{th}}$] who had heard me calling, met me & took the Louisianian. Fullerton being taller could just wade & thus easily got to where it was more shallow. He & I then carried [the] young man to shore. He was almost insensible & [. . .]thly sick for a few minutes. The poor fellow made [a] narrow escape—I very glad of having been the mean [. . .] of saving him, & truly thankful that both of us were not drowned, for I was in great danger myself.

May 24, Wednesday

SP: A 2 horse wagon drove up our street to-day followed by a large crowd & when it stopped near my tent, was at once surrounded & thronged. I went out & found that it was an agent of "Baltimore Sanitary or Christian Commission["] with of 1250 testaments for distribution amongst the prisoners. I also found that it was impossible for me to get up to the wagon but Farrier came out with some & gave me one. In the eveng a crowd was gathered on the street to see a fellow eat [for] a wager. He was to eat 2 pones of loaf bread & 3 rations of pickled pork, wh. was to be furnished him [. . .] gratis—but in the event of his failing to eat all [he] was to pay for it. I am told he ate it. The same fellow [. . .] a few evenings ago, ate 2.5 - 5et. pies in [ad]dition to a large quantity of bread & meat. 2 loaves [. . .] day's rations at 1 meal & 3 of meat.

May 25, Thursday

SP: The [bloc]kade of all Southern Ports except those of Texas has [bee]n raised. Pres. Davis is in close confinement at [Fort] Monroe; Alex Stephens is in Ft. Delaware—Gov. Vance [is] also held as a prisoner. I took a nap after bathing [th]is P.M. & on waking found many changes had [t]aken place—viz. all the white troops, including [cor]porals of Divisions & all are going away, & Sheb. [has] been promoted to Sergt of the Camp & will stay [. . .]ice outside. Briggs takes Sheb's place as Sergt. [. . .]is.

May 26, Friday

SP: Negro police came in last night [carry]ing pistols about, halted every one on street—cursed [&] ordered them back to their tents. I hear the report of [pisto]ls—one of which was fired at a man in the street, but the [. . .]iped missed him & passed thro' thigh of a poor fellow was ly[ing] asleep in a tent & caused the amputation of his leg. [The] behaviour of negroes was perfectly outrageous—& I propos[ed] that we should hold an indignation meeting to-day & demand that the negroes be taken out of the Camp, but it rained all day. This evening several Yankee officers came in & inquired into the affair & said the negroes would be severely punished. After wounding the man the negro was terribly alarmed & declared the pistol fired accidentally. The ig[norant] wretches were excited & scared any how & some did not [know] how to use a pistol.

May 27, Saturday

SP: All day yesterday [and] to-day it has rained incessantly—with a cold wind blowing all the time. Every one has kept closely in his tent both days—I slipped out a minute or 2 & was chilled thro' & thro. The old Chesapeake is lashed into fury—the waves running 4 or 5 ft. high, & backing water up in ditches in the Camp—

May 28, Sunday

SP: The rain has at last ceased after 48 hours' duration, & we are all "monstrous proud of it,["] for we were thoroughly worn out with the very disagreeable spell we have just had. The Yankee officer of the day rode thro' camp to-day escorted by 2 negroes armed with sabre & pistol. The Negro Soldiers were sent off from here to-day as they belong to Burnside's Corps. wh. is to be sent to Texas. Their place was taken by other black troops who came fr. Washington. The darkies were bitterly opposed to being sent to Texas & some said they had no intention of going t[here.] In Herald & Chronicle of 25$\underline{th}$ there is some Y. news fr. Trans Miss Dept. 'Twas said Kirby Smith had 60 or 80,000 veteran troops which no. was to be increased by 30,000 recruits [. . .]000 negroes. Magruder was preparing vigorously to ne[. . .] the expected invasion of Texas—whites & blacks between [. . .] of 13 to 60 were to be called out. Texans were holding ma[ss] meeting & passing the most patriotic resolutions—but they had not then heard of our misfortune on this side [of the] River! Had they done their duty & lent us some asista[nce] here where the tug of war was, it might have availed so[me]thing.

May 29, Monday

SP: To-day it is officially announced in Y. [pa]pers that K. Smith has surrendered all military & naval [offic]ers west of Miss. Rather a sensation was produced, late this afternoon by 3 ambulances driving about Camp in 1 of which 'twas s[aid] was Gen. Grant & staff. Have no idea though that it was so. [. . .]ed afterwards 'twas Gov. Peirpoint Holden of N.C. several na[val of]ficers, citizens & 2 women. Rebels sold a good many [. . .] etc. Bob Price opened a Faro bank to-day & met with [no] better success than ordinarily falls to his lot. T[here is] a mania for gambling here, which is carried on o[utside] the gates on the bay. There are more than 20 chuck a [luck] banks in operation—a dozen or 2 of Keno (?) & I noticed [Wheel] of Fortune—anything to gamble on.

NOTE: William Woods (not Pierpoint) Holden succeeded Zebulon Vance as governor of North Carolina.

May 30, Tuesday

SP: I've re[ad] several trash novels—viz—"Mand of the Miss, or Gra[. . . ,"] "The 7 (Doans)* or Brigands of the Revolution" "Jenny Diver, [or The Fe]male highway man" & a no. of "Graham's Magazine" & 1 of Har[pers.] The negro guards within the Camp have been taken out & Rebels substituted. A Co. of 40 or 50 has been formed with Morgan, the Preacher, teacher, clothing agent etc. etc. as Captain, & Glover as 1 of the Corporals. The[y] are unarmed but I suppose the men will willingly obey them rather than have "old Cuffy" in here. These men doing Guard duty get extra rations, Sugar, Coffee & tobacco. Young Idom & M<u>c</u>Diarmid belong to the Co.

*(Brothers of Wyoming).

NOTE: M. M. Huet, *The Seven Brothers of Wyoming, or The Brigands of the Revolution* (New York: H. Long & Brother, 1850).

James Pilgrim, *The Female Highwayman, or The Blighted Lily. A Drama in Three Acts* (New York, 1852).

May 31, Wednesday

SP: Andy Johnson long looked for Amnesty Proclamation has at last been promulgated & everybody is discussing it, but no body understands it. It is rather enigmatical, or at least not clearly expressed. From one section, in which are excluded fr. benefits of the amnesty "all officers above the rank of Col. in Army & (those above the rank of) Lieut. in Navy," one would infer that the balance of us were "pardoned", but in 12<u>th</u> Section it certainly seems that we are in the class of "exceptions": But if we are not "pardoned" who are?—certainly comparatively few in the Confederacy. We are becoming very impatient to get out—"Hope deferred maketh the heart sick". In talking over our imprisonment we all agree that we would never again cage a bird, for now we can fully appreciate their condition & know well how to sympathise with them.

June 1, Thursday

SP: The opening of Summer finds us still in prison, & we've been expecting to be released "very soon" ever since the surrender of Gen. Lee. The weather is very warm & were it not for the delightful bathing every evening in the bay I don't know how we'd manage to get along. A large party of us went in together this evening & enjoyed ourselves exceedingly in swimming, diving & playing about. Glover brings the news from Morgan that orders have certainly arrived for our release; & there are rumors that some are to be sent off tomorrow—the sick first. A man was badly stabbed yesterday & it was thought it would prove fatal, but he is still living. The man who cut him was handcuffed & taken out by a negro. "O tempora, O mores!["] (To be written up to the 14th inst.)

NOTE: "Terry" is Terry Glover.

"O tempora, O mores!" means "Oh these times, Oh these ways!" John H. Cowin, who attended some of the same schools as Sam Pickens, used the same phrase in October 1861.

June 14, Wednesday

SP: The release still goes on—very slowly it seems to us who are so anxious to get out. Tho' today 704 went out which is best days work that has been done yet. I wrote a letter to Mama to be sent it by Sheb. Chadwick, who expects to start this eveng by Steamer to Mobile. Glover goes too. Dr. Sims, Bob Price, Jno. Williams, Odell, Conner & I had a fine time in bay this afternoon. The waves were running much higher than ever before, when we've been in. We found it very difficult to ride the waves, & it required great exertion to do so. Several ambulances of ladies were in this Camp purchasing rebel fans, watch chains, rings, etc.

June 15, Thursday

SP: The vessel for Mobile was detained till to-day & Sheb. came in to bid us good bye & took our letters. Bob Price & I went down & when a call was made for "Ps" for M. we went over, but business was closed for the day & after taking a list of our names we were dismissed.

McD: I am called on today. I swallowed the oath bravely and am aboard a steamer for Mobile, Ala. Farewell old Point Lookout. I am glad to get away from you.

June 16, Friday

SP: Price & I bundled up early & went down to the house where the cere- monies are performed—i.e. the machine where U.S. citizens are made out of rebel soldiers. The place was already thronged & after being wedged in the crowd a couple of hours our squad was called over dead line & in due time passed into the house 2 at the time where our name, rank, Co. & Regt were taken, also place where captured & date, date of arrival here & description list i.e. height— complexion, color of hair & eyes. Then a squad of 32 forming 3 sides hollow square—standing with hats off & right hand on bible [one] to every four men— had oath of allegiance to U.S. read to them, [. . . co]nclusion of which each one was required to kiss the bib[le . . .] having oath administered, stood under U.S. flag—dimensions of which were about 20×30 feet, which was stretched so as to form a canopy above their heads—a form of oath & parole was handed each man who then had to pass by 4 other clerks' tables & have it filled out sign his own name to it & register his name in 2 different books for purpose—giving his residence (places of) & occupation before war. We next passed out other end of house into yard where as soon as a squad of 50 was formed it was marched to Parole Camp. With all this form & ceremony I don't wonder at their only getting out only 700 a day. Bob & I were very hungry as they've been feeding us on crackers & Cod fish for the last week, but Terry came out from Hospital & brot us a nice snack of light bread & mutton—it was a great treat. Not having been outside our pen—where not a green leaf & scarcely a sprig of grass is to be seen, I felt like a bird out of a cage during short walk outside to Parole Camp. We could see the old Potomac & the Va shore—and the trees & grass etc. Oh, I hope will not be long ere we are free & can turn our backs on this miserable place.

June 17, Saturday

SP: The Steamer for Mobile returned to this place yesterday eveng. Some of her machinery got out of fix & she had to come back for repairs. I am more restless in here than I was in the other pen: for every evening the gate is opened & a crowd is called out & sent to Washington, Balt., Richmond, City Point &c, & seeing them [. . .] lying there ready makes us feel anxious to go too. Had it

June 19, Monday

SP: Crackers & Cod-fish were issued to us this morning. The former we received, the latter we refused. Not starved quite enough to eat them yet. Dr. Sims got through & came into the Parole pen this morning. We were very glad to see him as Bob. P. & I had fully determind on going this evening via Richmond. Men from Ala., Ga, Miss, &c. are going that way every day despite the statements of the Yankee authorities here that the Gov. will give us transportation only to R. & that we will have to shift for ourselves & get home the best way we can from there. So it will be some time before another load for Mobile will be made up. And besides I dread that long voyage crowded together in a transport. The fate too of the vessel which started there more than a week ago, is enough to make every one avoid that route; for she is still lying off the wharf & wagon loads of sick & dead men are hauled away daily. All who had not recd. their papers—oath of allegiance & of parole—were marched out to Provost Marshal's office to day where they were delivered to them: each mans in an envelope. Late in evening men were called for each of the points of landing & formed in separate squads. Altho' one was made up for Mobile—we waited, believing there was a trick in it & last of all a call for R. was made & we fell in. This squad alone was then marched out of the pen to the infinite disappointment of all the rest. How much relieved & how free we felt on getting out with no guards around us. Drew crackers & bacon & then marched to Pro. Mars. office where money (not Confed) watches &c were returned to owners. We then got aboard the "Monitor" & started about 11 P.M.

June 20, Tuesday

SP: Passed old Ft. Monroe early this morning.* Thence thro' Hampton Roads up James River. Met several Steamers loaded with Yankee Soldiers returning home, and great many barges in tow of steam tugs bearing North the Yankee war material—such as artillery—gun carriages—rail road cars etc. etc. There was a great change taken place in the appearance of things about City Point not the busy place it was in—with the crowds of gun boats, transports, & every variety of steam & sail vessels. The distance from City pt. to Richmond is 60 miles, the river being very crooked. Butler's Tower & 2 others were visible from the boat. Saw mouth of Buter's Dutch Gap canal—that monument of Yankee folly. Then a little higher up passed celebrated Howlett House where we had that formidable battery which commanded the River & used to play on the Canal to the infinite annoyance of Yankees who were at work on it. Saw a large lot of army horses & mules & a very large herd of Cattle grazing in an extensive meadow along the James. Next came Chaffin's Farm & Drewry's Bluff & the obstructions in the river—some of which have been removed. Then the bridges & places where pontoons formerly stretched across the river. From here to R. we safely glided along where a few months ago a similar craft bearing Yankee colors would have been blown to atoms by the many torpedoes which guarded the channel. Saw a few fields of luxuriant corn & wheat just harvested—grateful visions to our eyes. Showered all the evening. This seemed a very long day to me. When we landed at our late Capital city a strange & sad feeling came over me on seeing the blue coats on the wharf to receive us—& thinking of the great changes which have taken place since I was here last. We were marched under escort of cavalry to Chimborazo Hosp. where guard was dismissed & took up our quarters in the buildings & drew rations—of "hard tack" raw pickled pork & beans. Dr. Sims, Bob Price & I then walked down town to ~~hunt up~~ see if the Ellisons were still here & after some difficulty found them.

   *(Presdt. Davis is still in confinement here.)

June 21, Wednesday

   SP: An old lady cooked our meat for us & we gave her ⅓ of it all the beans—good many white people & negroes are occupying the old Hosp. buildings & living on Gov. rations. Carried our baggage down to Wm Ellisons—now corner 9th & Main & he invited us to stay with him during our stay. What an unfortunate affair the burning of Richmond was. Cary Street is burnt up & Main from about 13th to 8th with exception of P. Office & the block of Spotswood Hotel. Had a snack of crackers and Scotch herrings which was enjoyed amazingly. 1st herrings I've tasted since the war.* Our business here is to get a little money to help us along on our way home, but the way the Ellisons talk of the hard times—their heavy losses & great scarcity of money, I see it is going to be but little if any that they will let us have altho' I've assured them that I will endeavor to return it to them immediately after getting to Ala. & pay any interest, at all reasonable, that they ask. Made inquiry concerning the routes South & find that the one by Danville, Greensboro, Charlotte etc. is the only one open & some gaps in that. Went with Bob. Price to Mrs. Barnes' who was very glad to see us & thence to Dr. Jno Cunningham's. Here I overhauled my trunk & John's box & exchanged my worn army clothes for a new suit of Confederate Jeans—new hat & fine light shoes—which metamorphused my appearance & feelings considerably. I took out also all the shirts & drawers & socks, as they'd be useful on the journey home. Ellison did let me have $10 in gold this even'g—& I sold him 2 pr. new army shoes at $1. per pair. We then went to barber shop & had hair cut—shaved &c. & treated ourselves to glass iced lemonade. Richmond is full of good things again—such as cheese, wines, nuts, raisins, fruits—oranges, lemons, bananas, prunes—Ice-cream, soda water &c. &c. It was really tantalizing to see so many good things & not be able to indulge in any of them.

   *(This is the first time I've ever been in R. without a cent in my pocket—I'm nearly 1000 miles from home, too.)

June 22, Thursday

   SP: Dr. S., Bob & myself went to Chimborazo Hosp. at 9 A.M. & got our transportation to Greensboro', Ala. Passing the Market I saw a fine assortment of meats, vegetables & early fruits—as Plums, apricots, maddlers (?) apples, cherries, blackberries, gooseberries etc. We feel the want of a little money keenly enough. At 2 P.M. went up & ate a very nice vegetable dinner with Mrs. Barnes. Soon after we hired a little wagon & went to Petersbg. Depot which is now on South other side Manchester—cross river on Pontoon bridge. Had a hard drive to reach train and then they would not allow soldiers to go on it, but telegraphed for extra train, which will not go till to-morrow. So we put our baggage in a house & walked back to Ellisons.

June 23, Friday

SP: Got up at day light, went in the store & filled a large haversack with ginger cakes, took a toddy & walked over to Depot. Started at 5½ or 6 & ran to Petersburg—where we found the train already crowded but managed to get on—tho' most of the crowd had to lie over. Arrived at Burkesville at 12 M. The Danville train soon passed crowded—& we waited till a box train was made up & started at about 4 P.M. or 5. Yankee Brig. took train here going North. Met a son of Mr. Grigg who lives here & learned that Joe G. is at his father's in Amelia. There has been a great deal too much rain for crops in this section. For 2 weeks past it has rained every day. At Meherrin station we halted just after dark & the conductor being on a spree with some Yankee friends—telegraphed ahead for instructions & awaited orders. *Frid. 23ᵈ*. Here we lie still at Meherrins—Got off at 5 or 6, ran a few miles to clover sta. & lay over 3 or 4 hours. Got basket of nice plums here. (Bot. 15 plugs tobacco from a negro @ 10 cts each. We'll speculate on them & make our money last longer.) Arrived at Danville about 3 P.M. & after delay of an hour or 2 got off in box train.—a Regt. or 2 of Yankees passed us here—northward bound. I'm glad to see them going where they belong. Found Corn looking much better in N.C. Reached Greensboro' about 9 or 10 & had to lie over all night.

June 24, Saturday

SP: Had some cheese for brkfst—40 ct. lb. & some pies for which we bartered some tobacco. Left at 9A.M. At Salisbury the Depot, work-shops & everything at R.R. was burnt up.

July 2, Sunday

SP: Took a day light start & drove to Washington, 7 ms. Co. seat of [Wilkes] Co. Gen Toomb's resides here. Dr. Sims & Mall went to a house & made a pot of excellent Coffee & got a little milk & sugar—we then had brkfast & enjoyed it very much. At 8 O'clk we started & ran down on the branch road 18 miles to Barnett station on Ga. R.R. 58 ms. from Augusta & 113 from Atlanta. This is by far the best road I've been on & makes much better time. Saw some fine water-melons & peaches fully ripe—on train. Reached Atlanta or Ruins of At. (for the destruction of the Gate City was more complete than I ever saw before. No one could recognize it.) at 7.30 P.M. We are hungry & without rations—can't draw on Sunday. Dr. S. & I walked up Marietta Street of residences—trying to purchase bread but failed—a little corn bread was given us.

July 3, Monday

SP: Slept last night in Portico of Hotel (Gate City)—we have no blanket at all
now. Started at 6 A.M. & reached West Point about 10 P.M. crossed Chattahoochie
in Ferry boat. Distance 86 ms. Started again at 2 & stopped at Chehaw at sun
down. Hacks charged 8 & 10 $ a seat to Montgomery 41 ms. & we three had only
$2 in gold & 3.40 green backs, but manoeuvred so as to get seats in a carriage for
that amount cash—counting gold at 2 for 1-& $5.50 gb. to be paid in Montg. or
when we get home; equivalent to $5. gb. each.

July 4, Tuesday

SP: Came 9 ms. & stayed all night at house of owners of the hack—Mr. Gibson.
Started a little after light—how fortunate we are to be able to ride—for the weather
is intensely hot. Had to walk across 2 swamps & up several hills. The corn is not
as good in Ala. as in Ga. & the Carolinas. It has suffered for rain here & then it has
not in some cases been worked enough. I hear that on some plantations so many
negroes have left work & gone off to the Yankee military Posts, that a good deal
of corn will make nothing. This is a grand occasion with the Yankees & negroes.
at all Mil. Posts. salutes were fired, at dawn & 100 guns at noon. troops paraded
& declaration of Independence & Lincoln's Emancipation Proclamation read to
them. There was a large barbecue 3 ms. fr. Montg. & others in town. The road
was full of negroes returning to the country & Yankees. to their Camp 3 or 4
ms fr. town—some of latter drunk. Got in town about 6 P.M. Still thronged with
negroes. U.S. flag floats over the Capitol. Steamer Flirt was due this morning
& ought to have gone down this evening but she has just arrived at dark. Slight
pyrotechnic display—of sky rockets sent up in streets—good many guns firing
wh. sounds exactly like picket skirmishing.

July 5, Wednesday

SP: Slept on the floor of the hall of Exchange Hotel. We made known to Mr.
Bolger—Proprietor our situation—viz Prisoners of war just fr. Point Lookout,
Md on our way home without a cent of money in our pockets— (but would be
able to send him the mon[ey] on reaching home.) & without any hesitation he
very kindly told us we were welcome to stay here & gave us tickets for supper
& brkfast this morning. It is uncomfortable & disagreeable in the extreme to be
traveling without money, but fortune has favored us very much. We were hard at
work all the morning trying to get an order from Pro. Marshal for transportation,
but failed utterly. The boat left at 11 & so slow & trifling were the officers in
their Deptmts—that not a single man got off. It was a terrible disappointment. D^r
Cruse, McBride & others of our Regt. got a skiff by sleight of hand & transported
themselves. By a desperate effort & exercise of a great deal of patience I managed
to get our papers thro' Pro. Mar. Office & obtained an *order for* transportation.
We then went to Comm. Office in Capitol to draw rations, but he had *closed*—&
so it has been ever since we were in Abbeville S.C. on 30 ult. There we drew
2 days' rations. Late in afternoon met D^r Ed. Semple & borrowed $5. from

him. Immediately invested 50 cts. in cold bath & never enjoyed one more in my life—changed clothes & feel 1000 pr cent better.

July 6, Thursday

SP: at market this morning were water melons, musk m., Pears, apples, Peaches & cider in fruit line, & variety of Vegetables—including Green Corn. Drew rations of Pickled pork & hard tack. All day long we've been anxiously on lookout for a boat—but none has come. This is decidedly the hottest spell weather I ever experienced. I was told that thermometer was higher on 4th (6th Contin) in Ex. Hotel than ever before. And yesterday & to-day have been equally sultry. It's so hot at night too, that you cant sleep. Messrs. Giovanni—Italians & Confectioners nearly opp. Ex. treated us very well—to cheese & beer. Enough, (dixerunt) to know we were Confed. Soldiers.

July 7, Friday

SP: Well we have had a miserable time in Montgom[.] Never was so unpleasantly situated in all my life. Been sleeping in portico & eating one meal a day & that on credit

Biographical Dictionary

Information compiled from: muster rolls at the National Archives, Washington (June 30, August 31, September 1, October 31, December 31, 1861; February 8, 1862; March 30, June 30, August 31, October 31, 1864); Greensboro *Alabama Beacon,* May 24, 1861; 1850, 1860, and 1870 Manuscript Census; Compiled Service Records, National Archives; William Edward Wadsworth Yerby, *History of Greensboro, Alabama, from Its Earliest Settlement* (Montgomery: Paragon Press, 1908), 42–45; Jonathan W. Williams, "Company D, Fifth Alabama, C.S.A.: A Complete List of the Original Company," *Greensboro Record,* June 4, 1903; V. Gayle Snedecor, *A Directory of Greene County for 1855–1856* (Mobile: Strickland & Co., 1856); Thomas McAdory Owen, *History of Alabama and Dictionary of Alabama Biography,* 4 volumes (Chicago: S. J. Clarke, 1921); local marriage and will records; and from other sources. Special thanks to Alan Pitts for material that he willingly shared on Rodes' brigade, the Fifth Alabama Infantry, and other units.

An initial asterisk (*) denotes members of the Greensboro Guards, Fifth Alabama Infantry Regiment. Those names mentioned by the diarists but not found below are either ambiguous (in several instances multiple individuals with the same last name belonged to the same regiment or company) or eluded my ability to identify. Members of the clergy, in particular, often do not show up in official records because they were not official chaplains, but rather missionaries sent by various churches.

*ADAMS, Benjamin Carter ("Buck") (1838–). Student at the University of Virginia in 1856; enlisted May 6, 1861, in Uniontown, Alabama; assistant regimental commissary with rank of captain; brigade commissary in 1862; D. H. Hill's division commissary with the rank of major in 1863; cotton planter in 1878. Brother of Guards John M. Adams and Richard Henry Adams.

ADAMS, Charles (1840–). From Grenada, Mississippi; student at the University of Virginia 1858–1860; captain during the war and Richmond merchant afterward.

ADAMS, Daniel Weisiger. Colonel of First Louisiana Infantry; promoted brigadier general in 1862; wounded and captured at Chickamauga; commanded troops in north Alabama until the end of the war.

*ADAMS, John M. Enlisted May 18, 1861, in Pensacola, Florida; discharged in September or October 1861 for a disability; later an assistant surgeon with the rank of captain. Brother of Guards Benjamin Carter Adams and Richard Henry Adams.

*ADAMS, Richard Henry (Jr.) (April 21, 1841, Alabama–October 8, 1896). Enlisted May 6, 1861, in Uniontown, Alabama; wounded May 31, 1862; joined Partisan Rangers, Fifty-first Alabama Infantry; captured in Nashville and remained a prisoner for twenty-one months; civil engineer, postmaster. Brother of Guards Benjamin Carter Adams and John M. Adams.

ALEXANDER, Charles M. Colonel of the Second District of Columbia Volunteers.

ALLEN, Mary H. Mother of Guard Henry Allen and wife of a Havanna, Alabama, merchant.

*ALLEN, W. Henry (c. 1844, Alabama–). In 1860 a student; son of a Havanna, Alabama, merchant reporting $1,000 in real estate and $5,800 in personal estate, including five slaves, in 1850; enlisted August 8 or 14, 1861, in Union Mills, Virginia; had typhoid fever April 23–June 3, 1862; appointed fourth corporal in March 1864; appointed third corporal in August 1864; wounded in the thigh October 19, 1864, and sent home.

ANDERSON, Richard Heron. South Carolina field officer who succeeded P. G. T. Beauregard as commander in South Carolina; later commanded Longstreet's Corps at Spotsylvania and Cold Harbor.

*ARRINGTON, James Portis (died during war). From Forkland, Alabama; Warrior Guard who transferred in April 1862; appointed aide-de-camp to Rodes with the rank of lieutenant in 1863.

ATKINS, Joseph. Greensboro druggist and former Greensboro Guard.

AVERELL, William Woods. Union cavalry commander who eventually rose to major general.

AVERY, Carrie. Married Jonathan W. Williams in 1864.

*AVERY, Robert (c. 1844, Alabama–during war). In 1860 a student at the Greene Springs School; enlisted March 11, 1862, in Greensboro.

*BADENHAUSEN, Charles von (c. 1834, Germany–). Imperial cadet in the Austrian army 1852–1854, lieutenant 1854–1859; in 1860 a teacher at Faunsdale plantation, Marengo County, Alabama; enlisted May 6, 1861, in Uniontown, Alabama; chief musician; lost his left arm and a finger of his right hand July 1, 1862; discharged July 28, 1862.

BAILEY, D. E. *See* BAYLEY, D. E.

BAKER, Edward Dickinson. U.S. Senator from Oregon 1860–1861; Union general killed in the Battle of Balls Bluff in 1861.

BAKER, La Fayette Curry. Union provost marshal in charge of tracking Booth and his conspirators.

BALL, J. D. Corporal in the Pickensville Blues, Fifth Alabama Infantry.

BALLS, P. D. *See* BOWLES, P. D.

BANKS, Nathaniel Prentiss. Unsuccessful Union commander who led the dismal Red River Campaign in 1864.

BARBER, James. Soldier in Forty-third Alabama Infantry, a regiment made up of companies from Greene, Marengo, and Tuscaloosa Counties.

BARNES, Mrs. Proprietor of the Richmond boardinghouse (on Franklin Street, about three hundred yards from the Capital Square) frequented by the Greensboro Guards.

*BARNUM, David (c. 1843, Alabama–). Enlisted August 23, 1861, in Union Mills, Virginia; captured September 14, 1862; appointed acting master, CS Navy at Charleston Harbor in August 1863. Son of former Guard Dr. Augustus Barnum.

BARTOW, Francis S. Colonel of Eighth Georgia Infantry killed at First Manassas.

BATTLE, Cullen Andrews. Colonel of the Third Alabama Infantry; promoted to brigadier general in command of Rodes' former brigade in August 1863.

*BAYLEY, D. E. Enlisted August 25, 1862, in Pike County, Alabama; sick with: sciatica (February 1863), chronic rheumatism (January 1864), diabetes (June 1864); wounded May 5, 1864; in Lynchburg, Virginia, hospital (September and October 1864); in camp in February 1865; captured April 2, 1865.

BAYOL, Adele, Francis, Josephine, and Sylvanie. Sisters of Ned and Jules Bayol.

*BAYOL, Francis Edward ("Ned") (c. 1835, Alabama–September 1900). Enlisted August 9, 1861, in Greensboro; wounded in the right leg September 14, 1862, in the right leg and hip May 3, 1863; detailed to the quartermaster department, Demopolis, Alabama; in 1880 a dancing instructor, married with five children. Son of former Guard Edward Bayol and brother of Guard Jules Honoré Bayol.

*BAYOL, Jules Honoré (c. 1837, Alabama–July 1, 1862, at Malvern Hill). Enlisted August 9, 1861, in Greensboro; never married. Son of former Guard Edward Bayol and brother of Guard Francis Edward Bayol.

BEAUREGARD, Pierre Gustave Toutant (1818–1893). Commander of Confederate forces at battles of Fort Sumter and First Manassas; temporarily retired in late 1862, then commanded Confederate forces at Charleston, South Carolina.

BECK, Francis. Younger sister of Henry Beck.

*BECK, Henry (April 24, 1839, Germany–). Arrived in Greensboro in 1857; in 1860 a merchant, married; enlisted April 18, 1861, in Greensboro but moved to the Jeff Davis Legion; exchanged with John S. Tucker to become brigade commissary clerk April 1, 1864; Mason 1870–1871; officer, Knights of Pythias; in 1870 a merchant with three children, reporting $30,000 in personal estate; moved to Birmingham in 1887; although he attended Christian services during the war, his son is described as Jewish in an 1892 issue of the *Greensboro Alabama Beacon*.

BEE, Barnard Elliott. Native South Carolinian and Mexican War veteran; brigadier general at the Battle of First Manassas, where he was fatally injured, but not before imparting to Thomas J. Jackson the nickname "Stonewall."

BELCHER or BELSHER, Thaddeus C. Captain of the Pickensville Blues, Fifth Alabama Infantry.

BENNERS, Augustus. Prominent Greensboro planter and politician.

BERNEY or BIRNEY, John W. Brigade lieutenant and aide-de-camp in August 1862; later assigned to General Simon Bolivar Buckner, Department of the Gulf.

BISCOE, Thomas H. From Greene County, Alabama, but a New Orleans resident when enlisted at age twenty-two; clerk; single; captain of Company K, Fifth Louisiana Infantry; captured at Fredericksburg May 3, 1863; killed May 5, 1864.

BLACK, Harvey. In 1864, surgeon in charge of the Second Corps' field hospital.

BLACKFORD, Eugene (1845–1904). A Marylander and student at the University of Virginia; teaching in Clayton, Alabama, when the war broke out; resumed his teaching career after the war, first in Virginia and then in Maryland.

BLACKFORD, William T. Greensboro physician who served as unofficial surgeon to the Fifth Alabama; a Republican probate judge after the war.

BLAIR, Francis Preston, Sr. Prominent Democratic newspaper editor in the 1830s; an adviser to presidents from Andrew Jackson through Abraham Lincoln; organized the 1865 Hampton Roads Peace Conference in an unsuccessful effort to end the Civil War; his Maryland home was burned by Confederates in July 1864.

BLOUNT, Robert P. Captain of the Sumter Rifle Guards, Fifth Alabama Infantry; later lieutenant colonel of the Ninth Alabama Infantry Battalion.

*BOARDMAN, James L. (c. 1841, Alabama–1876, Waco, Texas). His father was a silversmith and planter who owned twenty-two slaves in 1850 and more than forty-one slaves in 1860; enlisted April 13, 1861, in Greensboro; left in Montgomery with measles; third corporal in October 1861; clerk for Major Adams; division commissary clerk in 1864.

BONHAM, Milledge Luke. South Carolina politician and military figure; a brigadier general under Beauregard during the Battle of First Manassas.

BOOTH, Edwin T. Noted Shakespearean actor and Unionist brother of Lincoln's assassin, John Wilkes Booth.

BOOTH, John Wilkes. Assassin of Lincoln.

*BORDEN, Frederick A. (c. 1839, Alabama–). In 1860 a student living in Newbern, Alabama, with his mother, who reported $80,000 in real estate and $9,000 in personal estate; enlisted April 18, 1861, in Greensboro; left in Knoxville with measles; transferred to the Jeff Davis Legion to be with his brothers in August 1862.

*BORDEN, Joseph (January 27, 1828, North Carolina–1913, California). Married his stepsister Frances S. Gray ("Fannie") in 1851; in 1860 reported thirty-two slaves; member of the Greensboro Cavalry; enlisted in the Guards April 13, 1861, in Greensboro; third sergeant in April 1861; second sergeant in August 1861; second lieutenant in April 1862; wounded in July 1862; resigned December 12, 1863. Cousin of Guard James M. Jack.

*BORDEN, William W. In 1860 a student; enlisted April 20, 1861, in Greensboro; typhoid fever in August 1861; discharged August 13, 1862, for being underage; in 1880 a farmer, married with four or five children.

*BOSTICK, Lewis S. (died September 1862 while unloading a wagon of muskets). Enlisted March 10, 1862, in Greensboro; wagoner.

BOTTS, John Minor. Richmond lawyer and U.S. congressman; delegate to the 1866 Southern Loyalists' Convention.

BOWLES, P. D. Captain of the Conecuh Guards, Fourth Alabama Infantry.

BRAGG, Braxton. Succeeded Beauregard as commander of the Army of Tennessee; victor at Chickamauga, but replaced by Johnston at Chattanooga.

BRAME, Charles E. Professor at Southern University, Greensboro.

Braxton. Slave of Matthew Jones.

BRECKINRIDGE, John C. Vice president of the United States, 1857–1861; presidential candidate in 1860; commanded the Orphan Brigade in the West; transferred to Virginia and won the Battle of New Market as division commander; fled to Canada after the war.

*BRIDGES, D. J. Enlisted August 21, 1862, in Henry County, Virginia; wounded May 5, 1864; captured September 19, 1864, in Winchester, Virginia.

BRIGGS, Ann. Married William A. Sims in 1864.

*BRIGGS, Charles T. (c. 1842, Alabama–after 1906). In 1860 living at home; enlisted April 13, 1861, in Greensboro; discharged August 2, 1861, due to a disability; reenlisted November 20, 1862, in Middletown, Virginia; captured at Gettysburg; wounded May 8, 1864; typhoid fever in July 1864; sick in camp in February 1865; captured at

Petersburg April 2, 1865; in 1870 a dry goods clerk. Son of former Guard Samuel G. Briggs.

BRIGHTMAN, William M. Sergeant in the Haymouth Guards, Fifth Alabama Infantry.

*BRITTON, William G. (c. 1843–after 1910). Enlisted April 13, 1861, in Greensboro; third corporal in August 1861; wounded in the shoulder May 3, 1863; first sergeant in 1864; wounded July 13, 1864; wounded and captured September 19, 1864, right arm amputated; in 1870 a farmer reporting $500 in personal estate; in 1880 a tax collector, married with five children.

BROWN, F. A. Lieutenant in the Monroe Guards, Fifth Alabama Infantry.

BROWN, James. Wounded at Chattanooga; identity ambiguous.

BROWN, John. Planter from Hollow Square precinct.

BROWN, John Calvin. Tennesseean, enlisted as a private but by 1862 had been promoted to brigadier general; division commander under Hood; wounded at Fort Donelson, Perryville, Chickamauga, and Franklin, where his military career ended.

BROWN, Joseph Emerson. Governor of Georgia and opponent of Jefferson Davis.

*BROWN, Josiah McKendre (January 22, 1828, Greene County, Alabama–August 5, 1870). Enlisted April 16, 1861, in Greensboro; wounded in 1862; wounded and right leg amputated below the knee July 2, 1863; captured July 3, 1863; paroled September 25, 1863; married in 1868; farmer; Methodist.

BROWNLOW, William Gannaway. East Tennessee minister, vitriolic journalist, and impassioned Unionist; imprisoned and then expelled from the Confederacy; succeeded Andrew Johnson as governor in 1865.

BRYAN or BRYANT, James C. Quartermaster of Rodes' brigade and division 1862–1865 with the rank of major.

BUFORD, Abraham. Confederate general from Kentucky.

*BULGER, W. F. (died July 15, 1861, in Culpeper Court House, Virginia, of typhoid fever). Enlisted April 13, 1861, in Greensboro.

BURNSIDE, Ambrose Everett. Union general defeated at Fredericksburg.

BURTON, Horace. Member of Company K, Third Alabama Infantry.

*BURTON, James (c. 1838, Kentucky–November 3, 1863, in prison of smallpox). Member of Greensboro Cavalry; in 1860 a coach maker, married, and a Democrat; enlisted March 6, 1862, in Greensboro; captured at South Mountain and at Gettysburg.

*BUTLER, B. A. ("Bunk"). Enlisted March 8, 1862, in Greensboro; teamster in 1863; captured at Gettysburg; wounded and captured May 8, 1864.

BUTLER, Benjamin Franklin ("the Beast"). Controversial war Democrat who declared escaped slaves "contraband"; clashed with the women in occupied New Orleans; removed from command after a botched operation against Fort Fisher; after the war became a Radical who sought to remove Andrew Johnson.

BUTTS, Ben. Probably a member of the Ninth Alabama Infantry.

CADWALLADER, George. Federal general mustered out of service with Patterson after a failed attempt to hold Johnston's troops in the Valley during First Manassas.

CAMERON, Simon. Lincoln's secretary of war until his forced resignation in January 1862.

CAMPBELL, John Archibald. Former U.S. Supreme Court justice from Alabama; represented the Confederacy at Hampton Roads Peace Conference.

*CARBERRY, John. Enlisted April 13, 1861, in Greensboro; pioneer March–December 31, 1863; sick in camp in February 1865; captured April 2, 1865.

Carey. A slave of Jack Wynne.

*CARROLL, D. L. (died May 14, 1863, following a gunshot wound and an amputated arm after Chancellorsville). Enlisted before December 1862; wounded and captured May 3, 1863.

CARSON, Thomas K. Greensboro merchant; member of the Greensboro Guards from 1838 at least through 1846.

*CARTER, Benjamin A. (c. 1827, North Carolina–1870). Mason 1858–1870; in 1860 an overseer; enlisted April 13, 1861, in Greensboro; wounded May 3, 1863; surgical assistant.

CARTER, Thomas H. Captain of the King William Artillery.

*CHADWICK, Hanson M. Enlisted April 16, 1861, in Greensboro; captured November 21, 1863; released on oath of allegiance January 8, 1864.

CHADWICK, Mary A. Mother of Guards Shelby W. and Robert A. Chadwick.

*CHADWICK, Robert A. (c. 1845–). In 1860 a student; married Mary Willingham July 24, 1861; enlisted August 9, 1861, in Greensboro; discharged August 13, 1862, for being underage, but captured May 3, 1863, and on wounded furlough in 1864; moved to Austin, Texas, after the war. Brother of Guard Shelby W. Chadwick (Jr.).

*CHADWICK, Shelby W. (Jr.) (September 26, 1842, Alabama–1897). Enlisted in the Cahaba Rifles, Fifth Alabama Infantry June 16, 1861; transferred to the Greensboro Guards August 1, 1861; wounded in the right hand in 1862; promoted from fourth sergeant to sergeant major in February 1864; taken prisoner April 2, 1865; Mason; clerk, merchant, surveyor, county treasurer; Methodist. Son of former Guard Shelby W. Chadwick Sr., brother of Guard Robert A. Chadwick.

CHADWICK, William H. Member of Fifth Texas.

*CHAPMAN, Alonzo B. (c. 1840–May 31, 1862 at Seven Pines). Enlisted April 13, 1861, in Greensboro after recent move from Dallas County, Alabama.

CHARLES, Harriet J. Stickney. Daughter of early Greensboro settler Joseph B. Stickney.

CHASE, Salmon Portland. Lincoln's secretary of treasury.

CHENEY, Mrs. Ann. Aunt of John H. Cowin.

*CHILDRESS, Henry R. (c. 1844, Alabama–). Enlisted March 6, 1862, in Greensboro; captured September 19, 1864, in Winchester, Virginia; exchanged October 30, 1864; captured April 2, 1865. Brother of Guard Jeff Childress.

*CHILDRESS, Jeff. Left on thirty-day furlough March 11, 1864; in camp in February 1865. Brother of Guard Henry Childress.

*CHILES, J. W. (c. 1840, Alabama–March 19, 1864). His father owned fifty-one slaves in 1860; enlisted August 26, 1862, in Pike County, Alabama; captured July 14, 1863; may have joined the federal service January 25, 1864. (*Note:* Ambiguous records may refer to two individuals.)

*CHRISTIAN, Henry (c. 1820, Virginia–). Enlisted August 9, 1861, in Greensboro; discharged July 22, 1862, due to inability to perform duty.

*CHRISTIAN, John F. (c. 1839, Alabama–). In 1860 a hotelier living with his widowed mother and six siblings, reporting $3,500 in personal estate, including five slaves; fourth corporal at Fort Morgan; enlisted April 13, 1861, in Greensboro; first sergeant May 13, 1861; brevet second lieutenant May 28, 1861; captured September 14, 1862, and May 3, 1863; elected third lieutenant March 30, 1863; wounded July 18, 1864; in camp February 23, 1865; captured April 2, 1865.

CLANTON, James Holt. Colonel of the First Alabama Cavalry; commissioned brigadier in the spring of 1863, serving under Polk.

CLEBURNE, Patrick Ronayne. Irish-born colonel of Arkansas troops; wounded as a division commander; prominent at Chickamauga and Chattanooga; killed in action in 1864; a respected general most noted for advocating Confederate use of black troops.

*CLEMENTS, J. W. (1835–). Student at the University of Virginia in 1854; from Eutaw, Alabama; Warrior Guard who transferred to the Greensboro Guards in April 1862.

*CLIFTON, William (c. 1819, South Carolina–). From Tuscaloosa, Alabama; enlisted February 16, 1863, in Grace Church, Virginia; detailed as a blacksmith in Carter's Battery in 1863; sick in camp in February 1865; captured April 2, 1865.

CLOWER, Joe. John H. Cowin's friend from Woodstock, Virginia.

COBB, Thomas Reade Rootes. Georgian politician and brigade commander killed at Fredericksburg.

*COBBS, William Addison. Captured April 2, 1865.

COCHRANE, John. Outspoken Democratic congressman from New York who believed that the North had acted unfairly to the South; served as colonel of the Sixty-fifth New York Infantry in 1861; resigned as brigadier general in 1863.

*COLEMAN, Alonzo G. ("Lonnie") (1837, Alabama–March 1899). Student at the University of Virginia in 1856; enlisted May 6, 1861, in Uniontown, Alabama; wounded May 31, 1862, and discharged; joined Partisan Rangers, Fifty-first Alabama Infantry; captured, escaped to Canada; cotton planter after the war.

COLEMAN, S. C. ("Cruse"). Orderly sergeant in the Sumter Rifle Guard, Fifth Alabama Infantry; former student at the Greene Springs School.

COLQUITT, Alfred Holt. Colonel of the Sixth Georgia Infantry; promoted to brigadier in 1862; won the Battle of Olustee, Florida.

COOKE, Philip. Colonel of the Fourth Georgia Infantry who succeeded Brigadier General George Pierce Doles upon his death at Bethesda Church.

COOLIDGE, Richard H. Union army medical inspector.

COOPER, Samuel. Adjutant and inspector general of the Confederate army.

*COWIN, John Henry. (1839, Alabama–May 3, 1863, at Chancellorsville). Attended the Greene Springs School; student at the University of Virginia in 1858; graduated from Jefferson Medical College in 1860; enlisted April 13, 1861, in Greensboro; corporal, orderly sergeant. Son of Guard Samuel C. Cowin and brother of Guard William S. Cowin.

COWIN, Martha. Wife of Guard Samuel Cowin and mother of Guards John H. Cowin and William S. Cowin.

*COWIN, Samuel C. (c. 1813, Maryland–1886). In 1830 reported two slaves; married in 1836; enlisted February 22, 1836; first corporal in 1846; in 1850 reported fifteen slaves; in 1860 a planter and hotelier with three sons reporting $19,665 in real estate and $60,000 in personal estate, including fifty slaves; enlisted in the Guards April 13, 1861, in Greensboro; second lieutenant in October 1861; resigned in April 1862. Father of Guards John H. Cowin and William S. Cowin.

COWIN, Thomas. Son of Guard Samuel Cowin and brother of Guards John Henry and William S. Cowin.

*COWIN, William S. ("Tood") (c. 1842, Alabama–). Student at the University of Alabama; enlisted April 13, 1861, in Greensboro; wounded in October 1862; brigade courier in May 1863; division commissary clerk in October 1864. Son of Guard Samuel C. Cowin and brother of Guard John H. Cowin.

COX, William Ruffin. North Carolinian promoted to brigadier general after Spotsylvania.

*CRADDOCK, J. N. Warrior Guard who transferred to the Greensboro Guards in April 1862.

CREWS, Octavius L. *See* CRUSE, Octavius L.

CROOM, Isaac. Greensboro planter.

*CROOM, Wiley G. (c. 1844, Alabama–). In 1850 his parents in Newbern, Alabama, reported $10,000 in real estate and thirty-seven slaves; in 1860 reported $32,000 in real estate and $100,000 in personal estate, including fifty-nine slaves; enlisted April 22, 1861, in Greensboro.

*CROWELL, J. W. Enlisted April 13, 1861, in Greensboro; musician; wounded May 31, 1862; transferred to Thirtieth North Carolina Infantry April 7, 1863.

CRUSE or CREWS, Octavius L. Druggist; member of the Livingston Rifles, Fifth Alabama Infantry.

CUMMINGS, Chesley or Jesse D. Member of the Pickensville Blues, Fifth Alabama Infantry.

CUMMINGS, Thomas B. Member of the Livingston Rifles, Fifth Alabama Infantry.

CURRY, Jabez Lamar Monroe. Alabama congressman who initially supported Davis but became increasingly critical of his conduct of the war; after the war, president of Howard College and Richmond College, minister to Spain.

CURRY, William Green. Former member of the Monroe Guards; color corporal; ordained as a Baptist minister; appointed chaplain for the Fifth Alabama Infantry in 1863.

CURTIN, Andrew Gregg. Republican governor of Pennsylvania (1861–1867).

DAMER (sometimes DAMAR), Juliet M. Virginian. Fiancée of James Pickens, whom he married April 1, 1865.

DANIEL, Junius. North Carolina brigadier in Rodes' division; served with distinction at Gettysburg; mortally wounded at Spottsylvania.

DANIELS, John Moncure. Editor of the *Richmond Examiner*.

Dave. Slave of William Shelden.

DAWSON, N. H. R. Captain of the Magnolia Cadets, Fourth Alabama Infantry.

*DEDMAN, Marcus L. (c. 1822, Virginia–c. 1867). In 1860 a marshal and mechanic, married with two children, reporting $1,000 in real estate, and a Democrat; enlisted April 13, 1861, in Greensboro; second lieutenant in April 1861; second lieutenant in May 1861; resigned in October 1861 to form his own company.

DEJARNETTE, Daniel Coleman. Confederate congressman from Virginia who consistently supported the Davis administration.

DELOACH, William R. Member of the Livingston Rifles, Fifth Alabama Infantry.

DENT, George. Brother of John Hubbard Dent; entered the Fifth Alabama Infantry in August 1861.

DENT, John Hubbard. Captain of the Livingston Rifles, Fifth Alabama Infantry (1861).

DESHLER, James. Alabama artillerist; brigadier killed at Chickamauga.

DOLES, George Pierce. Colonel of the Fourth Georgia Infantry; promoted to brigadier after the Seven Days' battles; killed at Bethesda Church during the Cold Harbor campaign.

DORROH, Belinda. Mother of Samuel J., John, and Guard William Gayle Dorroh.

DORROH, James. Father of Samuel J., John, and Guard William Gayle Dorroh; died May 8, 1864.

DORROH, John. Brother of Guard Samuel Dorroh.

*DORROH, Samuel J. (c. 1840, Alabama–September 25, 1861, of typhoid). In 1860 living with his mother (Belinda) and father, who reported $12,500 in real estate and $50,000 in personal estate, including thirty-one slaves; enlisted April 20, 1861, in Greensboro. Cousin of Guards John J. Wright and Joseph L. Wright.

DORROH, William Gayle. Son of James and Belinda Hyle Dorroh, planters in Hollow Square precinct, near the Pickens family; University of Alabama cadet 1863–1864. Younger brother of Guard Samuel J. Dorroh.

DOUGHDELL, J. L. Lieutenant in Captain Tayloe's Cavalry company, Jeff Davis Legion.

Douglas. Slave of Richard H. Adams.

*DUFPHEY, London. Slave who drummed in the Creek War, for the Greensboro Volunteers in Mexico, and for the Guards in the early part of the Civil War.

DUFPHEY, Samuel. A Forkland planter and cousin to the Pickens.

*DUFPHEY, William L. (1832–). In 1860 his mother reported $30,000 in real estate and $45,000 in personal estate, including forty-eight slaves; member of the Greensboro Cavalry; enlisted April 18, 1861, in Greensboro; discharged December 19, 1861, due to a disability. Probably the son of the early Greensboro Guard William L. Dufphey.

DUNLAP, George. Member of the Sumter Rifle Guard, Fifth Alabama Infantry.

DUNLAP, George H., Jr. Lieutenant in Company K, Third Alabama Infantry; acting assistant adjutant general in 1865.

DUNLAP, William, and daughter Mollie. Middlebrook, Virginia, residents.

DUNOVANT, John. South Carolina brigadier general killed October 1, 1864, south of James River.

EARLY, Jubal Anderson. Virginian who in 1864 commanded the Army of the Valley, in which the Guards served, that threatened Washington.

EHART, Andrew J. Captain in the Thirteenth Virginia Infantry.

*ELIAS, Lewis. Enlisted July 18, 1861, in Montgomery; baker; wounded May 5, 1864; returned to his company under guard in December 1864; in camp in February 1865; deserted March 20, 1865.

*ELLIOTT, Joseph Knox ("Old Elliott"). Warrior Guard who transferred to the Greensboro Guards in April 1862; discharged July 22, 1862, as unable to perform duty and detailed to quartermaster department.

*ELLIOTT, William. Warrior Guard from Havanna, Alabama, who transferred to the Greensboro Guards in April 1862.

*ELLISON, William B. (c. 1838–June 27, 1862, at Gaines' Mill). Mason 1860–1862; enlisted August 9, 1861, in Greensboro; sutler.

ELZEY, Arnold. Maryland-born commander of the Department of Richmond during 1863 and most of 1864.

EUSTIS or EUSTIC, James L. Member of the Livingston Rifles, Fifth Alabama Infantry.

EVANS, Abner. Planter living in Hollow Square, west of Greensboro.

EWELL, Richard Stoddert. Commanded the Second Virginia Infantry Brigade at First Manassas; lost a leg at Groveton in August 1862; succeeded Stonewall Jackson as commander of the Second Corps.

FARLEY, Charles K. Cahaba physician appointed first commissary to the Fifth Alabama Infantry.

*FARRIER, J. A. Enlisted August 23, 1862, in Washington County, Alabama; wounded in the arm and captured May 3, 1863; wounded May 5, 1864; in camp in February 1865; captured April 2, 1865.

FEN or FENN, Matthew M. C. Member of the Barbour Greys, Fifth Alabama Infantry.

FERGUSON, Sampson Noland. Captain of the Pickensville Blues, Fifth Alabama Infantry (1861).

FIELD, Charles William. As commander of Hood's Texas division, saved Lee's right wing at the Wilderness.

FINKLEY, Julius C. Sergeant in the Monroe Guards, Fifth Alabama Infantry.

FIQUET, Dominique Deux. Member of the Warrior Guards, Fifth Alabama Infantry.

FLEMING, James W. Lieutenant in the Grove Hill Guards, Fifth Alabama Infantry.

FLOWERS, T. C. Lieutenant in the Talladega Artillery, Fifth Alabama Infantry.

FLOYD, John B. Uncooperative Confederate commander in western Virginia; relieved of command in March 1862.

FONTAINE, J. B. Surgeon in Wade Hampton's cavalry when killed October 1, 1864.

FOOTE, Henry Stuart. Confederate congressman from Tennessee who opposed the Davis administration on several issues.

FORNEY, John H. Colonel of the Tenth Alabama Infantry.

FORREST, Nathan Bedford. Tennessee-born Confederate cavalry leader in the West; began as a private and was promoted to lieutenant general in 1865.

FORSYTH, Charles M. Colonel of the Third Alabama Infantry during the spring of 1864.

*FOSTER, Ezra. Warrior Guard who transferred to the Greensboro Guards in April 1862; wounded May 31, 1862.

FOUNTAIN. *See* FONTAINE, J. B.

*FOWLER, Henry. Enlisted May 25, 1861, in Coffee County, Alabama; wounded in the arm May 3, 1863; discharged June 30, 1864.

FOWLER, William Henry (June 15, 1826–August 10, 1867). Editor; Greensboro Guard during the 1840s; succeeded Rodes as captain of the Warrior Guards, Fifth Alabama Infantry (1861); raised Fowler's Battery in Tuscaloosa; commissioned colonel of artillery; kept statistics of Alabama troops through the end of the war.

*FRIERSON, Thomas McRea. Warrior Guard who transferred to the Greensboro Guards in April 1862; fourth corporal; captured September 14, 1862; transferred to cavalry in October 1862.

FULLERTON, William R. Member of the Pickensville Blues, Fifth Alabama Infantry.

FULTON, William. Member of the North Sumter Rifles Infantry.

GARLAND, Samuel. One of the prominent Garland brothers (Augustus Hill, Landon Cabell, and Rufus King Jr.); killed at the Battle of South Mountain.

*GAWICKI, Stan (c. 1836, Poland or Germany-). In 1860 a tailor reporting $1,000 in personal estate; enlisted August 9, 1861, in Greensboro; musician; discharged October 27, 1862.

GAYLE, Bristor B. Colonel of the Twelfth Alabama Infantry; killed at South Mountain.

*GEDDIE, H. Enlisted April 22, 1861, in Greensboro; wounded in August 1862; captured May 20, 1864; exchanged October 29, 1864; in camp in February 1865.

GILLMORE, Quincy Adams. Union major general and engineer who directed the siege of Charleston.

GIOVANNI, A. F. Montgomery, Alabama, confectioner.

*GIVENS, John J. (c. 1827, Alabama–November or December 1862 of pneumonia). Enlisted September 28, 1862, in Henry County, Alabama; farmer.

GLOVER, Alfred. Brother of Guard Walton N. Glover.

GLOVER, Terry. Brother of Guard Walton N. Glover.

*GLOVER, Walton N. (c. 1841, Alabama-). In 1860 living with his father, who reported $91,200 in real estate and $193,000 in personal estate, including 148 slaves; enlisted August 14, 1861, in Union Mills, Virginia; brigade commissary clerk; broke a leg in February 1863.

GOFF, James M. Lieutenant in the Grove Hill Guards, Fifth Alabama Infantry.

GOODE, Giles. Captain of the Monroe Guards, Fifth Alabama Infantry; died September 25, 1861.

GOODGAME, John Chapman. Lieutenant colonel of the Twelfth Alabama Infantry.

GORDON, James. Member of the Eleventh Alabama Infantry; an ambiguous name.

GORDON, John Brown. Colonel of the Sixth Alabama who rose to command the Second Corps in 1865.

*GOSLIN, A. J. Enlisted September 10, 1862, in Virginia.

GRANT, Ulysses S. As commander in chief of the U.S. Army beginning in March 1864, Grant made his headquarters with Meade's Army of the Potomac.

GREEN, John S. Sergeant major in the Mobile Continentals, Fifth Alabama Infantry; resigned in September 1861.

GREEN, R. M. Captain of the Russell County company in the Sixth Alabama Infantry.

GREGG, John. Born in Alabama but moved to Texas in 1861; Confederate congressman before raising an infantry regiment; routed Rosecrans at Chickamauga; killed in 1864 near Richmond.

GREGG, Maxcy. South Carolinian general killed at Fredericksburg.

*GRIGG, Joe A. Enlisted April 16, 1861, in Greensboro; wagon master and division courier for Rodes; captured September 14, 1862.

*GRIGGS, James E. ("Squire") (c. 1813, Virginia–October 11, 1873). In 1860 a deputy sheriff; enlisted April 13, 1861, in Greensboro; fourth corporal in April 1861; wagon master in August 1861; discharged August 13, 1862, for being overage.

GRIMES, Bryan. North Carolinian promoted to brigadier general following critical service at the Wilderness; promoted to major general in February 1865.

GRISWOLD, E. Richmond provost marshal with the rank of major; prison camp commander.

*HADEN, W. B. Warrior Guard who transferred to the Greensboro Guards in April 1862; wounded May 31, 1862.

*HAFNER, Charles W. (1843–December 4, 1864, after Cedar Creek). In 1860 living with his father, a blacksmith who owned two slaves; enlisted March 16, 1862, in Greensboro; slightly wounded May 31, 1862; fifth sergeant; fourth sergeant in 1862; wounded September 14, 1862; fractured his left arm and captured May 3, 1863; fatally shot through the colon and rectum October 19, 1864. Brother of Guard William G. Hafner.

*HAFNER, William G. (December 17, 1842, South Carolina–). In 1861 a clerk living with his mother and father, a Forkland, Alabama, blacksmith; enlisted August 9, 1861, in Greensboro; wounded May 19, 1864; in 1868 an officer in Greensboro Fire Company 1. Brother of Guard Charles W. Hafner.

HAGINS, George W. Newbern planter and father of Guard Peter Hagins.

*HAGINS, Peter (c. 1838–). In 1860 an overseer in Newbern, Alabama, living with his father, also an overseer, who reported $4,000 in personal estate, including five slaves; enlisted April 22, 1861, in Greensboro; captured May 3, 1863; acting regimental commissary sergeant in camp in February 1865.

HAGUE, ———. Minister from Richmond.

HALL, Josephus M. Captain of the Grove Hill Guards, Fifth Alabama Infantry in 1861; elected lieutenant colonel of the Fifth Alabama Infantry in 1862; colonel when his arm was removed at Spotsylvania; retired in December 1864.

HAMPTON, Wade. Cavalry general under J. E. B. Stuart, whom he succeeded as corps commander upon the latter's death; after the war elected governor of South Carolina and U.S. senator.

HARDAWAY, James. Member of the Cahaba Rifles, Fifth Alabama Infantry.

HARDAWAY, M. L. Wife of William Hardaway.

*HARDAWAY, Robert H. (c. 1827, Virginia–). In 1860 a deputy sheriff and clerk reporting $300 in personal estate; enlisted April 13, 1861, in Greensboro; discharged March 31, 1862.

HARDAWAY, William R. Sheriff and former Guard.

*HARGROVE, Andrew Coleman. Warrior Guard who transferred to the Greensboro Guards in April 1862; discharged for a disability, then raised his own company.

HARRIS, John Gideon. Wealthy Greensboro lawyer and planter; former Greensboro Guard; later captain of the Planters' Guards (Company I), Twentieth Alabama Infantry, from which he was promoted to major.

HARRISON, James. Popular actor in Richmond.

HARVEY, John G. Editor of the *Greensboro Alabama Beacon;* West Point graduate variously called captain or colonel.

*HAUSMAN, Christopher Jacob. Warrior Guard who transferred to the Greensboro Guards in April 1862; wounded May 2, 1863, and May 6, 1864.

HAYS, Harry Thompson. Colonel of the Seventh Louisiana Infantry; promoted to brigadier in 1862; distinguished service at Sharpsburg, Fredericksburg, Chancellorsville, and Gettysburg; severely wounded at Spottsylvania.

HECKMAN, Charles Adam. Pennsylvania brigadier general captured at Drewry's Bluff, a Union defeat for which he was largely blamed.

HELLER, Lucy. Daughter of Moritez and future wife of Henry Beck.

HELLER, Moritez. Father of Lucy, living in Harrisonburg, Virginia.

HELM, Benjamin Hardin. Kentucky brigadier killed at Chickamauga.

HENDON, Benj. F. Newbern, Alabama, physician.

HERNDON, Thomas Hord. With J. D. Webb, successful secessionist candidate for the Alabama Convention; colonel of the Thirty-sixth Alabama Infantry; wounded at Chickamauga and Atlanta.

*HERRAN, J. C. N. (c. 1843, Alabama–December 16, 1861, in Richmond of disease). In 1860 living with his mother and father, a small farmer in Havanna, Alabama; enlisted April 25, 1861, in Greensboro.

HETH, Henry. Division commander in A. P. Hill's Corps; wounded at Chancellorsville and Gettysburg.

HIGH, Isaiah. Overseer for the Pickens family's Canebrake plantation.

HILL, Ambrose Powell. Commanded well during the Peninsula campaign and at Fredericksburg and Chancellorsville; commanded the Third Corps; killed in April 1865.

HILL, Charles. *See* HILL, Thomas Carter.

HILL, Daniel Harvey. Division commander in the Army of Northern Virginia until after Fredericksburg, when transferred to the Department of North Carolina; after Hill voiced disgust with Bragg's actions at Chickamauga, Davis withdrew his support.

HILL, Louis H. Lieutenant colonel of the Sixty-first Alabama Infantry; from Coosa County.

*HILL, Thomas Charles or Carter (c. 1847, Alabama–). In 1860 a Newbern, Alabama, physician and farmer who reported $20,000 in personal estate, including thirteen slaves; enlisted April 22, 1861, in Greensboro; first sergeant in August 1861; appointed assistant surgeon in the Fifth Alabama Infantry in 1863; later a surgeon; assigned to Lomax's cavalry division in 1864.

*HOBSON, Edwin Lafayette (1835, Alabama–November 2, 1901, Virginia). Attended the Greene Springs School; student at the University of Virginia in 1852; part of the Guards' 1857 reorganization; in 1860 a planter reporting $20,000 in real estate and $25,000 in personal estate, including twenty-seven slaves; with his mother reporting $20,000 in personal estate and other family members reporting ninety-five slaves; enlisted April 13, 1861, in Greensboro; elected captain May 13, 1861; elected major of the Fifth Alabama Infantry in April 1862; wounded in the left thigh May 2, 1863; wounded in the thigh May 8, 1864; colonel November 29, 1864; married daughter of J. R. Anderson of Tredegar Iron Works, where he worked after the war; ten children; Episcopalian.

HOFFMAN, William. Brevetted Union brigadier general at Point Lookout prison camp.

HOKE, Robert Frederick. North Carolinian promoted to brigadier general in early 1863 and major general a few months later; sent to North Carolina the next year to drive out Federal forces.

HOLDEN, William Woods. Successor to Zebulon Vance as governor of North Carolina; appointed provisional governor by President Johnson and later elected in his own right as a Republican.

*HOLLAND, H. T. (c. 1829–February 16 or 17, 1863, of disease). Enlisted September 21, 1862, in Henry County, Alabama; farmer.

HOLLBURG, ———. Physician with the Fifth Alabama Infantry.

HOLMES, Theophilus Hunter. Promoted to lieutenant general after the Seven Days' battles and commanded the Trans-Mississippi West until March 1863, when given command of the District of Arkansas.

HOOD, John Bell. General who lost an arm at Gettysburg and a leg at Chickamauga; succeeded Johnston in Georgia and lost his army at Nashville and Franklin.

HOOD, Samuel W. Member of the Pickensville Blues, Fifth Alabama Infantry.

*HOOPER, William R. (c. 1845, Alabama–). In 1860 a student; enlisted April 13, 1861, in Greensboro; wagoner; discharged August 13, 1862, for inability.

HOPKINS, Abner C. Chaplain of the Second Virginia Infantry.

*HUGGINS, Fred L. (c. 1844, Alabama–). In 1860 a student living in Newbern, Alabama, with his mother and father, who reported $2,500 in real estate and $10,000 in personal estate, including six slaves; enlisted April 22, 1861, in Greensboro; captured September 14, 1862; wounded September 3, 1864; captured September 25, 1864; wounded in the leg and captured October 19, 1864; in 1880 an unmarried store clerk.

*HUGGINS, Noah F. Member of the Guards in 1864.

*HUGGINS, Peter. *See* HAGINS, Peter.

HUMPHREYS, Benjamin Grubb. Mississippian promoted to brigadier general following distinguished action at Fredericksburg, Chancellorsville, and Gettysburg; participated in Wilderness campaign and the Valley campaign before being sent to Mississippi.

HUNTER, Robert Mercer Taliaferro. Confederate senator who, along with Alexander Stephens and John A. Campbell, met with Lincoln in early 1865 to discuss ending the war.

HUNTER, Thomas. Physician; member of the Cahaba Rifles, Fifth Alabama Infantry; served as regimental surgeon; resigned as lieutenant in 1862.

*HUTCHINSON, Edward T. (January 20, 1844–December 3, 1927). Enlisted April 20, 1863, in Grace Court House, Virginia; captured May 3, 1863; wounded May 8, 1864, and October 19, 1864; sick in camp in February 1865; reputed to be the only Guard present at Appomattox; in 1870 a dry goods clerk and an officer of Greensboro Fire Company 1; married in 1875. Son of the Reverend J. J. Hutchinson.

HUTCHINSON, James. Lieutenant and aide-de-camp to General Rodes; killed at the Bloody Angle May 12, 1864. Son of the Reverend J. J. Hutchinson.

HUTCHINSON, Joseph Johnston. Prominent secessionist Methodist minister from Greensboro whose four sons all served in the army, one as a Greensboro Guard.

HUTTON, Aquila. Greene County member of Company C, Thirty-sixth Alabama Infantry.

*IDOM, Edwin Young (c. 1843, Alabama–). In 1860 living with his mother and father, a well digger who reported $300 in real estate and $100 in personal estate; enlisted April 16, 1861, in Greensboro; brigade and division butcher; in 1870 a farmer, married with one son. Nephew of Guard William Young Idom.

*IDOM, William Young (c. 1825, Alabama–). Married in 1843; in 1860 a well digger with four children, reporting $1,300 in real estate and $1,600 in personal estate; enlisted April 13, 1861, in Greensboro; butcher, ambulance driver; discharged August 13, 1862, as overage but on duty again by May 1863; wounded in the thigh and back October 19, 1864; in camp in February 1865. Uncle of Guard Edwin Young Idom.

INGE, Richard Freer. Law partner of J. D. Webb; lieutenant colonel of the Eighteenth Alabama Infantry; killed at Chickamauga.

IVERSON, Alfred, Jr. Colonel of the Twentieth North Carolina Infantry; promoted to brigadier in 1862; sent to Georgia after Gettysburg.

JACK, James. Planter and father of Guard James M. Jack.

*JACK, James M. (c. 1830, Alabama–). Attended the Greene Springs School; in 1860 attending the Havanna, Alabama, plantation of his father, who reported $23,000 in real estate and $100,000 in personal estate, including seventy slaves; enlisted April 20, 1861, in Greensboro; lost his left leg July 1, 1862; captain of home guards; married in 1867; in 1870 a Havanna farmer with one child reporting $6,000 in real estate and $1,600 in personal estate; legislator in 1876; tax assessor in 1884. Cousin of Guard Joseph Borden.

*JACKSON, Andrew. Enlisted October 15, 1862, in Macon County, Alabama; prisoner of war in March 1864; captured October 19, 1864; exchanged January 17, 1865; illiterate. Brother of Guard Samuel B. Jackson.

*JACKSON, John F. (c. 1847–). Enlisted May 12, 1861, in Montgomery; ambulance driver; captured September 14, 1862.

*JACKSON, Norborne H. T. (c. 1843–). In 1860 a student at the Greene Springs School; enlisted April 17, 1861, in Greensboro; discharged October 5, 1861, for a disability; in 1870 a druggist, married with one child. Son of former Guard John T. Jackson.

*JACKSON, Samuel B. From Linden, Marengo County, Alabama; enlisted May 12, 1861, in Montgomery; wounded May 2 and 3, 1863, and had three toes amputated. Brother of Guard Andrew Jackson.

JACKSON, Thomas Jonathan ("Stonewall"). Commander of the Second Division (in which the Guards fought) until his death at Chancellorsville.

*JAMES, Cunningham ("Cunny") (c. 1842, Virginia–). In 1850 his father owned twenty-two slaves; enlisted April 25, 1861, in Greensboro; discharged November 28, 1862, due to typhoid, pneumonia, and chronic diarrhea; joined the Jeff Davis Legion.

*JAMES, Gilliam (c. 1835, Virginia–). Enlisted April 25, 1861, in Greensboro; division courier cited by Rodes for great service at Chancellorsville; left company in December 1864 after an exchange with Private Wesson of the Jeff Davis Legion; in 1880 an unmarried farmer.

*JEFFRIES, Robert H. (c. 1840–). In 1860 owned thirteen slaves and was attending the farm of his father, Algernon S. Jeffries, an 1861 Cooperationist candidate, who reported $51,900 in real estate and $57,000 in personal estate, including fifty slaves; enlisted April 13, 1861, in Greensboro; wounded July 1, 1862; foot and leg amputated.

JENKINS, Albert Gallatin. Lawyer from western Virginia who commanded a cavalry brigade during the Gettysburg campaign.

JENKINS, John T. Member of the Livingston Rifles, Fifth Alabama Infantry; died October 28, 1861.

John. Slave of Pickens family who accompanied Sam to Virginia.

JOHNSON, A. P. Member of the Talladega Artillery, Fifth Alabama Infantry.

JOHNSON, Andrew. Greensboro carriage maker.

JOHNSON, Andrew. Lincoln's vice president, thought to have been targeted in the 1865 assassination of Lincoln.

JOHNSON, Bushrod Rust. After a successful career in the West, including division commander at Chickamauga and in east Tennessee under Longstreet, promoted to major general and fought in Virginia; surrendered with Lee at Appomattox.

JOHNSON, Edward ("Allegheny"). Division commander in Ewell's Second Corps; led an 1863 assault on Culp's Hill.

*JOHNSON, James M. Enlisted in April or May 1861; deserted June 30, 1861.

JOHNSTON, Ed. *See* JOHNSON, Edward.

JOHNSTON, Joseph Eggleston. Confederate general who assisted Beauregard at First Manassas; commanded Confederate forces in the Peninsula campaign before being wounded and replaced by Robert E. Lee; commanded the Army of Tennessee against William T. Sherman until July 1864.

*JONES, Allen Cadwallader (c. 1812, North Carolina–January 9, 1894). Commissioner of free schools in 1854, legislator, agriculturalist, member of the Joint Military Committee; in 1860 a planter, married with five children, reporting $30,000 in real estate and $78,000 in personal estate, including seventy-two slaves; reorganized the Guards and served as captain February 1857–April 1861; lieutenant colonel of the Fifth Alabama Infantry in May 1861; colonel in November 1861; resigned in April 1862; in 1870 reported $34,000 in real estate and $15,000 in personal estate. Brother-in-law of former Guard George W. Erwin.

JONES, Dan. Member of the Selma Blues, Eighth Alabama Infantry.

*JONES, Edwin Pompey (c. 1841, Alabama–). Enlisted April 13, 1861, in Greensboro; corporal in June 1861; fourth sergeant in August 1861; orderly sergeant in April 1862; wounded in the right side and hand July 1, 1862; captured May 3, 1863; second lieutenant in May 1863; first lieutenant in 1864; captured July 18, 1864. Son of former Guard Claudius Jones.

JONES, Egbert J. Colonel of the Fourth Alabama Infantry; mortally wounded at First Manassas.

JONES, John M. Brigadier general killed on the first day of the Battle of the Wilderness.

JONES, Madison. Younger brother of Guard Napoleon Jones.

*JONES, Matthew H. (July 15, 1845–). From Mobile; enlisted April 20, 1863, in Santee, Virginia; wounded in the hand and foot May 2, 1863; appointed CSA cadet September 18, 1863.

*JONES, Napoleon B. (c. 1831, Alabama–after 1910). In 1860 living as a planter with or near his father, a planter and physician, who reported $121,357 in real estate and

$250,000 in personal estate; enlisted April 25, 1861, in Greensboro; appointed first corporal of a company of mounted infantry in May 1863.

JONES, Samuel. Virginia general whose uneven career included service in Pensacola, east Tennessee, West Virginia, and finally as head of the Department of South Carolina, Georgia, and Florida.

JONES, William G. Judge and father of Guard Matthew H. Jones.

*JONES, William J. (c. 1842, Alabama–). Enlisted April 20, 1861, in Greensboro; second corporal in 1863.

Keeley. Slave in a Richmond hospital.

KELLER, Jonas. Friend of Henry Beck living in Mount Crawford, Virginia.

*KENNEDY, William L. ("Tink") (c. 1842, Alabama–). In 1860 a student; enlisted April 13, 1861, in Greensboro; color corporal in August 1861; color sergeant May 31, 1862; wounded in September 1862; wounded September 19, 1864; exchanged October 30, 1864; captured at Amelia Court House April 5, 1865. Son of former Guard Warren E. Kennedy.

KERR, Ann Locke. Wife of William Kerr and mother of Guard James W. Locke by a former marriage; established hospitals for the Guards in Pensacola and Culpeper Court House, Virginia.

KERR, William. Major general in the Alabama militia; former captain of the Greensboro Cavalry; successful merchant and farmer.

KERSHAW, Joseph Brevard. Brigade commander who led a division in a crucial assault at the Wilderness.

KETCHUM, George Augustus. Surgeon in the Fifth Alabama Infantry.

KETCHUM, William H. Mobile physician; among the founders of the Medical College of Alabama; delegate to the Secession Convention; Captain of the Mobile Continental State Artillery, Fifth Alabama Infantry, in 1861.

KILPATRICK, Judson. Union cavalry commander assigned to Sherman during the March to the Sea and afterward.

KING, Mrs. Elisha. Wife of a prominent Hamburg, Alabama, planter.

KING, Porter. Marion lawyer and captain of the Marion Light Infantry, Fourth Alabama Infantry.

KIRKLAND, William Whedbee. In 1864, brigadier general in Hoke's division.

*KNIGHT, Sam. Enlisted September 22, 1862, in Washington County, Alabama; declared deserted in August 1863 after a furlough for typhoid fever.

*KNIGHT, William N. (c. 1840, Alabama–after 1910). Enlisted May 8, 1861, in Pensacola, Florida; discharged for a disability in October 1861; reenlisted and made captain of another company; Mason 1867–1903; in 1870 a farmer, married with two sons, reporting $33,000 in real estate and $7,000 in personal estate.

*KNOWLEN or KNOWLES or KNOLAND, John T. (c. 1824, Washington, D.C.–). In 1850 a painter, married, with one slave; enlisted May 13, 1861, in Pensacola, Florida; wounded May 31, 1861; captured July 2, 1863.

LACY, William Sterling. Distinguished Presbyterian minister and artillery commander in Jackson's corps.

LANE, Joseph. Senator from Oregon, 1859–1861; ran unsuccessfully for vice president with John C. Breckinridge in 1861.

LANGHAM, Sarah. Cousin of John H. Cowin.

*LANIER, Robert B. (c. 1840, North Carolina–). In 1860 living with his mother and father, a farmer reporting $10,735 in real estate and $25,000 in personal estate; enlisted April 22, 1861, in Greensboro; discharged for a constricted urethra January 11, 1862. Brother of Guard William A. Lanier.

*LANIER, William A. (c. 1841, North Carolina–November 17, 1864, from chest wound at Cedar Creek). In 1860 a student living with his parents; enlisted April 22, 1861, in Greensboro; wounded May 31, 1862; wounded in the head and captured July 2, 1863; exchanged April 27, 1864; shot in the lung and captured October 19, 1864. Brother of Guard Robert B. Lanier.

*LAVENDER, Paul H. (c. 1833, Alabama–May 27, 1883). In 1860 a merchant clerk reporting $2,500 in personal estate, including one slave; enlisted April 13, 1861, in Greensboro; wounded in the thigh July 1, 1863; detailed as a clerk in Richmond in June 1864; represented a New York firm in Mobile by 1879.

LAW, Evander McIvor. Lieutenant colonel of the Fourth Alabama Infantry at First Manassas; later general.

*LAWRENCE, Elijah (died during the war). In the hospital with scurvy in May 1863.

LAWTON, Alexander Robert. General wounded at Sharpsburg; named quartermaster general in 1864.

*LAYNE, G. W. (c. 1838, Tennessee–). In 1860 owner of a livery stable, reporting $1,600 in real estate and $5,000 in personal estate; enlisted March 6, 1862, in Greensboro.

LEE, Fitzhugh. Commanded a division of cavalry under J. E. B. Stuart.

LEE, George Washington Custis. Son of Robert E. Lee; engineer, general, and member of Davis' staff.

*LEE, James H. Enlisted in June 1861 in Linden, Alabama; musician; fractured his right leg in July 1863.

LEE, Robert Edward. Commander of the Army of Northern Virginia after Joseph E. Johnston's injury at Seven Pines.

LEE, William Henry Fitzhugh ("Rooney"). Son of Robert E. Lee; promoted to brigadier general of cavalry in 1862; eventually rose to second in command of all cavalry.

*LENIER, William A. *See* LANIER, William A.

*LESTER, James A. (c. 1843, Virginia–). In 1860 a clerk in Newbern, Alabama; enlisted April 13, 1861, in Greensboro; discharged in July 1861 for a disability.

LETCHER, John. Wartime governor of Virginia.

*LEWIS, Elias. *See* ELIAS, Lewis.

LEWIS, I. F. Major in the Jeff Davis Legion.

LIGHTFOOT, James N. Colonel of the Sixth Alabama Infantry during the spring of 1864.

LINCOLN, Robert Todd. Son of Abraham Lincoln; rumored to have been killed with his father.

LIPSCOMB, Alice. Died September 18, 1861, age eighteen, at the home of P. May.

*LITTLE, W. J. A. In the Guards in January 1863.

LIVERMAN, Miles Benson. Warrior Guard who died July 11, 1861.

LIVINGSTON, George. A Greene County planter.

*LOCKE, James W. (c. 1842, Alabama–). Enlisted April 13, 1861, in Greensboro; discharged August 9, 1862, due to a disability; second corporal of a company of mounted infantry in 1863; in 1870 a farmer reporting $4,000 in real estate and $500 in personal estate; in 1880 a tax collector, married with two children. Son of Mrs. William (Anne Locke) Kerr. Probably nephew or son of former Guards John Locke and William Locke.

LOMAX, Lunsford Lindsay. Confederate cavalry general who distinguished himself in Early's Valley campaign.

LONG, Alexander. Northern congressman; peace Democrat from Pennsylvania.

*LONG, W. W. ("Old Man") (c. 1820, South Carolina–1865). In 1860 a planter, married with two children, reporting $7,200 in real estate and $50,000 in personal estate, including forty-six slaves; enlisted February 8, 1864, in Eutaw, Alabama; in camp in February 1865.

LONGSTREET, James. Brigadier at First Manassas; during the Peninsula campaign, moved up to divisional leadership; corps commander at Second Manassas and thereafter.

LOVING, William Wing. Contentious Confederate general who served in various Western theaters with mixed results.

LOWE, Thaddeus Sobieski Coulincourt. New Hampshire native and instigator of the Union balloon corps.

*LYLES, William (c. 1841, Alabama–). In 1860 a farmer, married with six children, reporting $1,000 in real estate; entered the Guards from the Forty-third Alabama in February 1865 after an exchange with J. Sterling Speed; captured April 2, 1865; illiterate.

LYNCH, Sam. Slave in a prison camp in 1865.

LYON, Francis Strother. Lawyer and political rival of John Erwin credited with saving Alabama's banking system in the late 1840s; served in the Confederate Congress.

MACAFIE. *See* McAFEE, Nicholas Scales.

*MADISON, John W. (c. 1825, Alabama–). Enlisted April 22, 1861, in Greensboro; discharged in September or October 1861 for a disability; in 1870 a farmer in Havanna, Alabama, married with three children, reporting $800 in real estate and $2,000 in personal estate.

*MADISON, William J. (c. 1830, Alabama–). His Nova Scotia–born illiterate father owned twenty-eight slaves in 1850 and thirty-two in 1860; enlisted March 2, 1863, in Greensboro; by 1863 detailed to provost guard in Selma, Alabama; in 1870 a farmer, married, reporting $195 in real estate and $150 in personal estate.

MAFFITT, John Newland. Commander of the CSS *Florida*.

MAGRUDER, John Bankhead. Confederate major general transferred to Texas following ineffective command during the Peninsula campaign and the Seven Days' battles.

*MARKSTEIN, Max (c. 1842, Germany–). Clerk; enlisted April 22, 1861, in Greensboro; discharged August 14, 1862; in 1880 a merchant, married with three children.

MARSCHALL, Nicola. Prussian-born artist residing in Marion, Alabama, about seventeen miles east of Greensboro; designer of the Stars and Bars, the first Confederate national flag.

MARSHAL, ———. Surgeon.

*MARTIN, Edward Thomas (c. 1829, Alabama–). In 1860 a farmer, married with five children, reporting $2,000 in real estate and $3,000 in personal estate; enlisted April 20, 1861, in Greensboro; regimental butcher in 1863; wounded and captured May 5, 1864.

*MARTIN, John M. Warrior Guard who transferred to the Greensboro Guards in April 1862; sergeant major; later raised his own company.

MARVIN, Robert H. Sergeant in the Haymouth Guards, Fifth Alabama Infantry.

MASON, Wylie W. Lawyer, judge, and state legislator from Tuskegee, Alabama.

MAURY, Dabney Herndon. After May 1863, commander of the District of the Gulf, headquartered in Mobile.

MAY, Laura and Mary. Former schoolmates of Sam Pickens in Sawyerville, Alabama, in the Hollow Square precinct, west of Greensboro.

MAY, Philip P. Lieutenant in the Sumter Rifle Guard, Fifth Alabama Infantry.

MAY, Sydenham M. Member of Company C, Fourth Alabama Infantry.

MAY, William V. Member of Company C, Fourth Alabama Infantry.

McAFEE, Nicholas Scales. Captain of the Talladega Artillery, Fifth Alabama Infantry.

McBRIDE, Marion. Member of the Sumter Rifle Guard, Fifth Alabama Infantry.

McCALL, Pinkney L. Sergeant in the Talladega Artillery, Fifth Alabama Infantry.

*McCALL, Robert Scott (c. 1845, Alabama–). In 1860 living with his mother and father, a trader with four children reporting $2,200 in real estate; enlisted April 13, 1861, in Greensboro; wounded May 31, 1862; discharged August 13, 1862, for being underage. Brother of Guard W. Alexander McCall.

*McCALL, W. Alexander (c. 1843–). Enlisted April 13, 1861, in Greensboro; second sergeant in 1864; in command of the Guards October 19, 1864. Brother of Guard Robert Scott McCall.

McCHESNEY, ———. Middlebrook, Virginia, doctor.

McCLELLAN, George Brinton. Arrogant and cautious successor to Winfield Scott as general in chief of the Union army; finally removed by Lincoln following Sharpsburg; 1864 Democratic nominee for president.

McCOMBS, ———. Captain, probably in the commissary.

*McCRARY, Budd (c. 1840, Alabama–). In 1860 a farmer in Havanna, Alabama, married; enlisted March 11, 1862, in Greensboro; discharged for a disability April 1, 1864. Brother of Guard William H. McCrary.

*McCRARY, William H. (c. 1843, Alabama–). In 1860 living with his mother and father, a farmer in Havanna, Alabama, who reported $2,000 in real estate; enlisted March 13, 1862, in Greensboro; wounded in the arm in July 1864; guarding baggage in February 1865. Brother of Guard Budd McCrary.

*McDIARMID, McDIERMAID, or McDIERMID, Joel Calvin (October 30, 1836, North Carolina–October 25, 1900, Goodwater, Alabama). In 1838 his family moved to Talladega County, Alabama; in 1860 a clerk in Havanna, Alabama; enlisted April 13, 1861, in Greensboro; court-martialed for leaving the battlefield at Fredericksburg; wounded October 19, 1864; on work detail February 23, 1865; captured April 2, 1865. Married in 1880.

*McDONALD, William Jackson (c. 1825, Alabama–). Joined the Guards June 6, 1846; in 1850 a clerk, married with two children; in 1860 an architect, married with six children, reporting $20,000 in real estate and $12,000 in personal estate; enlisted April 13, 1861, in Greensboro; third sergeant; discharged August 2, 1861; in 1870 a merchant reporting $5,000 in real estate and $140 in personal estate, his wife reporting $2,500 in real estate and $1,500 in personal estate.

*McGEE or McGEHEE, James C. Warrior Guard who transferred to the Greensboro Guards in April 1862; captured September 14, 1862.

*McNEIL, W. W. (died January 7 or 8, 1863, in Richmond of pneumonia).

McRAE, John Jones. Former governor of Mississippi; supported Jefferson Davis while a member of the Confederate House of Representatives.

MELTON, Andrew J. Member of the Sumter Rifle Guard, Fifth Alabama Infantry.

*MILLER, William D. (c. 1838, Alabama–). Enlisted April 13, 1861, in Greensboro; discharged for a disability August 2, 1861.

MILROY, Robert Huston. Union general repeatedly defeated in the Valley, including Winchester June 14, 1863.

MINNEGERODE, C. Rector of St. Paul's (Episcopal) Church, Richmond.

MITCHELL, William S. Surgeon of the Third Alabama Infantry; appointed chief medical officer of Rodes' brigade in May 1863.

Mom Lindy. Slave of the Pickens family.

MONETTE, Wilkes. Member of a Hollow Square planter family.

*MOORE, Augustus H. ("Gus") (c. 1836, Alabama–May 31, 1862, at Seven Pines). Attended the Greene Springs School; in 1860 a physician living with his mother and father, a planter reporting $36,000 in real estate and $55,000 in personal estate; enlisted April 13, 1861, in Greensboro; color corporal. Brother of Guards James Pickens Moore and Thomas G. Moore.

MOORE, H. D. Chaplain of the Twelfth Alabama Infantry.

*MOORE, James Pickens ("Pick") (c. 1839, Alabama–). Student at the University of Virginia in 1858; in 1860 a merchant living with his parents; enlisted April 13, 1861, in Greensboro; corporal in January 1863, division courier for Rodes in 1864; in 1878 a cotton planter. Brother of Guards Augustus H. Moore and Thomas G. Moore.

*MOORE, Rick. *See* MOORE, James Pickens.

MOORE, Rittenhouse. Son of Sydenham Moore; in 1864 a lieutenant of ordnance at the Selma arsenal.

MOORE, Sydenham. Greensboro lawyer, Mexican War captain, judge, and U.S. congressman; colonel of the Eleventh Alabama Infantry (1861); killed at Seven Pines.

*MOORE, Thomas G. (c. 1842, Alabama–July 2, 1907). Attended the Greene Springs School; in 1860 a student living with his parents; enlisted April 13, 1861, in Greensboro; brigade courier in April 1863. Brother of Guards Augustus H. Moore and James Pickens Moore.

*MOORMAN, W. B. (died September 14, 1862, at South Mountain). Enlisted May 6, 1861, in Uniontown, Alabama; captured at Williamsburg, Virginia.

MORGAN, John Hunt. Confederate cavalry commander whose daring raids rallied the South.

MORGAN, John Tyler (1824–June 11, 1907). Secessionist supporter of W. L. Yancey; captain of the Cahaba Rifles; major, Fifth Alabama Infantry in 1861; resigned to create

with J. D. Webb the Partisan Rangers, Fifty-first Alabama Infantry; upon the death
of Webb, commanded the regiment and then the brigade; served in the U.S. Senate
1876–1907 and promoted a canal through Nicaragua.

*MORRIS, A. R. On the Guards' muster roll in January 1863.

MOSELEY, Elijah B. Captain of the Cahaba Rifles, Fifth Alabama Infantry.

MULLIGAN, James. Federal colonel who surrendered to General Sterling Price at
Lexington, Missouri.

MUSHAT, John Patrick. Former Haymouth Guard; appointed assistant surgeon in the
Fifth Alabama Infantry in 1863.

NAPOLEON, Prince (Napoleon Joseph Charles Paul Bonaparte, of France). Toured
the Civil War in 1861; met with President Lincoln August 3.

*NELSON, Gideon E. (c. 1824, Alabama–June 1867). In 1850 a planter reporting
$9,700 in real estate and 46 slaves; Mason 1855–1867; commissioned first lieutenant
April 27, 1857; in 1860 a planter, married with six children, reporting $10,000 in
real estate and $165,000 in personal estate, including 145 slaves; commissioned first
lieutenant April 27, 1857; enlisted April 13, 1861, in Greensboro; resigned May 28,
1861, due to a disability. Brother of former Guard Algernon Sidney Nelson.

NELSON, William ("Bull"). Federal Brigadier General engaged at the Battle of Richmond, Kentucky; killed a month later in a quarrel with another brigadier.

NEWSOM, John W. ("Bill"). *See* NUSUM, John W.

NICHOLSON, John Joseph. Captain of Company I, Twelfth Alabama Infantry.

*NOLAND, John T. *See* KNOWLEN, John T.

NUSUM or NEWSOM, John W. ("Bill"). Member of the Cahaba Rifles, Fifth Alabama
Infantry.

*NUTTING, Edwin (c. 1841, Alabama–). In 1860 living with his mother and father,
a master carpenter reporting $2,000 in real estate and $7,000 in personal estate,
including seven slaves; enlisted March 6, 1862, in Greensboro; wounded May 31,
1862; discharged December 5, 1862. Brother of Guard George Nutting; brother-in-
law of Guard John S. Tucker.

*NUTTING, George ("Tean") (c. 1843, Alabama–July 1, 1863, at Gettysburg). In
1860 living with his parents; enlisted April 13, 1861, in Greensboro; color corporal;
wounded May 31, 1862; captured May 3, 1863. Brother of Guard Edwin Nutting;
brother-in-law of Guard John S. Tucker.

NUTTING, Louise (c. 1818–1911). Mother of Guards Edwin and George Nutting,
mother-in-law of Guard John S. Tucker.

O'NEAL, Edward Asbury. Colonel of the Twenty-sixth Alabama Infantry; wounded at
South Mountain; commanded Rodes' brigade at Chancellorsville, where wounded a
second time; division commander at Gettysburg.

*ORRICK, John C. (1844, Alabama–1923, Texas). In 1860 living with his mother and
father, a dentist reporting $1,000 in real estate; enlisted April 13, 1861, in Greensboro;
discharged for being underage; joined Mosby's guerrillas as a scout; in 1867 killed
freedman Alex Webb and escaped to Central America and Mexico; changed his name
to Arrington and served as a captain in the Rangers and later as sheriff of Wheeler,
Texas, and attached counties; retired as a rancher near Canadian, Texas.

*OWENS, F. E. Warrior Guard who transferred to the Greensboro Guards in April 1862.

OWENS, Stephen D. Greensboro broker.

PALMER, William M. Greensboro postmaster.

PARK or PARKE, Robert W. Surgeon in the Fifth Alabama Infantry; reassigned to Mobile in 1863.

PARK or PARKE, W. T. Member of the Barbour Greys, Fifth Alabama Infantry.

PARKE, Robert W. *See* PARK, Robert W.

*PARKER, J. W. Enlisted in April or May 1861.

*PARRISH, R. C. Warrior Guard who transferred to the Greensboro Guards in April 1862.

*PASTEUR, Edward T. (c. 1836, Alabama–September 1, 1904). In 1860 living with his mother, a planter reporting $25,000 in real estate and $40,000 in personal estate, including thirty-three slaves; enlisted April 13, 1861, in Greensboro; corporal in January 1863; wounded and captured May 3, 1863; declared unfit for battle and detailed to the quartermaster department in Greensboro in 1864; in 1870 a farmer, married with two children, reporting $3,000 in real estate and $2,000 in personal estate; Episcopalian.

PATTERSON, Douglas. Member of a Greene County brick-making family.

PATTERSON, Robert. Federal general whose failure to hold Johnston's troops in the Valley during First Manassas resulted in his being mustered out of the service.

*PAULDING, Robert. Enlisted May 6, 1861, in Uniontown, Alabama; captured July 12, 1861.

*PEARSON, Tom. Warrior Guard who transferred to the Greensboro Guards in April 1862.

PEGRAM, John. Division commander under Forrest, Early, and Gordon; commanded Rodes' division at Winchester, Fisher's Hill, and Cedar Creek; killed near Petersburg in February 1865.

PEGUES, Charles. Lieutenant in the Cahaba Rifles, Fifth Alabama Infantry; appointed acting adjutant general in 1864.

PEGUES, Christopher Claudius (August 3, 1823–July 15, 1862). Cahaba lawyer; captain of the Cahaba Rifles, Fifth Alabama Infantry; elected colonel of the Fifth Alabama Infantry in 1862; fatally wounded at Gaines' Mill.

PELHAM, John. Alabama-born major of artillery killed at Kelly's Ford and immortalized by the South.

PENDLETON, George Hunt. Ohio copperhead who was the 1864 Democratic nominee for vice president.

PENDLETON, William Nelson. Chief of artillery for the Army of Northern Virginia.

*PERRIN, Robert. Unsuccessful candidate for the Alabama state house of representatives in 1861.

Perry. Slave of William Shelden.

PEYTON, Green. Served as adjutant general in the Fifth Alabama Infantry; drill instructor; promoted from lieutenant in 1862 to major in 1863 on Rodes' staff.

PHILIPS, George. Sergeant in the Livingston Rifles, Fifth Alabama Infantry.

PICKENS, Israel. Brother of Guards James and Samuel Pickens.

*PICKENS, James ("Jamie") (July 30, 1842, Alabama–). Attended the Greene Springs School; student at the University of Virginia in 1859; in 1860 living in Sawyerville, Alabama, with his mother, who reported \$209,600 in real estate and \$250,000 in personal estate, including 201 slaves; enlisted January 22, 1864, in Eutaw, Alabama; in 1870, married with one child. Brother of Guard Samuel Pickens.

PICKENS, Louisa ("Lou," "Louty," or "Loutie"). Sister of Guards James Pickens and Samuel Pickens.

PICKENS, Mary Gaillard. Sister of Guards James Pickens and Samuel Pickens.

PICKENS, Mary Gaillard Thomas. Mother of Guards James Pickens and Samuel Pickens.

PICKENS, Miles. Quartermaster of the Twelfth Alabama Infantry with the rank of captain. Brother of Samuel B. Pickens.

*PICKENS, Samuel (June 9, 1841, Alabama–September 9, 1890). Student at the University of Virginia in 1859; in 1860 living with his mother; enlisted September 3, 1862, in Gainesville, Alabama; captured May 3, 1863; first corporal in April 1864; wounded September 19, 1864; captured April 2, 1865. Brother of Guard James Pickens.

PICKENS, Samuel B. Colonel of the Twelfth Alabama Infantry wounded at Spotsylvania and Winchester.

PICKENS, William Carrigan ("Willy" or "Willie"). Brother of Guards James Pickens and Samuel Pickens.

*PICKERING, Robert (died during the war). Enlisted in March 1862 in Greensboro.

PICKETT, Alexander H. Lieutenant in the Third Alabama Infantry; captain and assistant adjutant general of Battle's brigade.

PICKETT, George Edward. Major general whose name is linked to the assault on the Union center at Gettysburg; sent to North Carolina in the fall of 1863; saved Petersburg the following spring.

POLK, Leonidas. Episcopal bishop who in 1843 consecrated St. Paul's Church in Greensboro; appointed major general in 1861 with command over much of the West; promoted to lieutenant general the following year; had command over the Department of Alabama in early 1864; killed in June of that year.

POLLARD, Charles. Officer in the Sixty-first Alabama Infantry.

POORE, Robert. Classmate of the Pickens brothers at Dr. Harrison's school in Virginia.

POPE, John. Union commander defeated at Second Manassas.

*POPE, William M. (c. 1829–June 20, 1863, of typhoid). In 1850 an overseer; division blacksmith in 1863.

PORTER, David Dixon. Union rear admiral who successfully captured New Orleans, ran past Vicksburg, and attacked Fort Fisher.

PORTER, Joseph D. Chaplain in the Fifth Alabama Infantry in 1861.

POTTS, S. M. Lieutenant in the Livingston Rifles, Fifth Alabama Infantry.

PRESTON, A. T. Assistant commissary of the Fifth Alabama Infantry with the rank of captain.

PRESTON, William. Kentucky division commander at Chickamauga; later envoy to Maximilian, emperor of Mexico.

*PRICE, George T. (1838, North Carolina–June 27, 1862, at Gaines' Mill). Enlisted April 18, 1861, in Greensboro; sergeant; unmarried.

*PRICE, Robert Belton (died 1865). Enlisted April 18, 1861, in Greensboro; captured September 14, 1862; wounded in the leg and hip May 2, 1863; detailed to South Carolina Conscript Bureau in 1864; returned to the Guards February 2, 1865; captured April 2, 1865.

PRICE, Sterling. Confederate general and former Missouri governor.

PRICE, ———. Married Dr. Fountain in 1863.

PRIEST, Robert L. Commissary for the Twenty-sixth Alabama Infantry.

PROSCO or PROSCOW. *See* PROSKAUER, Adolph.

PROSKAUER, Adolph. Major in the Twelfth Alabama Infantry; from Mobile.

PROSKOW. *See* PROSKAUER, Adolph.

PULLER, John W. Major in the Fifth Virginia Cavalry killed at Kelly's Ford.

*QUARLES, W. R. Warrior Guard who transferred to the Greensboro Guards in April 1862.

RAGSDALE, Felix. Soldier in the Livingston Rifles, Fifth Alabama Infantry.

RAMSEUR, Stephen Dodson. Brigadier in Rodes' division, wounded at Chancellorsville; promoted to major general following Spottsylvania; killed at Cedar Creek.

RAMSEY, Ed. Brother of Matthew Ramsey.

*RAMSEY, Matthew S. (died June 27, 1862, at Gaines' Mill). Physician just settled in Greensboro when he enlisted there April 16, 1861; third lieutenant in 1861; second lieutenant in October 1861; first lieutenant in April 1862.

RAMSON, Matt Whitaker. North Carolina brigadier general.

RANDOLPH, R. Carter. Lieutenant in Tayloe's Cavalry company, Jeff Davis Legion.

*RAY, John C. Enlisted August 17, 1862, in Tallapoosa County, Alabama; captured July 2, 1863; exchanged February 18, 1865.

RAYFORD, William. Member of the Livingston Rifles, Fifth Alabama Infantry.

REED or REID, George. Captain of the Sumter Rifle Guard, Fifth Alabama Infantry.

*RENCKE, Jacob (died December 11, 1864, of pneumonia). Enlisted March 27, 1863, in Grace Church, Virginia; captured July 12, 1864.

RENFREW, RENFRO, or RENFROE, William Thomas. Captain of the Talladega Artillery, Fifth Alabama Infantry.

RENKI. *See* RENCKE, Jacob.

REYNOLDS, James. Friend and neighbor of James Pickens, soldier in the Third Alabama Infantry.

*RHODES, Thomas Marshall (died September 11, 1863). Shot May 3, 1863, in the groin. Cousin of former Guard Alva Rhodes.

RILEY, Thomas. Captain of the Monroe Guards, Fifth Alabama Infantry.

RINKE or RINKEY. *See* RENCKE, Jacob.

RIPLEY, Roswell Sabine. Brigadier under D. H. Hill's division until wounded at Sharpsburg; then reassigned to artillery in Charleston, South Carolina.

*ROBERTS, J. C. Enlisted August 17, 1862, in Choctaw County, Alabama; reported deserted in August 1863 while on furlough for typhoid fever.

RODDEY, Philip Dale. Alabama cavalry commander; promoted to brigadier general in 1863; defeated, along with Nathan Bedford Forrest, at Selma in 1865.

RODES, Robert Emmett (1829–September 19, 1864). Virginia Military Institute graduate and professor, engineer; captain of the Warrior Guards in 1861; elected colonel of the Fifth Alabama Infantry; promoted to brigadier general; wounded at Fair Oaks and Sharpsburg; promoted to major general for his performance at Chancellorsville; killed at Winchester.

RODES, Virginia Hortense Woodruff. Wife of Robert Rodes; from Tuscaloosa.

ROSECRANS, William S. Union general whose successes in the West were overshadowed by his rout at Chickamauga.

ROSS, Polemon D. Captain of Company G, Twelfth Alabama Infantry.

ROSSER, T. H. Recruiting colonel in command of the Gainesville post.

ROSSER, Thomas Lafayette. Commander of the Fifth Virginia Cavalry in 1862; promoted to brigadier general after Gettysburg, to major general after Cedar Creek.

*ROWLAND, T. B. (died September 16, 1863, of fever in prison). Enlisted April 18, 1861, in Greensboro; wagon and forage master; captured in July 1863.

RUDOLPH, James Murry. Member of the Haymouth Guards, Fifth Alabama Infantry.

RUSSELL, William Howard. Correspondent to the *London Times.*

RUTLEDGE, Thomas J. Chaplain of the Third Alabama Infantry.

*SADLER, Benjamin F. (c. 1838, Ireland–). In 1860 a clerk; enlisted April 18, 1861, in Greensboro; ward master, Charlottesville, Virginia, hospital in 1864; chronic eye problems.

SADLER, William G. Planter in Hollow Square precinct, west of Greensboro.

*SAMPLE, Joseph (c. 1825, Alabama–). In 1850 a student and farmer living with his father, who reported $6,500 in real estate and thirty-two slaves; enlisted April 18, 1861, in Greensboro; discharged in October 1861 for a disability.

*SANDERS, J. W. Warrior Guard who transferred to the Greensboro Guards in April 1862; badly wounded May 31 or June 1, 1862.

SCHOFIELD, John McAllister. Victor over Hood's Army of Tennessee at Franklin November 30, 1864.

SCOTT, John S. Colonel of the First Louisiana Cavalry.

SCOTT, Winfield. Veteran of the War of 1812, Indian wars, and the Mexican War; 1852 Whig nominee for president; general in chief of the army since 1841; devised the Anaconda Plan; retired November 1, 1861.

SEIBELS, John H. Colonel of the Sixth Alabama Infantry; commanded Alabama troops in the Mexican War.

SEIBLES. *See* SEIBELS, John H.

SELDEN, Chris. *See* SHELDEN, Christopher.

*SELDEN, William M. (February 20, 1844, Virginia–). Student of medicine; enlisted May 6, 1861, in Uniontown, Alabama; discharged in September 1861 for a disability.

*SELLERS, James D. Enlisted August 23, 1862, in Pike County, Alabama; wounded in June 1864; sick in camp in February 1865.

SEMPLE, Edward A. Montgomery, Alabama, physician.

*SEMPLE, John P. (c. 1830, Virginia–). Druggist; enlisted May 6, 1861, in Selma, Alabama; on detached service in December 1861; transferred to CS Navy April 4, 1864.

Seve. John H. Cowin's personal slave and mess cook.

SEWARD, William Henry. Lincoln's secretary of state.

SEYMOUR, Isaac Gurden. Colonel of the Sixth Louisiana Infantry.

SHA[C]KELFORD, Edward. Son of Robert Shackelford, Greensboro Guard during the 1830s and 1840s.

*SHELDEN, Charles A. (c. 1847, Alabama–). In 1860 a student living with his mother and father, a merchant in Havanna, Alabama, who reported $5,000 in real estate and $10,000 in personal estate; enlisted March 11, 1862, in Greensboro; discharged due to underage and delicate constitution; Mason 1879–1903. Brother of Guards Christopher C. Shelden and William H. H. Shelden.

*SHELDEN, Christopher C. (c. 1844, Alabama–). In 1860 a student living with his parents; enlisted April 18, 1861, in Greensboro; wounded in 1862 and 1863; transferred to the Jeff Davis Legion in 1863; candidate for sheriff in 1867; in 1880 a farmer, married, reporting $500 in personal estate. Brother of Guards Charles A. Shelden and William H. H. Shelden.

*SHELDEN, William H. H. (c. 1841, North Carolina–). In 1860 a student living with his parents; enlisted April 18, 1861, in Greensboro; in camp in February 1865; in 1870 no occupation listed, married with two children. Brother of Guards Charles A. Shelden and Christopher C. Shelden.

SHELDON or SHELTON, John. Member of Company H, Sixth Alabama Infantry.

SHELLEY, Charles Miller (December 28, 1833–January 19, 1907). Lawyer; captain of the Talladega Artillery, Fifth Alabama Infantry; appointed colonel of the Thirtieth Alabama Infantry and eventually achieved brigadier general; entered the U.S. Congress after the war.

SHELTON, John. *See* SHELDON, John

SHERIDAN, Philip Henry. Union cavalry general notorious for destroying crops in the Shenandoah Valley.

SHERMAN, William Tecumseh. Famed for his "March to the Sea" and excellent working relationship with Grant; finally promoted to major general in August 1864.

*SHERRON, Patrick H. (c. 1821, New York–). In 1860 a gin maker, married with four children; enlisted August 9, 1861, in Greensboro; detailed to make artillery wagons; discharged in August 1862 for being overage.

SIGEL, Franz. German-born Union commander of the Department of West Virginia when he lost to Breckinridge at the Battle of New Market.

SIMMS, James H. A Greensboro merchant and Confederate government agent.

*SIMONDS, Richard H. (c. 1843, Alabama–). In 1860 a student living with his father, a physician who reported $2,000 in real estate and $28,000 in personal estate, including twenty-six slaves; enlisted March 6, 1862, in Greensboro; severely wounded May 3, 1863; applied for a cadet appointment in February 1864; discharged in March 1864 due to a gunshot wound.

SIMS, Eliza. Younger sister of Guard William A. Sims.

SIMS, Frank. Older brother of Guard William A. Sims.

*SIMS, William A. (c. 1839, Alabama–). In 1860 living with his father, a farmer reporting $12,260 in real estate and $30,000 in personal estate; enlisted April 13, 1861, in Greensboro; wounded in May or June 1862; captured May 3, 1863; division courier for Rodes, teamster, and forage master; hospitalized in 1864 with syphilis; married to Ann Briggs in 1864; in camp in February 1865; captured April 2, 1865; illiterate; in 1870 reported one child and $2,200 in real estate and $800 in personal estate.

SINGLETON, James W. Unofficial envoy whom Lincoln allowed to seek a settlement to the war in early 1865.

SLAUGHTER, John Fletcher. Sergeant in the Talladega Artillery, Fifth Alabama Infantry.

*SLEDGE, Alexander A. (1787, North Carolina–August 12, 1861). Physician who graduated from the University of Pennsylvania; married in 1817; moved to Alabama in 1822; moved to Marengo County in 1827; Methodist; enlisted in the Guards in April or May 1861 and went to Pensacola, Florida; and Virginia. (*Note:* Alexander Sledge is an ambiguous name in Greene County; another Alexander Sledge is mentioned by Samuel Pickens March 8, 1864.)

SMITH, Edmund Kirby. Confederate commander of the Department of East Tennessee in March 1862 and, beginning in February 1863, the Trans-Mississippi Department.

SMITH, Gustavus Woodson. Commissioned major general in September 1861; briefly succeeded Johnston upon the latter's injury at Seven Pines; resigned in January 1863.

SMITH, James P. In 1863 appointed captain and assistant inspector general (AIG) assigned to Battle's brigade.

SMITH, Pickens. Minister and cousin of Miles and Samuel B. Pickens.

SMITH, Preston. Tennessee brigadier killed at Chickamauga.

SMITH, Robert Hardy. Colonel of the Thirty-sixth Alabama Infantry from May 1862 until April 1863.

SMITH, William. General, Confederate congressman, and governor of Virginia during the war's last year.

SMITH, William Cuttino. Friend of James and Samuel Pickens from Pendleton, South Carolina; later served as a Confederate colporteur (a religious missionary) and became a Presbyterian minister.

SMITH, William Lundie. Lieutenant in the Talladega Artillery, Fifth Alabama Infantry.

*SOUTHWORTH, Larrison D. (c. 1839, Alabama–). In 1860 living with his father, an illiterate farmer who reported $400 in personal estate; enlisted in April 1861.

*SPEED, J. Sterling (c. 1824, North Carolina–). In 1850 an unmarried farmer; Mason 1861–1874; enlisted September 2, 1864, in Greensboro; exchanged with William Lyles; in 1870 a farmer, married with five children, reporting $280 in real estate and $1,000 in personal estate.

STANDENMEYER, Mr. and Mrs. Incompetent teachers hired and then fired by Mrs. Pickens during the war.

STEELE, Frederick. Union general who successfully captured Little Rock.

STEPHENS, Alexander Hamilton. Vice president of the Confederacy who, along with Robert Hunter and John A. Campbell, met with Lincoln in early 1865 to discuss ending the war.

*STEPHENSON, H. C. Enlisted September 6, 1862, in Pike County, Alabama; wounded May 12, 1864.

STEUART, George Hume. Maryland-born brigadier general who distinguished himself at Gettysburg and Spotsylvania, where he was taken prisoner.

*STEVENSON. *See* STEPHENSON, H. C.

STEWART. *See* STUART, J. E. B. or STEUART, George Hume.

STICKNEY, Charles. A Greensboro planter.

*STOKES, William (c. 1840, Alabama–August 27 or 28, 1863, of measles). In 1860 an overseer, reporting $300 in real estate; wounded in the leg and captured July 1 or 2, 1863; married with four children in 1863.

STOLLENWERCK, Alf. Greensboro druggist and town leader.

STREIGHT, Abel D. Captured in Alabama with his four hundred raiders mounted on mules; escaped from Richmond's Libby Prison.

STRINGFELLOW. Planter family in the Canebrake (the fertile plantation region south of Greensboro).

STUART, George. *See* STEUART, George Hume.

STUART, J. E. B. Famed commander of all cavalry under Lee; mortally wounded at Yellow Tavern.

Suckey. Wife to John and slave of the Pickens family.

SWANSON, William G. Colonel of the Sixty-first Alabama Infantry during the spring of 1864.

SWOPE, Sally Ann. Eutaw, Greene County, resident living in Richmond.

TALIAFERRO, William Booth. Virginian brigadier general wounded at Second Manassas; in 1863 given command of District of Savannah, East Florida, and South Carolina.

TALLMAN, James A. A Greensboro merchant.

TARRANT, Edward Williams. Member of the Tuscaloosa Warrior Guards, Fifth Alabama Infantry.

TAYLOR, G. W. or James A. Member of the Pickensville Blues, Fifth Alabama Infantry.

TAYLOR, Richard. Beginning in 1862, given several commands in the West; promoted from brigadier to lieutenant general.

TERRY, William. Virginia brigadier general after May 1864.

THOMAS, George Henry. "The Rock of Chickamauga" who destroyed John Bell Hood's Army of Tennessee at the Battle of Nashville December 15–16, 1864.

*THOMAS, Wade R. Transferred to the Greensboro Guards in August 1863 from the Livingston Rifles, Fifth Alabama Infantry.

THORNTON, George. Forkland physician and planter; former University of Virginia student.

*TINKER, William (1838–). Student at the University of Virginia 1856–1857; in 1860 living with his mother, who reported $100,000 in real estate and $125,000 in personal estate, including 232 slaves; enlisted April 13, 1861, in Greensboro; Mason 1864–1870; in 1870 a farmer reporting $12,500 in real estate and $2,000 in personal estate.

TOOMBS, Robert Augustus. Georgia secessionist, Confederate secretary of state, brigadier general who challenged D. H. Hill to a duel after Malvern Hill.

*TRAWICK, R. J. Enlisted August 28, 1862, in Dale or Pike County, Alabama; admitted to a hospital in May 1863; severely wounded October 19, 1864.

TUCKER, A. E. Sister of Guard John S. Tucker.

TUCKER, Annie Nutting. Wife of Guard John S. Tucker, whom she married in 1860, and sister of Guards Edwin Nutting and George Nutting.

TUCKER, Frances ("Fannie"). Sister of Guard John S. Tucker.

*TUCKER, John S. (died June 18, 1880). Mason 1858–1880; in 1860 a clerk, married to Annie Nutting; enlisted March 6, 1862, in Greensboro; regimental and division commissary clerk; entered the Jeff Davis Legion after an exchange with Henry Beck April 1, 1864; in 1870 a dry goods merchant with two children living with his in-laws, reported $2,000 in real estate and $150 in personal estate; murdered in a Newbern, Alabama, robbery. Brother-in-law of Guards George Nutting and Edwin Nutting.

TUCKER, Maria L. Mother of Guard John S. Tucker.

TUCKER, "Tun." Guard John S. Tucker's younger brother; killed at Gettysburg.

TUCKER, Walter. Infant son of Guard John S. Tucker.

*TUNSTALL, Wiley C. (c. 1840, Alabama–1916). In 1860 living with his mother, who reported $40,000 in real estate and $90,000 in personal estate, including eighty-six slaves; enlisted April 25, 1861, in Greensboro; third lieutenant in April 1862; resigned in October 1862, citing chronic diarrhea; in 1880 married with five children.

TUTWILER, Henry. Respected educational reformer whose Greene Springs School for Boys, which several Guards had attended, was the finest in Alabama.

*ULLMAN, L. Warrior Guard who transferred to the Greensboro Guards in April 1862; captured September 14, 1862.

USTICK, James. Member of the Livingston Rifles, Fifth Alabama Infantry, and killer of Dr. John T. Jenkins.

VALLANDIGHAM, Clement Laird. Prominent peace Democrat from Ohio; arrested in 1863 and expelled to the Confederacy before running the blockade to Canada.

VANCE, Zebulon Baird. Entered the war as a colonel; elected governor of North Carolina in 1862 and reelected in 1864.

VAN DORN, Earl. Confederate general who, after service in Virginia, was sent to a command in the West; killed by a jealous husband in 1863.

VENABLE, Nathaniel. Assistant surgeon in the Fifth Alabama Infantry.

*WADDELL, Abner C. (c. 1833, Virginia–). In 1860 a saddler, married; enlisted August 9, 1861, in Greensboro; ambulance driver and teamster; brigade quartermaster department; in camp in February 1865; in 1870 reported $1,500 in real estate and $250 in personal estate.

WADSWORTH, Edward. Professor of moral philosophy (1859–1870) and president of Southern University (1868–1870).

WAKEFIELD, Martin F. Sergeant in the Pickensville Blues, Fifth Alabama Infantry.

WALKER, J. S. Member of the Pickensville Blues, Fifth Alabama Infantry, taken prisoner July 31, 1861.

*WALKER, William T. (1832, Alabama–). Druggist; enlisted May 18, 1861, in Pensacola, Florida; discharged June 15, 1862, due to a bladder stone.

*WALL, L. P. Enlisted May 6, 1861, in Uniontown, Alabama; discharged August 2, 1861, for a disability.

WALTHALL, Edward Cary. Mississippi brigadier wounded, but not killed, at Chicka-mauga.

*WARD, Alfred G. (c. 1841–November 1908). In 1860 a clerk living with an upholsterer; Knight of Pythias; enlisted August 9, 1861, in Greensboro; sergeant major; wounded May 31, 1862; head fractured by a minié ball at Chancellorsville, where he was captured and cited for gallantry.

*WARD, Thomas R., Sr. (1826, North Carolina–November 14, 1897). Student at Charleston Medical College and Cincinnati Medical College; Mason 1854–1897; married in 1858; in 1860 a physician with one child, reporting $3,800 in real estate; enlisted March 6, 1862, in Greensboro; wounded and captured May 3, 1863; third corporal in August 1863; wounded and captured May 5, 1864; in camp in February 1865; in 1870 reported $6,000 in real estate and $2,500 in personal estate.

*WARREN, John H. (c. 1839, North Carolina–). In 1860 a clerk living with a shoemaker; enlisted April 13, 1861, in Greensboro; wounded May 31, 1862; in camp in February 1865; in 1870 a merchant, married with one child.

WATTS, Jesse A. Lieutenant in the Sumter Rifle Guard, Fifth Alabama Infantry.

WATTS, Thomas Hill. Colonel of the Seventeenth Alabama Infantry; Confederate attorney general (April 1862–December 1863); Alabama governor (December 1863–April 1864).

WEAVER, Phil. Schoolmate of Samuel Pickens at Henry Tutwiler's Greene Springs School.

*WEBB, James Daniel (Jr., to distinguish from distant relative of same name) (c. 1839–February 26, 1865, following Cedar Creek). In 1860 a clerk living with his father and reporting $2,000 in real estate; enlisted April 13, 1861, in Greensboro; cap-tured September 14, 1862; corporal; wounded and captured October 19, 1864; a leg amputated above the knee October 20, 1864. Probably son of former Guard Henry Webb.

*WEBB, James Daniel ("J. D.") (February 26, 1818, North Carolina–July 19, 1863). Mason 1839–1854; married in 1853; in 1860 a lawyer with five children, reporting $7,000 in real estate and $20,400 in personal estate, including nineteen slaves; enlisted in the Guards December 7, 1844; ensign in 1846; enlisted April 1861 in Greensboro; quartermaster of the Fifth Alabama Infantry with the rank of captain; with J. T. Morgan established Partisan Rangers, Fifty-first Alabama Infantry.

*WEBB, James Ed. (c. 1841, Alabama–). Student at the University of Alabama in 1859; in 1860 a law student living in Eutaw, Alabama, with his father, who reported $5,000 in real estate and $26,600 in personal estate; enlisted April 18, 1861, in Greensboro; promoted to lieutenant and division ordnance officer in 1863; assigned to W. H. F. Lee's cavalry division; after the war became a Birmingham lawyer.

WEBB, Joseph. Major in the Twenty-seventh North Carolina Infantry.

*WEBB, Sydney V. (c. 1832, Alabama–). In 1860 a physician reporting $5,000 in personal estate; enlisted April 20, 1861, in Greensboro.

*WEBSTER, Daniel T. (c. 1838, Alabama–). In 1860 a clerk living with his father, who reported $18,360 in real estate and $48,570 in personal estate, including forty-five slaves; enlisted April 18, 1861, in Greensboro; brigade commissary with the rank of major; married Bettie Wynne in 1865; cotton factor in 1866.

WEMYSS, James A. Captain of Company C, Thirty-sixth Alabama Infantry.

*WESSON, ———. Transferred into the Guards December 29, 1864, from the Jeff Davis Legion after an exchange with Gilliam James.

*WESTCOTT, Gideon G. (c. 1834, Rhode Island–). In 1860 living with Guard Charles Shelden; enlisted April 13, 1861, in Greensboro; corporal in August 1861; brigade commissary clerk; Mason 1867–1870; in 1870 a dry goods clerk, married with two children, reporting $500 in real estate and $300 in personal estate.

WHARTON, John Austin. Texas major general, retired from field duty in 1864.

*WHEELER, John E. (c. 1843, Alabama–). Enlisted April 13, 1861, in Greensboro; discharged in July 1861 due to a disability. Son of former Guard Isaac C. Wheeler.

WHEELER, Joseph. Storied cavalry general who participated in 127 battles in the West; later served in the Spanish-American War.

WHELAN, Charles, Jr. Greene County friend of John H. Cowin and Sam Pickens.

*WHELAN, Lee T. (c. 1840, Alabama–). In 1860 living with his mother and father, a grocery merchant reporting $1,700 in personal estate; enlisted August 9, 1861, in Greensboro; discharged June 8, 1862, for a disability brought on by disease; in 1870 a druggist.

WHITING, Henry A. Lieutenant in the Tuscaloosa Warrior Guards in 1861; assistant adjutant general and division inspector; elected major of the Fifth Alabama Infantry in January 1862.

WIGFALL, Louis Trezevant. Former U.S. senator and avowed Texas secessionist; brigadier general in the Texas Brigade; Confederate senator and opponent of Jefferson Davis.

WILCOX, Cadmus Marcellus. Colonel of the Ninth Alabama Infantry, but quickly promoted to brigadier; after conspicuous service promoted to major general in August 1863.

*WILDER, Lott M. (died after 1907). Enlisted August 14, 1862, in Montgomery; repeatedly in the hospital; in camp in February 1865.

WILEY, Josephine, Francis, or Adele. One of the older Bayol sisters, married and living in Selma, Alabama.

William. Slave of William S. Cowin.

William, Willie, or Willy. Slave of the Pickens family.

*WILLIAMS, Charles L. (c. 1837, Alabama–). Mason 1859–1867; in 1860 married and attending a farm; enlisted February 1, 1864, in Eutaw, Alabama; discharged June 1864 for a disability. Brother of Guard Jonathan W. Williams.

*WILLIAMS, Davis G. (c. 1842, Alabama–). Student at the Greene Springs School; in 1860 living with his mother and father, a farmer reporting $6,000 in real estate and $8,000 in personal estate; enlisted April 13, 1861, in Greensboro; wounded May 31, 1862; courier and division commissary department; wounded October 19, 1864.

*WILLIAMS, Jonathan W. (c. 1840, Alabama–April 24, 1908). In 1860 living with his brother Charles; Mason 1861–1885; enlisted April 13, 1861, in Greensboro; corporal in April 1861; second lieutenant in June 1861; first lieutenant in October 1861; captain in April 1862; captured September 14, 1862; wounded in the shoulder and captured May 3, 1863; wounded May 10, 1864; married Carrie Avery in 1864; resigned February 8, 1865, because of chronic diarrhea; in 1880 attending to his father's Havanna, Alabama, farm with seven children; ran the county poor farm. Brother of Guard Charles L. Williams.

WILLINGHAM, A. G. Sister of Guard William H. Willingham.

WILLINGHAM, Mary. Married Guard Robert Chadwick July 24, 1861.

WILLINGHAM, Philip. Overseer and father of Guard William H. Willingham.

*WILLINGHAM, Samuel M. (c. 1838, South Carolina–). In 1860 living with his mother and father, a planter reporting $5,000 in real estate and $20,000 in personal estate, including twenty-one slaves; enlisted April 13, 1861, in Greensboro; captured September 14, 1862; skull fractured in 1864; in 1880 a farmer, married with three children.

WILLINGHAM, Thomas. Member of a Texas battalion and son of Philip Willingham.

*WILLINGHAM, William H. (c. 1841, Alabama–October 3, 1861, of typhoid pneumonia). In 1860 living with his mother and father, an overseer reporting $2,000 in personal estate; enlisted April 29, 1861, in Greensboro.

WILMER, Richard Hooker. Second Protestant Episcopal bishop of Alabama and the only Confederate bishop; spent much of the war as an exile in Greensboro.

*WILSON, George W. (c. 1841, Alabama–). Enlisted April 13, 1861, in Greensboro; in 1860 farming with his father, who reported $3,000 in real estate and $12,000 in personal estate; in 1860 reported twelve slaves.

*WILSON, James Ezra (c. 1835, South Carolina–June 1884). In 1860 a farmer reporting $11,000 in real estate and $50,000 in personal estate; enlisted August 14, 1861, in Union Mills, Virginia; suffered broken thigh in July 1862; Knight of Pythias; in 1880 a dry goods clerk; died without family.

WILSON, William. Commander of Wilson's Zouaves, Sixth New York Infantry.

WINDER, John Henry. Brigadier general in charge of military prisons in Richmond; provost marshal general of Richmond; command eventually extended to all prison camps east of the Mississippi.

WINSTON, John R. Colonel of the Forty-fifth North Carolina.

*WITHERSPOON, William Dick. Warrior Guard who transferred to the Greensboro Guards in April 1862; assistant surgeon with the rank of captain; captured September 14, 1862; wounded in the shoulder May 3, 1863; transferred to the Eleventh Alabama in 1864 as assistant surgeon.

WITZ, Isaac. Staunton, Virginia, resident and friend of Henry Beck.

WOMACK, Lowndes. Former classmate of John H. Cowin.

WOODARD, Simeon. Captain of the Grove Hill Guards, Fifth Alabama Infantry.

*WOODRUFF, Daniel W. Warrior Guard who transferred to the Greensboro Guards in April 1862; clerk for R. E. Rodes.

WRIGHT, Ambrose Ransom. Colonel of the Third Georgia Infantry; promoted to brigadier following Seven Pines.

*WRIGHT, Joseph L. (c. 1841, Alabama–September 16, 1863, of congestion). In 1860 living with his father; tavern keeper; enlisted April 13, 1861, in Greensboro; fourth corporal in October 1861; regimental drummer; captured May 3, 1863; wounded in the shoulder July 2, 1863; promoted to fourth corporal in August 1863. Brother of Guard John J. Wright and cousin of Guard Samuel J. Dorroh.

*WRIGHT, John J. (c. 1839, Alabama–January 3, 1862, of pneumonia). In 1860 a printer/tinner living with his father, also a tinner; enlisted April 13, 1861, in Greensboro. Brother of Guard James L. Wright and cousin of Guard Samuel J. Dorroh.

*WRIGHT, Sam (c. 1846, Alabama–). Enlisted March 11, 1862, in Greensboro; discharged June 23, 1862, due to disability caused by chronic diarrhea.

WYNNE, Augustus J. Member of Company H., Fourth Texas Infantry.

WYNNE, Elizabeth J. ("Bettie"). Sister of Guard John W. Wynne; married Guard Daniel Webster in 1865.

*WYNNE, John W. ("Jack") (c. 1838, South Carolina–). In 1860 owned eight slaves and farmed with his father, a planter who reported $15,000 in real estate and $100,000 in personal estate, including eighty-five slaves; enlisted April 13, 1861, in Greensboro; wounded in June 1864; sergeant commanding the Guards in February 1865. Brother of former Guard William A. Wynne.

YANCEY, William Lowndes. Leading Alabama secessionist; diplomat to England and France.

*YOUNGBLOOD, Jacob B. Enlisted August 23, 1862, in Pike County, Alabama; wounded May 3, 1863, and May 12, 1864; in camp in February 1865; captured April 2, 1865.

*YOUNGBLOOD, John L. ("Jack"). Enlisted August 23, 1862, in Pike County, Alabama; wounded and captured May 5, 1864; in camp in February 1865; captured April 2, 1865.

Index

This index primarily lists those particular people and places encountered by the eight diarists. Secondary references, such as comments on Union politicians or names mentioned in letters from home, are only listed when interesting. By the same token, the commonplaces of a soldier's life (such as food, the mail, marching, and contempt for the enemy) did not necessarily warrant listing every time. All place names refer to Virginia or West Virginia unless otherwise noted, and military units larger than a brigade are generally excluded.

Also by G. W. Hubbs

Guarding Greensboro

A Confederate Company in the Making of a Southern Community

Now available from The University of Georgia Press